FREE Study Skills DVD Offer

Dear Customer,

Thank you for your purchase from Mometrix! We consider it an honor and privilege that you have purchased our product and want to ensure your satisfaction.

As a way of showing our appreciation and to help us better serve you, we have developed a Study Skills DVD that we would like to give you for <u>FREE</u>. **This DVD covers our "best practices" for studying for your exam, from using our study materials to preparing for the day of the test.**

All that we ask is that you email us your feedback that would describe your experience so far with our product. Good, bad or indifferent, we want to know what you think!

To get your **FREE Study Skills DVD**, email <u>freedvd@mometrix.com</u> with "FREE STUDY SKILLS DVD" in the subject line and the following information in the body of the email:

   a. The name of the product you purchased.

   b. Your product rating on a scale of 1-5, with 5 being the highest rating.

   c. Your feedback. It can be long, short, or anything in-between, just your impressions and experience so far with our product. Good feedback might include how our study material met your needs and will highlight features of the product that you found helpful.

   d. Your full name and shipping address where you would like us to send your free DVD.

If you have any questions or concerns, please don't hesitate to contact me directly.

Thanks again!

Sincerely,

Jay Willis
Vice President
jay.willis@mometrix.com
1-800-673-8175

Ham Radio License Manual

30 Ham Radio Practice Tests

Includes all 1500+ Technician, General, and Extra Class Exam Questions

Ham Radio Practice Questions and Test Review for All Ham Radio Class Exams

Copyright © 2018 by Mometrix Media LLC

All rights reserved. This product, or parts thereof, may not be reproduced, stored in a retrieval system, or transmitted in any form or by any means—electronic, mechanical, photocopy, recording, scanning, or other—except for brief quotations in critical reviews or articles, without the prior written permission of the publisher.

Written and edited by the Ham Radio Exam Test Prep Staff

Printed in the United States of America

This paper meets the requirements of ANSI/NISO Z39.48-1992 (Permanence of Paper).

Mometrix offers volume discount pricing to institutions. For more information or a price quote, please contact our sales department at sales@mometrix.com or 888-248-1219.

Mometrix Media LLC is not affiliated with or endorsed by any official testing organization. All organizational and test names are trademarks of their respective owners.

ISBN 13: 978-1-5167-0696-9
ISBN 10: 1-5167-0696-X

TABLE OF CONTENTS

Introduction

The FCC (Federal Communications Commission) has three levels of licensure: Technician class, General class, and Extra class. Each class provides further permissions. The Technician class allows for basic amateur radio use. The General class allows for a greater amount of freedom in amateur radio use, such as the ability to take part in world-wide communications. The Extra class allows for the greatest freedom of amateur radio use.

To aid in the process of studying, the FCC releases the full question pool for each exam. The question pools for the Technician and General class exams are made up of 35 topics each. The Extra class question pool has 50 topics. Each test will contain one question from each topic. The question pools contain enough questions to provide for at least 10 unique tests per class.

Because this guide contains the full question pool and 10 practice tests for each class, it is possible to familiarize yourself with the questions to a point where you can pass the exams on rote memory alone. However, to do so would be to miss out on a great opportunity to discover what knowledge gaps you have in the field of amateur radio and address them. We recommend that you study for memory and comprehension simultaneously. One possible strategy is outlined below:

1. Read through the question bank once to understand the full scope of the topics.
2. Address any obvious knowledge gaps with supplemental research.
3. Take a practice test and score yourself.
4. Examine each question you answered incorrectly and research its topic until you feel confident with that content.
5. Reread the question bank.
6. Repeat steps 3-5 until you comprehend each topic and its questions.

Of course, you should optimize any study plan for your individual strengths. No matter what study plan you follow, if you study diligently, you can be prepared and confident on your test day.

Copyright © Mometrix Media. You have been licensed one copy of this document for personal use only. Any other reproduction or redistribution is strictly prohibited. All rights reserved.

Technician Question Pool

T1 – FCC Rules

T1A – Amateur Radio Service: Purpose and Permissible Use of the Amateur Radio Service; Operator/Primary Station License Grant; Where FCC Rules Are Codified; Basis and Purpose of FCC Rules; Meanings of Basic Terms Used in FCC Rules; Interference; Spectrum Management

Which of the following is a purpose of the Amateur Radio Service as stated in the FCC rules and regulations?
  A. Providing personal radio communications for as many citizens as possible
  B. Providing communications for international non-profit organizations
  C. Advancing skills in the technical and communication phases of the radio art
  D. All of these choices are correct

T1A01 (C) [97.1]
Answer: C. As stated in the FCC rules, advancing skills in the technical and communication phases of the radio art is a purpose of the Amateur Radio Service

Which agency regulates and enforces the rules for the Amateur Radio Service in the United States?
  A. FEMA
  B. The ITU
  C. The FCC
  D. Homeland Security

T1A02 (C) [97.1]
Answer: C. The Federal Communications Commission (FCC) is the agency that regulates and enforces the rules for the Amateur Radio Service in the United States.

Which part of the FCC regulations contains the rules governing the Amateur Radio Service?
  A. Part 73
  B. Part 95
  C. Part 90
  D. Part 97

T1A03 (D)
Answer: D. Part 97 of the FCC rules contains the rules and regulations governing the Amateur Radio Service.

Which of the following meets the FCC definition of harmful interference?
  A. Radio transmissions that annoy users of a repeater
  B. Unwanted radio transmissions that cause costly harm to radio station apparatus
  C. That which seriously degrades, obstructs, or repeatedly interrupts a radio communication service operating in accordance with the Radio Regulations
  D. Static from lightning storms

Copyright © Mometrix Media. You have been licensed one copy of this document for personal use only. Any other reproduction or redistribution is strictly prohibited. All rights reserved.

T1A04 (C) [97.3(A)(23)]
Answer: C. According to the FCC, harmful interference is defined as that which seriously degrades, obstructs, or repeatedly interrupts a radiocommunication service operating in accordance with the radio regulations.

Which of the following is a purpose of the Amateur Radio Service rules and regulations as defined by the FCC?
    A. Enhancing international goodwill
    B. Providing inexpensive communication for local emergency organizations
    C. Training of operators in military radio operating procedures
    D. All of these choices are correct

T1A05 (A) [97.1 (e)]
Answer: A. According to the FCC, enhancing international goodwill is one of the purposes of the Amateur Radio Service rules and regulations.

Which of the following services are protected from interference by amateur signals under all circumstances?
    A. Citizens Radio Service
    B. Broadcast Service
    C. Land Mobile Radio Service
    D. Radionavigation Service

T1A06 (D) [97.101 (D), 97.303 (o)(2)]
Answer: D. The FCC states that amateur signals shall not cause harmful interference to, and must accept interference from, stations authorized by the FCC in the aeronautical radio navigation service.

What is the FCC Part 97 definition of telemetry?
    A. An information bulletin issued by the FCC
    B. A one-way transmission to initiate, modify or terminate functions of a device at a distance
    C. A one-way transmission of measurements at a distance from the measuring instrument
    D. An information bulletin from a VEC

T1A07 (C) [97.3(A)(46)]
Answer: C. FCC Part 97 defines telemetry as a one-way transmission of measurements at a distance from the measuring instrument.

Which of the following entities recommends transmit/receive channels and other parameters for auxiliary and repeater stations?
    A. Frequency Spectrum Manager
    B. Frequency Coordinator
    C. FCC Regional Field Office
    D. International Telecommunications Union

T1A08 (B) [97.3(A)(22)]
Answer: B. A frequency coordinator recommends transmit/receive channels and other parameters for auxiliary and repeater stations. A frequency coordinator is a person or group of people who advise users of the appropriate repeater frequencies, with the intention of diminishing interference between repeaters who are operating in roughly the same frequency in the same geographical area.

Copyright © Mometrix Media. You have been licensed one copy of this document for personal use only. Any other reproduction or redistribution is strictly prohibited. All rights reserved.

Who selects a Frequency Coordinator?
    A. The FCC Office of Spectrum Management and Coordination Policy
    B. The local chapter of the Office of National Council of Independent Frequency Coordinators
    C. Amateur operators in a local or regional area whose stations are eligible to be auxiliary or repeater stations
    D. FCC Regional Field Office

T1A09 (C) [97.3(A)(22)]
Answer: C. Amateur operators in a local or regional area whose stations are eligible to be auxiliary or repeater stations may select a frequency coordinator.

What is the FCC Part 97 definition of an amateur station?
    A. A station in an Amateur Radio Service consisting of the apparatus necessary for carrying on radio communications
    B. A building where Amateur Radio receivers, transmitters, and RF power amplifiers are installed
    C. Any radio station operated by a non-professional
    D. Any radio station for hobby use

T1A10 (A) [97.3(A)(5)]
Answer: A. An amateur station is a station licensed in the Amateur Radio Service and used for amateur communication. It includes any equipment that is necessary for such communication.

When is willful interference to other amateur radio stations permitted?
    A. Only if the station being interfered with is expressing extreme religious or political views
    B. At no time
    C. Only during a contest
    D. At any time, amateurs are not protected from willful interference

T1A11 (B) [97.101 (D)]
Answer: B. No amateur operator shall at no time willfully or maliciously interfere with or cause interference to any radio communication or signal

Which of the following is a permissible use of the Amateur Radio Service?
    A. Broadcasting music and videos to friends
    B. Providing a way for amateur radio operators to earn additional income by using their stations to pass messages
    C. Providing low-cost communications for start-up businesses
    D. Allowing a person to conduct radio experiments and to communicate with other licensed hams around the world

T1A12 (D)
Answer: D. Allowing a person to conduct radio experiments and to communicate with other licensed hams around the world is a permissible use of the Amateur Radio Service.

What is the FCC Part 97 definition of telecommand?
    A. An instruction bulletin issued by the FCC
    B. A one-way radio transmission of measurements at a distance from the measuring instrument
    C. A one-way transmission to initiate, modify or terminate functions of a device at a distance
    D. An instruction from a VEC

Copyright © Mometrix Media. You have been licensed one copy of this document for personal use only. Any other reproduction or redistribution is strictly prohibited. All rights reserved.

T1A13 (C) [97.3(A)(45)]
Answer: C. A telecommand is a one-way transmission to initiate, modify, or terminate functions of a device at a distance.

What must you do if you are operating on the 23 cm band and learn that you are interfering with a radiolocation station outside the United States?
    A. Stop operating or take steps to eliminate the harmful interference
    B. Nothing, because this band is allocated exclusively to the amateur service
    C. Establish contact with the radiolocation station and ask them to change frequency
    D. Change to CW mode, because this would not likely cause interference

T1A14 (A) [97.303(D)]
Answer: A. Amateur stations transmitting in the 23 cm band must not cause harmful interference to, and must accept interference from, stations authorized by the United States Government in the radiolocation service.

T1B – Authorized Frequencies: Frequency Allocations; ITU Regions; Emission Modes; Restricted Sub-Bands; Spectrum Sharing; Transmissions near Band Edges

What is the ITU?
    A. An agency of the United States Department of Telecommunications Management
    B. A United Nations agency for information and communication technology issues
    C. An independent frequency coordination agency
    D. A department of the FCC

T1B01 [B]
Answer: B. The ITU is a United Nations agency for information and communication technology issues.

Why are the frequency assignments for some U.S. Territories different from those in the 50 U.S. States?
    A. Some U. S. Territories are located in ITU regions other than region 2
    B. Territorial governments are allowed to select their own frequency allocations
    C. Territorial frequency allocations must also include those of adjacent countries
    D. Any territory that was in existence before the ratification of the Communications Act of 1934 is exempt from FCC frequency regulations

T1B02 (A) [97.301]
Answer: A. Some U.S. territories are located in ITU regions other than region 2 where the U.S. is located, making the frequency assignments different.

Which frequency is within the 6 meter band?
    A. 49.00 MHz
    B. 52.525 MHz
    C. 28.50 MHz
    D. 222.15 MHz

T1B03 (B) [97.301(A)]
Answer: B. 52.525 MHz is within the 6 meter band.

Copyright © Mometrix Media. You have been licensed one copy of this document for personal use only. Any other reproduction or redistribution is strictly prohibited. All rights reserved.

Which amateur band are you using when your station is transmitting on 146.52 MHz?
    A. 2 meter band
    B. 20 meter band
    C. 14 meter band
    D. 6 meter band

T1B04 (A) [97.301(A)]
Answer: A. If your station is transmitting on 146.52 MHz, it is using the 2-meter amateur band.

Which 70 cm frequency is authorized to a Technician Class license holder operating in ITU Region 2?
    A. 53.350 MHz
    B. 146.520 MHz
    C. 443.350 MHz
    D. 222.520 MHz

T1B05 (C) [97.301(A)]
Answer: C. 443.350 MHz is the 70 cm frequency authorized to a technician class license holder operating in ITU Region 2.

Which 23 cm frequency is authorized to a Technician Class licensee?
    A. 2315 MHz
    B. 1296 MHz
    C. 3390 MHz
    D. 146.52 MHz

T1B06 (B) [97.301(A)]
Answer: B. The 1296 MHz frequency is the 23 cm frequency authorized to a Technician Class operator.

What amateur band are you using if you are transmitting on 223.50 MHz?
    A. 15 meter band
    B. 10 meter band
    C. 2 meter band
    D. 1.25 meter band

T1B07 (D) [97.301(A)]
Answer: D. If you are transmitting on the 223.50 MHz, you are using the 1.25 meter amateur band.

Which of the following is a result of the fact that the amateur service is secondary in some portions of the 70 cm band?
    A. U.S. amateurs may find non-amateur stations in the bands, and must avoid interfering with them
    B. U.S. amateurs must give foreign amateur stations priority in those portions
    C. International communications are not permitted on 70 cm
    D. Digital transmissions are not permitted on 70 cm

T1B08 (A) [97.303]
Answer: A. The amateur service is secondary in some portions of the 70 cm band because U.S. amateurs my find non-amateur stations in the bands and must avoid interfering with them.

Copyright © Mometrix Media. You have been licensed one copy of this document for personal use only. Any other reproduction or redistribution is strictly prohibited. All rights reserved.

Why should you not set your transmit frequency to be exactly at the edge of an amateur band or sub-band?
    A. To allow for calibration error in the transmitter frequency display
    B. So that modulation sidebands do not extend beyond the band edge
    C. To allow for transmitter frequency drift
    D. All of these choices are correct

T1B09 (D) [97.101(A), 97.301(a-e)]
Answer: D. There are several reasons why an operator should not set the transmit frequency to be exactly at the edge of an amateur band or sub-band. To begin with, this allows for calibration error in the transmitter frequency display. It also ensures that modulation sidebands do not extend beyond the band edge. Finally, it allows for transmitter frequency drift.

Which of the bands above 30 MHz that are available to Technician Class operators have mode-restricted sub-bands?
    A. The 6 meter, 2 meter, and 70 cm bands
    B. The 2 meter and 13 cm bands
    C. The 6 meter, 2 meter, and 1.25 meter bands
    D. The 2 meter and 70 cm bands

T1B10 (C) [97.301(e), 97.305(C)]
Answer: C. Of the bands available to Technician Class operators, the 6 meter, 2 meter, and 1.25 meter bands have mode-restricted sub-bands.

What emission modes are permitted in the mode-restricted sub-bands at 50.0 to 50.1 MHz and 144.0 to 144.1 MHz?
    A. CW only
    B. CW and RTTY
    C. SSB only
    D. CW and SSB

T1B11 (A) [97.305 (A)(C)]
Answer: A. Only CW emission modes are permitted in the mode-restricted sub-bands at 50.0 to 50.1 MHz and 144.0 to 144.1 MHz.

Why are frequency assignments for U.S. stations operating maritime mobile not the same everywhere in the world?
    A. Amateur maritime mobile stations in international waters must conform to the frequency assignments of the country nearest to their vessel
    B. Amateur frequency assignments can vary among the three ITU regions
    C. Frequency assignments are determined by the captain of the vessel
    D. Amateur frequency assignments are different in each of the 90 ITU zones

T1B12 (B) [97.301]
Answer: B. Frequency assignments for U.S. stations operating maritime mobile are not the same everywhere in the world because the frequency assignment depends on which ITU region the operation is taking place in.

Copyright © Mometrix Media. You have been licensed one copy of this document for personal use only. Any other reproduction or redistribution is strictly prohibited. All rights reserved.

Which emission may be used between 219 and 220 MHz?
   A. Spread spectrum
   B. Data
   C. SSB voice
   D. Fast-scan television

T1B13 (B) [97.305(C)]
Answer: B. As stated by the FCC, only data emission may be used between 219and 220 MHz.

T1C – Operator Licensing: Operator Classes; Sequential, Special Event, and Vanity Call Sign Systems; International Communications; Reciprocal Operation; Station License and Licensee; Places where the Amateur Service is Regulated by the FCC; Name and Address on FCC License Database; License Term; Renewal; Grace Period

Which type of call sign has a single letter in both its prefix and suffix?
   A. Vanity
   B. Sequential
   C. Special event
   D. In-memoriam

T1C01 (C) [97.3(A)(11)(iii)]
Answer: C. The special event call sign has a single letter in both the prefix and suffix. Each license issued by the FCC comes with a unique call sign. Typically, the prefix of a call sign contains one or two letters and one number. It indicates the location of the operator.

Which of the following is a valid US amateur radio station call sign?
   A. KMA3505
   B. W3ABC
   C. KDKA
   D. 11Q1176

T1C02 (B)
Answer: B. W3ABC is a valid US amateur radio station call sign. Amateurs may have what are called 1 x 3 call signs, so long as the prefix is W, K, or N, and so long as the suffix is composed of three letters. Amateurs may also have a 2 x 3 call sign with a prefix of K through KG, K through KK, KM through K0, or KR through KZ. The 2 x 3 call signs may have any three letters in the suffix. Amateurs may also have 2 x 1 call sign, with the prefix beginning with A, K, N, or W, or a 1 x 2 call sign, with a prefix of K, N, or W.

What types of international communications are permitted by an FCC-licensed amateur station?
   A. Communications incidental to the purposes of the amateur service and remarks of a personal character
   B. Communications incidental to conducting business or remarks of a personal nature
   C. Only communications incidental to contest exchanges, all other communications are prohibited
   D. Any communications that would be permitted by an international broadcast station

T1C03 (A) [97.117]
Answer: A. FCC-licensed amateur stations are permitted to make international communications incidental to the purposes of the amateur service and remarks of a personal character.

Copyright © Mometrix Media. You have been licensed one copy of this document for personal use only. Any other reproduction or redistribution is strictly prohibited. All rights reserved.

When are you allowed to operate your amateur station in a foreign country?
  A. When the foreign country authorizes it
  B. When there is a mutual agreement allowing third party communications
  C. When authorization permits amateur communications in a foreign language
  D. When you are communicating with non-licensed individuals in another country

T1C04 (A) [97.107]
Answer: A. One is allowed to operate an amateur station in a foreign country when the foreign country authorizes it.

Which of the following is a vanity call sign which a technician class amateur operator might select if available?
  A. K1XXX
  B. KA1X
  C. W1XX
  D. All of these choices are correct

T1C05 (A)
Answer: A. Of the choices listed, only the K1XXX series of call signs is available to technician class amateur operators. The other two series listed are available only to extra class amateur operators.

From which of the following locations may an FCC-licensed amateur station transmit, in addition to places where the FCC regulates communications?
  A. From within any country that belongs to the International Telecommunications Union
  B. From within any country that is a member of the United Nations
  C. From anywhere within in ITU Regions 2 and 3
  D. From any vessel or craft located in international waters and documented or registered in the United States

T1C06 (D) [97.5(A)(2)]
Answer: D. In addition to those places where the FCC regulates communications, an FCC-licensed amateur station may transmit from any vessel or craft located in international waters and documented or registered in the United States.

What may result when correspondence from the FCC is returned as undeliverable because the grantee failed to provide the correct mailing address?
  A. Fine or imprisonment
  B. Revocation of the station license or suspension of the operator license
  C. Require the licensee to be re-examined
  D. A reduction of one rank in operator class

T1C07 (B) [97.23]
Answer: B. When correspondence from the FCC is returned as undeliverable because the grantee failed to provide the correct mailing address, the station license may be revoked, or the operator license may be suspended.

What is the normal term for an FCC-issued primary station/operator amateur radio license grant?
  A. Five years
  B. Life
  C. Ten years
  D. Twenty years

Copyright © Mometrix Media. You have been licensed one copy of this document for personal use only. Any other reproduction or redistribution is strictly prohibited. All rights reserved.

T1C08 (C) [97.25]
Answer: C. The normal term for an FCC-issued primary station/operator license grant is 10 years.

What is the grace period following the expiration of an amateur license within which the license may be renewed?
    A. Two years
    B. Three years
    C. Five years
    D. Ten years

T1C09 (A) [97.21(A)(B)]
Answer: A. The grace period following the expiration of an amateur license, within which the license may be renewed, is two years.

How soon after passing the examination for your first amateur radio license may you operate a transmitter on an amateur service frequency

    A. Immediately
    B. 30 days after the test date
    C. As soon as your operator/station license grant appears in the FCC's license database
    D. You must wait until you receive your license in the mail from the FCC

T1C10 (C) [97.5a]
Answer: C. After you pass the examination required for your first amateur radio license, you may operate a transmitter on an amateur service frequency as soon as your name and call sign appear in the FCC's ULS database.

If your license has expired and is still within the allowable grace period, may you continue to operate a transmitter on amateur service frequencies?
    A. No, transmitting is not allowed until the FCC license database shows that the license has been renewed
    B. Yes, but only if you identify using the suffix "GP"
    C. Yes, but only during authorized nets
    D. Yes, for up to two years

T1C11 (A) [97.21(B)]
Answer: A. An operator whose license has expired but who is still within the allowable grace period may not continue to operate a transmitter on amateur service frequencies until the ULS database shows that the license has been renewed.

Who may select a desired call sign under the vanity call sign rules?
    A. Only licensed amateurs with general or extra class licenses
    B. Only licensed amateurs with an extra class license
    C. Only an amateur licensee who has been licensed continuously for more than 10 years
    D. Any licensed amateur

T1C12 (D) [97.19]
Answer: D. Any licensed amateur is eligible to make application for modification of the license grant, or the renewal thereof, to show a call sign selected by the vanity call sign system.

Copyright © Mometrix Media. You have been licensed one copy of this document for personal use only. Any other reproduction or redistribution is strictly prohibited. All rights reserved.

For which licenses classes are new licenses currently available from the FCC?
A. Novice, Technician, General, Advanced
B. Technician, Technician Plus, General, Advanced
C. Novice, Technician Plus, General, Advanced
D. Technician, General, Amateur Extra

T1C13 (D) [97.9(A), 97.17(A)]
Answer: D. No new license grant will be issued for a Novice or Advanced Class operator/primary station.

Who may select a vanity call sign for a club station?
A. Any Extra Class member of the club
B. Any member of the club
C. Any officer of the club
D. Only the person named as trustee on the club station license grant

T1C14 (D) [97.21(A) (1)]
Answer: D. A Club Station Call Sign Administrator shall not file with the Commission any application to modify a club station license grant that was submitted by a person other than the trustee as shown on the license grant, except an application to change the club station license trustee.

T1D – Authorized and Prohibited Transmission: Communications with Other Countries; Music; Exchange of Information with Other Services; Indecent Language; Compensation for Use of Station; Retransmission of Other Amateur Signals; Codes and Ciphers; Sale of Equipment; Unidentified Transmissions; Broadcasting

With which countries are FCC-licensed amateur stations prohibited from exchanging communications?
A. Any country whose administration has notified the ITU that it objects to such communications
B. Any country whose administration has notified the United Nations that it objects to such communications
C. Any country engaged in hostilities with another country
D. Any country in violation of the War Powers Act of 1934

T1D01 (A) [97.111(A)(1)]
Answer: A. FCC-licensed amateur stations are prohibited from exchanging communications with any country whose administration has notified the ITU that it objects to such communications.

On which of the following occasions may an FCC-licensed amateur station exchange messages with a U.S. military station?
A. During an Armed Forces Day Communications Test
B. During a Memorial Day Celebration
C. During an Independence Day celebration
D. During a propagation test

T1D02 (A) [97.111(A)(5)]
Answer: A. An FCC-licensed amateur station may exchange messages with a US military station during an Armed Forces Day communications test.

Copyright © Mometrix Media. You have been licensed one copy of this document for personal use only. Any other reproduction or redistribution is strictly prohibited. All rights reserved.

When is the transmission of codes or ciphers that hide the meaning of a message allowed by an amateur station?

    A. Only during contests

    B. Only when operating mobile

    C. Only when transmitting control commands to space stations or radio control craft

    D. Only when frequencies above 1280 MHz are used

T1D03 (C) [97.211(B), 97.215]

Answer: C. An amateur station is allowed to hide the meaning of a transmitted message with codes or ciphers only when transmitting control commands to space stations or radio control craft.

What is the only time an amateur station is authorized to transmit music?

    A. When incidental to an authorized retransmission of manned spacecraft communications

    B. When the music produces no spurious emissions

    C. When the purpose is to interfere with an illegal transmission

    D. When the music is transmitted above 1280 MHz

T1D04 (A) [97.113(A)(4), 97.113(C)]

Answer: A. The only time an amateur station is authorized to transmit music is when it is incidental to unauthorized retransmission of manned spacecraft communications.

When may amateur radio operators use their stations to notify other amateurs of the availability of equipment for sale or trade?

    A. When the equipment is normally used in an amateur station and such activity is not conducted on a regular basis

    B. When the asking price is $100.00 or less

    C. When the asking price is less than its appraised value

    D. When the equipment is not the personal property of either the station licensee or the control operator or their close relatives

T1D05 (A) [97.113(A)(3)(ii)]

Answer: A. Amateur radio operators may use their stations to notify other amateurs of the availability of equipment for sale or trade when the equipment is normally used in an amateur station and such activity is not conducted on a regular basis.

What, if any, are the restrictions concerning transmission of language that may be considered indecent or obscene?

    A. The FCC maintains a list of words that are not permitted to be used on amateur frequencies

    B. Any such language is prohibited

    C. The ITU maintains a list of words that are not permitted to be used on amateur frequencies

    D. There is no such prohibition

T1D06 (B) [97.113(A)(4)]

Answer: B. As stated by the FCC, no amateur station shall transmit obscene or indecent words or language.

What types of amateur stations can automatically retransmit the signals of other amateur stations?

    A. Auxiliary, beacon, or Earth stations

    B. Auxiliary, repeater, or space stations

    C. Beacon, repeater, or space stations

    D. Earth, repeater, or space stations

Copyright © Mometrix Media. You have been licensed one copy of this document for personal use only. Any other reproduction or redistribution is strictly prohibited. All rights reserved.

T1D07 (B) [97.113(D)]
Answer: B. No amateur station, except an auxiliary, repeater, or space station, may automatically retransmit the radio signals of other amateur station.

In which of the following circumstances may the control operator of an amateur station receive compensation for operating the station?
    A. When engaging in communications on behalf of their employer
    B. When the communication is incidental to classroom instruction at an educational institution
    C. When re-broadcasting weather alerts during a RACES net
    D. When notifying other amateur operators of the availability for sale or trade of apparatus

T1D08 (B) [97.113]
Answer: B. The control operator of an amateur station may receive compensation for operating the station when the communication is incidental to classroom instruction at an educational institution.

Under which of the following circumstances are amateur stations authorized to transmit signals related to broadcasting, program production, or news gathering, assuming no other means is available?
    A. Only where such communications directly relate to the immediate safety of human life or protection of property
    B. Only when broadcasting communications to or from the space shuttle.
    C. Only where noncommercial programming is gathered and supplied exclusively to the National Public Radio network
    D. Only when using amateur repeaters linked to the Internet

T1D09 (A) [97.113(5)(B)]
Answer: A. Assuming no other means is available, amateur stations are authorized to transmit signals related to broadcasting, program production, or news gathering only where such communications directly relate to the immediate safety of human life or protection of property.

What is the meaning of the term "broadcasting" in the FCC rules for the amateur services?
    A. Two-way transmissions by amateur stations
    B. Transmission of music
    C. Transmission of messages directed only to amateur operators
    D. Transmissions intended for reception by the general public

T1D10 (D) [97.3(A)(10)]
Answer: D. In the FCC rules for the amateur services, broadcasting refers to transmissions intended for reception by the general public. Broadcasting refers to transmissions that are meant to be received by the general public, either on relay or directly.

When may an amateur station transmit without identifying?
    A. When the transmissions are of a brief nature to make station adjustments
    B. When the transmissions are unmodulated
    C. When the transmitted power level is below 1 watt
    D. When transmitting signals to control a model craft

T1D11 (D) [97.119(A)]
Answer: D. The station identification procedure is not required for an amateur station's transmissions directed only to the model craft, provided that a la bel indicating the station call sign and the station licensee's name and address is affixed to the station transmitter.

Copyright © Mometrix Media. You have been licensed one copy of this document for personal use only. Any other reproduction or redistribution is strictly prohibited. All rights reserved.

Under which of the following circumstances may an amateur radio station engage in broadcasting?
A. Under no circumstances
B. When transmitting code practice, information bulletins, or transmissions necessary to provide emergency communications
C. At any time as long as no music is transmitted
D. At any time as long as the material being transmitted did not originate from a commercial broadcast station

T1D12 (B) [97.111(B)(4,5,6)]
Answer: B. In addition to one-way transmissions specifically authorized elsewhere in this part, an amateur station may transmit the following types of one-way communications: transmissions necessary to providing emergency communications, transmissions necessary to assisting persons learning, or improving proficiency in, the international Morse code, and transmissions necessary to disseminate information bulletins.

T1E – Control Operator and Control Types: Control Operator Required; Eligibility; Designation of Control Operator; Privileges and Duties; Control Point; Local, Automatic and Remote Control; Location of Control Operator

When is an amateur station permitted to transmit without a control operator?
A. When using automatic control, such as in the case of a repeater
B. When the station licensee is away and another licensed amateur is using the station
C. When the transmitting station is an auxiliary station
D. Never

T1E01 (D) [97.7(A)]
Answer: D. When transmitting, each amateur station must have a control operator.

Who may a station licensee designate to be the control operator of an amateur station?
A. Any U.S. citizen or registered alien
B. Any family member of the station licensee
C. Any person over the age of 18
D. Only a person for whom an amateur operator/primary station license grant appears in the FCC database or who is authorized for alien reciprocal operation

T1E02 (D) [97.7(A)]
Answer: D. Only a person for whom an amateur operator/primary station license grant appears in the FCC database or who is authorized for alien reciprocal operation is eligible to be the control operator of an amateur station.

Who must designate the station control operator?
A. The station licensee
B. The FCC
C. The frequency coordinator
D. The ITU

T1E03 (A) [97.103(B)]
Answer: A. The station licensee must designate the station control operator.

Copyright © Mometrix Media. You have been licensed one copy of this document for personal use only. Any other reproduction or redistribution is strictly prohibited. All rights reserved.

What determines the transmitting privileges of an amateur station?
    A. The frequency authorized by the frequency coordinator
    B. The class of operator license held by the station licensee
    C. The highest class of operator license held by anyone on the premises
    D. The class of operator license held by the control operator

T1E04 (D) [97.103(B)]
Answer: D. The transmitting privileges of an amateur station are determined by the class of operator license held by the control operator.

What is an amateur station control point?
    A. The location of the station's transmitting antenna
    B. The location of the station transmitting apparatus
    C. The location at which the control operator function is performed
    D. The mailing address of the station licensee

T1E05 (C) [97.3(A)(14)]
Answer: C. An amateur station control point is the location at which the control operator function is performed. The control point is the set of locations at which the control operator functions are carried out.

Under what type of control do APRS network digipeaters operate?
    A. Automatic
    B. Remote
    C. Local
    D. Manual

T1E06 (A) [97.109(D)]
Answer: A. APRS digipeaters operate automatically, receiving the packets and propagating them without requiring any input from a human operator.

When the control operator is not the station licensee, who is responsible for the proper operation of the station?
    A. All licensed amateurs who are present at the operation
    B. Only the station licensee
    C. Only the control operator
    D. The control operator and the station licensee are equally responsible

T1E07 (D) [97.103(A)]
Answer: D. When the control operator is not the station licensee, the control operator and the station licensee are equally responsible for the proper operation of the station.

Which of the following is an example of automatic control?
    A. Repeater operation
    B. Controlling the station over the Internet
    C. Using a computer or other device to automatically send CW
    D. Using a computer or other device to automatically identify

T1E08 (A) [97.3(A)(6), 97.205(D)]
Answer: A. A repeater operation may be automatically controlled.

Copyright © Mometrix Media. You have been licensed one copy of this document for personal use only. Any other reproduction or redistribution is strictly prohibited. All rights reserved.

What type of control is being used when the control operator is at the control point?
    A. Radio control
    B. Unattended control
    C. Automatic control
    D. Local control

T1E09 (D) [97.109(B)]
Answer: D. Local control is used for transmissions from a handheld radio.

Which of the following is an example of remote control as defined in Part 97?
    A. Repeater operation
    B. Operating the station over the Internet
    C. Controlling a model aircraft, boat or car by amateur radio
    D. All of these choices are correct

T1E10 (B) [97.3(A)(39)]
Answer: B. Operating the station over the internet is an example of remote control.

Who does the FCC presume to be the control operator of an amateur station, unless documentation to the contrary is in the station records?
    A. The station custodian
    B. The third party participant
    C. The person operating the station equipment
    D. The station licensee

T1E11 (D) [97.103(A)]
Answer: D. Unless documentation to the contrary is in the station records, the FCC presumes the station licensee to be the control operator of an amateur station.

When, under normal circumstances, may a Technician Class licensee be the control operator of a station operating in an exclusive Extra Class operator segment of the amateur bands?
    A. At no time
    B. When operating a special event station
    C. As part of a multi-operator contest team
    D. When using a club station whose trustee is an Extra Class operator licensee

T1E12 (A) [97.119(e)]
Answer: A. At no time may a Technician Class licensee be the control operator of a station operating in an exclusive Extra Class operator segment of the amateur bands.

T1F – Station Identification; Repeaters; Third Party Communications; Club Stations; FCC Inspection

What type of identification is being used when identifying a station on the air as "Race Headquarters"?
    A. Tactical call
    B. Self-assigned designator
    C. SSID
    D. Broadcast station

Copyright © Mometrix Media. You have been licensed one copy of this document for personal use only. Any other reproduction or redistribution is strictly prohibited. All rights reserved.

T1F01 (A)
Answer: A. Tactical call identification is being used when identifying a station on the air as "race headquarters." Tactical call signs are the names that identify locations or functions during local emergency communications.

When using tactical identifiers such as "Race Headquarters" during a community service net operation, how often must your station transmit the station's FCC-assigned call sign?
    A. Never, the tactical call is sufficient
    B. Once during every hour
    C. At the end of each communication and every ten minutes during a communication
    D. At the end of every transmission

T1F02 (C) [97.119 (A)]
Answer: C. When using tactical identifiers, a station must transmit its FCC-assigned call sign every 10 minutes.

When is an amateur station required to transmit its assigned call sign?
    A. At the beginning of each contact, and every 10 minutes thereafter
    B. At least once during each transmission
    C. At least every 15 minutes during and at the end of a communication
    D. At least every 10 minutes during and at the end of a communication

T1F03 (D) [97.119(A)]
Answer: D. An amateur station is required to transmit its assigned call sign at least every 10 minutes during and at the end of a communication.

Which of the following is an acceptable language to use for station identification when operating in a phone sub-band?
    A. Any language recognized by the United Nations
    B. Any language recognized by the ITU
    C. The English language
    D. English, French, or Spanish

T1F04 (C) [97.119(B)(2)]
Answer: C. English is an acceptable language for station identification use when operating in a phone sub-band.

What method of call sign identification is required for a station transmitting phone signals?
    A. Send the call sign followed by the indicator RPT
    B. Send the call sign using CW or phone emission
    C. Send the call sign followed by the indicator R
    D. Send the call sign using only phone emission

T1F05 (B) [97.119(B)(2)]
Answer: B. When a station is transmitting phone signals, it should use the call sign identification system of sending the call sign using CW or phone emission.

Copyright © Mometrix Media. You have been licensed one copy of this document for personal use only. Any other reproduction or redistribution is strictly prohibited. All rights reserved.

Which of the following formats of a self-assigned indicator is acceptable when identifying using a phone transmission?

    A. KL7CC stroke W3
    B. KL7CC slant W3
    C. KL7CC slash W3
    D. All of these choices are correct

T1F06 (D) [97.119(C)]
Answer: D. For identification during a phone transmission, KL7CC stroke W3, KL7CC slant W3, and KL7CC slash W3 would all be acceptable formats for a self-assigned indicator.

Which of the following restrictions apply when a non-licensed person is allowed to speak to a foreign station using a station under the control of a Technician Class control operator?

    A. The person must be a U.S. citizen
    B. The foreign station must be one with which the U.S. has a third party agreement
    C. The licensed control operator must do the station identification
    D. All of these choices are correct

T1F07 (B) [97.115(A)(2)]
Answer: B. An amateur station may transmit messages for a third party to any station within the jurisdiction of any foreign government when transmitting emergency or disaster relief communications and any station within the jurisdiction of any foreign government whose administration has made arrangements with the United States to allow amateur stations to be used for transmitting international communications on behalf of third parties. No station shall transmit messages for a third party to any station within the jurisdiction of any foreign government whose administration has not made such an arrangement.

Which indicator is required by the FCC to be transmitted after a station call sign?

    A. /M when operating mobile
    B. /R when operating a repeater
    C. / followed the FCC Region number when operating out of the region in which the license was issued
    D. /KT, /AE or /AG when using new license privileges earned by CSCE while waiting for an upgrade to a previously issued license to appear in the FCC license database

T1F08 (D) [97.119(f)]
Answer: D. If you plan to use newly acquired privileges from a license upgrade in the time between your passing the exam and the FCC acknowledging your achievement in the ULS license database, you must transmit the appropriate indicator after your station call sign.

What type of amateur station simultaneously retransmits the signal of another amateur station on a different channel or channels?

    A. Beacon station
    B. Earth station
    C. Repeater station
    D. Message forwarding station

T1F09 (C) [97.3(A)(40)]
Answer: C. A repeater station is an amateur station that simultaneously retransmits the signal of another amateur station on a different channel or channels.

Copyright © Mometrix Media. You have been licensed one copy of this document for personal use only. Any other reproduction or redistribution is strictly prohibited. All rights reserved.

Who is accountable should a repeater inadvertently retransmit communications that violate the FCC rules?
    A. The control operator of the originating station
    B. The control operator of the repeater
    C. The owner of the repeater
    D. Both the originating station and the repeater owner

T1F10 (A) [97.205(g)]
Answer: A. If a repeater inadvertently retransmits communications that violate the FCC rules, the control operator of the originating station is accountable.

To which foreign stations do the FCC rules authorize the transmission of non-emergency third party communications?
    A. Any station whose government permits such communications
    B. Those in ITU Region 2 only
    C. Those in ITU Regions 2 and 3 only
    D. Those in ITU Region 3 only

T1F11 (A) [97.115(A)]
Answer: A. The FCC authorizes the transmission of non-emergency third party communications to any foreign station whose government permits such communications.

How many persons are required to be members of a club for a club station license to be issued by the FCC?
    A. At least 5
    B. At least 4
    C. A trustee and 2 officers
    D. At least 2

T1F12 (B) [97.5(B)(2)]
Answer: B. A club must have at least four members to be issued a club station licensed by the FCC. There are a large number of general and specialty clubs for ham radio operators.

When must the station licensee make the station and its records available for FCC inspection?
    A. At any time ten days after notification by the FCC of such an inspection
    B. At any time upon request by an FCC representative
    C. Only after failing to comply with an FCC notice of violation
    D. Only when presented with a valid warrant by an FCC official or government agent

T1F13 (B) [97.103(C)]
Answer: B. A station licensee must make the station and its records available for FCC inspection any time upon request by an FCC representative.

Copyright © Mometrix Media. You have been licensed one copy of this document for personal use only. Any other reproduction or redistribution is strictly prohibited. All rights reserved.

T2 – Operating Procedures

T2A – Station Operation: Choosing an Operating Frequency; Calling Another Station; Test Transmissions; Procedural Signs; Use of Minimum Power; Choosing an Operating Frequency; Band Plans; Calling Frequencies; Repeater Offsets

What is the most common repeater frequency offset in the 2 meter band?
A. Plus 500 kHz
B. Plus or minus 600 kHz
C. Minus 500 kHz
D. Only plus 600 kHz

T2A01 (B)
Answer: B. The most common repeater frequency offset in the 2 meter band is plus or minus 600 kHz.

What is the national calling frequency for FM simplex operations in the 70 cm band?
A. 146.520 MHz
B. 145.000 MHz
C. 432.100 MHz
D. 446.000 MHz

T2A02 (D)
Answer: D. The national calling frequency for FM simplex operations in the 70 cm band is 446.000 MHz. A simplex communication occurs when one station calls another without assistance from a repeater. This means that both stations transmit and receive over the same frequency. The other national FM simplex calling frequencies are 52.525, 146.52, 223.50, and 1294.5 MHz.

What is a common repeater frequency offset in the 70 cm band?
A. Plus or minus 5 MHz
B. Plus or minus 600 kHz
C. Minus 600 kHz
D. Plus 600 kHz

T2A03 (A)
Answer: A. A common repeater frequency offset in the 70 cm band is plus or minus 5 MHz.

What is an appropriate way to call another station on a repeater if you know the other station's call sign?
A. Say "break, break" then say the station's call sign
B. Say the station's call sign then identify with your call sign
C. Say "CQ" three times then the other station's call sign
D. Wait for the station to call "CQ" then answer it

T2A04 (B)
Answer: B. An appropriate way to call another station on a repeater if you know the other station's call sign is to say the station's call sign and then identify with your call sign.

How should you respond to a station calling CQ?
A. Transmit CQ followed by the other station's call sign
B. Transmit your call sign followed by the other station's call sign
C. Transmit the other station's call sign followed by your call sign
D. Transmit a signal report followed by your call sign

Copyright © Mometrix Media. You have been licensed one copy of this document for personal use only. Any other reproduction or redistribution is strictly prohibited. All rights reserved.

T2A05 (C)
Answer: C. When responding to a call of CQ, you should transmit the other station's call sign followed by your call sign.

What must an amateur operator do when making on-air transmissions to test equipment or antennas?
    A. Properly identify the transmitting station
    B. Make test transmissions only after 10:00 p.m. local time
    C. Notify the FCC of the test transmission
    D. State the purpose of the test during the test procedure

T2A06 (A)
Answer: A. When making on-air transmissions to test equipment or antennas, an amateur operator must properly identify the transmitting station.

Which of the following is true when making a test transmission?
    A. Station identification is not required if the transmission is less than 15 seconds
    B. Station identification is not required if the transmission is less than 1 watt
    C. Station identification is only required once an hour when the transmissions are for test purposes only
    D. Station identification is required at least every ten minutes during the test and at the end of the test

T2A07 (D)
Answer: D. When making a test transmission, station identification is required at least every 10 minutes during the test and at the end.

What is the meaning of the procedural signal "CQ"?
    A. Call on the quarter hour
    B. A new antenna is being tested (no station should answer)
    C. Only the called station should transmit
    D. Calling any station

T2A08 (D)
Answer: D. The meaning of the procedural signal CQ is "calling any station."

What brief statement is transmitted used in place of "CQ" to indicate that you are listening on a repeater?
    A. The words "Hello test" followed by your call sign
    B. Your call sign
    C. The repeater call sign followed by your call sign
    D. The letters "QSY" followed by your call sign

T2A09 (B)
Answer: B. A call sign is often used in place of CQ to indicate that you are listening on a repeater.

What is a band plan, beyond the privileges established by the FCC?
    A. A voluntary guideline for using different modes or activities within an amateur band
    B. A mandated list of operating schedules
    C. A list of scheduled net frequencies
    D. A plan devised by a club to indicate frequency band usage

Copyright © Mometrix Media. You have been licensed one copy of this document for personal use only. Any other reproduction or redistribution is strictly prohibited. All rights reserved.

T2A10 (A)
Answer: A. A band plan, beyond the privileges established by the FCC, is a voluntary guideline for using different modes or activities within an amateur band.

Which of the following is an FCC rule regarding power levels used in the amateur bands, under normal, non-distress circumstances?
A. There is no limit to power as long as there is no interference with other services
B. No more than 200 watts PEP may be used
C. Up to 1500 watts PEP may be used on any amateur frequency without restriction
D. While not exceeding the maximum power permitted on a given band, use the minimum power necessary to carry out the desired communication

T2A11 (D) [97.313(A)]
Answer: D. The FCC rules regarding power levels used in the amateur bands are that an amateur must use the minimum transmitter power necessary to carry out the desired communication.

Which of the following is a guideline to use when choosing an operating frequency for calling CQ?
A. Listen first to be sure that no one else is using the frequency
B. Ask if the frequency is in use
C. Make sure you are in your assigned band
D. All of these choices are correct

T2A12 (D)
Answer: D Before calling CQ, always make sure you are in your assigned band. Listen to see if the frequency is already in use. Finally, if there is no sign of anyone operating on the frequency, ask if it is in use. If you do not receive any response, the frequency is clear for you to use.

T2B – VHF/UHF Operating Practices: SSB Phone; FM Repeater; Simplex; Splits and Shifts; CTCSS; DTMF; Tone Squelch; Carrier Squelch; Phonetics; Operational Problem Resolution; Q Signals

What is the term used to describe an amateur station that is transmitting and receiving on the same frequency?
A. Full duplex communication
B. Diplex communication
C. Simplex communication
D. Multiplex communication

T2B01 (C)
Answer: C. The term used to describe an amateur station that is transmitting and receiving on the same frequency is simplex communication.

What is the term used to describe the use of a sub-audible tone transmitted with normal voice audio to open the squelch of a receiver?
A. Carrier squelch
B. Tone burst
C. DTMF
D. CTCSS

Copyright © Mometrix Media. You have been licensed one copy of this document for personal use only. Any other reproduction or redistribution is strictly prohibited. All rights reserved.

T2B02 (D)
Answer: D. CT CSS is the use of a sub-audible tone transmitted with normal voice audio to open the squelch of the receiver.

Which of the following describes the muting of receiver audio controlled solely by the presence or absence of an RF signal?
    A. Tone squelch
    B. Carrier squelch
    C. CTCSS
    D. Modulated carrier

T2B03 (B)
Answer: B. Carrier squelch is the muting of receiver audio controlled solely by the presence or absence of an RF signal.

Which of the following common problems might cause you to be able to hear but not access a repeater even when transmitting with the proper offset?
    A. The repeater receiver may require an audio tone burst for access
    B. The repeater receiver may require a CTCSS tone for access
    C. The repeater receiver may require a DCS tone sequence for access
    D. All of these choices are correct

T2B04 (D)
Answer: D. There are several common problems that might cause you to be able to hear but not access a repeater even when transmitting with the proper offset. This may occur when the repeater receiver requires audio tone burst, a CTCSS tone, or a DCS tone sequence for access.

What determines the amount of deviation of an FM (as opposed to PM) signal?
    A. Both the frequency and amplitude of the modulating signal
    B. The frequency of the modulating signal
    C. The amplitude of the modulating signal
    D. The relative phase of the modulating signal and the carrier

T2B05 (C)
Answer: C. The amplitude of the modulating signal determines the amount of deviation of an FM signal.

What happens when the deviation of an FM transmitter is increased?
    A. Its signal occupies more bandwidth
    B. Its output power increases
    C. Its output power and bandwidth increases
    D. Asymmetric modulation occurs

T2B06 (A)
Answer: A. When the deviation of an FM transmitter is increased, its signal occupies more bandwidth.

What could cause your FM signal to interfere with stations on nearby frequencies?
    A. Microphone gain too high, causing over-deviation
    B. SWR too high
    C. Incorrect CTCSS Tone
    D. All of these choices are correct

Copyright © Mometrix Media. You have been licensed one copy of this document for personal use only. Any other reproduction or redistribution is strictly prohibited. All rights reserved.

T2B07 (A)
Answer: A. Having your microphone gain turned up too high can cause over-deviation and result in your signal interfering with stations on nearby frequencies.

Which of the following applies when two stations transmitting on the same frequency interfere with each other?
    A. Common courtesy should prevail, but no one has absolute right to an amateur frequency
    B. Whoever has the strongest signal has priority on the frequency
    C. Whoever has been on the frequency the longest has priority on the frequency
    D. The station which has the weakest signal has priority on the frequency

T2B08 (A)
Answer: A. If two stations transmitting on the same frequency begin to interfere with one another, it is up to the participants to resolve the issue. There is no absolute right to any amateur frequency, so operators are encouraged to remain courteous and work out a solution.

Which of the following methods is encouraged by the FCC when identifying your station when using phone?
    A. Use of a phonetic alphabet
    B. Send your call sign in CW as well as voice
    C. Repeat your call sign three times
    D. Increase your signal to full power when identifying

T2B09 (A) [97.119(B)(2)]
Answer: A. When identifying your station while using the phone, one should use the phonetic alphabet.

Which "Q" signal indicates that you are receiving interference from other stations?
    A. QRM
    B. QRN
    C. QTH
    D. QSB

T2B10 (A)
Answer: A. The Q signal used to indicate that you are receiving interference from other stations is QRM. Q signals are useful methods for accelerating communication. A Q signal may be issued as a question or as a response. For example, QRG may mean "What is my exact frequency?" or "Your exact frequency is."

Which "Q" signal indicates that you are changing frequency?
    A. QRU
    B. QSY
    C. QSL
    D. QRZ

T2B11 (B)
Answer: B. The Q signal used to indicate that you're changing frequency is QSY. This Q signal can also be used to request a shift to another frequency.

Under what circumstances should you consider communicating via simplex rather than a repeater?
    A. When the stations can communicate directly without using a repeater
    B. Only when you have an endorsement for simplex operation on your license
    C. Only when third party traffic is not being passed
    D. Only if you have simplex modulation capability

Copyright © Mometrix Media. You have been licensed one copy of this document for personal use only. Any other reproduction or redistribution is strictly prohibited. All rights reserved.

T2B12 (A)
Answer: A. If two stations can communicate directly via simplex, without the need for a repeater, they should do so.

Which of the following is true of the use of SSB phone in amateur bands above 50 MHz?
    A. It is permitted only by holders of a General Class or higher license
    B. It is permitted only on repeaters
    C. It is permitted in at least some portion of all the amateur bands above 50 MHz
    D. It is permitted only on when power is limited to no more than 100 watts

T2B13 (C)
Answer: C. SSB phone may be used in at least some portion of all amateur bands above 50 MHz.

T2C – Public Service: Emergency and Non-Emergency Operations; Applicability of FCC Rules; RACES and ARES; Net and Traffic Procedures; Emergency Restrictions

When do the FCC rules NOT apply to the operation of an amateur station?
    A. When operating a RACES station
    B. When operating under special FEMA rules
    C. When operating under special ARES rules
    D. Never, FCC rules always apply

T2C01 (D) [97.103(A)]
Answer: D. FCC rules always apply to the operation of an amateur station.

What is one way to recharge a 12-volt lead-acid station battery if the commercial power is out?
    A. Cool the battery in ice for several hours
    B. Add acid to the battery
    C. Connect the battery in parallel with a vehicle's battery and run the engine
    D. All of these choices are correct

T2C02 (C)
Answer: C. One way to recharge a 12-volt lead-acid station battery when the commercial power is out is to connect the battery in parallel with a vehicle's battery and run the engine.

What should be done to ensure that voice message traffic containing proper names and unusual words are copied correctly by the receiving station?
    A. The entire message should be repeated at least four times
    B. Such messages must be limited to no more than 10 words
    C. Such words and terms should be spelled out using a standard phonetic alphabet
    D. All of these choices are correct

T2C03 (C)
Answer: C. To ensure that any proper names and unusual words are copied correctly by the receiving station, it is good practice to spell them out using a standard phonetic alphabet.

Copyright © Mometrix Media. You have been licensed one copy of this document for personal use only. Any other reproduction or redistribution is strictly prohibited. All rights reserved.

What do RACES and ARES have in common?

    A. They represent the two largest ham clubs in the United States

    B. Both organizations broadcast road and weather information

    C. Neither may handle emergency traffic supporting public service agencies

    D. Both organizations may provide communications during emergencies

T2C04 (D)

Answer: D. RACES (Radio Amateur Civil Emergency Service) and ARES (Amateur Radio Emergency Service) both may provide communications during emergencies. RACES is managed by the Federal Emergency Management Agency. Both RACES and ARES are open to any amateur radio operator.

Which of the following describes the Radio Amateur Civil Emergency Service (RACES)?

    A. A radio service using amateur frequencies for emergency management or civil defense communications

    B. A radio service using amateur stations for emergency management or civil defense communications

    C. An emergency service using amateur operators certified by a civil defense organization as being enrolled in that organization

    D. All of these choices are correct

T2C05 (D) [97.3(A)(38), 97.407]

Answer: D. The Radio Amateur Civil Emergency Service (RACES) is a radio service involving certified amateur operators using amateur stations and frequencies for emergency management or civil defense communications.

Which of the following is an accepted practice to get the immediate attention of a net control station when reporting an emergency?

    A. Repeat the words SOS three times followed by the call sign of the reporting station

    B. Press the push-to-talk button three times

    C. Begin your transmission by saying "Priority" or "Emergency" followed by your call sign

    D. Play a pre-recorded emergency alert tone followed by your call sign

T2C06 (C)

Answer: C. To get the immediate attention of the net control station when reporting an emergency, it is common practice to begin your transmission with "Priority" or "Emergency" followed by your call sign.

What should you do to minimize disruptions to an emergency traffic net once you have checked in?

    A. Whenever the net frequency is quiet, announce your call sign and location

    B. Move 5 kHz away from the net's frequency and use high power to ask other hams to keep clear of the net frequency

    C. Do not transmit on the net frequency until asked to do so by the net control station

    D. Wait until the net frequency is quiet, then ask for any emergency traffic for your area

T2C07 (C)

Answer: C. To minimize disruptions to an emergency traffic net once you have checked in, do not transmit on the net frequency until asked to do so by the net control station.

Which of the following is a characteristic of good emergency traffic handling?

    A. Passing messages exactly as received

    B. Making decisions as to whether or not messages should be relayed or delivered

    C. Communicating messages to the news media for broadcast outside the disaster area

    D. All of these choices are correct

Copyright © Mometrix Media. You have been licensed one copy of this document for personal use only. Any other reproduction or redistribution is strictly prohibited. All rights reserved.

T2C08 (A)
Answer: A. The most important job of an amateur operator when handling emergency traffic messages is usually considered to be passing messages exactly as received.

Are amateur station control operators ever permitted to operate outside the frequency privileges of their license class?
    A. No
    B. Yes, but only when part of a FEMA emergency plan
    C. Yes, but only when part of a RACES emergency plan
    D. Yes, but only if necessary in situations involving the immediate safety of human life or protection of property

T2C09 (D)
Answer: D. Amateur station control operator are permitted to operate outside the frequency privileges of their license class only if necessary in situations involving the immediate safety of human life or protection of property

What is the preamble in a formal traffic message?
    A. The first paragraph of the message text
    B. The message number
    C. The priority handling indicator for the message
    D. The information needed to track the message as it passes through the amateur radio traffic handling system

T2C10 (D)
Answer: D. The preamble in a formal traffic message is information needed to track the message as it passes through the amateur radio traffic handling system. The preamble is the first part of a radiogram. It identifies the source and some basic information about the message.

What is meant by the term "check" in reference to a formal traffic message?
    A. The check is a count of the number of words or word equivalents in the text portion of the message
    B. The check is the value of a money order attached to the message
    C. The check is a list of stations that have relayed the message
    D. The check is a box on the message form that tells you the message was received

T2C11 (A)
Answer: A. The term "check" in reference to a formal traffic message is a count of the number of words or word equivalents in the text portion of the message. It is important to confirm the word count with the receiving station, as an incorrect word count will suggest to relaying stations that there is an error in the message.

What is the Amateur Radio Emergency Service (ARES)?
    A. Licensed amateurs who have voluntarily registered their qualifications and equipment for communications duty in the public service
    B. Licensed amateurs who are members of the military and who voluntarily agreed to provide message handling services in the case of an emergency
    C. A training program that provides licensing courses for those interested in obtaining an amateur license to use during emergencies
    D. A training program that certifies amateur operators for membership in the Radio Amateur Civil Emergency Service

Copyright © Mometrix Media. You have been licensed one copy of this document for personal use only. Any other reproduction or redistribution is strictly prohibited. All rights reserved.

T2C12 (A)
Answer: A. Amateur Radio Emergency Service (ARES) are licensed amateurs who have voluntarily registered their qualifications and equipment for communications duty in the public service

T3 – Radio Wave Characteristics

T3A – Radio Wave Characteristics: How a Radio Signal Travels; Fading; Multipath; Wavelength vs. Penetration; Antenna Orientation

What should you do if another operator reports that your station's 2 meter signals were strong just a moment ago, but now they are weak or distorted?
    A. Change the batteries in your radio to a different type
    B. Turn on the CTCSS tone
    C. Ask the other operator to adjust his squelch control
    D. Try moving a few feet or changing the direction of your antenna if possible, as reflections may be causing multi-path distortion

T3A01 (D)
Answer: D. If another operator reports that your station's 2 meter signals were strong just a moment ago, but now they are weak or distorted, try moving a few feet, as random reflections may be causing multipath distortion.

Why are UHF signals often more effective from inside buildings than VHF signals?
    A. VHF signals lose power faster over distance
    B. The shorter wavelength allows them to more easily penetrate the structure of buildings
    C. This is incorrect; VHF works better than UHF inside buildings
    D. UHF antennas are more efficient than VHF antennas

T3A02 (B)
Answer: B. UHF signals are often more effective from inside buildings than VHF signals because the shorter wavelength allows them to more easily penetrate the structure of buildings.

What antenna polarization is normally used for long-distance weak-signal CW and SSB contacts using the VHF and UHF bands?
    A. Right-hand circular
    B. Left-hand circular
    C. Horizontal
    D. Vertical

T3A03 (C)
Answer: C. A horizontal antenna polarization is normally used for long-distance weak-signal CW and SSB contacts using the VHF and UHF bands.

What can happen if the antennas at opposite ends of a VHF or UHF line of sight radio link are not using the same polarization?
    A. The modulation sidebands might become inverted
    B. Signals could be significantly weaker
    C. Signals have an echo effect on voices
    D. Nothing significant will happen

Copyright © Mometrix Media. You have been licensed one copy of this document for personal use only. Any other reproduction or redistribution is strictly prohibited. All rights reserved.

T3A04 (B)
Answer: B. If the antennas at opposite ends of a VHF or UHF line of sight radio link are not using the same polarization, the signals could be significantly weaker.

When using a directional antenna, how might your station be able to access a distant repeater if buildings or obstructions are blocking the direct line of sight path?
    A. Change from vertical to horizontal polarization
    B. Try to find a path that reflects signals to the repeater
    C. Try the long path
    D. Increase the antenna SWR

T3A05 (B)
Answer: B. When using a directional antenna, a station might be able to access a distant repeater if buildings or obstructions are blocking the direct line of sight path by trying to find a path that reflects signals to the repeater.

What term is commonly used to describe the rapid fluttering sound sometimes heard from mobile stations that are moving while transmitting?
    A. Flip-flopping
    B. Picket fencing
    C. Frequency shifting
    D. Pulsing

T3A06 (B)
Answer: B. Picket fencing is a term used to describe the rapid fluttering sound sometimes heard from mobile stations that are moving while transmitting.

What type of wave carries radio signals between transmitting and receiving stations?
    A. Electromagnetic
    B. Electrostatic
    C. Surface acoustic
    D. Magnetostrictive

T3A07 (A)
Answer: A. Electromagnetic waves carry radio signals between transmitting and receiving stations.

Which of the following is a likely cause of irregular fading of signals received by ionospheric reflection?
    A. Frequency shift due to Faraday rotation
    B. Interference from thunderstorms
    C. Random combining of signals arriving via different paths
    D. Intermodulation distortion

T3A08 (C)
Answer: C. The cause of irregular fading of signals from distant stations during times of generally good reception is the random combining of signals arriving via different path lengths.

Copyright © Mometrix Media. You have been licensed one copy of this document for personal use only. Any other reproduction or redistribution is strictly prohibited. All rights reserved.

Which of the following results from the fact that skip signals refracted from the ionosphere are elliptically polarized?
    A. Digital modes are unusable
    B. Either vertically or horizontally polarized antennas may be used for transmission or reception
    C. FM voice is unusable
    D. Both the transmitting and receiving antennas must be of the same polarization

T3A09 (B)
Answer: B. Because skip signals refracted from the ionosphere are elliptically polarized, either vertically or horizontally polarized antennas can be used to transmit and receive them.

What may occur if data signals propagate over multiple paths?
    A. Transmission rates can be increased by a factor equal to the number of separate paths observed
    B. Transmission rates must be decreased by a factor equal to the number of separate paths observed
    C. No significant changes will occur if the signals are transmitting using FM
    D. Error rates are likely to increase

T3A10 (D)
Answer: D. If the data signals propagate over multiple paths, error rates are likely to increase.

Which part of the atmosphere enables the propagation of radio signals around the world?
    A. The stratosphere
    B. The troposphere
    C. The ionosphere
    D. The magnetosphere

T3A11 (C)
Answer: C. The ionosphere is the part of the atmosphere that enables the propagation of radio signals around the world. The paths of waves reflecting off the ionosphere may be as long as 2000 miles. In the case of HF signals, the waves may bounce in between the surface of the Earth and the ionosphere several times before reaching their destination.

T3B – Radio and Electromagnetic Wave Properties: The Electromagnetic Spectrum; Wavelength vs. Frequency; Velocity of Electromagnetic Waves; Calculating Wavelength

What is the name for the distance a radio wave travels during one complete cycle?
    A. Wave speed
    B. Waveform
    C. Wavelength
    D. Wave spread

T3B01 (C)
Answer: C. Wavelength is the distance a radio wave travels during one complete cycle. Another way of putting it is that wavelength is the distance between successive crests or troughs.

What property of a radio wave is used to describe its polarization?
    A. The orientation of the electric field
    B. The orientation of the magnetic field
    C. The ratio of the energy in the magnetic field to the energy in the electric field
    D. The ratio of the velocity to the wavelength

Copyright © Mometrix Media. You have been licensed one copy of this document for personal use only. Any other reproduction or redistribution is strictly prohibited. All rights reserved.

T3B02 (A)
Answer: A. The orientation of a radio wave's electric field is used to describe its polarization.

What are the two components of a radio wave?
 A. AC and DC
 B. Voltage and current
 C. Electric and magnetic fields
 D. Ionizing and non-ionizing radiation

T3B03 (C)
Answer: C. The two components of a radio wave are electric and magnetic fields. This is because a radio wave is an electromagnetic wave.

How fast does a radio wave travel through free space?
 A. At the speed of light
 B. At the speed of sound
 C. Its speed is inversely proportional to its wavelength
 D. Its speed increases as the frequency increases

T3B04 (A)
Answer: A. A radio wave travels through free space at the speed of light. In a vacuum, the speed of light is roughly 300,000,000 km/s.

How does the wavelength of a radio wave relate to its frequency?
 A. The wavelength gets longer as the frequency increases
 B. The wavelength gets shorter as the frequency increases
 C. There is no relationship between wavelength and frequency
 D. The wavelength depends on the bandwidth of the signal

T3B05 (B)
Answer: B. The wavelength of a radio wave gets shorter as the frequency increases. That is, these two characteristics are inversely proportional. If the wavelength grows longer, the frequency will decrease.

What is the formula for converting frequency to approximate wavelength in meters?
 A. Wavelength in meters equals frequency in hertz multiplied by 300
 B. Wavelength in meters equals frequency in hertz divided by 300
 C. Wavelength in meters equals frequency in megahertz divided by 300
 D. Wavelength in meters equals 300 divided by frequency in megahertz

T3B06 (D)
Answer: D. The formula for converting frequency to wavelength in meters is 300 divided by frequency in megahertz.

What property of radio waves is often used to identify the different frequency bands?
 A. The approximate wavelength
 B. The magnetic intensity of waves
 C. The time it takes for waves to travel one mile
 D. The voltage standing wave ratio of waves

Copyright © Mometrix Media. You have been licensed one copy of this document for personal use only. Any other reproduction or redistribution is strictly prohibited. All rights reserved.

T3B07 (A)
Answer: A. The approximate wavelength of radio waves is often used to identify the different frequency bands.

What are the frequency limits of the VHF spectrum?
    A. 30 to 300 kHz
    B. 30 to 300 MHz
    C. 300 to 3000 kHz
    D. 300 to 3000 MHz

T3B08 (B)
Answer: B. The frequency limits of the VHF spectrum are 30 to 300 MHz.

What are the frequency limits of the UHF spectrum?
    A. 30 to 300 kHz
    B. 30 to 300 MHz
    C. 300 to 3000 kHz
    D. 300 to 3000 MHz

T3B09 (D)
Answer: D. The frequency limits of the UHF spectrum are 300 to 3000 MHz.

What frequency range is referred to as HF?
    A. 300 to 3000 MHz
    B. 30 to 300 MHz
    C. 3 to 30 MHz
    D. 300 to 3000 kHz

T3B10 (C)
Answer: C. The frequency range of 3 to 30 MHz is referred to as HF.

What is the approximate velocity of a radio wave as it travels through free space?
    A. 3000 kilometers per second
    B. 300,000,000 meters per second
    C. 300,000 miles per hour
    D. 186,000 miles per hour

T3B11 (B)
Answer: B. The approximate velocity of a radio wave as it travels through free space is 300,000,000 m/s.

T3C – Propagation Modes: Line of Sight; Sporadic E; Meteor and Auroral Scatter and Reflections; Tropospheric Ducting; F Layer Skip; Radio Horizon

Why are "direct" (not via a repeater) UHF signals rarely heard from stations outside your local coverage area?
    A. They are too weak to go very far
    B. FCC regulations prohibit them from going more than 50 miles
    C. UHF signals are usually not reflected by the ionosphere
    D. They collide with trees and shrubbery and fade out

Copyright © Mometrix Media. You have been licensed one copy of this document for personal use only. Any other reproduction or redistribution is strictly prohibited. All rights reserved.

T3C01 (C).
Answer: C. Direct (that is, not by means of a repeater) UHF signals are rarely heard from stations outside the local coverage area because UHF signals are usually not reflected by the ionosphere.

Which of the following might be happening when VHF signals are being received from long distances?
A. Signals are being reflected from outer space
B. Signals are arriving by sub-surface ducting
C. Signals are being reflected by lightning storms in your area
D. Signals are being refracted from a sporadic E layer

T3C02 (D)
Answer: D. When VHF signals are being received from long distances, the signals might be being refracted from a sporadic E layer. The sporadic E layer is a region of heavy ionization that occurs in various places throughout the E layer of the atmosphere. The ionization density, height, time, and penetration frequency of the sporadic E layer are inconsistent.

What is a characteristic of VHF signals received via auroral reflection?
A. Signals from distances of 10,000 or more miles are common
B. The signals exhibit rapid fluctuations of strength and often sound distorted
C. These types of signals occur only during winter nighttime hours
D. These types of signals are generally strongest when your antenna is aimed west

T3C03 (B)
Answer: B. A characteristic of VHF signals received via auroral reflection is that the signals exhibit rapid fluctuations of strength and often sound distorted.

Which of the following propagation types is most commonly associated with occasional strong over-the-horizon signals on the 10, 6, and 2 meter bands?
A. Backscatter
B. Sporadic E
C. D layer absorption
D. Gray-line propagation

T3C04 (B)
Answer: B. The sporadic E propagation type is most commonly associated with occasional strong over-the-horizon signals on the 10, 6, and 2 meter bands.

Which of the following effects might cause radio signals to be heard despite obstructions between the transmitting and receiving stations?
A. Knife-edge diffraction
B. Faraday rotation
C. Quantum tunneling
D. Doppler shift

T3C05 (A)
Answer: A. A knife-edge diffraction might cause radio signals to be heard despite obstructions between the transmitting and receiving systems.

Copyright © Mometrix Media. You have been licensed one copy of this document for personal use only. Any other reproduction or redistribution is strictly prohibited. All rights reserved.

What mode is responsible for allowing over-the-horizon VHF and UHF communications to ranges of approximately 300 miles on a regular basis?
A. Tropospheric scatter
B. D layer refraction
C. F2 layer refraction
D. Faraday rotation

T3C06 (A)
Answer: A. The tropospheric scatter mode is responsible for allowing over-the-horizon VHF and UHF communications to ranges of approximately 300 miles on a regular basis.

What band is best suited for communicating via meteor scatter?
A. 10 meters
B. 6 meters
C. 2 meters
D. 70 cm

T3C07 (B)
Answer: B. The 6 meter band is best suited to communicating via meteor scatter.

What causes tropospheric ducting?
A. Discharges of lightning during electrical storms
B. Sunspots and solar flares
C. Updrafts from hurricanes and tornadoes
D. Temperature inversions in the atmosphere

T3C08 (D)
Answer: D. Tropospheric ducting is caused by temperature inversions in the atmosphere. This is a type of very high frequency propagation that occurs when warm air passes over cold air.

What is generally the best time for long-distance 10 meter band propagation via the F layer?
A. From dawn to shortly after sunset during periods of high sunspot activity
B. From shortly after sunset to dawn during periods of high sunspot activity
C. From dawn to shortly after sunset during periods of low sunspot activity
D. From shortly after sunset to dawn during periods of low sunspot activity

T3C09 (A)
Answer: A. Long-distance 10 meter band propagation via the F layer is best conducted between dawn and shortly after sunset during periods of high sunspot activity.

What is the radio horizon?
A. The distance over which two stations can communicate direct path
B. The distance from the ground to a horizontally mounted antenna
C. The farthest point you can see when standing at the base of your antenna tower
D. The shortest distance between two points on the Earth's surface

T3C10 (A)
Answer: A. A radio horizon is the distance over which two stations can communicate direct path

Copyright © Mometrix Media. You have been licensed one copy of this document for personal use only. Any other reproduction or redistribution is strictly prohibited. All rights reserved.

Why do VHF and UHF radio signals usually travel somewhat farther than the visual line of sight distance between two stations?

A. Radio signals move somewhat faster than the speed of light
B. Radio waves are not blocked by dust particles
C. The Earth seems less curved to radio waves than to light
D. Radio waves are blocked by dust particles

T3C11 (C).
Answer: C. VHF and UHF radio signals usually travel somewhat farther than the visual line of sight distance between two stations because the Earth seems less curved to radio waves than to light.

Which of the following bands may provide long distance communications during the peak of the sunspot cycle?

A. Six or ten meters
B. 23 centimeters
C. 70 centimeters or 1.25 meters
D. All of these choices are correct

T3C12 (A)
Answer: A. During periods of high sunspot activity, the 6 meter and 10 meter bands may be used for long-distance communication.

T4 – Amateur Radio Practices and Station Set Up

T4A – Station Setup: Connecting Microphones; Reducing Unwanted Emissions; Power Source; Connecting a Computer; RF Grounding; Connecting Digital Equipment; Connecting an SWR Meter

Which of the following is true concerning the microphone connectors on amateur transceivers?

A. All transceivers use the same microphone connector type
B. Some connectors include push-to-talk and voltages for powering the microphone
C. All transceivers using the same connector type are wired identically
D. Un-keyed connectors allow any microphone to be connected

T4A01 (B)
Answer: B. Some microphone connectors on amateur transceivers include push-to-talk and voltages for powering the microphone.

How might a computer be used as part of an amateur radio station?

A. For logging contacts and contact information
B. For sending and/or receiving CW
C. For generating and decoding digital signals
D. All of these choices are correct

T4A02 (D)
Answer: D. Computers may be integrated into an amateur radio station for a variety of purposes, including logging contacts and contact information, sending/receiving CW, and generating and decoding signals.

Copyright © Mometrix Media. You have been licensed one copy of this document for personal use only. Any other reproduction or redistribution is strictly prohibited. All rights reserved.

Which is a good reason to use a regulated power supply for communications equipment?
  A. It prevents voltage fluctuations from reaching sensitive circuits
  B. A regulated power supply has FCC approval
  C. A fuse or circuit breaker regulates the power
  D. Power consumption is independent of load

T4A03 (A)
Answer: A. One good reason to use a regulated power supply for communications equipment is that it prevents voltage fluctuations from reaching sensitive circuits.

Where must a filter be installed to reduce harmonic emissions?
  A. Between the transmitter and the antenna
  B. Between the receiver and the transmitter
  C. At the station power supply
  D. At the microphone

T4A04 (A)
Answer: A. To reduce harmonic emissions, a filter must be installed between the transmitter and the antenna. Harmonics are those signals from a transmitter or oscillator that occur on whole-number multiples of the operating frequency in use.

Where should an in-line SWR meter be connected to monitor the standing wave ratio of the station antenna system?
  A. In series with the feed line, between the transmitter and antenna
  B. In series with the station's ground
  C. In parallel with the push-to-talk line and the antenna
  D. In series with the power supply cable, as close as possible to the radio

T4A05 (A)
Answer: A. To monitor the standing wave ratio of a station antenna system, an in-line SWR meter should be connected in series with the feed line, between the transmitter and antenna.

Which of the following would be connected between a transceiver and computer in a packet radio station?
  A. Transmatch
  B. Mixer
  C. Terminal node controller
  D. Antenna

T4A06 (C)
Answer: C. A terminal node controller would be connected between a transceiver and computer in a packet radio station. A terminal node controller consists of microprocessor, software, and a modem that converts baseband digital signals into audio tones.

How is a computer's sound card used when conducting digital communications using a computer?
  A. The sound card communicates between the computer CPU and the video display
  B. The sound card records the audio frequency for video display
  C. The sound card provides audio to the microphone input and converts received audio to digital form
  D. All of these choices are correct

- 36 -

Copyright © Mometrix Media. You have been licensed one copy of this document for personal use only. Any other reproduction or redistribution is strictly prohibited. All rights reserved.

T4A07 (C)
Answer: C. When conducting digital communications using a computer, the sound card provides audio to the microphone input and converts received audio to digital form.

Which type of conductor is best to use for RF grounding?
    A. Round stranded wire
    B. Round copper-clad steel wire
    C. Twisted-pair cable
    D. Flat strap

T4A08 (D)
Answer: D. A flat strap conductor is the best to use for RF grounding. Most ham radio systems have a special terminal for grounding. Copper strap is most often used for grounding.

Which of the following could you use to cure distorted audio caused by RF current flowing on the shield of a microphone cable?
    A. Band-pass filter
    B. Low-pass filter
    C. Preamplifier
    D. Ferrite choke

T4A09 (D)
Answer: D. A ferrite choke can be used to cure distorted audio caused by RF current flowing on the shield of a microphone cable.

What is the source of a high-pitched whine that varies with engine speed in a mobile transceiver's receive audio?
    A. The ignition system
    B. The alternator
    C. The electric fuel pump
    D. Anti-lock braking system controllers

T4A10 (B)
Answer: B. The alternator is the source of a high-pitched whine that varies with engine speed in a mobile transceiver's receive audio. An alternator is an electric generator that creates an alternating current.

Where should a mobile transceiver's power the negative return connection a mobile transceiver's power cable be connected?
    A. At the battery or engine block ground strap
    B. At the antenna mount
    C. To any metal part of the vehicle
    D. Through the transceiver's mounting bracket

T4A11 (A)
Answer: A. A mobile transceiver's power negative connection should be made at the battery or engine block ground strap.

Copyright © Mometrix Media. You have been licensed one copy of this document for personal use only. Any other reproduction or redistribution is strictly prohibited. All rights reserved.

What could be happening if another operator reports a variable high-pitched whine on the audio from your mobile transmitter?
>   A. Your microphone is picking up noise from an open window
>   B. You have the volume on your receiver set too high
>   C. You need to adjust your squelch control
>   D. Noise on the vehicle's electrical system is being transmitted along with your speech audio

T4A12 (D)
Answer: D. If another operator reports a variable high-pitched whine on the audio from your mobile transmitter, the most likely source of this whine is noise from your vehicle's electrical system being transmitted along with your speech audio.

T4B – Operating Controls: Tuning; Use of Filters; Squelch Function; AGC; Repeater Offset; Memory Channels

What may happen if a transmitter is operated with the microphone gain set too high?
>   A. The output power might be too high
>   B. The output signal might become distorted
>   C. The frequency might vary
>   D. The SWR might increase

T4B01 (B)
Answer: B. If a transmitter is operated with the microphone gain set too high, the output signal might become distorted.

Which of the following can be used to enter the operating frequency on a modern transceiver?
>   A. The keypad or VFO knob
>   B. The CTCSS or DTMF encoder
>   C. The Automatic Frequency Control
>   D. All of these choices are correct

T4B02 (A)
Answer: A. The keypad or the FO knob can be used to enter the operating frequency on a modern transceiver. A transceiver is a single unit that contains both a radio transmitter and receiver.

What is the purpose of the squelch control on a transceiver?
>   A. To set the highest level of volume desired
>   B. To set the transmitter power level
>   C. To adjust the automatic gain control
>   D. To mute receiver output noise when no signal is being received

T4B03 (D)
Answer: D. The purpose of the squelch control on a transceiver is to mute receiver output noise when no signal is being received. The squelch control makes interpersonal communications more comprehensible.

What is a way to enable quick access to a favorite frequency on your transceiver?
>   A. Enable the CTCSS tones
>   B. Store the frequency in a memory channel
>   C. Disable the CTCSS tones
>   D. Use the scan mode to select the desired frequency

Copyright © Mometrix Media. You have been licensed one copy of this document for personal use only. Any other reproduction or redistribution is strictly prohibited. All rights reserved.

T4B04 (B)
Answer: B. One way to enable quick access to a favorite frequency on your transceiver is to store the frequency in a memory channel.

Which of the following would reduce ignition interference to a receiver?
    A. Change frequency slightly
    B. Decrease the squelch setting
    C. Turn on the noise blanker
    D. Use the RIT control

T4B05 (C)
Answer: C. Turning on the noise blinker would reduce ignition interference to a receiver.

Which of the following controls could be used if the voice pitch of a single-sideband signal seems too high or low?
    A. The AGC or limiter
    B. The bandwidth selection
    C. The tone squelch
    D. The receiver RIT or clarifier

T4B06 (D)
Answer: D. The receiver RIT or clarifier controls could be used if the voice pitch of a single-sideband signal seems too high or low. Receiver incremental tuning allows the receiver to be tuned up to 3 kilohertz on either side of the transmitter frequency.

What does the term "RIT" mean?
    A. Receiver Input Tone
    B. Receiver Incremental Tuning
    C. Rectifier Inverter Test
    D. Remote Input Transmitter

T4B07 (B)
Answer: B. The term RIT means Receiver Incremental Tuning. This is a transceiver control that enables the frequency of the receiver to be changed a little bit without requiring the frequency of the transmitter to be changed. Receiver Incremental Tuning is sometimes called a clarifier control.

What is the advantage of having multiple receive bandwidth choices on a multimode transceiver?
    A. Permits monitoring several modes at once
    B. Permits noise or interference reduction by selecting a bandwidth matching the mode
    C. Increases the number of frequencies that can be stored in memory
    D. Increases the amount of offset between receive and transmit frequencies

T4B08 (B)
Answer: B. The advantage of having multiple receive bandwidth choices on a multimode transceiver is that it permits noise or interference reduction by selecting a bandwidth matching the mode. A multimode transceiver transmits a signal in which the electromagnetic wave is accompanied by a waveguide, which has a much larger cross-section than the electromagnetic wave.

Copyright © Mometrix Media. You have been licensed one copy of this document for personal use only. Any other reproduction or redistribution is strictly prohibited. All rights reserved.

Which of the following is an appropriate receive filter bandwidth to select in order to minimize noise and interference for SSB reception?
    A. 500 Hz
    B. 1000 Hz
    C. 2400 Hz
    D. 5000 Hz

T4B09 (C)
Answer: C. 2400 Hz is an appropriate receive filter for minimizing noise and interference for SSB reception.

Which of the following is an appropriate receive filter bandwidth to select in order to minimize noise and interference for CW reception?
    A. 500 Hz
    B. 1000 Hz
    C. 2400 Hz
    D. 5000 Hz

T4B10 (A)
Answer: A. 500 Hz is an appropriate receive filter to select in order to minimize noise and interference for CW reception.

Which of the following describes the common meaning of the term "repeater offset"?
    A. The distance between the repeater's transmit and receive antennas
    B. The time delay before the repeater timer resets
    C. The difference between the repeater's transmit and receive frequencies
    D. Matching the antenna impedance to the feed line impedance

T4B11 (C)
Answer: C. The common meaning of the term "repeater offset" is the difference between the repeater's transmit and receive frequencies.

What is the function of automatic gain control or AGC?
    A. To keep received audio relatively constant
    B. To protect an antenna from lightning
    C. To eliminate RF on the station cabling
    D. An asymmetric goniometer control used for antenna matching

T4B12 (A)
Answer: A. The function of automatic gain control is to keep the volume of the received audio relatively constant.

Copyright © Mometrix Media. You have been licensed one copy of this document for personal use only. Any other reproduction or redistribution is strictly prohibited. All rights reserved.

T5 – Electrical Principles

T5A – Electrical Principles, Units, and Terms: Current and Voltage; Conductors and Insulators; Alternating and Direct Current

Electrical current is measured in which of the following units?
A. Volts
B. Watts
C. Ohms
D. Amperes

T5A01 (D)
Answer: D. Electrical current is measured in amperes, usually referred to as amps. Current is the amount of electrons flowing through a circuit.

Electrical power is measured in which of the following units?
A. Volts
B. Watts
C. Ohms
D. Amperes

T5A02 (B)
Answer B. Electrical power is measured in watts. Electrical power is the rate at which electricity can be converted into other types of energy. It is calculated by multiplying the current and the voltage drop. A watt is equal to one joule per second.

What is the name for the flow of electrons in an electric circuit?
A. Voltage
B. Resistance
C. Capacitance
D. Current

T5A03 (D)
Answer: D. The flow of electrons in an electric circuit is the current. Current is measured in amperes, also known as amps.

What is the name for a current that flows only in one direction?
A. Alternating current
B. Direct current
C. Normal current
D. Smooth current

T5A04 (B)
Answer: B. A current that flows in only one direction is called a direct current. Modern technological advances have made it possible to transmit direct current over long distances, though it typically must be converted into alternating current before it reaches its final destination.

Copyright © Mometrix Media. You have been licensed one copy of this document for personal use only. Any other reproduction or redistribution is strictly prohibited. All rights reserved.

What is the electrical term for the electromotive force (EMF) that causes electron flow?
    A. Voltage
    B. Ampere-hours
    C. Capacitance
    D. Inductance

T5A05 (A)
Answer: A. The electrical term for the electromotive force (EMF) that causes electron flow is voltage. It is useful to think of voltage as the electrical equivalent of water pressure.

How much voltage does a mobile transceiver usually require?
    A. About 12 volts
    B. About 30 volts
    C. About 120 volts
    D. About 240 volts

T5A06 (A)
Answer: A. A mobile transceiver usually requires about 12 V.

Which of the following is a good electrical conductor?
    A. Glass
    B. Wood
    C. Copper
    D. Rubber

T5A07 (C)
Answer: C. Copper is a good electrical conductor.

Which of the following is a good electrical insulator?
    A. Copper
    B. Glass
    C. Aluminum
    D. Mercury

T5A08 (B)
Answer: B. Glass is a good electrical insulator.

What is the name for a current that reverses direction on a regular basis?
    A. Alternating current
    B. Direct current
    C. Circular current
    D. Vertical current

T5A09 (A)
Answer: A. A current that reverses direction on a regular basis is called alternating current. One of the main advantages of alternating current is that a transformer may be used to increase or decrease the voltage, which makes it easier to transmit the current over a long distance.

Copyright © Mometrix Media. You have been licensed one copy of this document for personal use only. Any other reproduction or redistribution is strictly prohibited. All rights reserved.

Which term describes the rate at which electrical energy is used?
  A. Resistance
  B. Current
  C. Power
  D. Voltage

T5A10 (C)
Answer: C. The rate at which electrical energy is used is power.

What is the basic unit of electromotive force?
  A. The volt
  B. The watt
  C. The ampere
  D. The ohm

T5A11 (A)
Answer: A. The basic unit of electromotive force is the volt.

What term describes the number of times per second that an alternating current reverses direction?
  A. Pulse rate
  B. Speed
  C. Wavelength
  D. Frequency

T5A12 (D)
Answer: D. With regard to alternating current (AC), frequency is the number of times per second that the current direction alternates, measured in hertz, or cycles per second.

T5B – Math for Electronics: Conversion of Electrical Units; Decibels; The Metric System

How many milliamperes is 1.5 amperes?
  A. 15 milliamperes
  B. 150 milliamperes
  C. 1,500 milliamperes
  D. 15,000 milliamperes

T5B01 (C)
Answer: C. 1.5 amperes is equivalent to 1500 mA. The prefix milli- means thousandth, so a milliampere is a thousandth of an ampere. Therefore, 1.5 amperes can be converted to milliamperes by multiplying by a thousand: 1.5 x 1000 = 1500.

What is another way to specify a radio signal frequency of 1,500,000 hertz?
  A. 1500 kHz
  B. 1500 MHz
  C. 15 GHz
  D. 150 kHz

Copyright © Mometrix Media. You have been licensed one copy of this document for personal use only. Any other reproduction or redistribution is strictly prohibited. All rights reserved.

T5B02 (A)
Answer: A. Another way to specify a radio signal frequency of 1,500,000 Hz is 1500 kHz. In the metric system, the prefix kilo- means thousand, so a kilohertz is equal to 1000 hertz. Therefore, 1,500,000 Hz can be converted to kHz by dividing by a thousand: 1,500,000/1000 = 1500 kHz.

How many volts are equal to one kilovolt?
    A. One one-thousandth of a volt
    B. One hundred volts
    C. One thousand volts
    D. One million volts

T5B03 (C)
Answer: C. 1000 V is equal to 1 kV. The metric prefix kilo- means thousand, so a thousand volts is the same as one kilovolt. Therefore, V can be converted to kV by dividing by a thousand: 1000/1000 = 1.

How many volts are equal to one microvolt?
    A. One one-millionth of a volt
    B. One million volts
    C. One thousand kilovolts
    D. One one-thousandth of a volt

T5B04 (A)
Answer: A. 1/1,000,000 of a volt is equal to 1 µV. The metric prefix micro- means millionth, so 1,000,000 microvolts is equal to one volt. Volts can be converted to microvolts by dividing by a million: 1/1,000,000 = 1 µV.

Which of the following is equivalent to 500 milliwatts?
    A. 0.02 watts
    B. 0.5 watts
    C. 5 watts
    D. 50 watts

T5B05 (B)
Answer: B. 0.5 W is equivalent to 500 mW. The metric prefix milli- means thousandth, so 1000 mW is the same as 1 W. This conversion can be accomplished by multiplying by a thousand: 0.5 x 1000 = 500.

If an ammeter calibrated in amperes is used to measure a 3000-milliampere current, what reading would it show?
    A. 0.003 amperes
    B. 0.3 amperes
    C. 3 amperes
    D. 3,000,000 amperes

T5B06 (C)
Answer: C. If an ammeter calibrated in amperes is used to measure a 3000-milliampere current, it would show a reading of 3 amperes. The metric prefix milli- means thousandth, so milliamperes can be converted to amperes by multiplying by a thousand. An ammeter is an instrument used to measure electric current.

Copyright © Mometrix Media. You have been licensed one copy of this document for personal use only. Any other reproduction or redistribution is strictly prohibited. All rights reserved.

If a frequency readout calibrated in megahertz shows a reading of 3.525 MHz, what would it show if it were calibrated in kilohertz?
  A. 0.003525 kHz
  B. 35.25 kHz
  C. 3525 kHz
  D. 3,525,000 kHz

T5B07 (C)
Answer: C. If a frequency readout calibrated in megahertz shows a reading of 3.525 MHz, it would show 3525 kilohertz if it were calibrated in kilohertz. The metric prefix mega- means millions, and the prefix kilo- means thousands. Millions are the same as 106, while thousands are equal to 103. Megahertz can be converted into kilohertz, then, by multiplying by 103, or a thousand: 3.525 MHz x 1000 = 3525.

How many microfarads are 1,000,000 picofarads?
  A. 0.001 microfarads
  B. 1 microfarad
  C. 1000 microfarads
  D. 1,000,000,000 microfarads

T5B08 (B)
Answer: B. 1,000,000 picofarads is equivalent to 1 microfarad. The metric prefix pico- means trillionths (10-12), while the prefix micro-means millionths (10-6). Picofarads can be converted to microfarads, then, by dividing by 106, or one million: 1,000,000/1,000,000 = 1.

What is the approximate amount of change, measured in decibels (dB), of a power increase from 5 watts to 10 watts?
  A. 2 dB
  B. 3 dB
  C. 5 dB
  D. 10 dB

T5B09 (B)
Answer: B. A power increase from 5 to 10 watts creates approximately 3 dB of change. The relationship between power increases and changes in decibel levels is complex. Whenever the power is doubled, however, the decibel level will rise by three. If the power is quadrupled, the decibel level rises by 6. If the power increases by ten times, the decibel level also rises by ten.

What is the approximate amount of change, measured in decibels (dB), of a power decrease from 12 watts to 3 watts?
  A. 1 dB
  B. 3 dB
  C. 6 dB
  D. 9 dB

T5B10 (C)
Answer: C. A power decrease from 12 watts to 3 watts would result in approximately 6 dB of change. Just as a quadrupling of power would result in an extra 6 dB, so will a quartering of power cause the decibel level to drop by 6.

Copyright © Mometrix Media. You have been licensed one copy of this document for personal use only. Any other reproduction or redistribution is strictly prohibited. All rights reserved.

What is the approximate amount of change, measured in decibels (dB), of a power increase from 20 watts to 200 watts?
    A. 10 dB
    B. 12 dB
    C. 18 dB
    D. 28 dB

T5B11 (A)
Answer: A. A power increase from 20 W to 200 W would result in approximately 10 dB of change. When the power increases by ten times, the result is 10 dB of change.

Which of the following frequencies is equal to 28,400 kHz?
    A. 28.400 MHz
    B. 2.800 MHz
    C. 284.00 MHz
    D. 28.400 kHz

T5B12 (A)
Answer: A. One megahertz (MHz) is equivalent to one thousand kilohertz (kHz), so to convert a frequency from kilohertz to megahertz, divide the kilohertz number by one thousand.

If a frequency readout shows a reading of 2425 MHz, what frequency is that in GHz?
    A. 0.002425 GHZ
    B. 24.25 GHz
    C. 2.425 GHz
    D. 2425 GHz

T5B13 (C)
Answer: C. One gigahertz (GHz) is equivalent to one thousand megahertz (MHz), so to convert a frequency from megahertz to gigahertz, divide the megahertz number by one thousand.

T5C – Electronic Principles: Capacitance; Inductance; Current Flow in Circuits; Alternating Current; Definition of RF; DC Power Calculations; Impedance

What is the ability to store energy in an electric field called?
    A. Inductance
    B. Resistance
    C. Tolerance
    D. Capacitance

T5C01 (D)
Answer: D. The ability to store energy in an electric field is called capacitance. Capacitance can also be defined as the ratio of the electric charge that is shifted from one conductor to another to the resulting potential difference between them.

What is the basic unit of capacitance?
    A. The farad
    B. The ohm
    C. The volt
    D. The henry

Copyright © Mometrix Media. You have been licensed one copy of this document for personal use only. Any other reproduction or redistribution is strictly prohibited. All rights reserved.

T5C02 (A)
Answer: A. The basic unit of capacitance is the farad. One farad is equal to the capacitance of a capacitor that has an equal and opposite charge of 1 coulomb on each of its plates, and 1 V of potential difference between those plates.

What is the ability to store energy in a magnetic field called?
    A. Admittance
    B. Capacitance
    C. Resistance
    D. Inductance

T5C03 (D)
Answer: D. The ability to store energy in a magnetic field is called inductance. Inductance can also be defined as the characteristic of an electric circuit that enables electromagnetic force to be created in it through a varying magnetic flux.

What is the basic unit of inductance?
    A. The coulomb
    B. The farad
    C. The henry
    D. The ohm

T5C04 (C)
Answer: C. The basic unit of inductance is the henry.

What is the unit of frequency?
    A. Hertz
    B. Henry
    C. Farad
    D. Tesla

T5C05 (A)
Answer: A. The basic unit of frequency is the hertz. One hertz is an alternating-current frequency of one cycle per second.

What does the abbreviation "RF" refer to?
    A. Radio frequency signals of all types
    B. The resonant frequency of a tuned circuit
    C. The real frequency transmitted as opposed to the apparent frequency
    D. Reflective force in antenna transmission lines

T5C06 (A)
Answer: A. The abbreviation RF can be used to refer to radio frequency signals of all kinds.

What is a usual name for electromagnetic waves that travel through space?
    A. Gravity waves
    B. Sound waves
    C. Radio waves
    D. Pressure waves

T5C07 (C)
Answer: C. The usual name for electromagnetic waves that travel through space is radio waves.

Copyright © Mometrix Media. You have been licensed one copy of this document for personal use only. Any other reproduction or redistribution is strictly prohibited. All rights reserved.

What is the formula used to calculate electrical power in a DC circuit?
    A. Power (P) equals voltage (E) multiplied by current (I)
    B. Power (P) equals voltage (E) divided by current (I)
    C. Power (P) equals voltage (E) minus current (I)
    D. Power (P) equals voltage (E) plus current (I)

T5C08 (A)
Answer: A. The formula used to calculate electrical power in a DC circuit is power equals voltage multiplied by current.

How much power is being used in a circuit when the applied voltage is 13.8 volts DC and the current is 10 amperes?
    A. 138 watts
    B. 0.7 watts
    C. 23.8 watts
    D. 3.8 watts

T5C09 (A)
Answer: A. When the applied voltage is 13.8 volts DC and the current is 10 amperes, 138 watts of power is being used in the circuit. The power can be calculated by multiplying the voltage by the current: 13.8 x 10 = 138.

How much power is being used in a circuit when the applied voltage is 12 volts DC and the current is 2.5 amperes?
    A. 4.8 watts
    B. 30 watts
    C. 14.5 watts
    D. 0.208 watts

T5C10 (B)
Answer: B. When the applied voltage is 12 volts DC and the current is 2.5 amperes, 30 watts of power are being used in the circuit. The power can be calculated by multiplying the voltage by the current: 12 x 2.5 = 30.

How many amperes are flowing in a circuit when the applied voltage is 12 volts DC and the load is 120 watts?
    A. 0.1 amperes
    B. 10 amperes
    C. 12 amperes
    D. 132 amperes

T5C11 (B)
Answer: B. When the applied voltage is 12 volts DC and the load is 120 watts, 10 amperes are flowing in a circuit. The current can be calculated by dividing the load by the applied voltage: 120/12 = 10.

What is meant by the term impedance?
    A. It is a measure of the opposition to AC current flow in a circuit
    B. It is the inverse of resistance
    C. It is a measure of the Q or Quality Factor of a component
    D. It is a measure of the power handling capability of a component

Copyright © Mometrix Media. You have been licensed one copy of this document for personal use only. Any other reproduction or redistribution is strictly prohibited. All rights reserved.

T5C12 (A)
Answer: A. Impedance is a measure of the opposition to AC current flow in a circuit. It is analogous to resistance in a DC circuit.

What are the units of impedance?
  A. Volts
  B. Amperes
  C. Coulombs
  D. Ohms

T5C13 (D)
Answer: D. Impedance, like resistance, is measured in ohms (Ω).

T5D – Ohm's Law: Formulas and Usage

What formula is used to calculate current in a circuit?
  A. Current (I) equals voltage (E) multiplied by resistance (R)
  B. Current (I) equals voltage (E) divided by resistance (R)
  C. Current (I) equals voltage (E) added to resistance (R)
  D. Current (I) equals voltage (E) minus resistance (R)

T5D01 (B)
Answer: B. The formula for calculating current in a circuit is current equals voltage divided by resistance.

What formula is used to calculate voltage in a circuit?
  A. Voltage (E) equals current (I) multiplied by resistance (R)
  B. Voltage (E) equals current (I) divided by resistance (R)
  C. Voltage (E) equals current (I) added to resistance (R)
  D. Voltage (E) equals current (I) minus resistance (R)

T5D02 (A)
Answer: A. The formula for calculating voltage in a circuit is voltage equals current multiplied by resistance.

What formula is used to calculate resistance in a circuit?
  A. Resistance (R) equals voltage (E) multiplied by current (I)
  B. Resistance (R) equals voltage (E) divided by current (I)
  C. Resistance (R) equals voltage (E) added to current (I)
  D. Resistance (R) equals voltage (E) minus current (I)

T5D03 (B)
Answer: B. The formula for calculating resistance in a circuit is resistance (R) equals voltage (E) divided by current (I). Resistance is the opposition to the passage of current, the result of which is the conversion of electrical energy into heat or another type of energy.

Copyright © Mometrix Media. You have been licensed one copy of this document for personal use only. Any other reproduction or redistribution is strictly prohibited. All rights reserved.

What is the resistance of a circuit in which a current of 3 amperes flows through a resistor connected to 90 volts?

    A. 3 ohms

    B. 30 ohms

    C. 93 ohms

    D. 270 ohms

T5D04 (B)

Answer: B. The resistance of a circuit in which a current of 3 amperes flows through a resistor connected to 90 volts is 30 ohms. Resistance is calculated by dividing voltage by current. In this case, then, the resistance is found 90/3 = 30.

What is the resistance in a circuit for which the applied voltage is 12 volts and the current flow is 1.5 amperes?

    A. 18 ohms

    B. 0.125 ohms

    C. 8 ohms

    D. 13.5 ohms

T5D05 (C)

Answer: C. Resistance in a circuit for which the applied voltage is 12 volts and the current flow is 1.5 amperes is 8 ohms. Resistance is calculated by dividing voltage by current, so in this case the problem is solved 12/8 = 1.5.

What is the resistance of a circuit that draws 4 amperes from a 12-volt source?

    A. 3 ohms

    B. 16 ohms

    C. 48 ohms

    D. 8 Ohms

T5D06 (A)

Answer: A. The resistance of a circuit that draws 4 amperes from a 12-volt source is 3 ohms. Resistance is calculated by dividing voltage by current: 12/4 = 3.

What is the current flow in a circuit with an applied voltage of 120 volts and a resistance of 80 ohms?

    A. 9600 amperes

    B. 200 amperes

    C. 0.667 amperes

    D. 1.5 amperes

T5D07 (D)

Answer: D. The current flow in a circuit with an applied voltage of 120 V and a resistance of 80 ohms is 1.5 amperes. The current flow can be found by dividing the voltage by the resistance: 120/80 = 1.5.

What is the current flowing through a 100-ohm resistor connected across 200 volts?

    A. 20,000 amperes

    B. 0.5 amperes

    C. 2 amperes

    D. 100 amperes

Copyright © Mometrix Media. You have been licensed one copy of this document for personal use only. Any other reproduction or redistribution is strictly prohibited. All rights reserved.

T5D08 (C)
Answer: C. The current flowing through a 100-ohm resistor connected across 200 volts is 2 amperes. The current is found by dividing the voltage by the resistance: 200/100 = 2.

What is the current flowing through a 24-ohm resistor connected across 240 volts?
    A. 24,000 amperes
    B. 0.1 amperes
    C. 10 amperes
    D. 216 amperes

T5D09 (C)
Answer: C. The current flowing through a 24-ohm resistor connected across 240 volts is 10 amperes. The current is found by dividing the voltage by the resistance: 240/24 = 10.

What is the voltage across a 2-ohm resistor if a current of 0.5 amperes flows through it?
    A. 1 volt
    B. 0.25 volts
    C. 2.5 volts
    D. 1.5 volts

T5D10 (A)
Answer: A. The voltage across a 2-ohm resistor if a current of 0.5 amperes flows through it is 1 volt. The voltage can be calculated by multiplying the current by the resistance: 2 x 0.5 = 1.

What is the voltage across a 10-ohm resistor if a current of 1 ampere flows through it?
    A. 1 volt
    B. 10 volts
    C. 11 volts
    D. 9 volts

T5D11 (B)
Answer: B. The voltage across a 10-ohm resistor if a current of 1 ampere flows through it is 10 volts. The voltage can be calculated by multiplying the current by the resistance: 10 x 1 = 10.

What is the voltage across a 10-ohm resistor if a current of 2 amperes flows through it?
    A. 8 volts
    B. 0.2 volts
    C. 12 volts
    D. 20 volts

T5D12 (D)
Answer: D. The voltage across a 10-ohm resistor if a current of 2 amperes flows through it is 20 volts. The voltage can be calculated by multiplying the current by the resistance: 10 x 2 = 20.

Copyright © Mometrix Media. You have been licensed one copy of this document for personal use only. Any other reproduction or redistribution is strictly prohibited. All rights reserved.

T6 – Electrical Components

T6A – Electrical Components: Fixed and Variable Resistors; Capacitors and Inductors; Fuses; Switches; Batteries

What electrical component is used to oppose the flow of current in a DC circuit?
    A. Inductor
    B. Resistor
    C. Voltmeter
    D. Transformer

T6A01 (B)
Answer: B. The electrical component used to oppose the flow of current in a DC circuit is a resistor. For ham radio technicians, the most commonly required resistors are quarter- and half-watt fixed value resistors and 100, 500, 1k, 5k, 10k, and 100k ohm variable resistors.

What type of component is often used as an adjustable volume control?
    A. Fixed resistor
    B. Power resistor
    C. Potentiometer
    D. Transformer

T6A02 (C)
Answer: C. A potentiometer is often used as an adjustable volume control. A potentiometer is an instrument that measures an unknown voltage by comparing it to a standard voltage.

What electrical parameter is controlled by a potentiometer?
    A. Inductance
    B. Resistance
    C. Capacitance
    D. Field strength

T6A03 (B)
Answer: B. Resistance is controlled by a potentiometer. A potentiometer will typically have a resistance element connected to the circuit with three terminals. Two of these are attached to the two input voltage conductors of the circuit, and the third is connected to the circuit output. The third terminal is typically able to move across the resistance element, which enables the magnitude of the input voltage to be adjusted.

What electrical component stores energy in an electric field?
    A. Resistor
    B. Capacitor
    C. Inductor
    D. Diode

T6A04 (B)
Answer: B. The capacitor is the electrical component that stores energy in an electric field. Typically, a capacitor is composed of two metallic plates that are separated and insulated from one another by a dielectric.

Copyright © Mometrix Media. You have been licensed one copy of this document for personal use only. Any other reproduction or redistribution is strictly prohibited. All rights reserved.

What type of electrical component consists of two or more conductive surfaces separated by an insulator?
   A. Resistor
   B. Potentiometer
   C. Oscillator
   D. Capacitor

T6A05 (D)
Answer: D. A capacitor consists of two or more conductive surfaces separated by an insulator.

What type of electrical component stores energy in a magnetic field?
   A. Resistor
   B. Capacitor
   C. Inductor
   D. Diode

T6A06 (C)
Answer: C. An inductor stores energy in a magnetic field. Inductors are typically composed of at least one wire loop. An inductor may be fixed, adjustable, or variable, depending on whether the number of loops is able to be manipulated.

What electrical component is usually composed of a coil of wire?
   A. Switch
   B. Capacitor
   C. Diode
   D. Inductor

T6A07 (D)
Answer: D. An inductor is usually composed of a coil of wire.

What electrical component is used to connect or disconnect electrical circuits?
   A. Magnetron
   B. Switch
   C. Thermistor
   D. All of these choices are correct

T6A08 (B)
Answer: B. A switch is used to connect or disconnect electrical circuits.

What electrical component is used to protect other circuit components from current overloads?
   A. Fuse
   B. Capacitor
   C. Inductor
   D. All of these choices are correct

T6A09 (A)
Answer: A. A fuse is used to protect other circuit components from current overloads. It contains a metal element that will melt when the current exceeds a certain amperage. When the element melts, the circuit is broken.

Copyright © Mometrix Media. You have been licensed one copy of this document for personal use only. Any other reproduction or redistribution is strictly prohibited. All rights reserved.

Which of the following battery types is rechargeable?
    A. Nickel-metal hydride
    B. Lithium-ion
    C. Lead-acid gel-cell
    D. All of these choices are correct

T6A10 (D)
Answer: D. There are many different types of batteries that may be recharged, including nickel-metal hydride (NiMH), lithium-ion (Li-ion), and lead-acid gel cells.

Which of the following battery types is not rechargeable?
    A. Nickel-cadmium
    B. Carbon-zinc
    C. Lead-acid
    D. Lithium-ion

T6A11 (B)
Answer: B. The carbon-zinc battery is not rechargeable.

T6B – Semiconductors: Basic Principles and Applications of Solid State Devices; Diodes and Transistors

What class of electronic components is capable of using a voltage or current signal to control current flow?
    A. Capacitors
    B. Inductors
    C. Resistors
    D. Transistors

T6B01 (D)
Answer: D. Transistors are capable of using a voltage or current signal to control current flow. A transistor is an electronic device that includes a semiconductor and at least three electrical outlets. It may be used as a detector, amplifier, or switch.

What electronic component allows current to flow in only one direction?
    A. Resistor
    B. Fuse
    C. Diode
    D. Driven Element

T6B02 (C)
Answer: C. A diode allows current to flow in only one direction. A diode is an electronic device that includes two electrodes, an anode and a cathode. These devices are used to convert an alternating current into a direct current.

Which of these components can be used as an electronic switch or amplifier?
    A. Oscillator
    B. Potentiometer
    C. Transistor
    D. Voltmeter

Copyright © Mometrix Media. You have been licensed one copy of this document for personal use only. Any other reproduction or redistribution is strictly prohibited. All rights reserved.

T6B03 (C)
Answer: C. A transistor can be used as an electronic switch or amplifier. It may also be used as a detector.

Which of the following components can be made of three layers of semiconductor material?
    A. Alternator
    B. Transistor
    C. Triode
    D. Pentagrid converter

T6B04 (B)
Answer: B. A transistor is made of three layers of semiconductor material.

Which of the following electronic components can amplify signals?
    A. Transistor
    B. Variable resistor
    C. Electrolytic capacitor
    D. Multi-cell battery

T6B05 (A)
Answer: A. A transistor can amplify signals.

How is the cathode lead of a semiconductor diode usually identified?
    A. With the word "cathode"
    B. With a stripe
    C. With the letter "C"
    D. All of these choices are correct

T6B06 (B)
Answer: B. A semiconductor diode's cathode lead is usually identified with a stripe.

What does the abbreviation "LED" stand for?
    A. Low Emission Diode
    B. Light Emitting Diode
    C. Liquid Emission Detector
    D. Long Echo Delay

T6B07 (B)
Answer: B. The abbreviation LED stands for Light Emitting Diode. A LED is a semiconductor diode that, when a current passes through it, produces infrared or visible light. Each diode is only capable of producing a single primary color, though diodes may be combined to produce any color.

What does the abbreviation "FET" stand for?
    A. Field Effect Transistor
    B. Fast Electron Transistor
    C. Free Electron Transition
    D. Field Emission Thickness

T6B08 (A)
Answer: A. The abbreviation FET stands for Field Effect Transistor. In a field effect transistor, output current is controlled by a variable electric field.

Copyright © Mometrix Media. You have been licensed one copy of this document for personal use only. Any other reproduction or redistribution is strictly prohibited. All rights reserved.

What are the names of the two electrodes of a diode?
    A. Plus and minus
    B. Source and drain
    C. Anode and cathode
    D. Gate and base

T6B09 (C)
Answer: C. The names of the two electrodes of a diode are the anode and cathode. Electrons leave a system through the anode and return through the cathode.

What are the three electrodes of a PNP or NPN transistor?
    A. Emitter, base, and collector
    B. Source, gate, and drain
    C. Cathode, grid, and plate
    D. Cathode, drift cavity, and collector

T6B10 (A)
Answer: A. The three electrodes or terminals of a PNP or NPN transistor are the emitter, base, and collector.

What are the three electrodes of a field effect transistor?
    A. Emitter, base, and collector
    B. Source, gate, and drain
    C. Cathode, grid, and plate
    D. Cathode, gate, and anode

T6B11 (B)
Answer: B. The three electrodes or terminals of a field effect transistor are the source, gate, and drain.

What is the term that describes a transistor's ability to amplify a signal?
    A. Gain
    B. Forward resistance
    C. Forward voltage drop
    D. On resistance

T6B12 (A)
Answer: A. A transistor's ability to amplify the signal is referred to as its gain. Gain is typically expressed as the ratio of output to input.

T6C – Circuit Diagrams; Schematic Symbols

What is the name for standardized representations of components in an electrical wiring diagram?
    A. Electrical depictions
    B. Grey sketch
    C. Schematic symbols
    D. Component callouts

T6C01 (C)
Answer: C. Standardized representations of components in an electrical wiring diagram are known as schematic symbols.

Copyright © Mometrix Media. You have been licensed one copy of this document for personal use only. Any other reproduction or redistribution is strictly prohibited. All rights reserved.

What is component 1 in figure T1?
(figures found at the end of the guide)
    A. Resistor
    B. Transistor
    C. Battery
    D. Connector

T6C02 (A)
Answer: A. In figure T1, component 1 is a resistor.

What is component 2 in figure T1?
(figures found at the end of the guide)
    A. Resistor
    B. Transistor
    C. Indicator lamp
    D. Connector

T6C03 (B)
Answer: B. In figure T1, component 2 is a transistor.

What is component 3 in figure T1?
(figures found at the end of the guide)
    A. Resistor
    B. Transistor
    C. Lamp
    D. Ground symbol

T6C04 (C)
Answer: C. In figure T1, component 3 is a lamp.

What is component 4 in figure T1?
(figures found at the end of the guide)
    A. Resistor
    B. Transistor
    C. Battery
    D. Ground symbol

T6C05 (C)
Answer: C. In figure T1, component 4 is a battery.

What is component 6 in figure T2?
(figures found at the end of the guide)

    A. Resistor
    B. Capacitor
    C. Regulator IC
    D. Transistor

T6C06 (B)
Answer: B. In figure T2, component 6 is a capacitor.

Copyright © Mometrix Media. You have been licensed one copy of this document for personal use only. Any other reproduction or redistribution is strictly prohibited. All rights reserved.

What is component 8 in figure T2?
(figures found at the end of the guide)
    A. Resistor
    B. Inductor
    C. Regulator IC
    D. Light emitting diode

T6C07 (D)
Answer: D. In figure T2, component 8 is a light emitting diode.

What is component 9 in figure T2?
(figures found at the end of the guide)
    A. Variable capacitor
    B. Variable inductor
    C. Variable resistor
    D. Variable transformer

T6C08 (C)
Answer: C. In figure T2, component 9 is a variable resistor.

What is component 4 in figure T2?
(figures found at the end of the guide)
    A. Variable inductor
    B. Double-pole switch
    C. Potentiometer
    D. Transformer

T6C09 (D)
Answer: D. In figure T2, component 4 is a transformer.

What is component 3 in figure T3?
(figures found at the end of the guide)
    A. Connector
    B. Meter
    C. Variable capacitor
    D. Variable inductor

T6C10 (D)
Answer: D. In figure T3, component 3 is a variable inductor.

What is component 4 in figure T3?
(figures found at the end of the guide)
    A. Antenna
    B. Transmitter
    C. Dummy load
    D. Ground

T6C11 (A)
Answer: A. In figure T3, component 4 is for grounding.

Copyright © Mometrix Media. You have been licensed one copy of this document for personal use only. Any other reproduction or redistribution is strictly prohibited. All rights reserved.

What do the symbols on an electrical circuit schematic diagram represent?
  A. Electrical components
  B. Logic states
  C. Digital codes
  D. Traffic nodes

T6C12 (A)
Answer: A. The symbols on an electrical circuit schematic diagram represent electrical components. Moreover, the symbols have been standardized so that they can be easily understood around the world.

Which of the following is accurately represented in electrical circuit schematic diagrams?
  A. Wire lengths
  B. Physical appearance of components
  C. The way components are interconnected
  D. All of these choices are correct

T6C13 (C)
Answer: C. In electrical circuit schematic diagrams, the interconnections of components are accurately represented. The sizes in relative distances of the components, however, may not be to scale.

T6D – Component Functions: Rectification; Switches; Indicators; Power Supply Components; Resonant Circuit; Shielding; Power Transformers; Integrated Circuits

Which of the following devices or circuits changes an alternating current into a varying direct current signal?
  A. Transformer
  B. Rectifier
  C. Amplifier
  D. Reflector

T6D01 (B)
Answer: B. A rectifier changes an alternating current into a varying direct current signal. Specifically, it is a switch that blocks the current in one direction but permits it in the other.

What best describes a relay?
  A. A switch controlled by an electromagnet
  B. A current controlled amplifier
  C. An optical sensor
  D. A pass transistor

T6D02 (A)
Answer: A. A relay may best be described as a switch controlled by an electromagnet. When the device senses a miniscule voltage or current change, it activates a switch or another component in the electric circuit.

What type of switch is represented by component 3 in figure T2?
(figures found at the end of the guide)
  A. Single-pole single-throw
  B. Single-pole double-throw
  C. Double-pole single-throw
  D. Double-pole double-throw

- 59 -

Copyright © Mometrix Media. You have been licensed one copy of this document for personal use only. Any other reproduction or redistribution is strictly prohibited. All rights reserved.

T6D03 (A)
Answer: A. In figure T2, component 3 represents a single-pole, single-throw switch.

Which of the following can be used to display signal strength on a numeric scale?
    A. Potentiometer
    B. Transistor
    C. Meter
    D. Relay

T6D04 (C)
Answer: C. A meter is the best tool for displaying signal strength on a numeric scale.

What type of circuit controls the amount of voltage from a power supply?
    A. Regulator
    B. Oscillator
    C. Filter
    D. Phase inverter

T6D05 (A)
Answer: A. A regulator circuit controls the amount of voltage from a power supply.

What component is commonly used to change 120V AC house current to a lower AC voltage for other uses?
    A. Variable capacitor
    B. Transformer
    C. Transistor
    D. Diode

T6D06 (B)
Answer: B. A transformer is commonly used to change 120V AC house current to a lower AC voltage for other uses.

Which of the following is commonly used as a visual indicator?
    A. LED
    B. FET
    C. Zener diode
    D. Bipolar transistor

T6D07 (A)
Answer: A. LED is commonly used as a visual indicator.

Which of the following is used together with an inductor to make a tuned circuit?
    A. Resistor
    B. Zener diode
    C. Potentiometer
    D. Capacitor

T6D08 (D)
Answer: D. A capacitor is used along with an inductor to make a tuned circuit.

Copyright © Mometrix Media. You have been licensed one copy of this document for personal use only. Any other reproduction or redistribution is strictly prohibited. All rights reserved.

What is the name of a device that combines several semiconductors and other components into one package?
A. Transducer
B. Multi-pole relay
C. Integrated circuit
D. Transformer

T6D09 (C)
Answer: C. An integrated circuit combines several semiconductors and other components into one package. All of these semiconductors and other components are either imprinted or etched on a thin slice of a semiconducting material, as for instance silicon.

What is the function of component 2 in Figure T1?
(figures found at the end of the guide)
A. Give off light when current flows through it
B. Supply electrical energy
C. Control the flow of current
D. Convert electrical energy into radio waves

T6D10 (C)
Answer: C. In figure T1, the function of component 2 is to control the flow of current.

What is a simple resonant or tuned circuit?
A. An inductor and a capacitor connected in series or parallel to form a filter
B. A type of voltage regulator
C. A resistor circuit used for reducing standing wave ratio
D. A circuit designed to provide high fidelity audio

T6D11 (A)
Answer: A. A simple resonant or tuned circuit is a circuit containing an inductor and a capacitor, connected either in series or in parallel, which functions to filter out certain frequencies.

Which of the following is a common reason to use shielded wire?
A. To decrease the resistance of DC power connections
B. To increase the current carrying capability of the wire
C. To prevent coupling of unwanted signals to or from the wire
D. To couple the wire to other signals

T6D12 (C)
Answer: C. Shielding or insulating wires prevents the signal being carried by the wire from bleeding into other signals.

Copyright © Mometrix Media. You have been licensed one copy of this document for personal use only. Any other reproduction or redistribution is strictly prohibited. All rights reserved.

T7 – Station Equipment

T7A – Station Equipment: Receivers; Transmitters; Transceivers; Modulation; Transverters; Low Power and Weak Signal Operation; Transmit and Receive Amplifiers

Which term describes the ability of a receiver to detect the presence of a signal?
A. Linearity
B. Sensitivity
C. Selectivity
D. Total Harmonic Distortion

T7A01 (B)
Answer: B. The ability of a receiver to detect the presence of a signal is measured in terms of its sensitivity.

What is a transceiver?
A. A type of antenna switch
B. A unit combining the functions of a transmitter and a receiver
C. A component in a repeater which filters out unwanted interference
D. A type of antenna matching network

T7A02 (B)
Answer: B. A transceiver is a unit that combines the functions of a transmitter and a receiver.

Which of the following is used to convert a radio signal from one frequency to another?
A. Phase splitter
B. Mixer
C. Inverter
D. Amplifier

T7A03 (B)
Answer: B. A mixer is a device used to convert radio signals from one frequency to another.

Which term describes the ability of a receiver to discriminate between multiple signals?
A. Discrimination ratio
B. Sensitivity
C. Selectivity
D. Harmonic Distortion

T7A04 (C)
Answer: C. A receiver's ability to discriminate among multiple radio signals is referred to as its selectivity.

What is the name of a circuit that generates a signal of a desired frequency?
A. Reactance modulator
B. Product detector
C. Low-pass filter
D. Oscillator

Copyright © Mometrix Media. You have been licensed one copy of this document for personal use only. Any other reproduction or redistribution is strictly prohibited. All rights reserved.

T7A05 (D)
Answer: D. An oscillator is a circuit that produces an oscillating signal at a desired frequency.

What device takes the output of a low-powered 28 MHz SSB exciter and produces a 222 MHz output signal?
  A. High-pass filter
  B. Low-pass filter
  C. Transverter
  D. Phase converter

T7A06 (C)
Answer: C. A transverter takes the output of a low-powered 28 MHz SSB exciter and produces a 222 MHz output signal. Transverters are a single unit that includes both an upconverter and a downconverter. The transverter enables the transceiver to communicate over a broad range of frequencies.

What is meant by term "PTT"?
  A. Pre-transmission tuning to reduce transmitter harmonic emission
  B. Precise tone transmissions used to limit repeater access to only certain signals
  C. A primary transformer tuner use to match antennas
  D. The push to talk function which switches between receive and transmit

T7A07 (D)
Answer: D. The term PTT stands for push-to-talk, a setup in which the transceiver is set to receive when the button is not pushed, and transmit when the button is pushed.

Which of the following describes combining speech with an RF carrier signal?
  A. Impedance matching
  B. Oscillation
  C. Modulation
  D. Low-pass filtering

T7A08 (C)
Answer: C. The process of combining speech with an RF carrier signal is referred to as modulation.

Which of the following devices is most useful for VHF weak-signal communication?
  A. A quarter-wave vertical antenna
  B. A multi-mode VHF transceiver
  C. An omni-directional antenna
  D. A mobile VHF FM transceiver

T7A09 (B)
Answer: B. A multimode VHF transceiver would be most useful for VHF weak-signal communication.

What device increases the low-power output from a handheld transceiver?
  A. A voltage divider
  B. An RF power amplifier
  C. An impedance network
  D. All of these choices are correct

T7A10 (B)
Answer: B. An RF power amplifier increases the low-power output from a handheld transceiver.

- 63 -

Copyright © Mometrix Media. You have been licensed one copy of this document for personal use only. Any other reproduction or redistribution is strictly prohibited. All rights reserved.

Where is an RF preamplifier installed?
    A. Between the antenna and receiver
    B. At the output of the transmitter's power amplifier
    C. Between a transmitter and antenna tuner
    D. At the receiver's audio output

T7A11 (B)
Answer: A. An RF preamplifier is installed between the antenna and receiver. Preamplifiers increase the strength of radio signals, so that they may then be improved even more by subsequent amplification processes.

T7B – Common Transmitter and Receiver Problems: Symptoms of Overload and Overdrive; Distortion; Causes of Interference; Interference and Consumer Electronics; Part 15 Devices; Over and Under Modulation; RF Feedback; Off Frequency Signals; Fading and Noise; Problems with Digital Communications Interfaces

What can you do if you are told your FM handheld or mobile transceiver is over deviating?
    A. Talk louder into the microphone
    B. Let the transceiver cool off
    C. Change to a higher power level
    D. Talk farther away from the microphone

T7B01 (D)
Answer: D. If you are told your FM handheld or mobile transceiver is over deviating, you can talk farther away from the microphone.

What would cause a broadcast AM or FM radio to receive an amateur radio transmission unintentionally?
    A. The receiver is unable to reject strong signals outside the AM or FM band
    B. The microphone gain of the transmitter is turned up too high
    C. The audio amplifier of the transmitter is overloaded
    D. The deviation of an FM transmitter is set too low

T7B02 (A)
Answer: A. If a broadcast AM/FM radio is unintentionally receiving amateur radio transmissions, the most likely explanation is that the receiver is unable to reject strong signals outside of the AM/FM bands.

Which of the following may be a cause of radio frequency interference?
    A. Fundamental overload
    B. Harmonics
    C. Spurious emissions
    D. All of these choices are correct

T7B03 (D)
Answer: D. Radio frequency interference may be caused by fundamental overload, harmonics, or spurious emissions. A spurious emission is any radio frequency that was not created or transmitted on purpose.

Copyright © Mometrix Media. You have been licensed one copy of this document for personal use only. Any other reproduction or redistribution is strictly prohibited. All rights reserved.

Which of the following is a way to reduce or eliminate interference by an amateur transmitter to a nearby telephone?
    A. Put a filter on the amateur transmitter
    B. Reduce the microphone gain
    C. Reduce the SWR on the transmitter transmission line
    D. Put a RF filter on the telephone

T7B04 (D)
Answer: D. The best way to reduce or eliminate interference to a telephone from a nearby amateur transmitter is to install an RF filter on the telephone.

How can overload of a non-amateur radio or TV receiver by an amateur signal be reduced or eliminated?
    A. Block the amateur signal with a filter at the antenna input of the affected receiver
    B. Block the interfering signal with a filter on the amateur transmitter
    C. Switch the transmitter from FM to SSB
    D. Switch the transmitter to a narrow-band mode

T7B05 (A)
Answer: A. Filtering out an unwanted amateur radio signal at the receiver of the impacted device is the best way to reduce or eliminate overload on a TV or radio.

Which of the following actions should you take if a neighbor tells you that your station's transmissions are interfering with their radio or TV reception?
    A. Make sure that your station is functioning properly and that it does not cause interference to your own radio or television when it is tuned to the same channel
    B. Immediately turn off your transmitter and contact the nearest FCC office for assistance
    C. Tell them that your license gives you the right to transmit and nothing can be done to reduce the interference
    D. Install a harmonic doubler on the output of your transmitter and tune it until the interference is eliminated

T7B06 (A)
Answer: A. If someone tells you that your station's transmissions are interfering with their radio or TV reception, your first step should be to make sure that your station is functioning properly and that it does not cause interference to your own television.

Which of the following may be useful in correcting a radio frequency interference problem?
    A. Snap-on ferrite chokes
    B. Low-pass and high-pass filters
    C. Band-reject and band-pass filters
    D. All of these choices are correct

T7B07 (D)
Answers: D. A radio frequency interference problem may be corrected with snap-on ferrite chokes, low-pass and high-pass filters, or band-reject and band-pass filters.

Copyright © Mometrix Media. You have been licensed one copy of this document for personal use only. Any other reproduction or redistribution is strictly prohibited. All rights reserved.

What should you do if something in a neighbor's home is causing harmful interference to your amateur station?

    A. Work with your neighbor to identify the offending device

    B. Politely inform your neighbor about the rules that prohibit the use of devices which cause interference

    C. Check your station and make sure it meets the standards of good amateur practice

    D. All of these choices are correct

T7B08 (D)

Answer: D. If you believe something in your neighbor's house is causing harmful interference to your amateur station, there are a few things you can or should do. First, make sure that your station is set up properly and that a faulty setup is not causing the interference problems. If that is not successful, talk to your neighbor about the interference problems you are experiencing, and politely let him know about the FCC rules that govern harmful interference. If your neighbor is amenable, work with him to locate the source of the interference and find a solution. Always remain courteous.

What is a Part 15 device?

    A. An unlicensed device that may emit low powered radio signals on frequencies used by a licensed service

    B. A type of amateur radio that can legally be used in the citizen's band

    C. A device for long distance communications using special codes sanctioned by the International Amateur Radio Union

    D. A type of test set used to determine whether a transmitter is in compliance with FCC regulation 91.15

T7B09 (A)

Answer: A. A Part 15 device is an unlicensed device that may emit low powered radio signals on frequencies used by a licensed service.

What might be the problem if you receive a report that your audio signal through the repeater is distorted or unintelligible?

    A. Your transmitter may be slightly off frequency

    B. Your batteries may be running low

    C. You could be in a bad location

    D. All of these choices are correct

T7B10 (D)

Answer: D. If you receive a report that your audio signal through the repeater is distorted or unintelligible, this may be because your transmitter is slightly off frequency, your batteries are running low, or you're in a bad location.

What is a symptom of RF feedback in a transmitter or transceiver?

    A. Excessive SWR at the antenna connection

    B. The transmitter will not stay on the desired frequency

    C. Reports of garbled, distorted, or unintelligible transmissions

    D. Frequent blowing of power supply fuses

T7B11 (C)

Answer: C. One symptom of RF feedback in a transmitter or transceiver is reports of garbled, distorted, or unintelligible transmissions. Feedback is any portion of the radio output that is returned to the input. Feedback is often used to sustain or improve performance.

Copyright © Mometrix Media. You have been licensed one copy of this document for personal use only. Any other reproduction or redistribution is strictly prohibited. All rights reserved.

What might be the first step to resolve cable TV interference from your ham radio transmission?
    A. Add a low pass filter to the TV antenna input
    B. Add a high pass filter to the TV antenna input
    C. Add a preamplifier to the TV antenna input
    D. Be sure all TV coaxial connectors are installed properly

T7B12 (D)
Answer: D. The first step you should take when attempting to resolve interference from a cable TV is ensuring that all of your coaxial connectors on the TV are properly installed. If they are, and the interference persists, you may need to add a filter or preamplifier to help reduce the signal leakage.

T7C – Antenna Measurements and Troubleshooting: Measuring SWR; Dummy Loads; Coaxial Cables; Feed Line Failure Modes

What is the primary purpose of a dummy load?
    A. To prevent the radiation of signals when making tests
    B. To prevent over-modulation of your transmitter
    C. To improve the radiation from your antenna
    D. To improve the signal to noise ratio of your receiver

T7C01 (A)
Answer: A. The primary purpose of a dummy load is to prevent the radiation of signals when making tests. The dummy load, also known as a dummy antenna, is a station accessory that enables the user to test and fine-tune equipment without actually broadcasting a signal.

Which of the following instruments can be used to determine if an antenna is resonant at the desired operating frequency?
    A. A VTVM
    B. An antenna analyzer
    C. A "Q" meter
    D. A frequency counter

T7C02 (B)
Answer: B. An antenna analyzer can be used to determine if an antenna is resonant at the desired operating frequency. Antenna analyzers assess the efficiency of antenna systems.

What, in general terms, is standing wave ratio (SWR)?
    A. A measure of how well a load is matched to a transmission line
    B. The ratio of high to low impedance in a feed line
    C. The transmitter efficiency ratio
    D. An indication of the quality of your station's ground connection

T7C03 (A)
Answer: A. In general terms, standing wave ratio (SWR) is a measure of how well a load is matched to a transmission line. This is a measure of the impedance match between the antenna and the feedline. It is the ratio of the maximum voltage to the minimum voltage along the feedline. If a transmitter is being used, standing wave ratio is the impedance match between the feedline from the transmitter and the antenna system. If the antenna is a purely resistive load, the standing wave ratio is the ratio of antenna impedance to feedline impedance.

Copyright © Mometrix Media. You have been licensed one copy of this document for personal use only. Any other reproduction or redistribution is strictly prohibited. All rights reserved.

What reading on an SWR meter indicates a perfect impedance match between the antenna and the feed line?

    A. 2 to 1

    B. 1 to 3

    C. 1 to 1

    D. 10 to 1

T7C04 (C)

Answer: C. A reading of 1 to 1 on an SWR meter indicates a perfect impedance match between the antenna and the feed line. An SWR meter, also known as a watt meter, is a way to independently measure the power of a transmitter.

What is the approximate SWR value above which the protection circuits in most solid-state transmitters begin to reduce transmitter power?

    A. 2 to 1

    B. 1 to 2

    C. 6 to 1

    D. 10 to 1

T7C05 (A)

Answer: A. 2 to 1 is the approximate SWR value above which the protection circuits in most solid-state transmitters begin to reduce transmitter power.

What does an SWR reading of 4:1 indicate?

    A. Loss of -4dB

    B. Good impedance match

    C. Gain of +4dB

    D. Impedance mismatch

T7C06 (D)

Answer: D. An SWR reading of 4:1 indicates an impedance mismatch.

What happens to power lost in a feed line?

    A. It increases the SWR

    B. It comes back into your transmitter and could cause damage

    C. It is converted into heat

    D. It can cause distortion of your signal

T7C07 (C)

Answer: C. The power lost in a feed line is converted into heat. If the cable has cracks or dents, it will be more likely to lose power in this manner. A ham radio operator should always use the best feed line he or she can afford.

What instrument other than an SWR meter could you use to determine if a feed line and antenna are properly matched?

    A. Voltmeter

    B. Ohmmeter

    C. Iambic pentameter

    D. Directional wattmeter

Copyright © Mometrix Media. You have been licensed one copy of this document for personal use only. Any other reproduction or redistribution is strictly prohibited. All rights reserved.

T7C08 (D)
Answer: D. Besides an SWR meter, one could also use a directional wattmeter to determine if a feed line and antenna are properly matched. An SWR (standing wave ratio) meter can evaluate the effectiveness of impedance matching, and can also identify the degree of mismatch between a transmission line and its load. A directional wattmeter is capable of differentiating between the forward and reflected waves.

Which of the following is the most common cause for failure of coaxial cables?
    A. Moisture contamination
    B. Gamma rays
    C. The velocity factor exceeds 1.0
    D. Overloading

T7C09 (A)
Answer: A. The most common cause of failure in coaxial cables is moisture contamination. Coaxial cable, also known as coax, is composed of a central wire surrounded by hollow tube. The center wire is called the center conductor, and the outer conductor is known as the braid, or shield.

Why should the outer jacket of coaxial cable be resistant to ultraviolet light?
    A. Ultraviolet resistant jackets prevent harmonic radiation
    B. Ultraviolet light can increase losses in the cable's jacket
    C. Ultraviolet and RF signals can mix together, causing interference
    D. Ultraviolet light can damage the jacket and allow water to enter the cable

T7C10 (D)
Answer: D. The outer jacket of a coaxial cable should be resistant to ultraviolet light because this light can damage the jacket and allow water to enter the cable.

What is a disadvantage of "air core" coaxial cable when compared to foam or solid dielectric types?
    A. It has more loss per foot
    B. It cannot be used for VHF or UHF antennas
    C. It requires special techniques to prevent water absorption
    D. It cannot be used at below freezing temperatures

T7C11 (C)
Answer: C. One disadvantage of "air core" coaxial cable when compared to foam or solid dielectric-type cable is that it requires special techniques to prevent water absorption.

Which of the following is a common use of coaxial cable?
    A. Carrying DC power from a vehicle battery to a mobile radio
    B. Carrying RF signals between a radio and antenna
    C. Securing masts, tubing, and other cylindrical objects on towers
    D. Connecting data signals from a TNC to a computer

T7C12 (B)
Answer: B. Coaxial cables are most commonly used to transmit RF signals between various components within an amateur radio setup, such as between a radio and an antenna.

What does a dummy load consist of?
    A. A high-gain amplifier and a TR switch
    B. A non-inductive resistor and a heat sink
    C. A low voltage power supply and a DC relay
    D. A 50 ohm reactance used to terminate a transmission line

Copyright © Mometrix Media. You have been licensed one copy of this document for personal use only. Any other reproduction or redistribution is strictly prohibited. All rights reserved.

T7C13 (B)
Answer: B. A dummy load is a device used to simulate an electrical component, usually for testing purposes. It consists of a non-inductive resistor, and a heat sink to prevent overheating.

T7D – Basic Repair and Testing: Soldering; Using Basic Test Instruments; Connecting a Voltmeter, Ammeter, or Ohmmeter

Which instrument would you use to measure electric potential or electromotive force?
 A. An ammeter
 B. A voltmeter
 C. A wavemeter
 D. An ohmmeter

T7D01 (B)
Answer: B. A voltmeter is used to measure electric potential or electromotive force. It accomplishes this by identifying the electric potential difference between two conductors.

What is the correct way to connect a voltmeter to a circuit?
 A. In series with the circuit
 B. In parallel with the circuit
 C. In quadrature with the circuit
 D. In phase with the circuit

T7D02 (B)
Answer: B. The correct way to connect a voltmeter to a circuit is in parallel with the circuit. An analog voltmeter, on the other hand, is a moving coil galvanometer that works as a voltmeter after a resistor is installed in series with it.

How is an ammeter usually connected to a circuit?
 A. In series with the circuit
 B. In parallel with the circuit
 C. In quadrature with the circuit
 D. In phase with the circuit

T7D03 (A)
Answer: A. An ammeter is usually connected to a circuit in series with the circuit. In most cases, an ammeter is combined with a voltmeter and ohmmeter in a single instrument.

Which instrument is used to measure electric current?
 A. An ohmmeter
 B. A wavemeter
 C. A voltmeter
 D. An ammeter

T7D04 (D)
Answer: D. An ammeter is used to measure electric current. Typically, the current will need to be at least a few amperes to be susceptible to measurement by the ammeter.

Copyright © Mometrix Media. You have been licensed one copy of this document for personal use only. Any other reproduction or redistribution is strictly prohibited. All rights reserved.

What instrument is used to measure resistance?
- A. An oscilloscope
- B. A spectrum analyzer
- C. A noise bridge
- D. An ohmmeter

T7D05 (D)
Answer: D. An ohmmeter is used to measure resistance. These devices are capable of measuring very low levels of electrical resistance.

Which of the following might damage a multimeter?
- A. Measuring a voltage too small for the chosen scale
- B. Leaving the meter in the milliamps position overnight
- C. Attempting to measure voltage when using the resistance setting
- D. Not allowing it to warm up properly

T7D06 (C)
Answer: C. Attempting to measure voltage when using the resistance setting might damage a multimeter. Multimeters are capable of measuring the following values: current, resistance, and the current potential differences of alternating and direct current.

Which of the following measurements are commonly made using a multimeter?
- A. SWR and RF power
- B. Signal strength and noise
- C. Impedance and reactance
- D. Voltage and resistance

T7D07 (D)
Answer: D. Voltage and resistance measurements are commonly made using a multimeter. The multimeter is sometimes referred to as a volt-ohm meter.

Which of the following types of solder is best for radio and electronic use?
- A. Acid-core solder
- B. Silver solder
- C. Rosin-core solder
- D. Aluminum solder

T7D08 (C)
Answer: C. Rosin-core solder is best for radio and electronic use.

What is the characteristic appearance of a "cold" solder joint?
- A. Dark black spots
- B. A bright or shiny surface
- C. A grainy or dull surface
- D. A greenish tint

T7D09 (C)
Answer: C. The characteristic appearance of a "cold" solder joint is a grainy or dull surface.

Copyright © Mometrix Media. You have been licensed one copy of this document for personal use only. Any other reproduction or redistribution is strictly prohibited. All rights reserved.

What is probably happening when an ohmmeter, connected across an unpowered circuit, initially indicates a low resistance and then shows increasing resistance with time?
    A. The ohmmeter is defective
    B. The circuit contains a large capacitor
    C. The circuit contains a large inductor
    D. The circuit is a relaxation oscillator

T7D10 (B)
Answer: C. If an ohmmeter, connected across the circuit, initially indicates a low resistance and then shows increasing resistance with time, the circuit probably contains a large inductor.

Which of the following precautions should be taken when measuring circuit resistance with an ohmmeter?
    A. Ensure that the applied voltages are correct
    B. Ensure that the circuit is not powered
    C. Ensure that the circuit is grounded
    D. Ensure that the circuit is operating at the correct frequency

T7D11 (B)
Answer: B. When measuring circuit resistance with an ohmmeter, one should ensure that the circuit is not powered.

Which of the following precautions should be taken when measuring high voltages with a voltmeter?
    A. Ensure that the voltmeter has very low impedance
    B. Ensure that the voltmeter and leads are rated for use at the voltages to be measured
    C. Ensure that the circuit is grounded through the voltmeter
    D. Ensure that the voltmeter is set to the correct frequency

T7D12 (B)
Answer: B. When dealing with high voltages, safety should always be your foremost concern. If you need to measure the voltage on a high voltage circuit, always make sure that the voltmeter you are using and the attached leads are rated for use at the voltages you will be measuring.

T8 – Modulation Modes

T8A – Modulation Modes: Bandwidth of Various Signals; Choice of Emission Type

Which of the following is a form of amplitude modulation?
    A. Spread-spectrum
    B. Packet radio
    C. Single sideband
    D. Phase shift keying

T8A01 (C)
Answer: C. Single sideband is a form of amplitude modulation. Indeed, single sideband is the most common mode of voice transmission on the high-frequency bands. Unlike an a.m. transmission, in which two identical versions of the message are broadcast, an SSB transmission only broadcasts one. For this reason, single sideband communications are more efficient and are better at conserving space on the radio spectrum.

Copyright © Mometrix Media. You have been licensed one copy of this document for personal use only. Any other reproduction or redistribution is strictly prohibited. All rights reserved.

What type of modulation is most commonly used for VHF packet radio transmissions?
    A. FM
    B. SSB
    C. AM
    D. Spread Spectrum

T8A02 (A)
Answer: A. The type of modulation most commonly used for VHF packet radio transmission is FM.

Which type of voice mode is most often used for long-distance (weak signal) contacts on the VHF and UHF bands?
    A. FM
    B. DRM
    C. SSB
    D. PM

T8A03 (C)
Answer: C. The type of voice modulation most often used for long-distance or weak signal contacts on the VHF and UHF bands is SSB.

Which type of modulation is most commonly used for VHF and UHF voice repeaters?
    A. AM
    B. SSB
    C. PSK
    D. FM

T8A04 (D)
Answer: D. The type of modulation most commonly used for VHF and UHF voice repeaters is FM.

Which of the following types of emission has the narrowest bandwidth?
    A. FM voice
    B. SSB voice
    C. CW
    D. Slow-scan TV

T8A05 (C)
Answer: C. CW emission has a narrower bandwidth than FM voice, SSB voice, or slow-scan TV emission.

Which sideband is normally used for 10 meter HF, VHF and UHF single-sideband communications?
    A. Upper sideband
    B. Lower sideband
    C. Suppressed sideband
    D. Inverted sideband

T8A06 (A)
Answer: A. The upper sideband is normally used for 10 meter HF, VHF, and UHF single-sideband communications.

Copyright © Mometrix Media. You have been licensed one copy of this document for personal use only. Any other reproduction or redistribution is strictly prohibited. All rights reserved.

What is the primary advantage of single sideband over FM for voice transmissions?
    A. SSB signals are easier to tune
    B. SSB signals are less susceptible to interference
    C. SSB signals have narrower bandwidth
    D. All of these choices are correct

T8A07 (C)
Answer: C. The primary advantage of single sideband over FM for voice transmissions is that SSB signals have narrower bandwidth.

What is the approximate bandwidth of a single sideband voice signal?
    A. 1 kHz
    B. 3 kHz
    C. 6 kHz
    D. 15 kHz

T8A08 (B)
Answer: B. The approximate bandwidth of a single sideband voice signal is 3 kHz.

What is the approximate bandwidth of a VHF repeater FM phone signal?
    A. Less than 500 Hz
    B. About 150 kHz
    C. Between 10 and 15 kHz
    D. Between 50 and 125 kHz

T8A09 (C)
Answer: C. The approximate bandwidth of a VHF repeater FM phone signal is between 10 and 15 kHz.

What is the typical bandwidth of analog fast-scan TV transmissions on the 70 cm band?
    A. More than 10 MHz
    B. About 6 MHz
    C. About 3 MHz
    D. About 1 MHz

T8A10 (B)
Answer: B. The typical bandwidth of analog fast-scan TV transmissions on the 70 cm band is about 6 MHz.

What is the approximate maximum bandwidth required to transmit a CW signal?
    A. 2.4 kHz
    B. 150 Hz
    C. 1000 Hz
    D. 15 kHz

T8A11 (B)
Answer: B. The approximate maximum bandwidth required to transmit a CW signal is 150 Hz.

Copyright © Mometrix Media. You have been licensed one copy of this document for personal use only. Any other reproduction or redistribution is strictly prohibited. All rights reserved.

T8B – Amateur Satellite Operation; Doppler Shift, Basic Orbits, Operating Protocols; Control Operator, Transmitter Power Considerations; Satellite Tracking; Digital Modes

Who may be the control operator of a station communicating through an amateur satellite or space station?
    A. Only an Amateur Extra Class operator
    B. A General Class licensee or higher licensee who has a satellite operator certification
    C. Only an Amateur Extra Class operator who is also an AMSAT member
    D. Any amateur whose license privileges allow them to transmit on the satellite uplink frequency

T8B01 (D) [97.301, 97.207(C)]
Answer: D. Any amateur whose license privileges allow them to transmit on the satellite uplink frequency may be the control operator of a station communicating through an amateur satellite or space station.

How much transmitter power should be used on the uplink frequency of an amateur satellite or space station?
    A. The maximum power of your transmitter
    B. The minimum amount of power needed to complete the contact
    C. No more than half the rating of your linear amplifier
    D. Never more than 1 watt

T8B02 (B) [97.313]
Answer: B. The minimum amount of power needed to complete the contact should be used on the uplink frequency of an amateur satellite or space station.

Which of the following are provided by satellite tracking programs?
    A. Maps showing the real-time position of the satellite track over the earth
    B. The time, azimuth, and elevation of the start, maximum altitude, and end of a pass
    C. The apparent frequency of the satellite transmission, including effects of Doppler shift
    D. All of these answers are correct

T8B03 (D)
Answer: D. Satellite tracking programs provide a wealth of information about the path and position of orbiting satellites, as well as their operation.

Which amateur stations may make contact with an amateur station on the International Space Station using 2 meter and 70 cm band amateur radio frequencies?
    A. Only members of amateur radio clubs at NASA facilities
    B. Any amateur holding a Technician or higher class license
    C. Only the astronaut's family members who are hams
    D. You cannot talk to the ISS on amateur radio frequencies

T8B04 (B)) [97.301, 97.207(C)]
Answer: B. Any amateur holding a Technician or higher class license may make contact with an amateur station on the International Space Station using 2 meter and 70 cm band amateur radio frequencies.

Copyright © Mometrix Media. You have been licensed one copy of this document for personal use only. Any other reproduction or redistribution is strictly prohibited. All rights reserved.

What is a satellite beacon?
    A. The primary transmit antenna on the satellite
    B. An indicator light that that shows where to point your antenna
    C. A reflective surface on the satellite
    D. A transmission from a space station that contains information about a satellite

T8B05 (D)
Answer: D. A satellite beacon is a transmission from a space station that contains information about a satellite. These transmissions are used for maintenance and guidance.

Which of the following are inputs to a satellite tracking program?
    A. The weight of the satellite
    B. The Keplerian elements
    C. The last observed time of zero Doppler shift
    D. All of these answers are correct

T8B06 (B)
Answer: B. The six Keplerian elements precisely define the orbit of a satellite. The six elements are: (1) eccentricity, (2) semi-major axis, (3) inclination, (4) longitude of the ascending node, (5) argument of periapsis, and (6) mean anomaly at epoch.

With regard to satellite communications, what is Doppler shift?
    A. A change in the satellite orbit
    B. A mode where the satellite receives signals on one band and transmits on another
    C. An observed change in signal frequency caused by relative motion between the satellite and the earth station
    D. A special digital communications mode for some satellites

T8B07 (C)
Answer: C. With regard to satellite communications, Doppler shift is an observed change in signal frequency caused by relative motion between the satellite and the earth station. When the satellite is approaching the earth station, the wavelength will be shorter; as the satellite moves away from the earth station, the wave length will gradually expand.

What is meant by the statement that a satellite is operating in "mode U/V"?
    A. The satellite uplink is in the 15 meter band and the downlink is in the 10 meter band
    B. The satellite uplink is in the 70 cm band and the downlink is in the 2 meter band
    C. The satellite operates using ultraviolet frequencies
    D. The satellite frequencies are usually variable

T8B08 (B)
Answer: B. When it is said that a satellite is operating in "mode U/V," this means that the satellite uplink is in the 70 cm band and the downlink is in the 2 meter band. In ham radio, modes are particular types of modulation, and modulations are the systems for adding information to a radio signal to be broadcast over the air.

What causes "spin fading" when referring to satellite signals?
    A. Circular polarized noise interference radiated from the sun
    B. Rotation of the satellite and its antennas
    C. Doppler shift of the received signal
    D. Interfering signals within the satellite uplink band

Copyright © Mometrix Media. You have been licensed one copy of this document for personal use only. Any other reproduction or redistribution is strictly prohibited. All rights reserved.

T8B09 (B)
Answer: B. Spin fading with respect to satellite signals is caused by the rotation of the satellite and its antennas.

What do the initials LEO tell you about an amateur satellite?
    A. The satellite battery is in Low Energy Operation mode
    B. The satellite is performing a Lunar Ejection Orbit maneuver
    C. The satellite is in a Low Earth Orbit
    D. The satellite uses Light Emitting Optics

T8B10 (C)
Answer: C. The initials LEO indicate that an amateur satellite is in a Low Earth Orbit. This means that the path of the satellite is less than 1000 miles above the surface of the earth.

What is a commonly used method of sending signals to and from a digital satellite?
    A. USB AFSK
    B. PSK31
    C. FM Packet
    D. WSJT

T8B11 (C)
Answer: C. The FM packet is a commonly used method of sending signals to and from a digital satellite. Digital satellites function as store and forward or bulletin board systems, and are especially useful for ham radio operators in far-flung locations.

T8C – Operating Activities: Radio Direction Finding; Radio Control; Contests; Linking over the Internet; Grid Locators

Which of the following methods is used to locate sources of noise interference or jamming?
    A. Echolocation
    B. Doppler radar
    C. Radio direction finding
    D. Phase locking

T8C01 (C)
Answer: C. Radio direction finding is used to locate sources of noise interference or jamming.

Which of these items would be useful for a hidden transmitter hunt?
    A. Calibrated SWR meter
    B. A directional antenna
    C. A calibrated noise bridge
    D. All of these choices are correct

T8C02 (B)
Answer: B. A directional antenna would be useful for a hidden transmitter hunt. Directional antennas send and receive signals in some directions more than others. Therefore, these antennas are able to ascertain from which direction a signal is being broadcast.

Copyright © Mometrix Media. You have been licensed one copy of this document for personal use only. Any other reproduction or redistribution is strictly prohibited. All rights reserved.

What popular operating activity involves contacting as many stations as possible during a specified period of time?

- A. Contesting
- B. Net operations
- C. Public service events
- D. Simulated emergency exercises

T8C03 (A)
Answer: A. Contesting involves contacting as many stations as possible during a specified period of time.

Which of the following is good procedure when contacting another station in a radio contest?

- A. Be sure to sign only the last two letters of your call if there is a pileup calling the station
- B. Work the station twice to be sure that you are in his log
- C. Send only the minimum information needed for proper identification and the contest exchange
- D. All of these choices are correct

T8C04 (C)
Answer: C. Sending only the minimum information needed for proper identification and the contest exchange is good procedure when contacting another station in a radio contest.

What is a grid locator?

- A. A letter-number designator assigned to a geographic location
- B. A letter-number designator assigned to an azimuth and elevation
- C. An instrument for neutralizing a final amplifier
- D. An instrument for radio direction finding

T8C05 (A)
Answer: A. A grid locator is a letter-number designator assigned to a geographic location. The latitude and the longitude of the location are compressed into a brief string of characters, in alternating pairs of letters and numbers.

How is access to an IRLP node accomplished?

- A. By obtaining a password which is sent via voice to the node
- B. By using DTMF signals
- C. By entering the proper Internet password
- D. By using CTCSS tone codes

T8C06 (B)
Answer: B. Internet Radio Linking Project (IRLP) nodes consist of a radio attached to an internet-connected computer running specialized software. It allows amateur radio users to communicate with other users anywhere in the world near another IRLP node. Users access the node using Dual-Tone Multi-Frequency (DTMF) signals.

What is the maximum power allowed when transmitting telecommand signals to radio controlled models?

- A. 500 milliwatts
- B. 1 watt
- C. 25 watts
- D. 1500 watts

Copyright © Mometrix Media. You have been licensed one copy of this document for personal use only. Any other reproduction or redistribution is strictly prohibited. All rights reserved.

T8C07 (B) [97.215(C)]
Answer: B. The maximum power allowed when transmitting tele-command signals to radio controlled models is 1 watt.

What is required in place of on-air station identification when sending signals to a radio control model using amateur frequencies?
    A. Voice identification must be transmitted every 10 minutes
    B. Morse code ID must be sent once per hour
    C. A label indicating the licensee's name, call sign and address must be affixed to the transmitter
    D. A flag must be affixed to the transmitter antenna with the station call sign in 1 inch high letters or larger

T8C08 (C) [97.215(A)]
Answer: C. A label indicating the licensee's name, call sign, and address must be affixed to the transmitter instead of on-air station identification when sending signals to a radio control model using amateur frequencies.

How might you obtain a list of active nodes that use VoIP?
    A. From the FCC Rulebook
    B. From your local emergency coordinator
    C. From a repeater directory
    D. From the local repeater frequency coordinator

T8C09 (C)
Answer: C. A list of active nodes that use VoIP can be obtained from a repeater directory. Repeater directories are comprehensive lists of active ham repeater frequencies.

How do you select a specific IRLP node when using a portable transceiver?
    A. Choose a specific CTCSS tone
    B. Choose the correct DSC tone
    C. Access the repeater autopatch
    D. Use the keypad to transmit the IRLP node ID

T8C10 (D)
Answer: D. When using a portable transceiver, a specific IRLP node can be selected by using the keypad to transmit the IRLP node ID.

What name is given to an amateur radio station that is used to connect other amateur stations to the Internet?
    A. A gateway
    B. A repeater
    C. A digipeater
    D. A beacon

T8C11 (A)
Answer: A. A gateway is an amateur radio station that is used to connect other amateur stations to the Internet.

Copyright © Mometrix Media. You have been licensed one copy of this document for personal use only. Any other reproduction or redistribution is strictly prohibited. All rights reserved.

What is meant by Voice over Internet Protocol (VoIP) as used in amateur radio?
    A. A set of rules specifying how to identify your station when linked over the Internet to another station
    B. A set of guidelines for working DX during contests using Internet access
    C. A technique for measuring the modulation quality of a transmitter using remote sites monitored via the Internet
    D. A method of delivering voice communications over the Internet using digital techniques

T8C12 (D)
Answer: D. Voice-over-Internet Protocol (VoIP) is a method of delivering voice communications over the Internet. It is an integral part of the Internet Radio Linking Project (IRLP).

What is the Internet Radio Linking Project (IRLP)?
    A. A technique to connect amateur radio systems, such as repeaters, via the Internet using Voice over Internet Protocol
    B. A system for providing access to websites via amateur radio
    C. A system for informing amateurs in real time of the frequency of active DX stations
    D. A technique for measuring signal strength of an amateur transmitter via the Internet

T8C13 (A)
Answer: A. The IRLP is a project that makes use of the Internet to connect amateur radio stations to one another from all over the world.

T8D – Non-Voice Communications: Image Signals; Digital Modes; CW; Packet; PSK31; APRS; Error Detection and Correction; NTSC

Which of the following is an example of a digital communications method?
    A. Packet
    B. PSK31
    C. MFSK
    D. All of these choices are correct

T8D01 (D)
Answer: D. Packet, PSK 31s, and MFSKs are all examples of digital communications methods.

What does the term "APRS" mean?
    A. Automatic Packet Reporting System
    B. Associated Public Radio Station
    C. Auto Planning Radio Set-up
    D. Advanced Polar Radio System

T8D02 (A)
Answer: A. The term APRS means Automatic Packet Reporting System. This is a combination of GPS and packet radio. When a station uses this system, the operator takes the location data from the GPS receiver to a two-meter radio and sends out data packets announcing his or her presence. These packets may be received by other hams or by packet radio digipeaters.

Copyright © Mometrix Media. You have been licensed one copy of this document for personal use only. Any other reproduction or redistribution is strictly prohibited. All rights reserved.

Which of the following devices provides data to the transmitter when sending automatic position reports from a mobile amateur radio station?
    A. The vehicle speedometer
    B. A WWV receiver
    C. A connection to a broadcast FM sub-carrier receiver
    D. A Global Positioning System receiver

T8D03 (D)
Answer: D. A Global Positioning System receiver is normally used when sending automatic location reports via amateur radio.

What type of transmission is indicated by the term NTSC?
    A. A Normal Transmission mode in Static Circuit
    B. A special mode for earth satellite uplink
    C. An analog fast scan color TV signal
    D. A frame compression scheme for TV signals

T8D04 (C)
Answer: C. The term NTSC indicates an analog fast scan color TV signal.

Which of the following is an application of APRS (Automatic Packet Reporting System)?
    A. Providing real time tactical digital communications in conjunction with a map showing the locations of stations
    B. Showing automatically the number of packets transmitted via PACTOR during a specific time interval
    C. Providing voice over Internet connection between repeaters
    D. Providing information on the number of stations signed into a repeater

T8D05 (A)
Answer: A. The Automatic Packet Reporting System (APRS) is a system designed to provide real-time tactical digital communications along with a map indicating the sources of the signals carrying the communication.

What does the abbreviation PSK mean?
    A. Pulse Shift Keying
    B. Phase Shift Keying
    C. Packet Short Keying
    D. Phased Slide Keying

T8D06 (B)
Answer: B. The abbreviation PSK means phase shift keying. Phase shift keying is a strategy for digital modes in the high frequency spectrum. In this system, the components of code are indicated with shifts in the timing relationship between a continuously transmitted tone and a reference tone. This enables the user to transmit a signal in very limited space.

What is PSK31?
    A. A high-rate data transmission mode
    B. A method of reducing noise interference to FM signals
    C. A method of compressing digital television signals
    D. A low-rate data transmission mode

Copyright © Mometrix Media. You have been licensed one copy of this document for personal use only. Any other reproduction or redistribution is strictly prohibited. All rights reserved.

T8D07 (D)
Answer: D. PSK31 is a low-rate data transmission mode. This mode of phase shift keying only requires 31.25 Hz for its signal. It accomplishes this by using the Varicode system for characters, in which the constituent elements are distinguished by variations in a continuous tone rather than by separate tones.

Which of the following may be included in packet transmissions?
    A. A check sum which permits error detection
    B. A header which contains the call sign of the station to which the information is being sent
    C. Automatic repeat request in case of error
    D. All of these choices are correct

T8D08 (D)
Answer: D. Packet transmissions may include a check sum which permits error detection, a header which contains the call sign of the station to which the information is being sent, and an automatic repeat request in case of error.

What code is used when sending CW in the amateur bands?
    A. Baudot
    B. Hamming
    C. International Morse
    D. Gray

T8D09 (C)
Answer: C. International Morse code is used when sending CW in the amateur bands.

Which of the following can be used to transmit CW in the amateur bands?
    A. Straight Key
    B. Electronic Keyer
    C. Computer Keyboard
    D. All of these choices are correct

T8D10 (D)
Answer: D. Straight key, electronic keyer, and computer keyboard can be used to transmit CW in the amateur bands.

What is an ARQ transmission system?
    A. A special transmission format limited to video signals
    B. A system used to encrypt command signals to an amateur radio satellite
    C. A digital scheme whereby the receiving station detects errors and sends a request to the sending station to retransmit the information
    D. A method of compressing the data in a message so more information can be sent in a shorter time

T8D11 (C)
Answer: C. An Automatic Repeat Query (ARQ) transmission system is a system designed to catch errors in transmission. From the receiving station, it detects errors in the transmission and automatically sends a request to retransmit the information.

Copyright © Mometrix Media. You have been licensed one copy of this document for personal use only. Any other reproduction or redistribution is strictly prohibited. All rights reserved.

T9 – Antennas and Feed Lines

T9A – Antennas: Vertical and Horizontal Polarization; Concept of Gain; Common Portable and Mobile Antennas; Relationships Between Antenna Length and Frequency

What is a beam antenna?
- A. An antenna built from aluminum I-beams
- B. An omnidirectional antenna invented by Clarence Beam
- C. An antenna that concentrates signals in one direction
- D. An antenna that reverses the phase of received signals

T9A01 (C)
Answer: C. A beam antenna concentrates signals in one direction. Beam antennas, also known as beamforming antennas, are sometimes composed of a simple system made of two wires. The most popular beam antenna is the Yagi, which consists of two conducting elements running parallel to each other and 1/10 of a wavelength apart.

Which of the following is true regarding vertical antennas?
- A. The magnetic field is perpendicular to the Earth
- B. The electric field is perpendicular to the Earth
- C. The phase is inverted
- D. The phase is reversed

T9A02 (B)
Answer: B. When a vertical antenna is used, the electric field is perpendicular to the earth. The most common designs for vertical antennas are ¼ and ½ wavelength. Vertical antennas are known as omnidirectional antennas because they radiate in every direction equally.

Which of the following describes a simple dipole mounted so the conductor is parallel to the Earth's surface?
- A. A ground wave antenna
- B. A horizontally polarized antenna
- C. A rhombic antenna is
- D. A vertically polarized antenna

T9A03 (B)
Answer: B. When a simple dipole is mounted so that the conductor is parallel to the Earth's surface, this may be described as a horizontally polarized antenna.

What is a disadvantage of the "rubber duck" antenna supplied with most handheld radio transceivers?
- A. It does not transmit or receive as effectively as a full-sized antenna
- B. It transmits a circularly polarized signal
- C. If the rubber end cap is lost it will unravel very quickly
- D. All of these choices are correct

T9A04 (A)
Answer: A. One disadvantage of the "rubber duck" antenna supplied with most handheld radio transceivers is it does not transmit or receive as effectively as a full-sized antenna.

Copyright © Mometrix Media. You have been licensed one copy of this document for personal use only. Any other reproduction or redistribution is strictly prohibited. All rights reserved.

How would you change a dipole antenna to make it resonant on a higher frequency?
  A. Lengthen it
  B. Insert coils in series with radiating wires
  C. Shorten it
  D. Add capacitive loading to the ends of the radiating wires

T9A05 (C)
Answer: C. To make a dipole antenna resonant on a higher frequency, shorten it.

What type of antennas are the quad, Yagi, and dish?
  A. Non-resonant antennas
  B. Loop antennas
  C. Directional antennas
  D. Isotropic antennas

T9A06 . (C)
Answer: C. The quad, Yagi, and dish are three types of directional antenna.

What is a good reason not to use a "rubber duck" antenna inside your car?
  A. Signals can be significantly weaker than when it is outside of the vehicle
  B. It might cause your radio to overheat
  C. The SWR might decrease, decreasing the signal strength
  D. All of these choices are correct

T9A07 (A)
Answer: A. One good reason not to use a "rubber duck" antenna inside your car is that signals can be significantly weaker than when it is outside the vehicle.

What is the approximate length, in inches, of a quarter-wavelength vertical antenna for 146 MHz?
  A. 112
  B. 50
  C. 19
  D. 12

T9A08 (C)
Answer: C. The approximate length of a quarter-wavelength vertical antenna for 146 MHz is 19 inches.

What is the approximate length, in inches, of a 6 meter 1/2-wavelength wire dipole antenna?
  A. 6
  B. 50
  C. 112
  D. 236

T9A09 (C)
Answer: C. The approximate length of a 6 meter ½-wavelength wire dipole antenna is 112 inches.

In which direction is the radiation strongest from a half-wave dipole antenna in free space?
  A. Equally in all directions
  B. Off the ends of the antenna
  C. Broadside to the antenna
  D. In the direction of the feed line

Copyright © Mometrix Media. You have been licensed one copy of this document for personal use only. Any other reproduction or redistribution is strictly prohibited. All rights reserved.

T9A10 (C)
Answer: C. The radiation is strongest from a half-wave dipole antenna in free space broadside to the antenna.

What is meant by the gain of an antenna?
    A. The additional power that is added to the transmitter power
    B. The additional power that is lost in the antenna when transmitting on a higher frequency
    C. The increase in signal strength in a specified direction when compared to a reference antenna
    D. The increase in impedance on receive or transmit compared to a reference antenna

T9A11 (C)
Answer: C. The gain of an antenna is the increase in signal strength in a specified direction when compared to a reference antenna.

What is a reason to use a properly mounted 5/8 wavelength antenna for VHF or UHF mobile service?
    A. It offers a lower angle of radiation and more gain than a 1/4 wavelength antenna and usually provides improved coverage
    B. It features a very high angle of radiation and is better for communicating via a repeater
    C. The 5/8 wavelength antenna completely eliminates distortion caused by reflected signals
    D. The 5/8 wavelength antenna offers a 10-times power gain over a 1/4 wavelength design

T9A12 (A)
Answer: A. Because the 5/8 wavelength antenna provides a lower angle of radiation and more gain than a 1/4 wavelength antenna, usually resulting in superior coverage, the 5/8 is the preferred antenna for VHF and UHF mobile service.

Why are VHF and UHF mobile antennas often mounted in the center of the vehicle roof?
    A. Roof mounts have the lowest possible SWR of any mounting configuration
    B. Only roof mounting can guarantee a vertically polarized signal
    C. A roof mounted antenna normally provides the most uniform radiation pattern
    D. Roof mounted antennas are always the easiest to install

T9A13 (C)
Answer: C. VHF and UHF mobile antennas are most often mounted in the center of the vehicle roof since this configuration generally provides the most uniform radiation pattern.

Which of the following terms describes a type of loading when referring to an antenna?
    A. Inserting an inductor in the radiating portion of the antenna to make it electrically longer
    B. Inserting a resistor in the radiating portion of the antenna to make it resonant
    C. Installing a spring at the base of the antenna to absorb the effects of collisions with other objects
    D. Making the antenna heavier so it will resist wind effects when in motion

T9A14 (A)
Answer: A. One example of loading an antenna would be adding an inductor to the radiating portion of the antenna to make it electrically longer.

Copyright © Mometrix Media. You have been licensed one copy of this document for personal use only. Any other reproduction or redistribution is strictly prohibited. All rights reserved.

T9B – Feed Lines: Types of Feed Lines; Attenuation vs. Frequency; SWR Concepts; Matching; Weather Protection; Choosing RF Connectors and Feed Lines

Why is it important to have a low SWR in an antenna system that uses coaxial cable feed line?
- A. To reduce television interference
- B. To allow the efficient transfer of power and reduce losses
- C. To prolong antenna life
- D. All of these choices are correct

T9B01 (B)
Answer: B. It is important to have a low SWR in an antenna system that uses coaxial cable feed lines to allow the efficient transfer of power and reduce losses. Having a higher SWR can indicate impedance mismatching and thus significant energy loss.

What is the impedance of the most commonly used coaxial cable in typical amateur radio installations?
- A. 8 ohms
- B. 50 ohms
- C. 600 ohms
- D. 12 ohms

T9B02 (B)
Answer: B. The impedance of the most commonly used coaxial cable in typical amateur radio installations is 50 ohms. Impedance is the measure of the total opposition to current flow in an alternating current circuit, composed of reactance and ohmic resistance.

Why is coaxial cable used more often than any other feed line for amateur radio antenna systems?
- A. It is easy to use and requires few special installation considerations
- B. It has less loss than any other type of feed line
- C. It can handle more power than any other type of feed line
- D. It is less expensive than any other types of feed line

T9B03 (A)
Answer: A. Coaxial cable is used more often than any other feed lines for amateur radio antenna systems because it is easy to use and requires few special installation considerations.

What does an antenna tuner do?
- A. It matches the antenna system impedance to the transceiver's output impedance
- B. It helps a receiver automatically tune in weak stations
- C. It allows an antenna to be used on both transmit and receive
- D. It automatically selects the proper antenna for the frequency band being used

T9B04 (A)
Answer: A. An antenna tuner matches the antenna system impedance to the transceiver's output impedance.

What generally happens as the frequency of a signal passing through coaxial cable is increased?
- A. The apparent SWR increases
- B. The reflected power increases
- C. The characteristic impedance increases
- D. The loss increases

Copyright © Mometrix Media. You have been licensed one copy of this document for personal use only. Any other reproduction or redistribution is strictly prohibited. All rights reserved.

T9B05 (D)
Answer: D. As the frequency of a signal passing through coaxial cable is increased, the loss generally increases as well.

Which of the following connectors is most suitable for frequencies above 400 MHz?
    A. A UHF (PL-259/SO-239) connector
    B. A Type N connector
    C. An RS-213 connector
    D. A DB-25 connector

T9B06 (B)
Answer: B. A Type N connector is most suitable for frequencies above 400 MHz. Type N connectors are threaded RF connectors used to join coaxial cables. These cables are able to carry microwave frequency signals.

Which of the following is true of PL-259 type coax connectors?
    A. They are preferred for microwave operation
    B. They are water tight
    C. They are commonly used at HF frequencies
    D. They are a bayonet type connector

T9B07 (C)
Answer: C. PL–259 type coax connectors are commonly used at HF frequencies.

Why should coax connectors exposed to the weather be sealed against water intrusion?
    A. To prevent an increase in feed line loss
    B. To prevent interference to telephones
    C. To keep the jacket from becoming loose
    D. All of these choices are correct

T9B08 (A)
Answer: A. Coax connectors exposed to the weather should be sealed against water intrusion to prevent an increase in feed line loss.

What might cause erratic changes in SWR readings?
    A. The transmitter is being modulated
    B. A loose connection in an antenna or a feed line
    C. The transmitter is being over-modulated
    D. Interference from other stations is distorting your signal

T9B09 (B)
Answer: B. A loose connection in an antenna or a feed line might cause erratic changes in SWR readings.

What electrical difference exists between the smaller RG-58 and larger RG-8 coaxial cables?
    A. There is no significant difference between the two types
    B. RG-58 cable has less loss at a given frequency
    C. RG-8 cable has less loss at a given frequency
    D. RG-58 cable can handle higher power levels

T9B10 (C)
Answer: C. The electrical difference that exists between the smaller RG–58 and larger RG-8 coaxial cables is that the RG–8 cable has less loss at a given frequency.

Copyright © Mometrix Media. You have been licensed one copy of this document for personal use only. Any other reproduction or redistribution is strictly prohibited. All rights reserved.

Which of the following types of feed line has the lowest loss at VHF and UHF?
- A. 50-ohm flexible coax
- B. Multi-conductor unbalanced cable
- C. Air-insulated hard line
- D. 75-ohm flexible coax

T9B11 (C)
Answer: C. An air-insulated hard line has a lower loss at VHF and UHF than 50 ohm flexible callbacks, multi-conductor unbalanced cable, or 75 ohm flexible coax.

T0 – Electrical Safety

T0A – Power Circuits and Hazards: Hazardous Voltages; Fuses and Circuit Breakers; Grounding; Lightning Protection; Battery Safety; Electrical Code Compliance

Which of the following is a safety hazard of a 12-volt storage battery?
- A. Touching both terminals with the hands can cause electrical shock
- B. Shorting the terminals can cause burns, fire, or an explosion
- C. RF emissions from the battery
- D. All of these choices are correct

T0A01 (B)
Answer: B. In order for electrical shock from a 12-volt battery to be hazardous, the circuit would typically need to be connected on or near one's chest. The primary hazard associated with a 12-volt battery is shorting the terminals with low resistance materials such as metal wires or rods, potentially resulting in burns, fires, or explosions.

How does current flowing through the body cause a health hazard?
- A. By heating tissue
- B. It disrupts the electrical functions of cells
- C. It causes involuntary muscle contractions
- D. All of these choices are correct

T0A02 (D)
Answer: D. An electric current flowing through the body causes a health hazard by heating the tissue, disrupting the electrical functions of cells, and causing involuntary muscle contractions.

What is connected to the green wire in a three-wire electrical AC plug?
- A. Neutral
- B. Hot
- C. Safety ground
- D. The white wire

T0A03 (C)
Answer: C. In a three-wire electrical AC plug, the green wire is connected to the safety ground.

Copyright © Mometrix Media. You have been licensed one copy of this document for personal use only. Any other reproduction or redistribution is strictly prohibited. All rights reserved.

What is the purpose of a fuse in an electrical circuit?
    A. To prevent power supply ripple from damaging a circuit
    B. To interrupt power in case of overload
    C. To limit current to prevent shocks
    D. All of these choices are correct

T0A04 (B)
Answer: B. The purpose of a fuse in an electrical circuit is to interrupt power in case of overload.

Why is it unwise to install a 20-ampere fuse in the place of a 5-ampere fuse?
    A. The larger fuse would be likely to blow because it is rated for higher current
    B. The power supply ripple would greatly increase
    C. Excessive current could cause a fire
    D. All of these choices are correct

T0A05 (C)
Answer: C. It is unwise to install a 20-ampere fuse in the place of a 5-ampere fuse because the excessive current could cause a fire.

What is a good way to guard against electrical shock at your station?
    A. Use three-wire cords and plugs for all AC powered equipment
    B. Connect all AC powered station equipment to a common safety ground
    C. Use a circuit protected by a ground-fault interrupter
    D. All of these choices are correct

T0A06 (D)
Answer: D. There are a few good ways to guard against electrical shock at your station. To begin with, use three-wire cords and plugs for all AC powered equipment. Second, connect all AC powered station equipment to a common safety ground. Third, use a circuit protected by a ground-fault interrupter.

Which of these precautions should be taken when installing devices for lightning protection in a coaxial cable feed line?
    A. Include a parallel bypass switch for each protector so that it can be switched out of the circuit when running high power
    B. Include a series switch in the ground line of each protector to prevent RF overload from inadvertently damaging the protector
    C. Keep the ground wires from each protector separate and connected to station ground
    D. Ground all of the protectors to a common plate which is in turn connected to an external ground

T0A07 (D)
Answer: D. When installing devices for lightning protection in a coaxial cable feed line, one should ground all of the protectors to a common plate which is in turn connected to an external ground.

What safety equipment should always be included in home-built equipment that is powered from 120V AC power circuits?
    A. A fuse or circuit breaker in series with the AC hot conductor
    B. An AC voltmeter across the incoming power source
    C. An inductor in series with the AC power source
    D. A capacitor across the AC power source

Copyright © Mometrix Media. You have been licensed one copy of this document for personal use only. Any other reproduction or redistribution is strictly prohibited. All rights reserved.

T0A08 (A)
Answer: A. Home-built equipment that is powered with 120V AC power should always include a fuse or circuit breaker in series with the hot power line to reduce the risk of electrocution hazard.

What kind of hazard is presented by a conventional 12-volt storage battery?
    A. It emits ozone which can be harmful to the atmosphere
    B. Shock hazard due to high voltage
    C. Explosive gas can collect if not properly vented
    D. All of these choices are correct

T0A09 (C)
Answer: C. One hazard related to conventional 12-volt storage batteries is that explosive gas can collect if it is not properly vented.

What can happen if a lead-acid storage battery is charged or discharged too quickly?
    A. The battery could overheat and give off flammable gas or explode
    B. The voltage can become reversed
    C. The "memory effect" will reduce the capacity of the battery
    D. All of these choices are correct

T0A10 (A)
Answer: A. If a lead-acid storage battery is charged or discharged too quickly, the battery could overheat and give off flammable gas, or explode. Lead-acid batteries have a low energy-to-weight ratio and a low energy-to-volume ratio, but they nevertheless maintain a comparatively large power-to-weight ratio.

What kind of hazard might exist in a power supply when it is turned off and disconnected?
    A. Static electricity could damage the grounding system
    B. Circulating currents inside the transformer might cause damage
    C. The fuse might blow if you remove the cover
    D. You might receive an electric shock from the charged stored in large capacitors

T0A11 (D)
Answer: D. When a power supply is turned off and disconnected, a person still might receive an electric shock from the stored charge in large capacitors.

T0B – Antenna Safety: Tower Safety; Erecting an Antenna Support; Overhead Power Lines; Installing an Antenna

When should members of a tower work team wear a hard hat and safety glasses?
    A. At all times except when climbing the tower
    B. At all times except when belted firmly to the tower
    C. At all times when any work is being done on the tower
    D. Only when the tower exceeds 30 feet in height

T0B01 (C)
Answer: C. The members of the tower work team should wear a hard hat and safety glasses at all times when any work is being done on the tower.

Copyright © Mometrix Media. You have been licensed one copy of this document for personal use only. Any other reproduction or redistribution is strictly prohibited. All rights reserved.

What is a good precaution to observe before climbing an antenna tower?
    A. Make sure that you wear a grounded wrist strap
    B. Remove all tower grounding connections
    C. Put on a climbing harness and safety glasses
    D. All of these choices are correct

T0B02 (C)
Answer: C. Before climbing an antenna tower, one should put on a climbing harness and safety glasses.

Under what circumstances is it safe to climb a tower without a helper or observer?
    A. When no electrical work is being performed
    B. When no mechanical work is being performed
    C. When the work being done is not more than 20 feet above the ground
    D. Never

T0B03 (D)
Answer: D. It is never safe to climb a tower without a helper or observer.

Which of the following is an important safety precaution to observe when putting up an antenna tower?
    A. Wear a ground strap connected to your wrist at all times
    B. Insulate the base of the tower to avoid lightning strikes
    C. Look for and stay clear of any overhead electrical wires
    D. All of these choices are correct

T0B04 (C)
Answer: C. When putting up an antenna tower, it is important to look for and stay clear of any overhead electric wires.

What is the purpose of a gin pole?
    A. To temporarily replace guy wires
    B. To be used in place of a safety harness
    C. To lift tower sections or antennas
    D. To provide a temporary ground

T0B05 (C)
Answer: C. The purpose of a gin pole is to lift tower sections or antennas.

What is the minimum safe distance from a power line to allow when installing an antenna?
    A. Half the width of your property
    B. The height of the power line above ground
    C. 1/2 wavelength at the operating frequency
    D. So that if the antenna falls unexpectedly, no part of it can come closer than 10 feet to the power wires

T0B06 (D)
Answer: D. The minimum safe distance from a power line when installing an antenna is such that, if the antenna falls unexpectedly, no part of it can come closer than 10 feet to the power wires.

Copyright © Mometrix Media. You have been licensed one copy of this document for personal use only. Any other reproduction or redistribution is strictly prohibited. All rights reserved.

Which of the following is an important safety rule to remember when using a crank-up tower?
    A. This type of tower must never be painted
    B. This type of tower must never be grounded
    C. This type of tower must never be climbed unless it is in the fully retracted position
    D. All of these choices are correct

T0B07 (C)
Answer: C. An important safety rule to remember when using a crank-up tower is that this type of tower must never be climbed unless it is in the fully retracted position. Crank-up towers are kept stable by a concrete foundation rather than by guy wires.

What is considered to be a proper grounding method for a tower?
    A. A single four-foot ground rod, driven into the ground no more than 12 inches from the base
    B. A ferrite-core RF choke connected between the tower and ground
    C. Separate eight-foot long ground rods for each tower leg, bonded to the tower and each other
    D. A connection between the tower base and a cold water pipe

T0B08 (C)
Answer: C. Separate eight-foot long ground rods for each tower leg, bonded to the tower and each other, are considered to be a proper grounding method for a tower.

Why should you avoid attaching an antenna to a utility pole?
    A. The antenna will not work properly because of induced voltages
    B. The utility company will charge you an extra monthly fee
    C. The antenna could contact high-voltage power wires
    D. All of these choices are correct

T0B09 (C)
Answer: C. You should avoid attaching an antenna to a utility pole because the antenna could contact high-voltage power wires.

Which of the following is true concerning grounding conductors used for lightning protection?
    A. Only non-insulated wire must be used
    B. Wires must be carefully routed with precise right-angle bends
    C. Sharp bends must be avoided
    D. Common grounds must be avoided

T0B10 (C)
Answer: C. Sharp bends must be avoided in the grounding conductors used for lightning protection.

Which of the following establishes grounding requirements for an amateur radio tower or antenna?
    A. FCC Part 97 Rules
    B. Local electrical codes
    C. FAA tower lighting regulations
    D. Underwriters Laboratories' recommended practices

T0B11 (B)
Answer: B Local electrical codes establish grounding requirements for an amateur radio tower or antenna.

Copyright © Mometrix Media. You have been licensed one copy of this document for personal use only. Any other reproduction or redistribution is strictly prohibited. All rights reserved.

Which of the following is good practice when installing ground wires on a tower for lightning protection?
A. Put a loop in the ground connection to prevent water damage to the ground system
B. Make sure that all bends in the ground wires are clean, right angle bends
C. Ensure that connections are short and direct
D. All of these choices are correct

T0B12 (C)
Answer: C. When installing grounding wires for lightning protection purposes, you should always keep the wires short and direct to ensure that the electricity follows the desired path and reaches ground without causing damage.

T0C – RF Hazards: Radiation Exposure; Proximity to Antennas; Recognized Safe Power Levels; Exposure to Others; Radiation Types; Duty Cycle

What type of radiation are VHF and UHF radio signals?
A. Gamma radiation
B. Ionizing radiation
C. Alpha radiation
D. Non-ionizing radiation

T0C01 (D)
Answer: D. VHF and UHF radio signals are nonionizing radiation. That is, they are electromagnetic radiation without enough energy to knock electrons off of atoms or molecules, which would create an ion.

Which of the following frequencies has the lowest value for Maximum Permissible Exposure limit?
A. 3.5 MHz
B. 50 MHz
C. 440 MHz
D. 1296 MHz

T0C02 (B)
Answer: B. 50 MHz has a lower maximum permissible exposure limit then 3.5 MHz, 440 MHz, or 1296 MHz.

What is the maximum power level that an amateur radio station may use at VHF frequencies before an RF exposure evaluation is required?
A. 1500 watts PEP transmitter output
B. 1 watt forward power
C. 50 watts PEP at the antenna
D. 50 watts PEP reflected power

T0C03 (C)
Answer: C. The maximum power level that an amateur radio station may use at VHF frequencies before an RF exposure evaluation is required is 50 watts PEP at the antenna.

Copyright © Mometrix Media. You have been licensed one copy of this document for personal use only. Any other reproduction or redistribution is strictly prohibited. All rights reserved.

What factors affect the RF exposure of people near an amateur station antenna?
  A. Frequency and power level of the RF field
  B. Distance from the antenna to a person
  C. Radiation pattern of the antenna
  D. All of these choices are correct

T0C04 (D)
Answer: D. Several factors affect the RF exposure of people near an amateur station antenna. These factors include the frequency and power level of the RF field, the distance from the antenna to a person, and the radiation pattern of the antenna.

Why do exposure limits vary with frequency?
  A. Lower frequency RF fields have more energy than higher frequency fields
  B. Lower frequency RF fields do not penetrate the human body
  C. Higher frequency RF fields are transient in nature
  D. The human body absorbs more RF energy at some frequencies than at others

T0C05 (D)
Answer: D. Exposure limits vary with frequency because the human body absorbs more RF energy at some frequencies than at others.

Which of the following is an acceptable method to determine that your station complies with FCC RF exposure regulations?
  A. By calculation based on FCC OET Bulletin 65
  B. By calculation based on computer modeling
  C. By measurement of field strength using calibrated equipment
  D. All of these choices are correct

T0C06 (D)
Answer: D. It is acceptable to determine that your station complies with FCC RF exposure regulations by calculation based on FCC OET Bulletin 65, by calculation based on computer modeling, or by measurement of field strength using calibrated equipment.

What could happen if a person accidentally touched your antenna while you were transmitting?
  A. Touching the antenna could cause television interference
  B. They might receive a painful RF burn
  C. They might develop radiation poisoning
  D. All of these choices are correct

T0C07 (B)
Answer: B. If a person accidentally touched your antenna while you were transmitting, they might receive a painful RF burn.

Which of the following actions might amateur operators take to prevent exposure to RF radiation in excess of FCC-supplied limits?
  A. Relocate antennas
  B. Relocate the transmitter
  C. Increase the duty cycle
  D. All of these choices are correct

Copyright © Mometrix Media. You have been licensed one copy of this document for personal use only. Any other reproduction or redistribution is strictly prohibited. All rights reserved.

T0C08 (A)
Answer: A. Amateur operators might relocate antennas to prevent exposure to RF radiation in excess of FCC-supplied limits.

How can you make sure your station stays in compliance with RF safety regulations?
    A. By informing the FCC of any changes made in your station
    B. By re-evaluating the station whenever an item of equipment is changed
    C. By making sure your antennas have low SWR
    D. All of these choices are correct

T0C09 (B)
Answer: B. A station may ensure compliance by re-evaluating the station whenever an item of equipment is changed.

Why is duty cycle one of the factors used to determine safe RF radiation exposure levels?
    A. It affects the average exposure of people to radiation
    B. It affects the peak exposure of people to radiation
    C. It takes into account the antenna feedline loss
    D. It takes into account the thermal effects of the final amplifier

T0C10 (A)
Answer: A. Duty cycle is one of the factors used to determine safe RF radiation exposure levels because it affects the average exposure of people to radiation. If the duty cycle is lower, then there is less RF radiation exposure with no change in peak envelope power output.

What is the definition of duty cycle during the averaging time for RF exposure?
    A. The difference between the lowest power output and the highest power output of a transmitter
    B. The difference between the PEP and average power output of a transmitter
    C. The percentage of time that a transmitter is transmitting
    D. The percentage of time that a transmitter is not transmitting

T0C11 (C)
Answer: C. In the context of determining RF exposure, the duty cycle is the percentage of the time that the transmitter is actually transmitting.

How does RF radiation differ from ionizing radiation (radioactivity)?
    A. RF radiation does not have sufficient energy to cause genetic damage
    B. RF radiation can only be detected with an RF dosimeter
    C. RF radiation is limited in range to a few feet
    D. RF radiation is perfectly safe

T0C12 (A)
Answer: A. Unlike most ionizing radiation, RF radiation does not carry sufficient energy to cause genetic damage to living creatures.

If the averaging time for exposure is 6 minutes, how much power density is permitted if the signal is present for 3 minutes and absent for 3 minutes rather than being present for the entire 6 minutes?
    A. 3 times as much
    B. 1/2 as much
    C. 2 times as much
    D. There is no adjustment allowed for shorter exposure times

Copyright © Mometrix Media. You have been licensed one copy of this document for personal use only. Any other reproduction or redistribution is strictly prohibited. All rights reserved.

T0C13 (C)
Answer: C. If the signal is present for only half of the time period being considered, the allowed power density may be 2 times as high as if the signal were present for the entire time period.

Copyright © Mometrix Media. You have been licensed one copy of this document for personal use only. Any other reproduction or redistribution is strictly prohibited. All rights reserved.

Technician Class Practice Test 1

Practice Questions

1. Which of the following is a purpose of the Amateur Radio Service as stated in the FCC rules and regulations?
    a. Providing personal radio communications for as many citizens as possible
    b. Providing communications for international non-profit organizations
    c. Advancing skills in the technical and communication phases of the radio art
    d. All of these choices are correct

2. What is the ITU?
    a. An agency of the United States Department of Telecommunications Management
    b. A United Nations agency for information and communication technology issues
    c. An independent frequency coordination agency
    d. A department of the FCC

3. Which type of call sign has a single letter in both its prefix and suffix?
    a. Vanity
    b. Sequential
    c. Special event
    d. In-memoriam

4. With which countries are FCC-licensed amateur stations prohibited from exchanging communications?
    a. Any country whose administration has notified the ITU that it objects to such communications
    b. Any country whose administration has notified the United Nations that it objects to such communications
    c. Any country engaged in hostilities with another country
    d. Any country in violation of the War Powers Act of 1934

5. When is an amateur station permitted to transmit without a control operator?
    a. When using automatic control, such as in the case of a repeater
    b. When the station licensee is away and another licensed amateur is using the station
    c. When the transmitting station is an auxiliary station
    d. Never

6. What type of identification is being used when identifying a station on the air as "Race Headquarters"?
    a. Tactical call
    b. Self-assigned designator
    c. SSID
    d. Broadcast station

7. What is the most common repeater frequency offset in the 2 meter band?
    a. Plus 500 kHz
    b. Plus or minus 600 kHz
    c. Minus 500 kHz
    d. Only plus 600 kHz

Copyright © Mometrix Media. You have been licensed one copy of this document for personal use only. Any other reproduction or redistribution is strictly prohibited. All rights reserved.

8. What is the term used to describe an amateur station that is transmitting and receiving on the same frequency?
   a. Full duplex communication
   b. Diplex communication
   c. Simplex communication
   d. Multiplex communication

9. When do the FCC rules NOT apply to the operation of an amateur station?
   a. When operating a RACES station
   b. When operating under special FEMA rules
   c. When operating under special ARES rules
   d. Never, FCC rules always apply

10. What should you do if another operator reports that your station's 2 meter signals were strong just a moment ago, but now they are weak or distorted?
    a. Change the batteries in your radio to a different type
    b. Turn on the CTCSS tone
    c. Ask the other operator to adjust his squelch control
    d. Try moving a few feet or changing the direction of your antenna if possible, as reflections may be causing multi-path distortion

11. What is the name for the distance a radio wave travels during one complete cycle?
    a. Wave speed
    b. Waveform
    c. Wavelength
    d. Wave spread

12. Why are "direct" (not via a repeater) UHF signals rarely heard from stations outside your local coverage area?
    a. They are too weak to go very far
    b. FCC regulations prohibit them from going more than 50 miles
    c. UHF signals are usually not reflected by the ionosphere
    d. They collide with trees and shrubbery and fade out

13. Which of the following is true concerning the microphone connectors on amateur transceivers?
    a. All transceivers use the same microphone connector type
    b. Some connectors include push-to-talk and voltages for powering the microphone
    c. All transceivers using the same connector type are wired identically
    d. Un-keyed connectors allow any microphone to be connected

14. What may happen if a transmitter is operated with the microphone gain set too high?
    a. The output power might be too high
    b. The output signal might become distorted
    c. The frequency might vary
    d. The SWR might increase

15. Electrical current is measured in which of the following units?
    a. Volts
    b. Watts
    c. Ohms
    d. Amperes

Copyright © Mometrix Media. You have been licensed one copy of this document for personal use only. Any other reproduction or redistribution is strictly prohibited. All rights reserved.

16. How many milliamperes is 1.5 amperes?
    a. 15 milliamperes
    b. 150 milliamperes
    c. 1,500 milliamperes
    d. 15,000 milliamperes

17. What is the ability to store energy in an electric field called?
    a. Inductance
    b. Resistance
    c. Tolerance
    d. Capacitance

18. What formula is used to calculate current in a circuit?
    a. Current (I) equals voltage (E) multiplied by resistance (R)
    b. Current (I) equals voltage (E) divided by resistance (R)
    c. Current (I) equals voltage (E) added to resistance (R)
    d. Current (I) equals voltage (E) minus resistance (R)

19. What electrical component is used to oppose the flow of current in a DC circuit?
    a. Inductor
    b. Resistor
    c. Voltmeter
    d. Transformer

20. What class of electronic components is capable of using a voltage or current signal to control current flow?
    a. Capacitors
    b. Inductors
    c. Resistors
    d. Transistors

21. What is the name for standardized representations of components in an electrical wiring diagram?
    a. Electrical depictions
    b. Grey sketch
    c. Schematic symbols
    d. Component callouts

22. Which of the following devices or circuits changes an alternating current into a varying direct current signal?
    a. Transformer
    b. Rectifier
    c. Amplifier
    d. Reflector

23. Which term describes the ability of a receiver to detect the presence of a signal?
    a. Linearity
    b. Sensitivity
    c. Selectivity
    d. Total Harmonic Distortion

Copyright © Mometrix Media. You have been licensed one copy of this document for personal use only. Any other reproduction or redistribution is strictly prohibited. All rights reserved.

24. What can you do if you are told your FM handheld or mobile transceiver is over deviating?
    a. Talk louder into the microphone
    b. Let the transceiver cool off
    c. Change to a higher power level
    d. Talk farther away from the microphone

25. What is the primary purpose of a dummy load?
    a. To prevent the radiation of signals when making tests
    b. To prevent over-modulation of your transmitter
    c. To improve the radiation from your antenna
    d. To improve the signal to noise ratio of your receiver

26. Which instrument would you use to measure electric potential or electromotive force?
    a. An ammeter
    b. A voltmeter
    c. A wavemeter
    d. An ohmmeter

27. Which of the following is a form of amplitude modulation?
    a. Spread-spectrum
    b. Packet radio
    c. Single sideband
    d. Phase shift keying

28. Who may be the control operator of a station communicating through an amateur satellite or space station?
    a. Only an Amateur Extra Class operator
    b. A General Class licensee or higher licensee who has a satellite operator certification
    c. Only an Amateur Extra Class operator who is also an AMSAT member
    d. Any amateur whose license privileges allow them to transmit on the satellite uplink frequency

29. Which of the following methods is used to locate sources of noise interference or jamming?
    a. Echolocation
    b. Doppler radar
    c. Radio direction finding
    d. Phase locking

30. Which of the following is an example of a digital communications method?
    a. Packet
    b. PSK31
    c. MFSK
    d. All of these choices are correct

31. What is a beam antenna?
    a. An antenna built from aluminum I-beams
    b. An omnidirectional antenna invented by Clarence Beam
    c. An antenna that concentrates signals in one direction
    d. An antenna that reverses the phase of received signals

Copyright © Mometrix Media. You have been licensed one copy of this document for personal use only. Any other reproduction or redistribution is strictly prohibited. All rights reserved.

32. Why is it important to have a low SWR in an antenna system that uses coaxial cable feed line?
    a. To reduce television interference
    b. To allow the efficient transfer of power and reduce losses
    c. To prolong antenna life
    d. All of these choices are correct

33. Which of the following is a safety hazard of a 12-volt storage battery?
    a. Touching both terminals with the hands can cause electrical shock
    b. Shorting the terminals can cause burns, fire, or an explosion
    c. RF emissions from the battery
    d. All of these choices are correct

34. When should members of a tower work team wear a hard hat and safety glasses?
    a. At all times except when climbing the tower
    b. At all times except when belted firmly to the tower
    c. At all times when any work is being done on the tower
    d. Only when the tower exceeds 30 feet in height

35. What type of radiation are VHF and UHF radio signals?
    a. Gamma radiation
    b. Ionizing radiation
    c. Alpha radiation
    d. Non-ionizing radiation

- 101 -

Copyright © Mometrix Media. You have been licensed one copy of this document for personal use only. Any other reproduction or redistribution is strictly prohibited. All rights reserved.

Answers and Explanations

1. C: As stated in the FCC rules, advancing skills in the technical and communication phases of the radio art is a purpose of the Amateur Radio Service

2. B: The ITU is a United Nations agency for information and communication technology issues.

3. C: The special event call sign has a single letter in both the prefix and suffix. Each license issued by the FCC comes with a unique call sign. Typically, the prefix of a call sign contains one or two letters and one number. It indicates the location of the operator.

4. A: FCC-licensed amateur stations are prohibited from exchanging communications with any country whose administration has notified the ITU that it objects to such communications.

5. D: When transmitting, each amateur station must have a control operator.

6. A: Tactical call identification is being used when identifying a station on the air as "race headquarters." Tactical call signs are the names that identify locations or functions during local emergency communications.

7. B: The most common repeater frequency offset in the 2 meter band is plus or minus 600 kHz.

8. C: The term used to describe an amateur station that is transmitting and receiving on the same frequency is simplex communication.

9. D: FCC rules always apply to the operation of an amateur station.

10. D: If another operator reports that your station's 2 meter signals were strong just a moment ago, but now they are weak or distorted, try moving a few feet, as random reflections may be causing multipath distortion.

11. C: Wavelength is the distance a radio wave travels during one complete cycle. Another way of putting it is that wavelength is the distance between successive crests or troughs.

12. C: Direct (that is, not by means of a repeater) UHF signals are rarely heard from stations outside the local coverage area because UHF signals are usually not reflected by the ionosphere.

13. B: Some microphone connectors on amateur transceivers include push-to-talk and voltages for powering the microphone.

14. B: If a transmitter is operated with the microphone gain set too high, the output signal might become distorted.

15. D: Electrical current is measured in amperes, usually referred to as amps. Current is the amount of electrons flowing through a circuit.

16. C: 1.5 amperes is equivalent to 1500 mA. The prefix milli- means thousandth, so a milliampere is a thousandth of an ampere. Therefore, 1.5 amperes can be converted to milliamperes by multiplying by a thousand: 1.5 x 1000 = 1500.

17. D: The ability to store energy in an electric field is called capacitance. Capacitance can also be defined as the ratio of the electric charge that is shifted from one conductor to another to the resulting potential difference between them.

18. B: The formula for calculating current in a circuit is current equals voltage divided by resistance.

Copyright © Mometrix Media. You have been licensed one copy of this document for personal use only. Any other reproduction or redistribution is strictly prohibited. All rights reserved.

19. B: The electrical component used to oppose the flow of current in a DC circuit is a resistor. For ham radio technicians, the most commonly required resistors are quarter- and half-watt fixed value resistors and 100, 500, 1k, 5k, 10k, and 100k ohm variable resistors.

20. D: Transistors are capable of using a voltage or current signal to control current flow. A transistor is an electronic device that includes a semiconductor and at least three electrical outlets. It may be used as a detector, amplifier, or switch.

21. C: Standardized representations of components in an electrical wiring diagram are known as schematic symbols.

22. B: A rectifier changes an alternating current into a varying direct current signal. Specifically, it is a switch that blocks the current in one direction but permits it in the other.

23. B: The ability of a receiver to detect the presence of a signal is measured in terms of its sensitivity.

24. D: If you are told your FM handheld or mobile transceiver is over deviating, you can talk farther away from the microphone.

25. A: The primary purpose of a dummy load is to prevent the radiation of signals when making tests. The dummy load, also known as a dummy antenna, is a station accessory that enables the user to test and fine-tune equipment without actually broadcasting a signal.

26. B: A voltmeter is used to measure electric potential or electromotive force. It accomplishes this by identifying the electric potential difference between two conductors.

27. C: Single sideband is a form of amplitude modulation. Indeed, single sideband is the most common mode of voice transmission on the high-frequency bands. Unlike an a.m. transmission, in which two identical versions of the message are broadcast, an SSB transmission only broadcasts one. For this reason, single sideband communications are more efficient and are better at conserving space on the radio spectrum.

28. D: Any amateur whose license privileges allow them to transmit on the satellite uplink frequency may be the control operator of a station communicating through an amateur satellite or space station.

29. C: Radio direction finding is used to locate sources of noise interference or jamming.

30. D: Packet, PSK 31s, and MFSKs are all examples of digital communications methods.

31. C: A beam antenna concentrates signals in one direction. Beam antennas, also known as beamforming antennas, are sometimes composed of a simple system made of two wires. The most popular beam antenna is the Yagi, which consists of two conducting elements running parallel to each other and 1/10 of a wavelength apart.

32. B: It is important to have a low SWR in an antenna system that uses coaxial cable feed lines to allow the efficient transfer of power and reduce losses. Having a higher SWR can indicate impedance mismatching and thus significant energy loss.

33. B: In order for electrical shock from a 12-volt battery to be hazardous, the circuit would typically need to be connected on or near one's chest. The primary hazard associated with a 12-volt battery is shorting the terminals with low resistance materials such as metal wires or rods, potentially resulting in burns, fires, or explosions.

34. C: The members of the tower work team should wear a hard hat and safety glasses at all times when any work is being done on the tower.

Copyright © Mometrix Media. You have been licensed one copy of this document for personal use only. Any other reproduction or redistribution is strictly prohibited. All rights reserved.

35. D: VHF and UHF radio signals are nonionizing radiation. That is, they are electromagnetic radiation without enough energy to knock electrons off of atoms or molecules, which would create an ion.

Copyright © Mometrix Media. You have been licensed one copy of this document for personal use only. Any other reproduction or redistribution is strictly prohibited. All rights reserved.

Technician Class Practice Test 2

Practice Questions

1. Which agency regulates and enforces the rules for the Amateur Radio Service in the United States?
    a. FEMA
    b. The ITU
    c. The FCC
    d. Homeland Security

2. Why are the frequency assignments for some U.S. Territories different from those in the 50 U.S. States?
    a. Some U. S. Territories are located in ITU regions other than region 2
    b. Territorial governments are allowed to select their own frequency allocations
    c. Territorial frequency allocations must also include those of adjacent countries
    d. Any territory that was in existence before the ratification of the Communications Act of 1934 is exempt from FCC frequency regulations

3. Which of the following is a valid US amateur radio station call sign?
    a. KMA3505
    b. W3ABC
    c. KDKA
    d. 11Q1176

4. On which of the following occasions may an FCC-licensed amateur station exchange messages with a U.S. military station?
    a. During an Armed Forces Day Communications Test
    b. During a Memorial Day Celebration
    c. During an Independence Day celebration
    d. During a propagation test

5. Who may a station licensee designate to be the control operator of an amateur station?
    a. Any U.S. citizen or registered alien
    b. Any family member of the station licensee
    c. Any person over the age of 18
    d. Only a person for whom an amateur operator/primary station license grant appears in the FCC database or who is authorized for alien reciprocal operation

6. When using tactical identifiers such as "Race Headquarters" during a community service net operation, how often must your station transmit the station's FCC-assigned call sign?
    a. Never, the tactical call is sufficient
    b. Once during every hour
    c. At the end of each communication and every ten minutes during a communication
    d. At the end of every transmission

7. What is the national calling frequency for FM simplex operations in the 70 cm band?
    a. 146.520 MHz
    b. 145.000 MHz
    c. 432.100 MHz
    d. 446.000 MHz

Copyright © Mometrix Media. You have been licensed one copy of this document for personal use only. Any other reproduction or redistribution is strictly prohibited. All rights reserved.

8. What is the term used to describe the use of a sub-audible tone transmitted with normal voice audio to open the squelch of a receiver?
   a. Carrier squelch
   b. Tone burst
   c. DTMF
   d. CTCSS

9. What is one way to recharge a 12-volt lead-acid station battery if the commercial power is out?
   a. Cool the battery in ice for several hours
   b. Add acid to the battery
   c. Connect the battery in parallel with a vehicle's battery and run the engine
   d. All of these choices are correct

10. Why are UHF signals often more effective from inside buildings than VHF signals?
   a. VHF signals lose power faster over distance
   b. The shorter wavelength allows them to more easily penetrate the structure of buildings
   c. This is incorrect; VHF works better than UHF inside buildings
   d. UHF antennas are more efficient than VHF antennas

11. What property of a radio wave is used to describe its polarization?
   a. The orientation of the electric field
   b. The orientation of the magnetic field
   c. The ratio of the energy in the magnetic field to the energy in the electric field
   d. The ratio of the velocity to the wavelength

12. Which of the following might be happening when VHF signals are being received from long distances?
   a. Signals are being reflected from outer space
   b. Signals are arriving by sub-surface ducting
   c. Signals are being reflected by lightning storms in your area
   d. Signals are being refracted from a sporadic E layer

13. How might a computer be used as part of an amateur radio station?
   a. For logging contacts and contact information
   b. For sending and/or receiving CW
   c. For generating and decoding digital signals
   d. All of these choices are correct

14. Which of the following can be used to enter the operating frequency on a modern transceiver?
   a. The keypad or VFO knob
   b. The CTCSS or DTMF encoder
   c. The Automatic Frequency Control
   d. All of these choices are correct

15. Electrical power is measured in which of the following units?
   a. Volts
   b. Watts
   c. Ohms
   d. Amperes

Copyright © Mometrix Media. You have been licensed one copy of this document for personal use only. Any other reproduction or redistribution is strictly prohibited. All rights reserved.

16. What is another way to specify a radio signal frequency of 1,500,000 hertz?
    a. 1500 kHz
    b. 1500 MHz
    c. 15 GHz
    d. 150 kHz

17. What is the basic unit of capacitance?
    a. The farad
    b. The ohm
    c. The volt
    d. The henry

18. What formula is used to calculate voltage in a circuit?
    a. Voltage (E) equals current (I) multiplied by resistance (R)
    b. Voltage (E) equals current (I) divided by resistance (R)
    c. Voltage (E) equals current (I) added to resistance (R)
    d. Voltage (E) equals current (I) minus resistance (R)

19. What type of component is often used as an adjustable volume control?
    a. Fixed resistor
    b. Power resistor
    c. Potentiometer
    d. Transformer

20. What electronic component allows current to flow in only one direction?
    a. Resistor
    b. Fuse
    c. Diode
    d. Driven Element

21. What is component 1 in figure T1?
(figures found at the end of the guide)
    a. Resistor
    b. Transistor
    c. Battery
    d. Connector

22. What best describes a relay?
    a. A switch controlled by an electromagnet
    b. A current controlled amplifier
    c. An optical sensor
    d. A pass transistor

23. What is a transceiver?
    a. A type of antenna switch
    b. A unit combining the functions of a transmitter and a receiver
    c. A component in a repeater which filters out unwanted interference
    d. A type of antenna matching network

Copyright © Mometrix Media. You have been licensed one copy of this document for personal use only. Any other reproduction or redistribution is strictly prohibited. All rights reserved.

24. What would cause a broadcast AM or FM radio to receive an amateur radio transmission unintentionally?
    a. The receiver is unable to reject strong signals outside the AM or FM band
    b. The microphone gain of the transmitter is turned up too high
    c. The audio amplifier of the transmitter is overloaded
    d. The deviation of an FM transmitter is set too low

25. Which of the following instruments can be used to determine if an antenna is resonant at the desired operating frequency?
    a. A VTVM
    b. An antenna analyzer
    c. A "Q" meter
    d. A frequency counter

26. What is the correct way to connect a voltmeter to a circuit?
    a. In series with the circuit
    b. In parallel with the circuit
    c. In quadrature with the circuit
    d. In phase with the circuit

27. What type of modulation is most commonly used for VHF packet radio transmissions?
    a. FM
    b. SSB
    c. AM
    d. Spread Spectrum

28. How much transmitter power should be used on the uplink frequency of an amateur satellite or space station?
    a. The maximum power of your transmitter
    b. The minimum amount of power needed to complete the contact
    c. No more than half the rating of your linear amplifier
    d. Never more than 1 watt

29. Which of these items would be useful for a hidden transmitter hunt?
    a. Calibrated SWR meter
    b. A directional antenna
    c. A calibrated noise bridge
    d. All of these choices are correct

30. What does the term "APRS" mean?
    a. Automatic Packet Reporting System
    b. Associated Public Radio Station
    c. Auto Planning Radio Set-up
    d. Advanced Polar Radio System

31. Which of the following is true regarding vertical antennas?
    a. The magnetic field is perpendicular to the Earth
    b. The electric field is perpendicular to the Earth
    c. The phase is inverted
    d. The phase is reversed

Copyright © Mometrix Media. You have been licensed one copy of this document for personal use only. Any other reproduction or redistribution is strictly prohibited. All rights reserved.

32. What is the impedance of the most commonly used coaxial cable in typical amateur radio installations?
    a. 8 ohms
    b. 50 ohms
    c. 600 ohms
    d. 12 ohms

33. How does current flowing through the body cause a health hazard?
    a. By heating tissue
    b. It disrupts the electrical functions of cells
    c. It causes involuntary muscle contractions
    d. All of these choices are correct

34. What is a good precaution to observe before climbing an antenna tower?
    a. Make sure that you wear a grounded wrist strap
    b. Remove all tower grounding connections
    c. Put on a climbing harness and safety glasses
    d. All of these choices are correct

35. Which of the following frequencies has the lowest value for Maximum Permissible Exposure limit?
    a. 3.5 MHz
    b. 50 MHz
    c. 440 MHz
    d. 1296 MHz

Copyright © Mometrix Media. You have been licensed one copy of this document for personal use only. Any other reproduction or redistribution is strictly prohibited. All rights reserved.

Answers and Explanations

1. C: The Federal Communications Commission (FCC) is the agency that regulates and enforces the rules for the Amateur Radio Service in the United States.

2. A: Some U.S. territories are located in ITU regions other than region 2 where the U.S. is located, making the frequency assignments different.

3. B: W3ABC is a valid US amateur radio station call sign. Amateurs may have what are called 1 x 3 call signs, so long as the prefix is W, K, or N, and so long as the suffix is composed of three letters. Amateurs may also have a 2 x 3 call sign with a prefix of K through KG, K through KK, KM through K0, or KR through KZ. The 2 x 3 call signs may have any three letters in the suffix. Amateurs may also have 2 x 1 call sign, with the prefix beginning with A, K, N, or W, or a 1 x 2 call sign, with a prefix of K, N, or W.

4. A: An FCC-licensed amateur station may exchange messages with a US military station during an Armed Forces Day communications test.

5. D: Only a person for whom an amateur operator/primary station license grant appears in the FCC database or who is authorized for alien reciprocal operation is eligible to be the control operator of an amateur station.

6. C: When using tactical identifiers, a station must transmit its FCC-assigned call sign every 10 minutes.

7. D: The national calling frequency for FM simplex operations in the 70 cm band is 446.000 MHz. A simplex communication occurs when one station calls another without assistance from a repeater. This means that both stations transmit and receive over the same frequency. The other national FM simplex calling frequencies are 52.525, 146.52, 223.50, and 1294.5 MHz.

8. D: CT CSS is the use of a sub-audible tone transmitted with normal voice audio to open the squelch of the receiver.

9. C: One way to recharge a 12-volt lead-acid station battery when the commercial power is out is to connect the battery in parallel with a vehicle's battery and run the engine.

10. B: UHF signals are often more effective from inside buildings than VHF signals because the shorter wavelength allows them to more easily penetrate the structure of buildings.

11. A: The orientation of a radio wave's electric field is used to describe its polarization.

12. D: When VHF signals are being received from long distances, the signals might be being refracted from a sporadic E layer. The sporadic E layer is a region of heavy ionization that occurs in various places throughout the E layer of the atmosphere. The ionization density, height, time, and penetration frequency of the sporadic E layer are inconsistent.

13. D: Computers may be integrated into an amateur radio station for a variety of purposes, including logging contacts and contact information, sending/receiving CW, and generating and decoding signals.

14. A: The keypad or the FO knob can be used to enter the operating frequency on a modern transceiver. A transceiver is a single unit that contains both a radio transmitter and receiver.

15. B: Electrical power is measured in watts. Electrical power is the rate at which electricity can be converted into other types of energy. It is calculated by multiplying the current and the voltage drop. A watt is equal to one joule per second.

Copyright © Mometrix Media. You have been licensed one copy of this document for personal use only. Any other reproduction or redistribution is strictly prohibited. All rights reserved.

16. A: Another way to specify a radio signal frequency of 1,500,000 Hz is 1500 kHz. In the metric system, the prefix kilo- means thousand, so a kilohertz is equal to 1000 hertz. Therefore, 1,500,000 Hz can be converted to kHz by dividing by a thousand: 1,500,000/1000 = 1500 kHz.

17. A: The basic unit of capacitance is the farad. One farad is equal to the capacitance of a capacitor that has an equal and opposite charge of 1 coulomb on each of its plates, and 1 V of potential difference between those plates.

18. A: The formula for calculating voltage in a circuit is voltage equals current multiplied by resistance.

19. C: A potentiometer is often used as an adjustable volume control. A potentiometer is an instrument that measures an unknown voltage by comparing it to a standard voltage.

20. C: A diode allows current to flow in only one direction. A diode is an electronic device that includes two electrodes, an anode and a cathode. These devices are used to convert an alternating current into a direct current.

21. A: In figure T1, component 1 is a resistor.

22. A: A relay may best be described as a switch controlled by an electromagnet. When the device senses a miniscule voltage or current change, it activates a switch or another component in the electric circuit.

23. B: A transceiver is a unit that combines the functions of a transmitter and a receiver.

24. A: If a broadcast AM/FM radio is unintentionally receiving amateur radio transmissions, the most likely explanation is that the receiver is unable to reject strong signals outside of the AM/FM bands.

25. B: An antenna analyzer can be used to determine if an antenna is resonant at the desired operating frequency. Antenna analyzers assess the efficiency of antenna systems.

26. B: The correct way to connect a voltmeter to a circuit is in parallel with the circuit. An analog voltmeter, on the other hand, is a moving coil galvanometer that works as a voltmeter after a resistor is installed in series with it.

27. A: The type of modulation most commonly used for VHF packet radio transmission is FM.

28. B: The minimum amount of power needed to complete the contact should be used on the uplink frequency of an amateur satellite or space station.

29. B: A directional antenna would be useful for a hidden transmitter hunt. Directional antennas send and receive signals in some directions more than others. Therefore, these antennas are able to ascertain from which direction a signal is being broadcast.

30. A: The term APRS means Automatic Packet Reporting System. This is a combination of GPS and packet radio. When a station uses this system, the operator takes the location data from the GPS receiver to a two-meter radio and sends out data packets announcing his or her presence. These packets may be received by other hams or by packet radio digipeaters.

31. B: When a vertical antenna is used, the electric field is perpendicular to the earth. The most common designs for vertical antennas are ¼ and ½ wavelength. Vertical antennas are known as omnidirectional antennas because they radiate in every direction equally.

32. B: The impedance of the most commonly used coaxial cable in typical amateur radio installations is 50 ohms. Impedance is the measure of the total opposition to current flow in an alternating current circuit, composed of reactance and ohmic resistance.

Copyright © Mometrix Media. You have been licensed one copy of this document for personal use only. Any other reproduction or redistribution is strictly prohibited. All rights reserved.

33. D: An electric current flowing through the body causes a health hazard by heating the tissue, disrupting the electrical functions of cells, and causing involuntary muscle contractions.

34. C: Before climbing an antenna tower, one should put on a climbing harness and safety glasses.

35. B: 50 MHz has a lower maximum permissible exposure limit then 3.5 MHz, 440 MHz, or 1296 MHz.

Copyright © Mometrix Media. You have been licensed one copy of this document for personal use only. Any other reproduction or redistribution is strictly prohibited. All rights reserved.

Technician Class Practice Test 3

Practice Questions

1. Which part of the FCC regulations contains the rules governing the Amateur Radio Service?
   a. Part 73
   b. Part 95
   c. Part 90
   d. Part 97

2. Which frequency is within the 6 meter band?
   a. 49.00 MHz
   b. 52.525 MHz
   c. 28.50 MHz
   d. 222.15 MHz

3. What types of international communications are permitted by an FCC-licensed amateur station?
   a. Communications incidental to the purposes of the amateur service and remarks of a personal character
   b. Communications incidental to conducting business or remarks of a personal nature
   c. Only communications incidental to contest exchanges, all other communications are prohibited
   d. Any communications that would be permitted by an international broadcast station

4. When is the transmission of codes or ciphers that hide the meaning of a message allowed by an amateur station?
   a. Only during contests
   b. Only when operating mobile
   c. Only when transmitting control commands to space stations or radio control craft
   d. Only when frequencies above 1280 MHz are used

5. Who must designate the station control operator?
   a. The station licensee
   b. The FCC
   c. The frequency coordinator
   d. The ITU

6. When is an amateur station required to transmit its assigned call sign?
   a. At the beginning of each contact, and every 10 minutes thereafter
   b. At least once during each transmission
   c. At least every 15 minutes during and at the end of a communication
   d. At least every 10 minutes during and at the end of a communication

7. What is a common repeater frequency offset in the 70 cm band?
   a. Plus or minus 5 MHz
   b. Plus or minus 600 kHz
   c. Minus 600 kHz
   d. Plus 600 kHz

Copyright © Mometrix Media. You have been licensed one copy of this document for personal use only. Any other reproduction or redistribution is strictly prohibited. All rights reserved.

8. Which of the following describes the muting of receiver audio controlled solely by the presence or absence of an RF signal?
    a. Tone squelch
    b. Carrier squelch
    c. CTCSS
    d. Modulated carrier

9. What should be done to ensure that voice message traffic containing proper names and unusual words are copied correctly by the receiving station?
    a. The entire message should be repeated at least four times
    b. Such messages must be limited to no more than 10 words
    c. Such words and terms should be spelled out using a standard phonetic alphabet
    d. All of these choices are correct

10. What antenna polarization is normally used for long-distance weak-signal CW and SSB contacts using the VHF and UHF bands?
    a. Right-hand circular
    b. Left-hand circular
    c. Horizontal
    d. Vertical

11. What are the two components of a radio wave?
    a. AC and DC
    b. Voltage and current
    c. Electric and magnetic fields
    d. Ionizing and non-ionizing radiation

12. What is a characteristic of VHF signals received via auroral reflection?
    a. Signals from distances of 10,000 or more miles are common
    b. The signals exhibit rapid fluctuations of strength and often sound distorted
    c. These types of signals occur only during winter nighttime hours
    d. These types of signals are generally strongest when your antenna is aimed west

13. Which is a good reason to use a regulated power supply for communications equipment?
    a. It prevents voltage fluctuations from reaching sensitive circuits
    b. A regulated power supply has FCC approval
    c. A fuse or circuit breaker regulates the power
    d. Power consumption is independent of load

14. What is the purpose of the squelch control on a transceiver?
    a. To set the highest level of volume desired
    b. To set the transmitter power level
    c. To adjust the automatic gain control
    d. To mute receiver output noise when no signal is being received

15. What is the name for the flow of electrons in an electric circuit?
    a. Voltage
    b. Resistance
    c. Capacitance
    d. Current

Copyright © Mometrix Media. You have been licensed one copy of this document for personal use only. Any other reproduction or redistribution is strictly prohibited. All rights reserved.

16. How many volts are equal to one kilovolt?
    a. One one-thousandth of a volt
    b. One hundred volts
    c. One thousand volts
    d. One million volts

17. What is the ability to store energy in a magnetic field called?
    a. Admittance
    b. Capacitance
    c. Resistance
    d. Inductance

18. What formula is used to calculate resistance in a circuit?
    a. Resistance (R) equals voltage (E) multiplied by current (I)
    b. Resistance (R) equals voltage (E) divided by current (I)
    c. Resistance (R) equals voltage (E) added to current (I)
    d. Resistance (R) equals voltage (E) minus current (I)

19. What electrical parameter is controlled by a potentiometer?
    a. Inductance
    b. Resistance
    c. Capacitance
    d. Field strength

20. Which of these components can be used as an electronic switch or amplifier?
    a. Oscillator
    b. Potentiometer
    c. Transistor
    d. Voltmeter

21. What is component 2 in figure T1?
(figures found at the end of the guide)
    a. Resistor
    b. Transistor
    c. Indicator lamp
    d. Connector

22. What type of switch is represented by component 3 in figure T2?
(figures found at the end of the guide)
    a. Single-pole single-throw
    b. Single-pole double-throw
    c. Double-pole single-throw
    d. Double-pole double-throw

23. Which of the following is used to convert a radio signal from one frequency to another?
    a. Phase splitter
    b. Mixer
    c. Inverter
    d. Amplifier

- 115 -

Copyright © Mometrix Media. You have been licensed one copy of this document for personal use only. Any other reproduction or redistribution is strictly prohibited. All rights reserved.

24. Which of the following may be a cause of radio frequency interference?
    a. Fundamental overload
    b. Harmonics
    c. Spurious emissions
    d. All of these choices are correct

25. What, in general terms, is standing wave ratio (SWR)?
    a. A measure of how well a load is matched to a transmission line
    b. The ratio of high to low impedance in a feed line
    c. The transmitter efficiency ratio
    d. An indication of the quality of your station's ground connection

26. How is an ammeter usually connected to a circuit?
    a. In series with the circuit
    b. In parallel with the circuit
    c. In quadrature with the circuit
    d. In phase with the circuit

27. Which type of voice mode is most often used for long-distance (weak signal) contacts on the VHF and UHF bands?
    a. FM
    b. DRM
    c. SSB
    d. PM

28. Which of the following are provided by satellite tracking programs?
    a. Maps showing the real-time position of the satellite track over the earth
    b. The time, azimuth, and elevation of the start, maximum altitude, and end of a pass
    c. The apparent frequency of the satellite transmission, including effects of Doppler shift
    d. All of these answers are correct

29. What popular operating activity involves contacting as many stations as possible during a specified period of time?
    a. Contesting
    b. Net operations
    c. Public service events
    d. Simulated emergency exercises

30. Which of the following devices provides data to the transmitter when sending automatic position reports from a mobile amateur radio station?
    a. The vehicle speedometer
    b. A WWV receiver
    c. A connection to a broadcast FM sub-carrier receiver
    d. A Global Positioning System receiver

31. Which of the following describes a simple dipole mounted so the conductor is parallel to the Earth's surface?
    a. A ground wave antenna
    b. A horizontally polarized antenna
    c. A rhombic antenna is
    d. A vertically polarized antenna

Copyright © Mometrix Media. You have been licensed one copy of this document for personal use only. Any other reproduction or redistribution is strictly prohibited. All rights reserved.

32. Why is coaxial cable used more often than any other feed line for amateur radio antenna systems?
    a. It is easy to use and requires few special installation considerations
    b. It has less loss than any other type of feed line
    c. It can handle more power than any other type of feed line
    d. It is less expensive than any other types of feed line

33. What is connected to the green wire in a three-wire electrical AC plug?
    a. Neutral
    b. Hot
    c. Safety ground
    d. The white wire

34. Under what circumstances is it safe to climb a tower without a helper or observer?
    a. When no electrical work is being performed
    b. When no mechanical work is being performed
    c. When the work being done is not more than 20 feet above the ground
    d. Never

35. What is the maximum power level that an amateur radio station may use at VHF frequencies before an RF exposure evaluation is required?
    a. 1500 watts PEP transmitter output
    b. 1 watt forward power
    c. 50 watts PEP at the antenna
    d. 50 watts PEP reflected power

Copyright © Mometrix Media. You have been licensed one copy of this document for personal use only. Any other reproduction or redistribution is strictly prohibited. All rights reserved.

Answers and Explanations

1. D: Part 97 of the FCC rules contains the rules and regulations governing the Amateur Radio Service.

2. B: 52.525 MHz is within the 6 meter band.

3. A: FCC-licensed amateur stations are permitted to make international communications incidental to the purposes of the amateur service and remarks of a personal character.

4. C: An amateur station is allowed to hide the meaning of a transmitted message with codes or ciphers only when transmitting control commands to space stations or radio control craft.

5. A: The station licensee must designate the station control operator.

6. D: An amateur station is required to transmit its assigned call sign at least every 10 minutes during and at the end of a communication.

7. A: A common repeater frequency offset in the 70 cm band is plus or minus 5 MHz.

8. B: Carrier squelch is the muting of receiver audio controlled solely by the presence or absence of an RF signal.

9. C: To ensure that any proper names and unusual words are copied correctly by the receiving station, it is good practice to spell them out using a standard phonetic alphabet.

10. C: A horizontal antenna polarization is normally used for long-distance weak-signal CW and SSB contacts using the VHF and UHF bands.

11. C: The two components of a radio wave are electric and magnetic fields. This is because a radio wave is an electromagnetic wave.

12. B: A characteristic of VHF signals received via auroral reflection is that the signals exhibit rapid fluctuations of strength and often sound distorted.

13. A: One good reason to use a regulated power supply for communications equipment is that it prevents voltage fluctuations from reaching sensitive circuits.

14. D: The purpose of the squelch control on a transceiver is to mute receiver output noise when no signal is being received. The squelch control makes interpersonal communications more comprehensible.

15. D: The flow of electrons in an electric circuit is the current. Current is measured in amperes, also known as amps.

16. C: 1000 V is equal to 1 kV. The metric prefix kilo- means thousand, so a thousand volts is the same as one kilovolt. Therefore, V can be converted to kV by dividing by a thousand: 1000/1000 = 1.

17. D: The ability to store energy in a magnetic field is called inductance. Inductance can also be defined as the characteristic of an electric circuit that enables electromagnetic force to be created in it through a varying magnetic flux.

18. B: The formula for calculating resistance in a circuit is resistance (R) equals voltage (E) divided by current (I). Resistance is the opposition to the passage of current, the result of which is the conversion of electrical energy into heat or another type of energy.

Copyright © Mometrix Media. You have been licensed one copy of this document for personal use only. Any other reproduction or redistribution is strictly prohibited. All rights reserved.

19. B: Resistance is controlled by a potentiometer. A potentiometer will typically have a resistance element connected to the circuit with three terminals. Two of these are attached to the two input voltage conductors of the circuit, and the third is connected to the circuit output. The third terminal is typically able to move across the resistance element, which enables the magnitude of the input voltage to be adjusted.

20. C: A transistor can be used as an electronic switch or amplifier. It may also be used as a detector.

21. B: In figure T1, component 2 is a transistor.

22. A: In figure T2, component 3 represents a single-pole, single-throw switch.

23. B: A mixer is a device used to convert radio signals from one frequency to another.

24. D: Radio frequency interference may be caused by fundamental overload, harmonics, or spurious emissions. A spurious emission is any radio frequency that was not created or transmitted on purpose.

25. A: In general terms, standing wave ratio (SWR) is a measure of how well a load is matched to a transmission line. This is a measure of the impedance match between the antenna and the feedline. It is the ratio of the maximum voltage to the minimum voltage along the feedline. If a transmitter is being used, standing wave ratio is the impedance match between the feedline from the transmitter and the antenna system. If the antenna is a purely resistive load, the standing wave ratio is the ratio of antenna impedance to feedline impedance.

26. A: An ammeter is usually connected to a circuit in series with the circuit. In most cases, an ammeter is combined with a voltmeter and ohmmeter in a single instrument.

27. C: The type of voice modulation most often used for long-distance or weak signal contacts on the VHF and UHF bands is SSB.

28. D: Satellite tracking programs provide a wealth of information about the path and position of orbiting satellites, as well as their operation.

29. A: Contesting involves contacting as many stations as possible during a specified period of time.

30. D: A Global Positioning System receiver is normally used when sending automatic location reports via amateur radio.

31. B: When a simple dipole is mounted so that the conductor is parallel to the Earth's surface, this may be described as a horizontally polarized antenna.

32. A: Coaxial cable is used more often than any other feed lines for amateur radio antenna systems because it is easy to use and requires few special installation considerations.

33. C: In a three-wire electrical AC plug, the green wire is connected to the safety ground.

34. D: It is never safe to climb a tower without a helper or observer.

35. C: The maximum power level that an amateur radio station may use at VHF frequencies before an RF exposure evaluation is required is 50 watts PEP at the antenna.

Copyright © Mometrix Media. You have been licensed one copy of this document for personal use only. Any other reproduction or redistribution is strictly prohibited. All rights reserved.

Technician Class Practice Test 4

Practice Questions

1. Which of the following meets the FCC definition of harmful interference?
    a. Radio transmissions that annoy users of a repeater
    b. Unwanted radio transmissions that cause costly harm to radio station apparatus
    c. That which seriously degrades, obstructs, or repeatedly interrupts a radio communication service operating in accordance with the Radio Regulations
    d. Static from lightning storms

2. Which amateur band are you using when your station is transmitting on 146.52 MHz?
    a. 2 meter band
    b. 20 meter band
    c. 14 meter band
    d. 6 meter band

3. When are you allowed to operate your amateur station in a foreign country?
    a. When the foreign country authorizes it
    b. When there is a mutual agreement allowing third party communications
    c. When authorization permits amateur communications in a foreign language
    d. When you are communicating with non-licensed individuals in another country

4. What is the only time an amateur station is authorized to transmit music?
    a. When incidental to an authorized retransmission of manned spacecraft communications
    b. When the music produces no spurious emissions
    c. When the purpose is to interfere with an illegal transmission
    d. When the music is transmitted above 1280 MHz

5. What determines the transmitting privileges of an amateur station?
    a. The frequency authorized by the frequency coordinator
    b. The class of operator license held by the station licensee
    c. The highest class of operator license held by anyone on the premises
    d. The class of operator license held by the control operator

6. Which of the following is an acceptable language to use for station identification when operating in a phone sub-band?
    a. Any language recognized by the United Nations
    b. Any language recognized by the ITU
    c. The English language
    d. English, French, or Spanish

7. What is an appropriate way to call another station on a repeater if you know the other station's call sign?
    a. Say "break, break" then say the station's call sign
    b. Say the station's call sign then identify with your call sign
    c. Say "CQ" three times then the other station's call sign
    d. Wait for the station to call "CQ" then answer it

Copyright © Mometrix Media. You have been licensed one copy of this document for personal use only. Any other reproduction or redistribution is strictly prohibited. All rights reserved.

8. Which of the following common problems might cause you to be able to hear but not access a repeater even when transmitting with the proper offset?
   a. The repeater receiver may require an audio tone burst for access
   b. The repeater receiver may require a CTCSS tone for access
   c. The repeater receiver may require a DCS tone sequence for access
   d. All of these choices are correct

9. What do RACES and ARES have in common?
   a. They represent the two largest ham clubs in the United States
   b. Both organizations broadcast road and weather information
   c. Neither may handle emergency traffic supporting public service agencies
   d. Both organizations may provide communications during emergencies

10. What can happen if the antennas at opposite ends of a VHF or UHF line of sight radio link are not using the same polarization?
   a. The modulation sidebands might become inverted
   b. Signals could be significantly weaker
   c. Signals have an echo effect on voices
   d. Nothing significant will happen

11. How fast does a radio wave travel through free space?
   a. At the speed of light
   b. At the speed of sound
   d. Its speed is inversely proportional to its wavelength
   d. Its speed increases as the frequency increases

12. Which of the following propagation types is most commonly associated with occasional strong over-the-horizon signals on the 10, 6, and 2 meter bands?
   a. Backscatter
   b. Sporadic E
   c. D layer absorption
   d. Gray-line propagation

13. Where must a filter be installed to reduce harmonic emissions?
   a. Between the transmitter and the antenna
   b. Between the receiver and the transmitter
   c. At the station power supply
   d. At the microphone

14. What is a way to enable quick access to a favorite frequency on your transceiver?
   a. Enable the CTCSS tones
   b. Store the frequency in a memory channel
   c. Disable the CTCSS tones
   d. Use the scan mode to select the desired frequency

15. What is the name for a current that flows only in one direction?
   a. Alternating current
   b. Direct current
   c. Normal current
   d. Smooth current

Copyright © Mometrix Media. You have been licensed one copy of this document for personal use only. Any other reproduction or redistribution is strictly prohibited. All rights reserved.

16. How many volts are equal to one microvolt?
    a. One one-millionth of a volt
    b. One million volts
    c. One thousand kilovolts
    d. One one-thousandth of a volt

17. What is the basic unit of inductance?
    a. The coulomb
    b. The farad
    c. The henry
    d. The ohm

18. What is the resistance of a circuit in which a current of 3 amperes flows through a resistor connected to 90 volts?
    a. 3 ohms
    b. 30 ohms
    c. 93 ohms
    d. 270 ohms

19. What electrical component stores energy in an electric field?
    a. Resistor
    b. Capacitor
    c. Inductor
    d. Diode

20. Which of the following components can be made of three layers of semiconductor material?
    a. Alternator
    b. Transistor
    c. Triode
    d. Pentagrid converter

21. What is component 3 in figure T1?
(figures found at the end of the guide)
    a. Resistor
    b. Transistor
    c. Lamp
    d. Ground symbol

22. Which of the following can be used to display signal strength on a numeric scale?
    a. Potentiometer
    b. Transistor
    c. Meter
    d. Relay

23. Which term describes the ability of a receiver to discriminate between multiple signals?
    a. Discrimination ratio
    b. Sensitivity
    c. Selectivity
    d. Harmonic Distortion

Copyright © Mometrix Media. You have been licensed one copy of this document for personal use only. Any other reproduction or redistribution is strictly prohibited. All rights reserved.

24. Which of the following is a way to reduce or eliminate interference by an amateur transmitter to a nearby telephone?
    a. Put a filter on the amateur transmitter
    b. Reduce the microphone gain
    c. Reduce the SWR on the transmitter transmission line
    d. Put a RF filter on the telephone

25. What reading on an SWR meter indicates a perfect impedance match between the antenna and the feed line?
    a. 2 to 1
    b. 1 to 3
    c. 1 to 1
    d. 10 to 1

26. Which instrument is used to measure electric current?
    a. An ohmmeter
    b. A wavemeter
    c. A voltmeter
    d. An ammeter

27. Which type of modulation is most commonly used for VHF and UHF voice repeaters?
    a. AM
    b. SSB
    c. PSK
    d. FM

28. Which amateur stations may make contact with an amateur station on the International Space Station using 2 meter and 70 cm band amateur radio frequencies?
    a. Only members of amateur radio clubs at NASA facilities
    b. Any amateur holding a Technician or higher class license
    c. Only the astronaut's family members who are hams
    d. You cannot talk to the ISS on amateur radio frequencies

29. Which of the following is good procedure when contacting another station in a radio contest?
    a. Be sure to sign only the last two letters of your call if there is a pileup calling the station
    b. Work the station twice to be sure that you are in his log
    c. Send only the minimum information needed for proper identification and the contest exchange
    d. All of these choices are correct

30. What type of transmission is indicated by the term NTSC?
    a. A Normal Transmission mode in Static Circuit
    b. A special mode for earth satellite uplink
    c. An analog fast scan color TV signal
    d. A frame compression scheme for TV signals

31. What is a disadvantage of the "rubber duck" antenna supplied with most handheld radio transceivers?
    a. It does not transmit or receive as effectively as a full-sized antenna
    b. It transmits a circularly polarized signal
    c. If the rubber end cap is lost it will unravel very quickly
    d. All of these choices are correct

Copyright © Mometrix Media. You have been licensed one copy of this document for personal use only. Any other reproduction or redistribution is strictly prohibited. All rights reserved.

32. What does an antenna tuner do?
   a. It matches the antenna system impedance to the transceiver's output impedance
   b. It helps a receiver automatically tune in weak stations
   c. It allows an antenna to be used on both transmit and receive
   d. It automatically selects the proper antenna for the frequency band being used

33. What is the purpose of a fuse in an electrical circuit?
   a. To prevent power supply ripple from damaging a circuit
   b. To interrupt power in case of overload
   c. To limit current to prevent shocks
   d. All of these choices are correct

34. Which of the following is an important safety precaution to observe when putting up an antenna tower?
   a. Wear a ground strap connected to your wrist at all times
   b. Insulate the base of the tower to avoid lightning strikes
   c. Look for and stay clear of any overhead electrical wires
   d. All of these choices are correct

35. What factors affect the RF exposure of people near an amateur station antenna?
   a. Frequency and power level of the RF field
   b. Distance from the antenna to a person
   c. Radiation pattern of the antenna
   d. All of these choices are correct

Copyright © Mometrix Media. You have been licensed one copy of this document for personal use only. Any other reproduction or redistribution is strictly prohibited. All rights reserved.

Answers and Explanations

1. C: According to the FCC, harmful interference is defined as that which seriously degrades, obstructs, or repeatedly interrupts a radiocommunication service operating in accordance with the radio regulations.

2. A: If your station is transmitting on 146.52 MHz, it is using the 2-meter amateur band.

3. A: One is allowed to operate an amateur station in a foreign country when the foreign country authorizes it.

4. A: The only time an amateur station is authorized to transmit music is when it is incidental to unauthorized retransmission of manned spacecraft communications.

5. D: The transmitting privileges of an amateur station are determined by the class of operator license held by the control operator.

6. C: English is an acceptable language for station identification use when operating in a phone sub-band.

7. B: An appropriate way to call another station on a repeater if you know the other station's call sign is to say the station's call sign and then identify with your call sign.

8. D: There are several common problems that might cause you to be able to hear but not access a repeater even when transmitting with the proper offset. This may occur when the repeater receiver requires audio tone burst, a CTCSS tone, or a DCS tone sequence for access.

9. D: RACES (Radio Amateur Civil Emergency Service) and ARES (Amateur Radio Emergency Service) both may provide communications during emergencies. RACES is managed by the Federal Emergency Management Agency. Both RACES and ARES are open to any amateur radio operator.

10. B: If the antennas at opposite ends of a VHF or UHF line of sight radio link are not using the same polarization, the signals could be significantly weaker.

11. A: A radio wave travels through free space at the speed of light. In a vacuum, the speed of light is roughly 300,000,000 km/s.

12. B: The sporadic E propagation type is most commonly associated with occasional strong over-the-horizon signals on the 10, 6, and 2 meter bands.

13. A: To reduce harmonic emissions, a filter must be installed between the transmitter and the antenna. Harmonics are those signals from a transmitter or oscillator that occur on whole-number multiples of the operating frequency in use.

14. B: One way to enable quick access to a favorite frequency on your transceiver is to store the frequency in a memory channel.

15. B: A current that flows in only one direction is called a direct current. Modern technological advances have made it possible to transmit direct current over long distances, though it typically must be converted into alternating current before it reaches its final destination.

16. A: 1/1,000,000 of a volt is equal to 1 μV. The metric prefix micro- means millionth, so 1,000,000 microvolts is equal to one volt. Volts can be converted to microvolts by dividing by a million: $1/1,000,000 = 1$ μV.

17. C: The basic unit of inductance is the henry.

Copyright © Mometrix Media. You have been licensed one copy of this document for personal use only. Any other reproduction or redistribution is strictly prohibited. All rights reserved.

18. B: The resistance of a circuit in which a current of 3 amperes flows through a resistor connected to 90 volts is 30 ohms. Resistance is calculated by dividing voltage by current. In this case, then, the resistance is found 90/3 = 30.

19. B: The capacitor is the electrical component that stores energy in an electric field. Typically, a capacitor is composed of two metallic plates that are separated and insulated from one another by a dielectric.

20. B: A transistor is made of three layers of semiconductor material.

21. C: In figure T1, component 3 is a lamp.

22. C: A meter is the best tool for displaying signal strength on a numeric scale.

23. C: A receiver's ability to discriminate among multiple radio signals is referred to as its selectivity.

24. D: The best way to reduce or eliminate interference to a telephone from a nearby amateur transmitter is to install an RF filter on the telephone.

25. C: A reading of 1 to 1 on an SWR meter indicates a perfect impedance match between the antenna and the feed line. An SWR meter, also known as a watt meter, is a way to independently measure the power of a transmitter.

26. D: An ammeter is used to measure electric current. Typically, the current will need to be at least a few amperes to be susceptible to measurement by the ammeter.

27. D: The type of modulation most commonly used for VHF and UHF voice repeaters is FM.

28. B: Any amateur holding a Technician or higher class license may make contact with an amateur station on the International Space Station using 2 meter and 70 cm band amateur radio frequencies.

29. C: Sending only the minimum information needed for proper identification and the contest exchange is good procedure when contacting another station in a radio contest.

30. C: The term NTSC indicates an analog fast scan color TV signal.

31. A: One disadvantage of the "rubber duck" antenna supplied with most handheld radio transceivers is it does not transmit or receive as effectively as a full-sized antenna.

32. A: An antenna tuner matches the antenna system impedance to the transceiver's output impedance.

33. B: The purpose of a fuse in an electrical circuit is to interrupt power in case of overload.

34. C: When putting up an antenna tower, it is important to look for and stay clear of any overhead electric wires.

35. D: Several factors affect the RF exposure of people near an amateur station antenna. These factors include the frequency and power level of the RF field, the distance from the antenna to a person, and the radiation pattern of the antenna.

Copyright © Mometrix Media. You have been licensed one copy of this document for personal use only. Any other reproduction or redistribution is strictly prohibited. All rights reserved.

Technician Class Practice Test 5

Practice Questions

1. Which of the following is a purpose of the Amateur Radio Service rules and regulations as defined by the FCC?
    a. Enhancing international goodwill
    b. Providing inexpensive communication for local emergency organizations
    c. Training of operators in military radio operating procedures
    d. All of these choices are correct

2. Which 70 cm frequency is authorized to a Technician Class license holder operating in ITU Region 2?
    a. 53.350 MHz
    b. 146.520 MHz
    c. 443.350 MHz
    d. 222.520 MHz

3. Which of the following is a vanity call sign which a technician class amateur operator might select if available?
    a. K1XXX
    b. KA1X
    c. W1XX
    d. All of these choices are correct

4. When may amateur radio operators use their stations to notify other amateurs of the availability of equipment for sale or trade?
    a. When the equipment is normally used in an amateur station and such activity is not conducted on a regular basis
    b. When the asking price is $100.00 or less
    c. When the asking price is less than its appraised value
    d. When the equipment is not the personal property of either the station licensee or the control operator or their close relatives

5. What is an amateur station control point?
    a. The location of the station's transmitting antenna
    b. The location of the station transmitting apparatus
    c. The location at which the control operator function is performed
    d. The mailing address of the station licensee

6. What method of call sign identification is required for a station transmitting phone signals?
    a. Send the call sign followed by the indicator RPT
    b. Send the call sign using CW or phone emission
    c. Send the call sign followed by the indicator R
    d. Send the call sign using only phone emission

7. How should you respond to a station calling CQ?
    a. Transmit CQ followed by the other station's call sign
    b. Transmit your call sign followed by the other station's call sign
    c. Transmit the other station's call sign followed by your call sign
    d. Transmit a signal report followed by your call sign

Copyright © Mometrix Media. You have been licensed one copy of this document for personal use only. Any other reproduction or redistribution is strictly prohibited. All rights reserved.

8. What determines the amount of deviation of an FM (as opposed to PM) signal?
    a. Both the frequency and amplitude of the modulating signal
    b. The frequency of the modulating signal
    c. The amplitude of the modulating signal
    d. The relative phase of the modulating signal and the carrier

9. Which of the following describes the Radio Amateur Civil Emergency Service (RACES)?
    a. A radio service using amateur frequencies for emergency management or civil defense communications
    b. A radio service using amateur stations for emergency management or civil defense communications
    c. An emergency service using amateur operators certified by a civil defense organization as being enrolled in that organization
    d. All of these choices are correct

10. When using a directional antenna, how might your station be able to access a distant repeater if buildings or obstructions are blocking the direct line of sight path?
    a. Change from vertical to horizontal polarization
    b. Try to find a path that reflects signals to the repeater
    c. Try the long path
    d. Increase the antenna SWR

11. How does the wavelength of a radio wave relate to its frequency?
    a. The wavelength gets longer as the frequency increases
    b. The wavelength gets shorter as the frequency increases
    c. There is no relationship between wavelength and frequency
    d. The wavelength depends on the bandwidth of the signal

12. Which of the following effects might cause radio signals to be heard despite obstructions between the transmitting and receiving stations?
    a. Knife-edge diffraction
    b. Faraday rotation
    c. Quantum tunneling
    d. Doppler shift

13. Where should an in-line SWR meter be connected to monitor the standing wave ratio of the station antenna system?
    a. In series with the feed line, between the transmitter and antenna
    b. In series with the station's ground
    c. In parallel with the push-to-talk line and the antenna
    d. In series with the power supply cable, as close as possible to the radio

14. Which of the following would reduce ignition interference to a receiver?
    a. Change frequency slightly
    b. Decrease the squelch setting
    c. Turn on the noise blanker
    d. Use the RIT control

Copyright © Mometrix Media. You have been licensed one copy of this document for personal use only. Any other reproduction or redistribution is strictly prohibited. All rights reserved.

15. What is the electrical term for the electromotive force (EMF) that causes electron flow?
    a. Voltage
    b. Ampere-hours
    c. Capacitance
    d. Inductance

16. Which of the following is equivalent to 500 milliwatts?
    a. 0.02 watts
    b. 0.5 watts
    c. 5 watts
    d. 50 watts

17. What is the unit of frequency?
    a. Hertz
    b. Henry
    c. Farad
    d. Tesla

18. What is the resistance in a circuit for which the applied voltage is 12 volts and the current flow is 1.5 amperes?
    a. 18 ohms
    b. 0.125 ohms
    c. 8 ohms
    d. 13.5 ohms

19. What type of electrical component consists of two or more conductive surfaces separated by an insulator?
    a. Resistor
    b. Potentiometer
    c. Oscillator
    d. Capacitor

20. Which of the following electronic components can amplify signals?
    a. Transistor
    b. Variable resistor
    c. Electrolytic capacitor
    d. Multi-cell battery

21. What is component 4 in figure T1?
(figures found at the end of the guide)
    a. Resistor
    b. Transistor
    c. Battery
    d. Ground symbol

22. What type of circuit controls the amount of voltage from a power supply?
    a. Regulator
    b. Oscillator
    c. Filter
    d. Phase inverter

Copyright © Mometrix Media. You have been licensed one copy of this document for personal use only. Any other reproduction or redistribution is strictly prohibited. All rights reserved.

23. What is the name of a circuit that generates a signal of a desired frequency?
    a. Reactance modulator
    b. Product detector
    c. Low-pass filter
    d. Oscillator

24. How can overload of a non-amateur radio or TV receiver by an amateur signal be reduced or eliminated?
    a. Block the amateur signal with a filter at the antenna input of the affected receiver
    b. Block the interfering signal with a filter on the amateur transmitter
    c. Switch the transmitter from FM to SSB
    d. Switch the transmitter to a narrow-band mode

25. What is the approximate SWR value above which the protection circuits in most solid-state transmitters begin to reduce transmitter power?
    a. 2 to 1
    b. 1 to 2
    c. 6 to 1
    d. 10 to 1

26. What instrument is used to measure resistance?
    a. An oscilloscope
    b. A spectrum analyzer
    c. A noise bridge
    d. An ohmmeter

27. Which of the following types of emission has the narrowest bandwidth?
    a. FM voice
    b. SSB voice
    c. CW
    d. Slow-scan TV

28. What is a satellite beacon?
    a. The primary transmit antenna on the satellite
    b. An indicator light that that shows where to point your antenna
    c. A reflective surface on the satellite
    d. A transmission from a space station that contains information about a satellite

29. What is a grid locator?
    a. A letter-number designator assigned to a geographic location
    b. A letter-number designator assigned to an azimuth and elevation
    c. An instrument for neutralizing a final amplifier
    d. An instrument for radio direction finding

30. Which of the following is an application of APRS (Automatic Packet Reporting System)?
    a. Providing real time tactical digital communications in conjunction with a map showing the locations of stations
    b. Showing automatically the number of packets transmitted via PACTOR during a specific time interval
    c. Providing voice over Internet connection between repeaters
    d. Providing information on the number of stations signed into a repeater

Copyright © Mometrix Media. You have been licensed one copy of this document for personal use only. Any other reproduction or redistribution is strictly prohibited. All rights reserved.

31. How would you change a dipole antenna to make it resonant on a higher frequency?
    a. Lengthen it
    b. Insert coils in series with radiating wires
    c. Shorten it
    d. Add capacitive loading to the ends of the radiating wires

32. What generally happens as the frequency of a signal passing through coaxial cable is increased?
    a. The apparent SWR increases
    b. The reflected power increases
    c. The characteristic impedance increases
    d. The loss increases

33. Why is it unwise to install a 20-ampere fuse in the place of a 5-ampere fuse?
    a. The larger fuse would be likely to blow because it is rated for higher current
    b. The power supply ripple would greatly increase
    c. Excessive current could cause a fire
    d. All of these choices are correct

34. What is the purpose of a gin pole?
    a. To temporarily replace guy wires
    b. To be used in place of a safety harness
    c. To lift tower sections or antennas
    d. To provide a temporary ground

35. Why do exposure limits vary with frequency?
    a. Lower frequency RF fields have more energy than higher frequency fields
    b. Lower frequency RF fields do not penetrate the human body
    c. Higher frequency RF fields are transient in nature
    d. The human body absorbs more RF energy at some frequencies than at others

Copyright © Mometrix Media. You have been licensed one copy of this document for personal use only. Any other reproduction or redistribution is strictly prohibited. All rights reserved.

Answers and Explanations

1. A: According to the FCC, enhancing international goodwill is one of the purposes of the Amateur Radio Service rules and regulations.

2. C: 443.350 MHz is the 70 cm frequency authorized to a technician class license holder operating in ITU Region 2.

3. A: Of the choices listed, only the K1XXX series of call signs is available to technician class amateur operators. The other two series listed are available only to extra class amateur operators.

4. A: Amateur radio operators may use their stations to notify other amateurs of the availability of equipment for sale or trade when the equipment is normally used in an amateur station and such activity is not conducted on a regular basis.

5. C: An amateur station control point is the location at which the control operator function is performed. The control point is the set of locations at which the control operator functions are carried out.

6. B: When a station is transmitting phone signals, it should use the call sign identification system of sending the call sign using CW or phone emission.

7. C: When responding to a call of CQ, you should transmit the other station's call sign followed by your call sign.

8. C: The amplitude of the modulating signal determines the amount of deviation of an FM signal.

9. D: The Radio Amateur Civil Emergency Service (RACES) is a radio service involving certified amateur operators using amateur stations and frequencies for emergency management or civil defense communications.

10. B: When using a directional antenna, a station might be able to access a distant repeater if buildings or obstructions are blocking the direct line of sight path by trying to find a path that reflects signals to the repeater.

11. B: The wavelength of a radio wave gets shorter as the frequency increases. That is, these two characteristics are inversely proportional. If the wavelength grows longer, the frequency will decrease.

12. A: A knife-edge diffraction might cause radio signals to be heard despite obstructions between the transmitting and receiving systems.

13. A: To monitor the standing wave ratio of a station antenna system, an in-line SWR meter should be connected in series with the feed line, between the transmitter and antenna.

14. C: Turning on the noise blinker would reduce ignition interference to a receiver.

15. A: The electrical term for the electromotive force (EMF) that causes electron flow is voltage. It is useful to think of voltage as the electrical equivalent of water pressure.

16. B: 0.5 W is equivalent to 500 mW. The metric prefix milli- means thousandth, so 1000 mW is the same as 1 W. This conversion can be accomplished by multiplying by a thousand: 0.5 x 1000 = 500.

17. A: The basic unit of frequency is the hertz. One hertz is an alternating-current frequency of one cycle per second.

Copyright © Mometrix Media. You have been licensed one copy of this document for personal use only. Any other reproduction or redistribution is strictly prohibited. All rights reserved.

18. C: Resistance in a circuit for which the applied voltage is 12 volts and the current flow is 1.5 amperes is 8 ohms. Resistance is calculated by dividing voltage by current, so in this case the problem is solved 12/8 = 1.5.

19. D: A capacitor consists of two or more conductive surfaces separated by an insulator.

20. A: A transistor can amplify signals.

21. C: In figure T1, component 4 is a battery.

22. A: A regulator circuit controls the amount of voltage from a power supply.

23. D: An oscillator is a circuit that produces an oscillating signal at a desired frequency.

24. A: Filtering out an unwanted amateur radio signal at the receiver of the impacted device is the best way to reduce or eliminate overload on a TV or radio.

25. A: 2 to 1 is the approximate SWR value above which the protection circuits in most solid-state transmitters begin to reduce transmitter power.

26. D: An ohmmeter is used to measure resistance. These devices are capable of measuring very low levels of electrical resistance.

27. C: CW emission has a narrower bandwidth than FM voice, SSB voice, or slow-scan TV emission.

28. D: A satellite beacon is a transmission from a space station that contains information about a satellite. These transmissions are used for maintenance and guidance.

29. A: A grid locator is a letter-number designator assigned to a geographic location. The latitude and the longitude of the location are compressed into a brief string of characters, in alternating pairs of letters and numbers.

30. A: The Automatic Packet Reporting System (APRS) is a system designed to provide real-time tactical digital communications along with a map indicating the sources of the signals carrying the communication.

31. C: To make a dipole antenna resonant on a higher frequency, shorten it.

32. D: As the frequency of a signal passing through coaxial cable is increased, the loss generally increases as well.

33. C: It is unwise to install a 20-ampere fuse in the place of a 5-ampere fuse because the excessive current could cause a fire.

34. C: The purpose of a gin pole is to lift tower sections or antennas.

35. D: Exposure limits vary with frequency because the human body absorbs more RF energy at some frequencies than at others.

Copyright © Mometrix Media. You have been licensed one copy of this document for personal use only. Any other reproduction or redistribution is strictly prohibited. All rights reserved.

Technician Class Practice Test 6

Practice Questions

1. Which of the following services are protected from interference by amateur signals under all circumstances?
    a. Citizens Radio Service
    b. Broadcast Service
    c. Land Mobile Radio Service
    d. Radionavigation Service

2. Which 23 cm frequency is authorized to a Technician Class licensee?
    a. 2315 MHz
    b. 1296 MHz
    c. 3390 MHz
    d. 146.52 MHz

3. From which of the following locations may an FCC-licensed amateur station transmit, in addition to places where the FCC regulates communications?
    a. From within any country that belongs to the International Telecommunications Union
    b. From within any country that is a member of the United Nations
    c. From anywhere within in ITU Regions 2 and 3
    d. From any vessel or craft located in international waters and documented or registered in the United States

4. What, if any, are the restrictions concerning transmission of language that may be considered indecent or obscene?
    a. The FCC maintains a list of words that are not permitted to be used on amateur frequencies
    b. Any such language is prohibited
    c. The ITU maintains a list of words that are not permitted to be used on amateur frequencies
    d. There is no such prohibition

5. Under what type of control do APRS network digipeaters operate?
    a. Automatic
    b. Remote
    c. Local
    d. Manual

6. Which of the following formats of a self-assigned indicator is acceptable when identifying using a phone transmission?
    a. KL7CC stroke W3
    b. KL7CC slant W3
    c. KL7CC slash W3
    d. All of these choices are correct

7. What must an amateur operator do when making on-air transmissions to test equipment or antennas?
    a. Properly identify the transmitting station
    b. Make test transmissions only after 10:00 p.m. local time
    c. Notify the FCC of the test transmission
    d. State the purpose of the test during the test procedure

Copyright © Mometrix Media. You have been licensed one copy of this document for personal use only. Any other reproduction or redistribution is strictly prohibited. All rights reserved.

8. What happens when the deviation of an FM transmitter is increased?
    a. Its signal occupies more bandwidth
    b. Its output power increases
    c. Its output power and bandwidth increases
    d. Asymmetric modulation occurs

9. Which of the following is an accepted practice to get the immediate attention of a net control station when reporting an emergency?
    a. Repeat the words SOS three times followed by the call sign of the reporting station
    b. Press the push-to-talk button three times
    c. Begin your transmission by saying "Priority" or "Emergency" followed by your call sign
    d. Play a pre-recorded emergency alert tone followed by your call sign

10. What term is commonly used to describe the rapid fluttering sound sometimes heard from mobile stations that are moving while transmitting?
    a. Flip-flopping
    b. Picket fencing
    c. Frequency shifting
    d. Pulsing

11. What is the formula for converting frequency to approximate wavelength in meters?
    a. Wavelength in meters equals frequency in hertz multiplied by 300
    b. Wavelength in meters equals frequency in hertz divided by 300
    c. Wavelength in meters equals frequency in megahertz divided by 300
    d. Wavelength in meters equals 300 divided by frequency in megahertz

12. What mode is responsible for allowing over-the-horizon VHF and UHF communications to ranges of approximately 300 miles on a regular basis?
    a. Tropospheric scatter
    b. D layer refraction
    c. F2 layer refraction
    d. Faraday rotation

13. Which of the following would be connected between a transceiver and computer in a packet radio station?
    a. Transmatch
    b. Mixer
    c. Terminal node controller
    d. Antenna

14. Which of the following controls could be used if the voice pitch of a single-sideband signal seems too high or low?
    a. The AGC or limiter
    b. The bandwidth selection
    c. The tone squelch
    d. The receiver RIT or clarifier

Copyright © Mometrix Media. You have been licensed one copy of this document for personal use only. Any other reproduction or redistribution is strictly prohibited. All rights reserved.

15. How much voltage does a mobile transceiver usually require?
  a. About 12 volts
  b. About 30 volts
  c. About 120 volts
  d. About 240 volts

16. If an ammeter calibrated in amperes is used to measure a 3000-milliampere current, what reading would it show?
  a. 0.003 amperes
  b. 0.3 amperes
  c. 3 amperes
  d. 3,000,000 amperes

17. What does the abbreviation "RF" refer to?
  a. Radio frequency signals of all types
  b. The resonant frequency of a tuned circuit
  c. The real frequency transmitted as opposed to the apparent frequency
  d. Reflective force in antenna transmission lines

18. What is the resistance of a circuit that draws 4 amperes from a 12-volt source?
  a. 3 ohms
  b. 16 ohms
  c. 48 ohms
  d. 8 Ohms

19. What type of electrical component stores energy in a magnetic field?
  a. Resistor
  b. Capacitor
  c. Inductor
  d. Diode

20. How is the cathode lead of a semiconductor diode usually identified?
  a. With the word "cathode"
  b. With a stripe
  c. With the letter "C"
  d. All of these choices are correct

21. What is component 6 in figure T2?
(figures found at the end of the guide)
  a. Resistor
  b. Capacitor
  c. Regulator IC
  d. Transistor

22. What component is commonly used to change 120V AC house current to a lower AC voltage for other uses?
  a. Variable capacitor
  b. Transformer
  c. Transistor
  d. Diode

Copyright © Mometrix Media. You have been licensed one copy of this document for personal use only. Any other reproduction or redistribution is strictly prohibited. All rights reserved.

23. What device takes the output of a low-powered 28 MHz SSB exciter and produces a 222 MHz output signal?
    a. High-pass filter
    b. Low-pass filter
    c. Transverter
    d. Phase converter

24. Which of the following actions should you take if a neighbor tells you that your station's transmissions are interfering with their radio or TV reception?
    a. Make sure that your station is functioning properly and that it does not cause interference to your own radio or television when it is tuned to the same channel
    b. Immediately turn off your transmitter and contact the nearest FCC office for assistance
    c. Tell them that your license gives you the right to transmit and nothing can be done to reduce the interference
    d. Install a harmonic doubler on the output of your transmitter and tune it until the interference is eliminated

25. What does an SWR reading of 4:1 indicate?
    a. Loss of -4dB
    b. Good impedance match
    c. Gain of +4dB
    d. Impedance mismatch

26. Which of the following might damage a multimeter?
    a. Measuring a voltage too small for the chosen scale
    b. Leaving the meter in the milliamps position overnight
    c. Attempting to measure voltage when using the resistance setting
    d. Not allowing it to warm up properly

27. Which sideband is normally used for 10 meter HF, VHF and UHF single-sideband communications?
    a. Upper sideband
    b. Lower sideband
    c. Suppressed sideband
    d. Inverted sideband

28. Which of the following are inputs to a satellite tracking program?
    a. The weight of the satellite
    b. The Keplerian elements
    c. The last observed time of zero Doppler shift
    d. All of these answers are correct

29. How is access to an IRLP node accomplished?
    a. By obtaining a password which is sent via voice to the node
    b. By using DTMF signals
    c. By entering the proper Internet password
    d. By using CTCSS tone codes

30. What does the abbreviation PSK mean?
    a. Pulse Shift Keying
    b. Phase Shift Keying
    c. Packet Short Keying
    d. Phased Slide Keying

Copyright © Mometrix Media. You have been licensed one copy of this document for personal use only. Any other reproduction or redistribution is strictly prohibited. All rights reserved.

31. What type of antennas are the quad, Yagi, and dish?
    a. Non-resonant antennas
    b. Loop antennas
    c. Directional antennas
    d. Isotropic antennas

32. Which of the following connectors is most suitable for frequencies above 400 MHz?
    a. A UHF (PL-259/SO-239) connector
    b. A Type N connector
    c. An RS-213 connector
    d. A DB-25 connector

33. What is a good way to guard against electrical shock at your station?
    a. Use three-wire cords and plugs for all AC powered equipment
    b. Connect all AC powered station equipment to a common safety ground
    c. Use a circuit protected by a ground-fault interrupter
    d. All of these choices are correct

34. What is the minimum safe distance from a power line to allow when installing an antenna?
    a. Half the width of your property
    b. The height of the power line above ground
    c. 1/2 wavelength at the operating frequency
    d. So that if the antenna falls unexpectedly, no part of it can come closer than 10 feet to the power wires

35. Which of the following is an acceptable method to determine that your station complies with FCC RF exposure regulations?
    a. By calculation based on FCC OET Bulletin 65
    b. By calculation based on computer modeling
    c. By measurement of field strength using calibrated equipment
    d. All of these choices are correct

Copyright © Mometrix Media. You have been licensed one copy of this document for personal use only. Any other reproduction or redistribution is strictly prohibited. All rights reserved.

Answers and Explanations

1. D: The FCC states that amateur signals shall not cause harmful interference to, and must accept interference from, stations authorized by the FCC in the aeronautical radio navigation service.

2. B: The 1296 MHz frequency is the 23 cm frequency authorized to a Technician Class operator.

3. D: In addition to those places where the FCC regulates communications, an FCC-licensed amateur station may transmit from any vessel or craft located in international waters and documented or registered in the United States.

4. B: As stated by the FCC, no amateur station shall transmit obscene or indecent words or language.

5. A: APRS digipeaters operate automatically, receiving the packets and propagating them without requiring any input from a human operator.

6. D: For identification during a phone transmission, KL7CC stroke W3, KL7CC slant W3, and KL7CC slash W3 would all be acceptable formats for a self-assigned indicator.

7. A: When making on-air transmissions to test equipment or antennas, an amateur operator must properly identify the transmitting station.

8. A: When the deviation of an FM transmitter is increased, its signal occupies more bandwidth.

9. C: To get the immediate attention of the net control station when reporting an emergency, it is common practice to begin your transmission with "Priority" or "Emergency" followed by your call sign.

10. B: Picket fencing is a term used to describe the rapid fluttering sound sometimes heard from mobile stations that are moving while transmitting.

11. D: The formula for converting frequency to wavelength in meters is 300 divided by frequency in megahertz.

12. A: The tropospheric scatter mode is responsible for allowing over-the-horizon VHF and UHF communications to ranges of approximately 300 miles on a regular basis.

13. C: A terminal node controller would be connected between a transceiver and computer in a packet radio station. A terminal node controller consists of microprocessor, software, and a modem that converts baseband digital signals into audio tones.

14. D: The receiver RIT or clarifier controls could be used if the voice pitch of a single-sideband signal seems too high or low. Receiver incremental tuning allows the receiver to be tuned up to 3 kilohertz on either side of the transmitter frequency.

15. A: A mobile transceiver usually requires about 12 V.

16. C: If an ammeter calibrated in amperes is used to measure a 3000-milliampere current, it would show a reading of 3 amperes. The metric prefix milli- means thousandth, so milliamperes can be converted to amperes by multiplying by a thousand. An ammeter is an instrument used to measure electric current.

17. A: The abbreviation RF can be used to refer to radio frequency signals of all kinds.

Copyright © Mometrix Media. You have been licensed one copy of this document for personal use only. Any other reproduction or redistribution is strictly prohibited. All rights reserved.

18. A: The resistance of a circuit that draws 4 amperes from a 12-volt source is 3 ohms. Resistance is calculated by dividing voltage by current: 12/4 = 3.

19. C: An inductor stores energy in a magnetic field. Inductors are typically composed of at least one wire loop. An inductor may be fixed, adjustable, or variable, depending on whether the number of loops is able to be manipulated.

20. B: A semiconductor diode's cathode lead is usually identified with a stripe.

21. B: In figure T2, component 6 is a capacitor.

22. B: A transformer is commonly used to change 120V AC house current to a lower AC voltage for other uses.

23. C: A transverter takes the output of a low-powered 28 MHz SSB exciter and produces a 222 MHz output signal. Transverters are a single unit that includes both an upconverter and a downconverter. The transverter enables the transceiver to communicate over a broad range of frequencies.

24. A: If someone tells you that your station's transmissions are interfering with their radio or TV reception, your first step should be to make sure that your station is functioning properly and that it does not cause interference to your own television.

25. D: An SWR reading of 4:1 indicates an impedance mismatch.

26. C: Attempting to measure voltage when using the resistance setting might damage a multimeter. Multimeters are capable of measuring the following values: current, resistance, and the current potential differences of alternating and direct current.

27. A: The upper sideband is normally used for 10 meter HF, VHF, and UHF single-sideband communications.

28. B: The six Keplerian elements precisely define the orbit of a satellite. The six elements are: (1) eccentricity, (2) semi-major axis, (3) inclination, (4) longitude of the ascending node, (5) argument of periapsis, and (6) mean anomaly at epoch.

29. B: Internet Radio Linking Project (IRLP) nodes consist of a radio attached to an internet-connected computer running specialized software. It allows amateur radio users to communicate with other users anywhere in the world near another IRLP node. Users access the node using Dual-Tone Multi-Frequency (DTMF) signals.

30 B: The abbreviation PSK means phase shift keying. Phase shift keying is a strategy for digital modes in the high frequency spectrum. In this system, the components of code are indicated with shifts in the timing relationship between a continuously transmitted tone and a reference tone. This enables the user to transmit a signal in very limited space.

31. C: The quad, Yagi, and dish are three types of directional antenna.

32. B: A Type N connector is most suitable for frequencies above 400 MHz. Type N connectors are threaded RF connectors used to join coaxial cables. These cables are able to carry microwave frequency signals.

Copyright © Mometrix Media. You have been licensed one copy of this document for personal use only. Any other reproduction or redistribution is strictly prohibited. All rights reserved.

33. D: There are a few good ways to guard against electrical shock at your station. To begin with, use three-wire cords and plugs for all AC powered equipment. Second, connect all AC powered station equipment to a common safety ground. Third, use a circuit protected by a ground-fault interrupter.

34. D: The minimum safe distance from a power line when installing an antenna is such that, if the antenna falls unexpectedly, no part of it can come closer than 10 feet to the power wires.

35. D: It is acceptable to determine that your station complies with FCC RF exposure regulations by calculation based on FCC OET Bulletin 65, by calculation based on computer modeling, or by measurement of field strength using calibrated equipment.

Copyright © Mometrix Media. You have been licensed one copy of this document for personal use only. Any other reproduction or redistribution is strictly prohibited. All rights reserved.

Technician Class Practice Test 7

Practice Questions

1. What is the FCC Part 97 definition of telemetry?
    a. An information bulletin issued by the FCC
    b. A one-way transmission to initiate, modify or terminate functions of a device at a distance
    c. A one-way transmission of measurements at a distance from the measuring instrument
    d. An information bulletin from a VEC

2. What amateur band are you using if you are transmitting on 223.50 MHz?
    a. 15 meter band
    b. 10 meter band
    c. 2 meter band
    d. 1.25 meter band

3. What may result when correspondence from the FCC is returned as undeliverable because the grantee failed to provide the correct mailing address?
    a. Fine or imprisonment
    b. Revocation of the station license or suspension of the operator license
    c. Require the licensee to be re-examined
    d. A reduction of one rank in operator class

4. What types of amateur stations can automatically retransmit the signals of other amateur stations?
    a. Auxiliary, beacon, or Earth stations
    b. Auxiliary, repeater, or space stations
    c. Beacon, repeater, or space stations
    d. Earth, repeater, or space stations

5. When the control operator is not the station licensee, who is responsible for the proper operation of the station?
    a. All licensed amateurs who are present at the operation
    b. Only the station licensee
    c. Only the control operator
    d. The control operator and the station licensee are equally responsible

6. Which of the following restrictions apply when a non-licensed person is allowed to speak to a foreign station using a station under the control of a Technician Class control operator?
    a. The person must be a U.S. citizen
    b. The foreign station must be one with which the U.S. has a third party agreement
    c. The licensed control operator must do the station identification
    d. All of these choices are correct

7. Which of the following is true when making a test transmission?
    a. Station identification is not required if the transmission is less than 15 seconds
    b. Station identification is not required if the transmission is less than 1 watt
    c. Station identification is only required once an hour when the transmissions are for test purposes only
    d. Station identification is required at least every ten minutes during the test and at the end of the test

Copyright © Mometrix Media. You have been licensed one copy of this document for personal use only. Any other reproduction or redistribution is strictly prohibited. All rights reserved.

8. What could cause your FM signal to interfere with stations on nearby frequencies?
    a. Microphone gain too high, causing over-deviation
    b. SWR too high
    c. Incorrect CTCSS Tone
    d. All of these choices are correct

9. What should you do to minimize disruptions to an emergency traffic net once you have checked in?
    a. Whenever the net frequency is quiet, announce your call sign and location
    b. Move 5 kHz away from the net's frequency and use high power to ask other hams to keep clear of the net frequency
    c. Do not transmit on the net frequency until asked to do so by the net control station
    d. Wait until the net frequency is quiet, then ask for any emergency traffic for your area

10. What type of wave carries radio signals between transmitting and receiving stations?
    a. Electromagnetic
    b. Electrostatic
    c. Surface acoustic
    d. Magnetostrictive

11. What property of radio waves is often used to identify the different frequency bands?
    a. The approximate wavelength
    b. The magnetic intensity of waves
    c. The time it takes for waves to travel one mile
    d. The voltage standing wave ratio of waves

12. What band is best suited for communicating via meteor scatter?
    a. 10 meters
    b. 6 meters
    c. 2 meters
    d. 70 cm

13. How is a computer's sound card used when conducting digital communications using a computer?
    a. The sound card communicates between the computer CPU and the video display
    b. The sound card records the audio frequency for video display
    c. The sound card provides audio to the microphone input and converts received audio to digital form
    d. All of these choices are correct

14. What does the term "RIT" mean?
    a. Receiver Input Tone
    b. Receiver Incremental Tuning
    c. Rectifier Inverter Test
    d. Remote Input Transmitter

15. Which of the following is a good electrical conductor?
    a. Glass
    b. Wood
    c. Copper
    d. Rubber

Copyright © Mometrix Media. You have been licensed one copy of this document for personal use only. Any other reproduction or redistribution is strictly prohibited. All rights reserved.

16. If a frequency readout calibrated in megahertz shows a reading of 3.525 MHz, what would it show if it were calibrated in kilohertz?
    a. 0.003525 kHz
    b. 35.25 kHz
    c. 3525 kHz
    d. 3,525,000 kHz

17. What is a usual name for electromagnetic waves that travel through space?
    a. Gravity waves
    b. Sound waves
    c. Radio waves
    d. Pressure waves

18. What is the current flow in a circuit with an applied voltage of 120 volts and a resistance of 80 ohms?
    a. 9600 amperes
    b. 200 amperes
    c. 0.667 amperes
    d. 1.5 amperes

19. What electrical component is usually composed of a coil of wire?
    a. Switch
    b. Capacitor
    c. Diode
    d. Inductor

20. What does the abbreviation "LED" stand for?
    a. Low Emission Diode
    b. Light Emitting Diode
    c. Liquid Emission Detector
    d. Long Echo Delay

21. What is component 8 in figure T2?
(figures found at the end of the guide)
    a. Resistor
    b. Inductor
    c. Regulator IC
    d. Light emitting diode

22. Which of the following is commonly used as a visual indicator?
    a. LED
    b. FET
    c. Zener diode
    d. Bipolar transistor

23. What is meant by term "PTT"?
    a. Pre-transmission tuning to reduce transmitter harmonic emission
    b. Precise tone transmissions used to limit repeater access to only certain signals
    c. A primary transformer tuner use to match antennas
    d. The push to talk function which switches between receive and transmit

Copyright © Mometrix Media. You have been licensed one copy of this document for personal use only. Any other reproduction or redistribution is strictly prohibited. All rights reserved.

24. Which of the following may be useful in correcting a radio frequency interference problem?
    a. Snap-on ferrite chokes
    b. Low-pass and high-pass filters
    c. Band-reject and band-pass filters
    d. All of these choices are correct

25. What happens to power lost in a feed line?
    a. It increases the SWR
    b. It comes back into your transmitter and could cause damage
    c. It is converted into heat
    d. It can cause distortion of your signal

26. Which of the following measurements are commonly made using a multimeter?
    a. SWR and RF power
    b. Signal strength and noise
    c. Impedance and reactance
    d. Voltage and resistance

27. What is the primary advantage of single sideband over FM for voice transmissions?
    a. SSB signals are easier to tune
    b. SSB signals are less susceptible to interference
    c. SSB signals have narrower bandwidth
    d. All of these choices are correct

28. With regard to satellite communications, what is Doppler shift?
    a. A change in the satellite orbit
    b. A mode where the satellite receives signals on one band and transmits on another
    c. An observed change in signal frequency caused by relative motion between the satellite and the earth station
    d. A special digital communications mode for some satellites

29. What is the maximum power allowed when transmitting telecommand signals to radio controlled models?
    a. 500 milliwatts
    b. 1 watt
    c. 25 watts
    d. 1500 watts

30. What is PSK31?
    a. A high-rate data transmission mode
    b. A method of reducing noise interference to FM signals
    c. A method of compressing digital television signals
    d. A low-rate data transmission mode

31. What is a good reason not to use a "rubber duck" antenna inside your car?
    a. Signals can be significantly weaker than when it is outside of the vehicle
    b. It might cause your radio to overheat
    c. The SWR might decrease, decreasing the signal strength
    d. All of these choices are correct

Copyright © Mometrix Media. You have been licensed one copy of this document for personal use only. Any other reproduction or redistribution is strictly prohibited. All rights reserved.

32. Which of the following is true of PL-259 type coax connectors?
    a. They are preferred for microwave operation
    b. They are water tight
    c. They are commonly used at HF frequencies
    d. They are a bayonet type connector

33. Which of these precautions should be taken when installing devices for lightning protection in a coaxial cable feed line?
    a. Include a parallel bypass switch for each protector so that it can be switched out of the circuit when running high power
    b. Include a series switch in the ground line of each protector to prevent RF overload from inadvertently damaging the protector
    c. Keep the ground wires from each protector separate and connected to station ground
    d. Ground all of the protectors to a common plate which is in turn connected to an external ground

34. Which of the following is an important safety rule to remember when using a crank-up tower?
    a. This type of tower must never be painted
    b. This type of tower must never be grounded
    c. This type of tower must never be climbed unless it is in the fully retracted position
    d. All of these choices are correct

35. What could happen if a person accidentally touched your antenna while you were transmitting?
    a. Touching the antenna could cause television interference
    b. They might receive a painful RF burn
    c. They might develop radiation poisoning
    d. All of these choices are correct

Copyright © Mometrix Media. You have been licensed one copy of this document for personal use only. Any other reproduction or redistribution is strictly prohibited. All rights reserved.

Answers and Explanations

1. **C:** FCC Part 97 defines telemetry as a one-way transmission of measurements at a distance from the measuring instrument.

2. **D:** If you are transmitting on the 223.50 MHz, you are using the 1.25 meter amateur band.

3. **B:** When correspondence from the FCC is returned as undeliverable because the grantee failed to provide the correct mailing address, the station license may be revoked, or the operator license may be suspended.

4. **B:** No amateur station, except an auxiliary, repeater, or space station, may automatically retransmit the radio signals of other amateur station.

5. **D:** When the control operator is not the station licensee, the control operator and the station licensee are equally responsible for the proper operation of the station.

6. **B:** An amateur station may transmit messages for a third party to any station within the jurisdiction of any foreign government when transmitting emergency or disaster relief communications and any station within the jurisdiction of any foreign government whose administration has made arrangements with the United States to allow amateur stations to be used for transmitting international communications on behalf of third parties. No station shall transmit messages for a third party to any station within the jurisdiction of any foreign government whose administration has not made such an arrangement.

7. **D:** When making a test transmission, station identification is required at least every 10 minutes during the test and at the end.

8. **A:** Having your microphone gain turned up too high can cause over-deviation and result in your signal interfering with stations on nearby frequencies.

9. **C:** To minimize disruptions to an emergency traffic net once you have checked in, do not transmit on the net frequency until asked to do so by the net control station.

10. **A:** Electromagnetic waves carry radio signals between transmitting and receiving stations.

11. **A:** The approximate wavelength of radio waves is often used to identify the different frequency bands.

12. **B:** The 6 meter band is best suited to communicating via meteor scatter.

13. **C:** When conducting digital communications using a computer, the sound card provides audio to the microphone input and converts received audio to digital form.

14. **B:** The term RIT means Receiver Incremental Tuning. This is a transceiver control that enables the frequency of the receiver to be changed a little bit without requiring the frequency of the transmitter to be changed. Receiver Incremental Tuning is sometimes called a clarifier control.

15. **C:** Copper is a good electrical conductor.

16. **C:** If a frequency readout calibrated in megahertz shows a reading of 3.525 MHz, it would show 3525 kilohertz if it were calibrated in kilohertz. The metric prefix mega- means millions, and the prefix kilo- means thousands. Millions are the same as 106, while thousands are equal to 103. Megahertz can be converted into kilohertz, then, by multiplying by 103, or a thousand: 3.525 MHz x 1000 = 3525.

17. **C:** The usual name for electromagnetic waves that travel through space is radio waves.

Copyright © Mometrix Media. You have been licensed one copy of this document for personal use only. Any other reproduction or redistribution is strictly prohibited. All rights reserved.

18. D: The current flow in a circuit with an applied voltage of 120 V and a resistance of 80 ohms is 1.5 amperes. The current flow can be found by dividing the voltage by the resistance: 120/80 = 1.5.

19. D: An inductor is usually composed of a coil of wire.

20. B: The abbreviation LED stands for Light Emitting Diode. A LED is a semiconductor diode that, when a current passes through it, produces infrared or visible light. Each diode is only capable of producing a single primary color, though diodes may be combined to produce any color.

21. D: In figure T2, component 8 is a light emitting diode.

22. A: LED is commonly used as a visual indicator.

23. D: The term PTT stands for push-to-talk, a setup in which the transceiver is set to receive when the button is not pushed, and transmit when the button is pushed.

24. D: A radio frequency interference problem may be corrected with snap-on ferrite chokes, low-pass and high-pass filters, or band-reject and band-pass filters.

25. C: The power lost in a feed line is converted into heat. If the cable has cracks or dents, it will be more likely to lose power in this manner. A ham radio operator should always use the best feed line he or she can afford.

26. D: Voltage and resistance measurements are commonly made using a multimeter. The multimeter is sometimes referred to as a volt-ohm meter.

27. C: The primary advantage of single sideband over FM for voice transmissions is that SSB signals have narrower bandwidth.

28. C: With regard to satellite communications, Doppler shift is an observed change in signal frequency caused by relative motion between the satellite and the earth station. When the satellite is approaching the earth station, the wavelength will be shorter; as the satellite moves away from the earth station, the wave length will gradually expand.

29. B: The maximum power allowed when transmitting tele-command signals to radio controlled models is 1 watt.

30. D: PSK31 is a low-rate data transmission mode. This mode of phase shift keying only requires 31.25 Hz for its signal. It accomplishes this by using the Varicode system for characters, in which the constituent elements are distinguished by variations in a continuous tone rather than by separate tones.

31. A: One good reason not to use a "rubber duck" antenna inside your car is that signals can be significantly weaker than when it is outside the vehicle.

32. C: PL–259 type coax connectors are commonly used at HF frequencies.

33. D: When installing devices for lightning protection in a coaxial cable feed line, one should ground all of the protectors to a common plate which is in turn connected to an external ground.

34. C: An important safety rule to remember when using a crank-up tower is that this type of tower must never be climbed unless it is in the fully retracted position. Crank-up towers are kept stable by a concrete foundation rather than by guy wires.

35. B: If a person accidentally touched your antenna while you were transmitting, they might receive a painful RF burn.

Copyright © Mometrix Media. You have been licensed one copy of this document for personal use only. Any other reproduction or redistribution is strictly prohibited. All rights reserved.

Technician Class Practice Test 8

Practice Questions

1. Which of the following entities recommends transmit/receive channels and other parameters for auxiliary and repeater stations?
    a. Frequency Spectrum Manager
    b. Frequency Coordinator
    c. FCC Regional Field Office
    d. International Telecommunications Union

2. Which of the following is a result of the fact that the amateur service is secondary in some portions of the 70 cm band?
    a. U.S. amateurs may find non-amateur stations in the bands, and must avoid interfering with them
    b. U.S. amateurs must give foreign amateur stations priority in those portions
    c. International communications are not permitted on 70 cm
    d. Digital transmissions are not permitted on 70 cm

3. What is the normal term for an FCC-issued primary station/operator amateur radio license grant?
    a. Five years
    b. Life
    c. Ten years
    d. Twenty years

4. In which of the following circumstances may the control operator of an amateur station receive compensation for operating the station?
    a. When engaging in communications on behalf of their employer
    b. When the communication is incidental to classroom instruction at an educational institution
    c. When re-broadcasting weather alerts during a RACES net
    d. When notifying other amateur operators of the availability for sale or trade of apparatus

5. Which of the following is an example of automatic control?
    a. Repeater operation
    b. Controlling the station over the Internet
    c. Using a computer or other device to automatically send CW
    d. Using a computer or other device to automatically identify

6. Which indicator is required by the FCC to be transmitted after a station call sign?
    a. /M when operating mobile
    b. /R when operating a repeater
    c. / followed the FCC Region number when operating out of the region in which the license was issued
    d. /KT, /AE or /AG when using new license privileges earned by CSCE while waiting for an upgrade to a previously issued license to appear in the FCC license database

7. What is the meaning of the procedural signal "CQ"?
    a. Call on the quarter hour
    b. A new antenna is being tested (no station should answer)
    c. Only the called station should transmit
    d. Calling any station

Copyright © Mometrix Media. You have been licensed one copy of this document for personal use only. Any other reproduction or redistribution is strictly prohibited. All rights reserved.

8. Which of the following applies when two stations transmitting on the same frequency interfere with each other?
  a. Common courtesy should prevail, but no one has absolute right to an amateur frequency
  b. Whoever has the strongest signal has priority on the frequency
  c. Whoever has been on the frequency the longest has priority on the frequency
  d. The station which has the weakest signal has priority on the frequency

9. Which of the following is a characteristic of good emergency traffic handling?
  a. Passing messages exactly as received
  b. Making decisions as to whether or not messages should be relayed or delivered
  c. Communicating messages to the news media for broadcast outside the disaster area
  d. All of these choices are correct

10. Which of the following is a likely cause of irregular fading of signals received by ionospheric reflection?
  a. Frequency shift due to Faraday rotation
  b. Interference from thunderstorms
  c. Random combining of signals arriving via different paths
  d. Intermodulation distortion

11. What are the frequency limits of the VHF spectrum?
  a. 30 to 300 kHz
  b. 30 to 300 MHz
  c. 300 to 3000 kHz
  d. 300 to 3000 MHz

12. What causes tropospheric ducting?
  a. Discharges of lightning during electrical storms
  b. Sunspots and solar flares
  c. Updrafts from hurricanes and tornadoes
  d. Temperature inversions in the atmosphere

13. Which type of conductor is best to use for RF grounding?
  a. Round stranded wire
  b. Round copper-clad steel wire
  c. Twisted-pair cable
  d. Flat strap

14. What is the advantage of having multiple receive bandwidth choices on a multimode transceiver?
  a. Permits monitoring several modes at once
  b. Permits noise or interference reduction by selecting a bandwidth matching the mode
  c. Increases the number of frequencies that can be stored in memory
  d. Increases the amount of offset between receive and transmit frequencies

15. Which of the following is a good electrical insulator?
  a. Copper
  b. Glass
  c. Aluminum
  d. Mercury

Copyright © Mometrix Media. You have been licensed one copy of this document for personal use only. Any other reproduction or redistribution is strictly prohibited. All rights reserved.

16. How many microfarads are 1,000,000 picofarads?
    a. 0.001 microfarads
    b. 1 microfarad
    c. 1000 microfarads
    d. 1,000,000,000 microfarads

17. What is the formula used to calculate electrical power in a DC circuit?
    a. Power (P) equals voltage (E) multiplied by current (I)
    b. Power (P) equals voltage (E) divided by current (I)
    c. Power (P) equals voltage (E) minus current (I)
    d. Power (P) equals voltage (E) plus current (I)

18. What is the current flowing through a 100-ohm resistor connected across 200 volts?
    a. 20,000 amperes
    b. 0.5 amperes
    c. 2 amperes
    d. 100 amperes

19. What electrical component is used to connect or disconnect electrical circuits?
    a. Magnetron
    b. Switch
    c. Thermistor
    d. All of these choices are correct

20. What does the abbreviation "FET" stand for?
    a. Field Effect Transistor
    b. Fast Electron Transistor
    c. Free Electron Transition
    d. Field Emission Thickness

21. What is component 9 in figure T2?
(figures found at the end of the guide)
    a. Variable capacitor
    b. Variable inductor
    c. Variable resistor
    d. Variable transformer

22. Which of the following is used together with an inductor to make a tuned circuit?
    a. Resistor
    b. Zener diode
    c. Potentiometer
    d. Capacitor

23. Which of the following describes combining speech with an RF carrier signal?
    a. Impedance matching
    b. Oscillation
    c. Modulation
    d. Low-pass filtering

Copyright © Mometrix Media. You have been licensed one copy of this document for personal use only. Any other reproduction or redistribution is strictly prohibited. All rights reserved.

24. What should you do if something in a neighbor's home is causing harmful interference to your amateur station?
    a. Work with your neighbor to identify the offending device
    b. Politely inform your neighbor about the rules that prohibit the use of devices which cause interference
    c. Check your station and make sure it meets the standards of good amateur practice
    d. All of these choices are correct

25. What instrument other than an SWR meter could you use to determine if a feed line and antenna are properly matched?
    a. Voltmeter
    b. Ohmmeter
    c. Iambic pentameter
    d. Directional wattmeter

26. Which of the following types of solder is best for radio and electronic use?
    a. Acid-core solder
    b. Silver solder
    c. Rosin-core solder
    d. Aluminum solder

27. What is the approximate bandwidth of a single sideband voice signal?
    a. 1 kHz
    b. 3 kHz
    c. 6 kHz
    d. 15 kHz

28. What is meant by the statement that a satellite is operating in "mode U/V"?
    a. The satellite uplink is in the 15 meter band and the downlink is in the 10 meter band
    b. The satellite uplink is in the 70 cm band and the downlink is in the 2 meter band
    c. The satellite operates using ultraviolet frequencies
    d. The satellite frequencies are usually variable

29. What is required in place of on-air station identification when sending signals to a radio control model using amateur frequencies?
    a. Voice identification must be transmitted every 10 minutes
    b. Morse code ID must be sent once per hour
    c. A label indicating the licensee's name, call sign and address must be affixed to the transmitter
    d. A flag must be affixed to the transmitter antenna with the station call sign in 1 inch high letters or larger

30. Which of the following may be included in packet transmissions?
    a. A check sum which permits error detection
    b. A header which contains the call sign of the station to which the information is being sent
    c. Automatic repeat request in case of error
    d. All of these choices are correct

31. What is the approximate length, in inches, of a quarter-wavelength vertical antenna for 146 MHz?
    a. 112
    b. 50
    c. 19
    d. 12

Copyright © Mometrix Media. You have been licensed one copy of this document for personal use only. Any other reproduction or redistribution is strictly prohibited. All rights reserved.

32. Why should coax connectors exposed to the weather be sealed against water intrusion?
   a. To prevent an increase in feed line loss
   b. To prevent interference to telephones
   c. To keep the jacket from becoming loose
   d. All of these choices are correct

33. What safety equipment should always be included in home-built equipment that is powered from 120V AC power circuits?
   a. A fuse or circuit breaker in series with the AC hot conductor
   b. An AC voltmeter across the incoming power source
   c. An inductor in series with the AC power source
   d. A capacitor across the AC power source

34. What is considered to be a proper grounding method for a tower?
   a. A single four-foot ground rod, driven into the ground no more than 12 inches from the base
   b. A ferrite-core RF choke connected between the tower and ground
   c. Separate eight-foot long ground rods for each tower leg, bonded to the tower and each other
   d. A connection between the tower base and a cold water pipe

35. Which of the following actions might amateur operators take to prevent exposure to RF radiation in excess of FCC-supplied limits?
   a. Relocate antennas
   b. Relocate the transmitter
   c. Increase the duty cycle
   d. All of these choices are correct

Copyright © Mometrix Media. You have been licensed one copy of this document for personal use only. Any other reproduction or redistribution is strictly prohibited. All rights reserved.

Answers and Explanations

1. B: A frequency coordinator recommends transmit/receive channels and other parameters for auxiliary and repeater stations. A frequency coordinator is a person or group of people who advise users of the appropriate repeater frequencies, with the intention of diminishing interference between repeaters who are operating in roughly the same frequency in the same geographical area.

2. A: The amateur service is secondary in some portions of the 70 cm band because U.S. amateurs my find non-amateur stations in the bands and must avoid interfering with them.

3. C: The normal term for an FCC-issued primary station/operator license grant is 10 years.

4. B: The control operator of an amateur station may receive compensation for operating the station when the communication is incidental to classroom instruction at an educational institution.

5. A: A repeater operation may be automatically controlled.

6. D: If you plan to use newly acquired privileges from a license upgrade in the time between your passing the exam and the FCC acknowledging your achievement in the ULS license database, you must transmit the appropriate indicator after your station call sign.

7. D: The meaning of the procedural signal CQ is "calling any station."

8. A: If two stations transmitting on the same frequency begin to interfere with one another, it is up to the participants to resolve the issue. There is no absolute right to any amateur frequency, so operators are encouraged to remain courteous and work out a solution.

9. A: The most important job of an amateur operator when handling emergency traffic messages is usually considered to be passing messages exactly as received.

10. C: The cause of irregular fading of signals from distant stations during times of generally good reception is the random combining of signals arriving via different path lengths.

11. B: The frequency limits of the VHF spectrum are 30 to 300 MHz.

12. D: Tropospheric ducting is caused by temperature inversions in the atmosphere. This is a type of very high frequency propagation that occurs when warm air passes over cold air.

13. D: A flat strap conductor is the best to use for RF grounding. Most ham radio systems have a special terminal for grounding. Copper strap is most often used for grounding.

14. B: The advantage of having multiple receive bandwidth choices on a multimode transceiver is that it permits noise or interference reduction by selecting a bandwidth matching the mode. A multimode transceiver transmits a signal in which the electromagnetic wave is accompanied by a waveguide, which has a much larger cross-section than the electromagnetic wave.

15. B: Glass is a good electrical insulator.

16. B: 1,000,000 picofarads is equivalent to 1 microfarad. The metric prefix pico- means trillionths (10-12), while the prefix micro-means millionths (10-6). Picofarads can be converted to microfarads, then, by dividing by 106, or one million: 1,000,000/1,000,000 = 1.

17. A: The formula used to calculate electrical power in a DC circuit is power equals voltage multiplied by current.

Copyright © Mometrix Media. You have been licensed one copy of this document for personal use only. Any other reproduction or redistribution is strictly prohibited. All rights reserved.

18. C: The current flowing through a 100-ohm resistor connected across 200 volts is 2 amperes. The current is found by dividing the voltage by the resistance: 200/100 = 2.

19. B: A switch is used to connect or disconnect electrical circuits.

20. A: The abbreviation FET stands for Field Effect Transistor. In a field effect transistor, output current is controlled by a variable electric field.

21. C: In figure T2, component 9 is a variable resistor.

22. D: A capacitor is used along with an inductor to make a tuned circuit.

23. C: The process of combining speech with an RF carrier signal is referred to as modulation.

24. D: If you believe something in your neighbor's house is causing harmful interference to your amateur station, there are a few things you can or should do. First, make sure that your station is set up properly and that a faulty setup is not causing the interference problems. If that is not successful, talk to your neighbor about the interference problems you are experiencing, and politely let him know about the FCC rules that govern harmful interference. If your neighbor is amenable, work with him to locate the source of the interference and find a solution. Always remain courteous.

25. D: Besides an SWR meter, one could also use a directional wattmeter to determine if a feed line and antenna are properly matched. An SWR (standing wave ratio) meter can evaluate the effectiveness of impedance matching, and can also identify the degree of mismatch between a transmission line and its load. A directional wattmeter is capable of differentiating between the forward and reflected waves.

26. C: Rosin-core solder is best for radio and electronic use.

27: B: The approximate bandwidth of a single sideband voice signal is 3 kHz.

28. B: When it is said that a satellite is operating in "mode U/V," this means that the satellite uplink is in the 70 cm band and the downlink is in the 2 meter band. In ham radio, modes are particular types of modulation, and modulations are the systems for adding information to a radio signal to be broadcast over the air.

29. C: A label indicating the licensee's name, call sign, and address must be affixed to the transmitter instead of on-air station identification when sending signals to a radio control model using amateur frequencies.

30. D: Packet transmissions may include a check sum which permits error detection, a header which contains the call sign of the station to which the information is being sent, and an automatic repeat request in case of error.

31. C: The approximate length of a quarter-wavelength vertical antenna for 146 MHz is 19 inches.

32. A: Coax connectors exposed to the weather should be sealed against water intrusion to prevent an increase in feed line loss.

33. A: Home-built equipment that is powered with 120V AC power should always include a fuse or circuit breaker in series with the hot power line to reduce the risk of electrocution hazard.

34. C: Separate eight-foot long ground rods for each tower leg, bonded to the tower and each other, are considered to be a proper grounding method for a tower.

35. A: Amateur operators might relocate antennas to prevent exposure to RF radiation in excess of FCC-supplied limits.

Copyright © Mometrix Media. You have been licensed one copy of this document for personal use only. Any other reproduction or redistribution is strictly prohibited. All rights reserved.

Technician Class Practice Test 9

Practice Questions

1. Who selects a Frequency Coordinator?
    a. The FCC Office of Spectrum Management and Coordination Policy
    b. The local chapter of the Office of National Council of Independent Frequency Coordinators
    c. Amateur operators in a local or regional area whose stations are eligible to be auxiliary or repeater stations
    d. FCC Regional Field Office

2. Why should you not set your transmit frequency to be exactly at the edge of an amateur band or sub-band?
    a. To allow for calibration error in the transmitter frequency display
    b. So that modulation sidebands do not extend beyond the band edge
    c. To allow for transmitter frequency drift
    d. All of these choices are correct

3. What is the grace period following the expiration of an amateur license within which the license may be renewed?
    a. Two years
    b. Three years
    c. Five years
    d. Ten years

4. Under which of the following circumstances are amateur stations authorized to transmit signals related to broadcasting, program production, or news gathering, assuming no other means is available?
    a. Only where such communications directly relate to the immediate safety of human life or protection of property
    b. Only when broadcasting communications to or from the space shuttle.
    c. Only where noncommercial programming is gathered and supplied exclusively to the National Public Radio network
    d. Only when using amateur repeaters linked to the Internet

5. What type of control is being used when the control operator is at the control point?
    a. Radio control
    b. Unattended control
    c. Automatic control
    d. Local control

6. What type of amateur station simultaneously retransmits the signal of another amateur station on a different channel or channels?
    a. Beacon station
    b. Earth station
    c. Repeater station
    d. Message forwarding station

Copyright © Mometrix Media. You have been licensed one copy of this document for personal use only. Any other reproduction or redistribution is strictly prohibited. All rights reserved.

7. What brief statement is transmitted used in place of "CQ" to indicate that you are listening on a repeater?
    a. The words "Hello test" followed by your call sign
    b. Your call sign
    c. The repeater call sign followed by your call sign
    d. The letters "QSY" followed by your call sign

8. Which of the following methods is encouraged by the FCC when identifying your station when using phone?
    a. Use of a phonetic alphabet
    b. Send your call sign in CW as well as voice
    c. Repeat your call sign three times
    d. Increase your signal to full power when identifying

9. Are amateur station control operators ever permitted to operate outside the frequency privileges of their license class?
    a. No
    b. Yes, but only when part of a FEMA emergency plan
    c. Yes, but only when part of a RACES emergency plan
    d. Yes, but only if necessary in situations involving the immediate safety of human life or protection of property

10. Which of the following results from the fact that skip signals refracted from the ionosphere are elliptically polarized?
    a. Digital modes are unusable
    b. Either vertically or horizontally polarized antennas may be used for transmission or reception
    c. FM voice is unusable
    d. Both the transmitting and receiving antennas must be of the same polarization

11. What are the frequency limits of the UHF spectrum?
    a. 30 to 300 kHz
    b. 30 to 300 MHz
    c. 300 to 3000 kHz
    d. 300 to 3000 MHz

12. What is generally the best time for long-distance 10 meter band propagation via the F layer?
    a. From dawn to shortly after sunset during periods of high sunspot activity
    b. From shortly after sunset to dawn during periods of high sunspot activity
    c. From dawn to shortly after sunset during periods of low sunspot activity
    d. From shortly after sunset to dawn during periods of low sunspot activity

13. Which of the following could you use to cure distorted audio caused by RF current flowing on the shield of a microphone cable?
    a. Band-pass filter
    b. Low-pass filter
    c. Preamplifier
    d. Ferrite choke

Copyright © Mometrix Media. You have been licensed one copy of this document for personal use only. Any other reproduction or redistribution is strictly prohibited. All rights reserved.

14. Which of the following is an appropriate receive filter bandwidth to select in order to minimize noise and interference for SSB reception?
   a. 500 Hz
   b. 1000 Hz
   c. 2400 Hz
   d. 5000 Hz

15. What is the name for a current that reverses direction on a regular basis?
   a. Alternating current
   b. Direct current
   c. Circular current
   d. Vertical current

16. What is the approximate amount of change, measured in decibels (dB), of a power increase from 5 watts to 10 watts?
   a. 2 dB
   b. 3 dB
   c. 5 dB
   d. 10 dB

17. How much power is being used in a circuit when the applied voltage is 13.8 volts DC and the current is 10 amperes?
   a. 138 watts
   b. 0.7 watts
   c. 23.8 watts
   d. 3.8 watts

18. What is the current flowing through a 24-ohm resistor connected across 240 volts?
   a. 24,000 amperes
   b. 0.1 amperes
   c. 10 amperes
   d. 216 amperes

19. What electrical component is used to protect other circuit components from current overloads?
   a. Fuse
   b. Capacitor
   c. Inductor
   d. All of these choices are correct

20. What are the names of the two electrodes of a diode?
   a. Plus and minus
   b. Source and drain
   c. Anode and cathode
   d. Gate and base

21. What is component 4 in figure T2?
   (figures found at the end of the guide)
   a. Variable inductor
   b. Double-pole switch
   c. Potentiometer
   d. Transformer

Copyright © Mometrix Media. You have been licensed one copy of this document for personal use only. Any other reproduction or redistribution is strictly prohibited. All rights reserved.

22. What is the name of a device that combines several semiconductors and other components into one package?
    a. Transducer
    b. Multi-pole relay
    c. Integrated circuit
    d. Transformer

23. Which of the following devices is most useful for VHF weak-signal communication?
    a. A quarter-wave vertical antenna
    b. A multi-mode VHF transceiver
    c. An omni-directional antenna
    d. A mobile VHF FM transceiver

24. What is a Part 15 device?
    a. An unlicensed device that may emit low powered radio signals on frequencies used by a licensed service
    b. A type of amateur radio that can legally be used in the citizen's band
    c. A device for long distance communications using special codes sanctioned by the International Amateur Radio Union
    d. A type of test set used to determine whether a transmitter is in compliance with FCC regulation 91.15

25. Which of the following is the most common cause for failure of coaxial cables?
    a. Moisture contamination
    b. Gamma rays
    c. The velocity factor exceeds 1.0
    d. Overloading

26. What is the characteristic appearance of a "cold" solder joint?
    a. Dark black spots
    b. A bright or shiny surface
    c. A grainy or dull surface
    d. A greenish tint

27. What is the approximate bandwidth of a VHF repeater FM phone signal?
    a. Less than 500 Hz
    b. About 150 kHz
    c. Between 10 and 15 kHz
    d. Between 50 and 125 kHz

28. What causes "spin fading" when referring to satellite signals?
    a. Circular polarized noise interference radiated from the sun
    b. Rotation of the satellite and its antennas
    c. Doppler shift of the received signal
    d. Interfering signals within the satellite uplink band

29. How might you obtain a list of active nodes that use VoIP?
    a. From the FCC Rulebook
    b. From your local emergency coordinator
    c. From a repeater directory
    d. From the local repeater frequency coordinator

Copyright © Mometrix Media. You have been licensed one copy of this document for personal use only. Any other reproduction or redistribution is strictly prohibited. All rights reserved.

30. What code is used when sending CW in the amateur bands?
    a. Baudot
    b. Hamming
    c. International Morse
    d. Gray

31. What is the approximate length, in inches, of a 6 meter 1/2-wavelength wire dipole antenna?
    a. 6
    b. 50
    c. 112
    d. 236

32. What might cause erratic changes in SWR readings?
    a. The transmitter is being modulated
    b. A loose connection in an antenna or a feed line
    c. The transmitter is being over-modulated
    d. Interference from other stations is distorting your signal

33. What kind of hazard is presented by a conventional 12-volt storage battery?
    a. It emits ozone which can be harmful to the atmosphere
    b. Shock hazard due to high voltage
    c. Explosive gas can collect if not properly vented
    d. All of these choices are correct

34. Why should you avoid attaching an antenna to a utility pole?
    a. The antenna will not work properly because of induced voltages
    b. The utility company will charge you an extra monthly fee
    c. The antenna could contact high-voltage power wires
    d. All of these choices are correct

35. How can you make sure your station stays in compliance with RF safety regulations?
    a. By informing the FCC of any changes made in your station
    b. By re-evaluating the station whenever an item of equipment is changed
    c. By making sure your antennas have low SWR
    d. All of these choices are correct

Copyright © Mometrix Media. You have been licensed one copy of this document for personal use only. Any other reproduction or redistribution is strictly prohibited. All rights reserved.

Answers and Explanations

1. C: Amateur operators in a local or regional area whose stations are eligible to be auxiliary or repeater stations may select a frequency coordinator.

2. D: There are several reasons why an operator should not set the transmit frequency to be exactly at the edge of an amateur band or sub-band. To begin with, this allows for calibration error in the transmitter frequency display. It also ensures that modulation sidebands do not extend beyond the band edge. Finally, it allows for transmitter frequency drift.

3. A: The grace period following the expiration of an amateur license, within which the license may be renewed, is two years.

4. A: Assuming no other means is available, amateur stations are authorized to transmit signals related to broadcasting, program production, or news gathering only where such communications directly relate to the immediate safety of human life or protection of property.

5. D: Local control is used for transmissions from a handheld radio.

6. C: A repeater station is an amateur station that simultaneously retransmits the signal of another amateur station on a different channel or channels.

7. B: A call sign is often used in place of CQ to indicate that you are listening on a repeater.

8. A: When identifying your station while using the phone, one should use the phonetic alphabet.

9. D: Amateur station control operator are permitted to operate outside the frequency privileges of their license class only if necessary in situations involving the immediate safety of human life or protection of property

10. B: Because skip signals refracted from the ionosphere are elliptically polarized, either vertically or horizontally polarized antennas can be used to transmit and receive them.

11. D: The frequency limits of the UHF spectrum are 300 to 3000 MHz.

12. A: Long-distance 10 meter band propagation via the F layer is best conducted between dawn and shortly after sunset during periods of high sunspot activity.

13. D: A ferrite choke can be used to cure distorted audio caused by RF current flowing on the shield of a microphone cable.

14. C: 2400 Hz is an appropriate receive filter for minimizing noise and interference for SSB reception.

15. A: A current that reverses direction on a regular basis is called alternating current. One of the main advantages of alternating current is that a transformer may be used to increase or decrease the voltage, which makes it easier to transmit the current over a long distance.

16. B: A power increase from 5 to 10 watts creates approximately 3 dB of change. The relationship between power increases and changes in decibel levels is complex. Whenever the power is doubled, however, the decibel level will rise by three. If the power is quadrupled, the decibel level rises by 6. If the power increases by ten times, the decibel level also rises by ten.

17. A: When the applied voltage is 13.8 volts DC and the current is 10 amperes, 138 watts of power is being used in the circuit. The power can be calculated by multiplying the voltage by the current: 13.8 x 10 = 138.

Copyright © Mometrix Media. You have been licensed one copy of this document for personal use only. Any other reproduction or redistribution is strictly prohibited. All rights reserved.

18. C: The current flowing through a 24-ohm resistor connected across 240 volts is 10 amperes. The current is found by dividing the voltage by the resistance: 240/24 = 10.

19. A: A fuse is used to protect other circuit components from current overloads. It contains a metal element that will melt when the current exceeds a certain amperage. When the element melts, the circuit is broken.

20. C: The names of the two electrodes of a diode are the anode and cathode. Electrons leave a system through the anode and return through the cathode.

21. D: In figure T2, component 4 is a transformer.

22. C: An integrated circuit combines several semiconductors and other components into one package. All of these semiconductors and other components are either imprinted or etched on a thin slice of a semiconducting material, as for instance silicon.

23. B: A multimode VHF transceiver would be most useful for VHF weak-signal communication.

24. A: A Part 15 device is an unlicensed device that may emit low powered radio signals on frequencies used by a licensed service.

25. A: The most common cause of failure in coaxial cables is moisture contamination. Coaxial cable, also known as coax, is composed of a central wire surrounded by hollow tube. The center wire is called the center conductor, and the outer conductor is known as the braid, or shield.

26. C: The characteristic appearance of a "cold" solder joint is a grainy or dull surface.

27. C: The approximate bandwidth of a VHF repeater FM phone signal is between 10 and 15 kHz.

28. B: Spin fading with respect to satellite signals is caused by the rotation of the satellite and its antennas.

29. C: A list of active nodes that use VoIP can be obtained from a repeater directory. Repeater directories are comprehensive lists of active ham repeater frequencies.

30. C: International Morse code is used when sending CW in the amateur bands.

31. C: The approximate length of a 6 meter ½-wavelength wire dipole antenna is 112 inches.

32. B: A loose connection in an antenna or a feed line might cause erratic changes in SWR readings.

33. C: One hazard related to conventional 12-volt storage batteries is that explosive gas can collect if it is not properly vented.

34. C: You should avoid attaching an antenna to a utility pole because the antenna could contact high-voltage power wires.

35. B: A station may ensure compliance by re-evaluating the station whenever an item of equipment is changed.

Copyright © Mometrix Media. You have been licensed one copy of this document for personal use only. Any other reproduction or redistribution is strictly prohibited. All rights reserved.

Technician Class Practice Test 10

Practice Questions

1. What is the FCC Part 97 definition of an amateur station?
   a. A station in an Amateur Radio Service consisting of the apparatus necessary for carrying on radio communications
   b. A building where Amateur Radio receivers, transmitters, and RF power amplifiers are installed
   c. Any radio station operated by a non-professional
   d. Any radio station for hobby use

2. Which of the bands above 30 MHz that are available to Technician Class operators have mode-restricted sub-bands?
   a. The 6 meter, 2 meter, and 70 cm bands
   b. The 2 meter and 13 cm bands
   c. The 6 meter, 2 meter, and 1.25 meter bands
   d. The 2 meter and 70 cm bands

3. How soon after passing the examination for your first amateur radio license may you operate a transmitter on an amateur service frequency
   a. Immediately
   b. 30 days after the test date
   c. As soon as your operator/station license grant appears in the FCC's license database
   d. You must wait until you receive your license in the mail from the FCC

4. What is the meaning of the term "broadcasting" in the FCC rules for the amateur services?
   a. Two-way transmissions by amateur stations
   b. Transmission of music
   c. Transmission of messages directed only to amateur operators
   d. Transmissions intended for reception by the general public

5. Which of the following is an example of remote control as defined in Part 97?
   a. Repeater operation
   b. Operating the station over the Internet
   c. Controlling a model aircraft, boat or car by amateur radio
   d. All of these choices are correct

6. Who is accountable should a repeater inadvertently retransmit communications that violate the FCC rules?
   a. The control operator of the originating station
   b. The control operator of the repeater
   c. The owner of the repeater
   d. Both the originating station and the repeater owner

7. What is a band plan, beyond the privileges established by the FCC?
   a. A voluntary guideline for using different modes or activities within an amateur band
   b. A mandated list of operating schedules
   c. A list of scheduled net frequencies
   d. A plan devised by a club to indicate frequency band usage

Copyright © Mometrix Media. You have been licensed one copy of this document for personal use only. Any other reproduction or redistribution is strictly prohibited. All rights reserved.

8. Which "Q" signal indicates that you are receiving interference from other stations?
   a. QRM
   b. QRN
   c. QTH
   d. QSB

9. What is the preamble in a formal traffic message?
   a. The first paragraph of the message text
   b. The message number
   c. The priority handling indicator for the message
   d. The information needed to track the message as it passes through the amateur radio traffic handling system

10. What may occur if data signals propagate over multiple paths?
   a. Transmission rates can be increased by a factor equal to the number of separate paths observed
   b. Transmission rates must be decreased by a factor equal to the number of separate paths observed
   c. No significant changes will occur if the signals are transmitting using FM
   d. Error rates are likely to increase

11. What frequency range is referred to as HF?
   a. 300 to 3000 MHz
   b. 30 to 300 MHz
   c. 3 to 30 MHz
   d. 300 to 3000 kHz

12. What is the radio horizon?
   a. The distance over which two stations can communicate direct path
   b. The distance from the ground to a horizontally mounted antenna
   c. The farthest point you can see when standing at the base of your antenna tower
   d. The shortest distance between two points on the Earth's surface

13. What is the source of a high-pitched whine that varies with engine speed in a mobile transceiver's receive audio?
   a. The ignition system
   b. The alternator
   c. The electric fuel pump
   d. Anti-lock braking system controllers

14. Which of the following is an appropriate receive filter bandwidth to select in order to minimize noise and interference for CW reception?
   a. 500 Hz
   b. 1000 Hz
   c. 2400 Hz
   d. 5000 Hz

15. Which term describes the rate at which electrical energy is used?
   a. Resistance
   b. Current
   c. Power
   d. Voltage

Copyright © Mometrix Media. You have been licensed one copy of this document for personal use only. Any other reproduction or redistribution is strictly prohibited. All rights reserved.

16. What is the approximate amount of change, measured in decibels (dB), of a power decrease from 12 watts to 3 watts?
    a. 1 dB
    b. 3 dB
    c. 6 dB
    d. 9 dB

17. How much power is being used in a circuit when the applied voltage is 12 volts DC and the current is 2.5 amperes?
    a. 4.8 watts
    b. 30 watts
    c. 14.5 watts
    d. 0.208 watts

18. What is the voltage across a 2-ohm resistor if a current of 0.5 amperes flows through it?
    a. 1 volt
    b. 0.25 volts
    c. 2.5 volts
    d. 1.5 volts

19. Which of the following battery types is rechargeable?
    a. Nickel-metal hydride
    b. Lithium-ion
    c. Lead-acid gel-cell
    d. All of these choices are correct

20. What are the three electrodes of a PNP or NPN transistor?
    a. Emitter, base, and collector
    b. Source, gate, and drain
    c. Cathode, grid, and plate
    d. Cathode, drift cavity, and collector

21. What is component 3 in figure T3?
(figures found at the end of the guide)
    a. Connector
    b. Meter
    c. Variable capacitor
    d. Variable inductor

22. What is the function of component 2 in Figure T1?
(figures found at the end of the guide)
    a. Give off light when current flows through it
    b. Supply electrical energy
    c. Control the flow of current
    d. Convert electrical energy into radio waves

23. What device increases the low-power output from a handheld transceiver?
    a. A voltage divider
    b. An RF power amplifier
    c. An impedance network
    d. All of these choices are correct

Copyright © Mometrix Media. You have been licensed one copy of this document for personal use only. Any other reproduction or redistribution is strictly prohibited. All rights reserved.

24. What might be the problem if you receive a report that your audio signal through the repeater is distorted or unintelligible?
   a. Your transmitter may be slightly off frequency
   b. Your batteries may be running low
   c. You could be in a bad location
   d. All of these choices are correct

25. Why should the outer jacket of coaxial cable be resistant to ultraviolet light?
   a. Ultraviolet resistant jackets prevent harmonic radiation
   b. Ultraviolet light can increase losses in the cable's jacket
   c. Ultraviolet and RF signals can mix together, causing interference
   d. Ultraviolet light can damage the jacket and allow water to enter the cable

26. What is probably happening when an ohmmeter, connected across an unpowered circuit, initially indicates a low resistance and then shows increasing resistance with time?
   a. The ohmmeter is defective
   b. The circuit contains a large capacitor
   c. The circuit contains a large inductor
   d. The circuit is a relaxation oscillator

27. What is the typical bandwidth of analog fast-scan TV transmissions on the 70 cm band?
   a. More than 10 MHz
   b. About 6 MHz
   c. About 3 MHz
   d. About 1 MHz

28. What do the initials LEO tell you about an amateur satellite?
   a. The satellite battery is in Low Energy Operation mode
   b. The satellite is performing a Lunar Ejection Orbit maneuver
   c. The satellite is in a Low Earth Orbit
   d. The satellite uses Light Emitting Optics

29. How do you select a specific IRLP node when using a portable transceiver?
   a. Choose a specific CTCSS tone
   b. Choose the correct DSC tone
   c. Access the repeater autopatch
   d. Use the keypad to transmit the IRLP node ID

30. Which of the following can be used to transmit CW in the amateur bands?
   a. Straight Key
   b. Electronic Keyer
   c. Computer Keyboard
   d. All of these choices are correct

31. In which direction is the radiation strongest from a half-wave dipole antenna in free space?
   a. Equally in all directions
   b. Off the ends of the antenna
   c. Broadside to the antenna
   d. In the direction of the feed line

Copyright © Mometrix Media. You have been licensed one copy of this document for personal use only. Any other reproduction or redistribution is strictly prohibited. All rights reserved.

32. What electrical difference exists between the smaller RG-58 and larger RG-8 coaxial cables?
   a. There is no significant difference between the two types
   b. RG-58 cable has less loss at a given frequency
   c. RG-8 cable has less loss at a given frequency
   d. RG-58 cable can handle higher power levels

33. What can happen if a lead-acid storage battery is charged or discharged too quickly?
   a. The battery could overheat and give off flammable gas or explode
   b. The voltage can become reversed
   c. The "memory effect" will reduce the capacity of the battery
   d. All of these choices are correct

34. Which of the following is true concerning grounding conductors used for lightning protection?
   a. Only non-insulated wire must be used
   b. Wires must be carefully routed with precise right-angle bends
   c. Sharp bends must be avoided
   d. Common grounds must be avoided

35. Why is duty cycle one of the factors used to determine safe RF radiation exposure levels?
   a. It affects the average exposure of people to radiation
   b. It affects the peak exposure of people to radiation
   c. It takes into account the antenna feedline loss
   d. It takes into account the thermal effects of the final amplifier

Copyright © Mometrix Media. You have been licensed one copy of this document for personal use only. Any other reproduction or redistribution is strictly prohibited. All rights reserved.

Answers and Explanations

1. A: An amateur station is a station licensed in the Amateur Radio Service and used for amateur communication. It includes any equipment that is necessary for such communication.

2. C: Of the bands available to Technician Class operators, the 6 meter, 2 meter, and 1.25 meter bands have mode-restricted sub-bands.

3. C: After you pass the examination required for your first amateur radio license, you may operate a transmitter on an amateur service frequency as soon as your name and call sign appear in the FCC's ULS database.

4. D: In the FCC rules for the amateur services, broadcasting refers to transmissions intended for reception by the general public. Broadcasting refers to transmissions that are meant to be received by the general public, either on relay or directly.

5. B: Operating the station over the internet is an example of remote control.

6. A: If a repeater inadvertently retransmits communications that violate the FCC rules, the control operator of the originating station is accountable.

7. A: A band plan, beyond the privileges established by the FCC, is a voluntary guideline for using different modes or activities within an amateur band.

8. A: The Q signal used to indicate that you are receiving interference from other stations is QRM. Q signals are useful methods for accelerating communication. A Q signal may be issued as a question or as a response. For example, QRG may mean "What is my exact frequency?" or "Your exact frequency is."

9. D: The preamble in a formal traffic message is information needed to track the message as it passes through the amateur radio traffic handling system. The preamble is the first part of a radiogram. It identifies the source and some basic information about the message.

10. D: If the data signals propagate over multiple paths, error rates are likely to increase.

11. C: The frequency range of 3 to 30 MHz is referred to as HF.

12. A: A radio horizon is the distance over which two stations can communicate direct path.

13. B: The alternator is the source of a high-pitched whine that varies with engine speed in a mobile transceiver's receive audio. An alternator is an electric generator that creates an alternating current.

14. A: 500 Hz is an appropriate receive filter to select in order to minimize noise and interference for CW reception.

15. C: The rate at which electrical energy is used is power.

16. C: A power decrease from 12 watts to 3 watts would result in approximately 6 dB of change. Just as a quadrupling of power would result in an extra 6 dB, so will a quartering of power cause the decibel level to drop by 6.

Copyright © Mometrix Media. You have been licensed one copy of this document for personal use only. Any other reproduction or redistribution is strictly prohibited. All rights reserved.

17. B: When the applied voltage is 12 volts DC and the current is 2.5 amperes, 30 watts of power are being used in the circuit. The power can be calculated by multiplying the voltage by the current: 12 x 2.5 = 30.

18. A: The voltage across a 2-ohm resistor if a current of 0.5 amperes flows through it is 1 volt. The voltage can be calculated by multiplying the current by the resistance: 2 x 0.5 = 1.

19. D: There are many different types of batteries that may be recharged, including nickel-metal hydride (NiMH), lithium-ion (Li-ion), and lead-acid gel cells.

20. A: The three electrodes or terminals of a PNP or NPN transistor are the emitter, base, and collector.

21. D: In figure T3, component 3 is a variable inductor.

22. C: In figure T1, the function of component 2 is to control the flow of current.

23. B: An RF power amplifier increases the low-power output from a handheld transceiver.

24. D: If you receive a report that your audio signal through the repeater is distorted or unintelligible, this may be because your transmitter is slightly off frequency, your batteries are running low, or you're in a bad location.

25. D: The outer jacket of a coaxial cable should be resistant to ultraviolet light because this light can damage the jacket and allow water to enter the cable.

26. C: If an ohmmeter, connected across the circuit, initially indicates a low resistance and then shows increasing resistance with time, the circuit probably contains a large inductor.

27. B: The typical bandwidth of analog fast-scan TV transmissions on the 70 cm band is about 6 MHz.

28. C: The initials LEO indicate that an amateur satellite is in a Low Earth Orbit. This means that the path of the satellite is less than 1000 miles above the surface of the earth.

29. D: When using a portable transceiver, a specific IRLP node can be selected by using the keypad to transmit the IRLP node ID.

30. D: Straight key, electronic keyer, and computer keyboard can be used to transmit CW in the amateur bands.

31. C: The radiation is strongest from a half-wave dipole antenna in free space broadside to the antenna.

32. C: The electrical difference that exists between the smaller RG–58 and larger RG-8 coaxial cables is that the RG-8 cable has less loss at a given frequency.

33. A: If a lead-acid storage battery is charged or discharged too quickly, the battery could overheat and give off flammable gas, or explode. Lead-acid batteries have a low energy-to-weight ratio and a low energy-to-volume ratio, but they nevertheless maintain a comparatively large power-to-weight ratio.

34. C: Sharp bends must be avoided in the grounding conductors used for lightning protection.

Copyright © Mometrix Media. You have been licensed one copy of this document for personal use only. Any other reproduction or redistribution is strictly prohibited. All rights reserved.

35. A: Duty cycle is one of the factors used to determine safe RF radiation exposure levels because it affects the average exposure of people to radiation. If the duty cycle is lower, then there is less RF radiation exposure with no change in peak envelope power output.

Copyright © Mometrix Media. You have been licensed one copy of this document for personal use only. Any other reproduction or redistribution is strictly prohibited. All rights reserved.

General Class Question Pool

G1 – Commission's Rules

G1A – Frequency Privileges; Primary and Secondary Allocations

On which of the following bands is a General Class license holder granted all amateur frequency privileges?
   A. 60, 20, 17, and 12 meters
   B. 160, 80, 40, and 10 meters
   C. 160, 60, 30, 17, 12, and 10 meters
   D. 160, 30, 17, 15, 12, and 10 meters

G1A01 (C) [97.301(d), 97.303(s)]
Answer: C. A General Class license holder is granted all amateur frequency privileges on the 160, 60, 30, 17, 12, and 10 meter bands. On all other bands, the operations of General Class license holders are restricted according to FCC regulations.

On which of the following bands is phone operation prohibited?
   A. 160 meters
   B. 30 meters
   C. 17 meters
   D. 12 meters

G1A02 (B) [97.305]
Answer: B. Phone operation is prohibited on the 30 meter band. In ham radio, phone operation is the generic term for voice communication. There are a number of different ways to communicate by voice using ham radio technology. However, this type of communication is considered to be too cumbersome for the 30 meter band.

On which of the following bands is image transmission prohibited?
   A. 160 meters
   B. 30 meters
   C. 20 meters
   D. 12 meters

G1A03 (B) [97.305]
Answer: B. Image transmission is prohibited on the 30-meter band. This is because the transmission of images requires an amount of traffic that would obstruct the band for other users.

Which of the following amateur bands is restricted to communication on only specific channels, rather than frequency ranges?
   A. 11 meters
   B. 12 meters
   C. 30 meters
   D. 60 meters

Copyright © Mometrix Media. You have been licensed one copy of this document for personal use only. Any other reproduction or redistribution is strictly prohibited. All rights reserved.

G1A04 (D) [97.303 (s)]
Answer: D. The 60-meter amateur band is restricted to communication on only specific channels, rather than frequency ranges. This is in constrast to the other amateur bands, on which frequency ranges rather than channels are restricted.

Which of the following frequencies is in the General Class portion of the 40-meter band?
    A. 7.250 MHz
    B. 7.500 MHz
    C. 40.200 MHz
    D. 40.500 MHz

G1A05 (A) [97.301(d)]
Answer: A. 7.250 MHz is in the General Class portion of the 40-meter band.

Which of the following frequencies is within the General Class portion of the 75-meter phone band?
    A. 1875 kHz
    B. 3750 kHz
    C. 3900 kHz
    D. 4005 kHz

G1A06 (C) [97.301(d)]
Answer: C. 3900 kHz is within the General Class portion of the 75 meter phone band.

Which of the following frequencies is within the General Class portion of the 20-meter phone band?
    A. 14005 kHz
    B. 14105 kHz
    C. 14305 kHz
    D. 14405 kHz

G1A07 (C) [97.301(d)]
Answer: C. The 14305 kHz is within the General Class portion of the 20-meter phone band.

Which of the following frequencies is within the General Class portion of the 80-meter band?
    A. 1855 kHz
    B. 2560 kHz
    C. 3560 kHz
    D. 3650 kHz

G1A08 (C) [97.301(d)]
Answer: C. The 3560 kHz frequenciy is within the General Class portion of the 80 meter band.

Which of the following frequencies is within the General Class portion of the 15-meter band?
    A. 14250 kHz
    B. 18155 kHz
    C. 21300 kHz
    D. 24900 kHz

G1A09 (C) [97.301(d)]
Answer: C. The 21300 kHz frequency is within the General Class portion of the 15-meter band.

Copyright © Mometrix Media. You have been licensed one copy of this document for personal use only. Any other reproduction or redistribution is strictly prohibited. All rights reserved.

Which of the following frequencies is available to a control operator holding a General Class license?
A. 28.020 MHz
B. 28.350 MHz
C. 28.550 MHz
D. All of these choices are correct

G1A10 (D) [97.301(d)]
Answer: D. The 28.020 MHz, 28.350 MHz, and 28.550 MHz frequencies are all available to a control operator holding a General Class license. A control operator is an amateur who has been assigned responsibility for the transmissions made by an amateur station. This assignation is made by the station.

When General Class licensees are not permitted to use the entire voice portion of a particular band, which portion of the voice segment is generally available to them?
A. The lower frequency end
B. The upper frequency end
C. The lower frequency end on frequencies below 7.3 MHz and the upper end on frequencies above 14.150 MHz
D. The upper frequency end on frequencies below 7.3 MHz and the lower end on frequencies above 14.150 MHz

G1A11 (B) [97.301]
Answer: B. When General Class licensees are not permitted to use the entire voice portion of a particular band, the upper frequency end of the voice segment is generally available to them.

Which of the following applies when the FCC rules designate the Amateur Service as a secondary user on a band?
A. Amateur stations must record the call sign of the primary service station before operating on a frequency assigned to that station
B. Amateur stations are allowed to use the band only during emergencies
C. Amateur stations are allowed to use the band only if they do not cause harmful interference to primary users
D. Amateur stations may only operate during specific hours of the day, while primary users are permitted 24 hour use of the band

G1A12 (C) [97.303]
Answer: C. When the FCC rules designate the Amateur Service as a secondary user on a band, amateur stations are allowed to use the band only if they do not cause harmful interference to primary users. The Amateur Service is reserved for people who are interested in improving their ham radio skills simply for personal reasons (that is, not for pecuniary gain). The Amateur Service can be used for self-training, communication, and technical inquiries.

What is the appropriate action if, when operating on either the 30-meter or 60-meter bands, a station in the primary service interferes with your contact?
A. Notify the FCC's regional Engineer in Charge of the interference
B. Increase your transmitter's power to overcome the interference
C. Attempt to contact the station and request that it stop the interference
D. Move to a clear frequency

G1A13 (D) [97.303(h)(2)(j)]
Answer: D. If, when operating on either the 30 or 60 meter bands, a station in the primary service interferes with your contact, move to a clear frequency. Stations in the primary service are not required to accommodate others.

In what ITU region is operation in the 7.175 to 7.300 MHz band permitted for a control operator holding an FCC-issued General Class license?

A. Region 1
B. Region 2
C. Region 3
D. All three regions

G1A14 (B) [97.301(d)]
Answer: B. Operation in the 7.175 to 7.300 MHz band is permitted for a control operator holding an FCC-issued General Class license in ITU Region 2. Frequency allocations are made by the International Telecommunications Union, an organization based in Geneva. The ITU divides the world into three regions: Region 1 includes Europe, Russia, and Africa; Region 2 consists of North and South America; and Region 3 includes Asia, Australia, and most of the Pacific island nations.

G1B – Antenna Structure Limitations; Good Engineering and Good Amateur Practice; Beacon Operation; Prohibited Transmissions; Retransmitting Radio Signals

What is the maximum height above ground to which an antenna structure may be erected without requiring notification to the FAA and registration with the FCC, provided it is not at or near a public use airport?

A. 50 feet
B. 100 feet
C. 200 feet
D. 300 feet

G1B01 (C) [97.15(a)]
Answer: C. The maximum height above ground to which an antenna structure may be erected without requiring notification to the FAA and registration with the FCC, provided it is not at or near a public use airport, is 200 feet. For most ham radio operators, this will not be a problem.

With which of the following conditions must beacon stations comply?

A. A beacon station may not use automatic control
B. The frequency must be coordinated with the National Beacon Organization
C. The frequency must be posted on the Internet or published in a national periodical
D. There must be no more than one beacon signal in the same band from a single location

G1B02 (D) [97.203(b)]
Answer: D. There must be no more than one beacon signal in the same band from a single location. The use of multiple beacon signals may confuse those whom the signals were intended to inform.

Which of the following is a purpose of a beacon station as identified in the FCC Rules?

A. Observation of propagation and reception
B. Automatic identification of repeaters
C. Transmission of bulletins of general interest to Amateur Radio licensees
D. Identifying net frequencies

Copyright © Mometrix Media. You have been licensed one copy of this document for personal use only. Any other reproduction or redistribution is strictly prohibited. All rights reserved.

G1B03 (A) [97.3(a)(9)]
Answer: A. The FCC Rules state that one purpose of a beacon station is the observation of propagation and reception. Beacon stations communicate only for experimental purposes, most often to observe propagation and reception. Ham radio operators often use these stations as reference points or to calibrate their equipment.

Which of the following must be true before amateur stations may provide communications to broadcasters for dissemination to the public?
    A. The communications must directly relate to the immediate safety of human life or protection of property and there must be no other means of communication reasonably available before or at the time of the event
    B. The communications must be approved by a local emergency preparedness official and conducted on officially designated frequencies
    C. The FCC must have declared a state of emergency
    D. All of these choices are correct

G1B04 (A) [97.113(b)]
Answer: A. In order for amateur stations to provide communications to broadcasters for dissemination to the public, the communications must directly relate to the immediate safety of human life or protection of property and there must be no other means of communication reasonably available before or at the time of the event. In general, the FCC is lenient with operators who act in good faith without knowing all of the circumstances surrounding a possible emergency.

When may music be transmitted by an amateur station?
    A. At any time, as long as it produces no spurious emissions
    B. When it is unintentionally transmitted from the background at the transmitter
    C. When it is transmitted on frequencies above 1215 MHz
    D. When it is an incidental part of a manned space craft retransmission

G1B05 (D) [97.113(c)]
Answer: D. Music may be transmitted by an amateur station when it is an incidental part of a manned space craft retransmission. Otherwise, amateur stations should avoid music broadcasting that could represent an infringement of copyright.

When is an amateur station permitted to transmit secret codes?
    A. During a declared communications emergency
    B. To control a space station
    C. Only when the information is of a routine, personal nature
    D. Only with Special Temporary Authorization from the FCC

G1B06 (B) [97.113(a)(4) and 97.207(f)]
Answer: B. Amateur stations are permitted to transmit secret codes to control a space station. Any amateur station that is positioned more than 50 km above the surface of the Earth is considered a space station.

What are the restrictions on the use of abbreviations or procedural signals in the Amateur Service?
    A. Only "Q" codes are permitted
    B. They may be used if they do not obscure the meaning of a message
    C. They are not permitted
    D. Only "10 codes" are permitted

Copyright © Mometrix Media. You have been licensed one copy of this document for personal use only. Any other reproduction or redistribution is strictly prohibited. All rights reserved.

G1B07 (B) [97.113(a)(4)]
Answer: B. In the Amateur Service, abbreviations or procedural signals may be used if they do not obscure the meaning of a message. Procedural signals, also known as prosigns, are shorthand messages that indicate the immediate intentions of the operator. A procedural signal may consist of a single letter or two letters transmitted as a single character.

When choosing a transmitting frequency, what should you do to comply with good amateur practice?
    A. Review FCC Part 97 Rules regarding permitted frequencies and emissions
    B. Follow generally accepted band plans agreed to by the Amateur Radio community
    C. Before transmitting, listen to avoid interfering with ongoing communication
    D. All of these choices are correct

G1B08 (D) [97.101(a)]
Answer: D. When choosing a transmitting frequency, there are a few things you should do to comply with good amateur practice. To begin with, review the FCC Part 97 Rules regarding permitted frequencies and emissions. Also, follow the generally accepted band plans agreed to by the Amateur Radio community. Finally, before transmitting, listen to avoid interfering with ongoing communication.

When may an amateur station transmit communications in which the licensee or control operator has a pecuniary (monetary) interest?
    A. When other amateurs are being notified of the sale of apparatus normally used in an amateur station and such activity is not done on a regular basis
    B. Only when there is no other means of communications readily available
    C. When other amateurs are being notified of the sale of any item with a monetary value less than $200 and such activity is not done on a regular basis
    D. Never

G1B09 (A) [97.113(a)(3)]
Answer: A. An amateur station may transmit communications in which the licensee or control operator has a pecuniary (monetary) interest when other amateurs are being notified of the sale of apparatus normally used in an amateur station and such activity is not done on a regular basis. A pecuniary interest is said to exist even when the promised compensation is goods besides money.

What is the power limit for beacon stations?
    A. 10 watts PEP output
    B. 20 watts PEP output
    C. 100 watts PEP output
    D. 200 watts PEP output

G1B10 (C) [97.203(c)]
Answer: C. The power limit for beacon stations is 100 watts PEP output.

How does the FCC require an amateur station to be operated in all respects not specifically covered by the Part 97 rules?
    A. In conformance with the rules of the IARU
    B. In conformance with Amateur Radio custom
    C. In conformance with good engineering and good amateur practice
    D. All of these choices are correct

Copyright © Mometrix Media. You have been licensed one copy of this document for personal use only. Any other reproduction or redistribution is strictly prohibited. All rights reserved.

G1B11 (C) [97.101(a)]
Answer: C. In all respects not specifically covered by the Part 97 rules, the FCC requires an amateur station to be operated in conformance with good engineering and good amateur practice. Part 97 of the FCC rules and regulations has to do with amateur radio. It contains the following subparts: general provisions; station operating standards; special operations; technical standards; emergency communications; and qualifying examination systems.

Who or what determines "good engineering and good amateur practice" as applied to the operation of an amateur station in all respects not covered by the Part 97 rules?
    A. The FCC
    B. The Control Operator
    C. The IEEE
    D. The ITU

G1B12 (A) [97.101(a)]
Answer: A. The FCC determines "good engineering and good amateur practice" as applied to the operation of an amateur station in all respects not covered by the Part 97 rules. The FCC is generally willing to respond to novice operators who are unsure whether their operations are in keeping with these standards.

G1C – Transmitter Power Regulations; Data Emission Standards

What is the maximum transmitting power an amateur station may use on 10.140 MHz?
    A. 200 watts PEP output
    B. 1000 watts PEP output
    C. 1500 watts PEP output
    D. 2000 watts PEP output

G1C01 (A) [97.313(c)(1)]
Answer: A. The maximum transmitting power an amateur station may use on 10.140 MHz is 200 watts PEP output.

What is the maximum transmitting power an amateur station may use on the 12-meter band?
    A. 50 watts PEP output
    B. 200 watts PEP output
    C. 1500 watts PEP output
    D. An effective radiated power equivalent to 100 watts from a half-wave dipole

G1C02 (C) [97.313(a),(b)]
Answer: C. The maximum transmitting power an amateur station may use on the 12 meter band is 1500 watts PEP output.

What is the maximum bandwidth permitted by FCC rules for Amateur Radio stations when transmitting on USB frequencies in the 60-meter band?
    A. 2.8 kHz
    B. 5.6 kHz
    C. 1.8 kHz
    D. 3 kHz

Copyright © Mometrix Media. You have been licensed one copy of this document for personal use only. Any other reproduction or redistribution is strictly prohibited. All rights reserved.

G1C03 (A) [97.303(h)(1)]
Answer: A. The maximum bandwidth permitted by FCC rules for Amateur Radio stations when transmitting on USB frequencies in the 60-meter band is 2.8 kHz.

Which of the following limitations apply to transmitter power on every amateur band?
    A. Only the minimum power necessary to carry out the desired communications should be used
    B. Power must be limited to 200 watts when transmitting between 14.100 MHz and 14.150 MHz
    C. Power should be limited as necessary to avoid interference to another radio service on the frequency
    D. Effective radiated power cannot exceed 1500 watts

G1C04 (A) [97.313(a)]
Answer: A. On the 14MHz band, only the minimum power necessary to carry out the desired communications should be used.

Which of the following is a limitation on transmitter power on the 28 MHz band for a General Class control operator?
    A. 100 watts PEP output
    B. 1000 watts PEP output
    C. 1500 watts PEP output
    D. 2000 watts PEP output

G1C05 (C) [97.313(c)(2)]
Answer: C. On the 28 MHz band, the limitation on transmitter power is 1500 watts PEP output.

Which of the following is a limitation on transmitter power on 1.8 MHz band?
    A. 200 watts PEP output
    B. 1000 watts PEP output
    C. 1200 watts PEP output
    D. 1500 watts PEP output

G1C06 (D) [97.313]
Answer: D. On the 1.8 MHz band, the limitation on transmitter power is 1500 watts PEP output.

What is the maximum symbol rate permitted for RTTY or data emission transmission on the 20-meter band?
    A. 56 kilobaud
    B. 19.6 kilobaud
    C. 1200 baud
    D. 300 baud

G1C07 (D) [97.305(c), 97.307(f)(3)]
Answer: D. The maximum symbol rate permitted for RTTY or data emission transmission on the 20-meter band is 300 baud. RTTY (short for radioteletype) is the process of sending radio signals between teleprinters. This was the first fully automated protocol for data transmission. It uses the 5-bit Baudot code, in which characters are converted into codes. The typical speed of character transmission is between 60 and 100 wpm. Though RTTY has become slightly less popular in recent years, it remains a common mode of communication.

Copyright © Mometrix Media. You have been licensed one copy of this document for personal use only. Any other reproduction or redistribution is strictly prohibited. All rights reserved.

What is the maximum symbol rate permitted for RTTY or data emission transmitted at frequencies below 28 MHz?
    A. 56 kilobaud
    B. 19.6 kilobaud
    C. 1200 baud
    D. 300 baud

G1C08 (D) [97.307(f)(3)]
Answer: D. The maximum symbol rate permitted for RTTY or data emission transmitted at frequencies below 28 MHz is 300 baud.

What is the maximum symbol rate permitted for RTTY or data emission transmitted on the 1.25 meter and 70 centimeter bands?
    A. 56 kilobaud
    B. 19.6 kilobaud
    C. 1200 baud
    D. 300 baud

G1C09 (A) [97.305(c) and 97.307(f)(5)]
Answer: A. The maximum symbol rate permitted for RTTY or data emission transmitted on the 1.25 meter and 70 centimeter bands is 56 kilobaud.

What is the maximum symbol rate permitted for RTTY or data emission transmissions on the 10-meter band?
    A. 56 kilobaud
    B. 19.6 kilobaud
    C. 1200 baud
    D. 300 baud

G1C10 (C) [97.305(c) and 97.307(f)(4)]
Answer: C. The maximum symbol rate permitted for RTTY or data emission transmissions on the 10 meter band is 1200 baud.

What is the maximum symbol rate permitted for RTTY or data emission transmissions on the 2-meter band?
    A. 56 kilobaud
    B. 19.6 kilobaud
    C. 1200 baud
    D. 300 baud

G1C11 (B) [97.305(c) and 97.307(f)(5)]
Answer: B. The maximum symbol rate permitted for RTTY or data emission transmissions on the 2-meter band is 19.6 kilobaud.

Copyright © Mometrix Media. You have been licensed one copy of this document for personal use only. Any other reproduction or redistribution is strictly prohibited. All rights reserved.

G1D – Volunteer Examiners and Volunteer Examiner Coordinators; temporary identification

Who may receive credit for the elements represented by an expired amateur radio license?
    A. Any person who can demonstrate that they once held an FCC issued General, Advanced, or Amateur Extra class license that was not revoked by the FCC
    B. Anyone who held an FCC issued amateur radio license that has been expired for not less than 5 years and not more than 15 years
    C. Any person who previously held an amateur license issued by another country, but only if that country has a current reciprocal licensing agreement with the FCC
    D. Only persons who once held an FCC issued Novice, Technician, or Technician Plus license

G1D01 (A) [97.501, 97.505(a)]
Answer: A. As long as you can demonstrate that you have previously held a General, Advanced, or Amateur Extra class licenseIssued by the FCC and that it was not revoked, you may receive credit for all the elements represented

What license examinations may you administer when you are an accredited VE holding a General Class operator license?
    A. General and Technician
    B. General only
    C. Technician only
    D. Extra, General and Technician

G1D02 (C) [97.509(b)(3)(i)]
Answer: C. When you are an accredited VE holding a General Class operator license, you may only administer the Technician license exam. Volunteer Examiners are only allowed to proctor exams at a level below their own level. Any licensed amateur may become a Volunteer Examiner by completing the qualification process administered by the VEC.

On which of the following band segments may you operate if you are a Technician Class operator and have a CSCE for General Class privileges?
    A. Only the Technician band segments until your upgrade is posted on the FCC database
    B. Only on the Technician band segments until your license arrives in the mail
    C. On any General or Technician Class band segment
    D. On any General or Technician Class band segment except 30 and 60 meters

G1D03 (C) [97.9(b)]
Answer: C. You may operate on any General or Technician Class band segment if you are a Technician Class operator and have a CSCE for General Class privileges.

Which of the following is a requirement for administering a Technician Class license examination?
    A. At least three General Class or higher VEs must observe the examination
    B. At least two General Class or higher VEs must be present
    C. At least two General Class or higher VEs must be present, but only one need be Extra Class
    D. At least three VEs of Technician Class or higher must observe the examination

G1D04 (A) [97.509(3)(i)(c)]
Answer: A. In order for a Technician Class operator examination to be administered, at least three VEC-accredited General Class or higher VEs must be present.

Copyright © Mometrix Media. You have been licensed one copy of this document for personal use only. Any other reproduction or redistribution is strictly prohibited. All rights reserved.

Which of the following must a person have before they can be an administering VE for a Technician Class license examination?
    A. Notification to the FCC that you want to give an examination
    B. Receipt of a CSCE for General Class
    C. Possession of a properly obtained telegraphy license
    D. An FCC General Class or higher license and VEC accreditation

G1D05 (D) [97.509(b)(3)(i)]
Answer: D. To be an administering VE for a Technician Class operator license examination, you must have an FCC General Class or higher license and VEC accreditation. Volunteer Examiners are allowed to proctor exams at or below the level at which they are licensed.

When must you add the special identifier "AG" after your call sign if you are a Technician Class licensee and have a CSCE for General Class operator privileges, but the FCC has not yet posted your upgrade on its website?
    A. Whenever you operate using General Class frequency privileges
    B. Whenever you operate on any amateur frequency
    C. Whenever you operate using Technician frequency privileges
    D. A special identifier is not required as long as your General Class license application has been filed with the FCC

G1D06 (A) [97.119(f)(2)]
Answer: A. You must add the special identifier "AG" after your call sign if you are a Technician Class licensee and have a CSCE for General Class operator privileges, but the FCC has not yet posted your upgrade on its Web site. This indicates that your actual status will not be reflected on the site.

Volunteer Examiners are accredited by what organization?
    A. The Federal Communications Commission
    B. The Universal Licensing System
    C. A Volunteer Examiner Coordinator
    D. The Wireless Telecommunications Bureau

G1D07 (C) [97.509(b)(1)]
Answer: C. Volunteer Examiners are accredited by the Volunteer Examiner Coordinator. VECs are recognized by the American Radio Relay League.

Which of the following criteria must be met for a non-U.S. citizen to be an accredited Volunteer Examiner?
    A. The person must be a resident of the U.S. for a minimum of 5 years
    B. The person must hold an FCC granted Amateur Radio license of General Class or above
    C. The person's home citizenship must be in ITU region 2
    D. None of these choices is correct; a non-U.S. citizen cannot be a Volunteer Examiner

G1D08 (B) [97.509(b)(3)]
Answer: B. For a non-U.S. citizen to be an accredited Volunteer Examiner, the person must hold an FCC granted Amateur Radio license of General Class or above.

How long is a Certificate of Successful Completion of Examination (CSCE) valid for exam element credit?
    A. 30 days
    B. 180 days
    C. 365 days
    D. For as long as your current license is valid

Copyright © Mometrix Media. You have been licensed one copy of this document for personal use only. Any other reproduction or redistribution is strictly prohibited. All rights reserved.

G1D09 (C) [97.9(b)]
Answer: C. A Certificate of Successful Completion of Examination (CSCE) is valid for exam element credit for 365 days.

What is the minimum age that one must be to qualify as an accredited Volunteer Examiner?
    A. 12 years
    B. 18 years
    C. 21 years
    D. There is no age limit

G1D10 (B) [97.509(b)(2)]
Answer: B. One must be at least 18 years old to qualify as an accredited Volunteer Examiner. Each licensing exam requires the presence of three Volunteer Examiners, each of which needs to sign the paperwork for the exam to be valid.

If a person has an expired FCC issued amateur radio license of General Class or higher, what is required before they can receive a new license?
    A. They must have a letter from the FCC showing they once held an amateur or commercial license
    B. There are no requirements other than being able to show a copy of the expired license
    C. The applicant must be able to produce a copy of a page from a call book published in the USA showing his or her name and address
    D. The applicant must pass the current element 2 exam

G1D11 (D)
Answer: D. A person with an expired FCC issued amatuer radio license of General Class or higher must pass the current element 2 exam before they can receive a new license.

G1E – Control Categories; Repeater Regulations; Harmful Interference; Third Party Rules; ITU Regions; Automatically Controlled Digital Station

Which of the following would disqualify a third party from participating in stating a message over an amateur station?
    A. The third party's amateur license has been revoked and not reinstated
    B. The third party is not a U.S. citizen
    C. The third party is a licensed amateur
    D. The third party is speaking in a language other than English

G1E01 (A) [97.115(b)(2)]
Answer: A. A third party would be disqualified from participating in stating a message over an amateur station if his or her amateur license had ever been revoked. Typically, third-party participation is the only way an unlicensed person can join in on amateur communications. The responsibility for ensuring that all communications follow the rules is held by the control operator.

When may a 10-meter repeater retransmit the 2-meter signal from a station having a Technician Class control operator?
    A. Under no circumstances
    B. Only if the station on 10 meters is operating under a Special Temporary Authorization allowing such retransmission
    C. Only during an FCC declared general state of communications emergency
    D. Only if the 10 meter repeater control operator holds at least a General Class license

- 182 -

Copyright © Mometrix Media. You have been licensed one copy of this document for personal use only. Any other reproduction or redistribution is strictly prohibited. All rights reserved.

G1E02 (D) [97.205(a)]
Answer: D. A 10 meter repeater may retransmit the 2 meter signal from a station having a Technican Class control operator only if the 10 meter repeater control operator holds at least a General Class license.

What is required to conduct communications with a digital station operating under automatic control outside the automatic control band segments?
    A. The station initiating the contact must be under local or remote control
    B. The interrogating transmission must be made by another automatically controlled station
    C. No third party traffic maybe be transmitted
    D. The control operator of the interrogating station must hold an Extra Class license

G1E03 (A) [97.221]
Answer: A. To communicate with a digital station operating under automatic control outside the automatic control band segments, the station initiating contact must be under local or remote control.

Which of the following conditions require an Amateur Radio station licensee to take specific steps to avoid harmful interference to other users or facilities?
    A. When operating within one mile of an FCC Monitoring Station
    B. When using a band where the Amateur Service is secondary
    C. When a station is transmitting spread spectrum emissions
    D. All of these choices are correct

G1E04 (D) [97.13(b),97.311(b),97.303]
Answer: D. An Amateur Radio station licensee is required to take specific steps to avoid harmful interference to other users or facilities when the following conditions apply: when operating within one mile of an FCC Monitoring Station; when using a band where the Amateur Service is secondary; and when a station is transmitting spread spectrum emissions. All of these conditions place the responsibility for avoiding interference on the shoulders of the amateur operator.

What types of messages for a third party in another country may be transmitted by an amateur station?
    A. Any message, as long as the amateur operator is not paid
    B. Only messages for other licensed amateurs
    C. Only messages relating to Amateur Radio or remarks of a personal character, or messages relating to emergencies or disaster relief
    D. Any messages, as long as the text of the message is recorded in the station log

G1E05 (C) [97.115(a)(2),97.117]
Answer: C. Only messages relating to Amateur Radio or remarks of a personal character, or messages relating to emergencies or disaster relief, may be transmitted by an amateur station for a third party in another country.

Which of the following applies in the event of interference between a coordinated repeater and an uncoordinated repeater?
    A. The licensee of the non-coordinated repeater has primary responsibility to resolve the interference
    B. The licensee of the coordinated repeater has primary responsibility to resolve the interference
    C. Both repeater licensees share equal responsibility to resolve the interference
    D. The frequency coordinator bears primary responsibility to resolve the interference

Copyright © Mometrix Media. You have been licensed one copy of this document for personal use only. Any other reproduction or redistribution is strictly prohibited. All rights reserved.

G1E06 (A) [97.205(c)]
Answer: A. In the event of interference between a coordinated repeater and an uncoordinated repeater, the licensee of the uncoordinated repeater has primary responsibility to resolve the interference.

With which foreign countries is third party traffic prohibited, except for messages directly involving emergencies or disaster relief communications?
    A. Countries in ITU Region 2
    B. Countries in ITU Region 1
    C. Every foreign country, unless there is a third party agreement in effect with that country
    D. Any country which is not a member of the International Amateur Radio Union (IARU)

G1E07 (C) [97.115(a)(2)] .
Answer: C. Except for messages directly involving emergencies or disaster relief communications, third party traffic is prohibited in every foreign country, unless there is a third party agreement in effect with that country.

Which of the following is a requirement for a non-licensed person to communicate with a foreign Amateur Radio station from a station with an FCC granted license at which a licensed control operator is present?
    A. Information must be exchanged in English
    B. The foreign amateur station must be in a country with which the United States has a third party agreement
    C. The control operator must have at least a General Class license
    D. All of these choices are correct

G1E08 (B) [97.115(a)(b)]
Answer: B. For a non-licensed person to communicate with a foreign Amateur Radio station from a station with an FCC granted license at which a licensed control operator is present, the foreign amateur station must be in a country with which the United States has a third party agreement.

What language must you use when identifying your station if you are using a language other than English in making a contact using phone emission?
    A. The language being used for the contact
    B. Any language recognized by the United Nations
    C. English only
    D. English, Spanish, French, or German

G1E09 (C) [97.119(b)(2)]
Answer: C. When identifying your station while using a language other than English when making a contact using phone emission, you must speak in English. English is the lingua franca for ham radio communication.

Which of the following is the FCC term for an unattended digital station that transfers messages to and from the Internet?
    A. Locally controlled station
    B. Robotically controlled station
    C. Automatically controlled digital station
    D. Fail-safe digital station

G1E11 (C) [97.221]
Answer: C. The FCC term for an unattended digital station that tranfers messages to and from the internet is called an automatically controled digital station.

Copyright © Mometrix Media. You have been licensed one copy of this document for personal use only. Any other reproduction or redistribution is strictly prohibited. All rights reserved.

Under what circumstances are messages that are sent via digital modes exempt from Part 97 third party rules that apply to other modes of communication?
    A. Under no circumstances
    B. When messages are encrypted
    C. When messages are not encrypted
    D. When under automatic control

G1E12 (A) [97.115]
Answer: A. Messages are never exempt from Part 97 third party rules.

On what bands may automatically controlled stations transmitting RTTY or data emissions communicate with other automatically controlled digital stations?
    A. On any band segment where digital operation is permitted
    B. Anywhere in the non-phone segments of the 10-meter or shorter wavelength bands
    C. Only in the non-phone Extra Class segments of the bands
    D. Anywhere in the 1.25-meter or shorter wavelength bands, and in specified segments of the 80-meter through 2-meter bands

G1E13 (D) [97.221, 97.305]
Answer: D. An automatically controlled stations transmitting RTTY or data emissions communicate with other automatically controlled digital stations anywhere in the 1.25-meter or shorter wavelength bands, and in specified segments of the 80-meter through 2-meter bands.

G2 – Operating Procedures

G2A – Phone Operating Procedures; USB/LSB Conventions; Procedural Signals; Breaking into a Contact; VOX Operation

Which sideband is most commonly used for voice communications on frequencies of 14 MHz or higher?
    A. Upper sideband
    B. Lower sideband
    C. Vestigial sideband
    D. Double sideband

G2A01 (A)
Answer: A. The upper sideband is the most commonly used for voice communications on frequencies of 14 MHz or higher.

Which of the following modes is most commonly used for voice communications on the 160-meter, 75-meter, and 40-meter bands?
    A. Upper sideband
    B. Lower sideband
    C. Vestigial sideband
    D. Double sideband

G2A02 (B)
Answer: B. The lower sideband is most commonly used for voice communications on the 160, 75, and 40 meter bands. It is also the preferred operating mode on the 80 meter amateur bands. For voice communication on the HF bands, ham operators are most likely to use single sideband. Signals are

Copyright © Mometrix Media. You have been licensed one copy of this document for personal use only. Any other reproduction or redistribution is strictly prohibited. All rights reserved.

designated as upper or lower sideband depending on whether they are above or below the carrier frequency displayed on the radio. According to tradition, voice operation on HF bands above 9 MHz is on the upper sideband, and voice operation below 9 MHz occurs on the lower sideband. The four basic steps for tuning in an SSB signal are as follows: set your rig to receive LSB or USB signals; select the widest SSB filter; adjust the tuning dial until the SSB frequency can be heard; and adjust the tuning until the voice sounds normal.

Which of the following is most commonly used for SSB voice communications in the VHF and UHF bands?
    A. Upper sideband
    B. Lower sideband
    C. Vestigial sideband
    D. Double sideband

G2A03 (A)
Answer: A. The upper sideband is most commonly used for SSB voice communications in the VHF and UHF bands.

Which mode is most commonly used for voice communications on the 17-meter and 12-meter bands?
    A. Upper sideband
    B. Lower sideband
    C. Vestigial sideband
    D. Double sideband

G2A04 (A)
Answer: A. The upper sideband is the mode most commonly used for voice communications on the 17 and 12 meter bands. Indeed, the upper sideband is the preferred operating mode on the 20, 17, 15, 12, and 10 meter HF amateur bands. In addition, the upper sideband is preferred on all the VHF and UHF bands.

Which mode of voice communication is most commonly used on the HF amateur bands?
    A. Frequency modulation
    B. Double sideband
    C. Single sideband
    D. Phase modulation

G2A05 (C)
Answer: C. The single-sideband mode of voice communication is most commonly used on the high frequency amateur bands. This is more because of convention than for any technical reasons.

Which of the following is an advantage when using single sideband as compared to other analog voice modes on the HF amateur bands?
    A. Very high fidelity voice modulation
    B. Less bandwidth used and higher power efficiency
    C. Ease of tuning on receive and immunity to impulse noise
    D. Less subject to interference atmospheric static crashes

G2A06 (B)
Answer: B. When using single sideband as compared to other analog voice modes on the HF amateur bands, less bandwidth used and higher power efficiency is an advantage.

Copyright © Mometrix Media. You have been licensed one copy of this document for personal use only. Any other reproduction or redistribution is strictly prohibited. All rights reserved.

Which of the following statements is true of the single sideband voice mode?
    A. Only one sideband and the carrier are transmitted; the other sideband is suppressed
    B. Only one sideband is transmitted; the other sideband and carrier are suppressed
    C. SSB voice transmissions have higher average power than any other mode
    D. SSB is the only mode that is authorized on the 160, 75 and 40 meter amateur bands

G2A07 (B)
Answer: B. In the single sideband (SSB) voice mode, only one sideband is transmitted; the other sideband and carrier are suppressed. This means that SSB voice transmission consumes considerably less power.

Which of the following is a recommended way to break into a conversation when using phone?
    A. Say "QRZ" several times followed by your call sign
    B. Say your call sign during a break between transmissions from the other stations
    C. Say "Break. Break. Break." and wait for a response
    D. Say "CQ" followed by the call sign of either station

G2A08 (B)
Answer: B. Saying your call sign during a break between transmissions from the other stations is a recommended way to break into a conversation when using phone. Another method is to say "Break" quickly when there is a gap in the conversation. Often, the best time to break in is when the other stations alternate the transmitting and receiving roles. Typically, if the break is heard, one of the other stations will respond by requesting more information. At this point, the breaker should respond as if he or she was answering a CQ.

Why do most amateur stations use lower sideband on the 160-meter, 75-meter and 40-meter bands?
    A. Lower sideband is more efficient than upper sideband at these frequencies
    B. Lower sideband is the only sideband legal on these frequency bands
    C. Because it is fully compatible with an AM detector
    D. Current amateur practice is to use lower sideband on these frequency bands

G2A09 (D)
Answer: D. Most amateur stations use lower sideband on the 160, 75, and 40 meter bands simply because this is current amateur practice. The separation between the bands used by the upper sideband and those used by the lower sideband is largely arbitrary and based on tradition.

Which of the following statements is true of voice VOX operation versus PTT operation?
    A. The received signal is more natural sounding
    B. It allows "hands free" operation
    C. It occupies less bandwidth
    D. It provides more power output

G2A10 (B)
Answer: B. SSB VOX allows "hands free" operation.

What does the expression "CQ DX" usually indicate?
    A. A general call for any station
    B. The caller is listening for a station in Germany
    C. The caller is looking for any station outside their own country
    D. A distress call

Copyright © Mometrix Media. You have been licensed one copy of this document for personal use only. Any other reproduction or redistribution is strictly prohibited. All rights reserved.

G2A11 (C)
Answer: C. The expression "CQ DX" usually indicates that the caller is looking for any station outside their own country.

G2B – Operating Courtesy; Band Plans; Emergencies, Including Drills and Emergency Communications

Which of the following is true concerning access to frequencies in non-emergency situations?
A. Nets always have priority
B. QSO's in process always have priority
C. Except during FCC declared emergencies, no one has priority access to frequencies
D. Contest operations must always yield to non-contest use of frequencies

G2B01 (C)
Answer: C. No one has priority access to frequencies, common courtesy should always be a guide.

What is the first thing you should do if you are communicating with another amateur station and hear a station in distress break in?
A. Continue your communication because you were on frequency first
B. Acknowledge the station in distress and determine what assistance may be needed
C. Change to a different frequency
D. Immediately cease all transmissions

G2B02 (B)
Answer: B. If you are communicating with another amateur station and hear a station in distress break in, the first thing you should do is acknowledge the station in distress and determine what assistance may be needed. You should note the time and frequency of the call as soon as possible. Specifically, it is important to note the address, or, if an address cannot be obtained, the latitude and longitude of the emergency. You should also try to learn the nature of the problem and the sort of assistance required. After obtaining this information, you should ask the station in distress to remain on frequency as you contact the appropriate emergency services.

If propagation changes during your contact and you notice increasing interference from other activity on the same frequency, what should you do?
A. Tell the interfering stations to change frequency
B. Report the interference to your local Amateur Auxiliary Coordinator
C. As a common courtesy, move your contact to another frequency
D. Increase power to overcome interference

G2B03 (C)
Answer: C. If propagation changes during your contact and you notice increasing interference from another activity on the same frequency, you should move your contact to another frequency as a common courtesy. There is no rule for which party should move, so the best thing to do is exercise discretion and courtesy to other users.

When selecting a CW transmitting frequency, what minimum frequency separation should you allow in order to minimize interference to stations on adjacent frequencies?
A. 5 to 50 Hz
B. 150 to 500 Hz
C. 1 to 3 kHz
D. 3 to 6 kHz

Copyright © Mometrix Media. You have been licensed one copy of this document for personal use only. Any other reproduction or redistribution is strictly prohibited. All rights reserved.

G2B04 (B)
Answer: B. When selecting a CW transmitting frequency, you should allow a minimum frequency separation of approximately 3 kHz in order to minimize interference to stations on adjacent frequencies. CW transmissions, otherwise known as Morse code, are a series of on and off keys.

What is the customary minimum frequency separation between SSB signals under normal conditions?
    A. Between 150 and 500 Hz
    B. Approximately 3 kHz
    C. Approximately 6 kHz
    D. Approximately 10 kHz

G2B05 (B)
Answer: A. The customary minimum frequency separation between SSB signals under normal conditions is between 150 and 500 Hz. This allows enough space to prevent interference in most cases.

What is a practical way to avoid harmful interference when selecting a frequency to call CQ on CW or phone?
    A. Send "QRL?" on CW, followed by your call sign; or, if using phone, ask if the frequency is in use, followed by your call sign
    B. Listen for 2 minutes before calling CQ
    C. Send the letter "V" in Morse code several times and listen for a response
    D. Send "QSY" on CW or if using phone, announce "the frequency is in use", then send your call and listen for a response

G2B06 (A)
Answer: A. A practical way to avoid harmful interference when selecting a frequency to call CQ on CW or phone is to send "QRL?" on CW, followed by your call sign; or if using phone, ask if the frequency is in use, followed by your call sign. The Q-signal QRL, when issued as a question, means "Is the frequency busy?" When this same Q-signal is issued as a response, it means, "The frequency is busy. Please do not interfere."

Which of the following complies with good amateur practice when choosing a frequency on which to initiate a call?
    A. Check to see if the channel is assigned to another station
    B. Identify your station by transmitting your call sign at least 3 times
    C. Follow the voluntary band plan for the operating mode you intend to use
    D. All of these choices are correct

G2B07 (C)
Answer: C. Following the voluntary band plan for the operating mode you intend to use complies with good amateur practice when choosing a frequency on which to initiate a call.

What is the "DX window" in a voluntary band plan?
    A. A portion of the band that should not be used for contacts between stations within the 48 contiguous United States
    B. An FCC rule that prohibits contacts between stations within the United States and possessions on that band segment
    C. An FCC rule that allows only digital contacts in that portion of the band
    D. A portion of the band that has been voluntarily set aside for digital contacts only

Copyright © Mometrix Media. You have been licensed one copy of this document for personal use only. Any other reproduction or redistribution is strictly prohibited. All rights reserved.

G2B08 (A)
Answer: A. The "DX window" in a voluntary band plan is a portion of the band that should not be used for contacts between stations within the 48 contiguous United States.

Who may be the control operator of an amateur station transmitting in RACES to assist relief operations during a disaster?
    A. Only a person holding an FCC issued amateur operator license
    B. Only a RACES net control operator
    C. A person holding an FCC issued amateur operator license or an appropriate government official
    D. Any control operator when normal communication systems are operational

G2B09 (A) [97.407(a)]
Answer: A. Only a person holding an FCC-issued amateur operator license may be the control operator of an amateur station transmitting in RACES to assist relief operations during a disaster. RACES (the Radio Amateur Civil Emergency Service) is administered by the Federal Emergency Management Agency (FEMA). In order to be a part of RACES, an operator must also have membership in the relevant local group charged with disaster relief. Ham radio operators may obtain membership in RACES by contacting their state's Auxiliary Communications Service.

When may the FCC restrict normal frequency operations of amateur stations participating in RACES?
    A. When they declare a temporary state of communication emergency
    B. When they seize your equipment for use in disaster communications
    C. Only when all amateur stations are instructed to stop transmitting
    D. When the President's War Emergency Powers have been invoked

G2B10 (D) [97.407(b)]
Answer: D. The FCC may restrict normal frequency operations of amateur stations participating in RACES when the President's War Emergency Powers have been invoked. In these stations, the military or emergency services groups may require extra frequency ranges for urgent communications.

What frequency should be used to send a distress call?
    A. Whichever frequency has the best chance of communicating the distress message
    B. Only frequencies authorized for RACES or ARES stations
    C. Only frequencies that are within your operating privileges
    D. Only frequencies used by police, fire or emergency medical services

G2B11 (A) [97.405]
Answer: A. Distress calls should be sent with whatever frequency has the best chance of communicating.

When is an amateur station allowed to use any means at its disposal to assist another station in distress?
    A. Only when transmitting in RACES
    B. At any time when transmitting in an organized net
    C. At any time during an actual emergency
    D. Only on authorized HF frequencies

G2B12 (C) [97.405(b)]
Answer: C. An amateur station is allowed to use any means at its disposal to assist another station in distress.

Copyright © Mometrix Media. You have been licensed one copy of this document for personal use only. Any other reproduction or redistribution is strictly prohibited. All rights reserved.

G2C – CW Operating Procedures and Procedural Signals; Q Signals and Common Abbreviations; Full Break In

Which of the following describes full break-in telegraphy (QSK)?
    A. Breaking stations send the Morse code prosign BK
    B. Automatic keyers are used to send Morse code instead of hand keys
    C. An operator must activate a manual send/receive switch before and after every transmission
    D. Transmitting stations can receive between code characters and elements

G2C01 (D)
Answer: D. In full break-in telegraphy (QSK), transmitting stations can receive between code characters and elements. This mode of operation is only possible when the radio rig has the ability to switch very quickly between transmit and receive. When using full break-in telegraphy, the operator has the ability to hear the activity on the band between code characters and elements. However, the VOX operation must be turned off in order for this mode to work properly.

What should you do if a CW station sends "QRS"?
    A. Send slower
    B. Change frequency
    C. Increase your power
    D. Repeat everything twice

G2C02 (A)
Answer: A. If a CW station sends "QRS," you should send slower. The Q-signal QRS, when issued as a question, means "Shall I send more slowly?" When it is issued as a response, it means "Please send more slowly." It is often accompanied by the requested rate in words per minute.

What does it mean when a CW operator sends "KN" at the end of a transmission?
    A. Listening for novice stations
    B. Operating full break-in
    C. Listening only for a specific station or stations
    D. Closing station now

G2C03 (C)
Answer: C. When a CW operator sends "KN" at the end of a transmission, it means that the operator is listening only for a specific station or stations.

What does the Q signal "QRL?" mean?
    A. "Will you keep the frequency clear?"
    B. "Are you operating full break-in" or "Can you operate full break-in?"
    C. "Are you listening only for a specific station?"
    D. "Are you busy?", or "Is this frequency in use?"

G2C04 (D)
Answer: D. When a CW operator sends "QRL?," he or she is either asking if a frequency is being used or if the receiver is busy.

Copyright © Mometrix Media. You have been licensed one copy of this document for personal use only. Any other reproduction or redistribution is strictly prohibited. All rights reserved.

What is the best speed to use answering a CQ in Morse Code?
    A. The fastest speed at which you are comfortable copying
    B. The speed at which the CQ was sent
    C. A slow speed until contact is established
    D. At the standard calling speed of 5 wpm

G2C05 (B)
Answer: B. The best speed to use when answering a CQ in Morse Code is the speed at which the CQ was sent. Similarly, an operator should send initial transmissions at the speed which he or she would be comfortable receiving. In addition, the operator should leave sufficient time after transmitting for the other station to answer. At least once per cycle, the operator should use standard phonetics for his or her call sign on voice modes.

What does the term "zero beat" mean in CW operation?
    A. Matching the speed of the transmitting station
    B. Operating split to avoid interference on frequency
    C. Sending without error
    D. Matching your transmit frequency to the frequency of a received signal

G2C06 (D)
Answer: D. In CW operation, the term "zero beat" means matching your transmit frequency to the frequency of a received signal.

When sending CW, what does a "C" mean when added to the RST report?
    A. Chirpy or unstable signal
    B. Report was read from S meter reading rather than estimated
    C. 100 percent copy
    D. Key clicks

G2C07 (A)
Answer: A. When sending CW, a "C" added to the RST report means chirpy or unstable signal. RST stands for readability, strength, and tone. When single-sideband phones are being used, only R and S reports are necessary. In an RST report, readability is measured on a scale from 1 to 5, with 1 being unreadable and 5 being perfectly readable. Strength, meanwhile, is measured on a scale from 1 to 9, with a 1 indicating a barely perceptible signal and a 9 indicating a very strong signal. Tone is measured on a scale from 1 to 9, with 1 indicating sixty cycle a.c. or less, and a 9 indicating perfect tone with no trace of ripple or modulation of any kind.

What prosign is sent to indicate the end of a formal message when using CW?
    A. SK
    B. BK
    C. AR
    D. KN

G2C08 (C)
Answer: C. The prosign AR is sent to indicate the end of a formal message when using CW. Prosigns, otherwise known as procedural signals, are one- or two-letter signals that indicate the intention of the operator. The prosign AR means "end of message." Some of the other common prosigns are AA (new line), AS (wait), BK (break), BT (space down two lines), CL (going off the air), CT (start of transmission), DO (shift to wabun code), K (go or over; that is, an invitation for another station to speak), KN (invitation to a specific station to transmit), SK (end of contact), SN (understood), and SOS (serious distress, assistance required).

Copyright © Mometrix Media. You have been licensed one copy of this document for personal use only. Any other reproduction or redistribution is strictly prohibited. All rights reserved.

What does the Q signal "QSL" mean?
    A. Send slower
    B. We have already confirmed by card
    C. I acknowledge receipt
    D. We have worked before

G2C09 (C)
Answer: C. The Q signal "QSL" means "I acknowledge receipt." If this Q-signal is issued as a question, it means "Did you receive and understand my transmission?"

What does the Q signal "QRN" mean?
    A. Send more slowly
    B. I am troubled by static
    C. Zero beat my signal
    D. Stop sending

G2C10 (B)
Answer: B. The Q signal "QRN" means "noise from natural sources." When issued as a query, this Q signal means "Are you troubled by static?"

What does the Q signal "QRV" mean?
    A. You are sending too fast
    B. There is interference on the frequency
    C. I am quitting for the day
    D. I am ready to receive messages

G2C11 (D)
Answer: D. The Q signal "QRV" means "I am ready to receive messages." When this Q signal is issued as a query, it means "Are you ready to receive messages?"

G2D – Amateur Auxiliary; Minimizing Interference; HF Operations

What is the Amateur Auxiliary to the FCC?
    A. Amateur volunteers who are formally enlisted to monitor the airwaves for rules violations
    B. Amateur volunteers who conduct amateur licensing examinations
    C. Amateur volunteers who conduct frequency coordination for amateur VHF repeaters
    D. Amateur volunteers who use their station equipment to help civil defense organizations in times of emergency

G2D01 (A)
Answer: A. The Amateur Auxiliary to the FCC is a group of amateur volunteers who are formally enlisted to monitor the airwaves for rules violations. This group is administered by the American Radio Relay League. In a typical scenario, a member of the Amateur Auxiliary will hear something suspicious and will send a postcard to the amateur station describing the infraction.

Which of the following are objectives of the Amateur Auxiliary?
    A. To conduct efficient and orderly amateur licensing examinations
    B. To encourage self-regulation and compliance with the rules by radio amateur operators
    C. To coordinate repeaters for efficient and orderly spectrum usage
    D. To provide emergency and public safety communications

Copyright © Mometrix Media. You have been licensed one copy of this document for personal use only. Any other reproduction or redistribution is strictly prohibited. All rights reserved.

G2D02 (B)
Answer: B. The objectives of the Amateur Auxiliary are to encourage amateur self regulation and compliance with the rules. The FCC recognizes that it cannot effectively patrol the airwaves at all times, and so it has attempted to establish a culture of self-policing within the amateur radio community. The Amateur Auxiliary is a major part of this effort.

What skills learned during hidden transmitter hunts are of help to the Amateur Auxiliary?
    A. Identification of out of band operation
    B. Direction finding used to locate stations violating FCC Rules
    C. Identification of different call signs
    D. Hunters have an opportunity to transmit on non-amateur frequencies

G2D03 (B)
Answer: B. During "hidden transmitter hunts," the Amateur Auxiliary members will learn the skills of direction finding used to locate stations violating FCC Rules. As the name suggests, a hidden transmitter hunt is a game in which participants try to identify the point of origin for a particular radio signal.

Which of the following describes an azimuthal projection map?
    A. A world map that shows accurate land masses
    B. A map that shows true bearings and distances from a particular location
    C. A map that shows the angle at which an amateur satellite crosses the equator
    D. A map that shows the number of degrees longitude that an amateur satellite appears to move westward at the equator with each orbit

G2D04 (B)
Answer: B. An azimuthal projection map is a world map projection centered on a particular location. When the operator's station is positioned at the center of the map, the path of any transmission to or from the station will be a radial line straight to the other station.

When is it permissible to communicate with amateur stations in countries outside the areas administered by the Federal Communications Commission?
    A. Only when the foreign country has a formal third party agreement filed with the FCC
    B. When the contact is with amateurs in any country except those whose administrations have notified the ITU that they object to such communications
    C. When the contact is with amateurs in any country as long as the communication is conducted in English
    D. Only when the foreign country is a member of the International Amateur Radio Union

G2D05 (B) [97.111(a)(1)]
Answer: B. It is permissible to communicate with amateur stations in countries outside the areas administered by the Federal Communications Commission when the contact is with amateurs in any country except those whose administrations have notified the ITU that they object to such communications.

How is a directional antenna pointed when making a "long-path" contact with another station?
    A. Toward the rising Sun
    B. Along the gray line
    C. 180 degrees from its short-path heading
    D. Toward the north

Copyright © Mometrix Media. You have been licensed one copy of this document for personal use only. Any other reproduction or redistribution is strictly prohibited. All rights reserved.

G2D06 (C)
Answer: C. When making a long-path contact with another station, a directional antenna should be pointed 180 degrees from its short-path heading.

Which of the following is required by the FCC rules when operating in the 60-meter band?
    A. If you are using other than a dipole antenna, you must keep a record of the gain of your antenna
    B. You must keep a log of the date, time, frequency, power level and stations worked
    C. You must keep a log of all third party traffic
    D. You must keep a log of the manufacturer of your equipment and the antenna used

G2D07 (A) [97.303(i)]
Answer: A. When operating in the 60-meter band, the FCC rules require that you keep a record of the gain of your antenna, if you are using other than a dipole antenna.

What is a reason why many amateurs keep a station log?
    A. The ITU requires a log of all international contacts
    B. The ITU requires a log of all international third party traffic
    C. The log provides evidence of operation needed to renew a license without retest
    D. To help with a reply if the FCC requests information

G2D08 (D)
Answer: D. Many amateurs keep a log even though the FCC doesn't require it to help with a reply if the FCC requests information.

What information is traditionally contained in a station log?
    A. Date and time of contact
    B. Band and/or frequency of the contact
    C. Call sign of station contacted and the signal report given
    D. All of these choices are correct

G2D09 (D)
Answer: D. A station log traditionally contains the date and time of contact; the band and/or frequency of the contact; and the call sign of the station contacted and the signal report given. Many operators also record the mode of communication that was used, the signal report sent and received, and any other relevant personal information about the other operator.

What is QRP operation?
    A. Remote piloted model control
    B. Low power transmit operation
    C. Transmission using Quick Response Protocol
    D. Traffic relay procedure net operation

G2D10 (B)
Answer: B. QRP operation is low power transmit operation. This method of operation is preferred by many because it requires incredible precision and skill. QRP means no more than 5 watts of transmitter output power for Morse code, and no more than 10 watts of peak power on voice transmission. For the most part, QRP occurs in Morse code and on HF.

Copyright © Mometrix Media. You have been licensed one copy of this document for personal use only. Any other reproduction or redistribution is strictly prohibited. All rights reserved.

Which HF antenna would be the best to use for minimizing interference?
    A. A quarter-wave vertical antenna
    B. An isotropic antenna
    C. A unidirectional antenna
    D. An omnidirectional antenna

G2D11 (C)
Answer: C. A unidirectional antenna would be the best HF antenna for minimizing interference. The unidirectional antenna concentrates its energy on a single direction, and therefore diminishes interference from other directions.

G2E – Digital Operating; Procedures, Procedural Signals and Common Abbreviations

Which mode is normally used when sending an RTTY signal via AFSK with an SSB transmitter?
    A. USB
    B. DSB
    C. CW
    D. LSB

G2E01 (D)
Answer: D. The LSB mode is normally used when sending an RTTY signal via AFSK with an SSB transmitter.

How can a PACTOR modem or controller be used to determine if the channel is in use by other PACTOR stations?
    A. Unplug the data connector temporarily and see if the channel-busy indication is turned off
    B. Put the modem or controller in a mode which allows monitoring communications without a connection
    C. Transmit UI packets several times and wait to see if there is a response from another PACTOR station
    D. Send the message: "Is this frequency in use?"

G2E02 (B)
Answer: B. A PACTOR modem or controller can be used to determine if a channel is in use by other PACTOR stations by putting the modem or controller in a mode which allows monitoring communications without a connection.

What symptoms may result from other signals interfering with a PACTOR or WINMOR transmission?
    A. Frequent retries or timeouts
    B. Long pauses in message transmission
    C. Failure to establish a connection between stations
    D. All of these choices are correct

G2E03 (D)
Answer: D. These are all possible symptoms of other signals interfering with a PACTOR or WINMOR transmission.

Copyright © Mometrix Media. You have been licensed one copy of this document for personal use only. Any other reproduction or redistribution is strictly prohibited. All rights reserved.

What segment of the 20-meter band is most often used for data transmissions?
    A. 14.000 - 14.050 MHz
    B. 14.070 - 14.100 MHz
    C. 14.150 - 14.225 MHz
    D. 14.275 - 14.350 MHz

G2E04 (B)
Answer: B. The 14.070 to 14.100 MHz segment of the 20-meter band is most often used for data transmissions.

What is the standard sideband used to generate a JT65 or JT9 digital signal when using AFSK in any amateur band?
    A. LSB
    B. USB
    C. DSB
    D. SSB

G2E05 (B)
Answer: B. USB is the typical sideband used to generate a JT65 or JT9 digital signal when using AFSK in any amatuer band.

What is the most common frequency shift for RTTY emissions in the amateur HF bands?
    A. 85 Hz
    B. 170 Hz
    C. 425 Hz
    D. 850 Hz

G2E06 (B)
Answer: B. 170 Hz is the most common frequency shift for RTTY emissions in the amateur HF bands.

What segment of the 80-meter band is most commonly used for digital transmissions?
    A. 3570 – 3600 kHz
    B. 3500 – 3525 kHz
    C. 3700 – 3750 kHz
    D. 3775 – 3825 kHz

G2E07 (A)
Answer: A. The 3570 to 3600 kHz segment of the 80 meter band is most commonly used for data transmissions.

In what segment of the 20-meter band are most PSK31 operations commonly found?
    A. At the bottom of the slow-scan TV segment, near 14.230 MHz
    B. At the top of the SSB phone segment near 14.325 MHz
    C. In the middle of the CW segment, near 14.100 MHz
    D. Below the RTTY segment, near 14.070 MHz

G2E08 (D)
Answer: D. Most PSK31 operations are commonly found below the RTTY segment of the 20-meter band, near 14.070 MHz.

Copyright © Mometrix Media. You have been licensed one copy of this document for personal use only. Any other reproduction or redistribution is strictly prohibited. All rights reserved.

How do you join a contact between two stations using the PACTOR protocol?
    A. Send broadcast packets containing your call sign while in MONITOR mode
    B. Transmit a steady carrier until the PACTOR protocol times out and disconnects
    C. Joining an existing contact is not possible, PACTOR connections are limited to two stations
    D. Send a NAK response continuously so that the sending station has to pause

G2E09 (C)
Answer: C. It is not possible to join a contact between two stations using a PACTOR protocol.

Which of the following is a way to establish contact with a digital messaging system gateway station?
    A. Send an email to the system control operator
    B. Send QRL in Morse code
    C. Respond when the station broadcasts its SSID
    D. Transmit a connect message on the station's published frequency

G2E10 (D)
Answer: D. To establish contact with a digital messaging system gateway station, just transmit a connect message on the station's published frequency.

What is indicated on a waterfall display by one or more vertical lines adjacent to a PSK31 signal?
    A. Long Path propagation
    B. Backscatter propagation
    C. Insufficient modulation
    D. Overmodulation

G2E11 (D)
Answer: D. Overmodulation is indicated on a waterfall display by one or more vertical lines adjacent to a PSK31 signal.

Which of the following describes a waterfall display?
    A. Frequency is horizontal, signal strength is vertical, time is intensity
    B. Frequency is vertical, signal strength is intensity, time is horizontal
    C. Frequency is horizontal, signal strength is intensity, time is vertical
    D. Frequency is vertical, signal strength is horizontal, time is intensity

G2E12 (C)
Answer: C. In a waterfall display the frequency is horizontal, the signal strength is intensity and the time is vertical.

Which communication system sometimes uses the Internet to transfer messages?
    A. Winlink
    B. RTTY
    C. ARES
    D. Skywarn

G2E13 (A)
Answer: A. Winlink sometimes uses the internet to transfer messages.

Copyright © Mometrix Media. You have been licensed one copy of this document for personal use only. Any other reproduction or redistribution is strictly prohibited. All rights reserved.

What could be wrong if you cannot decode an RTTY or other FSK signal even though it is apparently tuned in properly?
    A. The mark and space frequencies may be reversed
    B. You may have selected the wrong baud rate
    C. You may be listening on the wrong sideband
    D. All of these choices are correct

G2E14 (D)
Answer: D. All of these are possibly wrong of you cannot decode an RTTY or other FSK signal that is tuned properly.

G3 – Radio Wave Propogation

G3A – Sunspots and Solar Radiation; Ionospheric Disturbances; Propagation Forecasting and Indices

What is the significance of the sunspot number with regard to HF propagation?
    A. Higher sunspot numbers generally indicate a greater probability of good propagation at higher frequencies
    B. Lower sunspot numbers generally indicate greater probability of sporadic E propagation
    C. A zero sunspot number indicate radio propagation is not possible on any band
    D. All of these choices are correct.

G3A01 (A)
Answer: A. The sunspot number is a measure of solar activity based on counting sunspots and sunspot groups. This is a number used to indicate the general amount of sunspot activity. It is sometimes referred to as relative sunspot number, Zurich number, or Wolf number, It is calculated with the equation $R = k(10g + f)$, in which f is the number of distinct spots, g is the number of spot groups, and k is a factor based on the location and equipment of the observer.

What effect does a Sudden Ionospheric Disturbance have on the daytime ionospheric propagation of HF radio waves?
    A. It enhances propagation on all HF frequencies
    B. It disrupts signals on lower frequencies more than those on higher frequencies
    C. It disrupts communications via satellite more than direct communications
    D. None, because only areas on the night side of the Earth are affected

G3A02 (B)
Answer: B. A Sudden Ionospheric Disturbance disrupts signals on lower frequencies more than those on higher frequencies. A sudden ionospheric disturbance is a complicated set of rapid fluctuations in the ionosphere, typically occurring after a period of solar flares. This phenomenon, also known as the Dellinger effect or the Mogel-Dellinger effect, is observable as a rapid increase in the radio-wave absorption, particularly in the lower HF and upper MF ranges. Sudden ionospheric disturbance can be very disruptive to telecommunications systems, including ham radio. The effects are most dire in the regions around the equator, and may last from a few minutes to several hours.

Copyright © Mometrix Media. You have been licensed one copy of this document for personal use only. Any other reproduction or redistribution is strictly prohibited. All rights reserved.

Approximately how long does it take the increased ultraviolet and X-ray radiation from solar flares to affect radio-wave propagation on the Earth?

A. 28 days
B. 1 to 2 hours
C. 8 minutes
D. 20 to 40 hours

G3A03 (C)
Answer: C. It takes the increased ultraviolet and X-ray radiation from solar flares approximately eight minutes to affect radio-wave propagation on the Earth. A solar flare is a rapid increase in the brightness of a particular area of the sun, representing a release of up to one-sixth of the sun's normal energy output. The solar flare is typically followed by a coronal mass ejection.

Which of the following are least reliable for long distance communications during periods of low solar activity?

A. 80 meters and 160 meters
B. 60 meters and 40 meters
C. 30 meters and 20 meters
D. 15 meters, 12 meters and 10 meters

G3A04 (D)
Answer: D. During periods of low solar activity, the 15 meters, 12 meters, and 10 meters are least reliable for long distance communication.

What is the solar-flux index?

A. A measure of the highest frequency that is useful for ionospheric propagation between two points on the Earth
B. A count of sunspots which is adjusted for solar emissions
C. Another name for the American sunspot number
D. A measure of solar radiation at 10.7 cm

G3A05 (D)
Answer: D. The solar flux index is a measure of solar radiation at 10.7 cm. The measure of 10.7 cm is important because it is the wavelength of radio signals at 2800 MHz. Although the solar flux index is proportional to the amount of sunspot activity at any given time, the ionization levels in the ionosphere can now be more accurately measured by assessing the X-ray flux from the Sun.

What is a geomagnetic storm?

A. A sudden drop in the solar-flux index
B. A thunderstorm which affects radio propagation
C. Ripples in the ionosphere
D. A temporary disturbance in the Earth's magnetosphere

G3A06 (D)
Answer: D. A geomagnetic storm is a temporary disturbance in the Earth's magnetosphere. These storms may be caused by magnetic field clouds and solar wind shock waves. A geomagnetic storm may cause rapid fluctuations and unpredictable propagation paths for radio signals. Radio operators in the HF bands may utilize solar and geomagnetic alerts that will enable them to avoid major problems caused by geomagnetic storms.

Copyright © Mometrix Media. You have been licensed one copy of this document for personal use only. Any other reproduction or redistribution is strictly prohibited. All rights reserved.

At what point in the solar cycle does the 20-meter band usually support worldwide propagation during daylight hours?
    A. At the summer solstice
    B. Only at the maximum point of the solar cycle
    C. Only at the minimum point of the solar cycle
    D. At any point in the solar cycle

G3A07 (D)
Answer: D. The 20 meter band usually supports worldwide propagation during daylight hours at any point in the solar cycle.

Which of the following effects can a geomagnetic storm have on radio-wave propagation?
    A. Improved high-latitude HF propagation
    B. Degraded high-latitude HF propagation
    C. Improved ground-wave propagation
    D. Improved chances of UHF ducting

G3A08 (B)
Answer: B. A geomagnetic storm can degrade high-latitude HF propagation.

What effect do high sunspot numbers have on radio communications?
    A. High-frequency radio signals become weak and distorted
    B. Frequencies above 300 MHz become usable for long-distance communication
    C. Long-distance communication in the upper HF and lower VHF range is enhanced
    D. Microwave communications become unstable

G3A09 (C)
Answer: C. High sunspot numbers enhance long-distance radio communication in the upper HF and lower VHF range.

What causes HF propagation conditions to vary periodically in a 28-day cycle?
    A. Long term oscillations in the upper atmosphere
    B. Cyclic variation in the Earth's radiation belts
    C. The Sun's rotation on its axis
    D. The position of the Moon in its orbit

G3A10 (C)
Answer: C. The Sun's rotation on its axis causes HF propagation conditions to vary periodically in a 28-day cycle.

Approximately how long is the typical sunspot cycle?
    A. 8 minutes
    B. 40 hours
    C. 28 days
    D. 11 years

G3A11 (D)
Answer: D. The typical sunspot cycle is 11 years. This is part of an overall solar cycle, which includes variations in radiation and the ejection of solar material.

Copyright © Mometrix Media. You have been licensed one copy of this document for personal use only. Any other reproduction or redistribution is strictly prohibited. All rights reserved.

What does the K-index indicate?
    A. The relative position of sunspots on the surface of the Sun
    B. The short term stability of the Earth's magnetic field
    C. The stability of the Sun's magnetic field
    D. The solar radio flux at Boulder, Colorado

G3A12 (B)
Answer: B. The K-index indicates the short-term stability of the Earth's magnetic field. The level of disturbance in the Earth's magnetic field is described by an integer between 0 and 9. In this scale, values at either end indicate calm, while a value of 5 indicates a geomagnetic storm.

What does the A-index indicate?
    A. The relative position of sunspots on the surface of the Sun
    B. The amount of polarization of the Sun's electric field
    C. The long term stability of the Earth's geomagnetic field
    D. The solar radio flux at Boulder, Colorado

G3A13 (C)
Answer: C. The A-index indicates the long-term stability of the Earth's geomagnetic field. It provides a daily average level of geomagnetic activity.

How are radio communications usually affected by the charged particles that reach the Earth from solar coronal holes?
    A. HF communications are improved
    B. HF communications are disturbed
    C. VHF/UHF ducting is improved
    D. VHF/UHF ducting is disturbed

G3A14 (B)
Answer: B. HF radio communications are usually disturbed by the charged particles that reach the Earth from solar coronal holes. A coronal hole is a place on the Sun where the corona is darker and colder. The solar wind is able to travel faster along the open magnetic field lines that pass through coronal holes, which makes them likely to disturb HF radio communications.

How long does it take charged particles from coronal mass ejections to affect radio-wave propagation on the Earth?
    A. 28 days
    B. 14 days
    C. 4 to 8 minutes
    D. 20 to 40 hours

G3A15 (D)
Answer: D. It takes 20 to 40 hours for charged particles from coronal mass ejections to affect radio-wave propagation on the Earth. A coronal mass ejection is an enormous burst of solar wind and magnetic fields. It is most common for coronal mass ejections to occur in areas where there are flaring sunspots.

What is a possible benefit to radio communications resulting from periods of high geomagnetic activity?
    A. Aurora that can reflect VHF signals
    B. Higher signal strength for HF signals passing through the polar regions
    C. Improved HF long path propagation
    D. Reduced long delayed echoes

Copyright © Mometrix Media. You have been licensed one copy of this document for personal use only. Any other reproduction or redistribution is strictly prohibited. All rights reserved.

G3A16 (A)
Answer: A. One possible benefit to radio communications resulting from periods of high geomagnetic activity is an aurora that can reflect VHF signals.

G3B – Maximum Usable Frequency; Lowest Usable Frequency; Propagation

How might a sky-wave signal sound if it arrives at your receiver by both short path and long path propagation?
 A. Periodic fading approximately every 10 seconds
 B. Signal strength increased by 3 dB
 C. The signal might be cancelled causing severe attenuation
 D. A well-defined echo might be heard

G3B01 (D)
Answer: D. If a sky-wave signal sound arrives at your receiver by both short path and long path propagation, a well-defined echo might be heard. This is due to the slight variation in the time it takes for each signal to reach the receiver.

Which of the following is a good indicator of the possibility of sky-wave propagation on the 6-meter band?
 A. Short skip sky-wave propagation on the 10-meter band
 B. Long skip sky-wave propagation on the 10-meter band
 C. Severe attenuation of signals on the 10-meter band
 D. Long delayed echoes on the 10-meter band

G3B02 (A)
Answer: A. Short skip sky-wave propagation on the 10-meter band is a good indicator of the possibility of sky-wave propagation on the 6-meter band.

Which of the following applies when selecting a frequency for lowest attenuation when transmitting on HF?
 A. Select a frequency just below the MUF
 B. Select a frequency just above the LUF
 C. Select a frequency just below the critical frequency
 D. Select a frequency just above the critical frequency

G3B03 (A)
Answer: A. When selecting a frequency for lowest attenuation when transmitting on HF, select a frequency just below the MUF.

What is a reliable way to determine if the MUF is high enough to support skip propagation between your station and a distant location on frequencies between 14 and 30 MHz?
 A. Listen for signals from an international beacon in the frequency range you plan to use
 B. Send a series of dots on the band and listen for echoes from your signal
 C. Check the strength of TV signals from Western Europe
 D. Check the strength of signals in the MF AM broadcast band

Copyright © Mometrix Media. You have been licensed one copy of this document for personal use only. Any other reproduction or redistribution is strictly prohibited. All rights reserved.

G3B04 (A)
Answer: A. One reliable way to determine if the Maximum Usable Frequency (MUF) is high enough to support skip propagation between your station and a distant location on frequencies between 14 and 30 MHz is to listen for signals from an international beacon. Skip propagation, also known as skywave propagation, is the reflection or refraction of radio waves from the ionosphere back to the Earth. For the most part, skywave propagation is limited to the shortwave frequency bands, and can be employed for transmissions between continents. Skywave propagation enables extremely remote signals to be very clear. The majority of long-distance shortwave communications are the result of skip propagation.

What usually happens to radio waves with frequencies below the MUF and above the LUF when they are sent into the ionosphere?
    A. They are bent back to the Earth
    B. They pass through the ionosphere
    C. They are amplified by interaction with the ionosphere
    D. They are bent and trapped in the ionosphere to circle the Earth

G3B05 (A)
Answer: A. Radio waves with frequencies below the Maximum Usable Frequency (MUF) and above the Lowest Usable Frequency (LUF) are bent back to the Earth when they are sent into the ionosphere. The maximum usable frequency is the highest frequency at which a signal may still be transmitted between two points with skip reflection (that is, the reflection of waves from the ionosphere). When the frequency of a signal increases, the refractive index of the ionosphere decreases, which is why there is an upper limit to usable frequency. If a signal has a higher frequency than that, it will pass through the ionosphere into space rather than being reflected by it. Lowest usable frequency, on the other hand, is the HF band frequency that has a received field intensity high enough to create the necessary signal-to-noise ratio.

What usually happens to radio waves with frequencies below the LUF?
    A. They are bent back to the Earth
    B. They pass through the ionosphere
    C. They are completely absorbed by the ionosphere
    D. They are bent and trapped in the ionosphere to circle the Earth

G3B06 (C)
Answer: C. Radio waves with frequencies below the Lowest Usable Frequency (LUF) are completely absorbed by the ionosphere.

What does LUF stand for?
    A. The Lowest Usable Frequency for communications between two points
    B. The Longest Universal Function for communications between two points
    C. The Lowest Usable Frequency during a 24 hour period
    D. The Longest Universal Function during a 24 hour period

G3B07 (A)
Answer: A. LUF stands for the Lowest Usable Frequency for communications between two points.

What does MUF stand for?
    A. The Minimum Usable Frequency for communications between two points
    B. The Maximum Usable Frequency for communications between two points
    C. The Minimum Usable Frequency during a 24 hour period
    D. The Maximum Usable Frequency during a 24 hour period

Copyright © Mometrix Media. You have been licensed one copy of this document for personal use only. Any other reproduction or redistribution is strictly prohibited. All rights reserved.

G3B08 (B)
Answer: B. MUF stands for the Maximum Usable Frequency for communications between two points. The maximum usable frequency is the highest radio signal frequency that will reach a given destination using skip, or skywave, propagation. The maximum usable frequency will not be the same for all destinations with respect to the same transmitter.

What is the approximate maximum distance along the Earth's surface that is normally covered in one hop using the F2 region?
    A. 180 miles
    B. 1,200 miles
    C. 2,500 miles
    D. 12,000 miles

G3B09 (C)
Answer: C. The approximate maximum distance along the Earth's surface that is normally covered in one hop using the F2 region is 2,500 miles. The F2 region is part of the ionosphere's F layer, also known as the Appleton layer. The F layer lies in between the E region and the protonosphere. It is useful for the propagation of high frequency radio waves. The greatest concentration of free electrons and ions in the atmosphere is found in the F region. The F1 region lies below the F2 region during the day, but at night these regions are one and the same. The F2 region is found between 220 and 800 km above the surface of the Earth.

What is the approximate maximum distance along the Earth's surface that is normally covered in one hop using the E region?
    A. 180 miles
    B. 1,200 miles
    C. 2,500 miles
    D. 12,000 miles

G3B10 (B)
Answer: B. The approximate maximum distance along the Earth's surface that is normally covered in one hop using the E region is 1,200 miles. The E region, also known as the Kennelly-Heaviside layer, is the section of the ionosphere that lies approximately 90 to 150 kilometers above the Earth's surface. This layer can reflect medium frequency radio waves, particularly at night when the ionosphere is dragged further away from the Earth by solar wind. The distance which the E layer can transmit signals is also influenced by the season and the level of sunspot activity.

What happens to HF propagation when the Lowest Usable Frequency (LUF) exceeds the Maximum Usable Frequency (MUF)?
    A. No HF radio frequency will support ordinary skywave communications over the path
    B. HF communications over the path are enhanced
    C. Double hop propagation along the path is more common
    D. Propagation over the path on all HF frequencies is enhanced

G3B11 (A)
Answer: A. When the Lowest Usable Frequency exceeds the Maximum Usable Frequency, no HF radio frequency will support ordinary skywave communications over the path.

Copyright © Mometrix Media. You have been licensed one copy of this document for personal use only. Any other reproduction or redistribution is strictly prohibited. All rights reserved.

What factors affect the Maximum Usable Frequency (MUF)?
    A. Path distance and location
    B. Time of day and season
    C. Solar radiation and ionospheric disturbances
    D. All of these choices are correct

G3B12 (D)
Answer: D. Maximum Usable Frequency is affected by path distance and location; time of day and season; and solar radiation and ionospheric disturbances.

G3C – Ionospheric Layers; Critical Angle and Frequency; HF Scatter; Near-Vertical Incidence Skywave

Which ionospheric layer is closest to the surface of the Earth?
    A. The D layer
    B. The E layer
    C. The F1 layer
    D. The F2 layer

G3C01 (A)
Answer: A. The D layer of the ionosphere is closest to the surface of the Earth. The D layer extends from roughly 60 to 90 km above the surface of the Earth. Because of extensive electron collisions, high frequency radio waves are absorbed rather than reflected. That is, HF radio waves actually decrease in intensity as they pass through the D layer.

Where on the Earth do ionospheric layers reach their maximum height?
    A. Where the Sun is overhead
    B. Where the Sun is on the opposite side of the Earth
    C. Where the Sun is rising
    D. Where the Sun has just set

G3C02 (A)
Answer: A. On the Earth, ionospheric layers reach their maximum height where the Sun is overhead.

Why is the F2 region mainly responsible for the longest distance radio wave propagation?
    A. Because it is the densest ionospheric layer
    B. Because it does not absorb radio waves as much as other ionospheric regions
    C. Because it is the highest ionospheric region
    D. All of these choices are correct

G3C03 (C)
Answer: C. The F2 region is mainly responsible for the longest distance radio wave propagation because it is the highest ionospheric region. It lies approximately 220 to 800 km above the surface of the Earth. It is the primary reflecting layer for HF communications both at night and during the day.

Copyright © Mometrix Media. You have been licensed one copy of this document for personal use only. Any other reproduction or redistribution is strictly prohibited. All rights reserved.

What does the term "critical angle" mean as used in radio wave propagation?
    A. The long path azimuth of a distant station
    B. The short path azimuth of a distant station
    C. The lowest takeoff angle that will return a radio wave to the Earth under specific ionospheric conditions
    D. The highest takeoff angle that will return a radio wave to the Earth under specific ionospheric conditions

G3C04 (D)
Answer: D. In radio wave propagation, the term "critical angle" means the highest takeoff angle that will return a radio wave to the Earth under specific ionospheric conditions. The critical angle is the highest possible angle for successful radio wave transmission. At angles higher than this, the radio wave will be reflected back upon itself, and will therefore not reach its destination.

Why is long distance communication on the 40-meter, 60-meter, 80-meter and 160-meter bands more difficult during the day?
    A. The F layer absorbs signals at these frequencies during daylight hours
    B. The F layer is unstable during daylight hours
    C. The D layer absorbs signals at these frequencies during daylight hours
    D. The E layer is unstable during daylight hours

G3C05 (C)
Answer: C. Long distance communications on the 40, 60, 80, and 160 meter bands is more difficult during the day because the D layer absorbs signals at these frequencies during daylight hours.

What is a characteristic of HF scatter signals?
    A. They have high intelligibility
    B. They have a wavering sound
    C. They have very large swings in signal strength
    D. All of these choices are correct

G3C06 (B)
Answer: B. One characteristic of HF scatter signals is a wavering sound.

What makes HF scatter signals often sound distorted?
    A. The ionospheric layer involved is unstable
    B. Ground waves are absorbing much of the signal
    C. The E-region is not present
    D. Energy is scattered into the skip zone through several different radio wave paths

G3C07 (D)
Answer: D. HF scatter signals often sound distorted because energy is scattered into the skip zone through several different radio wave paths.

Why are HF scatter signals in the skip zone usually weak?
    A. Only a small part of the signal energy is scattered into the skip zone
    B. Signals are scattered from the magnetosphere which is not a good reflector
    C. Propagation is through ground waves which absorb most of the signal energy
    D. Propagations is through ducts in F region which absorb most of the energy

Copyright © Mometrix Media. You have been licensed one copy of this document for personal use only. Any other reproduction or redistribution is strictly prohibited. All rights reserved.

G3C08 (A)
Answer: A. HF scatter signals in the skip zone are usually weak because only a small part of the signal energy is scattered into the skip zone. A skip zone is an area in which radio transmissions cannot be received, even though reception is possible at locations both closer to and farther away from the skip zone. In radio transmission, the skip zone is the area in between the respective ranges of the ground waves and sky waves. In other words, the skip zone is beyond the reach of ground waves but too close for sky waves. The sky waves that would otherwise reach the skip zone penetrate the ionosphere and proceed into space. There is no way to eliminate a skip zone. The precise size of the zone is determined by the height and structure of the ionosphere, and therefore is variable.

What type of radio wave propagation allows a signal to be detected at a distance too far for ground wave propagation but too near for normal sky-wave propagation?
    A. Faraday rotation
    B. Scatter
    C. Sporadic-E skip
    D. Short-path skip

G3C09 (B)
Answer: B. Scatter radio wave propagation allows a signal to be detected at a distance too far for ground wave propagation but too near for normal sky-wave propagation.

Which of the following might be an indication that signals heard on the HF bands are being received via scatter propagation?
    A. The communication is during a sunspot maximum
    B. The communication is during a sudden ionospheric disturbance
    C. The signal is heard on a frequency below the Maximum Usable Frequency
    D. The signal is heard on a frequency above the Maximum Usable Frequency

G3C10 (D)
Answer: D. If the signal is heard on a frequency above the Maximum Usable Frequency, this might be an indication that signals heard on the HF bands are being received via scatter propagation.

Which of the following antenna types will be most effective for skip communications on 40-meters during the day?
    A. Vertical antennas
    B. Horizontal dipoles placed between 1/8 and 1/4 wavelength above the ground
    C. Left-hand circularly polarized antennas
    D. Right-hand circularly polarized antenna

G3C11 (B)
Answer: B. Horizontal dipoles placed between 1/8 and ¼ wavelength above the ground will be the most effective for skip communications on 40 meters during the day.

Which ionospheric layer is the most absorbent of long skip signals during daylight hours on frequencies below 10 MHz?
    A. The F2 layer
    B. The F1 layer
    C. The E layer
    D. The D layer

Copyright © Mometrix Media. You have been licensed one copy of this document for personal use only. Any other reproduction or redistribution is strictly prohibited. All rights reserved.

G3C12 (D)
Answer: D. The D layer of the ionosphere is the most absorbent of long skip signals during daylight hours on frequencies below 10 MHz.

What is Near Vertical Incidence Sky-wave (NVIS) propagation?
    A. Propagation near the MUF
    B. Short distance HF propagation using high elevation angles
    C. Long path HF propagation at sunrise and sunset
    D. Double hop propagation near the LUF

G3C13 (B)
Answer: B. Near Vertical Incidence Sky-wave propagation is short distance HF propagation using high elevation angles. Near Vertical Incidence Skywave propagation creates transmissions that reach farther than ground waves but not as far as skywaves. This technique is especially useful in the tropics, where skywave propagation is more problematic. In NVIS propagation, the frequency range is typically between 1.8 and 8 MHZ. When the frequency is too low, a great deal of the signal is absorbed by the ionosphere, and when the frequency is too high, the signal penetrates the ionosphere rather than being refracted by it.

G4 – Amateur Radio Practices

G4A – Station Operation and Set Up

What is the purpose of the "notch filter" found on many HF transceivers?
    A. To restrict the transmitter voice bandwidth
    B. To reduce interference from carriers in the receiver passband
    C. To eliminate receiver interference from impulse noise sources
    D. To enhance the reception of a specific frequency on a crowded band

G4A01 (B)
Answer: B. The purpose of the "notch filter" found on many HF transceivers is to reduce interference from carriers in the receiver passband. A notch filter is a form of band-stop filter in which the stopband is particularly narrow (that is, it has a high Q factor). A band-stop filter, also known as a band-rejection filter, minimizes the frequencies within a specific range. This sort of filter is effective for eliminating a single interfering tone.

What is one advantage of selecting the opposite or "reverse" sideband when receiving CW signals on a typical HF transceiver?
    A. Interference from impulse noise will be eliminated
    B. More stations can be accommodated within a given signal passband
    C. It may be possible to reduce or eliminate interference from other signals
    D. Accidental out of band operation can be prevented

G4A02 (C)
Answer: C. One advantage of selecting the opposite or "reverse" sideband when receiving CW signals on a typical HF transceiver is that it may be possible to reduce or eliminate interference from other signals.

Copyright © Mometrix Media. You have been licensed one copy of this document for personal use only. Any other reproduction or redistribution is strictly prohibited. All rights reserved.

What is normally meant by operating a transceiver in "split" mode?
    A. The radio is operating at half power
    B. The transceiver is operating from an external power source
    C. The transceiver is set to different transmit and receive frequencies
    D. The transmitter is emitting a SSB signal, as opposed to DSB operation

G4A03 (C)
Answer: C. When a transceiver is operated in split mode, this generally means that it is set to different transmit and receive frequencies. This mode is often used when a large number of stations are trying to contact one station. An observer can tell that another station is operating in split mode when outgoing transmissions can be overheard but the responses cannot.

What reading on the plate current meter of a vacuum tube RF power amplifier indicates correct adjustment of the plate tuning control?
    A. A pronounced peak
    B. A pronounced dip
    C. No change will be observed
    D. A slow, rhythmic oscillation

G4A04 (B)
Answer: B. A pronounced dip on the plate current meter of a vacuum tube RF power amplifier indicates correct adjustment of the plate tuning control. An RF power amplifier is used to change a low-power radio-frequency signal into a stronger signal. RF power amplifiers typically have excellent heat dissipation, output compression, gain, and return loss on the input and output.

What is a purpose of using Automatic Level Control (ALC) with a RF power amplifier?
    A. To balance the transmitter audio frequency response
    B. To reduce harmonic radiation
    C. To reduce distortion due to excessive drive
    D. To increase overall efficiency

G4A05 (C)
Answer: C. One purpose of using Automatic Level Control with a RF power amplifier is to reduce distortion due to excessive drive.

What type of device is often used to match transmitter output impedance to an impedance not equal to 50 ohms?
    A. Balanced modulator
    B. SWR Bridge
    C. Antenna coupler or antenna tuner
    D. Q Multiplier

G4A06 (C)
Answer: C. An antenna coupler is often used to enable matching the transmitter output to an impedance other than 50 ohms.

What condition can lead to permanent damage to a solid-state RF power amplifier?
    A. Insufficient drive power
    B. Low input SWR
    C. Shorting the input signal to ground
    D. Excessive drive power

Copyright © Mometrix Media. You have been licensed one copy of this document for personal use only. Any other reproduction or redistribution is strictly prohibited. All rights reserved.

G4A07 (D)
Answer: D. Excessive drive power can lead to permanent damage when using a solid-state RF power amplifier.

What is the correct adjustment for the load or coupling control of a vacuum tube RF power amplifier?
    A. Minimum SWR on the antenna
    B. Minimum plate current without exceeding maximum allowable grid current
    C. Highest plate voltage while minimizing grid current
    D. Maximum power output without exceeding maximum allowable plate current

G4A08 (D)
Answer: D. The correct adjustment for the load or coupling control of a vacuum tube RF power amplifier is maximum power output without exceeding maximum allowable plate current.

Why is a time delay sometimes included in a transmitter keying circuit?
    A. To prevent stations from talking over each other
    B. To allow the transmitter power regulators to charge properly
    C. To allow time for transmit-receive changeover operations to complete properly before RF output is allowed
    D. To allow time for a warning signal to be sent to other stations

G4A09 (C)
Answer: C. A time delay is sometimes included in a transmitter keying circuit to allow time for transmit-receive changeover operations to complete properly before RF output is allowed.

What is the purpose of an electronic keyer?
    A. Automatic transmit/receive switching
    B. Automatic generation of strings of dots and dashes for CW operation
    C. VOX operation
    D. Computer interface for PSK and RTTY operation

G4A10 (B)
Answer: B. The purpose of an electronic keyer is the automatic generation of strings of dots and dashes for CW operation.

Which of the following is a use for the IF shift control on a receiver?
    A. To avoid interference from stations very close to the receive frequency
    B. To change frequency rapidly
    C. To permit listening on a different frequency from that on which you are transmitting
    D. To tune in stations that are slightly off frequency without changing your transmit frequency

G4A11 (A)
Answer: A. One use for the IF shift control on a receiver is to avoid interference from stations very close to the receive frequency. The intermediate frequency (IF) is the output frequency of a mixing stage in a superheterodyne receiver. Each successive stage of the receiver will be tuned so as to achieve maximum efficiency at the intermediate frequency.

Which of the following is a common use for the dual VFO feature on a transceiver?
    A. To allow transmitting on two frequencies at once
    B. To permit full duplex operation, that is transmitting and receiving at the same time
    C. To permit ease of monitoring the transmit and receive frequencies when they are not the same
    D. To facilitate computer interface

-211-

Copyright © Mometrix Media. You have been licensed one copy of this document for personal use only. Any other reproduction or redistribution is strictly prohibited. All rights reserved.

G4A12 (C)
Answer: C. One common use for the dual VFO feature on a transceiver is to ease the process of monitoring the transmit and receive frequencies when they are not the same. The variable frequency oscillator (VFO) is the circuit in a transmitter or receiver that is used for controlling the operating frequency.

What is one reason to use the attenuator function that is present on many HF transceivers?
    A. To reduce signal overload due to strong incoming signals
    B. To reduce the transmitter power when driving a linear amplifier
    C. To reduce power consumption when operating from batteries
    D. To slow down received CW signals for better copy

G4A13 (A)
Answer: A. One reason to use the attenuator function that is present on many HF transceivers is to reduce signal overload due to strong incoming signals. An attenuator diminishes the power of the radio signal without altering its waveform significantly. One way to think of an attenuator is as the opposite of an amplifier.

What is likely to happen if a transceiver's ALC system is not set properly when transmitting AFSK signals with the radio using single sideband mode?
    A. ALC will invert the modulation of the AFSK mode
    B. Improper action of ALC distorts the signal and can cause spurious emissions
    C. When using digital modes, too much ALC activity can cause the transmitter to overheat
    D. All of these choices are correct

G4A14 (B)
Answer: B. If a transceiver's ALC system is not set properly when transmitting AFSK signals with the radio using single sideband mode, then it distorts the signal and can cause spurious emissions.

Which of the following can be a symptom of transmitted RF being picked up by an audio cable carrying AFSK data signals between a computer and a transceiver?
    A. The VOX circuit does not un-key the transmitter
    B. The transmitter signal is distorted
    C. Frequent connection timeouts
    D. All of these choices are correct

G4A15 (D)
Answer: D. All of these could be symptoms of transmitted RF being picked up by an audio cable carrying AFSK data signals between a computer and a transceiver.

G4B – Test and Monitoring Equipment; Two-Tone Test

What item of test equipment contains horizontal and vertical channel amplifiers?
    A. An ohmmeter
    B. A signal generator
    C. An ammeter
    D. An oscilloscope

Copyright © Mometrix Media. You have been licensed one copy of this document for personal use only. Any other reproduction or redistribution is strictly prohibited. All rights reserved.

G4B01 (D)
Answer: D. An oscilloscope contains horizontal and vertical channel amplifiers. An oscilloscope enables the user to observe a continuous variation of signal voltages. In most cases, this variation is displayed as a graph in which electrical potential difference is on the y-axis and time is on the x-axis.

Which of the following is an advantage of an oscilloscope versus a digital voltmeter?
    A. An oscilloscope uses less power
    B. Complex impedances can be easily measured
    C. Input impedance is much lower
    D. Complex waveforms can be measured

G4B02 (D)
Answer: D. One advantage of an oscilloscope versus a digital voltmeter is that complex waveforms can be measured. A digital voltmeter is an effective tool for measuring electrical potential difference between two distinct points in an electric circuit; it employs an analog-to-digital converter to create a numerical reading of voltage.

Which of the following is the best instrument to use when checking the keying waveform of a CW transmitter?
    A. An oscilloscope
    B. A field-strength meter
    C. A sidetone monitor
    D. A wavemeter

G4B03 (A)
Answer: A. An oscilloscope is the best instrument to use when checking the keying waveform of a CW transmitter. An oscilloscope assesses the change of an electrical signal over time, and creates a graphical representation of the alterations in voltage and time. The resulting shape is called a waveform.

What signal source is connected to the vertical input of an oscilloscope when checking the RF envelope pattern of a transmitted signal?
    A. The local oscillator of the transmitter
    B. An external RF oscillator
    C. The transmitter balanced mixer output
    D. The attenuated RF output of the transmitter

G4B04 (D)
Answer: D. When checking the RF envelope pattern of a transmitted signal, the attenuated RF output of the transmitter is connected to the vertical input of an oscilloscope.

Why is high input impedance desirable for a voltmeter?
    A. It improves the frequency response
    B. It decreases battery consumption in the meter
    C. It improves the resolution of the readings
    D. It decreases the loading on circuits being measured

G4B05 (D)
Answer: D. High input impedance is desirable for a voltmeter because it decreases the loading on circuits being measured.

Copyright © Mometrix Media. You have been licensed one copy of this document for personal use only. Any other reproduction or redistribution is strictly prohibited. All rights reserved.

What is an advantage of a digital voltmeter as compared to an analog voltmeter?
 A. Better for measuring computer circuits
 B. Better for RF measurements
 C. Better precision for most uses
 D. Faster response

G4B06 (C)
Answer: C. One advantage of a digital voltmeter as compared to an analog voltmeter is that a digital voltmeter has better precision for most uses. Voltmeters are used to measure the electrical potential difference between two distinct points in a circuit. An analog voltmeter may be accurate to within a few percent of full scale, assuming that the instrument is being used appropriately. There are analog voltmeters suited for voltages ranging from a few fractions of a volt up to thousands of volts. A digital voltmeter, on the other hand, can achieve accuracy within one percentage point. One recurrent problem with voltmeters is the difficulty of calibration.

What signals are used to conduct a two-tone test?
 A. Two audio signals of the same frequency shifted 90 degrees
 B. Two non-harmonically related audio signals
 C. Two swept frequency tones
 D. Two audio frequency range square wave signals of equal amplitude

G4B07 (B)
Answer: B. A two-tone test is conducted with two non-harmonically related audio signals.

Which of the following instruments may be used to monitor relative RF output when making antenna and transmitter adjustments?
 A. A field strength meter
 B. An antenna noise bridge
 C. A multimeter
 D. A Q meter

G4B08 (A)
Answer: A. A field strength meter may be used to monitor relative RF output when making antenna and transmitter adjustments. A field strength meter operates in the same way as a receiver: that is, it uses a tuner circuit to find signals and feed them into a microammeter. Of course, the field strength meter can only be effective when the antenna has been calibrated.

Which of the following can be determined with a field strength meter?
 A. The radiation resistance of an antenna
 B. The radiation pattern of an antenna
 C. The presence and amount of phase distortion of a transmitter
 D. The presence and amount of amplitude distortion of a transmitter

G4B09 (B)
Answer: B. The radiation pattern of an antenna can be determined with a field strength meter.

Which of the following can be determined with a directional wattmeter?
 A. Standing wave ratio
 B. Antenna front-to-back ratio
 C. RF interference
 D. Radio wave propagation

Copyright © Mometrix Media. You have been licensed one copy of this document for personal use only. Any other reproduction or redistribution is strictly prohibited. All rights reserved.

G4B10 (A)
Answer: A. Standing wave ratio can be determined with a directional wattmeter. The standing wave ratio is the relationship of the amplitude of a partial standing wave at an antinode to the amplitude at the next node. Standing wave ratio, or SWR, is often used as an indicator of the efficiency of a radio frequency transmission. The best possible SWR is 1:1, which would mean that the entirety of the power is reaching its destination, and no part of the signal is reflected.

Which of the following must be connected to an antenna analyzer when it is being used for SWR measurements?
    A. Receiver
    B. Transmitter
    C. Antenna and feed line
    D. All of these choices are correct

G4B11 (C)
Answer: C. An antenna and feed line must be connected to an antenna analyzer when it is being used for SWR measurements. Antenna analyzers are used for measuring the efficiency of antenna systems in radio electronics applications.

What problem can occur when making measurements on an antenna system with an antenna analyzer?
    A. SWR readings may be incorrect if the antenna is too close to the Earth
    B. Strong signals from nearby transmitters can affect the accuracy of measurements
    C. The analyzer can be damaged if measurements outside the ham bands are attempted
    D. Connecting the analyzer to an antenna can cause it to absorb harmonics

G4B12 (B)
Answer: B. When making measurements on an antenna system with an antenna analyzer, strong signals from nearby transmitters can affect the accuracy of measurements.

What is a use for an antenna analyzer other than measuring the SWR of an antenna system?
    A. Measuring the front to back ratio of an antenna
    B. Measuring the turns ratio of a power transformer
    C. Determining the impedance of an unknown or unmarked coaxial cable
    D. Determining the gain of a directional antenna

G4B13 (C)
Answer: C. Determining the impedance of an unknown or unmarked coaxial cable is one use for an antenna analyzer other than measuring the SWR of an antenna system.

What is an instance in which the use of an instrument with analog readout may be preferred over an instrument with a numerical digital readout?
    A. When testing logic circuits
    B. When high precision is desired
    C. When measuring the frequency of an oscillator
    D. When adjusting tuned circuits

G4B14 (D)
Answer: D. One instance in which the use of an instrument with analog readout may be preferred over an instrument with a numerical digital readout is when adjusting tuned circuits.

Copyright © Mometrix Media. You have been licensed one copy of this document for personal use only. Any other reproduction or redistribution is strictly prohibited. All rights reserved.

What type of transmitter performance does a two-tone test analyze?
  A. Linearity
  B. Carrier and undesired sideband suppression
  C. Percentage of frequency modulation
  D. Percentage of carrier phase shift

G4B15 (A)
Answer: A. A two-tone test analyzes the linearity of transmitter performance.

G4C – Interference with Consumer Electronics; Grounding; DSP

Which of the following might be useful in reducing RF interference to audio frequency devices?
  A. Bypass inductor
  B. Bypass capacitor
  C. Forward-biased diode
  D. Reverse-biased diode

G4C01 (B)
Answer: B. A bypass capacitor might be useful in reducing RF interference to audio-frequency devices. A bypass capacitor, otherwise known as a decoupling capacitor, is a device for separating the various parts of an electrical circuit. The result of using a bypass capacitor is that noise created in one part of the system can be removed from the other parts.

Which of the following could be a cause of interference covering a wide range of frequencies?
  A. Not using a balun or line isolator to feed balanced antennas
  B. Lack of rectification of the transmitter's signal in power conductors
  C. Arcing at a poor electrical connection
  D. The use of horizontal rather than vertical antennas

G4C02 (C)
Answer: C. One cause of interference over a wide range of frequencies could be arcing at a poor electrical connection. Arcing is the flow of current through media that normally do not conduct, as for instance air.

What sound is heard from an audio device or telephone if there is interference from a nearby single-sideband phone transmitter?
  A. A steady hum whenever the transmitter is on the air
  B. On-and-off humming or clicking
  C. Distorted speech
  D. Clearly audible speech

G4C03 (C)
Answer: C. An audio device or telephone will produce distorted speech if there is interference from a nearby single-sideband phone transmitter.

What is the effect on an audio device or telephone system if there is interference from a nearby CW transmitter?
  A. On-and-off humming or clicking
  B. A CW signal at a nearly pure audio frequency
  C. A chirpy CW signal
  D. Severely distorted audio

Copyright © Mometrix Media. You have been licensed one copy of this document for personal use only. Any other reproduction or redistribution is strictly prohibited. All rights reserved.

G4C04 (A)
Answer: A. An audio device or telephone system may present on-and-off humming or clicking if there is interference from a nearby CW transmitter.

What might be the problem if you receive an RF burn when touching your equipment while transmitting on an HF band, assuming the equipment is connected to a ground rod?
    A. Flat braid rather than round wire has been used for the ground wire
    B. Insulated wire has been used for the ground wire
    C. The ground rod is resonant
    D. The ground wire has high impedance on that frequency

G4C05 (D)
Answer: D. If you receive an RF burn when touching your equipment while transmitting on an HF band, one problem might be that the ground wire has high impedance on that frequency.

What effect can be caused by a resonant ground connection?
    A. Overheating of ground straps
    B. Corrosion of the ground rod
    C. High RF voltages on the enclosures of station equipment
    D. A ground loop

G4C06 (C)
Answer: C. A resonant ground connection may cause high RF voltages on the enclosures of station equipment. A ground connection is any connection made to the ground for the purposes of safety. A ham radio operator may establish indoor or outdoor ground connections.

What is one good way to avoid unwanted effects of stray RF energy in an amateur station?
    A. Connect all equipment grounds together
    B. Install an RF filter in series with the ground wire
    C. Use a ground loop for best conductivity
    D. Install a few ferrite beads on the ground wire where it connects to your station

G4C07 (A)
Answer: A. One good way to avoid unwanted effects of stray RF energy in an amateur station is to connect all equipment grounds together.

Which of the following would reduce RF interference caused by common-mode current on an audio cable?
    A. Placing a ferrite bead around the cable
    B. Adding series capacitors to the conductors
    C. Adding shunt inductors to the conductors
    D. Adding an additional insulating jacket to the cable

G4C08 (A)
Answer: A. Placing a ferrite bead around the cable would reduce RF interference caused by common-mode current on an audio cable. Ferrite beads are passive electric components capable of diminishing high frequency noise in electronic circuits. The bead itself is a ceramic cylinder, which operates by concentrating the magnetic field, which has the effect of increasing the inductance and thereby increasing the reactance. The increased reactance impedes the unwanted noise.

Copyright © Mometrix Media. You have been licensed one copy of this document for personal use only. Any other reproduction or redistribution is strictly prohibited. All rights reserved.

How can a ground loop be avoided?
    A. Connect all ground conductors in series
    B. Connect the AC neutral conductor to the ground wire
    C. Avoid using lock washers and star washers when making ground connections
    D. Connect all ground conductors to a single point

G4C09 (D)
Answer: D. A ground loop can be avoided by connecting all ground conductors to a single point. A ground loop is an unexpected and unwanted current flowing between two points that are incorrectly believed to have the same electric potential. The most common consequences of a ground loop are noise and interference, but there can also be a risk of electric shock. Some other strategies for reducing the risk of ground loop are to position the most powerful devices closest to the power source, to use differential signals, and to check isolated power supplies for component, parasitic, or internal PCB power plane capacitance.

What could be a symptom of a ground loop somewhere in your station?
    A. You receive reports of "hum" on your station's transmitted signal
    B. The SWR reading for one or more antennas is suddenly very high
    C. An item of station equipment starts to draw excessive amounts of current
    D. You receive reports of harmonic interference from your station

G4C10 (A)
Answer: A. If you receive reports of "hum" on your station's transmitted signal, this may be a symptom of a ground loop. Ground loops are often responsible for noise and interference, and in some cases may even present a risk of electric shock.

Which of the following is a function of a digital signal processor?
    A. To provide adequate grounding
    B. To remove noise from received signals
    C. To increase antenna gain
    D. To increase antenna bandwidth

G4C11 (B)
Answer: B. One use for a Digital Signal Processor in an amateur station is to remove noise from received signals. Digital signal processors are microprocessors that receive and transmit analog signals, but process these signals digitally, which increases accuracy and safety quite a bit. Digital signal processors are better when they can handle a larger number of bits.

Which of the following is an advantage of a receiver DSProcessor IF filter as compared to an analog filter?
    A. A wide range of filter bandwidths and shapes can be created
    B. Fewer digital components are required
    C. Mixing products are greatly reduced
    D. The DSP filter is much more effective at VHF frequencies

G4C12 (A)
Answer: A. One advantage of a receiver Digital Signal Processor IF filter as compared to an analog filter is that a wide range of filter bandwidths and shapes can be created.

Copyright © Mometrix Media. You have been licensed one copy of this document for personal use only. Any other reproduction or redistribution is strictly prohibited. All rights reserved.

Which of the following can perform automatic notching of interfering carriers?
A. Band-pass tuning
B. A Digital Signal Processor (DSP) filter
C. Balanced mixing
D. A noise limiter

G4C13 (B)
Answer: B. A Digital Signal Processor filter can perform automatic notching of interfering carriers.

G4D – Speech Processors; S Meters; Sideband Operation near Band Edges

What is the purpose of a speech processor as used in a modern transceiver?
A. Increase the intelligibility of transmitted phone signals during poor conditions
B. Increase transmitter bass response for more natural sounding SSB signals
C. Prevent distortion of voice signals
D. Decrease high-frequency voice output to prevent out of band operation

G4D01 (A)
Answer: A. The purpose of a speech processor as used in a modern transceiver is to increase the intelligibility of transmitted phone signals during poor conditions. A speech processor is able to clean up voice communications so that they are easier to understand.

Which of the following describes how a speech processor affects a transmitted single sideband phone signal?
A. It increases peak power
B. It increases average power
C. It reduces harmonic distortion
D. It reduces intermodulation distortion

G4D02 (B)
Answer: B. A speech processor increases the average power of a transmitted single sideband phone signal. This is one of the ways in which it improves the general clarity and intelligibility of the voice signal.

Which of the following can be the result of an incorrectly adjusted speech processor?
A. Distorted speech
B. Splatter
C. Excessive background pickup
D. All of these choices are correct

G4D03 (D)
Answer: D. Distorted speech, splatter, and excessive background pickup can all result from an incorrectly adjusted speech processor. In radio communication, splatter (also known as spectral splatter) is noise created by the stopping and starting of the transmission.

What does an S meter measure?
A. Conductance
B. Impedance
C. Received signal strength
D. Transmitter power output

Copyright © Mometrix Media. You have been licensed one copy of this document for personal use only. Any other reproduction or redistribution is strictly prohibited. All rights reserved.

G4D04 (C)
Answer: C. An S meter measures received signal strength. An S meter, otherwise known as a signal strength meter, indicates signal strength on an arbitrary scale ranging from S1 to S9. Ham radio operators will often use the expression "S unit" to describe the amount of change in signal strength required to move the S meter from one level to an adjacent level on the S meter.

How does an S meter reading of 20 dB over S9 compare to an S9 signal, assuming a properly calibrated S meter?
    A. It is 10 times less powerful
    B. It is 20 times less powerful
    C. It is 20 times more powerful
    D. It is 100 times more powerful

G4D05 (D)
Answer: D. Assuming a properly calibrated S meter, an S meter reading of 20 dB over S-9 is 100 times stronger than an S-9 signal.

Where is an S meter found?
    A. In a receiver
    B. In an SWR bridge
    C. In a transmitter
    D. In a conductance bridge

G4D06 (A)
Answer: A. An S meter is found in a receiver.

How much must the power output of a transmitter be raised to change the S- meter reading on a distant receiver from S8 to S9?
    A. Approximately 1.5 times
    B. Approximately 2 times
    C. Approximately 4 times
    D. Approximately 8 times

G4D07 (C)
Answer: C. The power output of a transmitter must be raised approximately four times to change the S-meter reading on a distant receiver from S8 to S9.

What frequency range is occupied by a 3 kHz LSB signal when the displayed carrier frequency is set to 7.178 MHz?
    A. 7.178 to 7.181 MHz
    B. 7.178 to 7.184 MHz
    C. 7.175 to 7.178 MHz
    D. 7.1765 to 7.1795 MHz

G4D08 (C)
Answer: C. A 3 kHz LSB signal occupies a frequency range of 7.175 to 7.178 MHz when the displayed carrier frequency is set to 7.178MHz.

Copyright © Mometrix Media. You have been licensed one copy of this document for personal use only. Any other reproduction or redistribution is strictly prohibited. All rights reserved.

What frequency range is occupied by a 3 kHz USB signal with the displayed carrier frequency set to 14.347 MHz?
- A. 14.347 to 14.647 MHz
- B. 14.347 to 14.350 MHz
- C. 14.344 to 14.347 MHz
- D. 14.3455 to 14.3485 MHz

G4D09 (B)
Answer: B. A 3 kHz USB signal with the displayed carrier frequency set to 14.347 MHz occupies a frequency range from 14.347 to 14.350 MHz.

How close to the lower edge of the 40-meter General Class phone segment should your displayed carrier frequency be when using 3 kHz wide LSB?
- A. 3 kHz above the edge of the segment
- B. 3 kHz below the edge of the segment
- C. Your displayed carrier frequency may be set at the edge of the segment
- D. Center your signal on the edge of the segment

G4D10 (A)
Answer: A. When using 3 kHz wide LSB, your displayed carrier frequency should be 3 kHz above the lower edge of the 40-meter General Class phone segment.

How close to the upper edge of the 20-meter General Class band should your displayed carrier frequency be when using 3 kHz wide USB?
- A. 3 kHz above the edge of the band
- B. 3 kHz below the edge of the band
- C. Your displayed carrier frequency may be set at the edge of the band
- D. Center your signal on the edge of the band

G4D11 (B)
Answer: B. When using 3 kHz wide USB, your displayed carrier frequency should be 3 kHz below the upper edge of the 20 meter General Class band,

G4E – HF Mobile Radio Installations; Emergency and Battery Powered Operation

What is the purpose of a capacitance hat on a mobile antenna?
- A. To increase the power handling capacity of a whip antenna
- B. To allow automatic band changing
- C. To electrically lengthen a physically short antenna
- D. To allow remote tuning

G4E01 (C)
Answer: C. When referring to a mobile antenna, a "capacitance hat" is a device to electrically lengthen a physically short antenna. Capacitance hats may be composed of a metal disk, a wire basket, or a pyramid of wires. The capacitance hat regulates the flow of current through the antenna, so that more of the signal will propagate at the top. This has the effect of increasing the functional length of the antenna.

Copyright © Mometrix Media. You have been licensed one copy of this document for personal use only. Any other reproduction or redistribution is strictly prohibited. All rights reserved.

What is the purpose of a corona ball on a HF mobile antenna?
    A. To narrow the operating bandwidth of the antenna
    B. To increase the "Q" of the antenna
    C. To reduce the chance of damage if the antenna should strike an object
    D. To reduce high voltage discharge from the tip of the antenna

G4E02 (D)
Answer: D. The purpose of a "corona ball" on an HF mobile antenna is to reduce high voltage discharge from the tip of the antenna. A corona ball is a spherical piece of metal placed at the end of the antenna rod.

Which of the following direct, fused power connections would be the best for a 100 watt HF mobile installation?
    A. To the battery using heavy gauge wire
    B. To the alternator or generator using heavy gauge wire
    C. To the battery using resistor wire
    D. To the alternator or generator using resistor wire

G4E03 (A)
Answer: A. A direct, fused power connection to the battery using heavy gauge wire would be better than a direct, fused connection to the alternator or generator using heavy gauge wire. It would also be better than direct, fused power connections to the battery or to the alternator or generator using resistor wire.

Why is it best NOT to draw the DC power for a 100 watt HF transceiver from an automobile's auxiliary power socket?
    A. The socket is not wired with an RF-shielded power cable
    B. The socket's wiring may be inadequate for the current being drawn by the transceiver
    C. The DC polarity of the socket is reversed from the polarity of modern HF transceivers
    D. Drawing more than 50 watts from this socket could cause the engine to overheat

G4E04 (B)
Answer: B. It is best NOT to draw the DC power for a 100-watt HF transceiver from an automobile's auxiliary power socket because the socket's wiring may be inadequate for the current being drawn by the transceiver.

Which of the following most limits the effectiveness of an HF mobile transceiver operating in the 75-meter band?
    A. "Picket Fencing" signal variation
    B. The wire gauge of the DC power line to the transceiver
    C. The antenna system
    D. FCC rules limiting mobile output power on the 75 meter band

G4E05 (C)
Answer: C. The antenna system most limits the effectiveness of an HF mobile transceiver operating in the 75-meter band.

What is one disadvantage of using a shortened mobile antenna as opposed to a full size antenna?
    A. Short antennas are more likely to cause distortion of transmitted signals
    B. Short antennas can only receive vertically polarized signals
    C. Operating bandwidth may be very limited
    D. Harmonic radiation may increase

Copyright © Mometrix Media. You have been licensed one copy of this document for personal use only. Any other reproduction or redistribution is strictly prohibited. All rights reserved.

G4E06 (C)
Answer: C. One disadvantage of using a shortened mobile antenna as opposed to a full size antenna is that operating bandwidth may be very limited.

Which of the following is the most likely to cause interfering signals to be heard in the receiver of an HF mobile installation in a recent model vehicle?
    A. The battery charging system
    B. The anti-lock braking system
    C. The anti-theft circuitry
    D. The vehicle control computer

G4E07 (D)
Answer: D. The vehicle control computer is more likely to cause interfering signals to be heard in the receiver of an HF mobile installation in a recent model vehicle than the battery charging system, the anti-lock braking system, or the anti-theft circuitry.

What is the name of the process by which sunlight is changed directly into electricity?
    A. Photovoltaic conversion
    B. Photon emission
    C. Photosynthesis
    D. Photon decomposition

G4E08 (A)
Answer: A. Photovoltaic conversion is the process by which sunlight is changed directly into electricity. Photovoltaic conversion is accomplished with a photovoltaic cell, also known as a photocell. A photovoltaic cell is capable of generating an electric current, though it needs an external load. When the light from the sun is absorbed by the cell, it creates electron-hole pairs or excitons. At the same time, charge carriers of opposite types are separated. Finally, these carriers are extracted and directed to an outside circuit.

What is the approximate open-circuit voltage from a modern, well-illuminated photovoltaic cell?
    A. 0.02 VDC
    B. 0.5 VDC
    C. 0.2 VDC
    D. 1.38 VDC

G4E09 (B)
Answer: B. The approximate open-circuit voltage from a modern, well-illuminated photovoltaic cell is 0.5 VDC.

What is the reason a series diode is connected between a solar panel and a storage battery that is being charged by the panel?
    A. The diode serves to regulate the charging voltage to prevent overcharge
    B. The diode prevents self discharge of the battery though the panel during times of low or no illumination
    C. The diode limits the current flowing from the panel to a safe value
    D. The diode greatly increases the efficiency during times of high illumination

Copyright © Mometrix Media. You have been licensed one copy of this document for personal use only. Any other reproduction or redistribution is strictly prohibited. All rights reserved.

G4E10 (B)
Answer: B. A series diode is connected between a solar panel and a storage battery that is being charged by the panel to prevent self discharge of the battery through the panel during times of low or no illumination. Diodes are two-terminal electronic components that offer little resistance in one direction and total resistance in the other.

Which of the following is a disadvantage of using wind as the primary source of power for an emergency station?
    A. The conversion efficiency from mechanical energy to electrical energy is less than 2 percent
    B. The voltage and current ratings of such systems are not compatible with amateur equipment
    C. A large energy storage system is needed to supply power when the wind is not blowing
    D. All of these choices are correct

G4E11 (C)
Answer: C. One disadvantage of using wind as the primary source of power for an emergency station is that a large energy storage system is needed to supply power when the wind is not blowing.

G5 – Electrical Principles

G5A – Reactance; Inductance; Capacitance; Impedance; Impedance Matching

What is impedance?
    A. The electric charge stored by a capacitor
    B. The inverse of resistance
    C. The opposition to the flow of current in an AC circuit
    D. The force of repulsion between two similar electric fields

G5A01 (C)
Answer: C. Impedance is the opposition to the flow of current in an AC circuit. Another way of describing impedance is as the ratio of the voltage to the current in an alternating current circuit. Whereas resistance has only magnitude, impedance has both magnitude and phase. The concept of impedance is necessary for alternating current because they have the electrostatic storage of charge induced by voltages between conductors, or capacitance, and the induction of voltages in conductors that is self induced by the magnetic fields of the currents, known as inductance.

What is reactance?
    A. Opposition to the flow of direct current caused by resistance
    B. Opposition to the flow of alternating current caused by capacitance or inductance
    C. A property of ideal resistors in AC circuits
    D. A large spark produced at switch contacts when an inductor is de-energized

G5A02 (B)
Answer: B. Reactance is opposition to the flow of alternating current caused by capacitance or inductance. The amount of reactance in a circuit element depends on the inductance or capacitance of the element. If there is an established electric field, it will work against the voltage change on the element. At the same time, a magnetic field will have a natural resistance to a change in current. A perfect resistor will have a reactance of zero, while perfect inductors and capacitors will be entirely composed of reactance. This is because an ideal inductor will have zero resistance, and an ideal capacitor will have infinite resistance.

Copyright © Mometrix Media. You have been licensed one copy of this document for personal use only. Any other reproduction or redistribution is strictly prohibited. All rights reserved.

Which of the following causes opposition to the flow of alternating current in an inductor?
- A. Conductance
- B. Reluctance
- C. Admittance
- D. Reactance

G5A03 (D)
Answer: D. Reactance causes opposition to the flow of alternating current in an inductor. Another way of expressing this is that reactance is the opposition to the change in current caused by inductance.

Which of the following causes opposition to the flow of alternating current in a capacitor?
- A. Conductance
- B. Reluctance
- C. Reactance
- D. Admittance

G5A04 (C)
Answer: C. Reactance causes opposition to the flow of alternating current in a capacitor. Another way of expressing this is that reactance is the opposition to the change in voltage caused by capacitance.

How does an inductor react to AC?
- A. As the frequency of the applied AC increases, the reactance decreases
- B. As the amplitude of the applied AC increases, the reactance increases
- C. As the amplitude of the applied AC increases, the reactance decreases
- D. As the frequency of the applied AC increases, the reactance increases

G5A05 (D)
Answer: D. As the frequency of the applied AC increases, the reactance of an inductor increases. An inductor is a passive electrical component with two terminals. Its function is to resist alterations in an electric current. The most common structure of an inductor is a coil of wire. The passage of current through the wire creates a magnetic field; when the current changes, a voltage is produced by the inductor. The inductance of the component is the ratio of the voltage to the rate of change of current.

How does a capacitor react to AC?
- A. As the frequency of the applied AC increases, the reactance decreases
- B. As the frequency of the applied AC increases, the reactance increases
- C. As the amplitude of the applied AC increases, the reactance increases
- D. As the amplitude of the applied AC increases, the reactance decreases

G5A06 (A)
Answer: A. As the frequency of the applied AC increases, the reactance of a capacitor decreases. A capacitor is a passive electrical component with two terminals. Its function is to store energy in an electrical field. The basic structure of a capacitor is a pair of conductors separated by a dielectric, or insulator. However, there are capacitors that are much more complex. The capacitor operates by creating a potential difference between the conductors, which produces an electric field across the dielectric. That is, one of the plates of the dielectric has a positive charge, and the other has a negative charge. This electrostatic field becomes a repository of energy.

Copyright © Mometrix Media. You have been licensed one copy of this document for personal use only. Any other reproduction or redistribution is strictly prohibited. All rights reserved.

What happens when the impedance of an electrical load is equal to the internal impedance of the power source?

A. The source delivers minimum power to the load

B. The electrical load is shorted

C. No current can flow through the circuit

D. The source can deliver maximum power to the load

G5A07 (D)
Answer: D. When the impedance of an electrical load is equal to the internal impedance of the power source, the source can deliver maximum power to the load. This is known as impedance matching.

Why is impedance matching important?

A. So the source can deliver maximum power to the load

B. So the load will draw minimum power from the source

C. To ensure that there is less resistance than reactance in the circuit

D. To ensure that the resistance and reactance in the circuit are equal

G5A08 (A)
Answer: A. Impedance matching is important so that the source can deliver maximum power to the load. Impedance matching is the technique of maximizing the power transfer from an electrical load by fine-tuning its input impedance. Impedance matching can also be used to minimize the reflections from the electrical load. It can also be accomplished by adjusting the output impedance of the signal corresponding to the electrical load.

What unit is used to measure reactance?

A. Farad

B. Ohm

C. Ampere

D. Siemens

G5A09 (B)
Answer: B. The ohm is used to measure reactance. Specifically, the ohm is equal to the resistance created between two points of a conductor when a continuous potential difference of one volt is applied and produces a current of one ampere. The multimeter is the standard instrument for measuring resistance in ohms.

What unit is used to measure impedance?

A. Volt

B. Ohm

C. Ampere

D. Watt

G5A10 (B)
Answer: B. The ohm is used to measure impedance. In an alternating current circuit, ohms are used as the unit of measure for electrical impedance. This is always the case when measuring the electrical impedance of an alternating current circuit.

Which of the following describes one method of impedance matching between two AC circuits?

A. Insert an LC network between the two circuits

B. Reduce the power output of the first circuit

C. Increase the power output of the first circuit

D. Insert a circulator between the two circuits

Copyright © Mometrix Media. You have been licensed one copy of this document for personal use only. Any other reproduction or redistribution is strictly prohibited. All rights reserved.

G5A11 (A)
Answer: A. One method of impedance matching between two AC circuits is to insert an LC network between the two circuits. An LC network is a circuit consisting of an inductor and a capacitor.

What is one reason to use an impedance matching transformer?
    A. To minimize transmitter power output
    B. To maximize the transfer of power
    C. To reduce power supply ripple
    D. To minimize radiation resistance

G5A12 (B)
Answer: B. One reason to use an impedance matching transformer is to maximize the transfer of power.

Which of the following devices can be used for impedance matching at radio frequencies?
    A. A transformer
    B. A Pi-network
    C. A length of transmission line
    D. All of these choices are correct

G5A13 (D)
Answer: D. A transformer, a Pi-network, and a length of transmission line can all be used for impedance matching at radio frequencies.

G5B – The Decibel; Current and Voltage Dividers; Electrical Power Calculations; Sine Wave Root-Mean-Square (RMS) Values; PEP Calculations

What dB change represents a two-times increase or decrease in power?
    A. Approximately 2 dB
    B. Approximately 3 dB
    C. Approximately 6 dB
    D. Approximately 12 dB

G5B01 (B)
Answer: B. A two-times increase or decrease in power results in a change of approximately 3 dB. The amount of decibel change produced by a change in power is a proportional relationship.

How does the total current relate to the individual currents in each branch of a parallel circuit?
    A. It equals the average of each branch current
    B. It decreases as more parallel branches are added to the circuit
    C. It equals the sum of the currents through each branch
    D. It is the sum of the reciprocal of each individual voltage drop

G5B02 (C)
Answer: C. The total current equals the sum of the individual currents in each branch of a parallel circuit.

How many watts of electrical power are used if 400 VDC is supplied to an 800 ohm load?
    A. 0.5 watts
    B. 200 watts
    C. 400 watts
    D. 3200 watts

Copyright © Mometrix Media. You have been licensed one copy of this document for personal use only. Any other reproduction or redistribution is strictly prohibited. All rights reserved.

G5B03 (B)
Answer: B. If 400 VDC is supplied to an 800-ohm load, 200 watts of electrical power are used. The amount of power used is calculated by dividing the voltage by the resistance and then multiplying by 100.

How many watts of electrical power are used by a 12 VDC light bulb that draws 0.2 amperes?
  A. 2.4 watts
  B. 24 watts
  C. 6 watts
  D. 60 watts

G5B04 (A)
Answer: A. A 12-VDC light bulb that draws 0.2 amperes uses 2.4 watts of electrical power. The amount of electrical power used is calculated by dividing the voltage by the amperage.

How many watts are dissipated when a current of 7.0 milliamperes flows through 1.25 kilohms?
  A. Approximately 61 milliwatts
  B. Approximately 61 watts
  C. Approximately 11 milliwatts
  D. Approximately 11 watts

G5B05 (A)
Answer: A. When a current of 7.0 milliamperes flows through 1.25 kilohms, approximately 61 milliwatts are dissipated.

What is the output PEP from a transmitter if an oscilloscope measures 200 volts peak-to-peak across a 50 ohm dummy load connected to the transmitter output?
  A. 1.4 watts
  B. 100 watts
  C. 353.5 watts
  D. 400 watts

G5B06 (B)
Answer: B. The output PEP from a transmitter is 100 watts if an oscilloscope measures 200 volts peak-to-peak across a 50-ohm dummy load connected to the transmitter output. Output peak envelope power is calculated by dividing the square of the voltage by the resistance.

Which value of an AC signal results in the same power dissipation as a DC voltage of the same value?
  A. The peak-to-peak value
  B. The peak value
  C. The RMS value
  D. The reciprocal of the RMS value

G5B07 (C)
Answer: C. The RMS value of an AC signal results in the same power dissipation as a DC voltage of the same value. RMS (root mean square) value is necessary for determining the amount of power being dissipated by an electrical resistance. The RMS value is only required for this purpose when the current is varying over time.

Copyright © Mometrix Media. You have been licensed one copy of this document for personal use only. Any other reproduction or redistribution is strictly prohibited. All rights reserved.

What is the RMS voltage of a sine wave with a value of 17 volts peak?
    A. 8.5 volts
    B. 12 volts
    C. 24 volts
    D. 34 volts

G5B09 (B)
Answer: B. The RMS voltage of a sine wave with a value of 17 volts peak is 12 volts. RMS voltage is calculated by dividing the peak voltage by 1.414.

What percentage of power loss would result from a transmission line loss of 1 dB?
    A. 10.9 percent
    B. 12.2 percent
    C. 20.5 percent
    D. 25.9 percent

G5B10 (C)
Answer: C. A transmission line loss of 1 dB would result in a power loss of 20.5%.

What is the ratio of peak envelope power to average power for an unmodulated carrier?
    A. .707
    B. 1.00
    C. 1.414
    D. 2.00

G5B11 (B)
Answer: B. The ratio of peak envelope power to average power for an unmodulated carrier is 1.00. Peak envelope power is the highest envelope power a transmitter can deliver to the antenna transmission line during an undistorted RF cycle.

What would be the RMS voltage across a 50 ohm dummy load dissipating 1200 watts?
    A. 173 volts
    B. 245 volts
    C. 346 volts
    D. 692 volts

G5B12 (B)
Answer: B. The RMS voltage across a 50-ohm dummy load dissipating 1200 watts would be 245 volts. The RMS voltage is calculated by finding the square root of the product of the load and the dissipated power.

What is the output PEP of an unmodulated carrier if an average reading wattmeter connected to the transmitter output indicates 1060 watts?
    A. 530 watts
    B. 1060 watts
    C. 1500 watts
    D. 2120 watts

G5B13 (B)
Answer: B. The output PEP of an unmodulated carrier if an average reading wattmeter connected to the transmitter output indicates 1060 watts is 1060 watts.

Copyright © Mometrix Media. You have been licensed one copy of this document for personal use only. Any other reproduction or redistribution is strictly prohibited. All rights reserved.

What is the output PEP from a transmitter if an oscilloscope measures 500 volts peak-to-peak across a 50 ohm resistive load connected to the transmitter output?

    A. 8.75 watts
    B. 625 watts
    C. 2500 watts
    D. 5000 watts

G5B14 (B)
Answer: B. The output PEP from a transmitter if an oscilloscope measures 500 volts peak-to-peak across a 50-ohm resistor connected to the transmitter output would be 625 watts. First, peak-to-peak voltage is converted to RMS voltage by multiplying peak voltage (or, peak-to-peak divided by 2) it by 0.707. Then, the output PEP is found by squaring the RMS voltage and dividing it by the resistance.

G5C – Resistors, Capacitors, and Inductors in Series and Parallel; Transformers

What causes a voltage to appear across the secondary winding of a transformer when an AC voltage source is connected across its primary winding?

    A. Capacitive coupling
    B. Displacement current coupling
    C. Mutual inductance
    D. Mutual capacitance

G5C01 (C)
Answer: C. Mutual inductance causes a voltage to appear across the secondary winding of a transformer when an AC voltage source is connected across its primary winding. Mutual inductance exists when the current change in one inductor initiates a voltage in some other inductor.

What happens if you reverse the primary and secondary windings of a 4:1 voltage step down transformer?

    A. The secondary voltage becomes 4 times the primary voltage
    B. The transformer no longer functions as it is a unidirectional device
    C. Additional resistance must be added in series with the primary to prevent overload
    D. Additional resistance must be added in parallel with the secondary to prevent overload

G5C02 (A)
Answer: A. If you reverse the primary and secondary windings of a 4:1 voltage step down transformer, then the secondary voltage becomes 4 times the primary voltage.

Which of the following components should be added to an existing resistor to increase the resistance?

    A. A resistor in parallel
    B. A resistor in series
    C. A capacitor in series
    D. A capacitor in parallel

G5C03 (B)
Answer: B. To increase resistance, a resistor in series should be added to an existing resistor. When resistors are arranged in a series, the level of current passing through each resistor will be the same. However, the voltage across each resistor will be in proportion to the resistance. The total resistance will be equal to the sum of all the individual resistances.

Copyright © Mometrix Media. You have been licensed one copy of this document for personal use only. Any other reproduction or redistribution is strictly prohibited. All rights reserved.

What is the total resistance of three 100 ohm resistors in parallel?
  A. 0.30 ohms
  B. 0.33 ohms
  C. 33.3 ohms
  D. 300 ohms

G5C04 (C)
Answer: C. The total resistance of three 100-ohm resistors in parallel is 33.3 ohms. When resistors are arranged in a parallel configuration, the voltage across each resistor will be the same, but the currents passing through the resistors will be equal to the sum of the respective currents passing through each resistor. As more resistors are placed in parallel, the collective amount of resistance will decrease. It should be noted that the resistance of the system can be no greater than the least resistant resistor.

If three equal value resistors in series produce 450 ohms, what is the value of each resistor?
  A. 1500 ohms
  B. 90 ohms
  C. 150 ohms
  D. 175 ohms

G5C05 (C)
Answer: C. If three equal value resistors in parallel produce 50 ohms of resistance, and the same three resistors in series produce 450 ohms, the value of each resistor is 150 ohms. Resistors in series produce a total resistance equal to the sum of the individual resistances.

What is the RMS voltage across a 500-turn secondary winding in a transformer if the 2250-turn primary is connected to 120 VAC?
  A. 2370 volts
  B. 540 volts
  C. 26.7 volts
  D. 5.9 volts

G5C06 (C)
Answer: C. If the 2250-turn primary winding of a transformer is connected to 120 VAC, the RMS voltage across a 500-turn secondary winding is 26.7 volts.

What is the turns ratio of a transformer used to match an audio amplifier having 600-ohm output impedance to a speaker having a 4 ohm impedance?
  A. 12.2 to 1
  B. 24.4 to 1
  C. 150 to 1
  D. 300 to 1

G5C07 (A)
Answer: A. The turns ratio of a transformer used to match an audio amplifier having a 600-ohm output to a speaker having a 4-ohm impedance is 12.2 to 1.

What is the equivalent capacitance of two 5.0 nanofarad capacitors and one 750 picofarad capacitor connected in parallel?
  A. 576.9 nanofarads
  B. 1733 picofarads
  C. 3583 picofarads
  D. 10.750 nanofarads

Copyright © Mometrix Media. You have been licensed one copy of this document for personal use only. Any other reproduction or redistribution is strictly prohibited. All rights reserved.

G5C08 (D)
Answer: D. The equivalent capacitance of two 5000 picofarad capacitors and one 750 picofarad capacitor connected in parallel would be 10,750 picofarads. The equivalent capacitance of capacitors in parallel is found by simply adding the individual capacitances.

What is the capacitance of three 100 microfarad capacitors connected in series?
    A. 0.30 microfarads
    B. 0.33 microfarads
    C. 33.3 microfarads
    D. 300 microfarads

G5C09 (C)
Answer: C. The capacitance of three 100 microfarad capacitors connected in series would be 33.3 microfarads. When all of the capacitors in a series have the same capacitance, the total capacitance can be calculated by dividing the capacitance of a single capacitor by the number of capacitors.

What is the inductance of three 10 millihenry inductors connected in parallel?
    A. .30 henrys
    B. 3.3 henrys
    C. 3.3 millihenrys
    D. 30 millihenrys

G5C10 (C)
Answer: C. The inductance of three 10 millihenry inductors connected in parallel would be 3.3 millihenrys. One divided by the total inductance is equal to the sum of one divided by each of the individual inductances.

What is the inductance of a 20 millihenry inductor in series with a 50 millihenry inductor?
    A. .07 millihenrys
    B. 14.3 millihenrys
    C. 70 millihenrys
    D. 1000 millihenrys

G5C11 (C)
Answer: C. The inductance of a 20 millihenry inductor in series with a 50 millihenry inductor would be 70 millihenrys. The total inductance of inductors connected in series is equal to the sum of the individual inductances.

What is the capacitance of a 20 microfarad capacitor in series with a 50 microfarad capacitor?
    A. .07 microfarads
    B. 14.3 microfarads
    C. 70 microfarads
    D. 1000 microfarads

G5C12 (B)
Answer: B. The capacitance of a 20 microfarad capacitor in series with a 50 microfarad capacitor would be 14.3 microfarads. One divided by the total capacitance is equal to the sums of one divided by each of the individual capacitances.

Copyright © Mometrix Media. You have been licensed one copy of this document for personal use only. Any other reproduction or redistribution is strictly prohibited. All rights reserved.

Which of the following components should be added to a capacitor to increase the capacitance?
    A. An inductor in series
    B. A resistor in series
    C. A capacitor in parallel
    D. A capacitor in series

G5C13 (C)
Answer: C. Adding a capacitor in parallel with another capacitor would increase capacitance.

Which of the following components should be added to an inductor to increase the inductance?
    A. A capacitor in series
    B. A resistor in parallel
    C. An inductor in parallel
    D. An inductor in series

G5C14 (D)
Answer: D. Adding an inductor in series to another inductor would increase the inductance.

What is the total resistance of a 10 ohm, a 20 ohm, and a 50 ohm resistor in parallel?
    A. 5.9 ohms
    B. 0.17 ohms
    C. 10000 ohms
    D. 80 ohms

G5C15 (A)
Answer: A. The total resistance of a 10-ohm, a 20-ohm, and a 50-ohm resistor in parallel is 5.9 ohms. When resistors are connected in parallel, the total resistance is calculated by dividing one by the sum of each resistance divided by one.

Why is the conductor of the primary winding of many voltage step up transformers larger in diameter than the conductor of the secondary winding?
    A. To improve the coupling between the primary and secondary
    B. To accommodate the higher current of the primary
    C. To prevent parasitic oscillations due to resistive losses in the primary
    D. To insure that the volume of the primary winding is equal to the volume of the secondary winding

G5C16 (B)
Answer: B. The conductor of the primary winding of many step up transformers is larger in diameter to accommodate the higher current of the primary.

What is the value in nanofarads (nF) of a 22,000 pF capacitor?
    A. 0.22 nF
    B. 2.2 nF
    C. 22 nF
    D. 220 nF

G5C17 (C)
Answer: C. A 22,000 pF capacitor is equivalent to 22 nF.

Copyright © Mometrix Media. You have been licensed one copy of this document for personal use only. Any other reproduction or redistribution is strictly prohibited. All rights reserved.

What is the value in microfarads of a 4700 nanofarad (nF) capacitor?
   A. 47 μF
   B. 0.47 μF
   C. 47,000 μF
   D. 4.7 μF

G5C18 (D)
Answer: D. A 4700 nanofarad capacitor is equivalent to 4.7 microfarads.

G6 – Circuit Components

G6A – Resistors; Capacitors; Inductors; Rectifiers; Solid State Diodes and Transistors; Vacuum Tubes; Batteries

What is the minimum allowable discharge voltage for maximum life of a standard 12 volt lead acid battery?
   A. 6 volts
   B. 8.5 volts
   C. 10.5 volts
   D. 12 volts

G6A01 (C)
Answer: C. The minimum allowable discharge voltage for maximum life of a standard 12-volt lead acid battery is 10.5 volts.

What is an advantage of the low internal resistance of nickel-cadmium batteries?
   A. Long life
   B. High discharge current
   C. High voltage
   D. Rapid recharge

G6A02 (B)
Answer: B. One advantage of the low internal resistance of nickel-cadmium batteries is a high discharge current. Batteries convert chemical energy into electrical energy.

What is the approximate junction threshold voltage of a germanium diode?
   A. 0.1 volt
   B. 0.3 volts
   C. 0.7 volts
   D. 1.0 volts

G6A03 (B)
Answer: B. The approximate junction threshold voltage of a germanium diode is 0.3 volts. The junction threshold voltage is the amount of voltage the diode can handle.

When is it acceptable to recharge a carbon-zinc primary cell?
   A. As long as the voltage has not been allowed to drop below 1.0 volt
   B. When the cell is kept warm during the recharging period
   C. When a constant current charger is used
   D. Never

Copyright © Mometrix Media. You have been licensed one copy of this document for personal use only. Any other reproduction or redistribution is strictly prohibited. All rights reserved.

G6A04 (D)
Answer: D. It is never acceptable to recharge a carbon-zinc primary cell.

What is the approximate junction threshold voltage of a conventional silicon diode?
    A. 0.1 volt
    B. 0.3 volts
    C. 0.7 volts
    D. 1.0 volts

G6A05 (C)
Answer: C. The approximate junction threshold voltage of a conventional silicon diode is 0.7 volts. The junction threshold voltage is the maximum amount of current that can be handled by a component without damage.

Which of the following is an advantage of using a Schottky diode in an RF switching circuit as compared to a standard silicon diode?
    A. Lower capacitance
    B. Lower inductance
    C. Longer switching times
    D. Higher breakdown voltage

G6A06 (A)
Answer: A. Lower capacitance is one advantage of using a Schottky diode in an RF switching circuit as compared to a standard silicon diode. A Schottky diode is a semiconductor diode that can switch very quickly and has a low forward voltage drop. Because the switching time is reduced, the overall system efficiency is improved. The main drawbacks of the Schottky diode are that it has a relatively low reverse voltage rating and a relatively high reverse leakage current. This is true of the typical silicon-metal diode; however, recently silicon carbide Schottky diodes have been constructed that have a much lower reverse leakage current.

What are the stable operating points for a bipolar transistor used as a switch in a logic circuit?
    A. Its saturation and cut-off regions
    B. Its active region (between the cut-off and saturation regions)
    C. Its peak and valley current points
    D. Its enhancement and deletion modes

G6A07 (A)
Answer: A. The stable operating points for a bipolar transistor used as a switch in a logic circuit are its saturation and cut-off regions.

Why must the cases of some large power transistors be insulated from ground?
    A. To increase the beta of the transistor
    B. To improve the power dissipation capability
    C. To reduce stray capacitance
    D. To avoid shorting the collector or drain voltage to ground

G6A08 (D)
Answer: D. The cases of some large power transistors must be insulated from the ground to avoid shorting the collector or drain voltage.

Copyright © Mometrix Media. You have been licensed one copy of this document for personal use only. Any other reproduction or redistribution is strictly prohibited. All rights reserved.

Which of the following describes the construction of a MOSFET?
    A. The gate is formed by a back-biased junction
    B. The gate is separated from the channel with a thin insulating layer
    C. The source is separated from the drain by a thin insulating layer
    D. The source is formed by depositing metal on silicon

G6A09 (B)
Answer: B. In a MOSFET, the gate is separated from the channel with a thin insulating layer. A MOSFET, or metal-oxide-semiconductor field effect transistor, is used to switch or amplify electronic signals. A MOSFET has four terminals: source, gate, drain, and body.

Which element of a triode vacuum tube is used to regulate the flow of electrons between cathode and plate?
    A. Control grid
    B. Heater
    C. Screen Grid
    D. Trigger electrode

G6A10 (A)
Answer: A. The control grid of a triode vacuum tube is used to regulate the flow of electrons between cathode and plate.

Which of the following solid state devices is most like a vacuum tube in its general operating characteristics?
    A. A bipolar transistor
    B. A Field Effect Transistor
    C. A tunnel diode
    D. A varistor

G6A11 (B)
Answer: B. A Field Effect Transistor is more like a vacuum in its general operating characteristics than a bipolar transistor, a tunnel diode, or a varistor. Field effect transistors use an electric field to alter the shape and conductivity of a semiconductor.

What is the primary purpose of a screen grid in a vacuum tube?
    A. To reduce grid-to-plate capacitance
    B. To increase efficiency
    C. To increase the control grid resistance
    D. To decrease plate resistance

G6A12 (A)
Answer: A. The primary purpose of a screen grid in a vacuum tube is to reduce grid-to-plate capacitance. It is typical for the screen grid to be connected to a positive DC voltage that is set slightly lower than the plate voltage. The screen grid will also be bypassed to the cathode with a capacitor.

Why is the polarity of applied voltages important for polarized capacitors?
    A. Incorrect polarity can cause the capacitor to short-circuit
    B. Reverse voltages can destroy the dielectric layer of an electrolytic capacitor
    C. The capacitor could overheat and explode
    D. All of these choices are correct

Copyright © Mometrix Media. You have been licensed one copy of this document for personal use only. Any other reproduction or redistribution is strictly prohibited. All rights reserved.

G6A13 (D)
Answer: D. These are all reasons why the polarity of applied voltages are important.

Which of the following is an advantage of ceramic capacitors as compared to other types of capacitors?
  A. Tight tolerance
  B. High stability
  C. High capacitance for given volume
  D. Comparatively low cost

G6A14 (D)
Answer: D. One advantage of ceramic capacitors as compared to other types of capacitors is the comparatively low cost.

Which of the following is an advantage of an electrolytic capacitor?
  A. Tight tolerance
  B. Much less leakage than any other type
  C. High capacitance for a given volume
  D. Inexpensive RF capacitor

G6A15 (C)
Answer: C. One advantage of an electrolytic capacitor is a high capacitance for a given volume.

What will happen to the resistance if the temperature of a resistor is increased?
  A. It will change depending on the resistor's reactance coefficient
  B. It will stay the same
  C. It will change depending on the resistor's temperature coefficient
  D. It will become time dependent

G6A16 (C)
Answer: C. If the temperature of a resistor is increased, the resistance will change depending on the resistor's temperature coefficient.

Which of the following is a reason not to use wire-wound resistors in an RF circuit?
  A. The resistor's tolerance value would not be adequate for such a circuit
  B. The resistor's inductance could make circuit performance unpredictable
  C. The resistor could overheat
  D. The resistor's internal capacitance would detune the circuit

G6A17 (B)
Answer: B. One reason not to use wire-wound resistors in an RF circuit is that the resistor's inductance could make circuit performance unpredictable.

What is an advantage of using a ferrite core toroidal inductor?
  A. Large values of inductance may be obtained
  B. The magnetic properties of the core may be optimized for a specific range of frequencies
  C. Most of the magnetic field is contained in the core
  D. All of these choices are correct

Copyright © Mometrix Media. You have been licensed one copy of this document for personal use only. Any other reproduction or redistribution is strictly prohibited. All rights reserved.

G6A18 (D)
Answer: D. There are several advantages of using a ferrite core toroidal inductor. To begin with, large values of inductance may be obtained. Also, the magnetic properties of the core may be optimized for a specific range of frequencies. Finally, most of the magnetic field is contained in the core. A toroidal inductor is a passive electronic component.

How should the winding axes of solenoid inductors be placed to minimize their mutual inductance?
    A. In line
    B. Parallel to each other
    C. At right angles
    D. Interleaved

G6A19 (C)
Answer: C. To minimize their mutual inductance, the winding axes of solenoid inductors should be placed at right angles.

G6B – Analog and Digital Integrated Circuits (ICs); Microprocessors; Memory; I/O Devices; Microwave ICs (MMICs); Display Devices

Which of the following is an analog integrated circuit?
    A. NAND Gate
    B. Microprocessor
    C. Frequency Counter
    D. Linear voltage regulator

G6B01 (D)
Answer: D. A linear voltage regulator is an analog integrated circuit. This device keeps the voltage of the circuit consistent. Any difference between the input and the regulated voltage is discharged by the regulator as heat. The regulator also has a voltage divider network that maintains a consistent output voltage.

What is meant by the term MMIC?
    A. Multi Megabyte Integrated Circuit
    B. Monolithic Microwave Integrated Circuit
    C. Military-specification Manufactured Integrated Circuit
    D. Mode Modulated Integrated Circuit

G6B02 (B)
Answer: B. The term MMIC means Monolithic Microwave Integrated Circuit. This is a type of integrated circuit that is capable of operating at microwave frequencies. The most common uses for these devices are high-frequency switching, low-noise amplification, power amplification, and microwave mixing.

Which of the following is an advantage of CMOS integrated circuits compared to TTL integrated circuits?
    A. Low power consumption
    B. High power handling capability
    C. Better suited for RF amplification
    D. Better suited for power supply regulation

Copyright © Mometrix Media. You have been licensed one copy of this document for personal use only. Any other reproduction or redistribution is strictly prohibited. All rights reserved.

G6B03 (A)
Answer: A. Low power consumption is one advantage of CMOS integrated circuits as compared to TTL integrated circuits. CMOS (complementary metal-oxide-semiconductor) circuits are commonly used in microcontrollers and microprocessors. These circuits also have a high noise immunity. They only use a little bit of power because at least one of the two transistors is always off. In a TTL (transistor-transistor logic) circuit, on the other hand, a great deal of power is wasted through the heat emission.

What is meant by the term ROM?
    A. Resistor Operated Memory
    B. Read Only Memory
    C. Random Operational Memory
    D. Resistant to Overload Memory

G6B04 (B)
Answer: B. The term ROM means Read Only Memory. This means that the information encoded in ROM cannot be altered, or can only be altered with great effort. For this reason, it is used to store only the most important and basic functions of the machine.

What is meant when memory is characterized as "non-volatile"?
    A. It is resistant to radiation damage
    B. It is resistant to high temperatures
    C. The stored information is maintained even if power is removed
    D. The stored information cannot be changed once written

G6B05 (C)
Answer: C. When memory is characterized as "non-volatile," this means that the stored information is maintained even if power is removed. Some of the most common examples of non-volatile memory are read-only memory (ROM), flash memory, optical disks, and hard disks.

What kind of device is an integrated circuit operational amplifier?
    A. Digital
    B. MMIC
    C. Programmable Logic
    D. Analog

G6B06 (D)
Answer: D. An integrated circuit operational amplifier is analog.

Which of the following is an advantage of an LED indicator compared to an incandescent indicator?
    A. Lower power consumption
    B. Faster response time
    C. Longer life
    D. All of these choices are correct

G6B07 (D)
Answer: D. Incandescent indicators consume more power than LEDs. An incandescent indicator produces light because of its temperature. For this reason, it tends to waste a great deal of power. An LED (light-emitting diode) indicator, on the other hand, produces light through electroluminescence.

Copyright © Mometrix Media. You have been licensed one copy of this document for personal use only. Any other reproduction or redistribution is strictly prohibited. All rights reserved.

How is an LED biased when emitting light?
    A. Beyond cutoff
    B. At the Zener voltage
    C. Reverse Biased
    D. Forward Biased

G6B08 (D)
Answer: D. An LED is forward biased when emitting light.

Which of the following is a characteristic of a liquid crystal display?
    A. It requires ambient or back lighting
    B. It offers a wide dynamic range
    C. It has a wide viewing angle
    D. All of these choices are correct

G6B09 (A)
Answer: A. One characteristic of a liquid crystal display is that it requires ambient or back lighting. A liquid crystal display (LCD) does not emit light directly, but rather relies on external light to create an image.

What two devices in an Amateur Radio station might be connected using a USB interface?
    A. Computer and transceiver
    B. Microphone and transceiver
    C. Amplifier and antenna
    D. Power supply and amplifier

G6B10 (A)
Answer: A. The computer and transceiver of an Amateur Radio station might be connected with a USB interface.

What is a microprocessor?
    A. A low power analog signal processor used as a microwave detector
    B. A computer on a single integrated circuit
    C. A microwave detector, amplifier, and local oscillator on a single integrated circuit
    D. A low voltage amplifier used in a microwave transmitter modulator stage

G6B11 (B)
Answer: B. A microprocessor is a computer on a single integrated circuit. Microprocessors are capable of performing basic arithmetic functions as well as conducting general programming functions.

Which of the following connectors would be a good choice for a serial data port?
    A. PL-259
    B. Type N
    C. Type SMA
    D. DE-9

G6B12 (D)
Answer: D. A DE-9 connector would be a good choice for a serial data port. These types of connectors derive their name from the characteristic D shape of the metal shield. The relative smallness of these connectors makes them ideal for computing tasks.

Copyright © Mometrix Media. You have been licensed one copy of this document for personal use only. Any other reproduction or redistribution is strictly prohibited. All rights reserved.

Which of these connector types is commonly used for RF service at frequencies up to 150 MHz?
   A. Octal
   B. RJ-11
   C. PL-259
   D. DB-25

G6B13 (C)
Answer: C. PL-259 connectors are commonly used for RF service at frequencies up to 150 MHz.

Which of these connector types is commonly used for audio signals in Amateur Radio stations?
   A. PL-259
   B. BNC
   C. RCA Phono
   D. Type N

G6B14 (C)
Answer: C. RCA Phono connectors are commonly used for audio signals in Amateur Radio stations.

What is the main reason to use keyed connectors instead of non-keyed types?
   A. Prevention of use by unauthorized persons
   B. Reduced chance of incorrect mating
   C. Higher current carrying capacity
   D. All of these choices are correct

G6B15 (B)
Answer: B. The main reason to use keyed connectors instead of non-keyed types is to reduce the chance of incorrect mating.

Which of the following describes a type N connector?
   A. A moisture-resistant RF connector useful to 10 GHz
   B. A small bayonet connector used for data circuits
   C. A threaded connector used for hydraulic systems
   D. An audio connector used in surround-sound installations

G6B16 (A)
Answer: A. A type-N connector is a moisture-resistant RF connector useful up to 10 GHz.

What is the general description of a DIN type connector?
   A. A special connector for microwave interfacing
   B. A DC power connector rated for currents between 30 and 50 amperes
   C. A family of multiple circuit connectors suitable for audio and control signals
   D. A special watertight connector for use in marine applications

G6B17 (C)
Answer: C. A DIN type connector is a family of multiple circuit connectors suitable for audio and control signals.

What is a type SMA connector?
   A. A large bayonet-type connector usable at power levels in excess of 1 KW
   B. A small threaded connector suitable for signals up to several GHz
   C. A connector designed for serial multiple access signals
   D. A type of push-on connector intended for high voltage applications

Copyright © Mometrix Media. You have been licensed one copy of this document for personal use only. Any other reproduction or redistribution is strictly prohibited. All rights reserved.

G6B18 (B)
Answer: B. A type SMA connector is a small threaded connector suitable for signals up to several GHz.

G7 – Practical Circuits

G7A – Power Supplies; and Schematic Symbols

What useful feature does a power supply bleeder resistor provide?
   A. It acts as a fuse for excess voltage
   B. It ensures that the filter capacitors are discharged when power is removed
   C. It removes shock hazards from the induction coils
   D. It eliminates ground loop current

G7A01 (B)
Answer: B. The power-supply bleeder resistor discharges the filter capacitors.

Which of the following components are used in a power supply filter network?
   A. Diodes
   B. Transformers and transducers
   C. Quartz crystals
   D. Capacitors and inductors

G7A02 (D)
Answer: D. Capacitors and inductors are used in a power-supply filter network.

What is the peak-inverse-voltage across the rectifiers in a full-wave bridge power supply?
   A. One-quarter the normal output voltage of the power supply
   B. Half the normal output voltage of the power supply
   C. Double the normal peak output voltage of the power supply
   D. Equal to the normal peak output voltage of the power supply

G7A03 (D)
Answer: D. The peak-inverse-voltage across the rectifiers in a full-wave bridge power supply is equal to the normal peak output voltage of the power supply.

What is the peak-inverse-voltage across the rectifier in a half-wave power supply?
   A. One-half the normal peak output voltage of the power supply
   B. One-half the normal output voltage of the power supply
   C. Equal to the normal output voltage of the power supply
   D. Two times the normal peak output voltage of the power supply

G7A04 (D)
Answer: D. In a half-wave power supply, the peak-inverse voltage across the rectifier is two times the normal peak output voltage of the power supply.

Copyright © Mometrix Media. You have been licensed one copy of this document for personal use only. Any other reproduction or redistribution is strictly prohibited. All rights reserved.

What portion of the AC cycle is converted to DC by a half-wave rectifier?
  A. 90 degrees
  B. 180 degrees
  C. 270 degrees
  D. 360 degrees

G7A05 (B)
Answer: B. 180 degrees of the AC cycle is converted to DC by a half-wave rectifier. This device earns its name by rectifying half of the sine wave.

What portion of the AC cycle is converted to DC by a full-wave rectifier?
  A. 90 degrees
  B. 180 degrees
  C. 270 degrees
  D. 360 degrees

G7A06 (D)
Answer: D. 360 degrees of the AC cycle is converted to DC by a full-wave rectifier. In other words, a full-wave rectifier operates on the entirety of the sine wave.

What is the output waveform of an unfiltered full-wave rectifier connected to a resistive load?
  A. A series of DC pulses at twice the frequency of the AC input
  B. A series of DC pulses at the same frequency as the AC input
  C. A sine wave at half the frequency of the AC input
  D. A steady DC voltage

G7A07 (A)
Answer: A. The output waveform of an unfiltered full-wave rectifier connected to a resistive load is a series of DC pulses at twice the frequency of the AC input.

Which of the following is an advantage of a switch-mode power supply as compared to a linear power supply?
  A. Faster switching time makes higher output voltage possible
  B. Fewer circuit components are required
  C. High frequency operation allows the use of smaller components
  D. All of these choices are correct

G7A08(C)
Answer: C. One advantage of a switch-mode power supply as compared to a linear power supply is that high frequency operation allows the use of smaller components.

Which symbol in figure G7-1 represents a field effect transistor?
(figure G7-1 found at the end of the guide)
  A. Symbol 2
  B. Symbol 5
  C. Symbol 1
  D. Symbol 4

G7A09 (C)
Answer: C. In figure G7-1, symbol 1 represents a field effect transistor.

Copyright © Mometrix Media. You have been licensed one copy of this document for personal use only. Any other reproduction or redistribution is strictly prohibited. All rights reserved.

Which symbol in figure G7-1 represents a Zener diode?
(figure G7-1 found at the end of the guide)
    A. Symbol 4
    B. Symbol 1
    C. Symbol 11
    D. Symbol 5

G7A10 (D)
Answer: D. In figure G7-1, symbol 5 represents a Zener diode. A Zener diode is a semiconductor made of silicon, primarily used to regulate voltage. The positive characteristic of this diode is that it can maintain a fairly consistent voltage through a broad range of currents.

Which symbol in figure G7-1 represents an NPN junction transistor?
(figure G7-1 found at the end of the guide)
    A. Symbol 1
    B. Symbol 2
    C. Symbol 7
    D. Symbol 11

G7A11 (B)
Answer: B. In figure G7-1, symbol 2 represents an NPN junction transistor.

Which symbol in figure G7-1 represents a multiple-winding transformer?
(figure G7-1 found at the end of the guide)
    A. Symbol 4
    B. Symbol 7
    C. Symbol 6
    D. Symbol 1

G7A12 (C)
Answer: C. In figure G7-1, symbol 6 represents a multiple-winding transformer.

Which symbol in figure G7-1 represents a tapped inductor?
(figure G7-1 found at the end of the guide)
    A. Symbol 7
    B. Symbol 11
    C. Symbol 6
    D. Symbol 1

G7A13 (A)
Answer: A. In figure G7-1, symbol 7 represents a tapped inductor.

G7B – Digital Circuits; Amplifiers and Oscillators

Complex digital circuitry can often be replaced by what type of integrated circuit?
    A. Microcontroller
    B. Charge-coupled device
    C. Phase detector
    D. Window comparator

Copyright © Mometrix Media. You have been licensed one copy of this document for personal use only. Any other reproduction or redistribution is strictly prohibited. All rights reserved.

G7B01 (A)
Answer: A. Complex digital circuitry can often be replaced by a microcontroller. A microcontroller contains all of the elements required for a basic computer: clock, I/O control unit, non-volatile memory (ROM), volatile memory (RAM), and a processor.

Which of the following is an advantage of using the binary system when processing digital signals?
    A. Binary "ones" and "zeros" are easy to represent with an "on" or "off" state
    B. The binary number system is most accurate
    C. Binary numbers are more compatible with analog circuitry
    D. All of these choices are correct

G7B02 (A)
Answer: A. One advantage of using the binary system when processing digital signals is that binary "ones" and "zeros" are easy to represent with an "on" or "off" state.

Which of the following describes the function of a two input AND gate?
    A. Output is high when either or both inputs are low
    B. Output is high only when both inputs are high
    C. Output is low when either or both inputs are high
    D. Output is low only when both inputs are high

G7B03 (B)
Answer: B. In a two input AND gate, output is high only when both inputs are high.

Which of the following describes the function of a two input NOR gate?
    A. Output is high when either or both inputs are low
    B. Output is high only when both inputs are high
    C. Output is low when either or both inputs are high
    D. Output is low only when both inputs are high

G7B04 (C)
Answer: C. In a two input NOR gate, output is low when either or both inputs are high.

How many states does a 3-bit binary counter have?
    A. 3
    B. 6
    C. 8
    D. 16

G7B05 (C)
Answer: C. A 3-bit binary counter has 8 states.

What is a shift register?
    A. A clocked array of circuits that passes data in steps along the array
    B. An array of operational amplifiers used for tri state arithmetic operations
    C. A digital mixer
    D. An analog mixer

G7B06 (A)
Answer: A. A shift register is a clocked array of circuits that passes data in steps along the array. Shift registers are used to perform timing functions, serial/parallel conversion, and multiplication and division.

Copyright © Mometrix Media. You have been licensed one copy of this document for personal use only. Any other reproduction or redistribution is strictly prohibited. All rights reserved.

What are the basic components of virtually all sine wave oscillators?
    A. An amplifier and a divider
    B. A frequency multiplier and a mixer
    C. A circulator and a filter operating in a feed-forward loop
    D. A filter and an amplifier operating in a feedback loop

G7B07 (D)
Answer: D. The basic componets of virtually all sine wave oscilllators are a filter and an amplifier operating in a feedback loop. A sine-wave oscillator produces an output voltage that is a sine-wave function of time.

How is the efficiency of an RF power amplifier determined?
    A. Divide the DC input power by the DC output power
    B. Divide the RF output power by the DC input power
    C. Multiply the RF input power by the reciprocal of the RF output power
    D. Add the RF input power to the DC output power

G7B08 (B)
Answer: B. The efficiency of an RF power amplifier is determined by dividing the RF output power by the DC input power.

What determines the frequency of an LC oscillator?
    A. The number of stages in the counter
    B. The number of stages in the divider
    C. The inductance and capacitance in the tank circuit
    D. The time delay of the lag circuit

G7B09 (C)
Answer: C. The frequency of an LC oscillator is determined by the inductance and capacitance in the tank circuit.

Which of the following is a characteristic of a Class A amplifier?
    A. Low standby power
    B. High Efficiency,
    C. No need for bias
    D. Low distortion

G7B10 (D)
Answer: D. Low distortion is a characteristic of a Class A amplifier. This type of linear amplifier is biased such that the active device conducts through 360 degrees of the input waveform.

For which of the following modes is a Class C power stage appropriate for amplifying a modulated signal?
    A. SSB
    B. CW
    C. AM
    D. All of these choices are correct

G7B11 (B)
Answer: B. A Class C power stage is appropriate for amplifying a CW modulated signal.

Copyright © Mometrix Media. You have been licensed one copy of this document for personal use only. Any other reproduction or redistribution is strictly prohibited. All rights reserved.

Which of these classes of amplifiers has the highest efficiency?
    A. Class A
    B. Class B
    C. Class AB
    D. Class C

G7B12 (D)
Answer: D. Class C amplifiers have the highest efficiency. A Class C amplifier is biased such that the active device conducts for less than 180 degrees of the input waveform.

What is the reason for neutralizing the final amplifier stage of a transmitter?
    A. To limit the modulation index
    B. To eliminate self-oscillations
    C. To cut off the final amplifier during standby periods
    D. To keep the carrier on frequency

G7B13 (B)
Answer: B. The final amplifier stage of a transmitter is neutralized to eliminate self-oscillations.

Which of the following describes a linear amplifier?
    A. Any RF power amplifier used in conjunction with an amateur transceiver
    B. An amplifier in which the output preserves the input waveform
    C. A Class C high efficiency amplifier
    D. An amplifier used as a frequency multiplier

G7B14 (B)
Answer: B. A linear amplifier is an amplifier in which the output preserves the input waveform. The Class A amplifier is a good example of a linear amplifier.

G7C – Receivers and Transmitters; Filters, Oscillators

Which of the following is used to process signals from the balanced modulator and send them to the mixer in a single sideband phone transmitter?
    A. Carrier oscillator
    B. Filter
    C. IF amplifier
    D. RF amplifier

G7C01 (B)
Answer: B. A filter is used to process signals from the balanced modulator and send them to the mixer in a single-sideband phone transmitter. Filters are circuits that allow some signals to pass through but greatly reduce the strength of other signals.

Which circuit is used to combine signals from the carrier oscillator and speech amplifier and send the result to the filter in a typical single-sideband phone transmitter?
    A. Discriminator
    B. Detector
    C. IF amplifier
    D. Balanced modulator

Copyright © Mometrix Media. You have been licensed one copy of this document for personal use only. Any other reproduction or redistribution is strictly prohibited. All rights reserved.

G7C02 (D)
Answer: D. A balanced modulator is used to combine signals from the carrier oscillator and speech amplifier and send the result to the filter in a typical single-sideband phone transmitter.

What circuit is used to process signals from the RF amplifier and local oscillator and send the result to the IF filter in a superheterodyne receiver?
    A. Balanced modulator
    B. IF amplifier
    C. Mixer
    D. Detector

G7C03 (C)
Answer: C. A mixer is used to process signals from the RF amplifier and local oscillator and send the result to the IF filter in a superheterodyne receiver.

What circuit is used to combine signals from the IF amplifier and BFO and send the result to the AF amplifier in a single-sideband receiver?
    A. RF oscillator
    B. IF filter
    C. Balanced modulator
    D. Product detector

G7C04 (D)
Answer: D. A product detector is used to combine signals from the IF amplifier and BFO and send the result to the AF amplifier in a single-sideband receiver. A product detector is a piece of equipment that gives a receiver the ability to process both CW and SSB signals.

Which of the following is an advantage of a transceiver controlled by a direct digital synthesizer (DDS)?
    A. Wide tuning range and no need for band switching
    B. Relatively high power output
    C. Relatively low power consumption
    D. Variable frequency with the stability of a crystal oscillator

G7C05 (D)
Answer: D. One advantage of a transceiver controlled by a direct digital synthesizer (DDS) is variable frequency with the stability of a crystal oscillator. A direct digital synthesizer can make arbitrary waveforms based on the inputs from a clock.

What should be the impedance of a low-pass filter as compared to the impedance of the transmission line into which it is inserted?
    A. Substantially higher
    B. About the same
    C. Substantially lower
    D. Twice the transmission line impedance

G7C06 (B)
Answer: B. The impedance of a low-pass filter should be about the same as the impedance of the transmission line into which it is compared. A low-pass filter permits signals below a certain cutoff frequency to be transmitted, but attenuates signals above the cutoff frequency.

Copyright © Mometrix Media. You have been licensed one copy of this document for personal use only. Any other reproduction or redistribution is strictly prohibited. All rights reserved.

What is the simplest combination of stages that implement a superheterodyne receiver?
    A. RF amplifier, detector, audio amplifier
    B. RF amplifier, mixer, IF discriminator
    C. HF oscillator, mixer, detector
    D. HF oscillator, pre-scaler, audio amplifier

G7C07 (C)
Answer: C. The simplest combination of stages that implement a superheterodyne receiver is HF oscillator, mixer, and detector.

What type of circuit is used in many FM receivers to convert signals coming from the IF amplifier to audio?
    A. Product detector
    B. Phase inverter
    C. Mixer
    D. Discriminator

G7C08 (D)
Answer: D. A discriminator is used in many FM receivers to convert signals coming from the IP amplifier to audio.

Which of the following is needed for a Digital Signal Processor IF filter?
    A. An analog to digital converter
    B. A digital to analog converter
    C. A digital processor chip
    D. All of these choices are correct

G7C09 (D)
Answer: D. A Digital Signal Processor IF filter requires an analog to digital converter, a digital to analog converter, and a digital processor chip. This type of filtering allows digital signal processing to reach levels of flexibility equal to those of high-quality fixed-width filters.

How is Digital Signal Processor filtering accomplished?
    A. By using direct signal phasing
    B. By converting the signal from analog to digital and using digital processing
    C. By differential spurious phasing
    D. By converting the signal from digital to analog and taking the difference of mixing products

G7C10 (B)
Answer: B. Digital Signal Processing filtering is accomplished by converting the signal from analog to digital and using digital processing.

What is meant by the term "software defined radio" (SDR)?
    A. A radio in which most major signal processing functions are performed by software
    B. A radio which provides computer interface for automatic logging of band and frequency
    C. A radio which uses crystal filters designed using software
    D. A computer model which can simulate performance of a radio to aid in the design process

G7C11 (A)
Answer: A. The term "software defined radio" (SDR) means a radio in which most major signal processing functions are performed by software.

Copyright © Mometrix Media. You have been licensed one copy of this document for personal use only. Any other reproduction or redistribution is strictly prohibited. All rights reserved.

G8 – Signals and Emissions

G8A – Carriers and Modulation; AM; FM; Single Sideband; Modulation Envelope; Digital Modulation; Over Modulation

How is an FSK signal generated?
    A. By keying an FM transmitter with a sub-audible tone
    B. By changing an oscillator's frequency directly with a digital control signal
    C. By using a transceiver's computer data interface protocol to change frequencies
    D. By reconfiguring the CW keying input to act as a tone generator

G8A01 (B)
Answer: B. An FSK signal is generated by changing an oscillator's frequency directly with a digital control signal.

What is the name of the process that changes the phase angle of an RF wave to convey information?
    A. Phase convolution
    B. Phase modulation
    C. Angle convolution
    D. Radian inversion

G8A02 (B)
Answer: B. Phase modulation is the process that changes the phase angle of an RF wave to convey information.

What is the name of the process which changes the instantaneous frequency of an RF wave to convey information?
    A. Frequency convolution
    B. Frequency transformation
    C. Frequency conversion
    D. Frequency modulation

G8A03 (D)
Answer: D. Frequency modulation is the process which changes the frequency of an RF wave to convey information. Most repeaters use frequency modulated phone signals to communicate via voice. When this is done, the RF carrier frequency is altered by the voice data.

What emission is produced by a reactance modulator connected to an RF power amplifier?
    A. Multiplex modulation
    B. Phase modulation
    C. Amplitude modulation
    D. Pulse modulation

G8A04 (B)
Answer: B. Phase modulation is the emission produced by a reactance modulator connected to an RF power amplifier.

Copyright © Mometrix Media. You have been licensed one copy of this document for personal use only. Any other reproduction or redistribution is strictly prohibited. All rights reserved.

What type of modulation varies the instantaneous power level of the RF signal?
    A. Frequency shift keying
    B. Phase modulation
    C. Frequency modulation
    D. Amplitude modulation

G8A05 (D)
Answer: D. Amplitude modulation varies the instantaneous power level of the RF signal.

What is one advantage of carrier suppression in a single sideband phone transmission versus full carrier amplitude modulation?
    A. Audio fidelity is improved
    B. Greater modulation percentage is obtainable with lower distortion
    C. Available transmitter power can be used more effectively
    D. Simpler receiving equipment can be used

G8A06 (C)
Answer: C. One advantage of carrier suppression in a single sideband phone transmission is that the available transmitter power can be used more effectively.

Which of the following phone emissions uses the narrowest bandwidth?
    A. Single sideband
    B. Double sideband
    C. Phase modulation
    D. Frequency modulation

G8A07 (A)
Answer: A. Single sideband phone emissions uses the narrowest frequency bandwidth. Unlike an AM transmission, which requires two matching copies of the voice information to be sent out, an SSB transmission only requires one. Therefore, it takes up considerably less of the radio spectrum.

Which of the following is an effect of overmodulation?
    A. Insufficient audio
    B. Insufficient bandwidth
    C. Frequency drift
    D. Excessive bandwidth

G8A08 (D)
Answer: D. Excessive bandwidth is an effect of over-modulation.

What control is typically adjusted for proper ALC setting on an amateur single sideband transceiver?
    A. The RF clipping level
    B. Transmit audio or microphone gain
    C. Antenna inductance or capacitance
    D. Attenuator level

G8A09 (B)
Answer: B. The transmit audio or microphone gain is typically adjusted for proper ALC setting on an amateur single sideband transceiver.

Copyright © Mometrix Media. You have been licensed one copy of this document for personal use only. Any other reproduction or redistribution is strictly prohibited. All rights reserved.

What is meant by flat-topping of a single-sideband phone transmission?
   A. Signal distortion caused by insufficient collector current
   B. The transmitter's automatic level control is properly adjusted
   C. Signal distortion caused by excessive drive
   D. The transmitter's carrier is properly suppressed

G8A10 (C)
Answer: C. In single sideband phone transmission, flat-topping is signal distortion caused by excessive drive.

What is the modulation envelope of an AM signal?
   A. The waveform created by connecting the peak values of the modulated signal
   B. The carrier frequency that contains the signal
   C. Spurious signals that envelop nearby frequencies
   D. The bandwidth of the modulated signal

G8A11 (A)
Answer: A. The modulation envelope of an AM signal is the waveform created by connecting the peak values of the modulated signal.

G8B – Frequency Mixing; Multiplication; Bandwidths of Various Modes; Deviation

What receiver stage combines a 14.250 MHz input signal with a 13.795 MHz oscillator signal to produce a 455 kHz intermediate frequency (IF) signal?
   A. Mixer
   B. BFO
   C. VFO
   D. Discriminator

G8B01 (A)
Answer: A. The mixer combines a 14.250 MHz input signal with a 13.795 MHz oscillator signal to produce a 455 kHz intermediate frequency (IF) signal.

If a receiver mixes a 13.800 MHz VFO with a 14.255 MHz received signal to produce a 455 kHz intermediate frequency (IF) signal, what type of interference will a 13.345 MHz signal produce in the receiver?
   A. Quadrature noise
   B. Image response
   C. Mixer interference
   D. Intermediate interference

G8B02 (B)
Answer: B. If a receiver mixes a 13.800 MHz VFO with a 14.255 MHz received signal to produce a 455 kHz intermediate frequency (IF) signal, a 13.345 MHz signal will produce image response interference in the receiver.

What is another term for the mixing of two RF signals?
   A. Heterodyning
   B. Synthesizing
   C. Cancellation
   D. Phase inverting

Copyright © Mometrix Media. You have been licensed one copy of this document for personal use only. Any other reproduction or redistribution is strictly prohibited. All rights reserved.

G8B03 (A)
Answer: A. Heterodyning is another term for the mixing of two RF signals. In this process, an electronic circuit is used to combine an input radio frequency with a generated frequency: the result is one frequency that is a sum of the frequencies and one frequency that is the difference between the frequencies.

What is the stage in a VHF FM transmitter that generates a harmonic of a lower frequency signal to reach the desired operating frequency?
  A. Mixer
  B. Reactance modulator
  C. Pre-emphasis network
  D. Multiplier

G8B04 (D)
Answer: D. The multiplier stage in a VHF FM transmitter generates a harmonic of a lower frequency signal to reach the desired operating frequency.

What is the approximate bandwidth of a PACTOR3 signal at maximum data rate?

  A. 31.5 Hz
  B. 500 Hz
  C. 1800 Hz
  D. 2300 Hz

G8B05 (D)
Answer: D. The approximate bandwidth of a PACTOR3 signal at maximum data rate is 2300Hz.

What is the total bandwidth of an FM-phone transmission having a 5 kHz deviation and a 3 kHz modulating frequency?
  A. 3 kHz
  B. 5 kHz
  C. 8 kHz
  D. 16 kHz

G8B06 (D)
Answer: D. The total bandwidth of an FM-phone transmission having a 5 kHz deviation and a 3 kHz modulating frequency is 16 kHz.

What is the frequency deviation for a 12.21-MHz reactance modulated oscillator in a 5 kHz deviation, 146.52 MHz FM phone transmitter?
  A. 101.75 Hz
  B. 416.7 Hz
  C. 5 kHz
  D. 60 kHz

G8B07 (B)
Answer: B. The frequency deviation for a 12.21-MHz reactance-modulated oscillator in a 5-kHz deviation, 146.52-MHz FM-phone transmitter is 416.7 Hz.

Copyright © Mometrix Media. You have been licensed one copy of this document for personal use only. Any other reproduction or redistribution is strictly prohibited. All rights reserved.

Why is it important to know the duty cycle of the data mode you are using when transmitting?
    A. To aid in tuning your transmitter
    B. Some modes have high duty cycles which could exceed the transmitter's average power rating.
    C. To allow time for the other station to break in during a transmission
    D. All of these choices are correct

G8B08 (B)
Answer: B. It is important to know the duty cycle of the data mode you are using when transmitting because some modes have high duty cycles which could exceed the transmitter's average power rating. The duty cycle of a transmitter is the amount of time it spends operating at full output power during each transmission. When a transmitter has a higher duty cycle, this means that it creates more RF radiation exposure for an equivalent PEP output.

Why is it good to match receiver bandwidth to the bandwidth of the operating mode?
    A. It is required by FCC rules
    B. It minimizes power consumption in the receiver
    C. It improves impedance matching of the antenna
    D. It results in the best signal to noise ratio

G8B09 (D)
Answer: D. Matching receiver bandwidth to the bandwidth of the operating mode results in the best signal to noise ratio. The receiver is the piece of equipment that converts radio waves into signals that can be heard or seen by the operator.

What is the relationship between transmitted symbol rate and bandwidth?
    A. Symbol rate and bandwidth are not related
    B. Higher symbol rates require wider bandwidth
    C. Lower symbol rates require wider bandwidth
    D. Bandwidth is always half the symbol rate

G8B10 (B)
Answer: B. The relationship between transmitted symbol rate and bandwidth is the higher symbol rates require wider bandwidth.

G8C – Digital Emission Modes

Which of the following digital modes is designed to operate at extremely low signal strength on the HF bands?
    A. FSK441 and Hellschreiber
    B. JT9 and JT65
    C. Clover
    D. RTTY

G8C01 (B)
Answer: B. JT9 and JT65 are designed to operate at extremely low signal strength on the HF bands.

How many data bits are sent in a single PSK31 character?
    A. The number varies
    B. 5
    C. 7
    D. 8

Copyright © Mometrix Media. You have been licensed one copy of this document for personal use only. Any other reproduction or redistribution is strictly prohibited. All rights reserved.

G8C02 (A)
Answer: A. The number of data bits sent in a single PSK31 character varies. Phase shift keying is a highly sophisticated method for digital transmission in the HF spectrum. PSK31 is named after the tiny 31.25 Hz used by its signal. The coding system for characters is called Varicode: much like Morse code, it employs a different number of bits for different characters. The signal is a continuous tone, and the characters are indicated by shifts in the timing relationship with a reference signal.

What part of a data packet contains the routing and handling information?
    A. Directory
    B. Preamble
    C. Header
    D. Footer

G8C03 (C)
Answer: C. The header of a data packet contains the routing and handling information. The trailer of a data packet may also contain the routing and handling information, which is also known as the control information. The main content of the message is called the user data, or payload.

Which of the following describes Baudot code?
    A. A 7-bit code with start, stop and parity bits
    B. A code using error detection and correction
    C. A 5-bit code with additional start and stop bits
    D. A code using SELCAL and LISTEN

G8C04 (C)
Answer: C. Baudot code is a five-bit code with additional start and stop bits. It is used in RTTY (radioteletype) communications. In Baudot code, characters of plain text are sent as five-bit codes composed of patterns of marks and spaces. The modulation created by this succession of frequencies is called frequency shift keying.

In the PACTOR protocol, what is meant by an NAK response to a transmitted packet?
    A. The receiver is requesting the packet be re-transmitted
    B. The receiver is reporting the packet was received without error
    C. The receiver is busy decoding the packet
    D. The entire file has been received correctly

G8C05 (A)
Answer: A. In the PACTOR protocol, an NAK response to a transmitted packet means that the receiver is requesting the packet be retransmitted. PACTOR is a system for teleprinting over radio (TOR), or transmitting text characters. This program improved the structure of the TOR and AMTOR programs.

How does the receiving station respond to an ARQ data mode packet containing errors?
    A. Terminates the contact
    B. Requests the packet be retransmitted
    C. Sends the packet back to the transmitting station
    D. Requests a change in transmitting protocol

G8C07 (B)
Answer: B. The receiving station responds to an ARQ data mode packet containing errors by requesting the packet be retransmitted.

Copyright © Mometrix Media. You have been licensed one copy of this document for personal use only. Any other reproduction or redistribution is strictly prohibited. All rights reserved.

Which of the following statements is true about PSK31?
A. Upper case letters make the signal stronger
B. Upper case letters use longer Varicode signals and thus slow down transmission
C. Varicode Error Correction is used to ensure accurate message reception
D. Higher power is needed as compared to RTTY for similar error rates

G8C08 (B)
Answer: B. In PSK31 the upper case letters use longer Varicode signals and thus slow down transmission.

What does the number 31 represent in PSK31?
A. The approximate transmitted symbol rate
B. The version of the PSK protocol
C. The year in which PSK31 was invented
D. The number of characters that can be represented by PSK31

G8C09 (A)
Answer: A. In PSK31, the number 31 represents the approximate transmitted symbol rate. Specifically, it refers to the 31.25 Hz taken up by the PSK31 signal: this is a comparatively tiny portion of the bandwidth.

How does forward error correction (FEC) allow the receiver to correct errors in received data packets?
A. By controlling transmitter output power for optimum signal strength
B. By using the varicode character set
C. By transmitting redundant information with the data
D. By using a parity bit with each character

G8C10 (C)
Answer: C. FEC allows the receiver to correct errors in received data packets by transmitting redundant information with the data.

How are the two separate frequencies of a Frequency Shift Keyed (FSK) signal identified?
A. Dot and Dash
B. On and Off
C. High and Low
D. Mark and Space

G8C11 (D)
Answer: D. The two separate frequencies of a FSK signal are identified by a mark and space.

Which type of code is used for sending characters in a PSK31 signal?
A. Varicode
B. Viterbi
C. Volumetric
D. Binary

G8C12 (A)
Answer: A. In a PSK31 signal Varicode is used to send characters.

Copyright © Mometrix Media. You have been licensed one copy of this document for personal use only. Any other reproduction or redistribution is strictly prohibited. All rights reserved.

G9 – Antennas and Feed Lines

G9A – Antenna Feed Lines; Characteristic Impedance, and Attenuation; SWR Calculation, Measurement and Effects; Matching Networks

Which of the following factors determine the characteristic impedance of a parallel conductor antenna feed line?
A. The distance between the centers of the conductors and the radius of the conductors
B. The distance between the centers of the conductors and the length of the line
C. The radius of the conductors and the frequency of the signal
D. The frequency of the signal and the length of the line

G9A01 (A)
Answer: A. The distance between the centers of the conductors and the radius of the conductors determines the characteristic impedance of a parallel conductor antenna feed line.

What are the typical characteristic impedances of coaxial cables used for antenna feed lines at amateur stations?
A. 25 and 30 ohms
B. 50 and 75 ohms
C. 80 and 100 ohms
D. 500 and 750 ohms

G9A02 (B)
Answer: B. The typical characteristic impedances of coaxial cables used for antenna feed lines at amateur stations is between 50 and 75 ohms.

What is the characteristic impedance of flat ribbon TV type twinlead?
A. 50 ohms
B. 75 ohms
C. 100 ohms
D. 300 ohms

G9A03 (D)
Answer: D. The characteristic impedance of flat ribbon TV type twinlead is 300 ohms.

What might cause reflected power at the point where a feed line connects to an antenna?
A. Operating an antenna at its resonant frequency
B. Using more transmitter power than the antenna can handle
C. A difference between feed line impedance and antenna feed point impedance
D. Feeding the antenna with unbalanced feed line

G9A04 (C)
Answer: C. At the point where a feed line connects to an antenna, a difference between feed-line impedance and antenna feed-point impedance results in reflected power.

Copyright © Mometrix Media. You have been licensed one copy of this document for personal use only. Any other reproduction or redistribution is strictly prohibited. All rights reserved.

How does the attenuation of coaxial cable change as the frequency of the signal it is carrying increases?
    A. It is independent of frequency
    B. It increases
    C. It decreases
    D. It reaches a maximum at approximately 18 MHz

G9A05 (B)
Answer: B. The attenuation of coaxial cable increases as the frequency of the signal it is carrying increases. A coaxial cable is a type of feedline in which one conductor is entirely inside another.

In what units is RF feed line loss usually expressed?
    A. Ohms per 1000 feet
    B. Decibels per 1000 feet
    C. Ohms per 100 feet
    D. Decibels per 100 feet

G9A06 (D)
Answer: D. RF feed line losses are usually expressed in dB per 100 ft.

What must be done to prevent standing waves on an antenna feed line?
    A. The antenna feed point must be at DC ground potential
    B. The feed line must be cut to a length equal to an odd number of electrical quarter wavelengths
    C. The feed line must be cut to a length equal to an even number of physical half wavelengths
    D. The antenna feed point impedance must be matched to the characteristic impedance of the feed line

G9A07 (D)
Answer: D. To prevent standing waves on an antenna feed line, the antenna feed point impedance must be matched to the characteristic impedance of the feed line.

If the SWR on an antenna feed line is 5 to 1, and a matching network at the transmitter end of the feed line is adjusted to 1 to 1 SWR, what is the resulting SWR on the feed line?
    A. 1 to 1
    B. 5 to 1
    C. Between 1 to 1 and 5 to 1 depending on the characteristic impedance of the line
    D. Between 1 to 1 and 5 to 1 depending on the reflected power at the transmitter

G9A08 (B)
Answer: B. If the SWR on an antenna line is 5 to 1, and a matching network at the transmitter end of the feed line is adjusted to 1 to 1 SWR, the resulting SWR on the feed line is 5 to 1. The standing wave ratio, also known as the voltage standing wave ratio, is an indication of the impedance match between the feedline and the antenna.

What standing wave ratio will result from the connection of a 50 ohm feed line to a non-reactive load having a 200 ohm impedance?
    A. 4:1
    B. 1:4
    C. 2:1
    D. 1:2

Copyright © Mometrix Media. You have been licensed one copy of this document for personal use only. Any other reproduction or redistribution is strictly prohibited. All rights reserved.

G9A09 (A)
Answer: A. The connection of a 50-ohm feed line to a non-reactive load having a 200-ohm impedance will result in a standing wave ratio of 4:1.

What standing wave ratio will result from the connection of a 50 ohm feed line to a non-reactive load having a 10 ohm impedance?
    A. 2:1
    B. 50:1
    C. 1:5
    D. 5:1

G9A10 (D)
Answer: D. The connection of a 50-ohm feed line to a non-reactive load with a 10-ohm impedance will result in a standing wave ratio of 5:1.

What standing wave ratio will result from the connection of a 50 ohm feed line to a non-reactive load having a 50 ohm impedance?
    A. 2:1
    B. 1:1
    C. 50:50
    D. 0:0

G9A11 (B)
Answer: B. The connection of a 50-ohm feed line to a non-reactive load having a 50-ohm impedance will result in a standing wave ratio of 1:1.

What standing wave ratio will result when connecting a 50 ohm feed line to a non-reactive load having 25 ohm impedance?
    A. 2:1
    B. 2.5:1
    C. 1.25:1
    D. You cannot determine SWR from impedance values

G9A12 (A)
Answer: A. If you feed a vertical antenna that has a 25-ohm feed-point impedance with 50-ohm coaxial cable, the standing wave ratio would be 2:1.

What standing wave ratio will result when connecting a 50 ohm feed line to an antenna that has a purely resistive 300 ohm feed point impedance?
    A. 1.5:1
    B. 3:1
    C. 6:1
    D. You cannot determine SWR from impedance values

G9A13 (C)
Answer: C. If you feed an antenna that has 300-ohm feed-point impedance with 50-ohm coaxial cable, the standing wave ratio would be 6:1.

Copyright © Mometrix Media. You have been licensed one copy of this document for personal use only. Any other reproduction or redistribution is strictly prohibited. All rights reserved.

What is the interaction between high standing wave ratio (SWR) and transmission line loss?
- A. There is no interaction between transmission line loss and SWR
- B. If a transmission line is lossy, high SWR will increase the loss
- C. High SWR makes it difficult to measure transmission line loss
- D. High SWR reduces the relative effect of transmission line loss

G9A14 (B)
Answer: B. If a transmission line is lossy, high SWR will increase the loss.

What is the effect of transmission line loss on SWR measured at the input to the line?
- A. The higher the transmission line loss, the more the SWR will read artificially low
- B. The higher the transmission line loss, the more the SWR will read artificially high
- C. The higher the transmission line loss, the more accurate the SWR measurement will be
- D. Transmission line loss does not affect the SWR measurement

G9A15 (A)
Answer: A. The effect is the higher the transmission line loss, the more the SWR will read artificially low.

G9B – Basic Antennas

What is one disadvantage of a directly fed random-wire antenna?
- A. It must be longer than 1 wavelength
- B. You may experience RF burns when touching metal objects in your station
- C. It produces only vertically polarized radiation
- D. It is not effective on the higher HF bands

G9B01 (B)
Answer: B. One disadvantage of a directly fed random-wire antenna is that you may experience RF burns when touching metal objects in your station.

Which of the following is a common way to adjust the feed point impedance of a quarter wave ground plane vertical antenna to be approximately 50 ohms?
- A. Slope the radials upward
- B. Slope the radials downward
- C. Lengthen the radials
- D. Shorten the radials

G9B02 (B)
Answer: B. A common way to adjust the feed point impedance of a quarter wave ground plane vertical antenna is to slope the radials downward.

What happens to the feed point impedance of a ground plane antenna when its radials are changed from horizontal to sloping downward?
- A. It decreases
- B. It increases
- C. It stays the same
- D. It reaches a maximum at an angle of 45 degrees

G9B03 (B)
Answer: B. The feed-point impedance of a ground-plane antenna increases when its radials are changed from horizontal to downward-sloping.

Copyright © Mometrix Media. You have been licensed one copy of this document for personal use only. Any other reproduction or redistribution is strictly prohibited. All rights reserved.

What is the radiation pattern of a dipole antenna in free space in the plane of the conductor?
    A. It is a figure-eight at right angles to the antenna
    B. It is a figure-eight off both ends of the antenna
    C. It is a circle (equal radiation in all directions)
    D. It has a pair of lobes on one side of the antenna and a single lobe on the other side

G9B04 (A)
Answer: A. The low angle azimuthal radiation pattern of an ideal half-wavelength dipole antenna installed 1/2 wavelength high and parallel to the Earth is a figure-eight at right angles to the antenna.

How does antenna height affect the horizontal (azimuthal) radiation pattern of a horizontal dipole HF antenna?
    A. If the antenna is too high, the pattern becomes unpredictable
    B. Antenna height has no effect on the pattern
    C. If the antenna is less than 1/2 wavelength high, the azimuthal pattern is almost omnidirectional
    D. If the antenna is less than 1/2 wavelength high, radiation off the ends of the wire is eliminated

G9B05 (C)
Answer: C. If a horizontal dipole HF antenna is less than 1.2 wavelengths high, the horizontal (azimuthal) pattern is almost omnidirectional.

Where should the radial wires of a ground-mounted vertical antenna system be placed?
    A. As high as possible above the ground
    B. Parallel to the antenna element
    C. On the surface or buried a few inches below the ground
    D. At the top of the antenna

G9B06 (C)
Answer: C. The radial wires of a ground-mounted vertical antenna system should be placed on the surface or buried a few inches below the ground.

How does the feed point impedance of a ½ wave dipole antenna change as the antenna is lowered from ¼ wave above ground?
    A. It steadily increases
    B. It steadily decreases
    C. It peaks at about 1/8 wavelength above ground
    D. It is unaffected by the height above ground

G9B07 (B)
Answer: B. The feed-point impedance of a 1/2 wave dipole antenna steadily decreases as the antenna is lowered from ¼ wave above ground.

How does the feed point impedance of a ½ wave dipole change as the feed-point location is moved from the center toward the ends?
    A. It steadily increases
    B. It steadily decreases
    C. It peaks at about 1/8 wavelength from the end
    D. It is unaffected by the location of the feed point

Copyright © Mometrix Media. You have been licensed one copy of this document for personal use only. Any other reproduction or redistribution is strictly prohibited. All rights reserved.

G9B08 (A)
Answer: A. The feed-point impedance of a ½ wave dipole steadily increases as the feed-point location is moved from the center toward the ends.

Which of the following is an advantage of a horizontally polarized as compared to vertically polarized HF antenna?
A. Lower ground reflection losses
B. Lower feed point impedance
C. Shorter Radials
D. Lower radiation resistance

G9B09 (A)
Answer: A. Horizontally polarized HF antennas have lower ground reflection losses than vertically polarized HF antennas.

What is the approximate length for a ½ wave dipole antenna cut for 14.250 MHz?
A. 8 feet
B. 16 feet
C. 24 feet
D. 32 feet

G9B10 (D)
Answer: D. The approximate length for a ½ wave dipole antenna cut for 14.250 MHz is 32 feet.

What is the approximate length for a ½ wave dipole antenna cut for 3.550 MHz?
A. 42 feet
B. 84 feet
C. 131 feet
D. 263 feet

G9B11 (C)
Answer: C. The approximate length for a ½ wave dipole antenna cut for 3.550 MHz is 131 feet.

What is the approximate length for a ¼ wave vertical antenna cut for 28.5 MHz?
A. 8 feet
B. 11 feet
C. 16 feet
D. 21 feet

G9B12 (A)
Answer: A. The approximate length for a ¼ wave vertical antenna cut for 28.5 MHz is 8 feet.

G9C – Directional Antennas

Which of the following would increase the bandwidth of a Yagi antenna?
A. Larger diameter elements
B. Closer element spacing
C. Loading coils in series with the element
D. Tapered-diameter elements

Copyright © Mometrix Media. You have been licensed one copy of this document for personal use only. Any other reproduction or redistribution is strictly prohibited. All rights reserved.

G9C01 (A)
Answer: A. Larger diameter elements would increase the bandwidth of a Yagi antenna. The Yagi antenna is the most popular form of amateur directional antenna. It has one driven element and additional elements.

What is the approximate length of the driven element of a Yagi antenna?
    A. 1/4 wavelength
    B. 1/2 wavelength
    C. 3/4 wavelength
    D. 1 wavelength

G9C02 (B)
Answer: B. The approximate length of the driven element of a Yagi antenna is ½ wavelength.

Which statement about a three-element, single-band Yagi antenna is true?
    A. The reflector is normally the shortest element
    B. The director is normally the shortest element
    C. The driven element is the longest element
    D. Low feed-point impedance increases bandwidth

G9C03 (B)
Answer: B. The director is normally the shortest parasitic element of a three-element, single-band Yagi antenna.

Which statement about a three-element; single-band Yagi antenna is true?
    A. The reflector is normally the longest parasitic element
    B. The director is normally the longest parasitic element
    C. The reflector is normally the shortest parasitic element
    D. All of the elements must be the same length

G9C04 (A)
Answer: A. The reflector is normally the longest parasitic element of a three-element, single-band Yagi antenna.

How does increasing boom length and adding directors affect a Yagi antenna?
    A. Gain increases
    B. Beamwidth increases
    C. Weight decreases
    D. Wind load decreases

G9C05 (A)
Answer: A. Increasing the boom length and adding directors increases the gain of a Yagi antenna.

What configuration of the loops of a two-element quad antenna must be used for the antenna to operate as a beam antenna, assuming one of the elements is used as a reflector?
    A. The driven element must be fed with a balun transformer
    B. There must be an open circuit in the driven element at the point opposite the feed point
    C. The reflector element must be approximately 5 percent shorter than the driven element
    D. The reflector element must be approximately 5 percent longer than the driven element

Copyright © Mometrix Media. You have been licensed one copy of this document for personal use only. Any other reproduction or redistribution is strictly prohibited. All rights reserved.

G9C06 (D)
Answer: D. The reflector element must be approximately 5 percent longer than the driven element to operate as a beam antenna.

What does "front-to-back ratio" mean in reference to a Yagi antenna?
    A. The number of directors versus the number of reflectors
    B. The relative position of the driven element with respect to the reflectors and directors
    C. The power radiated in the major radiation lobe compared to the power radiated in exactly the opposite direction
    D. The ratio of forward gain to dipole gain

G9C07 (C)
Answer: C. In reference to a Yagi antenna, the "front-to-back ratio" is the power radiated in the major radiation lobe compared to the power radiated in exactly the opposite direction.

What is meant by the "main lobe" of a directive antenna?
    A. The magnitude of the maximum vertical angle of radiation
    B. The point of maximum current in a radiating antenna element
    C. The maximum voltage standing wave point on a radiating element
    D. The direction of maximum radiated field strength from the antenna

G9C08 (D)
Answer: D. The "main lobe" of a directive antenna is the direction of maximum radiated field strength from the antenna.

How does the gain of two 3-element horizontally polarized Yagi antennas spaced vertically 1/2 wavelength apart typically compare to the gain of a single 3-element Yagi?
    A. Approximately 1.5 dB higher
    B. Approximately 3 dB higher
    C. Approximately 6 dB higher
    D. Approximately 9 dB higher

G9C09 (B)
Answer: B. The gain of two 3-element horizontally polarized Yagi antennas spaced vertically 1/2 wavelength apart is approximately 3 dB higher than the gain of a single 3-element Yagi.

Which of the following is a Yagi antenna design variable that could be adjusted to optimize forward gain, front-to-back ratio, or SWR bandwidth?
    A. The physical length of the boom
    B. The number of elements on the boom
    C. The spacing of each element along the boom
    D. All of these choices are correct

G9C10 (D)
Answer: D. The forward gain, front-to-back ratio, or SWR bandwidth of a Yagi antenna could be optimized by adjusting the physical length of the boom, the number of elements on the boom, or the spacing of each element along the boom.

Copyright © Mometrix Media. You have been licensed one copy of this document for personal use only. Any other reproduction or redistribution is strictly prohibited. All rights reserved.

What is the purpose of a gamma match used with Yagi antennas?
    A. To match the relatively low feed-point impedance to 50 ohms
    B. To match the relatively high feed-point impedance to 50 ohms
    C. To increase the front to back ratio
    D. To increase the main lobe gain

G9C11 (A)
Answer: A. The purpose of the gamma match used with Yagi antennas is to match the relatively low feed-point impedance to 50 ohms.

Which of the following is an advantage of using a gamma match for impedance matching of a Yagi antenna to 50 ohm coax feed line?
    A. It does not require that the elements be insulated from the boom
    B. It does not require any inductors or capacitors
    C. It is useful for matching multiband antennas
    D. All of these choices are correct

G9C12 (A)
Answer: A. One advantage of using a gamma match for impedance matching of a Yagi antenna to 50-ohm coax feed line is that it does not require that the elements be insulated from the boom.

Approximately how long is each side of the driven element of a quad antenna?
    A. 1/4 wavelength
    B. 1/2 wavelength
    C. 3/4 wavelength
    D. 1 wavelength

G9C13 (A)
Answer: A. Each side of a quad antenna driven element is approximately ¼ wavelength.

How does the forward gain of a two-element quad antenna compare to the forward gain of a three-element Yagi antenna?
    A. About 2/3 as much
    B. About the same
    C. About 1.5 times as much
    D. About twice as much

G9C14 (B)
Answer: B. The forward gain of a two-element quad antenna is about the same as the forward gain of a three-element Yagi antenna.

Approximately how long is each side of the reflector element of a quad antenna?
    A. Slightly less than 1/4 wavelength
    B. Slightly more than 1/4 wavelength
    C. Slightly less than 1/2 wavelength
    D. Slightly more than 1/2 wavelength

G9C15 (B)
Answer: B. Each side of a quad antenna reflector element is slightly more than ¼ wavelength.

Copyright © Mometrix Media. You have been licensed one copy of this document for personal use only. Any other reproduction or redistribution is strictly prohibited. All rights reserved.

How does the gain of a two-element delta-loop beam compare to the gain of a two-element quad antenna?

    A. 3 dB higher

    B. 3 dB lower

    C. 2.54 dB higher

    D. About the same

G9C16 (D)

Answer: D. The gain of a two-element delta-loop beam is about the same as the gain of a two-element quad antenna. A delta loop antenna is similar to the cubical quad antenna, except it has triangular elements.

Approximately how long is each leg of a symmetrical delta-loop antenna?

    A. 1/4 wavelength

    B. 1/3 wavelength

    C. 1/2 wavelength

    D. 2/3 wavelength

G9C17 (B)

Answer: B. Each leg of a symmetrical delta-loop antenna is approximately 1/3 wavelength.

What happens when the feed point of a quad antenna of any shape is moved from the midpoint of the top or bottom to the midpoint of either side?

    A. The polarization of the radiated signal changes from horizontal to vertical

    B. The polarization of the radiated signal changes from vertical to horizontal

    C. There is no change in polarization

    D. The radiated signal becomes circularly polarized

G9C18 (A)

Answer: A. When the feed point of a quad antenna is changed from the center of either horizontal wire to the center of either vertical wire, the polarization of the radiated signal changes from horizontal to vertical.

How does antenna gain stated in dBi compare to gain stated in dBd for the same antenna?

    A. dBi gain figures are 2.15 dB lower then dBd gain figures

    B. dBi gain figures are 2.15 dB higher than dBd gain figures

    C. dBi gain figures are the same as the square root of dBd gain figures multiplied by 2.15

    D. dBi gain figures are the reciprocal of dBd gain figures + 2.15 dB

G9C19 (B)

Answer: B. The antenna gain in dBi are 2.15 dB higher than the same antenna gain stated in dBd.

What is meant by the terms dBi and dBd when referring to antenna gain?

    A. dBi refers to an isotropic antenna, dBd refers to a dipole antenna

    B. dBi refers to an ionospheric reflecting antenna, dBd refers to a dissipative antenna

    C. dBi refers to an inverted-vee antenna, dBd refers to a downward reflecting antenna

    D. dBi refers to an isometric antenna, dBd refers to a discone antenna

G9C20 (A)

Answer: A. The term dBi refers to an isometric antenna, and the term dBd refers to a dipole antenna.

Copyright © Mometrix Media. You have been licensed one copy of this document for personal use only. Any other reproduction or redistribution is strictly prohibited. All rights reserved.

G9D – Specialized Antennas

What does the term NVIS mean as related to antennas?
    A. Nearly Vertical Inductance System
    B. Non-Varying Indicated SWR
    C. Non-Varying Impedance Smoothing
    D. Near Vertical Incidence sky-wave

G9D01 (D)
Answer: D. As related to antennas, the term "NVIS" means Near Vertical Incidence Sky wave. This technique is often used for amateur radio transmissions that must reach the space between groundwave and skywave distance. In an NVIS transmission, the waves are sent into the ionosphere and then refracted back down into a circular region.

Which of the following is an advantage of an NVIS antenna?
    A. Low vertical angle radiation for working stations out to ranges of several thousand kilometers
    B. High vertical angle radiation for working stations within a radius of a few hundred kilometers
    C. High forward gain
    D. All of these choices are correct

G9D02 (B)
Answer: B. One advantage of an NVIS antenna is high vertical angle radiation for working stations within a radius of a few hundred kilometers.

At what height above ground is an NVIS antenna typically installed?
    A. As close to one-half wave as possible
    B. As close to one wavelength as possible
    C. Height is not critical as long as it is significantly more than 1/2 wavelength
    D. Between 1/10 and 1/4 wavelength

G9D03 (D)
Answer: D. An NVIS antenna is typically installed between 1/10 and ¼ wavelength above the ground.

What is the primary purpose of antenna traps?
    A. To permit multiband operation
    B. To notch spurious frequencies
    C. To provide balanced feed-point impedance
    D. To prevent out of band operation

G9D04 (A)
Answer: A. The primary purpose of antenna traps is to permit multiband operation.

What is the advantage of vertical stacking of horizontally polarized Yagi antennas?
    A. It allows quick selection of vertical or horizontal polarization
    B. It allows simultaneous vertical and horizontal polarization
    C. It narrows the main lobe in azimuth
    D. It narrows the main lobe in elevation

G9D05 (D)
Answer: D. One advantage of vertically stacking horizontally polarized Yagi antennas is that it narrows the main lobe in elevation.

Copyright © Mometrix Media. You have been licensed one copy of this document for personal use only. Any other reproduction or redistribution is strictly prohibited. All rights reserved.

Which of the following is an advantage of a log periodic antenna?
    A. Wide bandwidth
    B. Higher gain per element than a Yagi antenna
    C. Harmonic suppression
    D. Polarization diversity

G9D06 (A)
Answer: A. Wide bandwidth is one advantage of a log periodic antenna. A log periodic antenna resembles a large TV antenna, with several angled elements. These antennas have several elements so that they can function over all of the bands within a particular range. For instance, a ham radio operator may use a log periodic antenna so that a single antenna can be used to cover the 20, 17, 15, 12, and 10 meter bands.

Which of the following describes a log periodic antenna?
    A. Length and spacing of the elements increases logarithmically from one end of the boom to the other
    B. Impedance varies periodically as a function of frequency
    C. Gain varies logarithmically as a function of frequency
    D. SWR varies periodically as a function of boom length

G9D07 (A)
Answer: A. In a log periodic antenna, the length and spacing of the elements increases logarithmically from one end of the boom to the other.

Why is a Beverage antenna not used for transmitting?
    A. Its impedance is too low for effective matching
    B. It has high losses compared to other types of antennas
    C. It has poor directivity
    D. All of these choices are correct

G9D08 (B)
Answer: B. A Beverage antenna is not used for transmitting because it has high losses compared to other types of antennas. However, the Beverage antenna is an inexpensive and effective receiving antenna. The Beverage antenna is extremely directional and large, so it cannot be rotated very easily.

Which of the following is an application for a Beverage antenna?
    A. Directional transmitting for low HF bands
    B. Directional receiving for low HF bands
    C. Portable direction finding at higher HF frequencies
    D. Portable direction finding at lower HF frequencies

G9D09 (B)
Answer: B. One application for a Beverage antenna is directional receiving for low HF bands.

Which of the following describes a Beverage antenna?
    A. A vertical antenna constructed from beverage cans
    B. A broad-band mobile antenna
    C. A helical antenna for space reception
    D. A very long and low directional receiving antenna

G9D10 (D)
Answer: D. A Beverage antenna is a very long and low directional receiving antenna.

Copyright © Mometrix Media. You have been licensed one copy of this document for personal use only. Any other reproduction or redistribution is strictly prohibited. All rights reserved.

Which of the following is a disadvantage of multiband antennas?
   A. They present low impedance on all design frequencies
   B. They must be used with an antenna tuner
   C. They must be fed with open wire line
   D. They have poor harmonic rejection

G9D11 (D)
Answer: D. One disadvantage of multiband antennas is that they have poor harmonic rejection.

G0 – Electrical and RF Safety

G0A – RF Safety Principles, Rules and Guidelines; Routine Station Evaluation

What is one way that RF energy can affect human body tissue?
   A. It heats body tissue
   B. It causes radiation poisoning
   C. It causes the blood count to reach a dangerously low level
   D. It cools body tissue

G0A01 (A)
Answer: A. RF energy can heat human body tissue.

Which of the following properties is important in estimating whether an RF signal exceeds the maximum permissible exposure (MPE)?
   A. Its duty cycle
   B. Its frequency
   C. Its power density
   D. All of these choices are correct

G0A02 (D)
Answer: D. The duty cycle, frequency, and power density are all important when estimating whether an RF signal exceeds the maximum permissible exposure (MPE).

How can you determine that your station complies with FCC RF exposure regulations?
   A. By calculation based on FCC OET Bulletin 65
   B. By calculation based on computer modeling
   C. By measurement of field strength using calibrated equipment
   D. All of these choices are correct

G0A03 (D) [97.13(c)(1)]
Answer: D. You can determine that your station complies with FCC RF exposure regulations by calculation based on FCC OET Bulletin 65; by calculation based on computer modeling; or by measurement of field strength using calibrated equipment.

What does "time averaging" mean in reference to RF radiation exposure?
   A. The average time of day when the exposure occurs
   B. The average time it takes RF radiation to have any long-term effect on the body
   C. The total time of the exposure
   D. The total RF exposure averaged over a certain time

Copyright © Mometrix Media. You have been licensed one copy of this document for personal use only. Any other reproduction or redistribution is strictly prohibited. All rights reserved.

G0A04 (D)
Answer: D. In reference to RF radiation exposure, "time averaging" means the total RF exposure averaged over a certain time.

What must you do if an evaluation of your station shows RF energy radiated from your station exceeds permissible limits?
   A. Take action to prevent human exposure to the excessive RF fields
   B. File an Environmental Impact Statement (EIS-97) with the FCC
   C. Secure written permission from your neighbors to operate above the controlled MPE limits
   D. All of these choices are correct

G0A05 (A)
Answer: A. If an evaluation shows that the RF energy radiated from your station exceeds permissible limits, you must take action to prevent human exposure to the excessive RF fields.

What precaution should be taken when installing a ground-mounted antenna?
   A. It should not be installed higher than you can reach
   B. It should not be installed in a wet area
   C. It should limited to 10 feet in height
   D. It should be installed so no one can be exposed to RF radiation in excess of maximum permissible limits

G0A06 (A)
Answer: A. A ground-mounted antenna should not be installed higher than you can reach.

What effect does transmitter duty cycle have when evaluating RF exposure?
   A. A lower transmitter duty cycle permits greater short-term exposure levels
   B. A higher transmitter duty cycle permits greater short-term exposure levels
   C. Low duty cycle transmitters are exempt from RF exposure evaluation requirements
   D. High duty cycle transmitters are exempt from RF exposure requirements

G0A07 (A)
Answer: A. When evaluating RF exposure, a lower transmitter duty cycle permits greater short-term exposure levels.

Which of the following steps must an amateur operator take to ensure compliance with RF safety regulations when transmitter power exceeds levels specified in part 97.13?
   A. Post a copy of FCC Part 97.13 in the station
   B. Post a copy of OET Bulletin 65 in the station
   C. Perform a routine RF exposure evaluation
   D. All of these choices are correct

G0A08 (C)
Answer: C. To ensure compliance with RF safety regulations when transmitter power exceeds specified in part 97.13, an amateur operator should perform a routine RF exposure evaluation.

What type of instrument can be used to accurately measure an RF field?
   A. A receiver with an S meter
   B. A calibrated field strength meter with a calibrated antenna
   C. An SWR meter with a peak-reading function
   D. An oscilloscope with a high-stability crystal marker generator

Copyright © Mometrix Media. You have been licensed one copy of this document for personal use only. Any other reproduction or redistribution is strictly prohibited. All rights reserved.

G0A09 (B)
Answer: B. A calibrated field-strength meter with a calibrated antenna can be used to accurately measure an RF field.

What is one thing that can be done if evaluation shows that a neighbor might receive more than the allowable limit of RF exposure from the main lobe of a directional antenna?
    A. Change to a non-polarized antenna with higher gain
    B. Post a warning sign that is clearly visible to the neighbor
    C. Use an antenna with a higher front-to-back ratio
    D. Take precautions to ensure that the antenna cannot be pointed in their direction

G0A10 (D)
Answer: D. If evaluation shows that a neighbor might receive more than the allowable limit of RF exposure from the main lobe of a directional antenna, the operator can take precautions to ensure that the antenna cannot be pointed in his or her direction.

What precaution should you take if you install an indoor transmitting antenna?
    A. Locate the antenna close to your operating position to minimize feed line radiation
    B. Position the antenna along the edge of a wall to reduce parasitic radiation
    C. Make sure that MPE limits are not exceeded in occupied areas
    D. Make sure the antenna is properly shielded

G0A11 (C)
Answer: C. If you install an indoor transmitting antenna, you should make sure that MPE limits are not exceeded in occupied areas.

What precaution should you take whenever you make adjustments or repairs to an antenna?
    A. Ensure that you and the antenna structure are grounded
    B. Turn off the transmitter and disconnect the feed line
    C. Wear a radiation badge
    D. All of these choices are correct

G0A12 (B)
Answer: B. Whenever you make adjustments or repairs to an antenna, turn off the transmitter and disconnect the feed line.

G0B – Safety in the Ham Shack; Electrical Shock and Treatment, Safety Grounding, Fusing, Interlocks, Wiring, Antenna and Tower Safety

Which wire or wires in a four-conductor line cord should be attached to fuses or circuit breakers in a device operated from a 240 VAC single phase source?
    A. Only the hot wires
    B. Only the neutral wire
    C. Only the ground wire
    D. All wires

G0B01 (A)
Answer: A. Only the hot wires in a four-conductor line cord should be attached to fuses or circuit breakers in a device operated from a 240-VAC single-phase source.

Copyright © Mometrix Media. You have been licensed one copy of this document for personal use only. Any other reproduction or redistribution is strictly prohibited. All rights reserved.

What is the minimum wire size that may be safely used for a circuit that draws up to 20 amperes of continuous current?
    A. AWG number 20
    B. AWG number 16
    C. AWG number 12
    D. AWG number 8

G0B02 (C)
Answer: C. The minimum wire size that may be safely used for a circuit that draws up to 20 amperes of continuous current is AWG number 12.

Which size of fuse or circuit breaker would be appropriate to use with a circuit that uses AWG number 14 wiring?
    A. 100 amperes
    B. 60 amperes
    C. 30 amperes
    D. 15 amperes

G0B03 (D)
Answer: D. A fuse or circuit breaker of 15 amperes would be appropriate to use with a circuit that uses AWG number 14 wiring.

Which of the following is a primary reason for not placing a gasoline-fueled generator inside an occupied area?
    A. Danger of carbon monoxide poisoning
    B. Danger of engine over torque
    C. Lack of oxygen for adequate combustion
    D. Lack of nitrogen for adequate combustion

G0B04 (A)
Answer: A. The danger of carbon monoxide poisoning is a primary reason for not placing a gasoline-fueled generator inside an occupied area.

Which of the following conditions will cause a Ground Fault Circuit Interrupter (GFCI) to disconnect the 120 or 240 Volt AC line power to a device?
    A. Current flowing from one or more of the hot wires to the neutral wire
    B. Current flowing from one or more of the hot wires directly to ground
    C. Over-voltage on the hot wire
    D. All of these choices are correct

G0B05 (B)
Answer: B. Current flowing from one or more of the hot wires directly to ground will cause a Ground Fault Circuit Interrupter (GFCI) to disconnect the 120 or 240 Volt AC line power to a device.

Why must the metal enclosure of every item of station equipment be grounded?
    A. It prevents blowing of fuses in case of an internal short circuit
    B. It prevents signal overload
    C. It ensures that the neutral wire is grounded
    D. It ensures that hazardous voltages cannot appear on the chassis

Copyright © Mometrix Media. You have been licensed one copy of this document for personal use only. Any other reproduction or redistribution is strictly prohibited. All rights reserved.

G0B06 (D)
Answer: D. The metal enclosure of every item of station equipment must be grounded because it ensures that hazardous voltages cannot appear on the chassis.

Which of these choices should be observed when climbing a tower using a safety belt or harness?
    A. Never lean back and rely on the belt alone to support your weight
    B. Confirm that the belt is rated for the weight of the climber and that it is within its allowable service life
    C. Ensure that all heavy tools are securely fastened to the belt D-ring
    D. All of these choices are correct

G0B07 (B)
Answer: B. When climbing on a tower using a safety belt or harness, always attach the belt safety hook to the belt D-ring with the hook opening away from the tower.

What should be done by any person preparing to climb a tower that supports electrically powered devices?
    A. Notify the electric company that a person will be working on the tower
    B. Make sure all circuits that supply power to the tower are locked out and tagged
    C. Unground the base of the tower
    D. All of these choices are correct

G0B08 (B)
Answer: B. Any person preparing to climb a tower that supports electrically powered devices should make sure all circuits that supply power to the tower are locked out and tagged.

Why should soldered joints not be used with the wires that connect the base of a tower to a system of ground rods?
    A. The resistance of solder is too high
    B. Solder flux will prevent a low conductivity connection
    C. Solder has too high a dielectric constant to provide adequate lightning protection
    D. A soldered joint will likely be destroyed by the heat of a lightning strike

G0B09 (D)
Answer: D. Soldered joints should not be used with the wires that connect the base of a tower to a system of ground rods because a soldered joint will likely be destroyed by the heat of a lightning strike.

Which of the following is a danger from lead-tin solder?
    A. Lead can contaminate food if hands are not washed carefully after handling the solder
    B. High voltages can cause lead-tin solder to disintegrate suddenly
    C. Tin in the solder can "cold flow" causing shorts in the circuit
    D. RF energy can convert the lead into a poisonous gas

G0B10 (A)
Answer: A. One danger of lead-tin solder is that the lead can contaminate food if hands are not washed carefully after handling.

Which of the following is good engineering practice for lightning protection grounds?
    A. They must be bonded to all buried water and gas lines
    B. Bends in ground wires must be made as close as possible to a right angle
    C. Lightning grounds must be connected to all ungrounded wiring
    D. They must be bonded together with all other grounds

Copyright © Mometrix Media. You have been licensed one copy of this document for personal use only. Any other reproduction or redistribution is strictly prohibited. All rights reserved.

G0B11 (D)
Answer: D. It is good engineering practice for lightning protection grounds to be bonded together with all other grounds.

What is the purpose of a transmitter power supply interlock?
    A. To prevent unauthorized access to a transmitter
    B. To guarantee that you cannot accidentally transmit out of band
    C. To ensure that dangerous voltages are removed if the cabinet is opened
    D. To shut off the transmitter if too much current is drawn

G0B12 (C)
Answer: C. The purpose of a transmitter power supply interlock is to ensure that dangerous voltages are removed if the cabinet is opened.

What must you do when powering your house from an emergency generator?
    A. Disconnect the incoming utility power feed
    B. Insure that the generator is not grounded
    C. Insure that all lightning grounds are disconnected
    D. All of these choices are correct

G0B13 (A)
Answer: A. When powering your house from an emergency generator, you must disconnect the incoming utility power feed.

Which of the following is covered by the National Electrical Code?
    A. Acceptable bandwidth limits
    B. Acceptable modulation limits
    C. Electrical safety inside the ham shack
    D. RF exposure limits of the human body

G0B14 (C)
Answer: C. Electrical safety inside the ham shack is covered by the National Electrical Code. The National Electrical Code is a set of guidelines that govern electrical safety, including the use of antennas.

Which of the following is true of an emergency generator installation?
    A. The generator should be located in a well ventilated area
    B. The generator should be insulated from ground
    C. Fuel should be stored near the generator for rapid refueling in case of an emergency
    D. All of these choices are correct

G0B15 (A)
Answer: A. In an emergency generator installation, the generator should be located in a well-ventilated area. This is also true when the ham radio rig is to be powered by an automobile battery.

Copyright © Mometrix Media. You have been licensed one copy of this document for personal use only. Any other reproduction or redistribution is strictly prohibited. All rights reserved.

General Class Practice Test 1

Practice Questions

1. On which of the following bands is a General Class license holder granted all amateur frequency privileges?
   a. 60, 20, 17, and 12 meters
   b. 160, 80, 40, and 10 meters
   c. 160, 60, 30, 17, 12, and 10 meters
   d. 160, 30, 17, 15, 12, and 10 meters

2. What is the maximum height above ground to which an antenna structure may be erected without requiring notification to the FAA and registration with the FCC, provided it is not at or near a public use airport?
   a. 50 feet
   b. 100 feet
   c. 200 feet
   d. 300 feet

3. What is the maximum transmitting power an amateur station may use on 10.140 MHz?
   a. 200 watts PEP output
   b. 1000 watts PEP output
   c. 1500 watts PEP output
   d. 2000 watts PEP output

4. Who may receive credit for the elements represented by an expired amateur radio license?
   a. Any person who can demonstrate that they once held an FCC issued General, Advanced, or Amateur Extra class license that was not revoked by the FCC
   b. Anyone who held an FCC issued amateur radio license that has been expired for not less than 5 years and not more than 15 years
   c. Any person who previously held an amateur license issued by another country, but only if that country has a current reciprocal licensing agreement with the FCC
   d. Only persons who once held an FCC issued Novice, Technician, or Technician Plus license

5. Which of the following would disqualify a third party from participating in stating a message over an amateur station?
   a. The third party's amateur license has been revoked and not reinstated
   b. The third party is not a U.S. citizen
   c. The third party is a licensed amateur
   d. The third party is speaking in a language other than English

6. Which sideband is most commonly used for voice communications on frequencies of 14 MHz or higher?
   a. Upper sideband
   b. Lower sideband
   c. Vestigial sideband
   d. Double sideband

Copyright © Mometrix Media. You have been licensed one copy of this document for personal use only. Any other reproduction or redistribution is strictly prohibited. All rights reserved.

7. Which of the following is true concerning access to frequencies in non-emergency situations?
    a. Nets always have priority
    b. QSO's in process always have priority
    c. Except during FCC declared emergencies, no one has priority access to frequencies
    d. Contest operations must always yield to non-contest use of frequencies

8. Which of the following describes full break-in telegraphy (QSK)?
    a. Breaking stations send the Morse code prosign BK
    b. Automatic keyers are used to send Morse code instead of hand keys
    c. An operator must activate a manual send/receive switch before and after every transmission
    d. Transmitting stations can receive between code characters and elements

9. What is the Amateur Auxiliary to the FCC?
    a. Amateur volunteers who are formally enlisted to monitor the airwaves for rules violations
    b. Amateur volunteers who conduct amateur licensing examinations
    c. Amateur volunteers who conduct frequency coordination for amateur VHF repeaters
    d. Amateur volunteers who use their station equipment to help civil defense organizations in times of emergency

10. Which mode is normally used when sending an RTTY signal via AFSK with an SSB transmitter?
    a. USB
    b. DSB
    c. CW
    d. LSB

11. What is the significance of the sunspot number with regard to HF propagation?
    a. Higher sunspot numbers generally indicate a greater probability of good propagation at higher frequencies
    b. Lower sunspot numbers generally indicate greater probability of sporadic E propagation
    c. A zero sunspot number indicate radio propagation is not possible on any band
    d. All of these choices are correct.

12. How might a sky-wave signal sound if it arrives at your receiver by both short path and long path propagation?
    a. Periodic fading approximately every 10 seconds
    b. Signal strength increased by 3 dB
    c. The signal might be cancelled causing severe attenuation
    d. A well-defined echo might be heard

13. Which ionospheric layer is closest to the surface of the Earth?
    a. The D layer
    b. The E layer
    c. The F1 layer
    d. The F2 layer

14. What is the purpose of the "notch filter" found on many HF transceivers?
    a. To restrict the transmitter voice bandwidth
    b. To reduce interference from carriers in the receiver passband
    c. To eliminate receiver interference from impulse noise sources
    d. To enhance the reception of a specific frequency on a crowded band

Copyright © Mometrix Media. You have been licensed one copy of this document for personal use only. Any other reproduction or redistribution is strictly prohibited. All rights reserved.

15. What item of test equipment contains horizontal and vertical channel amplifiers?
    a. An ohmmeter
    b. A signal generator
    c. An ammeter
    d. An oscilloscope

16. Which of the following might be useful in reducing RF interference to audio frequency devices?
    a. Bypass inductor
    b. Bypass capacitor
    c. Forward-biased diode
    d. Reverse-biased diode

17. What is the purpose of a speech processor as used in a modern transceiver?
    a. Increase the intelligibility of transmitted phone signals during poor conditions
    b. Increase transmitter bass response for more natural sounding SSB signals
    c. Prevent distortion of voice signals
    d. Decrease high-frequency voice output to prevent out of band operation

18. What is the purpose of a capacitance hat on a mobile antenna?
    a. To increase the power handling capacity of a whip antenna
    b. To allow automatic band changing
    c. To electrically lengthen a physically short antenna
    d. To allow remote tuning

19. What is impedance?
    a. The electric charge stored by a capacitor
    b. The inverse of resistance
    c. The opposition to the flow of current in an AC circuit
    d. The force of repulsion between two similar electric fields

20. What dB change represents a two-times increase or decrease in power?
    a. Approximately 2 dB
    b. Approximately 3 dB
    c. Approximately 6 dB
    d. Approximately 12 dB

21. What causes a voltage to appear across the secondary winding of a transformer when an AC voltage source is connected across its primary winding?
    a. Capacitive coupling
    b. Displacement current coupling
    c. Mutual inductance
    d. Mutual capacitance

22. What is the minimum allowable discharge voltage for maximum life of a standard 12 volt lead acid battery?
    a. 6 volts
    b. 8.5 volts
    c. 10.5 volts
    d. 12 volts

Copyright © Mometrix Media. You have been licensed one copy of this document for personal use only. Any other reproduction or redistribution is strictly prohibited. All rights reserved.

23. Which of the following is an analog integrated circuit?
 a. NAND Gate
 b. Microprocessor
 c. Frequency Counter
 d. Linear voltage regulator

24. What useful feature does a power supply bleeder resistor provide?
 a. It acts as a fuse for excess voltage
 b. It ensures that the filter capacitors are discharged when power is removed
 c. It removes shock hazards from the induction coils
 d. It eliminates ground loop current

25. Complex digital circuitry can often be replaced by what type of integrated circuit?
 a. Microcontroller
 b. Charge-coupled device
 c. Phase detector
 d. Window comparator

26. Which of the following is used to process signals from the balanced modulator and send them to the mixer in a single sideband phone transmitter?
 a. Carrier oscillator
 b. Filter
 c. IF amplifier
 d. RF amplifier

27. How is an FSK signal generated?
 a. By keying an FM transmitter with a sub-audible tone
 b. By changing an oscillator's frequency directly with a digital control signal
 c. By using a transceiver's computer data interface protocol to change frequencies
 d. By reconfiguring the CW keying input to act as a tone generator

28. What receiver stage combines a 14.250 MHz input signal with a 13.795 MHz oscillator signal to produce a 455 kHz intermediate frequency (IF) signal?
 a. Mixer
 b. BFO
 c. VFO
 d. Discriminator

29. Which of the following digital modes is designed to operate at extremely low signal strength on the HF bands?
 a. FSK441 and Hellschreiber
 b. JT9 and JT65
 c. Clover
 d. RTTY

30. Which of the following factors determine the characteristic impedance of a parallel conductor antenna feed line?
 a. The distance between the centers of the conductors and the radius of the conductors
 b. The distance between the centers of the conductors and the length of the line
 c. The radius of the conductors and the frequency of the signal
 d. The frequency of the signal and the length of the line

Copyright © Mometrix Media. You have been licensed one copy of this document for personal use only. Any other reproduction or redistribution is strictly prohibited. All rights reserved.

31. What is one disadvantage of a directly fed random-wire antenna?
    a. It must be longer than 1 wavelength
    b. You may experience RF burns when touching metal objects in your station
    c. It produces only vertically polarized radiation
    d. It is not effective on the higher HF bands

32. Which of the following would increase the bandwidth of a Yagi antenna?
    a. Larger diameter elements
    b. Closer element spacing
    c. Loading coils in series with the element
    d. Tapered-diameter elements

33. What does the term NVIS mean as related to antennas?
    a. Nearly Vertical Inductance System
    b. Non-Varying Indicated SWR
    c. Non-Varying Impedance Smoothing
    d. Near Vertical Incidence sky-wave

34. What is one way that RF energy can affect human body tissue?
    a. It heats body tissue
    b. It causes radiation poisoning
    c. It causes the blood count to reach a dangerously low level
    d. It cools body tissue

35. Which wire or wires in a four-conductor line cord should be attached to fuses or circuit breakers in a device operated from a 240 VAC single phase source?
    a. Only the hot wires
    b. Only the neutral wire
    c. Only the ground wire
    d. All wires

- 279 -

Copyright © Mometrix Media. You have been licensed one copy of this document for personal use only. Any other reproduction or redistribution is strictly prohibited. All rights reserved.

Answers and Explanations

1. C: A General Class license holder is granted all amateur frequency privileges on the 160, 60, 30, 17, 12, and 10 meter bands. On all other bands, the operations of General Class license holders are restricted according to FCC regulations.

2. C: The maximum height above ground to which an antenna structure may be erected without requiring notification to the FAA and registration with the FCC, provided it is not at or near a public use airport, is 200 feet. For most ham radio operators, this will not be a problem.

3. A: The maximum transmitting power an amateur station may use on 10.140 MHz is 200 watts PEP output.

4. A: As long as you can demonstrate that you have previously held a General, Advanced, or Amateur Extra class licenseIssued by the FCC and that it was not revoked, you may receive credit for all the elements represented

5. A: A third party would be disqualified from participating in stating a message over an amateur station if his or her amateur license had ever been revoked. Typically, third-party participation is the only way an unlicensed person can join in on amateur communications. The responsibility for ensuring that all communications follow the rules is held by the control operator.

6. A: The upper sideband is the most commonly used for voice communications on frequencies of 14 MHz or higher.

7. C: No one has priority access to frequencies, common courtesy should always be a guide.

8. D: In full break-in telegraphy (QSK), transmitting stations can receive between code characters and elements. This mode of operation is only possible when the radio rig has the ability to switch very quickly between transmit and receive. When using full break-in telegraphy, the operator has the ability to hear the activity on the band between code characters and elements. However, the VOX operation must be turned off in order for this mode to work properly.

9. A: The Amateur Auxiliary to the FCC is a group of amateur volunteers who are formally enlisted to monitor the airwaves for rules violations. This group is administered by the American Radio Relay League. In a typical scenario, a member of the Amateur Auxiliary will hear something suspicious and will send a postcard to the amateur station describing the infraction.

10. D: The LSB mode is normally used when sending an RTTY signal via AFSK with an SSB transmitter.

11. A: The sunspot number is a measure of solar activity based on counting sunspots and sunspot groups. This is a number used to indicate the general amount of sunspot activity. It is sometimes referred to as relative sunspot number, Zurich number, or Wolf number, It is calculated with the equation $R = k(10g + f)$, in which f is the number of distinct spots, g is the number of spot groups, and k is a factor based on the location and equipment of the observer.

12. D: If a sky-wave signal sound arrives at your receiver by both short path and long path propagation, a well-defined echo might be heard. This is due to the slight variation in the time it takes for each signal to reach the receiver.

13. A: The D layer of the ionosphere is closest to the surface of the Earth. The D layer extends from roughly 60 to 90 km above the surface of the Earth. Because of extensive electron collisions, high frequency radio waves are absorbed rather than reflected. That is, HF radio waves actually decrease in intensity as they pass through the D layer.

Copyright © Mometrix Media. You have been licensed one copy of this document for personal use only. Any other reproduction or redistribution is strictly prohibited. All rights reserved.

14. B: The purpose of the "notch filter" found on many HF transceivers is to reduce interference from carriers in the receiver passband. A notch filter is a form of band-stop filter in which the stopband is particularly narrow (that is, it has a high Q factor). A band-stop filter, also known as a band-rejection filter, minimizes the frequencies within a specific range. This sort of filter is effective for eliminating a single interfering tone.

15. D: An oscilloscope contains horizontal and vertical channel amplifiers. An oscilloscope enables the user to observe a continuous variation of signal voltages. In most cases, this variation is displayed as a graph in which electrical potential difference is on the y-axis and time is on the x-axis.

16. B: A bypass capacitor might be useful in reducing RF interference to audio-frequency devices. A bypass capacitor, otherwise known as a decoupling capacitor, is a device for separating the various parts of an electrical circuit. The result of using a bypass capacitor is that noise created in one part of the system can be removed from the other parts.

17. A: The purpose of a speech processor as used in a modern transceiver is to increase the intelligibility of transmitted phone signals during poor conditions. A speech processor is able to clean up voice communications so that they are easier to understand.

18. C: When referring to a mobile antenna, a "capacitance hat" is a device to electrically lengthen a physically short antenna. Capacitance hats may be composed of a metal disk, a wire basket, or a pyramid of wires. The capacitance hat regulates the flow of current through the antenna, so that more of the signal will propagate at the top. This has the effect of increasing the functional length of the antenna.

19. C: Impedance is the opposition to the flow of current in an AC circuit. Another way of describing impedance is as the ratio of the voltage to the current in an alternating current circuit. Whereas resistance has only magnitude, impedance has both magnitude and phase. The concept of impedance is necessary for alternating current because they have the electrostatic storage of charge induced by voltages between conductors, or capacitance, and the induction of voltages in conductors that is self induced by the magnetic fields of the currents, known as inductance.

20. B: A two-times increase or decrease in power results in a change of approximately 3 dB. The amount of decibel change produced by a change in power is a proportional relationship.

21. C: Mutual inductance causes a voltage to appear across the secondary winding of a transformer when an AC voltage source is connected across its primary winding. Mutual inductance exists when the current change in one inductor initiates a voltage in some other inductor.

22. C: The minimum allowable discharge voltage for maximum life of a standard 12-volt lead acid battery is 10.5 volts.

23. D: A linear voltage regulator is an analog integrated circuit. This device keeps the voltage of the circuit consistent. Any difference between the input and the regulated voltage is discharged by the regulator as heat. The regulator also has a voltage divider network that maintains a consistent output voltage.

24. B: The power-supply bleeder resistor discharges the filter capacitors.

25. A: Complex digital circuitry can often be replaced by a microcontroller. A microcontroller contains all of the elements required for a basic computer: clock, I/O control unit, non-volatile memory (ROM), volatile memory (RAM), and a processor.

26. B: A filter is used to process signals from the balanced modulator and send them to the mixer in a single-sideband phone transmitter. Filters are circuits that allow some signals to pass through but greatly reduce the strength of other signals.

27. B: An FSK signal is generated by changing an oscillator's frequency directly with a digital control signal.

Copyright © Mometrix Media. You have been licensed one copy of this document for personal use only. Any other reproduction or redistribution is strictly prohibited. All rights reserved.

28. A: The mixer combines a 14.250 MHz input signal with a 13.795 MHz oscillator signal to produce a 455 kHz intermediate frequency (IF) signal.

29. B: JT9 and JT65 are designed to operate at extremely low signal strength on the HF bands.

30. A: The distance between the centers of the conductors and the radius of the conductors determines the characteristic impedance of a parallel conductor antenna feed line.

31. B: One disadvantage of a directly fed random-wire antenna is that you may experience RF burns when touching metal objects in your station.

32. A: Larger diameter elements would increase the bandwidth of a Yagi antenna. The Yagi antenna is the most popular form of amateur directional antenna. It has one driven element and additional elements.

33. D: As related to antennas, the term "NVIS" means Near Vertical Incidence Sky wave. This technique is often used for amateur radio transmissions that must reach the space between groundwave and skywave distance. In an NVIS transmission, the waves are sent into the ionosphere and then refracted back down into a circular region.

34. A: RF energy can heat human body tissue.

35. A: Only the hot wires in a four-conductor line cord should be attached to fuses or circuit breakers in a device operated from a 240-VAC single-phase source.

Copyright © Mometrix Media. You have been licensed one copy of this document for personal use only. Any other reproduction or redistribution is strictly prohibited. All rights reserved.

General Class Practice Test 2

Practice Questions

1. On which of the following bands is phone operation prohibited?
    a. 160 meters
    b. 30 meters
    c. 17 meters
    d. 12 meters

2. With which of the following conditions must beacon stations comply?
    a. A beacon station may not use automatic control
    b. The frequency must be coordinated with the National Beacon Organization
    c. The frequency must be posted on the Internet or published in a national periodical
    d. There must be no more than one beacon signal in the same band from a single location

3. What is the maximum transmitting power an amateur station may use on the 12-meter band?
    a. 50 watts PEP output
    b. 200 watts PEP output
    c. 1500 watts PEP output
    d. An effective radiated power equivalent to 100 watts from a half-wave dipole

4. What license examinations may you administer when you are an accredited VE holding a General Class operator license?
    a. General and Technician
    b. General only
    c. Technician only
    d. Extra, General and Technician

5. When may a 10-meter repeater retransmit the 2-meter signal from a station having a Technician Class control operator?
    a. Under no circumstances
    b. Only if the station on 10 meters is operating under a Special Temporary Authorization allowing such retransmission
    c. Only during an FCC declared general state of communications emergency
    d. Only if the 10 meter repeater control operator holds at least a General Class license

6. Which of the following modes is most commonly used for voice communications on the 160-meter, 75-meter, and 40-meter bands?
    a. Upper sideband
    b. Lower sideband
    c. Vestigial sideband
    d. Double sideband

7. What is the first thing you should do if you are communicating with another amateur station and hear a station in distress break in?
    a. Continue your communication because you were on frequency first
    b. Acknowledge the station in distress and determine what assistance may be needed
    c. Change to a different frequency
    d. Immediately cease all transmissions

- 283 -

Copyright © Mometrix Media. You have been licensed one copy of this document for personal use only. Any other reproduction or redistribution is strictly prohibited. All rights reserved.

8. What should you do if a CW station sends "QRS"?
   a. Send slower
   b. Change frequency
   c. Increase your power
   d. Repeat everything twice

9. Which of the following are objectives of the Amateur Auxiliary?
   a. To conduct efficient and orderly amateur licensing examinations
   b. To encourage self-regulation and compliance with the rules by radio amateur operators
   c. To coordinate repeaters for efficient and orderly spectrum usage
   d. To provide emergency and public safety communications

10. How can a PACTOR modem or controller be used to determine if the channel is in use by other PACTOR stations?
   a. Unplug the data connector temporarily and see if the channel-busy indication is turned off
   b. Put the modem or controller in a mode which allows monitoring communications without a connection
   c. Transmit UI packets several times and wait to see if there is a response from another PACTOR station
   d. Send the message: "Is this frequency in use?"

11. What effect does a Sudden Ionospheric Disturbance have on the daytime ionospheric propagation of HF radio waves?
   a. It enhances propagation on all HF frequencies
   b. It disrupts signals on lower frequencies more than those on higher frequencies
   c. It disrupts communications via satellite more than direct communications
   d. None, because only areas on the night side of the Earth are affected

12. Which of the following is a good indicator of the possibility of sky-wave propagation on the 6-meter band?
   a. Short skip sky-wave propagation on the 10-meter band
   b. Long skip sky-wave propagation on the 10-meter band
   c. Severe attenuation of signals on the 10-meter band
   d. Long delayed echoes on the 10-meter band

13. Where on the Earth do ionospheric layers reach their maximum height?
   a. Where the Sun is overhead
   b. Where the Sun is on the opposite side of the Earth
   c. Where the Sun is rising
   d. Where the Sun has just set

14. What is one advantage of selecting the opposite or "reverse" sideband when receiving CW signals on a typical HF transceiver?
   a. Interference from impulse noise will be eliminated
   b. More stations can be accommodated within a given signal passband
   c. It may be possible to reduce or eliminate interference from other signals
   d. Accidental out of band operation can be prevented

Copyright © Mometrix Media. You have been licensed one copy of this document for personal use only. Any other reproduction or redistribution is strictly prohibited. All rights reserved.

15. Which of the following is an advantage of an oscilloscope versus a digital voltmeter?
    a. An oscilloscope uses less power
    b. Complex impedances can be easily measured
    c. Input impedance is much lower
    d. Complex waveforms can be measured

16. Which of the following could be a cause of interference covering a wide range of frequencies?
    a. Not using a balun or line isolator to feed balanced antennas
    b. Lack of rectification of the transmitter's signal in power conductors
    c. Arcing at a poor electrical connection
    d. The use of horizontal rather than vertical antennas

17. Which of the following describes how a speech processor affects a transmitted single sideband phone signal?
    a. It increases peak power
    b. It increases average power
    c. It reduces harmonic distortion
    d. It reduces intermodulation distortion

18. What is the purpose of a corona ball on a HF mobile antenna?
    a. To narrow the operating bandwidth of the antenna
    b. To increase the "Q" of the antenna
    c. To reduce the chance of damage if the antenna should strike an object
    d. To reduce high voltage discharge from the tip of the antenna

19. What is reactance?
    a. Opposition to the flow of direct current caused by resistance
    b. Opposition to the flow of alternating current caused by capacitance or inductance
    c. A property of ideal resistors in AC circuits
    d. A large spark produced at switch contacts when an inductor is de-energized

20. How does the total current relate to the individual currents in each branch of a parallel circuit?
    a. It equals the average of each branch current
    b. It decreases as more parallel branches are added to the circuit
    c. It equals the sum of the currents through each branch
    d. It is the sum of the reciprocal of each individual voltage drop

21. What happens if you reverse the primary and secondary windings of a 4:1 voltage step down transformer?
    a. The secondary voltage becomes 4 times the primary voltage
    b. The transformer no longer functions as it is a unidirectional device
    c. Additional resistance must be added in series with the primary to prevent overload
    d. Additional resistance must be added in parallel with the secondary to prevent overload

22. What is an advantage of the low internal resistance of nickel-cadmium batteries?
    a. Long life
    b. High discharge current
    c. High voltage
    d. Rapid recharge

Copyright © Mometrix Media. You have been licensed one copy of this document for personal use only. Any other reproduction or redistribution is strictly prohibited. All rights reserved.

23. What is meant by the term MMIC?
    a. Multi Megabyte Integrated Circuit
    b. Monolithic Microwave Integrated Circuit
    c. Military-specification Manufactured Integrated Circuit
    d. Mode Modulated Integrated Circuit

24. Which of the following components are used in a power supply filter network?
    a. Diodes
    b. Transformers and transducers
    c. Quartz crystals
    d. Capacitors and inductors

25. Which of the following is an advantage of using the binary system when processing digital signals?
    a. Binary "ones" and "zeros" are easy to represent with an "on" or "off" state
    b. The binary number system is most accurate
    c. Binary numbers are more compatible with analog circuitry
    d. All of these choices are correct

26. Which circuit is used to combine signals from the carrier oscillator and speech amplifier and send the result to the filter in a typical single-sideband phone transmitter?
    a. Discriminator
    b. Detector
    c. IF amplifier
    d. Balanced modulator

27. What is the name of the process that changes the phase angle of an RF wave to convey information?
    a. Phase convolution
    b. Phase modulation
    c. Angle convolution
    d. Radian inversion

28. If a receiver mixes a 13.800 MHz VFO with a 14.255 MHz received signal to produce a 455 kHz intermediate frequency (IF) signal, what type of interference will a 13.345 MHz signal produce in the receiver?
    a. Quadrature noise
    b. Image response
    c. Mixer interference
    d. Intermediate interference

29. How many data bits are sent in a single PSK31 character?
    a. The number varies
    b. 5
    c. 7
    d. 8

30. What are the typical characteristic impedances of coaxial cables used for antenna feed lines at amateur stations?
    a. 25 and 30 ohms
    b. 50 and 75 ohms
    c. 80 and 100 ohms
    d. 500 and 750 ohms

Copyright © Mometrix Media. You have been licensed one copy of this document for personal use only. Any other reproduction or redistribution is strictly prohibited. All rights reserved.

31. Which of the following is a common way to adjust the feed point impedance of a quarter wave ground plane vertical antenna to be approximately 50 ohms?
    a. Slope the radials upward
    b. Slope the radials downward
    c. Lengthen the radials
    d. Shorten the radials

32. What is the approximate length of the driven element of a Yagi antenna?
    a. 1/4 wavelength
    b. 1/2 wavelength
    c. 3/4 wavelength
    d. 1 wavelength

33. Which of the following is an advantage of an NVIS antenna?
    a. Low vertical angle radiation for working stations out to ranges of several thousand kilometers
    b. High vertical angle radiation for working stations within a radius of a few hundred kilometers
    c. High forward gain
    d. All of these choices are correct

34. Which of the following properties is important in estimating whether an RF signal exceeds the maximum permissible exposure (MPE)?
    a. Its duty cycle
    b. Its frequency
    c. Its power density
    d. All of these choices are correct

35. What is the minimum wire size that may be safely used for a circuit that draws up to 20 amperes of continuous current?
    a. AWG number 20
    b. AWG number 16
    c. AWG number 12
    d. AWG number 8

Copyright © Mometrix Media. You have been licensed one copy of this document for personal use only. Any other reproduction or redistribution is strictly prohibited. All rights reserved.

Answers and Explanations

1. B: Phone operation is prohibited on the 30 meter band. In ham radio, phone operation is the generic term for voice communication. There are a number of different ways to communicate by voice using ham radio technology. However, this type of communication is considered to be too cumbersome for the 30 meter band.

2. D: There must be no more than one beacon signal in the same band from a single location. The use of multiple beacon signals may confuse those whom the signals were intended to inform.

3. C: The maximum transmitting power an amateur station may use on the 12 meter band is 1500 watts PEP output.

4. C: When you are an accredited VE holding a General Class operator license, you may only administer the Technician license exam. Volunteer Examiners are only allowed to proctor exams at a level below their own level. Any licensed amateur may become a Volunteer Examiner by completing the qualification process administered by the VEC.

5. D: A 10 meter repeater may retransmit the 2 meter signal from a station having a Technican Class control operator only if the 10 meter repeater control operator holds at least a General Class license.

6. B: The lower sideband is most commonly used for voice communications on the 160, 75, and 40 meter bands. It is also the preferred operating mode on the 80 meter amateur bands. For voice communication on the HF bands, ham operators are most likely to use single sideband. Signals are designated as upper or lower sideband depending on whether they are above or below the carrier frequency displayed on the radio. According to tradition, voice operation on HF bands above 9 MHz is on the upper sideband, and voice operation below 9 MHz occurs on the lower sideband. The four basic steps for tuning in an SSB signal are as follows: set your rig to receive LSB or USB signals; select the widest SSB filter; adjust the tuning dial until the SSB frequency can be heard; and adjust the tuning until the voice sounds normal.

7. B: If you are communicating with another amateur station and hear a station in distress break in, the first thing you should do is acknowledge the station in distress and determine what assistance may be needed. You should note the time and frequency of the call as soon as possible. Specifically, it is important to note the address, or, if an address cannot be obtained, the latitude and longitude of the emergency. You should also try to learn the nature of the problem and the sort of assistance required. After obtaining this information, you should ask the station in distress to remain on frequency as you contact the appropriate emergency services.

8. A: If a CW station sends "QRS," you should send slower. The Q-signal QRS, when issued as a question, means "Shall I send more slowly?" When it is issued as a response, it means "Please send more slowly." It is often accompanied by the requested rate in words per minute.

9. B: The objectives of the Amateur Auxiliary are to encourage amateur self regulation and compliance with the rules. The FCC recognizes that it cannot effectively patrol the airwaves at all times, and so it has attempted to establish a culture of self-policing within the amateur radio community. The Amateur Auxiliary is a major part of this effort.

10. B: A PACTOR modem or controller can be used to determine if a channel is in use by other PACTOR stations by putting the modem or controller in a mode which allows monitoring communications without a connection.

Copyright © Mometrix Media. You have been licensed one copy of this document for personal use only. Any other reproduction or redistribution is strictly prohibited. All rights reserved.

11. B: A Sudden Ionospheric Disturbance disrupts signals on lower frequencies more than those on higher frequencies. A sudden ionospheric disturbance is a complicated set of rapid fluctuations in the ionosphere, typically occurring after a period of solar flares. This phenomenon, also known as the Dellinger effect or the Mogel-Dellinger effect, is observable as a rapid increase in the radio-wave absorption, particularly in the lower HF and upper MF ranges. Sudden ionospheric disturbance can be very disruptive to telecommunications systems, including ham radio. The effects are most dire in the regions around the equator, and may last from a few minutes to several hours.

12. A: Short skip sky-wave propagation on the 10-meter band is a good indicator of the possibility of sky-wave propagation on the 6-meter band.

13. A: On the Earth, ionospheric layers reach their maximum height where the Sun is overhead.

14. C: One advantage of selecting the opposite or "reverse" sideband when receiving CW signals on a typical HF transceiver is that it may be possible to reduce or eliminate interference from other signals.

15. D: One advantage of an oscilloscope versus a digital voltmeter is that complex waveforms can be measured. A digital voltmeter is an effective tool for measuring electrical potential difference between two distinct points in an electric circuit; it employs an analog-to-digital converter to create a numerical reading of voltage.

16. C: One cause of interference over a wide range of frequencies could be arcing at a poor electrical connection. Arcing is the flow of current through media that normally do not conduct, as for instance air.

17. B: A speech processor increases the average power of a transmitted single sideband phone signal. This is one of the ways in which it improves the general clarity and intelligibility of the voice signal.

18. D: The purpose of a "corona ball" on an HF mobile antenna is to reduce high voltage discharge from the tip of the antenna. A corona ball is a spherical piece of metal placed at the end of the antenna rod.

19. B: Reactance is opposition to the flow of alternating current caused by capacitance or inductance. The amount of reactance in a circuit element depends on the inductance or capacitance of the element. If there is an established electric field, it will work against the voltage change on the element. At the same time, a magnetic field will have a natural resistance to a change in current. A perfect resistor will have a reactance of zero, while perfect inductors and capacitors will be entirely composed of reactance. This is because an ideal inductor will have zero resistance, and an ideal capacitor will have infinite resistance.

20. C: The total current equals the sum of the individual currents in each branch of a parallel circuit.

21. A: If you reverse the primary and secondary windings of a 4:1 voltage step down transformer, then the secondary voltage becomes 4 times the primary voltage.

22. B: One advantage of the low internal resistance of nickel-cadmium batteries is a high discharge current. Batteries convert chemical energy into electrical energy.

23. B: The term MMIC means Monolithic Microwave Integrated Circuit. This is a type of integrated circuit that is capable of operating at microwave frequencies. The most common uses for these devices are high-frequency switching, low-noise amplification, power amplification, and microwave mixing.

24. D: Capacitors and inductors are used in a power-supply filter network.

Copyright © Mometrix Media. You have been licensed one copy of this document for personal use only. Any other reproduction or redistribution is strictly prohibited. All rights reserved.

25. A: One advantage of using the binary system when processing digital signals is that binary "ones" and "zeros" are easy to represent with an "on" or "off" state.

26. D: A balanced modulator is used to combine signals from the carrier oscillator and speech amplifier and send the result to the filter in a typical single-sideband phone transmitter.

27. B: Phase modulation is the process that changes the phase angle of an RF wave to convey information.

28. B: If a receiver mixes a 13.800 MHz VFO with a 14.255 MHz received signal to produce a 455 kHz intermediate frequency (IF) signal, a 13.345 MHz signal will produce image response interference in the receiver.

29. A: The number of data bits sent in a single PSK31 character varies. Phase shift keying is a highly sophisticated method for digital transmission in the HF spectrum. PSK31 is named after the tiny 31.25 Hz used by its signal. The coding system for characters is called Varicode: much like Morse code, it employs a different number of bits for different characters. The signal is a continuous tone, and the characters are indicated by shifts in the timing relationship with a reference signal.

30. B: The typical characteristic impedances of coaxial cables used for antenna feed lines at amateur stations is between 50 and 75 ohms.

31. B: A common way to adjust the feed point impedance of a quarter wave ground plane vertical antenna is to slope the radials downward.

32. B: The approximate length of the driven element of a Yagi antenna is ½ wavelength.

33. B: One advantage of an NVIS antenna is high vertical angle radiation for working stations within a radius of a few hundred kilometers.

34. D: The duty cycle, frequency, and power density are all important when estimating whether an RF signal exceeds the maximum permissible exposure (MPE).

35. C: The minimum wire size that may be safely used for a circuit that draws up to 20 amperes of continuous current is AWG number 12.

Copyright © Mometrix Media. You have been licensed one copy of this document for personal use only. Any other reproduction or redistribution is strictly prohibited. All rights reserved.

General Class Practice Test 3

Practice Questions

1. On which of the following bands is image transmission prohibited?
   a. 160 meters
   b. 30 meters
   c. 20 meters
   d. 12 meters

2. Which of the following is a purpose of a beacon station as identified in the FCC Rules?
   a. Observation of propagation and reception
   b. Automatic identification of repeaters
   c. Transmission of bulletins of general interest to Amateur Radio licensees
   d. Identifying net frequencies

3. What is the maximum bandwidth permitted by FCC rules for Amateur Radio stations when transmitting on USB frequencies in the 60-meter band?
   a. 2.8 kHz
   b. 5.6 kHz
   c. 1.8 kHz
   d. 3 kHz

4. On which of the following band segments may you operate if you are a Technician Class operator and have a CSCE for General Class privileges?
   a. Only the Technician band segments until your upgrade is posted on the FCC database
   b. Only on the Technician band segments until your license arrives in the mail
   c. On any General or Technician Class band segment
   d. On any General or Technician Class band segment except 30 and 60 meters

5. What is required to conduct communications with a digital station operating under automatic control outside the automatic control band segments?
   a. The station initiating the contact must be under local or remote control
   b. The interrogating transmission must be made by another automatically controlled station
   c. No third party traffic maybe be transmitted
   d. The control operator of the interrogating station must hold an Extra Class license

6. Which of the following is most commonly used for SSB voice communications in the VHF and UHF bands?
   a. Upper sideband
   b. Lower sideband
   c. Vestigial sideband
   d. Double sideband

7. If propagation changes during your contact and you notice increasing interference from other activity on the same frequency, what should you do?
   a. Tell the interfering stations to change frequency
   b. Report the interference to your local Amateur Auxiliary Coordinator
   c. As a common courtesy, move your contact to another frequency
   d. Increase power to overcome interference

Copyright © Mometrix Media. You have been licensed one copy of this document for personal use only. Any other reproduction or redistribution is strictly prohibited. All rights reserved.

8. What does it mean when a CW operator sends "KN" at the end of a transmission?
   a. Listening for novice stations
   b. Operating full break-in
   c. Listening only for a specific station or stations
   d. Closing station now

9. What skills learned during hidden transmitter hunts are of help to the Amateur Auxiliary?
   a. Identification of out of band operation
   b. Direction finding used to locate stations violating FCC Rules
   c. Identification of different call signs
   d. Hunters have an opportunity to transmit on non-amateur frequencies

10. What symptoms may result from other signals interfering with a PACTOR or WINMOR transmission?
    a. Frequent retries or timeouts
    b. Long pauses in message transmission
    c. Failure to establish a connection between stations
    d. All of these choices are correct

11. Approximately how long does it take the increased ultraviolet and X-ray radiation from solar flares to affect radio-wave propagation on the Earth?
    a. 28 days
    b. 1 to 2 hours
    c. 8 minutes
    d. 20 to 40 hours

12. Which of the following applies when selecting a frequency for lowest attenuation when transmitting on HF?
    a. Select a frequency just below the MUF
    b. Select a frequency just above the LUF
    c. Select a frequency just below the critical frequency
    d. Select a frequency just above the critical frequency

13. Why is the F2 region mainly responsible for the longest distance radio wave propagation?
    a. Because it is the densest ionospheric layer
    b. Because it does not absorb radio waves as much as other ionospheric regions
    c. Because it is the highest ionospheric region
    d. All of these choices are correct

14. What is normally meant by operating a transceiver in "split" mode?
    a. The radio is operating at half power
    b. The transceiver is operating from an external power source
    c. The transceiver is set to different transmit and receive frequencies
    d. The transmitter is emitting a SSB signal, as opposed to DSB operation

15. Which of the following is the best instrument to use when checking the keying waveform of a CW transmitter?
    a. An oscilloscope
    b. A field-strength meter
    c. A sidetone monitor
    d. A wavemeter

Copyright © Mometrix Media. You have been licensed one copy of this document for personal use only. Any other reproduction or redistribution is strictly prohibited. All rights reserved.

16. What sound is heard from an audio device or telephone if there is interference from a nearby single-sideband phone transmitter?
    a. A steady hum whenever the transmitter is on the air
    b. On-and-off humming or clicking
    c. Distorted speech
    d. Clearly audible speech

17. Which of the following can be the result of an incorrectly adjusted speech processor?
    a. Distorted speech
    b. Splatter
    c. Excessive background pickup
    d. All of these choices are correct

18. Which of the following direct, fused power connections would be the best for a 100 watt HF mobile installation?
    a. To the battery using heavy gauge wire
    b. To the alternator or generator using heavy gauge wire
    c. To the battery using resistor wire
    d. To the alternator or generator using resistor wire

19. Which of the following causes opposition to the flow of alternating current in an inductor?
    a. Conductance
    b. Reluctance
    c. Admittance
    d. Reactance

20. How many watts of electrical power are used if 400 VDC is supplied to an 800 ohm load?
    a. 0.5 watts
    b. 200 watts
    c. 400 watts
    d. 3200 watts

21. Which of the following components should be added to an existing resistor to increase the resistance?
    a. A resistor in parallel
    b. A resistor in series
    c. A capacitor in series
    d. A capacitor in parallel

22. What is the approximate junction threshold voltage of a germanium diode?
    a. 0.1 volt
    b. 0.3 volts
    c. 0.7 volts
    d. 1.0 volts

23. Which of the following is an advantage of CMOS integrated circuits compared to TTL integrated circuits?
    a. Low power consumption
    b. High power handling capability
    c. Better suited for RF amplification
    d. Better suited for power supply regulation

Copyright © Mometrix Media. You have been licensed one copy of this document for personal use only. Any other reproduction or redistribution is strictly prohibited. All rights reserved.

24. What is the peak-inverse-voltage across the rectifiers in a full-wave bridge power supply?
    a. One-quarter the normal output voltage of the power supply
    b. Half the normal output voltage of the power supply
    c. Double the normal peak output voltage of the power supply
    d. Equal to the normal peak output voltage of the power supply

25. Which of the following describes the function of a two input AND gate?
    a. Output is high when either or both inputs are low
    b. Output is high only when both inputs are high
    c. Output is low when either or both inputs are high
    d. Output is low only when both inputs are high

26. What circuit is used to process signals from the RF amplifier and local oscillator and send the result to the IF filter in a superheterodyne receiver?
    a. Balanced modulator
    b. IF amplifier
    c. Mixer
    d. Detector

27. What is the name of the process which changes the instantaneous frequency of an RF wave to convey information?
    a. Frequency convolution
    b. Frequency transformation
    c. Frequency conversion
    d. Frequency modulation

28. What is another term for the mixing of two RF signals?
    a. Heterodyning
    b. Synthesizing
    c. Cancellation
    d. Phase inverting

29. What part of a data packet contains the routing and handling information?
    a. Directory
    b. Preamble
    c. Header
    d. Footer

30. What is the characteristic impedance of flat ribbon TV type twinlead?
    a. 50 ohms
    b. 75 ohms
    c. 100 ohms
    d. 300 ohms

31. What happens to the feed point impedance of a ground plane antenna when its radials are changed from horizontal to sloping downward?
    a. It decreases
    b. It increases
    c. It stays the same
    d. It reaches a maximum at an angle of 45 degrees

Copyright © Mometrix Media. You have been licensed one copy of this document for personal use only. Any other reproduction or redistribution is strictly prohibited. All rights reserved.

32. Which statement about a three-element, single-band Yagi antenna is true?
   a. The reflector is normally the shortest element
   b. The director is normally the shortest element
   c. The driven element is the longest element
   d. Low feed-point impedance increases bandwidth

33. At what height above ground is an NVIS antenna typically installed?
   a. As close to one-half wave as possible
   b. As close to one wavelength as possible
   c. Height is not critical as long as it is significantly more than 1/2 wavelength
   d. Between 1/10 and 1/4 wavelength

34. How can you determine that your station complies with FCC RF exposure regulations?
   a. By calculation based on FCC OET Bulletin 65
   b. By calculation based on computer modeling
   c. By measurement of field strength using calibrated equipment
   d. All of these choices are correct

35. Which size of fuse or circuit breaker would be appropriate to use with a circuit that uses AWG number 14 wiring?
   a. 100 amperes
   b. 60 amperes
   c. 30 amperes
   d. 15 amperes

Copyright © Mometrix Media. You have been licensed one copy of this document for personal use only. Any other reproduction or redistribution is strictly prohibited. All rights reserved.

Answers and Explanations

1. B: Image transmission is prohibited on the 30-meter band. This is because the transmission of images requires an amount of traffic that would obstruct the band for other users.

2. A: The FCC Rules state that one purpose of a beacon station is the observation of propagation and reception. Beacon stations communicate only for experimental purposes, most often to observe propagation and reception. Ham radio operators often use these stations as reference points or to calibrate their equipment.

3. A: The maximum bandwidth permitted by FCC rules for Amateur Radio stations when transmitting on USB frequencies in the 60-meter band is 2.8 kHz.

4. C: You may operate on any General or Technician Class band segment if you are a Technician Class operator and have a CSCE for General Class privileges.

5. A: To communicate with a digital station operating under automatic control outside the automatic control band segments, the station initiating contact must be under local or remote control.

6. A: The upper sideband is most commonly used for SSB voice communications in the VHF and UHF bands.

7. C: If propagation changes during your contact and you notice increasing interference from another activity on the same frequency, you should move your contact to another frequency as a common courtesy. There is no rule for which party should move, so the best thing to do is exercise discretion and courtesy to other users.

8. C: When a CW operator sends "KN" at the end of a transmission, it means that the operator is listening only for a specific station or stations.

9. B: During "hidden transmitter hunts," the Amateur Auxiliary members will learn the skills of direction finding used to locate stations violating FCC Rules. As the name suggests, a hidden transmitter hunt is a game in which participants try to identify the point of origin for a particular radio signal.

10. D: These are all possible symptoms of other signals interfering with a PACTOR or WINMOR transmission.

11. C: It takes the increased ultraviolet and X-ray radiation from solar flares approximately eight minutes to affect radio-wave propagation on the Earth. A solar flare is a rapid increase in the brightness of a particular area of the sun, representing a release of up to one-sixth of the sun's normal energy output. The solar flare is typically followed by a coronal mass ejection.

12. A: When selecting a frequency for lowest attenuation when transmitting on HF, select a frequency just below the MUF.

13. C: The F2 region is mainly responsible for the longest distance radio wave propagation because it is the highest ionospheric region. It lies approximately 220 to 800 km above the surface of the Earth. It is the primary reflecting layer for HF communications both at night and during the day.

14. C: When a transceiver is operated in split mode, this generally means that it is set to different transmit and receive frequencies. This mode is often used when a large number of stations are trying to contact one station. An observer can tell that another station is operating in split mode when outgoing transmissions can be overheard but the responses cannot.

15. A: An oscilloscope is the best instrument to use when checking the keying waveform of a CW transmitter. An oscilloscope assesses the change of an electrical signal over time, and creates a graphical representation of the alterations in voltage and time. The resulting shape is called a waveform.

Copyright © Mometrix Media. You have been licensed one copy of this document for personal use only. Any other reproduction or redistribution is strictly prohibited. All rights reserved.

16. C: An audio device or telephone will produce distorted speech if there is interference from a nearby single-sideband phone transmitter.

17. D: Distorted speech, splatter, and excessive background pickup can all result from an incorrectly adjusted speech processor. In radio communication, splatter (also known as spectral splatter) is noise created by the stopping and starting of the transmission.

18. A: A direct, fused power connection to the battery using heavy gauge wire would be better than a direct, fused connection to the alternator or generator using heavy gauge wire. It would also be better than direct, fused power connections to the battery or to the alternator or generator using resistor wire.

19. D: Reactance causes opposition to the flow of alternating current in an inductor. Another way of expressing this is that reactance is the opposition to the change in current caused by inductance.

20. B: If 400 VDC is supplied to an 800-ohm load, 200 watts of electrical power are used. The amount of power used is calculated by dividing the voltage by the resistance and then multiplying by 100.

21. B: To increase resistance, a resistor in series should be added to an existing resistor. When resistors are arranged in a series, the level of current passing through each resistor will be the same. However, the voltage across each resistor will be in proportion to the resistance. The total resistance will be equal to the sum of all the individual resistances.

22. B: The approximate junction threshold voltage of a germanium diode is 0.3 volts. The junction threshold voltage is the amount of voltage the diode can handle.

23. A: Low power consumption is one advantage of CMOS integrated circuits as compared to TTL integrated circuits. CMOS (complementary metal-oxide-semiconductor) circuits are commonly used in microcontrollers and microprocessors. These circuits also have a high noise immunity. They only use a little bit of power because at least one of the two transistors is always off. In a TTL (transistor-transistor logic) circuit, on the other hand, a great deal of power is wasted through the heat emission.

24. D: The peak-inverse-voltage across the rectifiers in a full-wave bridge power supply is equal to the normal peak output voltage of the power supply.

25. B: In a two input AND gate, output is high only when both inputs are high.

26. C: A mixer is used to process signals from the RF amplifier and local oscillator and send the result to the IF filter in a superheterodyne receiver.

27. D: Frequency modulation is the process which changes the frequency of an RF wave to convey information. Most repeaters use frequency modulated phone signals to communicate via voice. When this is done, the RF carrier frequency is altered by the voice data.

28. A: Heterodyning is another term for the mixing of two RF signals. In this process, an electronic circuit is used to combine an input radio frequency with a generated frequency: the result is one frequency that is a sum of the frequencies and one frequency that is the difference between the frequencies.

29. C: The header of a data packet contains the routing and handling information. The trailer of a data packet may also contain the routing and handling information, which is also known as the control information. The main content of the message is called the user data, or payload.

30. D: The characteristic impedance of flat ribbon TV type twinlead is 300 ohms.

Copyright © Mometrix Media. You have been licensed one copy of this document for personal use only. Any other reproduction or redistribution is strictly prohibited. All rights reserved.

31. B: The feed-point impedance of a ground-plane antenna increases when its radials are changed from horizontal to downward-sloping.

32. B: The director is normally the shortest parasitic element of a three-element, single-band Yagi antenna.

33. D: An NVIS antenna is typically installed between 1/10 and ¼ wavelength above the ground.

34. D: You can determine that your station complies with FCC RF exposure regulations by calculation based on FCC OET Bulletin 65; by calculation based on computer modeling; or by measurement of field strength using calibrated equipment.

35. D: A fuse or circuit breaker of 15 amperes would be appropriate to use with a circuit that uses AWG number 14 wiring.

Copyright © Mometrix Media. You have been licensed one copy of this document for personal use only. Any other reproduction or redistribution is strictly prohibited. All rights reserved.

General Class Practice Test 4

Practice Questions

1. Which of the following amateur bands is restricted to communication on only specific channels, rather than frequency ranges?
    a. 11 meters
    b. 12 meters
    c. 30 meters
    d. 60 meters

2. Which of the following must be true before amateur stations may provide communications to broadcasters for dissemination to the public?
    a. The communications must directly relate to the immediate safety of human life or protection of property and there must be no other means of communication reasonably available before or at the time of the event
    b. The communications must be approved by a local emergency preparedness official and conducted on officially designated frequencies
    c. The FCC must have declared a state of emergency
    d. All of these choices are correct

3. Which of the following limitations apply to transmitter power on every amateur band?
    a. Only the minimum power necessary to carry out the desired communications should be used
    b. Power must be limited to 200 watts when transmitting between 14.100 MHz and 14.150 MHz
    c. Power should be limited as necessary to avoid interference to another radio service on the frequency
    d. Effective radiated power cannot exceed 1500 watts

4. Which of the following is a requirement for administering a Technician Class license examination?
    a. At least three General Class or higher VEs must observe the examination
    b. At least two General Class or higher VEs must be present
    c. At least two General Class or higher VEs must be present, but only one need be Extra Class
    d. At least three VEs of Technician Class or higher must observe the examination

5. Which of the following conditions require an Amateur Radio station licensee to take specific steps to avoid harmful interference to other users or facilities?
    a. When operating within one mile of an FCC Monitoring Station
    b. When using a band where the Amateur Service is secondary
    c. When a station is transmitting spread spectrum emissions
    d. All of these choices are correct

6. Which mode is most commonly used for voice communications on the 17-meter and 12-meter bands?
    a. Upper sideband
    b. Lower sideband
    c. Vestigial sideband
    d. Double sideband

Copyright © Mometrix Media. You have been licensed one copy of this document for personal use only. Any other reproduction or redistribution is strictly prohibited. All rights reserved.

7. When selecting a CW transmitting frequency, what minimum frequency separation should you allow in order to minimize interference to stations on adjacent frequencies?
    a. 5 to 50 Hz
    b. 150 to 500 Hz
    c. 1 to 3 kHz
    d. 3 to 6 kHz

8. What does the Q signal "QRL?" mean?
    a. "Will you keep the frequency clear?"
    b. "Are you operating full break-in" or "Can you operate full break-in?"
    c. "Are you listening only for a specific station?"
    d. "Are you busy?", or "Is this frequency in use?"

9. Which of the following describes an azimuthal projection map?
    a. A world map that shows accurate land masses
    b. A map that shows true bearings and distances from a particular location
    c. A map that shows the angle at which an amateur satellite crosses the equator
    d. A map that shows the number of degrees longitude that an amateur satellite appears to move westward at the equator with each orbit

10. What segment of the 20-meter band is most often used for data transmissions?
    a. 14.000 - 14.050 MHz
    b. 14.070 - 14.100 MHz
    c. 14.150 - 14.225 MHz
    d. 14.275 - 14.350 MHz

11. Which of the following are least reliable for long distance communications during periods of low solar activity?
    a. 80 meters and 160 meters
    b. 60 meters and 40 meters
    c. 30 meters and 20 meters
    d. 15 meters, 12 meters and 10 meters

12. What is a reliable way to determine if the MUF is high enough to support skip propagation between your station and a distant location on frequencies between 14 and 30 MHz?
    a. Listen for signals from an international beacon in the frequency range you plan to use
    b. Send a series of dots on the band and listen for echoes from your signal
    c. Check the strength of TV signals from Western Europe
    d. Check the strength of signals in the MF AM broadcast band

13. What does the term "critical angle" mean as used in radio wave propagation?
    a. The long path azimuth of a distant station
    b. The short path azimuth of a distant station
    c. The lowest takeoff angle that will return a radio wave to the Earth under specific ionospheric conditions
    d. The highest takeoff angle that will return a radio wave to the Earth under specific ionospheric conditions

Copyright © Mometrix Media. You have been licensed one copy of this document for personal use only. Any other reproduction or redistribution is strictly prohibited. All rights reserved.

14. What reading on the plate current meter of a vacuum tube RF power amplifier indicates correct adjustment of the plate tuning control?
   a. A pronounced peak
   b. A pronounced dip
   c. No change will be observed
   d. A slow, rhythmic oscillation

15. What signal source is connected to the vertical input of an oscilloscope when checking the RF envelope pattern of a transmitted signal?
   a. The local oscillator of the transmitter
   b. An external RF oscillator
   c. The transmitter balanced mixer output
   d. The attenuated RF output of the transmitter

16. What is the effect on an audio device or telephone system if there is interference from a nearby CW transmitter?
   a. On-and-off humming or clicking
   b. A CW signal at a nearly pure audio frequency
   c. A chirpy CW signal
   d. Severely distorted audio

17. What does an S meter measure?
   a. Conductance
   b. Impedance
   c. Received signal strength
   d. Transmitter power output

18. Why is it best NOT to draw the DC power for a 100 watt HF transceiver from an automobile's auxiliary power socket?
   a. The socket is not wired with an RF-shielded power cable
   b. The socket's wiring may be inadequate for the current being drawn by the transceiver
   c. The DC polarity of the socket is reversed from the polarity of modern HF transceivers
   d. Drawing more than 50 watts from this socket could cause the engine to overheat

19. Which of the following causes opposition to the flow of alternating current in a capacitor?
   a. Conductance
   b. Reluctance
   c. Reactance
   d. Admittance

20. How many watts of electrical power are used by a 12 VDC light bulb that draws 0.2 amperes?
   a. 2.4 watts
   b. 24 watts
   c. 6 watts
   d. 60 watts

21. What is the total resistance of three 100 ohm resistors in parallel?
   a. 0.30 ohms
   b. 0.33 ohms
   c. 33.3 ohms
   d. 300 ohms

Copyright © Mometrix Media. You have been licensed one copy of this document for personal use only. Any other reproduction or redistribution is strictly prohibited. All rights reserved.

22. When is it acceptable to recharge a carbon-zinc primary cell?
    a. As long as the voltage has not been allowed to drop below 1.0 volt
    b. When the cell is kept warm during the recharging period
    c. When a constant current charger is used
    d. Never

23. What is meant by the term ROM?
    a. Resistor Operated Memory
    b. Read Only Memory
    c. Random Operational Memory
    d. Resistant to Overload Memory

24. What is the peak-inverse-voltage across the rectifier in a half-wave power supply?
    a. One-half the normal peak output voltage of the power supply
    b. One-half the normal output voltage of the power supply
    c. Equal to the normal output voltage of the power supply
    d. Two times the normal peak output voltage of the power supply

25. Which of the following describes the function of a two input NOR gate?
    a. Output is high when either or both inputs are low
    b. Output is high only when both inputs are high
    c. Output is low when either or both inputs are high
    d. Output is low only when both inputs are high

26. What circuit is used to combine signals from the IF amplifier and BFO and send the result to the AF amplifier in a single-sideband receiver?
    a. RF oscillator
    b. IF filter
    c. Balanced modulator
    d. Product detector

27. What emission is produced by a reactance modulator connected to an RF power amplifier?
    a. Multiplex modulation
    b. Phase modulation
    c. Amplitude modulation
    d. Pulse modulation

28. What is the stage in a VHF FM transmitter that generates a harmonic of a lower frequency signal to reach the desired operating frequency?
    a. Mixer
    b. Reactance modulator
    c. Pre-emphasis network
    d. Multiplier

29. Which of the following describes Baudot code?
    a. A 7-bit code with start, stop and parity bits
    b. A code using error detection and correction
    c. A 5-bit code with additional start and stop bits
    d. A code using SELCAL and LISTEN

Copyright © Mometrix Media. You have been licensed one copy of this document for personal use only. Any other reproduction or redistribution is strictly prohibited. All rights reserved.

30. What might cause reflected power at the point where a feed line connects to an antenna?
    a. Operating an antenna at its resonant frequency
    b. Using more transmitter power than the antenna can handle
    c. A difference between feed line impedance and antenna feed point impedance
    d. Feeding the antenna with unbalanced feed line

31. What is the radiation pattern of a dipole antenna in free space in the plane of the conductor?
    a. It is a figure-eight at right angles to the antenna
    b. It is a figure-eight off both ends of the antenna
    c. It is a circle (equal radiation in all directions)
    d. It has a pair of lobes on one side of the antenna and a single lobe on the other side

32. Which statement about a three-element; single-band Yagi antenna is true?
    a. The reflector is normally the longest parasitic element
    b. The director is normally the longest parasitic element
    c. The reflector is normally the shortest parasitic element
    d. All of the elements must be the same length

33. What is the primary purpose of antenna traps?
    a. To permit multiband operation
    b. To notch spurious frequencies
    c. To provide balanced feed-point impedance
    d. To prevent out of band operation

34. What does "time averaging" mean in reference to RF radiation exposure?
    a. The average time of day when the exposure occurs
    b. The average time it takes RF radiation to have any long-term effect on the body
    c. The total time of the exposure
    d. The total RF exposure averaged over a certain time

35. Which of the following is a primary reason for not placing a gasoline-fueled generator inside an occupied area?
    a. Danger of carbon monoxide poisoning
    b. Danger of engine over torque
    c. Lack of oxygen for adequate combustion
    d. Lack of nitrogen for adequate combustion

Copyright © Mometrix Media. You have been licensed one copy of this document for personal use only. Any other reproduction or redistribution is strictly prohibited. All rights reserved.

Answers and Explanations

1. **D:** The 60-meter amateur band is restricted to communication on only specific channels, rather than frequency ranges. This is in constrast to the other amateur bands, on which frequency ranges rather than channels are restricted.

2. **A:** In order for amateur stations to provide communications to broadcasters for dissemination to the public, the communications must directly relate to the immediate safety of human life or protection of property and there must be no other means of communication reasonably available before or at the time of the event. In general, the FCC is lenient with operators who act in good faith without knowing all of the circumstances surrounding a possible emergency.

3. **A:** On the 14MHz band, only the minimum power necessary to carry out the desired communications should be used.

4. **A:** In order for a Technician Class operator examination to be administered, at least three VEC-accredited General Class or higher VEs must be present.

5. **D:** An Amateur Radio station licensee is required to take specific steps to avoid harmful interference to other users or facilities when the following conditions apply: when operating within one mile of an FCC Monitoring Station; when using a band where the Amateur Service is secondary; and when a station is transmitting spread spectrum emissions. All of these conditions place the responsibility for avoiding interference on the shoulders of the amateur operator.

6. **A:** The upper sideband is the mode most commonly used for voice communications on the 17 and 12 meter bands. Indeed, the upper sideband is the preferred operating mode on the 20, 17, 15, 12, and 10 meter HF amateur bands. In addition, the upper sideband is preferred on all the VHF and UHF bands.

7. **B:** When selecting a CW transmitting frequency, you should allow a minimum frequency separation of 150 to 500 Hz in order to minimize interference to stations on adjacent frequencies. CW transmissions, otherwise known as Morse code, are a series of on and off keys.

8. **D:** When a CW operator sends "QRL?," he or she is either asking if a frequency is being used or if the receiver is busy.

9. **B:** An azimuthal projection map is a world map projection centered on a particular location. When the operator's station is positioned at the center of the map, the path of any transmission to or from the station will be a radial line straight to the other station.

10. **B:** The 14.070 to 14.100 MHz segment of the 20-meter band is most often used for data transmissions.

11. **D:** During periods of low solar activity, the 15 meters, 12 meters, and 10 meters are least reliable for long distance communication.

12. **A:** One reliable way to determine if the Maximum Usable Frequency (MUF) is high enough to support skip propagation between your station and a distant location on frequencies between 14 and 30 MHz is to listen for signals from an international beacon. Skip propagation, also known as skywave propagation, is the reflection or refraction of radio waves from the ionosphere back to the Earth. For the most part, skywave propagation is limited to the shortwave frequency bands, and can be employed for transmissions between continents. Skywave propagation enables extremely remote signals to be very clear. The majority of long-distance shortwave communications are the result of skip propagation.

Copyright © Mometrix Media. You have been licensed one copy of this document for personal use only. Any other reproduction or redistribution is strictly prohibited. All rights reserved.

13. D: In radio wave propagation, the term "critical angle" means the highest takeoff angle that will return a radio wave to the Earth under specific ionospheric conditions. The critical angle is the highest possible angle for successful radio wave transmission. At angles higher than this, the radio wave will be reflected back upon itself, and will therefore not reach its destination.

14. B: A pronounced dip on the plate current meter of a vacuum tube RF power amplifier indicates correct adjustment of the plate tuning control. An RF power amplifier is used to change a low-power radio-frequency signal into a stronger signal. RF power amplifiers typically have excellent heat dissipation, output compression, gain, and return loss on the input and output.

15. D: When checking the RF envelope pattern of a transmitted signal, the attenuated RF output of the transmitter is connected to the vertical input of an oscilloscope.

16. A: An audio device or telephone system may present on-and-off humming or clicking if there is interference from a nearby CW transmitter.

17. C: An S meter measures received signal strength. An S meter, otherwise known as a signal strength meter, indicates signal strength on an arbitrary scale ranging from S1 to S9. Ham radio operators will often use the expression "S unit" to describe the amount of change in signal strength required to move the S meter from one level to an adjacent level on the S meter.

18. B: It is best NOT to draw the DC power for a 100-watt HF transceiver from an automobile's auxiliary power socket because the socket's wiring may be inadequate for the current being drawn by the transceiver.

19. C: Reactance causes opposition to the flow of alternating current in a capacitor. Another way of expressing this is that reactance is the opposition to the change in voltage caused by capacitance.

20. A: A 12-VDC light bulb that draws 0.2 amperes uses 2.4 watts of electrical power. The amount of electrical power used is calculated by dividing the voltage by the amperage.

21. C: The total resistance of three 100-ohm resistors in parallel is 33.3 ohms. When resistors are arranged in a parallel configuration, the voltage across each resistor will be the same, but the currents passing through the resistors will be equal to the sum of the respective currents passing through each resistor. As more resistors are placed in parallel, the collective amount of resistance will decrease. It should be noted that the resistance of the system can be no greater than the least resistant resistor.

22. D: It is never acceptable to recharge a carbon-zinc primary cell.

23. B: The term ROM means Read Only Memory. This means that the information encoded in ROM cannot be altered, or can only be altered with great effort. For this reason, it is used to store only the most important and basic functions of the machine.

24. D: In a half-wave power supply, the peak-inverse voltage across the rectifier is two times the normal peak output voltage of the power supply.

25. C: In a two input NOR gate, output is low when either or both inputs are high.

26. D: A product detector is used to combine signals from the IF amplifier and BFO and send the result to the AF amplifier in a single-sideband receiver. A product detector is a piece of equipment that gives a receiver the ability to process both CW and SSB signals.

Copyright © Mometrix Media. You have been licensed one copy of this document for personal use only. Any other reproduction or redistribution is strictly prohibited. All rights reserved.

27. B: Phase modulation is the emission produced by a reactance modulator connected to an RF power amplifier.

28. D: The multiplier stage in a VHF FM transmitter generates a harmonic of a lower frequency signal to reach the desired operating frequency.

29. C: Baudot code is a five-bit code with additional start and stop bits. It is used in RTTY (radioteletype) communications. In Baudot code, characters of plain text are sent as five-bit codes composed of patterns of marks and spaces. The modulation created by this succession of frequencies is called frequency shift keying.

30. C: At the point where a feed line connects to an antenna, a difference between feed-line impedance and antenna feed-point impedance results in reflected power.

31. A: The low angle azimuthal radiation pattern of an ideal half-wavelength dipole antenna installed 1/2 wavelength high and parallel to the Earth is a figure-eight at right angles to the antenna.

32. A: The reflector is normally the longest parasitic element of a three-element, single-band Yagi antenna.

33. A: The primary purpose of antenna traps is to permit multiband operation.

34. D: In reference to RF radiation exposure, "time averaging" means the total RF exposure averaged over a certain time.

35. A: The danger of carbon monoxide poisoning is a primary reason for not placing a gasoline-fueled generator inside an occupied area.

Copyright © Mometrix Media. You have been licensed one copy of this document for personal use only. Any other reproduction or redistribution is strictly prohibited. All rights reserved.

General Class Practice Test 5

Practice Questions

1. Which of the following frequencies is in the General Class portion of the 40-meter band?
    a. 7.250 MHz
    b. 7.500 MHz
    c. 40.200 MHz
    d. 40.500 MHz

2. When may music be transmitted by an amateur station?
    a. At any time, as long as it produces no spurious emissions
    b. When it is unintentionally transmitted from the background at the transmitter
    c. When it is transmitted on frequencies above 1215 MHz
    d. When it is an incidental part of a manned space craft retransmission

3. Which of the following is a limitation on transmitter power on the 28 MHz band for a General Class control operator?
    a. 100 watts PEP output
    b. 1000 watts PEP output
    c. 1500 watts PEP output
    d. 2000 watts PEP output

4. Which of the following must a person have before they can be an administering VE for a Technician Class license examination?
    a. Notification to the FCC that you want to give an examination
    b. Receipt of a CSCE for General Class
    c. Possession of a properly obtained telegraphy license
    d. An FCC General Class or higher license and VEC accreditation

5. What types of messages for a third party in another country may be transmitted by an amateur station?
    a. Any message, as long as the amateur operator is not paid
    b. Only messages for other licensed amateurs
    c. Only messages relating to Amateur Radio or remarks of a personal character, or messages relating to emergencies or disaster relief
    d. Any messages, as long as the text of the message is recorded in the station log

6. Which mode of voice communication is most commonly used on the HF amateur bands?
    a. Frequency modulation
    b. Double sideband
    c. Single sideband
    d. Phase modulation

7. What is the customary minimum frequency separation between SSB signals under normal conditions?
    a. Between 150 and 500 Hz
    b. Approximately 3 kHz
    c. Approximately 6 kHz
    d. Approximately 10 kHz

Copyright © Mometrix Media. You have been licensed one copy of this document for personal use only. Any other reproduction or redistribution is strictly prohibited. All rights reserved.

8. What is the best speed to use answering a CQ in Morse Code?
   a. The fastest speed at which you are comfortable copying
   b. The speed at which the CQ was sent
   c. A slow speed until contact is established
   d. At the standard calling speed of 5 wpm

9. When is it permissible to communicate with amateur stations in countries outside the areas administered by the Federal Communications Commission?
   a. Only when the foreign country has a formal third party agreement filed with the FCC
   b. When the contact is with amateurs in any country except those whose administrations have notified the ITU that they object to such communications
   c. When the contact is with amateurs in any country as long as the communication is conducted in English
   d. Only when the foreign country is a member of the International Amateur Radio Union

10. What is the standard sideband used to generate a JT65 or JT9 digital signal when using AFSK in any amateur band?
    a. LSB
    b. USB
    c. DSB
    d. SSB

11. What is the solar-flux index?
    a. A measure of the highest frequency that is useful for ionospheric propagation between two points on the Earth
    b. A count of sunspots which is adjusted for solar emissions
    c. Another name for the American sunspot number
    d. A measure of solar radiation at 10.7 cm

12. What usually happens to radio waves with frequencies below the MUF and above the LUF when they are sent into the ionosphere?
    a. They are bent back to the Earth
    b. They pass through the ionosphere
    c. They are amplified by interaction with the ionosphere
    d. They are bent and trapped in the ionosphere to circle the Earth

13. Why is long distance communication on the 40-meter, 60-meter, 80-meter and 160-meter bands more difficult during the day?
    a. The F layer absorbs signals at these frequencies during daylight hours
    b. The F layer is unstable during daylight hours
    c. The D layer absorbs signals at these frequencies during daylight hours
    d. The E layer is unstable during daylight hours

14. What is a purpose of using Automatic Level Control (ALC) with a RF power amplifier?
    a. To balance the transmitter audio frequency response
    b. To reduce harmonic radiation
    c. To reduce distortion due to excessive drive
    d. To increase overall efficiency

Copyright © Mometrix Media. You have been licensed one copy of this document for personal use only. Any other reproduction or redistribution is strictly prohibited. All rights reserved.

15. Why is high input impedance desirable for a voltmeter?
    a. It improves the frequency response
    b. It decreases battery consumption in the meter
    c. It improves the resolution of the readings
    d. It decreases the loading on circuits being measured

16. What might be the problem if you receive an RF burn when touching your equipment while transmitting on an HF band, assuming the equipment is connected to a ground rod?
    a. Flat braid rather than round wire has been used for the ground wire
    b. Insulated wire has been used for the ground wire
    c. The ground rod is resonant
    d. The ground wire has high impedance on that frequency

17. How does an S meter reading of 20 dB over S9 compare to an S9 signal, assuming a properly calibrated S meter?
    a. It is 10 times less powerful
    b. It is 20 times less powerful
    c. It is 20 times more powerful
    d. It is 100 times more powerful

18. Which of the following most limits the effectiveness of an HF mobile transceiver operating in the 75-meter band?
    a. "Picket Fencing" signal variation
    b. The wire gauge of the DC power line to the transceiver
    c. The antenna system
    d. FCC rules limiting mobile output power on the 75 meter band

19. How does an inductor react to AC?
    a. As the frequency of the applied AC increases, the reactance decreases
    b. As the amplitude of the applied AC increases, the reactance increases
    c. As the amplitude of the applied AC increases, the reactance decreases
    d. As the frequency of the applied AC increases, the reactance increases

20. How many watts are dissipated when a current of 7.0 milliamperes flows through 1.25 kilohms?
    a. Approximately 61 milliwatts
    b. Approximately 61 watts
    c. Approximately 11 milliwatts
    d. Approximately 11 watts

21. If three equal value resistors in series produce 450 ohms, what is the value of each resistor?
    a. 1500 ohms
    b. 90 ohms
    c. 150 ohms
    d. 175 ohms

22. What is the approximate junction threshold voltage of a conventional silicon diode?
    a. 0.1 volt
    b. 0.3 volts
    c. 0.7 volts
    d. 1.0 volts

Copyright © Mometrix Media. You have been licensed one copy of this document for personal use only. Any other reproduction or redistribution is strictly prohibited. All rights reserved.

23. What is meant when memory is characterized as "non-volatile"?
   a. It is resistant to radiation damage
   b. It is resistant to high temperatures
   c. The stored information is maintained even if power is removed
   d. The stored information cannot be changed once written

24. What portion of the AC cycle is converted to DC by a half-wave rectifier?
   a. 90 degrees
   b. 180 degrees
   c. 270 degrees
   d. 360 degrees

25. How many states does a 3-bit binary counter have?
   a. 3
   b. 6
   c. 8
   d. 16

26. Which of the following is an advantage of a transceiver controlled by a direct digital synthesizer (DDS)?
   a. Wide tuning range and no need for band switching
   b. Relatively high power output
   c. Relatively low power consumption
   d. Variable frequency with the stability of a crystal oscillator

27. What type of modulation varies the instantaneous power level of the RF signal?
   a. Frequency shift keying
   b. Phase modulation
   c. Frequency modulation
   d. Amplitude modulation

28. What is the approximate bandwidth of a PACTOR3 signal at maximum data rate?]
   a. 31.5 Hz
   b. 500 Hz
   c. 1800 Hz
   d. 2300 Hz

29. In the PACTOR protocol, what is meant by an NAK response to a transmitted packet?
   a. The receiver is requesting the packet be re-transmitted
   b. The receiver is reporting the packet was received without error
   c. The receiver is busy decoding the packet
   d. The entire file has been received correctly

30. How does the attenuation of coaxial cable change as the frequency of the signal it is carrying increases?
   a. It is independent of frequency
   b. It increases
   c. It decreases
   d. It reaches a maximum at approximately 18 MHz

Copyright © Mometrix Media. You have been licensed one copy of this document for personal use only. Any other reproduction or redistribution is strictly prohibited. All rights reserved.

31. How does antenna height affect the horizontal (azimuthal) radiation pattern of a horizontal dipole HF antenna?
    a. If the antenna is too high, the pattern becomes unpredictable
    b. Antenna height has no effect on the pattern
    c. If the antenna is less than 1/2 wavelength high, the azimuthal pattern is almost omnidirectional
    d. If the antenna is less than 1/2 wavelength high, radiation off the ends of the wire is eliminated

32. How does increasing boom length and adding directors affect a Yagi antenna?
    a. Gain increases
    b. Beamwidth increases
    c. Weight decreases
    d. Wind load decreases

33. What is the advantage of vertical stacking of horizontally polarized Yagi antennas?
    a. It allows quick selection of vertical or horizontal polarization
    b. It allows simultaneous vertical and horizontal polarization
    c. It narrows the main lobe in azimuth
    d. It narrows the main lobe in elevation

34. What must you do if an evaluation of your station shows RF energy radiated from your station exceeds permissible limits?
    a. Take action to prevent human exposure to the excessive RF fields
    b. File an Environmental Impact Statement (EIS-97) with the FCC
    c. Secure written permission from your neighbors to operate above the controlled MPE limits
    d. All of these choices are correct

35. Which of the following conditions will cause a Ground Fault Circuit Interrupter (GFCI) to disconnect the 120 or 240 Volt AC line power to a device?
    a. Current flowing from one or more of the hot wires to the neutral wire
    b. Current flowing from one or more of the hot wires directly to ground
    c. Over-voltage on the hot wire
    d. All of these choices are correct

Copyright © Mometrix Media. You have been licensed one copy of this document for personal use only. Any other reproduction or redistribution is strictly prohibited. All rights reserved.

Answers and Questions

1. A: 7.250 MHz is in the General Class portion of the 40-meter band.

2. D: Music may be transmitted by an amateur station when it is an incidental part of a manned space craft retransmission. Otherwise, amateur stations should avoid music broadcasting that could represent an infringement of copyright.

3. C: On the 28 MHz band, the limitation on transmitter power is 1500 watts PEP output.

4. D: To be an administering VE for a Technician Class operator license examination, you must have an FCC General Class or higher license and VEC accreditation. Volunteer Examiners are allowed to proctor exams at or below the level at which they are licensed.

5. C: Only messages relating to Amateur Radio or remarks of a personal character, or messages relating to emergencies or disaster relief, may be transmitted by an amateur station for a third party in another country.

6. C: The single-sideband mode of voice communication is most commonly used on the high frequency amateur bands. This is more because of convention than for any technical reasons.

7. B: The customary minimum frequency separation between SSB signals under normal conditions is between 150 and 500 Hz. This allows enough space to prevent interference in most cases.

8. B: The best speed to use when answering a CQ in Morse Code is the speed at which the CQ was sent. Similarly, an operator should send initial transmissions at the speed which he or she would be comfortable receiving. In addition, the operator should leave sufficient time after transmitting for the other station to answer. At least once per cycle, the operator should use standard phonetics for his or her call sign on voice modes.

9. B: It is permissible to communicate with amateur stations in countries outside the areas administered by the Federal Communications Commission when the contact is with amateurs in any country except those whose administrations have notified the ITU that they object to such communications.

10. B: USB is the typical sideband used to generate a JT65 or JT9 digital signal when using AFSK in any amatuer band.

11. D: The solar flux index is a measure of solar radiation at 10.7 cm. The measure of 10.7 cm is important because it is the wavelength of radio signals at 2800 MHz. Although the solar flux index is proportional to the amount of sunspot activity at any given time, the ionization levels in the ionosphere can now be more accurately measured by assessing the X-ray flux from the Sun.

12. A: Radio waves with frequencies below the Maximum Usable Frequency (MUF) and above the Lowest Usable Frequency (LUF) are bent back to the Earth when they are sent into the ionosphere. The maximum usable frequency is the highest frequency at which a signal may still be transmitted between two points with skip reflection (that is, the reflection of waves from the ionosphere). When the frequency of a signal increases, the refractive index of the ionosphere decreases, which is why there is an upper limit to usable frequency. If a signal has a higher frequency than that, it will pass through the ionosphere into space rather than being reflected by it. Lowest usable frequency, on the other hand, is the HF band frequency that has a received field intensity high enough to create the necessary signal-to-noise ratio.

13. C: Long distance communications on the 40, 60, 80, and 160 meter bands is more difficult during the day because the D layer absorbs signals at these frequencies during daylight hours.

Copyright © Mometrix Media. You have been licensed one copy of this document for personal use only. Any other reproduction or redistribution is strictly prohibited. All rights reserved.

14. C: One purpose of using Automatic Level Control with a RF power amplifier is to reduce distortion due to excessive drive.

15. D: High input impedance is desirable for a voltmeter because it decreases the loading on circuits being measured.

16. D: If you receive an RF burn when touching your equipment while transmitting on an HF band, one problem might be that the ground wire has high impedance on that frequency.

17. D: Assuming a properly calibrated S meter, an S meter reading of 20 dB over S-9 is 100 times stronger than an S-9 signal.

18. C: The antenna system most limits the effectiveness of an HF mobile transceiver operating in the 75-meter band.

19. D: As the frequency of the applied AC increases, the reactance of an inductor increases. An inductor is a passive electrical component with two terminals. Its function is to resist alterations in an electric current. The most common structure of an inductor is a coil of wire. The passage of current through the wire creates a magnetic field; when the current changes, a voltage is produced by the inductor. The inductance of the component is the ratio of the voltage to the rate of change of current.

20. A: When a current of 7.0 milliamperes flows through 1.25 kilohms, approximately 61 milliwatts are dissipated.

21. C: If three equal value resistors in parallel produce 50 ohms of resistance, and the same three resistors in series produce 450 ohms, the value of each resistor is 150 ohms. Resistors in series produce a total resistance equal to the sum of the individual resistances.

22. C: The approximate junction threshold voltage of a conventional silicon diode is 0.7 volts. The junction threshold voltage is the maximum amount of current that can be handled by a component without damage.

23. C: When memory is characterized as "non-volatile," this means that the stored information is maintained even if power is removed. Some of the most common examples of non-volatile memory are read-only memory (ROM), flash memory, optical disks, and hard disks.

24. B: 180 degrees of the AC cycle is converted to DC by a half-wave rectifier. This device earns its name by rectifying half of the sine wave.

25. C: A 3-bit binary counter has 8 states.

26. D: One advantage of a transceiver controlled by a direct digital synthesizer (DDS) is variable frequency with the stability of a crystal oscillator. A direct digital synthesizer can make arbitrary waveforms based on the inputs from a clock.

27. D: Amplitude modulation varies the instantaneous power level of the RF signal.

28. D: The approximate bandwidth of a PACTOR3 signal at maximum data rate is 2300Hz.

29. A: In the PACTOR protocol, an NAK response to a transmitted packet means that the receiver is requesting the packet be retransmitted. PACTOR is a system for teleprinting over radio (TOR), or transmitting text characters. This program improved the structure of the TOR and AMTOR programs.

30. B: The attenuation of coaxial cable increases as the frequency of the signal it is carrying increases. A coaxial cable is a type of feedline in which one conductor is entirely inside another.

Copyright © Mometrix Media. You have been licensed one copy of this document for personal use only. Any other reproduction or redistribution is strictly prohibited. All rights reserved.

31. C: If a horizontal dipole HF antenna is less than 1.2 wavelengths high, the horizontal (azimuthal) pattern is almost omnidirectional.

32. A: Increasing the boom length and adding directors increases the gain of a Yagi antenna.

33. D: One advantage of vertically stacking horizontally polarized Yagi antennas is that it narrows the main lobe in elevation.

34. A: If an evaluation shows that the RF energy radiated from your station exceeds permissible limits, you must take action to prevent human exposure to the excessive RF fields.

35. B: Current flowing from one or more of the hot wires directly to ground will cause a Ground Fault Circuit Interrupter (GFCI) to disconnect the 120 or 240 Volt AC line power to a device.

Copyright © Mometrix Media. You have been licensed one copy of this document for personal use only. Any other reproduction or redistribution is strictly prohibited. All rights reserved.

General Class Practice Test 6

Practice Questions

1. Which of the following frequencies is within the General Class portion of the 75-meter phone band?
    a. 1875 kHz
    b. 3750 kHz
    c. 3900 kHz
    d. 4005 kHz

2. When is an amateur station permitted to transmit secret codes?
    a. During a declared communications emergency
    b. To control a space station
    c. Only when the information is of a routine, personal nature
    d. Only with Special Temporary Authorization from the FCC

3. Which of the following is a limitation on transmitter power on 1.8 MHz band?
    a. 200 watts PEP output
    b. 1000 watts PEP output
    c. 1200 watts PEP output
    d. 1500 watts PEP output

4. When must you add the special identifier "AG" after your call sign if you are a Technician Class licensee and have a CSCE for General Class operator privileges, but the FCC has not yet posted your upgrade on its website?
    a. Whenever you operate using General Class frequency privileges
    b. Whenever you operate on any amateur frequency
    c. Whenever you operate using Technician frequency privileges
    d. A special identifier is not required as long as your General Class license application has been filed with the FCC

5. Which of the following applies in the event of interference between a coordinated repeater and an uncoordinated repeater?
    a. The licensee of the non-coordinated repeater has primary responsibility to resolve the interference
    b. The licensee of the coordinated repeater has primary responsibility to resolve the interference
    c. Both repeater licensees share equal responsibility to resolve the interference
    d. The frequency coordinator bears primary responsibility to resolve the interference

6. Which of the following is an advantage when using single sideband as compared to other analog voice modes on the HF amateur bands?
    a. Very high fidelity voice modulation
    b. Less bandwidth used and higher power efficiency
    c. Ease of tuning on receive and immunity to impulse noise
    d. Less subject to interference atmospheric static crashes

Copyright © Mometrix Media. You have been licensed one copy of this document for personal use only. Any other reproduction or redistribution is strictly prohibited. All rights reserved.

7. What is a practical way to avoid harmful interference when selecting a frequency to call CQ on CW or phone?
  a. Send "QRL?" on CW, followed by your call sign; or, if using phone, ask if the frequency is in use, followed by your call sign
  b. Listen for 2 minutes before calling CQ
  c. Send the letter "V" in Morse code several times and listen for a response
  d. Send "QSY" on CW or if using phone, announce "the frequency is in use", then send your call and listen for a response

8. What does the term "zero beat" mean in CW operation?
  a. Matching the speed of the transmitting station
  b. Operating split to avoid interference on frequency
  c. Sending without error
  d. Matching your transmit frequency to the frequency of a received signal

9. How is a directional antenna pointed when making a "long-path" contact with another station?
  a. Toward the rising Sun
  b. Along the gray line
  c. 180 degrees from its short-path heading
  d. Toward the north

10. What is the most common frequency shift for RTTY emissions in the amateur HF bands?
  a. 85 Hz
  b. 170 Hz
  c. 425 Hz
  d. 850 Hz

11. What is a geomagnetic storm?
  a. A sudden drop in the solar-flux index
  b. A thunderstorm which affects radio propagation
  c. Ripples in the ionosphere
  d. A temporary disturbance in the Earth's magnetosphere

12. What usually happens to radio waves with frequencies below the LUF?
  a. They are bent back to the Earth
  b. They pass through the ionosphere
  c. They are completely absorbed by the ionosphere
  d. They are bent and trapped in the ionosphere to circle the Earth

13. What is a characteristic of HF scatter signals?
  a. They have high intelligibility
  b. They have a wavering sound
  c. They have very large swings in signal strength
  d. All of these choices are correct

14. What type of device is often used to match transmitter output impedance to an impedance not equal to 50 ohms?
  a. Balanced modulator
  b. SWR Bridge
  c. Antenna coupler or antenna tuner
  d. Q Multiplier

Copyright © Mometrix Media. You have been licensed one copy of this document for personal use only. Any other reproduction or redistribution is strictly prohibited. All rights reserved.

15. What is an advantage of a digital voltmeter as compared to an analog voltmeter?
   a. Better for measuring computer circuits
   b. Better for RF measurements
   c. Better precision for most uses
   d. Faster response

16. What effect can be caused by a resonant ground connection?
   a. Overheating of ground straps
   b. Corrosion of the ground rod
   c. High RF voltages on the enclosures of station equipment
   d. A ground loop

17. Where is an S meter found?
   a. In a receiver
   b. In an SWR bridge
   c. In a transmitter
   d. In a conductance bridge

18. What is one disadvantage of using a shortened mobile antenna as opposed to a full size antenna?
   a. Short antennas are more likely to cause distortion of transmitted signals
   b. Short antennas can only receive vertically polarized signals
   c. Operating bandwidth may be very limited
   d. Harmonic radiation may increase

19. How does a capacitor react to AC?
   a. As the frequency of the applied AC increases, the reactance decreases
   b. As the frequency of the applied AC increases, the reactance increases
   c. As the amplitude of the applied AC increases, the reactance increases
   d. As the amplitude of the applied AC increases, the reactance decreases

20. What is the output PEP from a transmitter if an oscilloscope measures 200 volts peak-to-peak across a 50 ohm dummy load connected to the transmitter output?
   a. 1.4 watts
   b. 100 watts
   c. 353.5 watts
   d. 400 watts

21. What is the RMS voltage across a 500-turn secondary winding in a transformer if the 2250-turn primary is connected to 120 VAC?
   a. 2370 volts
   b. 540 volts
   c. 26.7 volts
   d. 5.9 volts

22. Which of the following is an advantage of using a Schottky diode in an RF switching circuit as compared to a standard silicon diode?
   a. Lower capacitance
   b. Lower inductance
   c. Longer switching times
   d. Higher breakdown voltage

Copyright © Mometrix Media. You have been licensed one copy of this document for personal use only. Any other reproduction or redistribution is strictly prohibited. All rights reserved.

23. What kind of device is an integrated circuit operational amplifier?
    a. Digital
    b. MMIC
    c. Programmable Logic
    d. Analog

24. What portion of the AC cycle is converted to DC by a full-wave rectifier?
    a. 90 degrees
    b. 180 degrees
    c. 270 degrees
    d. 360 degrees

25. What is a shift register?
    a. A clocked array of circuits that passes data in steps along the array
    b. An array of operational amplifiers used for tri state arithmetic operations
    c. A digital mixer
    d. An analog mixer

26. What should be the impedance of a low-pass filter as compared to the impedance of the transmission line into which it is inserted?
    a. Substantially higher
    b. About the same
    c. Substantially lower
    d. Twice the transmission line impedance

27. What is one advantage of carrier suppression in a single sideband phone transmission versus full carrier amplitude modulation?
    a. Audio fidelity is improved
    b. Greater modulation percentage is obtainable with lower distortion
    c. Available transmitter power can be used more effectively
    d. Simpler receiving equipment can be used

28. What is the total bandwidth of an FM-phone transmission having a 5 kHz deviation and a 3 kHz modulating frequency?
    a. 3 kHz
    b. 5 kHz
    c. 8 kHz
    d. 16 kHz

29. How does the receiving station respond to an ARQ data mode packet containing errors?
    a. Terminates the contact
    b. Requests the packet be retransmitted
    c. Sends the packet back to the transmitting station
    d. Requests a change in transmitting protocol

30. In what units is RF feed line loss usually expressed?
    a. Ohms per 1000 feet
    b. Decibels per 1000 feet
    c. Ohms per 100 feet
    d. Decibels per 100 feet

Copyright © Mometrix Media. You have been licensed one copy of this document for personal use only. Any other reproduction or redistribution is strictly prohibited. All rights reserved.

31. Where should the radial wires of a ground-mounted vertical antenna system be placed?
   a. As high as possible above the ground
   b. Parallel to the antenna element
   c. On the surface or buried a few inches below the ground
   d. At the top of the antenna

32. What configuration of the loops of a two-element quad antenna must be used for the antenna to operate as a beam antenna, assuming one of the elements is used as a reflector?
   a. The driven element must be fed with a balun transformer
   b. There must be an open circuit in the driven element at the point opposite the feed point
   c. The reflector element must be approximately 5 percent shorter than the driven element
   d. The reflector element must be approximately 5 percent longer than the driven element

33. Which of the following is an advantage of a log periodic antenna?
   a. Wide bandwidth
   b. Higher gain per element than a Yagi antenna
   c. Harmonic suppression
   d. Polarization diversity

34. What precaution should be taken when installing a ground-mounted antenna?
   a. It should not be installed higher than you can reach
   b. It should not be installed in a wet area
   c. It should limited to 10 feet in height
   d. It should be installed so no one can be exposed to RF radiation in excess of maximum permissible limits

35. Why must the metal enclosure of every item of station equipment be grounded?
   a. It prevents blowing of fuses in case of an internal short circuit
   b. It prevents signal overload
   c. It ensures that the neutral wire is grounded
   d. It ensures that hazardous voltages cannot appear on the chassis

Answers and Explanations

1. C: 3900 kHz is within the General Class portion of the 75 meter phone band.

2. B: Amateur stations are permitted to transmit secret codes to control a space station. Any amateur station that is positioned more than 50 km above the surface of the Earth is considered a space station.

3. D: On the 1.8 MHz band, the limitation on transmitter power is 1500 watts PEP output.

4. A: You must add the special identifier "AG" after your call sign if you are a Technician Class licensee and have a CSCE for General Class operator privileges, but the FCC has not yet posted your upgrade on its Web site. This indicates that your actual status will not be reflected on the site.

5. A: In the event of interference between a coordinated repeater and an uncoordinated repeater, the licensee of the uncoordinated repeater has primary responsibility to resolve the interference.

6. B: When using single sideband as compared to other analog voice modes on the HF amateur bands, less bandwidth used and higher power efficiency is an advantage.

Copyright © Mometrix Media. You have been licensed one copy of this document for personal use only. Any other reproduction or redistribution is strictly prohibited. All rights reserved.

7. A: A practical way to avoid harmful interference when selecting a frequency to call CQ on CW or phone is to send "QRL?" on CW, followed by your call sign; or if using phone, ask if the frequency is in use, followed by your call sign. The Q-signal QRL, when issued as a question, means "Is the frequency busy?" When this same Q-signal is issued as a response, it means, "The frequency is busy. Please do not interfere."

8. D: In CW operation, the term "zero beat" means matching your transmit frequency to the frequency of a received signal.

9. C: When making a long-path contact with another station, a directional antenna should be pointed 180 degrees from its short-path heading.

10. B: 170 Hz is the most common frequency shift for RTTY emissions in the amateur HF bands.

11. D: A geomagnetic storm is a temporary disturbance in the Earth's magnetosphere. These storms may be caused by magnetic field clouds and solar wind shock waves. A geomagnetic storm may cause rapid fluctuations and unpredictable propagation paths for radio signals. Radio operators in the HF bands may utilize solar and geomagnetic alerts that will enable them to avoid major problems caused by geomagnetic storms.

12. C: Radio waves with frequencies below the Lowest Usable Frequency (LUF) are completely absorbed by the ionosphere.

13. B: One characteristic of HF scatter signals is a wavering sound.

14. C: An antenna coupler is often used to enable matching the transmitter output to an impedance other than 50 ohms.

15. C: One advantage of a digital voltmeter as compared to an analog voltmeter is that a digital voltmeter has better precision for most uses. Voltmeters are used to measure the electrical potential difference between two distinct points in a circuit. An analog voltmeter may be accurate to within a few percent of full scale, assuming that the instrument is being used appropriately. There are analog voltmeters suited for voltages ranging from a few fractions of a volt up to thousands of volts. A digital voltmeter, on the other hand, can achieve accuracy within one percentage point. One recurrent problem with voltmeters is the difficulty of calibration.

16. C: A resonant ground connection may cause high RF voltages on the enclosures of station equipment. A ground connection is any connection made to the ground for the purposes of safety. A ham radio operator may establish indoor or outdoor ground connections.

17. A: An S meter is found in a receiver.

18. C: One disadvantage of using a shortened mobile antenna as opposed to a full size antenna is that operating bandwidth may be very limited.

19. A: As the frequency of the applied AC increases, the reactance of a capacitor decreases. A capacitor is a passive electrical component with two terminals. Its function is to store energy in an electrical field. The basic structure of a capacitor is a pair of conductors separated by a dielectric, or insulator. However, there are capacitors that are much more complex. The capacitor operates by creating a potential difference between the conductors, which produces an electric field across the dielectric. That is, one of the plates of the dielectric has a positive charge, and the other has a negative charge. This electrostatic field becomes a repository of energy.

Copyright © Mometrix Media. You have been licensed one copy of this document for personal use only. Any other reproduction or redistribution is strictly prohibited. All rights reserved.

20. B: The output PEP from a transmitter is 100 watts if an oscilloscope measures 200 volts peak-to-peak across a 50-ohm dummy load connected to the transmitter output. Output peak envelope power is calculated by dividing the square of the voltage by the resistance.

21. C: If the 2250-turn primary winding of a transformer is connected to 120 VAC, the RMS voltage across a 500-turn secondary winding is 26.7 volts.

22. A: Lower capacitance is one advantage of using a Schottky diode in an RF switching circuit as compared to a standard silicon diode. A Schottky diode is a semiconductor diode that can switch very quickly and has a low forward voltage drop. Because the switching time is reduced, the overall system efficiency is improved. The main drawbacks of the Schottky diode are that it has a relatively low reverse voltage rating and a relatively high reverse leakage current. This is true of the typical silicon-metal diode; however, recently silicon carbide Schottky diodes have been constructed that have a much lower reverse leakage current.

23. D: An integrated circuit operational amplifier is analog.

24. D: 360 degrees of the AC cycle is converted to DC by a full-wave rectifier. In other words, a full-wave rectifier operates on the entirety of the sine wave.

25. A: A shift register is a clocked array of circuits that passes data in steps along the array. Shift registers are used to perform timing functions, serial/parallel conversion, and multiplication and division.

26. B: The impedance of a low-pass filter should be about the same as the impedance of the transmission line into which it is compared. A low-pass filter permits signals below a certain cutoff frequency to be transmitted, but attenuates signals above the cutoff frequency.

27. C: One advantage of carrier suppression in a single sideband phone transmission is that the available transmitter power can be used more effectively.

28. D: The total bandwidth of an FM-phone transmission having a 5 kHz deviation and a 3 kHz modulating frequency is 16 kHz.

29. B: The receiving station responds to an ARQ data mode packet containing errors by requesting the packet be retransmitted.

30. D: RF feed line losses are usually expressed in dB per 100 ft.

31. C: The radial wires of a ground-mounted vertical antenna system should be placed on the surface or buried a few inches below the ground.

32. D: The reflector element must be approximately 5 percent longer than the driven element to operate as a beam antenna.

33. A: Wide bandwidth is one advantage of a log periodic antenna. A log periodic antenna resembles a large TV antenna, with several angled elements. These antennas have several elements so that they can function over all of the bands within a particular range. For instance, a ham radio operator may use a log periodic antenna so that a single antenna can be used to cover the 20, 17, 15, 12, and 10 meter bands.

34. D: A ground-mounted antenna should not be installed higher than you can reach.

Copyright © Mometrix Media. You have been licensed one copy of this document for personal use only. Any other reproduction or redistribution is strictly prohibited. All rights reserved.

35. D: The metal enclosure of every item of station equipment must be grounded because it ensures that hazardous voltages cannot appear on the chassis.

Copyright © Mometrix Media. You have been licensed one copy of this document for personal use only. Any other reproduction or redistribution is strictly prohibited. All rights reserved.

General Class Practice Test 7

Practice Questions

1. Which of the following frequencies is within the General Class portion of the 20-meter phone band?
   a. 14005 kHz
   b. 14105 kHz
   c. 14305 kHz
   d. 14405 kHz

2. What are the restrictions on the use of abbreviations or procedural signals in the Amateur Service?
   a. Only "Q" codes are permitted
   b. They may be used if they do not obscure the meaning of a message
   c. They are not permitted
   d. Only "10 codes" are permitted

3. What is the maximum symbol rate permitted for RTTY or data emission transmission on the 20-meter band?
   a. 56 kilobaud
   b. 19.6 kilobaud
   c. 1200 baud
   d. 300 baud

4. Volunteer Examiners are accredited by what organization?
   a. The Federal Communications Commission
   b. The Universal Licensing System
   c. A Volunteer Examiner Coordinator
   d. The Wireless Telecommunications Bureau

5. With which foreign countries is third party traffic prohibited, except for messages directly involving emergencies or disaster relief communications?
   a. Countries in ITU Region 2
   b. Countries in ITU Region 1
   c. Every foreign country, unless there is a third party agreement in effect with that country
   d. Any country which is not a member of the International Amateur Radio Union (IARU)

6. Which of the following statements is true of the single sideband voice mode?
   a. Only one sideband and the carrier are transmitted; the other sideband is suppressed
   b. Only one sideband is transmitted; the other sideband and carrier are suppressed
   c. SSB voice transmissions have higher average power than any other mode
   d. SSB is the only mode that is authorized on the 160, 75 and 40 meter amateur bands

7. Which of the following complies with good amateur practice when choosing a frequency on which to initiate a call?
   a. Check to see if the channel is assigned to another station
   b. Identify your station by transmitting your call sign at least 3 times
   c. Follow the voluntary band plan for the operating mode you intend to use
   d. All of these choices are correct

Copyright © Mometrix Media. You have been licensed one copy of this document for personal use only. Any other reproduction or redistribution is strictly prohibited. All rights reserved.

8. When sending CW, what does a "C" mean when added to the RST report?
   a. Chirpy or unstable signal
   b. Report was read from S meter reading rather than estimated
   c. 100 percent copy
   d. Key clicks

9. Which of the following is required by the FCC rules when operating in the 60-meter band?
   a. If you are using other than a dipole antenna, you must keep a record of the gain of your antenna
   b. You must keep a log of the date, time, frequency, power level and stations worked
   c. You must keep a log of all third party traffic
   d. You must keep a log of the manufacturer of your equipment and the antenna used

10. What segment of the 80-meter band is most commonly used for digital transmissions?
   a. 3570 – 3600 kHz
   b. 3500 – 3525 kHz
   c. 3700 – 3750 kHz
   d. 3775 – 3825 kHz

11. At what point in the solar cycle does the 20-meter band usually support worldwide propagation during daylight hours?
   a. At the summer solstice
   b. Only at the maximum point of the solar cycle
   c. Only at the minimum point of the solar cycle
   d. At any point in the solar cycle

12. What does LUF stand for?
   a. The Lowest Usable Frequency for communications between two points
   b. The Longest Universal Function for communications between two points
   c. The Lowest Usable Frequency during a 24 hour period
   d. The Longest Universal Function during a 24 hour period

13. What makes HF scatter signals often sound distorted?
   a. The ionospheric layer involved is unstable
   b. Ground waves are absorbing much of the signal
   c. The E-region is not present
   d. Energy is scattered into the skip zone through several different radio wave paths

14. What condition can lead to permanent damage to a solid-state RF power amplifier?
   a. Insufficient drive power
   b. Low input SWR
   c. Shorting the input signal to ground
   d. Excessive drive power

15. What signals are used to conduct a two-tone test?
   a. Two audio signals of the same frequency shifted 90 degrees
   b. Two non-harmonically related audio signals
   c. Two swept frequency tones
   d. Two audio frequency range square wave signals of equal amplitude

Copyright © Mometrix Media. You have been licensed one copy of this document for personal use only. Any other reproduction or redistribution is strictly prohibited. All rights reserved.

16. What is one good way to avoid unwanted effects of stray RF energy in an amateur station?
    a. Connect all equipment grounds together
    b. Install an RF filter in series with the ground wire
    c. Use a ground loop for best conductivity
    d. Install a few ferrite beads on the ground wire where it connects to your station

17. How much must the power output of a transmitter be raised to change the S- meter reading on a distant receiver from S8 to S9?
    a. Approximately 1.5 times
    b. Approximately 2 times
    c. Approximately 4 times
    d. Approximately 8 times

18. Which of the following is the most likely to cause interfering signals to be heard in the receiver of an HF mobile installation in a recent model vehicle?
    a. The battery charging system
    b. The anti-lock braking system
    c. The anti-theft circuitry
    d. The vehicle control computer

19. What happens when the impedance of an electrical load is equal to the internal impedance of the power source?
    a. The source delivers minimum power to the load
    b. The electrical load is shorted
    c. No current can flow through the circuit
    d. The source can deliver maximum power to the load

20. Which value of an AC signal results in the same power dissipation as a DC voltage of the same value?
    a. The peak-to-peak value
    b. The peak value
    c. The RMS value
    d. The reciprocal of the RMS value

21. What is the turns ratio of a transformer used to match an audio amplifier having 600-ohm output impedance to a speaker having a 4 ohm impedance?
    a. 12.2 to 1
    b. 24.4 to 1
    c. 150 to 1
    d. 300 to 1

22. What are the stable operating points for a bipolar transistor used as a switch in a logic circuit?
    a. Its saturation and cut-off regions
    b. Its active region (between the cut-off and saturation regions)
    c. Its peak and valley current points
    d. Its enhancement and deletion modes

23. Which of the following is an advantage of an LED indicator compared to an incandescent indicator?
    a. Lower power consumption
    b. Faster response time
    c. Longer life
    d. All of these choices are correct

Copyright © Mometrix Media. You have been licensed one copy of this document for personal use only. Any other reproduction or redistribution is strictly prohibited. All rights reserved.

24. What is the output waveform of an unfiltered full-wave rectifier connected to a resistive load?
    a. A series of DC pulses at twice the frequency of the AC input
    b. A series of DC pulses at the same frequency as the AC input
    c. A sine wave at half the frequency of the AC input
    d. A steady DC voltage

25. What are the basic components of virtually all sine wave oscillators?
    a. An amplifier and a divider
    b. A frequency multiplier and a mixer
    c. A circulator and a filter operating in a feed-forward loop
    d. A filter and an amplifier operating in a feedback loop

26. What is the simplest combination of stages that implement a superheterodyne receiver?
    a. RF amplifier, detector, audio amplifier
    b. RF amplifier, mixer, IF discriminator
    c. HF oscillator, mixer, detector
    d. HF oscillator, pre-scaler, audio amplifier

27. Which of the following phone emissions uses the narrowest bandwidth?
    a. Single sideband
    b. Double sideband
    c. Phase modulation
    d. Frequency modulation

28. What is the frequency deviation for a 12.21-MHz reactance modulated oscillator in a 5 kHz deviation, 146.52 MHz FM phone transmitter?
    a. 101.75 Hz
    b. 416.7 Hz
    c. 5 kHz
    d. 60 kHz

29. Which of the following statements is true about PSK31?
    a. Upper case letters make the signal stronger
    b. Upper case letters use longer Varicode signals and thus slow down transmission
    c. Varicode Error Correction is used to ensure accurate message reception
    d. Higher power is needed as compared to RTTY for similar error rates

30. What must be done to prevent standing waves on an antenna feed line?
    a. The antenna feed point must be at DC ground potential
    b. The feed line must be cut to a length equal to an odd number of electrical quarter wavelengths
    c. The feed line must be cut to a length equal to an even number of physical half wavelengths
    d. The antenna feed point impedance must be matched to the characteristic impedance of the feed line

31. How does the feed point impedance of a ½ wave dipole antenna change as the antenna is lowered from ¼ wave above ground?
    a. It steadily increases
    b. It steadily decreases
    c. It peaks at about 1/8 wavelength above ground
    d. It is unaffected by the height above ground

Copyright © Mometrix Media. You have been licensed one copy of this document for personal use only. Any other reproduction or redistribution is strictly prohibited. All rights reserved.

32. What does "front-to-back ratio" mean in reference to a Yagi antenna?
   a. The number of directors versus the number of reflectors
   b. The relative position of the driven element with respect to the reflectors and directors
   c. The power radiated in the major radiation lobe compared to the power radiated in exactly the opposite direction
   d. The ratio of forward gain to dipole gain

33. Which of the following describes a log periodic antenna?
   a. Length and spacing of the elements increases logarithmically from one end of the boom to the other
   b. Impedance varies periodically as a function of frequency
   c. Gain varies logarithmically as a function of frequency
   d. SWR varies periodically as a function of boom length

34. What effect does transmitter duty cycle have when evaluating RF exposure?
   a. A lower transmitter duty cycle permits greater short-term exposure levels
   b. A higher transmitter duty cycle permits greater short-term exposure levels
   c. Low duty cycle transmitters are exempt from RF exposure evaluation requirements
   d. High duty cycle transmitters are exempt from RF exposure requirements

35. Which of these choices should be observed when climbing a tower using a safety belt or harness?
   a. Never lean back and rely on the belt alone to support your weight
   b. Confirm that the belt is rated for the weight of the climber and that it is within its allowable service life
   c. Ensure that all heavy tools are securely fastened to the belt D-ring
   d. All of these choices are correct

Copyright © Mometrix Media. You have been licensed one copy of this document for personal use only. Any other reproduction or redistribution is strictly prohibited. All rights reserved.

Answers and Explanations

1. C: The 14305 kHz is within the General Class portion of the 20-meter phone band.

2. B: In the Amateur Service, abbreviations or procedural signals may be used if they do not obscure the meaning of a message. Procedural signals, also known as prosigns, are shorthand messages that indicate the immediate intentions of the operator. A procedural signal may consist of a single letter or two letters transmitted as a single character.

3. D: The maximum symbol rate permitted for RTTY or data emission transmission on the 20-meter band is 300 baud. RTTY (short for radioteletype) is the process of sending radio signals between teleprinters. This was the first fully automated protocol for data transmission. It uses the 5-bit Baudot code, in which characters are converted into codes. The typical speed of character transmission is between 60 and 100 wpm. Though RTTY has become slightly less popular in recent years, it remains a common mode of communication.

4. C: Volunteer Examiners are accredited by the Volunteer Examiner Coordinator. VECs are recognized by the American Radio Relay League.

5. C: Except for messages directly involving emergencies or disaster relief communications, third party traffic is prohibited in every foreign country, unless there is a third party agreement in effect with that country.

6. B: In the single sideband (SSB) voice mode, only one sideband is transmitted; the other sideband and carrier are suppressed. This means that SSB voice transmission consumes considerably less power.

7. C: Following the voluntary band plan for the operating mode you intend to use complies with good amateur practice when choosing a frequency on which to initiate a call.

8. A: When sending CW, a "C" added to the RST report means chirpy or unstable signal. RST stands for readability, strength, and tone. When single-sideband phones are being used, only R and S reports are necessary. In an RST report, readability is measured on a scale from 1 to 5, with 1 being unreadable and 5 being perfectly readable. Strength, meanwhile, is measured on a scale from 1 to 9, with a 1 indicating a barely perceptible signal and a 9 indicating a very strong signal. Tone is measured on a scale from 1 to 9, with 1 indicating sixty cycle a.c. or less, and a 9 indicating perfect tone with no trace of ripple or modulation of any kind.

9. A: When operating in the 60-meter band, the FCC rules require that you keep a record of the gain of your antenna, if you are using other than a dipole antenna.

10. A: The 3570 to 3600 kHz segment of the 80 meter band is most commonly used for data transmissions.

11. D: The 20 meter band usually supports worldwide propagation during daylight hours at any point in the solar cycle.

12. A: LUF stands for the Lowest Usable Frequency for communications between two points.

13. D: HF scatter signals often sound distorted because energy is scattered into the skip zone through several different radio wave paths.

14. D: Excessive drive power can lead to permanent damage when using a solid-state RF power amplifier.

15. B: A two-tone test is conducted with two non-harmonically related audio signals.

16. A: One good way to avoid unwanted effects of stray RF energy in an amateur station is to connect all equipment grounds together.

Copyright © Mometrix Media. You have been licensed one copy of this document for personal use only. Any other reproduction or redistribution is strictly prohibited. All rights reserved.

17. C: The power output of a transmitter must be raised approximately four times to change the S-meter reading on a distant receiver from S8 to S9.

18. D: The vehicle control computer is more likely to cause interfering signals to be heard in the receiver of an HF mobile installation in a recent model vehicle than the battery charging system, the anti-lock braking system, or the anti-theft circuitry.

19. D: When the impedance of an electrical load is equal to the internal impedance of the power source, the source can deliver maximum power to the load. This is known as impedance matching.

20. C: The RMS value of an AC signal results in the same power dissipation as a DC voltage of the same value. RMS (root mean square) value is necessary for determining the amount of power being dissipated by an electrical resistance. The RMS value is only required for this purpose when the current is varying over time.

21. A: The turns ratio of a transformer used to match an audio amplifier having a 600-ohm output to a speaker having a 4-ohm impedance is 12.2 to 1.

22. A: The stable operating points for a bipolar transistor used as a switch in a logic circuit are its saturation and cut-off regions.

23. D: Incandescent indicators consume more power than LEDs. An incandescent indicator produces light because of its temperature. For this reason, it tends to waste a great deal of power. An LED (light-emitting diode) indicator, on the other hand, produces light through electroluminescence.

24. A: The output waveform of an unfiltered full-wave rectifier connected to a resistive load is a series of DC pulses at twice the frequency of the AC input.

25. D: The basic componets of virtually all sine wave oscilllators are a filter and an amplifier operating in a feedback loop. A sine-wave oscillator produces an output voltage that is a sine-wave function of time.

26. C: The simplest combination of stages that implement a superheterodyne receiver is HF oscillator, mixer, and detector.

27. A: Single sideband phone emissions uses the narrowest frequency bandwidth. Unlike an AM transmission, which requires two matching copies of the voice information to be sent out, an SSB transmission only requires one. Therefore, it takes up considerably less of the radio spectrum.

28. B: The frequency deviation for a 12.21-MHz reactance-modulated oscillator in a 5-kHz deviation, 146.52-MHz FM-phone transmitter is 416.7 Hz.

29. B: In PSK31 the upper case letters use longer Varicode signals and thus slow down transmission.

30. D: To prevent standing waves on an antenna feed line, the antenna feed point impedance must be matched to the characteristic impedance of the feed line.

31. B: The feed-point impedance of a 1/2 wave dipole antenna steadily decreases as the antenna is lowered from ¼ wave above ground.

32. C: In reference to a Yagi antenna, the "front-to-back ratio" is the power radiated in the major radiation lobe compared to the power radiated in exactly the opposite direction.

33. A: In a log periodic antenna, the length and spacing of the elements increases logarithmically from one end of the boom to the other.

Copyright © Mometrix Media. You have been licensed one copy of this document for personal use only. Any other reproduction or redistribution is strictly prohibited. All rights reserved.

34. A: When evaluating RF exposure, a lower transmitter duty cycle permits greater short-term exposure levels.

35. B: When climbing on a tower using a safety belt or harness, always attach the belt safety hook to the belt D-ring with the hook opening away from the tower.

Copyright © Mometrix Media. You have been licensed one copy of this document for personal use only. Any other reproduction or redistribution is strictly prohibited. All rights reserved.

General Class Practice Test 8

Practice Questions

1. Which of the following frequencies is within the General Class portion of the 80-meter band?
    a. 1855 kHz
    b. 2560 kHz
    c. 3560 kHz
    d. 3650 kHz

2. When choosing a transmitting frequency, what should you do to comply with good amateur practice?
    a. Review FCC Part 97 Rules regarding permitted frequencies and emissions
    b. Follow generally accepted band plans agreed to by the Amateur Radio community
    c. Before transmitting, listen to avoid interfering with ongoing communication
    d. All of these choices are correct

3. What is the maximum symbol rate permitted for RTTY or data emission transmitted at frequencies below 28 MHz?
    a. 56 kilobaud
    b. 19.6 kilobaud
    c. 1200 baud
    d. 300 baud

4. Which of the following criteria must be met for a non-U.S. citizen to be an accredited Volunteer Examiner?
    a. The person must be a resident of the U.S. for a minimum of 5 years
    b. The person must hold an FCC granted Amateur Radio license of General Class or above
    c. The person's home citizenship must be in ITU region 2
    d. None of these choices is correct; a non-U.S. citizen cannot be a Volunteer Examiner

5. Which of the following is a requirement for a non-licensed person to communicate with a foreign Amateur Radio station from a station with an FCC granted license at which a licensed control operator is present?
    a. Information must be exchanged in English
    b. The foreign amateur station must be in a country with which the United States has a third party agreement
    c. The control operator must have at least a General Class license
    d. All of these choices are correct

6. Which of the following is a recommended way to break into a conversation when using phone?
    a. Say "QRZ" several times followed by your call sign
    b. Say your call sign during a break between transmissions from the other stations
    c. Say "Break. Break. Break." and wait for a response
    d. Say "CQ" followed by the call sign of either station

Copyright © Mometrix Media. You have been licensed one copy of this document for personal use only. Any other reproduction or redistribution is strictly prohibited. All rights reserved.

7. What is the "DX window" in a voluntary band plan?
   a. A portion of the band that should not be used for contacts between stations within the 48 contiguous United States
   b. An FCC rule that prohibits contacts between stations within the United States and possessions on that band segment
   c. An FCC rule that allows only digital contacts in that portion of the band
   d. A portion of the band that has been voluntarily set aside for digital contacts only

8. What prosign is sent to indicate the end of a formal message when using CW?
   a. SK
   b. BK
   c. AR
   d. KN

9. What is a reason why many amateurs keep a station log?
   a. The ITU requires a log of all international contacts
   b. The ITU requires a log of all international third party traffic
   c. The log provides evidence of operation needed to renew a license without retest
   d. To help with a reply if the FCC requests information

10. In what segment of the 20-meter band are most PSK31 operations commonly found?
   a. At the bottom of the slow-scan TV segment, near 14.230 MHz
   b. At the top of the SSB phone segment near 14.325 MHz
   c. In the middle of the CW segment, near 14.100 MHz
   d. Below the RTTY segment, near 14.070 MHz

11. Which of the following effects can a geomagnetic storm have on radio-wave propagation?
   a. Improved high-latitude HF propagation
   b. Degraded high-latitude HF propagation
   c. Improved ground-wave propagation
   d. Improved chances of UHF ducting

12. What does MUF stand for?
   a. The Minimum Usable Frequency for communications between two points
   b. The Maximum Usable Frequency for communications between two points
   c. The Minimum Usable Frequency during a 24 hour period
   d. The Maximum Usable Frequency during a 24 hour period

13. Why are HF scatter signals in the skip zone usually weak?
   a. Only a small part of the signal energy is scattered into the skip zone
   b. Signals are scattered from the magnetosphere which is not a good reflector
   c. Propagation is through ground waves which absorb most of the signal energy
   d. Propagations is through ducts in F region which absorb most of the energy

14. What is the correct adjustment for the load or coupling control of a vacuum tube RF power amplifier?
   a. Minimum SWR on the antenna
   b. Minimum plate current without exceeding maximum allowable grid current
   c. Highest plate voltage while minimizing grid current
   d. Maximum power output without exceeding maximum allowable plate current

Copyright © Mometrix Media. You have been licensed one copy of this document for personal use only. Any other reproduction or redistribution is strictly prohibited. All rights reserved.

15. Which of the following instruments may be used to monitor relative RF output when making antenna and transmitter adjustments?
    a. A field strength meter
    b. An antenna noise bridge
    c. A multimeter
    d. A Q meter

16. Which of the following would reduce RF interference caused by common-mode current on an audio cable?
    a. Placing a ferrite bead around the cable
    b. Adding series capacitors to the conductors
    c. Adding shunt inductors to the conductors
    d. Adding an additional insulating jacket to the cable

17. What frequency range is occupied by a 3 kHz LSB signal when the displayed carrier frequency is set to 7.178 MHz?
    a. 7.178 to 7.181 MHz
    b. 7.178 to 7.184 MHz
    c. 7.175 to 7.178 MHz
    d. 7.1765 to 7.1795 MHz

18. What is the name of the process by which sunlight is changed directly into electricity?
    a. Photovoltaic conversion
    b. Photon emission
    c. Photosynthesis
    d. Photon decomposition

19. Why is impedance matching important?
    a. So the source can deliver maximum power to the load
    b. So the load will draw minimum power from the source
    c. To ensure that there is less resistance than reactance in the circuit
    d. To ensure that the resistance and reactance in the circuit are equal

20. What is the RMS voltage of a sine wave with a value of 17 volts peak?
    a. 8.5 volts
    b. 12 volts
    c. 24 volts
    d. 34 volts

21. What is the equivalent capacitance of two 5.0 nanofarad capacitors and one 750 picofarad capacitor connected in parallel?
    a. 576.9 nanofarads
    b. 1733 picofarads
    c. 3583 picofarads
    d. 10.750 nanofarads

22. Why must the cases of some large power transistors be insulated from ground?
    a. To increase the beta of the transistor
    b. To improve the power dissipation capability
    c. To reduce stray capacitance
    d. To avoid shorting the collector or drain voltage to ground

Copyright © Mometrix Media. You have been licensed one copy of this document for personal use only. Any other reproduction or redistribution is strictly prohibited. All rights reserved.

23. How is an LED biased when emitting light?
    a. Beyond cutoff
    b. At the Zener voltage
    c. Reverse Biased
    d. Forward Biased

24. Which of the following is an advantage of a switch-mode power supply as compared to a linear power supply?
    a. Faster switching time makes higher output voltage possible
    b. Fewer circuit components are required
    c. High frequency operation allows the use of smaller components
    d. All of these choices are correct

25. How is the efficiency of an RF power amplifier determined?
    a. Divide the DC input power by the DC output power
    b. Divide the RF output power by the DC input power
    c. Multiply the RF input power by the reciprocal of the RF output power
    d. Add the RF input power to the DC output power

26. What type of circuit is used in many FM receivers to convert signals coming from the IF amplifier to audio?
    a. Product detector
    b. Phase inverter
    c. Mixer
    d. Discriminator

27. Which of the following is an effect of overmodulation?
    a. Insufficient audio
    b. Insufficient bandwidth
    c. Frequency drift
    d. Excessive bandwidth

28. Why is it important to know the duty cycle of the data mode you are using when transmitting?
    a. To aid in tuning your transmitter
    b. Some modes have high duty cycles which could exceed the transmitter's average power rating.
    c. To allow time for the other station to break in during a transmission
    d. All of these choices are correct

29. What does the number 31 represent in PSK31?
    a. The approximate transmitted symbol rate
    b. The version of the PSK protocol
    c. The year in which PSK31 was invented
    d. The number of characters that can be represented by PSK31

30. If the SWR on an antenna feed line is 5 to 1, and a matching network at the transmitter end of the feed line is adjusted to 1 to 1 SWR, what is the resulting SWR on the feed line?
    a. 1 to 1
    b. 5 to 1
    c. Between 1 to 1 and 5 to 1 depending on the characteristic impedance of the line
    d. Between 1 to 1 and 5 to 1 depending on the reflected power at the transmitter

Copyright © Mometrix Media. You have been licensed one copy of this document for personal use only. Any other reproduction or redistribution is strictly prohibited. All rights reserved.

31. How does the feed point impedance of a ½ wave dipole change as the feed-point location is moved from the center toward the ends?
    a. It steadily increases
    b. It steadily decreases
    c. It peaks at about 1/8 wavelength from the end
    d. It is unaffected by the location of the feed point

32. What is meant by the "main lobe" of a directive antenna?
    a. The magnitude of the maximum vertical angle of radiation
    b. The point of maximum current in a radiating antenna element
    c. The maximum voltage standing wave point on a radiating element
    d. The direction of maximum radiated field strength from the antenna

33. Why is a Beverage antenna not used for transmitting?
    a. Its impedance is too low for effective matching
    b. It has high losses compared to other types of antennas
    c. It has poor directivity
    d. All of these choices are correct

34. Which of the following steps must an amateur operator take to ensure compliance with RF safety regulations when transmitter power exceeds levels specified in part 97.13?
    a. Post a copy of FCC Part 97.13 in the station
    b. Post a copy of OET Bulletin 65 in the station
    c. Perform a routine RF exposure evaluation
    d. All of these choices are correct

35. What should be done by any person preparing to climb a tower that supports electrically powered devices?
    a. Notify the electric company that a person will be working on the tower
    b. Make sure all circuits that supply power to the tower are locked out and tagged
    c. Unground the base of the tower
    d. All of these choices are correct

Copyright © Mometrix Media. You have been licensed one copy of this document for personal use only. Any other reproduction or redistribution is strictly prohibited. All rights reserved.

Answers and Explanations

1. C: The 3560 kHz frequenciy is within the General Class portion of the 80 meter band.

2. D: When choosing a transmitting frequency, there are a few things you should do to comply with good amateur practice. To begin with, review the FCC Part 97 Rules regarding permitted frequencies and emissions. Also, follow the generally accepted band plans agreed to by the Amateur Radio community. Finally, before transmitting, listen to avoid interfering with ongoing communication.

3. D: The maximum symbol rate permitted for RTTY or data emission transmitted at frequencies below 28 MHz is 300 baud.

4. B: For a non-U.S. citizen to be an accredited Volunteer Examiner, the person must hold an FCC granted Amateur Radio license of General Class or above.

5. B: For a non-licensed person to communicate with a foreign Amateur Radio station from a station with an FCC granted license at which a licensed control operator is present, the foreign amateur station must be in a country with which the United States has a third party agreement.

6. B: Saying your call sign during a break between transmissions from the other stations is a recommended way to break into a conversation when using phone. Another method is to say "Break" quickly when there is a gap in the conversation. Often, the best time to break in is when the other stations alternate the transmitting and receiving roles. Typically, if the break is heard, one of the other stations will respond by requesting more information. At this point, the breaker should respond as if he or she was answering a CQ.

7. A: The "DX window" in a voluntary band plan is a portion of the band that should not be used for contacts between stations within the 48 contiguous United States.

8. C: The prosign AR is sent to indicate the end of a formal message when using CW. Prosigns, otherwise known as procedural signals, are one- or two-letter signals that indicate the intention of the operator. The prosign AR means "end of message." Some of the other common prosigns are AA (new line), AS (wait), BK (break), BT (space down two lines), CL (going off the air), CT (start of transmission), DO (shift to wabun code), K (go or over; that is, an invitation for another station to speak), KN (invitation to a specific station to transmit), SK (end of contact), SN (understood), and SOS (serious distress, assistance required).

9. D: Many amateurs keep a log even though the FCC doesn't require it to help with a reply if the FCC requests information.

10. D: Most PSK31 operations are commonly found below the RTTY segment of the 20-meter band, near 14.070 MHz.

11. B: A geomagnetic storm can improve the chances of UHF ducting during radio-wave propagation.

12. B: MUF stands for the Maximum Usable Frequency for communications between two points. The maximum usable frequency is the highest radio signal frequency that will reach a given destination using skip, or skywave, propagation. The maximum usable frequency will not be the same for all destinations with respect to the same transmitter.

13. A: HF scatter signals in the skip zone are usually weak because only a small part of the signal energy is scattered into the skip zone. A skip zone is an area in which radio transmissions cannot be received,

Copyright © Mometrix Media. You have been licensed one copy of this document for personal use only. Any other reproduction or redistribution is strictly prohibited. All rights reserved.

even though reception is possible at locations both closer to and farther away from the skip zone. In radio transmission, the skip zone is the area in between the respective ranges of the ground waves and sky waves. In other words, the skip zone is beyond the reach of ground waves but too close for sky waves. The sky waves that would otherwise reach the skip zone penetrate the ionosphere and proceed into space. There is no way to eliminate a skip zone. The precise size of the zone is determined by the height and structure of the ionosphere, and therefore is variable.

14. D: The correct adjustment for the load or coupling control of a vacuum tube RF power amplifier is maximum power output without exceeding maximum allowable plate current.

15. A: A field strength meter may be used to monitor relative RF output when making antenna and transmitter adjustments. A field strength meter operates in the same way as a receiver: that is, it uses a tuner circuit to find signals and feed them into a microammeter. Of course, the field strength meter can only be effective when the antenna has been calibrated.

16. A:. Placing a ferrite bead around the cable would reduce RF interference caused by common-mode current on an audio cable. Ferrite beads are passive electric components capable of diminishing high frequency noise in electronic circuits. The bead itself is a ceramic cylinder, which operates by concentrating the magnetic field, which has the effect of increasing the inductance and thereby increasing the reactance. The increased reactance impedes the unwanted noise.

17. C: A 3 kHz LSB signal occupies a frequency range of 7.175 to 7.178 MHz when the displayed carrier frequency is set to 7.178MHz.

18. A: Photovoltaic conversion is the process by which sunlight is changed directly into electricity. Photovoltaic conversion is accomplished with a photovoltaic cell, also known as a photocell. A photovoltaic cell is capable of generating an electric current, though it needs an external load. When the light from the sun is absorbed by the cell, it creates electron-hole pairs or excitons. At the same time, charge carriers of opposite types are separated. Finally, these carriers are extracted and directed to an outside circuit.

19. A: Impedance matching is important so that the source can deliver maximum power to the load. Impedance matching is the technique of maximizing the power transfer from an electrical load by fine-tuning its input impedance. Impedance matching can also be used to minimize the reflections from the electrical load. It can also be accomplished by adjusting the output impedance of the signal corresponding to the electrical load.

20. B: The RMS voltage of a sine wave with a value of 17 volts peak is 12 volts. RMS voltage is calculated by dividing the peak voltage by 1.414.

21. D: The equivalent capacitance of two 5000 picofarad capacitors and one 750 picofarad capacitor connected in parallel would be 10,750 picofarads. The equivalent capacitance of capacitors in parallel is found by simply adding the individual capacitances.

22. D: The cases of some large power transistors must be insulated from the ground to avoid shorting the collector or drain voltage.

23: D: An LED is forward biased when emitting light.

24. C: One advantage of a switch-mode power supply as compared to a linear power supply is that high frequency operation allows the use of smaller components.

Copyright © Mometrix Media. You have been licensed one copy of this document for personal use only. Any other reproduction or redistribution is strictly prohibited. All rights reserved.

25. B: The efficiency of an RF power amplifier is determined by dividing the RF output power by the DC input power.

26. D: A discriminator is used in many FM receivers to convert signals coming from the IP amplifier to audio.

27. D: Excessive bandwidth is an effect of over-modulation.

28. B: It is important to know the duty cycle of the data mode you are using when transmitting because some modes have high duty cycles which could exceed the transmitter's average power rating. The duty cycle of a transmitter is the amount of time it spends operating at full output power during each transmission. When a transmitter has a higher duty cycle, this means that it creates more RF radiation exposure for an equivalent PEP output.

29. A: In PSK31, the number 31 represents the approximate transmitted symbol rate. Specifically, it refers to the 31.25 Hz taken up by the PSK31 signal: this is a comparatively tiny portion of the bandwidth.

30. B: If the SWR on an antenna line is 5 to 1, and a matching network at the transmitter end of the feed line is adjusted to 1 to 1 SWR, the resulting SWR on the feed line is 5 to 1. The standing wave ratio, also known as the voltage standing wave ratio, is an indication of the impedance match between the feedline and the antenna.

31. A: The feed-point impedance of a ½ wave dipole steadily increases as the feed-point location is moved from the center toward the ends.

32. D: The "main lobe" of a directive antenna is the direction of maximum radiated field strength from the antenna.

33. B: A Beverage antenna is not used for transmitting because it has high losses compared to other types of antennas. However, the Beverage antenna is an inexpensive and effective receiving antenna. The Beverage antenna is extremely directional and large, so it cannot be rotated very easily.

34. C: To ensure compliance with RF safety regulations when transmitter power exceeds specified in part 97.13, an amateur operator should perform a routine RF exposure evaluation.

35. B: Any person preparing to climb a tower that supports electrically powered devices should make sure all circuits that supply power to the tower are locked out and tagged.

Copyright © Mometrix Media. You have been licensed one copy of this document for personal use only. Any other reproduction or redistribution is strictly prohibited. All rights reserved.

General Class Practice Test 9

Practice Questions

1. Which of the following frequencies is within the General Class portion of the 15-meter band?
   a. 14250 kHz
   b. 18155 kHz
   c. 21300 kHz
   d. 24900 kHz

2. When may an amateur station transmit communications in which the licensee or control operator has a pecuniary (monetary) interest?
   a. When other amateurs are being notified of the sale of apparatus normally used in an amateur station and such activity is not done on a regular basis
   b. Only when there is no other means of communications readily available
   c. When other amateurs are being notified of the sale of any item with a monetary value less than $200 and such activity is not done on a regular basis
   d. Never

3. What is the maximum symbol rate permitted for RTTY or data emission transmitted on the 1.25 meter and 70 centimeter bands?
   a. 56 kilobaud
   b. 19.6 kilobaud
   c. 1200 baud
   d. 300 baud

4. How long is a Certificate of Successful Completion of Examination (CSCE) valid for exam element credit?
   a. 30 days
   b. 180 days
   c. 365 days
   d. For as long as your current license is valid

5. What language must you use when identifying your station if you are using a language other than English in making a contact using phone emission?
   a. The language being used for the contact
   b. Any language recognized by the United Nations
   c. English only
   d. English, Spanish, French, or German

6. Why do most amateur stations use lower sideband on the 160-meter, 75-meter and 40-meter bands?
   a. Lower sideband is more efficient than upper sideband at these frequencies
   b. Lower sideband is the only sideband legal on these frequency bands
   c. Because it is fully compatible with an AM detector
   d. Current amateur practice is to use lower sideband on these frequency bands

Copyright © Mometrix Media. You have been licensed one copy of this document for personal use only. Any other reproduction or redistribution is strictly prohibited. All rights reserved.

7. Who may be the control operator of an amateur station transmitting in RACES to assist relief operations during a disaster?
    a. Only a person holding an FCC issued amateur operator license
    b. Only a RACES net control operator
    c. A person holding an FCC issued amateur operator license or an appropriate government official
    d. Any control operator when normal communication systems are operational

8. What does the Q signal "QSL" mean?
    a. Send slower
    b. We have already confirmed by card
    c. I acknowledge receipt
    d. We have worked before

9. What information is traditionally contained in a station log?
    a. Date and time of contact
    b. Band and/or frequency of the contact
    c. Call sign of station contacted and the signal report given
    d. All of these choices are correct

10. How do you join a contact between two stations using the PACTOR protocol?
    a. Send broadcast packets containing your call sign while in MONITOR mode
    b. Transmit a steady carrier until the PACTOR protocol times out and disconnects
    c. Joining an existing contact is not possible, PACTOR connections are limited to two stations
    d. Send a NAK response continuously so that the sending station has to pause

11. What effect do high sunspot numbers have on radio communications?
    a. High-frequency radio signals become weak and distorted
    b. Frequencies above 300 MHz become usable for long-distance communication
    c. Long-distance communication in the upper HF and lower VHF range is enhanced
    d. Microwave communications become unstable

12. What is the approximate maximum distance along the Earth's surface that is normally covered in one hop using the F2 region?
    a. 180 miles
    b. 1,200 miles
    c. 2,500 miles
    d. 12,000 miles

13. What type of radio wave propagation allows a signal to be detected at a distance too far for ground wave propagation but too near for normal sky-wave propagation?
    a. Faraday rotation
    b. Scatter
    c. Sporadic-E skip
    d. Short-path skip

14. Why is a time delay sometimes included in a transmitter keying circuit?
    a. To prevent stations from talking over each other
    b. To allow the transmitter power regulators to charge properly
    c. To allow time for transmit-receive changeover operations to complete properly before RF output is allowed
    d. To allow time for a warning signal to be sent to other stations

Copyright © Mometrix Media. You have been licensed one copy of this document for personal use only. Any other reproduction or redistribution is strictly prohibited. All rights reserved.

15. Which of the following can be determined with a field strength meter?
    a. The radiation resistance of an antenna
    b. The radiation pattern of an antenna
    c. The presence and amount of phase distortion of a transmitter
    d. The presence and amount of amplitude distortion of a transmitter

16. How can a ground loop be avoided?
    a. Connect all ground conductors in series
    b. Connect the AC neutral conductor to the ground wire
    c. Avoid using lock washers and star washers when making ground connections
    d. Connect all ground conductors to a single point

17. What frequency range is occupied by a 3 kHz USB signal with the displayed carrier frequency set to 14.347 MHz?
    a. 14.347 to 14.647 MHz
    b. 14.347 to 14.350 MHz
    c. 14.344 to 14.347 MHz
    d. 14.3455 to 14.3485 MHz

18. What is the approximate open-circuit voltage from a modern, well-illuminated photovoltaic cell?
    a. 0.02 VDC
    b. 0.5 VDC
    c. 0.2 VDC
    d. 1.38 VDC

19. What unit is used to measure reactance?
    a. Farad
    b. Ohm
    c. Ampere
    d. Siemens

20. What percentage of power loss would result from a transmission line loss of 1 dB?
    a. 10.9 percent
    b. 12.2 percent
    c. 20.5 percent
    d. 25.9 percent

21. What is the capacitance of three 100 microfarad capacitors connected in series?
    a. 0.30 microfarads
    b. 0.33 microfarads
    c. 33.3 microfarads
    d. 300 microfarads

22. Which of the following describes the construction of a MOSFET?
    a. The gate is formed by a back-biased junction
    b. The gate is separated from the channel with a thin insulating layer
    c. The source is separated from the drain by a thin insulating layer
    d. The source is formed by depositing metal on silicon

Copyright © Mometrix Media. You have been licensed one copy of this document for personal use only. Any other reproduction or redistribution is strictly prohibited. All rights reserved.

23. Which of the following is a characteristic of a liquid crystal display?
    a. It requires ambient or back lighting
    b. It offers a wide dynamic range
    c. It has a wide viewing angle
    d. All of these choices are correct

24. Which symbol in figure G7-1 represents a field effect transistor?
(figure G7-1 found at the end of the guide)
    a. Symbol 2
    b. Symbol 5
    c. Symbol 1
    d. Symbol 4

25. What determines the frequency of an LC oscillator?
    a. The number of stages in the counter
    b. The number of stages in the divider
    c. The inductance and capacitance in the tank circuit
    d. The time delay of the lag circuit

26. Which of the following is needed for a Digital Signal Processor IF filter?
    a. An analog to digital converter
    b. A digital to analog converter
    c. A digital processor chip
    d. All of these choices are correct

27. What control is typically adjusted for proper ALC setting on an amateur single sideband transceiver?
    a. The RF clipping level
    b. Transmit audio or microphone gain
    c. Antenna inductance or capacitance
    d. Attenuator level

28. Why is it good to match receiver bandwidth to the bandwidth of the operating mode?
    a. It is required by FCC rules
    b. It minimizes power consumption in the receiver
    c. It improves impedance matching of the antenna
    d. It results in the best signal to noise ratio

29. How does forward error correction (FEC) allow the receiver to correct errors in received data packets?
    a. By controlling transmitter output power for optimum signal strength
    b. By using the varicode character set
    c. By transmitting redundant information with the data
    d. By using a parity bit with each character

30. What standing wave ratio will result from the connection of a 50 ohm feed line to a non-reactive load having a 200 ohm impedance?
    a. 4:1
    b. 1:4
    c. 2:1
    d. 1:2

Copyright © Mometrix Media. You have been licensed one copy of this document for personal use only. Any other reproduction or redistribution is strictly prohibited. All rights reserved.

31. Which of the following is an advantage of a horizontally polarized as compared to vertically polarized HF antenna?
    a. Lower ground reflection losses
    b. Lower feed point impedance
    c. Shorter Radials
    d. Lower radiation resistance

32. How does the gain of two 3-element horizontally polarized Yagi antennas spaced vertically 1/2 wavelength apart typically compare to the gain of a single 3-element Yagi?
    a. Approximately 1.5 dB higher
    b. Approximately 3 dB higher
    c. Approximately 6 dB higher
    d. Approximately 9 dB higher

33. Which of the following is an application for a Beverage antenna?
    a. Directional transmitting for low HF bands
    b. Directional receiving for low HF bands
    c. Portable direction finding at higher HF frequencies
    d. Portable direction finding at lower HF frequencies

34. What type of instrument can be used to accurately measure an RF field?
    a. A receiver with an S meter
    b. A calibrated field strength meter with a calibrated antenna
    c. An SWR meter with a peak-reading function
    d. An oscilloscope with a high-stability crystal marker generator

35. Why should soldered joints not be used with the wires that connect the base of a tower to a system of ground rods?
    a. The resistance of solder is too high
    b. Solder flux will prevent a low conductivity connection
    c. Solder has too high a dielectric constant to provide adequate lightning protection
    d. A soldered joint will likely be destroyed by the heat of a lightning strike

Copyright © Mometrix Media. You have been licensed one copy of this document for personal use only. Any other reproduction or redistribution is strictly prohibited. All rights reserved.

Answers and Explanations

1. C: The 21300 kHz frequency is within the General Class portion of the 15-meter band.

2. A: An amateur station may transmit communications in which the licensee or control operator has a pecuniary (monetary) interest when other amateurs are being notified of the sale of apparatus normally used in an amateur station and such activity is not done on a regular basis. A pecuniary interest is said to exist even when the promised compensation is goods besides money.

3. A: The maximum symbol rate permitted for RTTY or data emission transmitted on the 1.25 meter and 70 centimeter bands is 56 kilobaud.

4. C: A Certificate of Successful Completion of Examination (CSCE) is valid for exam element credit for 365 days.

5. C: When identifying your station while using a language other than English when making a contact using phone emission, you must speak in English. English is the lingua franca for ham radio communication.

6. D: Most amateur stations use lower sideband on the 160, 75, and 40 meter bands simply because this is current amateur practice. The separation between the bands used by the upper sideband and those used by the lower sideband is largely arbitrary and based on tradition.

7. A: Only a person holding an FCC-issued amateur operator license may be the control operator of an amateur station transmitting in RACES to assist relief operations during a disaster. RACES (the Radio Amateur Civil Emergency Service) is administered by the Federal Emergency Management Agency (FEMA). In order to be a part of RACES, an operator must also have membership in the relevant local group charged with disaster relief. Ham radio operators may obtain membership in RACES by contacting their state's Auxiliary Communications Service.

8. C: The Q signal "QSL" means "I acknowledge receipt." If this Q-signal is issued as a question, it means "Did you receive and understand my transmission?"

9. D: A station log traditionally contains the date and time of contact; the band and/or frequency of the contact; and the call sign of the station contacted and the signal report given. Many operators also record the mode of communication that was used, the signal report sent and received, and any other relevant personal information about the other operator.

10. C: It is not possible to join a contact between two stations using a PACTOR protocol.

11. C: High sunspot numbers enhance long-distance radio communication in the upper HF and lower VHF range.

12. C: The approximate maximum distance along the Earth's surface that is normally covered in one hop using the F2 region is 2,500 miles. The F2 region is part of the ionosphere's F layer, also known as the Appleton layer. The F layer lies in between the E region and the protonosphere. It is useful for the propagation of high frequency radio waves. The greatest concentration of free electrons and ions in the atmosphere is found in the F region. The F1 region lies below the F2 region during the day, but at night these regions are one and the same. The F2 region is found between 220 and 800 km above the surface of the Earth.

13. B: Scatter radio wave propagation allows a signal to be detected at a distance too far for ground wave propagation but too near for normal sky-wave propagation.

14. C: A time delay is sometimes included in a transmitter keying circuit to allow time for transmit-receive changeover operations to complete properly before RF output is allowed.

Copyright © Mometrix Media. You have been licensed one copy of this document for personal use only. Any other reproduction or redistribution is strictly prohibited. All rights reserved.

15. B: The radiation pattern of an antenna can be determined with a field strength meter.

16. D: A ground loop can be avoided by connecting all ground conductors to a single point. A ground loop is an unexpected and unwanted current flowing between two points that are incorrectly believed to have the same electric potential. The most common consequences of a ground loop are noise and interference, but there can also be a risk of electric shock. Some other strategies for reducing the risk of ground loop are to position the most powerful devices closest to the power source, to use differential signals, and to check isolated power supplies for component, parasitic, or internal PCB power plane capacitance.

17. B: A 3 kHz USB signal with the displayed carrier frequency set to 14.347 MHz occupies a frequency range from 14.347 to 14.350 MHz.

18. B: The approximate open-circuit voltage from a modern, well-illuminated photovoltaic cell is 0.5 VDC.

19. B: The ohm is used to measure reactance. Specifically, the ohm is equal to the resistance created between two points of a conductor when a continuous potential difference of one volt is applied and produces a current of one ampere. The multimeter is the standard instrument for measuring resistance in ohms.

20. C: A transmission line loss of 1 dB would result in a power loss of 20.5%.

21. C: The capacitance of three 100 microfarad capacitors connected in series would be 33.3 microfarads. When all of the capacitors in a series have the same capacitance, the total capacitance can be calculated by dividing the capacitance of a single capacitor by the number of capacitors.

22. B: In a MOSFET, the gate is separated from the channel with a thin insulating layer. A MOSFET, or metal-oxide-semiconductor field effect transistor, is used to switch or amplify electronic signals. A MOSFET has four terminals: source, gate, drain, and body.

23. A: One characteristic of a liquid crystal display is that it requires ambient or back lighting. A liquid crystal display (LCD) does not emit light directly, but rather relies on external light to create an image.

24. C: In figure G7-1, symbol 1 represents a field effect transistor.

25. C: The frequency of an LC oscillator is determined by the inductance and capacitance in the tank circuit.

26. D: A Digital Signal Processor IF filter requires an analog to digital converter, a digital to analog converter, and a digital processor chip. This type of filtering allows digital signal processing to reach levels of flexibility equal to those of high-quality fixed-width filters.

27. B: The transmit audio or microphone gain is typically adjusted for proper ALC setting on an amateur single sideband transceiver.

28. D: Matching receiver bandwidth to the bandwidth of the operating mode results in the best signal to noise ratio. The receiver is the piece of equipment that converts radio waves into signals that can be heard or seen by the operator.

29. C: FEC allows the receiver to correct errors in received data packets by transmitting redundant information with the data.

30. A: The connection of a 50-ohm feed line to a non-reactive load having a 200-ohm impedance will result in a standing wave ratio of 4:1.

31. A: Horizontally polarized HF antennas have lower ground reflection losses than vertically polarized HF antennas.

Copyright © Mometrix Media. You have been licensed one copy of this document for personal use only. Any other reproduction or redistribution is strictly prohibited. All rights reserved.

32. B: The gain of two 3-element horizontally polarized Yagi antennas spaced vertically 1/2 wavelength apart is approximately 3 dB higher than the gain of a single 3-element Yagi.

33. B: One application for a Beverage antenna is directional receiving for low HF bands.

34. B: A calibrated field-strength meter with a calibrated antenna can be used to accurately measure an RF field.

35. D: Soldered joints should not be used with the wires that connect the base of a tower to a system of ground rods because a soldered joint will likely be destroyed by the heat of a lightning strike.

Copyright © Mometrix Media. You have been licensed one copy of this document for personal use only. Any other reproduction or redistribution is strictly prohibited. All rights reserved.

General Class Practice Test 10

Practice Questions

1. Which of the following frequencies is available to a control operator holding a General Class license?
   a. 28.020 MHz
   b. 28.350 MHz
   c. 28.550 MHz
   d. All of these choices are correct

2. What is the power limit for beacon stations?
   a. 10 watts PEP output
   b. 20 watts PEP output
   c. 100 watts PEP output
   d. 200 watts PEP output

3. What is the maximum symbol rate permitted for RTTY or data emission transmissions on the 10-meter band?
   a. 56 kilobaud
   b. 19.6 kilobaud
   c. 1200 baud
   d. 300 baud

4. What is the minimum age that one must be to qualify as an accredited Volunteer Examiner?
   a. 12 years
   b. 18 years
   c. 21 years
   d. There is no age limit

5. Which of the following is the FCC term for an unattended digital station that transfers messages to and from the Internet?
   a. Locally controlled station
   b. Robotically controlled station
   c. Automatically controlled digital station
   d. Fail-safe digital station

6. Which of the following statements is true of voice VOX operation versus PTT operation?
   a. The received signal is more natural sounding
   b. It allows "hands free" operation
   c. It occupies less bandwidth
   d. It provides more power output

7. When may the FCC restrict normal frequency operations of amateur stations participating in RACES?
   a. When they declare a temporary state of communication emergency
   b. When they seize your equipment for use in disaster communications
   c. Only when all amateur stations are instructed to stop transmitting
   d. When the President's War Emergency Powers have been invoked

Copyright © Mometrix Media. You have been licensed one copy of this document for personal use only. Any other reproduction or redistribution is strictly prohibited. All rights reserved.

8. What does the Q signal "QRQ" mean?
    a. Send faster
    b. I am troubled by static
    c. Zero beat my signal
    d. Stop sending

9. What is QRP operation?
    a. Remote piloted model control
    b. Low power transmit operation
    c. Transmission using Quick Response Protocol
    d. Traffic relay procedure net operation

10. Which of the following is a way to establish contact with a digital messaging system gateway station?
    a. Send an email to the system control operator
    b. Send QRL in Morse code
    c. Respond when the station broadcasts its SSID
    d. Transmit a connect message on the station's published frequency

11. What causes HF propagation conditions to vary periodically in a 28-day cycle?
    a. Long term oscillations in the upper atmosphere
    b. Cyclic variation in the Earth's radiation belts
    c. The Sun's rotation on its axis
    d. The position of the Moon in its orbit

12. What is the approximate maximum distance along the Earth's surface that is normally covered in one hop using the E region?
    a. 180 miles
    b. 1,200 miles
    c. 2,500 miles
    d. 12,000 miles

13. Which of the following might be an indication that signals heard on the HF bands are being received via scatter propagation?
    a. The communication is during a sunspot maximum
    b. The communication is during a sudden ionospheric disturbance
    c. The signal is heard on a frequency below the Maximum Usable Frequency
    d. The signal is heard on a frequency above the Maximum Usable Frequency

14. What is the purpose of an electronic keyer?
    a. Automatic transmit/receive switching
    b. Automatic generation of strings of dots and dashes for CW operation
    c. VOX operation
    d. Computer interface for PSK and RTTY operation

15. Which of the following can be determined with a directional wattmeter?
    a. Standing wave ratio
    b. Antenna front-to-back ratio
    c. RF interference
    d. Radio wave propagation

Copyright © Mometrix Media. You have been licensed one copy of this document for personal use only. Any other reproduction or redistribution is strictly prohibited. All rights reserved.

16. What could be a symptom of a ground loop somewhere in your station?
    a. You receive reports of "hum" on your station's transmitted signal
    b. The SWR reading for one or more antennas is suddenly very high
    c. An item of station equipment starts to draw excessive amounts of current
    d. You receive reports of harmonic interference from your station

17. How close to the lower edge of the 40-meter General Class phone segment should your displayed carrier frequency be when using 3 kHz wide LSB?
    a. 3 kHz above the edge of the segment
    b. 3 kHz below the edge of the segment
    c. Your displayed carrier frequency may be set at the edge of the segment
    d. Center your signal on the edge of the segment

18. What is the reason a series diode is connected between a solar panel and a storage battery that is being charged by the panel?
    a. The diode serves to regulate the charging voltage to prevent overcharge
    b. The diode prevents self discharge of the battery though the panel during times of low or no illumination
    c. The diode limits the current flowing from the panel to a safe value
    d. The diode greatly increases the efficiency during times of high illumination

19. What unit is used to measure impedance?
    a. Volt
    b. Ohm
    c. Ampere
    d. Watt

20. What is the ratio of peak envelope power to average power for an unmodulated carrier?
    a. .707
    b. 1.00
    c. 1.414
    d. 2.00

21. What is the inductance of three 10 millihenry inductors connected in parallel?
    a. .30 henrys
    b. 3.3 henrys
    c. 3.3 millihenrys
    d. 30 millihenrys

22. Which element of a triode vacuum tube is used to regulate the flow of electrons between cathode and plate?
    a. Control grid
    b. Heater
    c. Screen Grid
    d. Trigger electrode

23. What two devices in an Amateur Radio station might be connected using a USB interface?
    a. Computer and transceiver
    b. Microphone and transceiver
    c. Amplifier and antenna
    d. Power supply and amplifier

Copyright © Mometrix Media. You have been licensed one copy of this document for personal use only. Any other reproduction or redistribution is strictly prohibited. All rights reserved.

24. Which symbol in figure G7-1 represents a Zener diode?
(figure G7-1 found at the end of the guide)
    a. Symbol 4
    b. Symbol 1
    c. Symbol 11
    d. Symbol 5

25. Which of the following is a characteristic of a Class A amplifier?
    a. Low standby power
    b. High Efficiency,
    c. No need for bias
    d. Low distortion

26. How is Digital Signal Processor filtering accomplished?
    a. By using direct signal phasing
    b. By converting the signal from analog to digital and using digital processing
    c. By differential spurious phasing
    d. By converting the signal from digital to analog and taking the difference of mixing products

27. What is meant by flat-topping of a single-sideband phone transmission?
    a. Signal distortion caused by insufficient collector current
    b. The transmitter's automatic level control is properly adjusted
    c. Signal distortion caused by excessive drive
    d. The transmitter's carrier is properly suppressed

28. What is the relationship between transmitted symbol rate and bandwidth?
    a. Symbol rate and bandwidth are not related
    b. Higher symbol rates require wider bandwidth
    c. Lower symbol rates require wider bandwidth
    d. Bandwidth is always half the symbol rate

29. How are the two separate frequencies of a Frequency Shift Keyed (FSK) signal identified?
    a. Dot and Dash
    b. On and Off
    c. High and Low
    d. Mark and Space

30. What standing wave ratio will result from the connection of a 50 ohm feed line to a non-reactive load having a 10 ohm impedance?
    a. 2:1
    b. 50:1
    c. 1:5
    d. 5:1

31. What is the approximate length for a ½ wave dipole antenna cut for 14.250 MHz?
    a. 8 feet
    b. 16 feet
    c. 24 feet
    d. 32 feet

Copyright © Mometrix Media. You have been licensed one copy of this document for personal use only. Any other reproduction or redistribution is strictly prohibited. All rights reserved.

32. Which of the following is a Yagi antenna design variable that could be adjusted to optimize forward gain, front-to-back ratio, or SWR bandwidth?
   a. The physical length of the boom
   b. The number of elements on the boom
   c. The spacing of each element along the boom
   d. All of these choices are correct

33. Which of the following describes a Beverage antenna?
   a. A vertical antenna constructed from beverage cans
   b. A broad-band mobile antenna
   c. A helical antenna for space reception
   d. A very long and low directional receiving antenna

34. What is one thing that can be done if evaluation shows that a neighbor might receive more than the allowable limit of RF exposure from the main lobe of a directional antenna?
   a. Change to a non-polarized antenna with higher gain
   b. Post a warning sign that is clearly visible to the neighbor
   c. Use an antenna with a higher front-to-back ratio
   d. Take precautions to ensure that the antenna cannot be pointed in their direction

35. Which of the following is a danger from lead-tin solder?
   a. Lead can contaminate food if hands are not washed carefully after handling the solder
   b. High voltages can cause lead-tin solder to disintegrate suddenly
   c. Tin in the solder can "cold flow" causing shorts in the circuit
   d. RF energy can convert the lead into a poisonous gas

Copyright © Mometrix Media. You have been licensed one copy of this document for personal use only. Any other reproduction or redistribution is strictly prohibited. All rights reserved.

Answers and Explanations

1. D: The 28.020 MHz, 28.350 MHz, and 28.550 MHz frequencies are all available to a control operator holding a General Class license. A control operator is an amateur who has been assigned responsibility for the transmissions made by an amateur station. This assignation is made by the station.

2. C: The power limit for beacon stations is 100 watts PEP output.

3. C: The maximum symbol rate permitted for RTTY or data emission transmissions on the 10 meter band is 1200 baud.

4. B: One must be at least 18 years old to qualify as an accredited Volunteer Examiner. Each licensing exam requires the presence of three Volunteer Examiners, each of which needs to sign the paperwork for the exam to be valid.

5. C: The FCC term for an unattended digital station that tranfers messages to and from the internet is called an automatically controlled digital station.

6. B: SSB VOX allows "hands free" operation.

7. D: The FCC may restrict normal frequency operations of amateur stations participating in RACES when the President's War Emergency Powers have been invoked. In these stations, the military or emergency services groups may require extra frequency ranges for urgent communications.

8. B: The Q signal "QRQ" means send faster. When issued as a query, this Q signal means "Shall I send faster?" This signal is often accompanied by a suggested rate of transmission in words per minute.

9. B: QRP operation is low power transmit operation. This method of operation is preferred by many because it requires incredible precision and skill. QRP means no more than 5 watts of transmitter output power for Morse code, and no more than 10 watts of peak power on voice transmission. For the most part, QRP occurs in Morse code and on HF.

10. D: To establish contact with a digital messaging system gateway station, just transmit a connect message on the station's published frequency.

11. C: The Sun's rotation on its axis causes HF propagation conditions to vary periodically in a 28-day cycle.

12. B: The approximate maximum distance along the Earth's surface that is normally covered in one hop using the E region is 1,200 miles. The E region, also known as the Kennelly-Heaviside layer, is the section of the ionosphere that lies approximately 90 to 150 kilometers above the Earth's surface. This layer can reflect medium frequency radio waves, particularly at night when the ionosphere is dragged further away from the Earth by solar wind. The distance which the E layer can transmit signals is also influenced by the season and the level of sunspot activity.

13. D: If the signal is heard on a frequency above the Maximum Usable Frequency, this might be an indication that signals heard on the HF bands are being received via scatter propagation.

14. B: The purpose of an electronic keyer is the automatic generation of strings of dots and dashes for CW operation.

Copyright © Mometrix Media. You have been licensed one copy of this document for personal use only. Any other reproduction or redistribution is strictly prohibited. All rights reserved.

15. A: Standing wave ratio can be determined with a directional wattmeter. The standing wave ratio is the relationship of the amplitude of a partial standing wave at an antinode to the amplitude at the next node. Standing wave ratio, or SWR, is often used as an indicator of the efficiency of a radio frequency transmission. The best possible SWR is 1:1, which would mean that the entirety of the power is reaching its destination, and no part of the signal is reflected.

16. A: If you receive reports of "hum" on your station's transmitted signal, this may be a symptom of a ground loop. Ground loops are often responsible for noise and interference, and in some cases may even present a risk of electric shock.

17. A: When using 3 kHz wide LSB, your displayed carrier frequency should be 3 kHz above the lower edge of the 40-meter General Class phone segment.

18. B: A series diode is connected between a solar panel and a storage battery that is being charged by the panel to prevent self discharge of the battery through the panel during times of low or no illumination. Diodes are two-terminal electronic components that offer little resistance in one direction and total resistance in the other.

19. B: The ohm is used to measure impedance. In an alternating current circuit, ohms are used as the unit of measure for electrical impedance. This is always the case when measuring the electrical impedance of an alternating current circuit.

20. B: The ratio of peak envelope power to average power for an unmodulated carrier is 1.00. Peak envelope power is the highest envelope power a transmitter can deliver to the antenna transmission line during an undistorted RF cycle.

21. C: The inductance of three 10 millihenry inductors connected in parallel would be 3.3 millihenrys. One divided by the total inductance is equal to the sum of one divided by each of the individual inductances.

22. A: The control grid of a triode vacuum tube is used to regulate the flow of electrons between cathode and plate.

23. A: The computer and transceiver of an Amateur Radio station might be connected with a USB interface.

24. D: In figure G7-1, symbol 5 represents a Zener diode. A Zener diode is a semiconductor made of silicon, primarily used to regulate voltage. The positive characteristic of this diode is that it can maintain a fairly consistent voltage through a broad range of currents.

25. D: Low distortion is a characteristic of a Class A amplifier. This type of linear amplifier is biased such that the active device conducts through 360 degrees of the input waveform.

26. B: Digital Signal Processing filtering is accomplished by converting the signal from analog to digital and using digital processing.

27. C: In single sideband phone transmission, flat-topping is signal distortion caused by excessive drive.

28. B: The relationship between transmitted symbol rate and bandwidth is the higher symbol rates require wider bandwidth.

29. D: The two separate frequencies of a FSK signal are identified by a mark and space.

Copyright © Mometrix Media. You have been licensed one copy of this document for personal use only. Any other reproduction or redistribution is strictly prohibited. All rights reserved.

30. D: The connection of a 50-ohm feed line to a non-reactive load with a 10-ohm impedance will result in a standing wave ratio of 5:1.

31. D: The approximate length for a ½ wave dipole antenna cut for 14.250 MHz is 32 feet.

32. D: The forward gain, front-to-back ratio, or SWR bandwidth of a Yagi antenna could be optimized by adjusting the physical length of the boom, the number of elements on the boom, or the spacing of each element along the boom.

33. D: A Beverage antenna is a very long and low directional receiving antenna.

34. D: If evaluation shows that a neighbor might receive more than the allowable limit of RF exposure from the main lobe of a directional antenna, the operator can take precautions to ensure that the antenna cannot be pointed in his or her direction.

35. A: One danger of lead-tin solder is that the lead can contaminate food if hands are not washed carefully after handling.

Copyright © Mometrix Media. You have been licensed one copy of this document for personal use only. Any other reproduction or redistribution is strictly prohibited. All rights reserved.

Extra Class Question Pool

E1 – Commission's Rules

E1A – Operating Standards: frequency privileges; emission standards; automatic message forwarding; frequency sharing; stations aboard ships or aircraft

When using a transceiver that displays the carrier frequency of phone signals, which of the following displayed frequencies represents the highest frequency at which a properly adjusted USB emission will be totally within the band?
- A. The exact upper band edge
- B. 300 Hz below the upper band edge
- C. 1 kHz below the upper band edge
- D. 3 kHz below the upper band edge

E1A01: D. The highest frequency at which a properly adjusted USB emission will be totally within the band is 3 kHz below the upper band edge. [97.301, 97.305]

When using a transceiver that displays the carrier frequency of phone signals, which of the following displayed frequencies represents the lowest frequency at which a properly adjusted LSB emission will be totally within the band?
- A. The exact lower band edge
- B. 300 Hz above the lower band edge
- C. 1 kHz above the lower band edge
- D. 3 kHz above the lower band edge

E1A02: D. The lowest frequency at which a properly adjusted LSB emission will be totally within the band is 3 kHz above the lower band edge. [97.301, 97.305]

With your transceiver displaying the carrier frequency of phone signals, you hear a station calling CQ on 14.349 MHz USB. Is it legal to return the call using upper sideband on the same frequency?
- A. Yes, because you were not the station calling CQ
- B. Yes, because the displayed frequency is within the 20 meter band
- C. No, the sideband will extend beyond the band edge
- D. No, U.S. stations are not permitted to use phone emissions above 14.340 MHz

E1A03: C. It is not legal respond using USB on 14.349 MHz because the sideband will extend beyond the band edge. [97.301, 97.305]

With your transceiver displaying the carrier frequency of phone signals, you hear a DX station calling CQ on 3.601 MHz LSB. Is it legal to return the call using lower sideband on the same frequency?
- A. Yes, because the DX station initiated the contact
- B. Yes, because the displayed frequency is within the 75 meter phone band segment
- C. No, the sideband will extend beyond the edge of the phone band segment
- D. No, U.S. stations are not permitted to use phone emissions below 3.610 MHz

E1A04: C. It is not legal to respond using LSB on 3.601 MHz because the sideband will extend beyond the edge of the phone band segment. [97.301, 97.305]

Copyright © Mometrix Media. You have been licensed one copy of this document for personal use only. Any other reproduction or redistribution is strictly prohibited. All rights reserved.

What is the maximum power output permitted on the 60-meter band?
   A. 50 watts PEP effective radiated power relative to an isotropic radiator
   B. 50 watts PEP effective radiated power relative to a dipole
   C. 100 watts PEP effective radiated power relative to the gain of a half-wave dipole
   D. 100 watts PEP effective radiated power relative to an isotropic radiator

E1A05: C. The maximum power output permitted on the 60-meter band is 100 W PEP relative to a half-wave dipole. Before March 3, 2012, the maximum was 50 W. [97.313]

Where must the carrier frequency of a CW signal be set to comply with FCC rules for 60-meter operation?
   A. At the lowest frequency of the channel
   B. At the center frequency of the channel
   C. At the highest frequency of the channel
   D. On any frequency where the signal's sidebands are within the channel

E1A06: B. The carrier frequency of a CW signal must be set at the center frequency of the channel to comply with FCC rules. [97.15]

Which amateur band requires transmission on specific channels rather than on a range of frequencies?
   A. 12 meter band
   B. 17 meter band
   C. 30 meter band
   D. 60 meter band

E1A07: D. The 60-meter band requires transmission on specific channels rather than on a range of frequencies. [97.303]

If a station in a message forwarding system inadvertently forwards a message that is in violation of FCC rules, who is primarily accountable for the rules violation?
   A. The control operator of the packet bulletin board station
   B. The control operator of the originating station
   C. The control operators of all the stations in the system
   D. The control operators of all the stations in the system not authenticating the source from which they accept communications

E1A08: B. The control operator of the originating station is primarily accountable if a forwarded message violates FCC rules. [97.219]

What is the first action you should take if your digital message forwarding station inadvertently forwards a communication that violates FCC rules?
   A. Discontinue forwarding the communication as soon as you become aware of it
   B. Notify the originating station that the communication does not comply with FCC rules
   C. Notify the nearest FCC Field Engineer's office
   D. Discontinue forwarding all messages

E1A09: A. If your digital message forwarding station inadvertently forwards a communication that violates FCC rules, the first thing you should do is stop forwarding the message. [97.219]

Copyright © Mometrix Media. You have been licensed one copy of this document for personal use only. Any other reproduction or redistribution is strictly prohibited. All rights reserved.

If an amateur station is installed aboard a ship or aircraft, what condition must be met before the station is operated?

A. Its operation must be approved by the master of the ship or the pilot in command of the aircraft

B. The amateur station operator must agree not to transmit when the main radio of the ship or aircraft is in use

C. The amateur station must have a power supply that is completely independent of the main ship or aircraft power supply

D. The amateur operator must have an FCC Marine or Aircraft endorsement on his or her amateur license

E1A10: A. Amateur stations aboard ships or aircraft do not need special endorsement so long as permission is obtained from the captain or pilot of the craft, and all applicable rules are followed. [97.11]

Which of the following describes authorization or licensing required when operating an amateur station aboard a U.S.-registered vessel in international waters?

A. Any amateur license with an FCC Marine or Aircraft endorsement

B. Any FCC-issued amateur license

C. Only General class or higher amateur licenses

D. An unrestricted Radiotelephone Operator Permit

E1A11: B. Any FCC-issued amateur license is suitable for operating an amateur station aboard a U.S.-registered vessel in international waters. [97.5]

With your transceiver displaying the carrier frequency of CW signals, you hear a DX station's CQ on 3.500 MHz. Is it legal to return the call using CW on the same frequency?

A. Yes, the DX station initiated the contact

B. Yes, the displayed frequency is within the 80 meter CW band segment

C. No, one of the sidebands of the CW signal will be out of the band

D. No, U.S. stations are not permitted to use CW emissions below 3.525 MHz

E1A12: C. It is not legal to respond using CW on the same frequency because one of the sidebands will be out of the band. [97.301, 97.305]

Who must be in physical control of the station apparatus of an amateur station aboard any vessel or craft that is documented or registered in the United States?

A. Only a person with an FCC Marine Radio

B. Any person holding an FCC issued amateur license or who is authorized for alien reciprocal operation

C. Only a person named in an amateur station license grant

D. Any person named in an amateur station license grant or a person holding an unrestricted Radiotelephone Operator Permit

E1A13: B. A person with an FCC issued amateur license or someone who is authorized for alien reciprocal operation must be in physical control of the station apparatus of an amateur station aboard any vessel or craft that is documented or registered in the United States. [97.5]

What is the maximum bandwidth for a data emission on 60 meters?

A. 60 Hz

B. 170 Hz

C. 1.5 kHz

D. 2.8 kHz

Copyright © Mometrix Media. You have been licensed one copy of this document for personal use only. Any other reproduction or redistribution is strictly prohibited. All rights reserved.

E1A14: D. The maximum bandwidth for a data emission on 60 meters is 2.8 kHz. [97.303]

E1B – Station restrictions and special operations: restrictions on station location; general operating restrictions, spurious emissions, control operator reimbursement; antenna structure restrictions; RACES operations; national quiet zone

Which of the following constitutes a spurious emission?
A. An amateur station transmission made at random without the proper call sign identification
B. A signal transmitted to prevent its detection by any station other than the intended recipient
C. Any transmitted signal that unintentionally interferes with another licensed radio station
D. An emission outside its necessary bandwidth that can be reduced or eliminated without affecting the information transmitted

E1B01: D. A spurious emission is an emission outside its necessary bandwidth that can be reduced or eliminated without affecting the information transmitted. [97.3]

Which of the following factors might cause the physical location of an amateur station apparatus or antenna structure to be restricted?
A. The location is near an area of political conflict
B. The location is of geographical or horticultural importance
C. The location is in an ITU Zone designated for coordination with one or more foreign governments
D. The location is of environmental importance or significant in American history, architecture, or culture

E1B02: D. If the location of an amateur station apparatus or antenna structure is of environmental importance or significant in American history, architecture, or culture, it may be restricted. [97.13]

Within what distance must an amateur station protect an FCC monitoring facility from harmful interference?
A. 1 mile
B. 3 miles
C. 10 miles
D. 30 miles

E1B03: A. An amateur station located within 1 mile (1600 m) of an FCC monitoring facility must protect it from harmful interference. [97.13]

What must be done before placing an amateur station within an officially designated wilderness area or wildlife preserve, or an area listed in the National Register of Historical Places?
A. A proposal must be submitted to the National Park Service
B. A letter of intent must be filed with the National Audubon Society
C. An Environmental Assessment must be submitted to the FCC
D. A form FSD-15 must be submitted to the Department of the Interior

E1B04: C. Before placing an amateur station within an officially designated wilderness area or wildlife preserve, or an area listed in the National Register of Historical Places, an Environmental Assessment must be submitted to the FCC. [97.13, 1.1305-1.1319]

Copyright © Mometrix Media. You have been licensed one copy of this document for personal use only. Any other reproduction or redistribution is strictly prohibited. All rights reserved.

What is the National Radio Quiet Zone?
    A. An area in Puerto Rico surrounding the Arecibo Radio Telescope
    B. An area in New Mexico surrounding the White Sands Test Area
    C. An area surrounding the National Radio Astronomy Observatory
    D. An area in Florida surrounding Cape Canaveral

E1B05: C. The National Radio Quiet Zone is an area surrounding the National Radio Astronomy Observatory. [97.3]

Which of the following additional rules apply if you are installing an amateur station antenna at a site at or near a public use airport?
    A. You may have to notify the Federal Aviation Administration and register it with the FCC as required by Part 17 of FCC rules
    B. No special rules apply if your antenna structure will be less than 300 feet in height
    C. You must file an Environmental Impact Statement with the EPA before construction begins
    D. You must obtain a construction permit from the airport zoning authority

E1B06: A. If installing an amateur station antenna at a site at or near a public use airport, you may have to notify the Federal Aviation Administration and register it with the FCC as required by Part 17 of FCC rules. [97.15]

What is the highest modulation index permitted at the highest modulation frequency for angle modulation below 29.0 MHz?
    A. 0.5
    B. 1.0
    C. 2.0
    D. 3.0

E1B07: B. The highest modulation index permitted at the highest modulation frequency for angle modulation below 29.0 MHz is 1.0. [97.307]

What limitations may the FCC place on an amateur station if its signal causes interference to domestic broadcast reception, assuming that the receivers involved are of good engineering design?
    A. The amateur station must cease operation
    B. The amateur station must cease operation on all frequencies below 30 MHz
    C. The amateur station must cease operation on all frequencies above 30 MHz
    D. The amateur station must avoid transmitting during certain hours on frequencies that cause the interference

E1B08: D. If an amateur station causes interference to domestic broadcast reception, the FCC may require that the station avoid transmitting during certain hours on frequencies that cause the interference. [97.121]

Which amateur stations may be operated under RACES rules?
    A. Only those club stations licensed to Amateur Extra class operators
    B. Any FCC-licensed amateur station except a Technician class
    C. Any FCC-licensed amateur station certified by the responsible civil defense organization for the area served
    D. Any FCC-licensed amateur station participating in the Military Auxiliary Radio System (MARS)

E1B09: C. Any FCC-licensed amateur station certified by the responsible civil defense organization for the area served may be operated under RACES rules. [97.407]

Copyright © Mometrix Media. You have been licensed one copy of this document for personal use only. Any other reproduction or redistribution is strictly prohibited. All rights reserved.

What frequencies are authorized to an amateur station operating under RACES rules?
- A. All amateur service frequencies authorized to the control operator
- B. Specific segments in the amateur service MF, HF, VHF and UHF bands
- C. Specific local government channels
- D. Military Auxiliary Radio System (MARS) channels

E1B10: A. An amateur station operating under RACES rules may use all amateur service frequencies authorized to the control operator. [97.407]

What is the permitted mean power of any spurious emission relative to the mean power of the fundamental emission from a station transmitter or external RF amplifier installed after January 1, 2003 and transmitting on a frequency below 30 MHZ?
- A. At least 43 dB below
- B. At least 53 dB below
- C. At least 63 dB below
- D. At least 73 dB below

E1B11: A. The mean power of any spurious emission from a station transmitter or external RF amplifier installed after January 1, 2003 and transmitting on a frequency below 30 MHZ must be at least 43 dB below the mean power of the fundamental emission from the station. [97.307]

E1C – Definitions and restrictions pertaining to local, automatic and remote control operation; control operator responsibilities for remote and automatically controlled stations; IARP and CEPT licenses; third party communications over automatically controlled stations

What is a remotely controlled station?
- A. A station operated away from its regular home location
- B. A station controlled by someone other than the licensee
- C. A station operating under automatic control
- D. A station controlled indirectly through a control link

E1C01: D. A remotely controlled station is a station controlled indirectly through a control link. [97.3]

What is meant by automatic control of a station?
- A. The use of devices and procedures for control so that the control operator does not have to be present at a control point
- B. A station operating with its output power controlled automatically
- C. Remotely controlling a station's antenna pattern through a directional control link
- D. The use of a control link between a control point and a locally controlled station

E1C02: A. Automatic control of a station is the use of devices and procedures for control so that the control operator does not have to be present at a control point. [97.3, 97.109]

How do the control operator responsibilities of a station under automatic control differ from one under local control?
- A. Under local control there is no control operator
- B. Under automatic control the control operator is not required to be present at the control point
- C. Under automatic control there is no control operator
- D. Under local control a control operator is not required to be present at a control point

Copyright © Mometrix Media. You have been licensed one copy of this document for personal use only. Any other reproduction or redistribution is strictly prohibited. All rights reserved.

E1C03: B. The control operator does not have to be present at a station under automatic control. [97.3, 97.109]

What is meant by IARP?
  A. An international amateur radio permit that allows U.S. amateurs to operate in certain countries of the Americas
  B. The internal amateur radio practices policy of the FCC
  C. An indication of increased antenna reflected power
  D. A forecast of intermittent aurora radio propagation

E1C04: A. IARP is an international amateur radio permit that allows U.S. amateurs to operate in certain countries of the Americas.

When may an automatically controlled station originate third party communications?
  A. Never
  B. Only when transmitting RTTY or data emissions
  C. When agreed upon by the sending or receiving station
  D. When approved by the National Telecommunication and Information Administration

E1C05: A. An automatically controlled station may never originate third party communications. [97.221(c)(1),[97.115(c)]

Which of the following statements concerning remotely controlled amateur stations is true?
  A. Only Extra Class operators may be the control operator of a remote station
  B. A control operator need not be present at the control point
  C. A control operator must be present at the control point
  D. Repeater and auxiliary stations may not be remotely controlled

E1C06: C. A control operator must be present at the control point of a remotely controlled amateur station. [97.109]

What is meant by local control?
  A. Controlling a station through a local auxiliary link
  B. Automatically manipulating local station controls
  C. Direct manipulation of the transmitter by a control operator
  D. Controlling a repeater using a portable handheld transceiver

E1C07: C. Local control is direct manipulation of the transmitter by a control operator. [97.3]

What is the maximum permissible duration of a remotely controlled station's transmissions if its control link malfunctions?
  A. 30 seconds
  B. 3 minutes
  C. 5 minutes
  D. 10 minutes

E1C08: B. The maximum permissible duration of a remotely controlled station's transmissions if its control link malfunctions is 3 minutes. [97.213]

Copyright © Mometrix Media. You have been licensed one copy of this document for personal use only. Any other reproduction or redistribution is strictly prohibited. All rights reserved.

Which of these ranges of frequencies is available for an automatically controlled repeater operating below 30 MHz?
    A. 18.110 MHz – 18.168 MHz
    B. 24.940 MHz – 24.990 MHz
    C. 10.100 MHz – 10.150 MHz
    D. 29.500 MHz – 29.700 MHz

E1C09: D. An automatically controlled repeater operating below 30 MHz may operate between 29.500 MHz and 29.700 MHz. [97.205]

What types of amateur stations may automatically retransmit the radio signals of other amateur stations?
    A. Only beacon, repeater or space stations
    B. Only auxiliary, repeater or space stations
    C. Only earth stations, repeater stations or model craft
    D. Only auxiliary, beacon or space stations

E1C10: B. Only auxiliary, repeater or space stations may automatically retransmit the radio signals of other amateur stations. [97.113]

Which of the following operating arrangements allows an FCC-licensed U.S. citizen to operate in many European countries, and alien amateurs from many European countries to operate in the U.S.?
    A. CEPT agreement
    B. IARP agreement
    C. ITU reciprocal license
    D. All of these choices are correct

E1C11: A. A CEPT agreement allows an FCC-licensed U.S. citizen to operate in many European countries, and alien amateurs from many European countries to operate in the U.S. [97.5]

What types of communications may be transmitted to amateur stations in foreign countries?
    A. Business-related messages for non-profit organizations
    B. Messages intended for connection to users of the maritime satellite service
    C. Communications incidental to the purpose of the amateur service and remarks of a personal nature
    D. All of these choices are correct

E1C12: C. Communications incidental to the purpose of the amateur service and remarks of a personal nature may be transmitted to amateur stations in foreign countries. [97.117]

Which of the following is required in order to operate in accordance with CEPT rules in foreign countries where permitted?
    A. You must identify in the official language of the country in which you are operating
    B. The U.S. embassy must approve of your operation
    C. You must bring a copy of FCC Public Notice DA 11-221
    D. You must append "/CEPT" to your call sign

E1C13: C. To operate in accordance with CEPT rules in foreign countries where permitted, you must bring a copy of FCC Public Notice DA 11-221.

Copyright © Mometrix Media. You have been licensed one copy of this document for personal use only. Any other reproduction or redistribution is strictly prohibited. All rights reserved.

E1D – Amateur satellites: definitions and purpose; license requirements for space stations; available frequencies and bands; telecommand and telemetry operations; restrictions, and special provisions; notification requirements

What is the definition of the term telemetry?
A. One-way transmission of measurements at a distance from the measuring instrument
B. Two-way radiotelephone transmissions in excess of 1000 feet
C. Two-way single channel transmissions of data
D. One-way transmission that initiates, modifies, or terminates the functions of a device at a distance

E1D01: A. Telemetry is one-way transmission of measurements at a distance from the measuring instrument. [97.3]

What is the amateur satellite service?
A. A radio navigation service using satellites for the purpose of self training, intercommunication and technical studies carried out by amateurs
B. A spacecraft launching service for amateur-built satellites
C. A radio communications service using amateur radio stations on satellites
D. A radio communications service using stations on Earth satellites for public service broadcast

E1D02: C. The amateur satellite service is a radio communications service using amateur radio stations on satellites. [97.3]

What is a telecommand station in the amateur satellite service?
A. An amateur station located on the Earth's surface for communication with other Earth stations by means of Earth satellites
B. An amateur station that transmits communications to initiate, modify or terminate functions of a space station
C. An amateur station located more than 50 km above the Earth's surface
D. An amateur station that transmits telemetry consisting of measurements of upper atmosphere

E1D03: B. A telecommand station in the amateur satellite service is an amateur station that transmits communications to initiate, modify or terminate functions of a space station. [97.3]

What is an Earth station in the amateur satellite service?
A. An amateur station within 50 km of the Earth's surface intended for communications with amateur stations by means of objects in space
B. An amateur station that is not able to communicate using amateur satellites
C. An amateur station that transmits telemetry consisting of measurement of upper atmosphere
D. Any amateur station on the surface of the Earth

E1D04: A. An Earth station in the amateur satellite service is an amateur station within 50 km of the Earth's surface intended for communications with amateur stations by means of objects in space. [97.3]

What class of licensee is authorized to be the control operator of a space station?
A. All except Technician Class
B. Only General, Advanced or Amateur Extra Class
C. Any class with appropriate operator privileges
D. Only Amateur Extra Class

Copyright © Mometrix Media. You have been licensed one copy of this document for personal use only. Any other reproduction or redistribution is strictly prohibited. All rights reserved.

E1D05: C. Any license class with appropriate operator privileges is authorized to be the control operator of a space station. [97.207]

Which of the following is a requirement of a space station?
A. The space station must be capable of terminating transmissions by telecommand when directed by the FCC
B. The space station must cease all transmissions after 5 years
C. The space station must be capable of changing its orbit whenever such a change is ordered by NASA
D. All of these choices are correct

E1D06: A. A space station must be capable of terminating transmissions by telecommand when directed by the FCC. [97.207]

Which amateur service HF bands have frequencies authorized for space stations?
A. Only the 40 m, 20 m, 17 m, 15 m, 12 m and 10 m bands
B. Only the 40 m, 20 m, 17 m, 15 m and 10 m bands
C. Only the 40 m, 30 m, 20 m, 15 m, 12 m and 10 m bands
D. All HF bands

E1D07: A. Only the 40 m, 20 m, 17 m, 15 m, 12 m and 10 m bands have frequencies authorized for space stations. [97.207]

Which VHF amateur service bands have frequencies available for space stations?
A. 6 meters and 2 meters
B. 6 meters, 2 meters, and 1.25 meters
C. 2 meters and 1.25 meters
D. 2 meters

E1D08: D. The 2-meter amateur service bands have frequencies available for space stations. [97.207]

Which UHF amateur service bands have frequencies available for a space station?
A. 70 cm only
B. 70 cm and 13 cm
C. 70 cm and 33 cm
D. 33 cm and 13 cm

E1D09: B. The 70 cm and 13 cm amateur service bands have frequencies available for space stations. [97.207]

Which amateur stations are eligible to be telecommand stations?
A. Any amateur station designated by NASA
B. Any amateur station so designated by the space station licensee, subject to the privileges of the class of operator license held by the control operator
C. Any amateur station so designated by the ITU
D. All of these choices are correct

E1D10: B. Any amateur station so designated by the space station licensee is eligible to be a telecommand station, subject to the privileges of the class of operator license held by the control operator. [97.211]

Copyright © Mometrix Media. You have been licensed one copy of this document for personal use only. Any other reproduction or redistribution is strictly prohibited. All rights reserved.

Which amateur stations are eligible to operate as Earth stations?
A. Any amateur station whose licensee has filed a pre-space notification with the FCC's International Bureau
B. Only those of General, Advanced or Amateur Extra Class operators
C. Only those of Amateur Extra Class operators
D. Any amateur station, subject to the privileges of the class of operator license held by the control operator

E1D11: D. Any amateur station is eligible to operate as an Earth station, subject to the privileges of the class of operator license held by the control operator. [97.209]

E1E – Volunteer examiner program: definitions; qualifications; preparation and administration of exams; accreditation; question pools; documentation requirements

What is the minimum number of qualified VEs required to administer an Element 4 amateur operator license examination?
A. 5
B. 2
C. 4
D. 3

E1E01: D. The minimum number of qualified VEs required to administer an Element 4 amateur operator license examination is 3. [97.509]

Where are the questions for all written U.S. amateur license examinations listed?
A. In FCC Part 97
B. In a question pool maintained by the FCC
C. In a question pool maintained by all the VECs
D. In the appropriate FCC Report and Order

E1E02: C. The questions for all written U.S. amateur license examinations listed are in a question pool maintained by all the VECs. [97.523]

What is a Volunteer Examiner Coordinator?
A. A person who has volunteered to administer amateur operator license examinations
B. A person who has volunteered to prepare amateur operator license examinations
C. An organization that has entered into an agreement with the FCC to coordinate amateur operator license examinations
D. The person who has entered into an agreement with the FCC to be the VE session manager

E1E03: C. A Volunteer Examiner Coordinator is an organization that has entered into an agreement with the FCC to coordinate amateur operator license examinations. [97.521]

Copyright © Mometrix Media. You have been licensed one copy of this document for personal use only. Any other reproduction or redistribution is strictly prohibited. All rights reserved.

Which of the following best describes the Volunteer Examiner accreditation process?
    A. Each General, Advanced and Amateur Extra Class operator is automatically accredited as a VE when the license is granted
    B. The amateur operator applying must pass a VE examination administered by the FCC Enforcement Bureau
    C. The prospective VE obtains accreditation from the FCC
    D. The procedure by which a VEC confirms that the VE applicant meets FCC requirements to serve as an examiner

E1E04: D. The Volunteer Examiner accreditation process is the procedure by which a VEC confirms that the VE applicant meets FCC requirements to serve as an examiner. [97.509, 97.525]

What is the minimum passing score on amateur operator license examinations?
    A. Minimum passing score of 70%
    B. Minimum passing score of 74%
    C. Minimum passing score of 80%
    D. Minimum passing score of 77%

E1E05: B. The minimum passing score on amateur operator license examinations is 74%. [97.503]

Who is responsible for the proper conduct and necessary supervision during an amateur operator license examination session?
    A. The VEC coordinating the session
    B. The FCC
    C. Each administering VE
    D. The VE session manager

E1E06: C. Each administering VE is responsible for the proper conduct and necessary supervision during an amateur operator license examination session. [97.509]

What should a VE do if a candidate fails to comply with the examiner's instructions during an amateur operator license examination?
    A. Warn the candidate that continued failure to comply will result in termination of the examination
    B. Immediately terminate the candidate's examination
    C. Allow the candidate to complete the examination, but invalidate the results
    D. Immediately terminate everyone's examination and close the session

E1E07: B. If a candidate fails to comply with the examiner's instructions during an amateur operator license examination, the VE should immediately terminate the candidate's examination. [97.509]

To which of the following examinees may a VE not administer an examination?
    A. Employees of the VE
    B. Friends of the VE
    C. Relatives of the VE as listed in the FCC rules
    D. All of these choices are correct

E1E08: C. A VE may not administer an examination to his or her own relatives, as listed in the FCC rules. [97.509]

Copyright © Mometrix Media. You have been licensed one copy of this document for personal use only. Any other reproduction or redistribution is strictly prohibited. All rights reserved.

What may be the penalty for a VE who fraudulently administers or certifies an examination?
A. Revocation of the VE's amateur station license grant and the suspension of the VE's amateur operator license grant
B. A fine of up to $1000 per occurrence
C. A sentence of up to one year in prison
D. All of these choices are correct

E1E09: A. A VE who fraudulently administers or certifies an examination may be subject to revocation of his or her amateur station license grant and suspension of his or her amateur operator license grant. [97.509]

What must the administering VEs do after the administration of a successful examination for an amateur operator license?
A. They must collect and send the documents to the NCVEC for grading
B. They must collect and submit the documents to the coordinating VEC for grading
C. They must submit the application document to the coordinating VEC according to the coordinating VEC instructions
D. They must collect and send the documents to the FCC according to instructions

E1E10: C. The administering VEs must submit the application document to the coordinating VEC according to the coordinating VEC's instructions after the administration of a successful examination for an amateur operator license. [97.509]

What must the VE team do if an examinee scores a passing grade on all examination elements needed for an upgrade or new license?
A. Photocopy all examination documents and forward them to the FCC for processing
B. Three VEs must certify that the examinee is qualified for the license grant and that they have complied with the administering VE requirements
C. Issue the examinee the new or upgrade license
D. All these choices are correct

E1E11: B. If an examinee scores a passing grade on all examination elements needed for an upgrade or new license, the VE team must certify that the examinee is qualified for the license grant and that they have complied with the administering VE requirements. [97.509]

What must the VE team do with the application form if the examinee does not pass the exam?
A. Return the application document to the examinee
B. Maintain the application form with the VEC's records
C. Send the application form to the FCC and inform the FCC of the grade
D. Destroy the application form

E1E12: A. If the examinee does not pass the exam the VE team must return the application document to the examinee. [97.509]

Which of these choices is an acceptable method for monitoring the applicants if a VEC opts to conduct an exam session remotely?
A. Record the exam session on video tape for later review by the
VE team
B. Use a real-time video link and the Internet to connect the exam session to the observing VEs
C. The exam proctor observes the applicants and reports any violations
D. Have each applicant sign an affidavit stating that all session rules were followed

Copyright © Mometrix Media. You have been licensed one copy of this document for personal use only. Any other reproduction or redistribution is strictly prohibited. All rights reserved.

E1E13: B. If a VEC opts to conduct an exam session remotely, they should use a real-time video link and the Internet to connect the exam session to the observing VEs. [97.509]

For which types of out-of-pocket expenses do the Part 97 rules state that VEs and VECs may be reimbursed?
    A. Preparing, processing, administering and coordinating an examination for an amateur radio license
    B. Teaching an amateur operator license examination preparation course
    C. No expenses are authorized for reimbursement
    D. Providing amateur operator license examination preparation training materials

E1E14: A. The Part 97 rules state that VEs and VECs may be reimbursed for preparing, processing, administering and coordinating an examination for an amateur radio license. [97.527]

E1F – Miscellaneous rules: external RF power amplifiers; business communications; compensated communications; spread spectrum; auxiliary stations; reciprocal operating privileges; special temporary authority

On what frequencies are spread spectrum transmissions permitted?
    A. Only on amateur frequencies above 50 MHz
    B. Only on amateur frequencies above 222 MHz
    C. Only on amateur frequencies above 420 MHz
    D. Only on amateur frequencies above 144 MHz

E1F01: B. spread spectrum transmissions are permitted only on amateur frequencies above 222 MHz. [97.305]

What privileges are authorized in the U.S. to persons holding an amateur service license granted by the Government of Canada?
    A. None, they must obtain a U.S. license
    B. All privileges of the Extra Class license
    C. The operating terms and conditions of the Canadian amateur service license, not to exceed U.S. Extra Class privileges
    D. Full privileges, up to and including those of the Extra Class License, on the 80, 40, 20, 15, and 10 meter bands

E1F02: C. Persons in the US holding an amateur service license granted by the Government of Canada are granted the operating terms and conditions of the Canadian amateur service license, not to exceed U.S. Extra Class privileges. [97.107]

Under what circumstances may a dealer sell an external RF power amplifier capable of operation below 144 MHz if it has not been granted FCC certification?
    A. It was purchased in used condition from an amateur operator and is sold to another amateur operator for use at that operator's station
    B. The equipment dealer assembled it from a kit
    C. It was imported from a manufacturer in a country that does not require certification of RF power amplifiers
    D. It was imported from a manufacturer in another country and was certificated by that country's government

Copyright © Mometrix Media. You have been licensed one copy of this document for personal use only. Any other reproduction or redistribution is strictly prohibited. All rights reserved.

E1F03: A. A dealer may sell an external RF power amplifier capable of operation below 144 MHz if it has not been granted FCC certification if it was purchased in used condition from an amateur operator and is sold to another amateur operator for use at that operator's station. [97.315]

Which of the following geographic descriptions approximately describes "Line A"?
    A. A line roughly parallel to and south of the U.S.-Canadian border
    B. A line roughly parallel to and west of the U.S. Atlantic coastline
    C. A line roughly parallel to and north of the U.S.-Mexican border and Gulf coastline
    D. A line roughly parallel to and east of the U.S. Pacific coastline

E1F04: A. "Line A" is a line roughly parallel to and south of the U.S.-Canadian border. [97.3]

Amateur stations may not transmit in which of the following frequency segments if they are located in the contiguous 48 states and north of Line A?
    A. 440 MHz – 450 MHz
    B. 53 MHz – 54 MHz
    C. 222 MHz – 223 MHz
    D. 420 MHz – 430 MHz

E1F05: D. Amateur stations may not transmit on frequencies between 222 MHz and 223 MHz if they are located in the contiguous 48 states and north of Line A. [97.303]

Under what circumstances might the FCC issue a Special Temporary Authority (STA) to an amateur station?
    A. To provide for experimental amateur communications
    B. To allow regular operation on Land Mobile channels
    C. To provide additional spectrum for personal use
    D. To provide temporary operation while awaiting normal licensing

E1F06: A. The FCC might issue a Special Temporary Authority (STA) to an amateur station to provide for experimental amateur communications. [1.931]

When may an amateur station send a message to a business?
    A. When the total money involved does not exceed $25
    B. When the control operator is employed by the FCC or another government agency
    C. When transmitting international third-party communications
    D. When neither the amateur nor his or her employer has a pecuniary interest in the communications

E1F07: D. An amateur station may send a message to a business when neither the amateur nor his or her employer has a pecuniary interest in the communications. [97.113]

Which of the following types of amateur station communications are prohibited?
    A. Communications transmitted for hire or material compensation, except as otherwise provided in the rules
    B. Communications that have a political content, except as allowed by the Fairness Doctrine
    C. Communications that have a religious content
    D. Communications in a language other than English

E1F08: A. Amateur station communications transmitted for hire or material compensation are prohibited, except as otherwise provided in the rules. [97.113]

Copyright © Mometrix Media. You have been licensed one copy of this document for personal use only. Any other reproduction or redistribution is strictly prohibited. All rights reserved

Which of the following conditions apply when transmitting spread spectrum emission?
A. A station transmitting SS emission must not cause harmful interference to other stations employing other authorized emissions
B. The transmitting station must be in an area regulated by the FCC or in a country that permits SS emissions
C. The transmission must not be used to obscure the meaning of any communication
D. All of these choices are correct

E1F09: D. When transmitting spread spectrum emission, the station must not cause harmful interference to other stations employing other authorized emissions, the transmitting station must be in an area regulated by the FCC or in a country that permits SS emissions, and the transmission must not be used to obscure the meaning of any communication. [97.311]

What is the maximum permitted transmitter peak envelope power for an amateur station transmitting spread spectrum communications?
A. 1 W
B. 1.5 W
C. 10 W
D. 1.5 kW

E1F10: C. The maximum permitted transmitter peak envelope power for an amateur station transmitting spread spectrum communications is 10 W. [97.313]

Which of the following best describes one of the standards that must be met by an external RF power amplifier if it is to qualify for a grant of FCC certification?
A. It must produce full legal output when driven by not more than 5 watts of mean RF input power
B. It must be capable of external RF switching between its input and output networks
C. It must exhibit a gain of 0 dB or less over its full output range
D. It must satisfy the FCC's spurious emission standards when operated at the lesser of 1500 watts or its full output power

E1F11: D. An external RF power amplifier must satisfy the FCC's spurious emission standards when operated at the lesser of 1500 watts or its full output power if it is to qualify for a grant of FCC certification. [97.317]

Who may be the control operator of an auxiliary station?
A. Any licensed amateur operator
B. Only Technician, General, Advanced or Amateur Extra Class operators
C. Only General, Advanced or Amateur Extra Class operators
D. Only Amateur Extra Class operators

E1F12: B. Only Technician, General, Advanced or Amateur Extra Class operators may be control operators of auxiliary stations. [97.201]

Copyright © Mometrix Media. You have been licensed one copy of this document for personal use only. Any other reproduction or redistribution is strictly prohibited. All rights reserved.

E2 – Operating Procedures

E2A – Amateur radio in space: amateur satellites; orbital mechanics; frequencies and modes; satellite hardware; satellite operations; experimental telemetry applications

What is the direction of an ascending pass for an amateur satellite?
   A. From west to east
   B. From east to west
   C. From south to north
   D. From north to south

E2A01: C. An amateur satellite goes from south to north in an ascending pass.

What is the direction of a descending pass for an amateur satellite?
   A. From north to south
   B. From west to east
   C. From east to west
   D. From south to north

E2A02: A. An amateur satellite goes from north to south in a descending pass.

What is the orbital period of an Earth satellite?
   A. The point of maximum height of a satellite's orbit
   B. The point of minimum height of a satellite's orbit
   C. The time it takes for a satellite to complete one revolution around the Earth
   D. The time it takes for a satellite to travel from perigee to apogee

E2A03: C. The orbital period of an Earth satellite is the time it takes for a satellite to complete one revolution around the Earth.

What is meant by the term mode as applied to an amateur radio satellite?
   A. The type of signals that can be relayed through the satellite
   B. The satellite's uplink and downlink frequency bands
   C. The satellite's orientation with respect to the Earth
   D. Whether the satellite is in a polar or equatorial orbit

E2A04: B. The term mode as applied to an amateur radio satellite refers to the satellite's uplink and downlink frequency bands.

What do the letters in a satellite's mode designator specify?
   A. Power limits for uplink and downlink transmissions
   B. The location of the ground control station
   C. The polarization of uplink and downlink signals
   D. The uplink and downlink frequency ranges

E2A05: D. The letters in a satellite's mode designator specify the uplink and downlink frequency ranges.

Copyright © Mometrix Media. You have been licensed one copy of this document for personal use only. Any other reproduction or redistribution is strictly prohibited. All rights reserved.

On what band would a satellite receive signals if it were operating in mode U/V?
    A. 435 MHz – 438 MHz
    B. 144 MHz – 146 MHz
    C. 50.0 MHz – 50.2 MHz
    D. 29.5 MHz – 29.7 MHz

E2A06: A. a satellite would receive signals between 435 MHz and 438 MHz if it were operating in mode U/V.

Which of the following types of signals can be relayed through a linear transponder?
    A. FM and CW
    B. SSB and SSTV
    C. PSK and Packet
    D. All of these choices are correct

E2A07: D. FM, CW, SSB, SSTV, PSK, and Packet signals can all be relayed through a linear transponder.

Why should effective radiated power to a satellite which uses a linear transponder be limited?
    A. To prevent creating errors in the satellite telemetry
    B. To avoid reducing the downlink power to all other users
    C. To prevent the satellite from emitting out-of-band signals
    D. To avoid interfering with terrestrial QSOs

E2A08: B. Effective radiated power should be limited to a satellite which uses a linear transponder to avoid reducing the downlink power to all other users.

What do the terms L band and S band specify with regard to satellite communications?
    A. The 23 centimeter and 13 centimeter bands
    B. The 2 meter and 70 centimeter bands
    C. FM and Digital Store-and-Forward systems
    D. Which sideband to use

E2A09: A. The terms L band and S band specify the 23 centimeter and 13 centimeter bands, respectively, with regard to satellite communications.

Why may the received signal from an amateur satellite exhibit a rapidly repeating fading effect?
    A. Because the satellite is spinning
    B. Because of ionospheric absorption
    C. Because of the satellite's low orbital altitude
    D. Because of the Doppler Effect

E2A10: A. The received signal from an amateur satellite may exhibit a rapidly repeating fading effect because the satellite is spinning.

What type of antenna can be used to minimize the effects of spin modulation and Faraday rotation?
    A. A linearly polarized antenna
    B. A circularly polarized antenna
    C. An isotropic antenna
    D. A log-periodic dipole array

E2A11:B. A circularly polarized antenna can be used to minimize the effects of spin modulation and Faraday rotation.

Copyright © Mometrix Media. You have been licensed one copy of this document for personal use only. Any other reproduction or redistribution is strictly prohibited. All rights reserved.

What is one way to predict the location of a satellite at a given time?
    A. By means of the Doppler data for the specified satellite
    B. By subtracting the mean anomaly from the orbital inclination
    C. By adding the mean anomaly to the orbital inclination
    D. By calculations using the Keplerian elements for the specified satellite

E2A12: D. One way to predict the location of a satellite at a given time is by using calculations with the Keplerian elements for the specified satellite.

What type of satellite appears to stay in one position in the sky?
    A. HEO
    B. Geostationary
    C. Geomagnetic
    D. LEO

E2A13: B. A geostationary satellite appears to stay in one position in the sky.

What technology is used to track, in real time, balloons carrying amateur radio transmitters?
    A. Radar
    B. Bandwidth compressed LORAN
    C. APRS
    D. Doppler shift of beacon signals

E2A14: C. APRS technology is used to track balloons carrying amateur radio transmitters in real time.

E2B – Television practices: fast scan television standards and techniques; slow scan television standards and techniques

How many times per second is a new frame transmitted in a fast-scan (NTSC) television system?
    A. 30
    B. 60
    C. 90
    D. 120

E2B01: A. A new frame transmitted 30 times per second in a fast-scan (NTSC) television system.

How many horizontal lines make up a fast-scan (NTSC) television frame?
    A. 30
    B. 60
    C. 525
    D. 1080

E2B02: C. There are 525 horizontal lines in a fast-scan (NTSC) television frame.

How is an interlaced scanning pattern generated in a fast-scan (NTSC) television system?
    A. By scanning two fields simultaneously
    B. By scanning each field from bottom to top
    C. By scanning lines from left to right in one field and right to left in the next
    D. By scanning odd numbered lines in one field and even numbered lines in the next

Copyright © Mometrix Media. You have been licensed one copy of this document for personal use only. Any other reproduction or redistribution is strictly prohibited. All rights reserved.

E2B03: D. In a fast-scan (NTSC) television system, an interlaced scanning pattern is generated by scanning odd numbered lines in one field and even numbered lines in the next.

What is blanking in a video signal?
A. Synchronization of the horizontal and vertical sync pulses
B. Turning off the scanning beam while it is traveling from right to left or from bottom to top
C. Turning off the scanning beam at the conclusion of a transmission
D. Transmitting a black and white test pattern

E2B04: B. Blanking in a video signal is turning off the scanning beam while it is traveling from right to left or from bottom to top.

Which of the following is an advantage of using vestigial sideband for standard fast- scan TV transmissions?
A. The vestigial sideband carries the audio information
B. The vestigial sideband contains chroma information
C. Vestigial sideband reduces bandwidth while allowing for simple video detector circuitry
D. Vestigial sideband provides high frequency emphasis to sharpen the picture

E2B05: C. An advantage of using vestigial sideband for standard fast- scan TV transmissions is reducing bandwidth while allowing for simple video detector circuitry.

What is vestigial sideband modulation?
A. Amplitude modulation in which one complete sideband and a portion of the other are transmitted
B. A type of modulation in which one sideband is inverted
C. Narrow-band FM modulation achieved by filtering one sideband from the audio before frequency modulating the carrier
D. Spread spectrum modulation achieved by applying FM modulation following single sideband amplitude modulation

E2B06: A. Vestigial sideband modulation is amplitude modulation in which one complete sideband and a portion of the other are transmitted.

What is the name of the signal component that carries color information in NTSC video?
A. Luminance
B. Chroma
C. Hue
D. Spectral Intensity

E2B07: B. The signal component that carries color information in NTSC video is chroma.

Which of the following is a common method of transmitting accompanying audio with amateur fast-scan television?
A. Frequency-modulated sub-carrier
B. A separate VHF or UHF audio link
C. Frequency modulation of the video carrier
D. All of these choices are correct

E2B08: D. Frequency-modulated sub-carriers, separate VHF or UHF audio links, and frequency modulation of the video carrier are all common methods of transmitting accompanying audio with amateur fast-scan television.

Copyright © Mometrix Media. You have been licensed one copy of this document for personal use only. Any other reproduction or redistribution is strictly prohibited. All rights reserved.

What hardware, other than a receiver with SSB capability and a suitable computer, is needed to decode SSTV using Digital Radio Mondiale (DRM)?
    A. A special IF converter
    B. A special front end limiter
    C. A special notch filter to remove synchronization pulses
    D. No other hardware is needed

E2B09: D. The only hardware required to decode SSTV using Digital Radio Mondiale (DRM) is a receiver with SSB capability and a suitable computer.

Which of the following is an acceptable bandwidth for Digital Radio Mondiale (DRM) based voice or SSTV digital transmissions made on the HF amateur bands?
    A. 3 KHz
    B. 10 KHz
    C. 15 KHz
    D. 20 KHz

E2B10: A. 3 KHz is an acceptable bandwidth for Digital Radio Mondiale (DRM) based voice or SSTV digital transmissions made on the HF amateur bands.

What is the function of the Vertical Interval Signaling (VIS) code sent as part of an SSTV transmission?
    A. To lock the color burst oscillator in color SSTV images
    B. To identify the SSTV mode being used
    C. To provide vertical synchronization
    D. To identify the call sign of the station transmitting

E2B11: B. The Vertical Interval Signaling (VIS) code is sent as part of an SSTV transmission to identify the SSTV mode being used.

How are analog SSTV images typically transmitted on the HF bands?
    A. Video is converted to equivalent Baudot representation
    B. Video is converted to equivalent ASCII representation
    C. Varying tone frequencies representing the video are transmitted using PSK
    D. Varying tone frequencies representing the video are transmitted using single sideband

E2B12: D. Analog SSTV images are typically transmitted on the HF bands using single sideband, with varying tone frequencies representing the video.

How many lines are commonly used in each frame of an amateur slow-scan color television picture?
    A. 30 or 60
    B. 60 or 100
    C. 128 or 256
    D. 180 or 360

E2B13: C. 128 or 256 lines are commonly used in each frame of an amateur slow-scan color television picture.

Copyright © Mometrix Media. You have been licensed one copy of this document for personal use only. Any other reproduction or redistribution is strictly prohibited. All rights reserved.

What aspect of an amateur slow-scan television signal encodes the brightness of the picture?
    A. Tone frequency
    B. Tone amplitude
    C. Sync amplitude
    D. Sync frequency

E2B14: A. The tone frequency encodes the brightness of the picture in an amateur slow-scan television signal.

What signals SSTV receiving equipment to begin a new picture line?
    A. Specific tone frequencies
    B. Elapsed time
    C. Specific tone amplitudes
    D. A two-tone signal

E2B15: A. Specific tone frequencies tell SSTV receiving equipment to begin a new picture line.

Which is a video standard used by North American Fast Scan ATV stations?
    A. PAL
    B. DRM
    C. Scottie
    D. NTSC

E2B16: D. NTSC is a video standard used by North American Fast Scan ATV stations.

What is the approximate bandwidth of a slow-scan TV signal?
    A. 600 Hz
    B. 3 kHz
    C. 2 MHz
    D. 6 MHz

E2B17: B. The approximate bandwidth of a slow-scan TV signal is 3 kHz.

On which of the following frequencies is one likely to find FM ATV transmissions?
    A. 14.230 MHz
    B. 29.6 MHz
    C. 52.525 MHz
    D. 1255 MHz

E2B18: D. One is likely to find FM ATV transmissions at 1255 MHz.

What special operating frequency restrictions are imposed on slow scan TV transmissions?
    A. None; they are allowed on all amateur frequencies
    B. They are restricted to 7.245 MHz, 14.245 MHz, 21.345 MHz, and 28.945 MHz
    C. They are restricted to phone band segments and their bandwidth can be no greater than that of a voice signal of the same modulation type
    D. They are not permitted above 54 MHz

E2B19: C. Slow scan TV transmissions are restricted to phone band segments and their bandwidth can be no greater than that of a voice signal of the same modulation type.

Copyright © Mometrix Media. You have been licensed one copy of this document for personal use only. Any other reproduction or redistribution is strictly prohibited. All rights reserved.

E2C – Operating methods: contest and DX operating; remote operation techniques; Cabrillo format; QSLing; RF network connected systems

Which of the following is true about contest operating?
A. Operators are permitted to make contacts even if they do not submit a log
B. Interference to other amateurs is unavoidable and therefore acceptable
C. It is mandatory to transmit the call sign of the station being worked as part of every transmission to that station
D. Every contest requires a signal report in the exchange

E2C01: A. In contest operating, operators are permitted to make contacts even if they do not submit a log.

Which of the following best describes the term self-spotting in regards to HF contest operating?
A. The generally prohibited practice of posting one's own call sign and frequency on a spotting network
B. The acceptable practice of manually posting the call signs of stations on a spotting network
C. A manual technique for rapidly zero beating or tuning to a station's frequency before calling that station
D. An automatic method for rapidly zero beating or tuning to a station's frequency before calling that station

E2C02: A. In HF contest operating, self-spotting is the generally prohibited practice of posting one's own call sign and frequency on a spotting network.

From which of the following bands is amateur radio contesting generally excluded?
A. 30 m
B. 6 m
C. 2 m
D. 33 cm

E2C03: A. amateur radio contesting is generally excluded from the 30 meter band.

What type of transmission is most often used for a ham radio mesh network?
A. Spread spectrum in the 2.4 GHz band
B. Multiple Frequency Shift Keying in the 10 GHz band
C. Store and forward on the 440 MHz band
D. Frequency division multiplex in the 24 GHz band

E2C04: A. Spread spectrum in the 2.4 GHz band is most often used for a ham radio mesh network.

What is the function of a DX QSL Manager?
A. To allocate frequencies for DXpeditions
B. To handle the receiving and sending of confirmation cards for a DX station
C. To run a net to allow many stations to contact a rare DX station
D. To relay calls to and from a DX station

E2C05: B. A DX QSL Manager handles the receiving and sending of confirmation cards for a DX station.

Copyright © Mometrix Media. You have been licensed one copy of this document for personal use only. Any other reproduction or redistribution is strictly prohibited. All rights reserved.

During a VHF/UHF contest, in which band segment would you expect to find the highest level of activity?
A. At the top of each band, usually in a segment reserved for contests
B. In the middle of each band, usually on the national calling frequency
C. In the weak signal segment of the band, with most of the activity near the calling frequency
D. In the middle of the band, usually 25 kHz above the national calling frequency

E2C06: C. During a VHF/UHF contest, you would expect to find the highest activity in the weak signal segment of the band, with most of the activity near the calling frequency.

What is the Cabrillo format?
A. A standard for submission of electronic contest logs
B. A method of exchanging information during a contest QSO
C. The most common set of contest rules
D. The rules of order for meetings between contest sponsors

E2C07: A. The Cabrillo format is a standard for submission of electronic contest logs.

Which of the following contacts may be confirmed through the U.S. QSL bureau system?
A. Special event contacts between stations in the U.S.
B. Contacts between a U.S. station and a non-U.S. station
C. Repeater contacts between U.S. club members
D. Contacts using tactical call signs

E2C08: B. Contacts between a U.S. station and a non-U.S. station may be confirmed through the U.S. QSL bureau system.

What type of equipment is commonly used to implement a ham radio mesh network?
A. A 2 meter VHF transceiver with a 1200 baud modem
B. An optical cable connection between the USB ports of 2 separate computers
C. A standard wireless router running custom software
D. A 440 MHz transceiver with a 9600 baud modem

E2C09: C. Standard wireless routers running custom software are commonly used to implement ham radio mesh networks.

Why might a DX station state that they are listening on another frequency?
A. Because the DX station may be transmitting on a frequency that is prohibited to some responding stations
B. To separate the calling stations from the DX station
C. To improve operating efficiency by reducing interference
D. All of these choices are correct

E2C10: D. A DX station may state that they are listening on another frequency for a number of reasons, including because they may be transmitting on a frequency that is prohibited to some responding stations, to separate the calling stations from the DX station, and to improve operating efficiency by reducing interference.

Copyright © Mometrix Media. You have been licensed one copy of this document for personal use only. Any other reproduction or redistribution is strictly prohibited. All rights reserved.

How should you generally identify your station when attempting to contact a DX station during a contest or in a pileup?
  A. Send your full call sign once or twice
  B. Send only the last two letters of your call sign until you make contact
  C. Send your full call sign and grid square
  D. Send the call sign of the DX station three times, the words "this is", then your call sign three times

E2C11: A. When attempting to contact a DX station during a contest or in a pileup, you should generally identify your station by sending your full call sign once or twice.

What might help to restore contact when DX signals become too weak to copy across an entire HF band a few hours after sunset?
  A. Switch to a higher frequency HF band
  B. Switch to a lower frequency HF band
  C. Wait 90 minutes or so for the signal degradation to pass
  D. Wait 24 hours before attempting another communication on the band

E2C12: B. When DX signals become too weak to copy across an entire HF band a few hours after sunset, you should switch to a lower frequency HF band.

What indicator is required to be used by U.S.-licensed operators when operating a station via remote control where the transmitter is located in the U.S.?
  A. / followed by the USPS two letter abbreviation for the state in which the remote station is located
  B. /R# where # is the district of the remote station
  C. The ARRL section of the remote station
  D. No additional indicator is required

E2C13: D. No additional indicator is required when U.S.-licensed operators operate a station via remote control where the transmitter is located in the U.S.

E2D – Operating methods: VHF and UHF digital modes and procedures; APRS; EME procedures, meteor scatter procedures

Which of the following digital modes is especially designed for use for meteor scatter signals?
  A. WSPR
  B. FSK441
  C. Hellschreiber
  D. APRS

E2D01: B. The FSK441 digital mode is especially designed for use for meteor scatter signals.

Which of the following is a good technique for making meteor scatter contacts?
  A. 15 second timed transmission sequences with stations alternating based on location
  B. Use of high speed CW or digital modes
  C. Short transmission with rapidly repeated call signs and signal reports
  D. All of these choices are correct

E2D02: D. Good techniques for making meteor scatter contacts include 15 second timed transmission sequences with stations alternating based on location, use of high speed CW or digital modes, and short transmissions with rapidly repeated call signs and signal reports.

Copyright © Mometrix Media. You have been licensed one copy of this document for personal use only. Any other reproduction or redistribution is strictly prohibited. All rights reserved.

Which of the following digital modes is especially useful for EME communications?
    A. FSK441
    B. PACTOR III
    C. Olivia
    D. JT65

E2D03: D. the JT65 digital mode is especially useful for EME communications.

What is the purpose of digital store-and-forward functions on an Amateur Radio satellite?
    A. To upload operational software for the transponder
    B. To delay download of telemetry between satellites
    C. To store digital messages in the satellite for later download by other stations
    D. To relay messages between satellites

E2D04: C. The purpose of digital store-and-forward functions on an Amateur Radio satellite is to store digital messages in the satellite for later download by other stations.

Which of the following techniques is normally used by low Earth orbiting digital satellites to relay messages around the world?
    A. Digipeating
    B. Store-and-forward
    C. Multi-satellite relaying
    D. Node hopping

E2D05: B. Store-and-forward is a technique used by low Earth orbiting digital satellites to relay messages around the world.

Which of the following describes a method of establishing EME contacts?
    A. Time synchronous transmissions alternately from each station
    B. Storing and forwarding digital messages
    C. Judging optimum transmission times by monitoring beacons reflected from the Moon
    D. High speed CW identification to avoid fading

E2D06: A. Establishing EME contacts can be done by timing synchronous transmissions alternately from each station.

What digital protocol is used by APRS?
    A. PACTOR
    B. 802.11
    C. AX.25
    D. AMTOR

E2D07: C. The AX.25 digital protocol is used by APRS.

What type of packet frame is used to transmit APRS beacon data?
    A. Unnumbered Information
    B. Disconnect
    C. Acknowledgement
    D. Connect

E2D08: A. Unnumbered Information packet frames are used to transmit APRS beacon data.

Copyright © Mometrix Media. You have been licensed one copy of this document for personal use only. Any other reproduction or redistribution is strictly prohibited. All rights reserved.

Which of these digital modes has the fastest data throughput under clear communication conditions?
   A. AMTOR
   B. 170 Hz shift, 45 baud RTTY
   C. PSK31
   D. 300 baud packet

E2D09: D. 300 baud packets are faster than PSK31, 170 Hz shift, 45 baud RTTY, and AMTOR under clear communication conditions.

How can an APRS station be used to help support a public service communications activity?
   A. An APRS station with an emergency medical technician can automatically transmit medical data to the nearest hospital
   B. APRS stations with General Personnel Scanners can automatically relay the participant numbers and time as they pass the check points
   C. An APRS station with a GPS unit can automatically transmit information to show a mobile station's position during the event
   D. All of these choices are correct

E2D10: C. An APRS station can help support a public service communications activity by automatically transmitting information to show a mobile station's position during the event.

Which of the following data are used by the APRS network to communicate your location?
   A. Polar coordinates
   B. Time and frequency
   C. Radio direction finding spectrum analysis
   D. Latitude and longitude

E2D11: D. Latitude and longitude data is used by the APRS network to communicate your location.

How does JT65 improve EME communications?
   A. It can decode signals many dB below the noise floor using FEC
   B. It controls the receiver to track Doppler shift
   C. It supplies signals to guide the antenna to track the Moon
   D. All of these choices are correct

E2D12: A. JT65 improves EME communications by decoding signals many dB below the noise floor using FEC.

What type of modulation is used for JT65 contacts?
   A. Multi-tone AFSK
   B. PSK
   C. RTTY
   D. IEEE 802.11

E2D13: A. JT65 contacts use multi-tone AFSK modulation.

What is one advantage of using JT65 coding?
   A. Uses only a 65 Hz bandwidth
   B. The ability to decode signals which have a very low signal to noise ratio
   C. Easily copied by ear if necessary
   D. Permits fast-scan TV transmissions over narrow bandwidth

Copyright © Mometrix Media. You have been licensed one copy of this document for personal use only. Any other reproduction or redistribution is strictly prohibited. All rights reserved.

E2D14: B. JT65 coding has the ability to decode signals which have a very low signal to noise ratio.

E2E – Operating methods: operating HF digital modes

Which type of modulation is common for data emissions below 30 MHz?
    A. DTMF tones modulating an FM signal
    B. FSK
    C. Pulse modulation
    D. Spread spectrum

E2E01: B. FSK modulation is common for data emissions below 30 MHz.

What do the letters FEC mean as they relate to digital operation?
    A. Forward Error Correction
    B. First Error Correction
    C. Fatal Error Correction
    D. Final Error Correction

E2E02: A. The letters FEC in digital operation mean Forward Error Correction.

How is the timing of JT65 contacts organized?
    A. By exchanging ACK/NAK packets
    B. Stations take turns on alternate days
    C. Alternating transmissions at 1 minute intervals
    D. It depends on the lunar phase

E2E03: C. The timing of JT65 contacts is organized by alternating transmissions at 1 minute intervals.

What is indicated when one of the ellipses in an FSK crossed-ellipse display suddenly disappears?
    A. Selective fading has occurred
    B. One of the signal filters is saturated
    C. The receiver has drifted 5 kHz from the desired receive frequency
    D. The mark and space signal have been inverted

E2E04: A. When one of the ellipses in an FSK crossed-ellipse display suddenly disappears, it means selective fading has occurred.

Which type of digital mode does not support keyboard-to-keyboard operation?
    A. Winlink
    B. RTTY
    C. PSK31
    D. MFSK

E2E05: A. Winlink does not support keyboard-to-keyboard operation.

Copyright © Mometrix Media. You have been licensed one copy of this document for personal use only. Any other reproduction or redistribution is strictly prohibited. All rights reserved.

What is the most common data rate used for HF packet?
   A. 48 baud
   B. 110 baud
   C. 300 baud
   D. 1200 baud

E2E06: C. The most common data rate used for HF packets is 300 baud.

What is the typical bandwidth of a properly modulated MFSK16 signal?
   A. 31 Hz
   B. 316 Hz
   C. 550 Hz
   D. 2.16 kHz

E2E07: B. The typical bandwidth of a properly modulated MFSK16 signal is 316 Hz.

Which of the following HF digital modes can be used to transfer binary files?
   A. Hellschreiber
   B. PACTOR
   C. RTTY
   D. AMTOR

E2E08: B. PACTOR can be used to transfer binary files.

Which of the following HF digital modes uses variable-length coding for bandwidth efficiency?
   A. RTTY
   B. PACTOR
   C. MT63
   D. PSK31

E2E09: D. PSK31 uses variable-length coding for bandwidth efficiency.

Which of these digital modes has the narrowest bandwidth?
   A. MFSK16
   B. 170 Hz shift, 45 baud RTTY
   C. PSK31
   D. 300-baud packet

E2E10: C. PSK31 has lower bandwidth than MFSK16, 170 Hz shift, 45 baud RTTY, and 300-baud packets.

What is the difference between direct FSK and audio FSK?
   A. Direct FSK applies the data signal to the transmitter VFO
   B. Audio FSK has a superior frequency response
   C. Direct FSK uses a DC-coupled data connection
   D. Audio FSK can be performed anywhere in the transmit chain

E2E11: A. The difference between direct FSK and audio FSK is that Direct FSK applies the data signal to the transmitter VFO.

Copyright © Mometrix Media. You have been licensed one copy of this document for personal use only. Any other reproduction or redistribution is strictly prohibited. All rights reserved.

Which type of control is used by stations using the Automatic Link Enable (ALE) protocol?
    A. Local
    B. Remote
    C. Automatic
    D. ALE can use any type of control

E2E12: C. Automatic control is used by stations using the Automatic Link Enable (ALE) protocol.

Which of the following is a possible reason that attempts to initiate contact with a digital station on a clear frequency are unsuccessful?
    A. Your transmit frequency is incorrect
    B. The protocol version you are using is not the supported by the digital station
    C. Another station you are unable to hear is using the frequency
    D. All of these choices are correct

E2E13: D. Possible reasons that attempts to initiate contact with a digital station on a clear frequency are unsuccessful can include an incorrect transmit frequency, an unsupported protocol version, and another station using the same frequency.

E3 – Radio Wave Propagation

E3A – Electromagnetic waves; Earth-Moon-Earth communications; meteor scatter; microwave tropospheric and scatter propagation; aurora propagation

What is the approximate maximum separation measured along the surface of the Earth between two stations communicating by Moon bounce?
    A. 500 miles, if the Moon is at perigee
    B. 2000 miles, if the Moon is at apogee
    C. 5000 miles, if the Moon is at perigee
    D. 12,000 miles, if the Moon is visible by both stations

E3A01: D. The approximate maximum separation measured along the surface of the Earth between two stations communicating by Moon bounce is 12,000 miles, if the Moon is visible by both stations.

What characterizes libration fading of an EME signal?
    A. A slow change in the pitch of the CW signal
    B. A fluttery irregular fading
    C. A gradual loss of signal as the Sun rises
    D. The returning echo is several Hertz lower in frequency than the transmitted signal

E3A02: B. A fluttery irregular fading characterizes libration fading of an EME signal.

When scheduling EME contacts, which of these conditions will generally result in the least path loss?
    A. When the Moon is at perigee
    B. When the Moon is full
    C. When the Moon is at apogee
    D. When the MUF is above 30 MHz

E3A03: A. Scheduling EME contacts when the Moon is at perigee will generally result in the least path loss.

Copyright © Mometrix Media. You have been licensed one copy of this document for personal use only. Any other reproduction or redistribution is strictly prohibited. All rights reserved.

What do Hepburn maps predict?
    A. Sporadic E propagation
    B. Locations of auroral reflecting zones
    C. Likelihood of rain-scatter along cold or warm fronts
    D. Probability of tropospheric propagation

E3A04: D. Hepburn maps predict the probability of tropospheric propagation.

Tropospheric propagation of microwave signals often occurs along what weather related structure?
    A. Gray-line
    B. Lightning discharges
    C. Warm and cold fronts
    D. Sprites and jets

E3A05: C. Tropospheric propagation of microwave signals often occurs along warm and cold fronts.

Which of the following is required for microwave propagation via rain scatter?
    A. Rain droplets must be electrically charged
    B. Rain droplets must be within the E layer
    C. The rain must be within radio range of both stations
    D. All of these choices are correct

E3A06: C. For microwave propagation via rain scatter, the rain must be within radio range of both stations.

Atmospheric ducts capable of propagating microwave signals often form over what geographic feature?
    A. Mountain ranges
    B. Forests
    C. Bodies of water
    D. Urban areas

E3A07: C. Atmospheric ducts capable of propagating microwave signals often form over bodies of water.

When a meteor strikes the Earth's atmosphere, a cylindrical region of free electrons is formed at what layer of the ionosphere?
    A. The E layer
    B. The F1 layer
    C. The F2 layer
    D. The D layer

E3A08: A. When a meteor strikes the Earth's atmosphere, a cylindrical region of free electrons is formed at the E layer of the ionosphere.

Which of the following frequency ranges is most suited for meteor scatter communications?
    A. 1.8 MHz – 1.9 MHz
    B. 10 MHz – 14 MHz
    C. 28 MHz – 148 MHz
    D. 220 MHz – 450 MHz

E3A09: C. The 28 MHz – 148 MHz range is better suited for meteor scatter communications than 1.8 MHz – 1.9 MHz, 10 MHz – 14 MHz, or 220 MHz – 450 MHz.

Copyright © Mometrix Media. You have been licensed one copy of this document for personal use only. Any other reproduction or redistribution is strictly prohibited. All rights reserved.

Which type of atmospheric structure can create a path for microwave propagation?
    A. The jet stream
    B. Temperature inversion
    C. Wind shear
    D. Dust devil

E3A10: B. Temperature inversion can create a path for microwave propagation.

What is a typical range for tropospheric propagation of microwave signals?
    A. 10 miles to 50 miles
    B. 100 miles to 300 miles
    C. 1200 miles
    D. 2500 miles

E3A11: B. 100 miles to 300 miles is a typical range for tropospheric propagation of microwave signals.

What is the cause of auroral activity?
    A. The interaction in the F2 layer between the solar wind and the Van Allen belt
    B. A low sunspot level combined with tropospheric ducting
    C. The interaction in the E layer of charged particles from the Sun with the Earth's magnetic field
    D. Meteor showers concentrated in the extreme northern and southern latitudes

E3A12: C. The cause of auroral activity is the interaction in the E layer of charged particles from the Sun with the Earth's magnetic field.

Which emission mode is best for aurora propagation?
    A. CW
    B. SSB
    C. FM
    D. RTTY

E3A13: FM is better for aurora propagation than CW, SSB, or RTTY.

From the contiguous 48 states, in which approximate direction should an antenna be pointed to take maximum advantage of aurora propagation?
    A. South
    B. North
    C. East
    D. West

E3A14: B. From the contiguous 48 states, an antenna be pointed north to take maximum advantage of aurora propagation.

What is an electromagnetic wave?
    A. A wave of alternating current, in the core of an electromagnet
    B. A wave consisting of two electric fields at parallel right angles to each other
    C. A wave consisting of an electric field and a magnetic field oscillating at right angles to each other
    D. A wave consisting of two magnetic fields at right angles to each other

E3A15: An electromagnetic wave is a wave consisting of an electric field and a magnetic field oscillating at right angles to each other

Copyright © Mometrix Media. You have been licensed one copy of this document for personal use only. Any other reproduction or redistribution is strictly prohibited. All rights reserved.

Which of the following best describes electromagnetic waves traveling in free space?
    A. Electric and magnetic fields become aligned as they travel
    B. The energy propagates through a medium with a high refractive index
    C. The waves are reflected by the ionosphere and return to their source
    D. Changing electric and magnetic fields propagate the energy

E3A16: D. For electromagnetic waves traveling in free space, changing electric and magnetic fields propagate the energy.

What is meant by circularly polarized electromagnetic waves?
    A. Waves with an electric field bent into a circular shape
    B. Waves with a rotating electric field
    C. Waves that circle the Earth
    D. Waves produced by a loop antenna

E3A17: B. Circularly polarized electromagnetic waves are waves with a rotating electric field.

E3B – Transequatorial propagation; long path; gray-line; multi-path; ordinary and extraordinary waves; chordal hop, sporadic E mechanisms

What is transequatorial propagation?
    A. Propagation between two mid-latitude points at approximately the same distance north and south of the magnetic equator
    B. Propagation between any two points located on the magnetic equator
    C. Propagation between two continents by way of ducts along the magnetic equator
    D. Propagation between two stations at the same latitude

E3B01: A. Transequatorial propagation is propagation between two mid-latitude points at approximately the same distance north and south of the magnetic equator.

What is the approximate maximum range for signals using transequatorial propagation?
    A. 1000 miles
    B. 2500 miles
    C. 5000 miles
    D. 7500 miles

E3B02: C. The approximate maximum range for signals using transequatorial propagation is 5000 miles.

What is the best time of day for transequatorial propagation?
    A. Morning
    B. Noon
    C. Afternoon or early evening
    D. Late at night

E3B03: C. the best time of day for transequatorial propagation is afternoon or early evening.

Copyright © Mometrix Media. You have been licensed one copy of this document for personal use only. Any other reproduction or redistribution is strictly prohibited. All rights reserved.

What is meant by the terms extraordinary and ordinary waves?
   A. Extraordinary waves describe rare long skip propagation compared to ordinary waves which travel shorter distances
   B. Independent waves created in the ionosphere that are elliptically polarized
   C. Long path and short path waves
   D. Refracted rays and reflected waves

E3B04: B. Extraordinary and ordinary waves are independent waves created in the ionosphere that are elliptically polarized.

Which amateur bands typically support long-path propagation?
   A. 160 meters to 40 meters
   B. 30 meters to 10 meters
   C. 160 meters to 10 meters
   D. 6 meters to 2 meters

E3B05: C. The amateur 160 m and 10 m bands typically support long-path propagation.

Which of the following amateur bands most frequently provides long-path propagation?
   A. 80 meters
   B. 20 meters
   C. 10 meters
   D. 6 meters

E3B06: B. The amateur 20 meter band supports long-path propagation more frequently than the 6, 10, or 80 meter bands.

Which of the following could account for hearing an echo on the received signal of a distant station?
   A. High D layer absorption
   B. Meteor scatter
   C. Transmit frequency is higher than the MUF
   D. Receipt of a signal by more than one path

E3B07: D. Receipt of a signal by more than one path could account for hearing an echo on the received signal of a distant station.

What type of HF propagation is probably occurring if radio signals travel along the terminator between daylight and darkness?
   A. Transequatorial
   B. Sporadic-E
   C. Long-path
   D. Gray-line

E3B08: D. Gray-line HF propagation is probably occurring if radio signals travel along the terminator between daylight and darkness.

At what time of year is Sporadic E propagation most likely to occur?
   A. Around the solstices, especially the summer solstice
   B. Around the solstices, especially the winter solstice
   C. Around the equinoxes, especially the spring equinox
   D. Around the equinoxes, especially the fall equinox

Copyright © Mometrix Media. You have been licensed one copy of this document for personal use only. Any other reproduction or redistribution is strictly prohibited. All rights reserved.

E3B09:A. Sporadic E propagation most likely to occur around the solstices, especially the summer solstice.

What is the cause of gray-line propagation?
    A. At midday, the Sun super heats the ionosphere causing increased refraction of radio waves
    B. At twilight and sunrise, D-layer absorption is low while E-layer and F-layer propagation remains high
    C. In darkness, solar absorption drops greatly while atmospheric ionization remains steady
    D. At mid-afternoon, the Sun heats the ionosphere decreasing radio wave refraction and the MUF

E3B10: B. The cause of gray-line propagation is low D-layer absorption and high E-layer and F-layer propagation at twilight and sunrise.

At what time of day is Sporadic-E propagation most likely to occur?
    A. Around sunset
    B. Around sunrise
    C. Early evening
    D. Any time

E3B11: D. Sporadic-E propagation can occur at any time of day.

What is the primary characteristic of chordal hop propagation?
    A. Propagation away from the great circle bearing between stations
    B. Successive ionospheric reflections without an intermediate reflection from the ground
    C. Propagation across the geomagnetic equator
    D. Signals reflected back toward the transmitting station

E3B12: B. Chordal hop propagation is characterized by successive ionospheric reflections without an intermediate reflection from the ground.

Why is chordal hop propagation desirable?
    A. The signal experiences less loss along the path compared to normal skip propagation
    B. The MUF for chordal hop propagation is much lower than for normal skip propagation
    C. Atmospheric noise is lower in the direction of chordal hop propagation
    D. Signals travel faster along ionospheric chords

E3B13: A. Chordal hop propagation is desirable because the signal experiences less loss along the path compared to normal skip propagation

What happens to linearly polarized radio waves that split into ordinary and extraordinary waves in the ionosphere?
    A. They are bent toward the magnetic poles
    B. Their polarization is randomly modified
    C. They become elliptically polarized
    D. They become phase-locked

E3B14: C. Linearly polarized radio waves that split into ordinary and extraordinary waves in the ionosphere become elliptically polarized.

Copyright © Mometrix Media. You have been licensed one copy of this document for personal use only. Any other reproduction or redistribution is strictly prohibited. All rights reserved.

E3C – Radio-path horizon; less common propagation modes; propagation prediction techniques and modeling; space weather parameters and amateur radio

What does the term ray tracing describe in regard to radio communications?
    A. The process in which an electronic display presents a pattern
    B. Modeling a radio wave's path through the ionosphere
    C. Determining the radiation pattern from an array of antennas
    D. Evaluating high voltage sources for X-Rays

E3C01: B. Ray tracing is modeling a radio wave's path through the ionosphere.

What is indicated by a rising A or K index?
    A. Increasing disruption of the geomagnetic field
    B. Decreasing disruption of the geomagnetic field
    C. Higher levels of solar UV radiation
    D. An increase in the critical frequency

E3C02: A. A rising A or K index indicates increasing disruption of the geomagnetic field.

Which of the following signal paths is most likely to experience high levels of absorption when the A index or K index is elevated?
    A. Transequatorial propagation
    B. Polar paths
    C. Sporadic-E
    D. NVIS

E3C03: B. Polar paths are more likely to experience high levels of absorption when the A index or K index is elevated than transequatorial propagation, sporadic-E propagation, and NVIS propagation.

What does the value of Bz (B sub Z) represent?
    A. Geomagnetic field stability
    B. Critical frequency for vertical transmissions
    C. Direction and strength of the interplanetary magnetic field
    D. Duration of long-delayed echoes

E3C04: C. Bz represents the direction and strength of the interplanetary magnetic field.

What orientation of Bz (B sub z) increases the likelihood that incoming particles from the Sun will cause disturbed conditions?
    A. Southward
    B. Northward
    C. Eastward
    D. Westward

E3C05: A. A southward orientation of Bz increases the likelihood that incoming particles from the Sun will cause disturbed conditions.

Copyright © Mometrix Media. You have been licensed one copy of this document for personal use only. Any other reproduction or redistribution is strictly prohibited. All rights reserved.

By how much does the VHF/UHF radio horizon distance exceed the geometric horizon?
    A. By approximately 15 percent of the distance
    B. By approximately twice the distance
    C. By approximately 50 percent of the distance
    D. By approximately four times the distance

E3C06: A. The VHF/UHF radio horizon distance exceeds the geometric horizon by approximately 15 percent of the distance.

Which of the following descriptors indicates the greatest solar flare intensity?
    A. Class A
    B. Class B
    C. Class M
    D. Class X

E3C07: D. A class X descriptor indicates the greatest solar flare intensity.

What does the space weather term G5 mean?
    A. An extreme geomagnetic storm
    B. Very low solar activity
    C. Moderate solar wind
    D. Waning sunspot numbers

E3C08: A. The space weather term G5 indicates an extreme geomagnetic storm.

How does the intensity of an X3 flare compare to that of an X2 flare?
    A. 10 percent greater
    B. 50 percent greater
    C. Twice as great
    D. Four times as great

E3C09: C. An X3 flare is twice as great as an X2 flare.

What does the 304A solar parameter measure?
    A. The ratio of X-Ray flux to radio flux, correlated to sunspot number
    B. UV emissions at 304 angstroms, correlated to solar flux index
    C. The solar wind velocity at 304 degrees from the solar equator, correlated to solar activity
    D. The solar emission at 304 GHz, correlated to X-Ray flare levels

E3C10: B. The 304A solar parameter measures UV emissions at 304 angstroms, correlated to solar flux index.

What does VOACAP software model?
    A. AC voltage and impedance
    B. VHF radio propagation
    C. HF propagation
    D. AC current and impedance

E3C11: C. VOACAP software models HF propagation.

Copyright © Mometrix Media. You have been licensed one copy of this document for personal use only. Any other reproduction or redistribution is strictly prohibited. All rights reserved.

How does the maximum distance of ground-wave propagation change when the signal frequency is increased?

A. It stays the same
B. It increases
C. It decreases
D. It peaks at roughly 14 MHz

E3C12: C. The maximum distance of ground-wave propagation decreases when the signal frequency is increased.

What type of polarization is best for ground-wave propagation?

A. Vertical
B. Horizontal
C. Circular
D. Elliptical

E3C13: A. Vertical polarization is best for ground-wave propagation.

Why does the radio-path horizon distance exceed the geometric horizon?

A. E-region skip
B. D-region skip
C. Downward bending due to aurora refraction
D. Downward bending due to density variations in the atmosphere

E3C14: D. The radio-path horizon distance exceeds the geometric horizon due to downward bending due to density variations in the atmosphere.

What might a sudden rise in radio background noise indicate?

A. A meteor ping
B. A solar flare has occurred
C. Increased transequatorial propagation likely
D. Long-path propagation is occurring

E3C15: B. A sudden rise in radio background noise might indicate that a solar flare has occurred.

E4 – Amateur Practices

E4A – Test equipment: analog and digital instruments; spectrum and network analyzers, antenna analyzers; oscilloscopes; RF measurements; computer aided measurements

Which of the following parameter determines the bandwidth of a digital or computer-based oscilloscope?

A. Input capacitance
B. Input impedance
C. Sampling rate
D. Sample resolution

E4A01: C. Sampling rate determines the bandwidth of a digital or computer-based oscilloscope.

Copyright © Mometrix Media. You have been licensed one copy of this document for personal use only. Any other reproduction or redistribution is strictly prohibited. All rights reserved.

Which of the following parameters would a spectrum analyzer display on the vertical and horizontal axes?
- A. RF amplitude and time
- B. RF amplitude and frequency
- C. SWR and frequency
- D. SWR and time

E4A02: B. a spectrum analyzer would display RF amplitude and frequency on the vertical and horizontal axes, respectively.

Which of the following test instrument is used to display spurious signals and/or intermodulation distortion products in an SSB transmitter?
- A. A wattmeter
- B. A spectrum analyzer
- C. A logic analyzer
- D. A time-domain reflectometer

E4A03: B. A spectrum analyzer is used to display spurious signals and/or intermodulation distortion products in an SSB transmitter.

What determines the upper frequency limit for a computer sound-card-based oscilloscope program?
- A. Analog-to-digital conversion speed of the soundcard
- B. Amount of memory on the soundcard
- C. Q of the interface of the interface circuit
- D. All of these choices are correct

E4A04: A. The analog-to-digital conversion speed of the sound card determines the upper frequency limit of a computer sound-card-based oscilloscope program.

What might be an advantage of a digital vs. an analog oscilloscope?
- A. Automatic amplitude and frequency numerical readout
- B. Storage of traces for future reference
- C. Manipulation of time base after trace capture
- D. All of these choices are correct

E4A05: D. Digital oscilloscopes have many advantages over analog oscilloscopes, including automatic amplitude and frequency readouts, onboard storage of traces, and manipulation of time bases after trace capture.

What is the effect of aliasing in a digital or computer-based oscilloscope?
- A. False signals are displayed
- B. All signals will have a DC offset
- C. Calibration of the vertical scale is no longer valid
- D. False triggering occurs

E4A06: A. Aliasing in a digital or computer-based oscilloscope means that false signals are being displayed.

Copyright © Mometrix Media. You have been licensed one copy of this document for personal use only. Any other reproduction or redistribution is strictly prohibited. All rights reserved.

Which of the following is an advantage of using an antenna analyzer compared to an SWR bridge to measure antenna SWR?
 A. Antenna analyzers automatically tune your antenna for resonance
 B. Antenna analyzers do not need an external RF source
 C. Antenna analyzers display a time-varying representation of the modulation envelope
 D. All of these choices are correct

E4A07: B. An advantage of using an antenna analyzer compared to an SWR bridge to measure antenna SWR is that antenna analyzers do not need an external RF source.

Which of the following instruments would be best for measuring the SWR of a beam antenna?
 A. A spectrum analyzer
 B. A Q meter
 C. An ohmmeter
 D. An antenna analyzer

E4A08: D. An antenna analyzer would be best for measuring the SWR of a beam antenna.

When using a computer's soundcard input to digitize signals, what is the highest frequency signal that can be digitized without aliasing?
 A. The same as the sample rate
 B. One-half the sample rate
 C. One-tenth the sample rate
 D. It depends on how the data is stored internally

E4A09: B. When using a computer's soundcard input to digitize signals, the highest frequency signal that can be digitized without aliasing is one-half the sample rate.

Which of the following displays multiple digital signal states simultaneously?
 A. Network analyzer
 B. Bit error rate tester
 C. Modulation monitor
 D. Logic analyzer

E4A10: D. A logic analyzer displays multiple digital signal states simultaneously.

Which of the following is good practice when using an oscilloscope probe?
 A. Keep the signal ground connection of the probe as short as possible
 B. Never use a high impedance probe to measure a low impedance circuit
 C. Never use a DC-coupled probe to measure an AC circuit
 D. All of these choices are correct

E4A11: A. When using an oscilloscope probe, you should keep the signal ground connection of the probe as short as possible.

Which of the following procedures is an important precaution to follow when connecting a spectrum analyzer to a transmitter output?
 A. Use high quality double shielded coaxial cables to reduce signal losses
 B. Attenuate the transmitter output going to the spectrum analyzer
 C. Match the antenna to the load
 D. All of these choices are correct

Copyright © Mometrix Media. You have been licensed one copy of this document for personal use only. Any other reproduction or redistribution is strictly prohibited. All rights reserved.

E4A12: B. When connecting a spectrum analyzer to a transmitter output, you should attenuate the transmitter output going to the spectrum analyzer

How is the compensation of an oscilloscope probe typically adjusted?
A. A square wave is displayed and the probe is adjusted until the horizontal portions of the displayed wave are as nearly flat as possible
B. A high frequency sine wave is displayed and the probe is adjusted for maximum amplitude
C. A frequency standard is displayed and the probe is adjusted until the deflection time is accurate
D. A DC voltage standard is displayed and the probe is adjusted until the displayed voltage is accurate

E4A13: A. An oscilloscope probe is typically adjusted by displaying a square wave and adjusting the probe until the horizontal portions of the displayed wave are as nearly flat as possible.

What is the purpose of the prescaler function on a frequency counter?
A. It amplifies low level signals for more accurate counting
B. It multiplies a higher frequency signal so a low-frequency counter can display the operating frequency
C. It prevents oscillation in a low-frequency counter circuit
D. It divides a higher frequency signal so a low-frequency counter can display the input frequency

E4A14: D. The prescaler function on a frequency counter divides a higher frequency signal so a low-frequency counter can display the input frequency.

What is an advantage of a period-measuring frequency counter over a direct-count type?
A. It can run on battery power for remote measurements
B. It does not require an expensive high-precision time base
C. It provides improved resolution of low-frequency signals within a comparable time period
D. It can directly measure the modulation index of an FM transmitter

E4A15: C. An advantage of a period-measuring frequency counter over a direct-count type is that it provides improved resolution of low-frequency signals within a comparable time period.

E4B – Measurement technique and limitations: instrument accuracy and performance limitations; probes; techniques to minimize errors; measurement of "Q"; instrument calibration; S parameters; vector network analyzers

Which of the following factors most affects the accuracy of a frequency counter?
A. Input attenuator accuracy
B. Time base accuracy
C. Decade divider accuracy
D. Temperature coefficient of the logic

E4B01: B. Time base accuracy most affects the overall accuracy of a frequency counter.

What is an advantage of using a bridge circuit to measure impedance?
A. It provides an excellent match under all conditions
B. It is relatively immune to drift in the signal generator source
C. It is very precise in obtaining a signal null
D. It can display results directly in Smith chart format

Copyright © Mometrix Media. You have been licensed one copy of this document for personal use only. Any other reproduction or redistribution is strictly prohibited. All rights reserved.

E4B02: C. An advantage of using a bridge circuit to measure impedance is that it is very precise in obtaining a signal null.

If a frequency counter with a specified accuracy of +/- 1.0 ppm reads 146,520,000 Hz, what is the most the actual frequency being measured could differ from the reading?
    A. 165.2 Hz
    B. 14.652 kHz
    C. 146.52 Hz
    D. 1.4652 MHz

E4B03: C. The most the actual frequency being measured could differ from the reading would be 146.52 Hz.

If a frequency counter with a specified accuracy of +/- 0.1 ppm reads 146,520,000 Hz, what is the most the actual frequency being measured could differ from the reading?
    A. 14.652 Hz
    B. 0.1 MHz
    C. 1.4652 Hz
    D. 1.4652 kHz

E4B04: A. The most the actual frequency being measured could differ from the reading would be 14.652 Hz.

If a frequency counter with a specified accuracy of +/- 10 ppm reads 146,520,000 Hz, what is the most the actual frequency being measured could differ from the reading?
    A. 146.52 Hz
    B. 10 Hz
    C. 146.52 kHz
    D. 1465.20 Hz

E4B05: D. The most the actual frequency being measured could differ from the reading would be 1465.20 Hz.

How much power is being absorbed by the load when a directional power meter connected between a transmitter and a terminating load reads 100 watts forward power and 25 watts reflected power?
    A. 100 watts
    B. 125 watts
    C. 25 watts
    D. 75 watts

E4B06: D. 75 watts of power are being absorbed by the load when a directional power meter connected between a transmitter and a terminating load reads 100 watts forward power and 25 watts reflected power.

What do the subscripts of S parameters represent?
    A. The port or ports at which measurements are made
    B. The relative time between measurements
    C. Relative quality of the data
    D. Frequency order of the measurements

E4B07: A. The subscripts of S parameters represent the port or ports at which measurements are made.

Copyright © Mometrix Media. You have been licensed one copy of this document for personal use only. Any other reproduction or redistribution is strictly prohibited. All rights reserved.

Which of the following is a characteristic of a good DC voltmeter?
- A. High reluctance input
- B. Low reluctance input
- C. High impedance input
- D. Low impedance input

E4B08: C. High impedance input is a characteristic of a good DC voltmeter.

What is indicated if the current reading on an RF ammeter placed in series with the antenna feed line of a transmitter increases as the transmitter is tuned to resonance?
- A. There is possibly a short to ground in the feed line
- B. The transmitter is not properly neutralized
- C. There is an impedance mismatch between the antenna and feed line
- D. There is more power going into the antenna

E4B09: D. If the current reading on an RF ammeter placed in series with the antenna feed line of a transmitter increases as the transmitter is tuned to resonance, it indicates there is more power going into the antenna.

Which of the following describes a method to measure intermodulation distortion in an SSB transmitter?
- A. Modulate the transmitter with two non-harmonically related radio frequencies and observe the RF output with a spectrum analyzer
- B. Modulate the transmitter with two non-harmonically related audio frequencies and observe the RF output with a spectrum analyzer
- C. Modulate the transmitter with two harmonically related audio frequencies and observe the RF output with a peak reading wattmeter
- D. Modulate the transmitter with two harmonically related audio frequencies and observe the RF output with a logic analyzer

E4B10: B. Intermodulation distortion in an SSB transmitter can be measured by modulating the transmitter with two non-harmonically related audio frequencies and observing the RF output with a spectrum analyzer.

How should an antenna analyzer be connected when measuring antenna resonance and feed point impedance?
- A. Loosely couple the analyzer near the antenna base
- B. Connect the analyzer via a high-impedance transformer to the antenna
- C. Loosely couple the antenna and a dummy load to the analyzer
- D. Connect the antenna feed line directly to the analyzer's connector

E4B11: D. An antenna analyzer should be connected directly to the antenna feed line when measuring antenna resonance and feed point impedance.

Copyright © Mometrix Media. You have been licensed one copy of this document for personal use only. Any other reproduction or redistribution is strictly prohibited. All rights reserved.

What is the significance of voltmeter sensitivity expressed in ohms per volt?
  A. The full scale reading of the voltmeter multiplied by its ohms per volt rating will indicate the input impedance of the voltmeter
  B. When used as a galvanometer, the reading in volts multiplied by the ohms per volt rating will determine the power drawn by the device under test
  C. When used as an ohmmeter, the reading in ohms divided by the ohms per volt rating will determine the voltage applied to the circuit
  D. When used as an ammeter, the full scale reading in amps divided by ohms per volt rating will determine the size of shunt needed

E4B12: A. Voltmeter sensitivity is expressed in ohms per volt because the full scale reading of the voltmeter multiplied by its ohms per volt rating will indicate the input impedance of the voltmeter.

Which S parameter is equivalent to forward gain?
  A. S11
  B. S12
  C. S21
  D. S22

E4B13: C. The S21 parameter is equivalent to forward gain.

What happens if a dip meter is too tightly coupled to a tuned circuit being checked?
  A. Harmonics are generated
  B. A less accurate reading results
  C. Cross modulation occurs
  D. Intermodulation distortion occurs

E4B14: B. If a dip meter is too tightly coupled to a tuned circuit being checked, a less accurate reading results.

Which of the following can be used as a relative measurement of the Q for a series-tuned circuit?
  A. The inductance to capacitance ratio
  B. The frequency shift
  C. The bandwidth of the circuit's frequency response
  D. The resonant frequency of the circuit

E4B15: C. The bandwidth of the circuit's frequency response can be used as a relative measurement of the Q for a series-tuned circuit.

Which S parameter represents return loss or SWR?
  A. S11
  B. S12
  C. S21
  D. S22

E4B16: A. The S11 parameter represents return loss or SWR.

What three test loads are used to calibrate a standard RF vector network analyzer?
  A. 50 ohms, 75 ohms, and 90 ohms
  B. Short circuit, open circuit, and 50 ohms
  C. Short circuit, open circuit, and resonant circuit
  D. 50 ohms through 1/8 wavelength, 1/4 wavelength, and 1/2 wavelength of coaxial cable

Copyright © Mometrix Media. You have been licensed one copy of this document for personal use only. Any other reproduction or redistribution is strictly prohibited. All rights reserved.

E4B17: B. Short circuit, open circuit, and 50 ohms test loads are used to calibrate a standard RF vector network analyzer.

E4C – Receiver performance characteristics, phase noise, noise floor, image rejection, MDS, signal-to-noise-ratio; selectivity; effects of SDR receiver non-linearity

What is an effect of excessive phase noise in the local oscillator section of a receiver?
A. It limits the receiver's ability to receive strong signals
B. It reduces receiver sensitivity
C. It decreases receiver third-order intermodulation distortion dynamic range
D. It can cause strong signals on nearby frequencies to interfere with reception of weak signals

E4C01: D. Excessive phase noise in the local oscillator section of a receiver can cause strong signals on nearby frequencies to interfere with reception of weak signals.

Which of the following portions of a receiver can be effective in eliminating image signal interference?
A. A front-end filter or pre-selector
B. A narrow IF filter
C. A notch filter
D. A properly adjusted product detector

E4C02: A. A front-end filter or pre-selector can be effective in eliminating image signal interference.

What is the term for the blocking of one FM phone signal by another, stronger FM phone signal?
A. Desensitization
B. Cross-modulation interference
C. Capture effect
D. Frequency discrimination

E4C03: C. Capture effect is the term for the blocking of one FM phone signal by another, stronger FM phone signal.

How is the noise figure of a receiver defined?
A. The ratio of atmospheric noise to phase noise
B. The ratio of the noise bandwidth in Hertz to the theoretical bandwidth of a resistive network
C. The ratio of thermal noise to atmospheric noise
D. The ratio in dB of the noise generated by the receiver to the theoretical minimum noise

E4C04: D. The noise figure of a receiver is defined as the ratio in dB of the noise generated by the receiver to the theoretical minimum noise.

What does a value of -174 dBm/Hz represent with regard to the noise floor of a receiver?
A. The minimum detectable signal as a function of receive frequency
B. The theoretical noise at the input of a perfect receiver at room temperature
C. The noise figure of a 1 Hz bandwidth receiver
D. The galactic noise contribution to minimum detectable signal

E4C05: B. A value of -174 dBm/Hz represents the theoretical noise at the input of a perfect receiver at room temperature.

Copyright © Mometrix Media. You have been licensed one copy of this document for personal use only. Any other reproduction or redistribution is strictly prohibited. All rights reserved.

A CW receiver with the AGC off has an equivalent input noise power density of -174 dBm/Hz. What would be the level of an unmodulated carrier input to this receiver that would yield an audio output SNR of 0 dB in a 400 Hz noise bandwidth?
- A. -174 dBm
- B. -164 dBm
- C. -155 dBm
- D. -148 dBm

E4C06: D. -148 dBm is the level of an unmodulated carrier input to this receiver that would yield an audio output SNR of 0 dB in a 400 Hz noise bandwidth.

What does the MDS of a receiver represent?
- A. The meter display sensitivity
- B. The minimum discernible signal
- C. The multiplex distortion stability
- D. The maximum detectable spectrum

E4C07: B. The MDS of a receiver represents the minimum discernible signal.

An SDR receiver is overloaded when input signals exceed what level?
- A. One-half the maximum sample rate
- B. One-half the maximum sampling buffer size
- C. The maximum count value of the analog-to-digital converter
- D. The reference voltage of the analog-to-digital converter

E4C08: C. An SDR receiver is overloaded when input signals exceed the maximum count value of the analog-to-digital converter.

Which of the following choices is a good reason for selecting a high frequency for the design of the IF in a conventional HF or VHF communications receiver?
- A. Fewer components in the receiver
- B. Reduced drift
- C. Easier for front-end circuitry to eliminate image responses
- D. Improved receiver noise figure

E4C09: C. It is a good reason to select a high frequency for the design of the IF in a conventional HF or VHF communications receiver because it makes it easier for front-end circuitry to eliminate image responses.

Which of the following is a desirable amount of selectivity for an amateur RTTY HF receiver?
- A. 100 Hz
- B. 300 Hz
- C. 6000 Hz
- D. 2400 Hz

E4C10: B. 300 Hz is a desirable amount of selectivity for an amateur RTTY HF receiver.

Copyright © Mometrix Media. You have been licensed one copy of this document for personal use only. Any other reproduction or redistribution is strictly prohibited. All rights reserved.

Which of the following is a desirable amount of selectivity for an amateur SSB phone receiver?
  A. 1 kHz
  B. 2.4 kHz
  C. 4.2 kHz
  D. 4.8 kHz

E4C11: B. 2.4 kHz is a desirable amount of selectivity for an amateur SSB phone receiver.

What is an undesirable effect of using too wide a filter bandwidth in the IF section of a receiver?
  A. Output-offset overshoot
  B. Filter ringing
  C. Thermal-noise distortion
  D. Undesired signals may be heard

E4C12: D. Using too wide a filter bandwidth in the IF section of a receiver may result in undesired signals being heard.

How does a narrow-band roofing filter affect receiver performance?
  A. It improves sensitivity by reducing front end noise
  B. It improves intelligibility by using low Q circuitry to reduce ringing
  C. It improves dynamic range by attenuating strong signals near the receive frequency
  D. All of these choices are correct

E4C13: C. A narrow-band roofing filter affects receiver performance improving dynamic range by attenuating strong signals near the receive frequency.

What transmit frequency might generate an image response signal in a receiver tuned to 14.300 MHz and which uses a 455 kHz IF frequency?
  A. 13.845 MHz
  B. 14.755 MHz
  C. 14.445 MHz
  D. 15.210 MHz

E4C14: D. A 15.210 MHz transmit frequency might generate an image response signal in a receiver tuned to 14.300 MHz and which uses a 455 kHz IF frequency.

What is usually the primary source of noise that is heard from an HF receiver with an antenna connected?
  A. Detector noise
  B. Induction motor noise
  C. Receiver front-end noise
  D. Atmospheric noise

E4C15: D. Atmospheric noise is usually the primary source of noise that is heard from an HF receiver with an antenna connected.

Which of the following is caused by missing codes in an SDR receiver's analog-to-digital converter?
  A. Distortion
  B. Overload
  C. Loss of sensitivity
  D. Excess output level

Copyright © Mometrix Media. You have been licensed one copy of this document for personal use only. Any other reproduction or redistribution is strictly prohibited. All rights reserved.

E4C16: A. Distortion is caused by missing codes in an SDR receiver's analog-to-digital converter.

Which of the following has the largest effect on an SDR receiver's linearity?
    A. CPU register width in bits
    B. Anti-aliasing input filter bandwidth
    C. RAM speed used for data storage
    D. Analog-to-digital converter sample width in bits

E4C17: D. Analog-to-digital converter sample width in bits has the largest effect on an SDR receiver's linearity.

E4D – Receiver performance characteristics: blocking dynamic range; intermodulation and cross-modulation interference; 3rd order intercept; desensitization; preselector

What is meant by the blocking dynamic range of a receiver?
    A. The difference in dB between the noise floor and the level of an incoming signal which will cause 1 dB of gain compression
    B. The minimum difference in dB between the levels of two FM signals which will cause one signal to block the other
    C. The difference in dB between the noise floor and the third order intercept point
    D. The minimum difference in dB between two signals which produce third order intermodulation products greater than the noise floor

E4D01: A. The blocking dynamic range of a receiver is the difference in dB between the noise floor and the level of an incoming signal which will cause 1 dB of gain compression

Which of the following describes two problems caused by poor dynamic range in a communications receiver?
    A. Cross-modulation of the desired signal and desensitization from strong adjacent signals
    B. Oscillator instability requiring frequent retuning and loss of ability to recover the opposite sideband
    C. Cross-modulation of the desired signal and insufficient audio power to operate the speaker
    D. Oscillator instability and severe audio distortion of all but the strongest received signals

E4D02: A. Cross-modulation of the desired signal and desensitization from strong adjacent signals are both problems caused by poor dynamic range in a communications receiver.

How can intermodulation interference between two repeaters occur?
    A. When the repeaters are in close proximity and the signals cause feedback in the final amplifier of one or both transmitters
    B. When the repeaters are in close proximity and the signals mix in the final amplifier of one or both transmitters
    C. When the signals from the transmitters are reflected out of phase from airplanes passing overhead
    D. When the signals from the transmitters are reflected in phase from airplanes passing overhead

E4D03: B. Intermodulation interference between two repeaters can occur when the repeaters are in close proximity and the signals mix in the final amplifier of one or both transmitters.

Copyright © Mometrix Media. You have been licensed one copy of this document for personal use only. Any other reproduction or redistribution is strictly prohibited. All rights reserved.

Which of the following may reduce or eliminate intermodulation interference in a repeater caused by another transmitter operating in close proximity?
    A. A band-pass filter in the feed line between the transmitter and receiver
    B. A properly terminated circulator at the output of the transmitter
    C. A Class C final amplifier
    D. A Class D final amplifier

E4D04: B. A properly terminated circulator at the output of the transmitter may reduce or eliminate intermodulation interference in a repeater caused by another transmitter operating in close proximity.

What transmitter frequencies would cause an intermodulation-product signal in a receiver tuned to 146.70 MHz when a nearby station transmits on 146.52 MHz?
    A. 146.34 MHz and 146.61 MHz
    B. 146.88 MHz and 146.34 MHz
    C. 146.10 MHz and 147.30 MHz
    D. 173.35 MHz and 139.40 MHz

E4D05: A. 146.34 MHz and 146.61 MHz frequencies would cause an intermodulation-product signal in a receiver tuned to 146.70 MHz when a nearby station transmits on 146.52 MHz.

What is the term for unwanted signals generated by the mixing of two or more signals?
    A. Amplifier desensitization
    B. Neutralization
    C. Adjacent channel interference
    D. Intermodulation interference

E4D06: D. Intermodulation interference is an unwanted signal generated by the mixing of two or more signals.

Which describes the most significant effect of an off-frequency signal when it is causing cross-modulation interference to a desired signal?
    A. A large increase in background noise
    B. A reduction in apparent signal strength
    C. The desired signal can no longer be heard
    D. The off-frequency unwanted signal is heard in addition to the desired signal

E4D07: D. When an off-frequency signal is causing cross-modulation interference to a desired signal, the off-frequency signal is heard in addition to the desired signal.

What causes intermodulation in an electronic circuit?
    A. Too little gain
    B. Lack of neutralization
    C. Nonlinear circuits or devices
    D. Positive feedback

E4D08: C. Nonlinear circuits or devices cause intermodulation in an electronic circuit.

What is the purpose of the preselector in a communications receiver?
    A. To store often-used frequencies
    B. To provide a range of AGC time constants
    C. To increase rejection of unwanted signals
    D. To allow selection of the optimum RF amplifier device

Copyright © Mometrix Media. You have been licensed one copy of this document for personal use only. Any other reproduction or redistribution is strictly prohibited. All rights reserved.

E4D09: C. The purpose of the preselector in a communications receiver is to increase rejection of unwanted signals.

What does a third-order intercept level of 40 dBm mean with respect to receiver performance?
    A. Signals less than 40 dBm will not generate audible third-order intermodulation products
    B. The receiver can tolerate signals up to 40 dB above the noise floor without producing third-order intermodulation products
    C. A pair of 40 dBm signals will theoretically generate a third-order intermodulation product with the same level as the input signals
    D. A pair of 1 mW input signals will produce a third-order intermodulation product which is 40 dB stronger than the input signal

E4D10: C. A third-order intercept level of 40 dBm means that a pair of 40 dBm signals will theoretically generate a third-order intermodulation product with the same level as the input signals.

Why are third-order intermodulation products created within a receiver of particular interest compared to other products?
    A. The third-order product of two signals which are in the band of interest is also likely to be within the band
    B. The third-order intercept is much higher than other orders
    C. Third-order products are an indication of poor image rejection
    D. Third-order intermodulation produces three products for every input signal within the band of interest

E4D11: A. Third-order intermodulation products created within a receiver of particular interest are often compared to other products because the third-order product of two signals which are in the band of interest is also likely to be within the band.

What is the term for the reduction in receiver sensitivity caused by a strong signal near the received frequency?
    A. Desensitization
    B. Quieting
    C. Cross-modulation interference
    D. Squelch gain rollback

E4D12: A. Desensitization is the reduction in receiver sensitivity caused by a strong signal near the received frequency.

Which of the following can cause receiver desensitization?
    A. Audio gain adjusted too low
    B. Strong adjacent channel signals
    C. Audio bias adjusted too high
    D. Squelch gain misadjusted

E4D13: B. Strong adjacent channel signals can cause receiver desensitization.

Which of the following is a way to reduce the likelihood of receiver desensitization?
    A. Decrease the RF bandwidth of the receiver
    B. Raise the receiver IF frequency
    C. Increase the receiver front end gain
    D. Switch from fast AGC to slow AGC

Copyright © Mometrix Media. You have been licensed one copy of this document for personal use only. Any other reproduction or redistribution is strictly prohibited. All rights reserved.

E4D14: A. Decreasing the RF bandwidth of the receiver is a way to reduce the likelihood of receiver desensitization.

E4E – Noise suppression: system noise; electrical appliance noise; line noise; locating noise sources; DSP noise reduction; noise blankers; grounding for signals

Which of the following types of receiver noise can often be reduced by use of a receiver noise blanker?
    A. Ignition noise
    B. Broadband white noise
    C. Heterodyne interference
    D. All of these choices are correct

E4E01: A. Ignition noise can often be reduced by use of a receiver noise blanker.

Which of the following types of receiver noise can often be reduced with a DSP noise filter?
    A. Broadband white noise
    B. Ignition noise
    C. Power line noise
    D. All of these choices are correct

E4E02: D. Broadband white noise, ignition noise, and power line noise can often be reduced with a DSP noise filter.

Which of the following signals might a receiver noise blanker be able to remove from desired signals?
    A. Signals which are constant at all IF levels
    B. Signals which appear across a wide bandwidth
    C. Signals which appear at one IF but not another
    D. Signals which have a sharply peaked frequency distribution

E4E03: B. A receiver noise blanker might be able to remove signals which appear across a wide bandwidth from desired signals.

How can conducted and radiated noise caused by an automobile alternator be suppressed?
    A. By installing filter capacitors in series with the DC power lead and a blocking capacitor in the field lead
    B. By installing a noise suppression resistor and a blocking capacitor in both leads
    C. By installing a high-pass filter in series with the radio's power lead and a low-pass filter in parallel with the field lead
    D. By connecting the radio's power leads directly to the battery and by installing coaxial capacitors in line with the alternator leads

E4E04: D. Conducted and radiated noise caused by an automobile alternator can be suppressed by connecting the radio's power leads directly to the battery and by installing coaxial capacitors in line with the alternator leads.

How can noise from an electric motor be suppressed?
    A. By installing a high pass filter in series with the motor's power leads
    B. By installing a brute-force AC-line filter in series with the motor leads
    C. By installing a bypass capacitor in series with the motor leads
    D. By using a ground-fault current interrupter in the circuit used to power the motor

Copyright © Mometrix Media. You have been licensed one copy of this document for personal use only. Any other reproduction or redistribution is strictly prohibited. All rights reserved.

E4E05: B. Noise from an electric motor can be suppressed by installing a brute-force AC-line filter in series with the motor leads.

What is a major cause of atmospheric static?
    A. Solar radio frequency emissions
    B. Thunderstorms
    C. Geomagnetic storms
    D. Meteor showers

E4E06: B. Thunderstorms are a major cause of atmospheric static.

How can you determine if line noise interference is being generated within your home?
    A. By checking the power line voltage with a time domain reflectometer
    B. By observing the AC power line waveform with an oscilloscope
    C. By turning off the AC power line main circuit breaker and listening on a battery operated radio
    D. By observing the AC power line voltage with a spectrum analyzer

E4E07: You can determine if line noise interference is being generated within your home by turning off the AC power line main circuit breaker and listening on a battery operated radio.

What type of signal is picked up by electrical wiring near a radio antenna?
    A. A common-mode signal at the frequency of the radio transmitter
    B. An electrical-sparking signal
    C. A differential-mode signal at the AC power line frequency
    D. Harmonics of the AC power line frequency

E4E08: A. A common-mode signal at the frequency of the radio transmitter is picked up by electrical wiring near a radio antenna.

What undesirable effect can occur when using an IF noise blanker?
    A. Received audio in the speech range might have an echo effect
    B. The audio frequency bandwidth of the received signal might be compressed
    C. Nearby signals may appear to be excessively wide even if they meet emission standards
    D. FM signals can no longer be demodulated

E4E09: C. When using an IF noise blanker, nearby signals may appear to be excessively wide even if they meet emission standards.

What is a common characteristic of interference caused by a touch controlled electrical device?
    A. The interfering signal sounds like AC hum on an AM receiver or a carrier modulated by 60 Hz hum on a SSB or CW receiver
    B. The interfering signal may drift slowly across the HF spectrum
    C. The interfering signal can be several kHz in width and usually repeats at regular intervals across a HF band
    D. All of these choices are correct

E4E10: D. Touch-controlled electrical devices may cause interference that sounds like AC hum on an AM receiver or a carrier modulated by 60 Hz hum on a SSB or CW receiver, interference that drifts slowly across the HF spectrum, and interference that can be several kHz in width and repeats at regular intervals across a HF band.

Copyright © Mometrix Media. You have been licensed one copy of this document for personal use only. Any other reproduction or redistribution is strictly prohibited. All rights reserved.

Which is the most likely cause if you are hearing combinations of local AM broadcast signals within one or more of the MF or HF ham bands?

A. The broadcast station is transmitting an over-modulated signal
B. Nearby corroded metal joints are mixing and re-radiating the broadcast signals
C. You are receiving sky wave signals from a distant station
D. Your station receiver IF amplifier stage is defective

E4E11: B. If you are hearing combinations of local AM broadcast signals within one or more of the MF or HF ham bands, it is likely that nearby corroded metal joints are mixing and re-radiating the broadcast signals.

What is one disadvantage of using some types of automatic DSP notch-filters when attempting to copy CW signals?

A. A DSP filter can remove the desired signal at the same time as it removes interfering signals
B. Any nearby signal passing through the DSP system will overwhelm the desired signal
C. Received CW signals will appear to be modulated at the DSP clock frequency
D. Ringing in the DSP filter will completely remove the spaces between the CW characters

E4E12: A. A disadvantage of using some types of automatic DSP notch-filters when attempting to copy CW signals is that a DSP filter can remove the desired signal at the same time as it removes interfering signals.

What might be the cause of a loud roaring or buzzing AC line interference that comes and goes at intervals?

A. Arcing contacts in a thermostatically controlled device
B. A defective doorbell or doorbell transformer inside a nearby residence
C. A malfunctioning illuminated advertising display
D. All of these choices are correct

E4E13: D. Loud roaring or buzzing AC line interference that comes and goes at intervals could be caused by a number of things, including arcing contacts in a thermostatically controlled device, a defective doorbell or doorbell transformer inside a nearby residence, or a malfunctioning illuminated advertising display.

What is one type of electrical interference that might be caused by the operation of a nearby personal computer?

A. A loud AC hum in the audio output of your station receiver
B. A clicking noise at intervals of a few seconds
C. The appearance of unstable modulated or unmodulated signals at specific frequencies
D. A whining type noise that continually pulses off and on

E4E14: C. The appearance of unstable modulated or unmodulated signals at specific frequencies could be caused by the operation of a nearby personal computer.

Which of the following can cause shielded cables to radiate or receive interference?

A. Low inductance ground connections at both ends of the shield
B. Common mode currents on the shield and conductors
C. Use of braided shielding material
D. Tying all ground connections to a common point resulting in differential mode currents in the shield

Copyright © Mometrix Media. You have been licensed one copy of this document for personal use only. Any other reproduction or redistribution is strictly prohibited. All rights reserved.

E4E15: B. Common mode currents on the shield and conductors can cause shielded cables to radiate or receive interference.

What current flows equally on all conductors of an unshielded multi-conductor cable?
    A. Differential-mode current
    B. Common-mode current
    C. Reactive current only
    D. Return current

E4E16: B. Common-mode current flows equally on all conductors of an unshielded multi-conductor cable.

E5 – Electrical Principles

E5A – Resonance and Q: characteristics of resonant circuits: series and parallel resonance; definitions and effects of Q; half-power bandwidth; phase relationships in reactive circuits

What can cause the voltage across reactances in series to be larger than the voltage applied to them?
    A. Resonance
    B. Capacitance
    C. Conductance
    D. Resistance

E5A01: A. Resonance can cause the voltage across reactances in series to be larger than the voltage applied to them.

What is resonance in an electrical circuit?
    A. The highest frequency that will pass current
    B. The lowest frequency that will pass current
    C. The frequency at which the capacitive reactance equals the inductive reactance
    D. The frequency at which the reactive impedance equals the resistive impedance

E5A02: C. Resonance in an electrical circuit is the frequency at which the capacitive reactance equals the inductive reactance.

What is the magnitude of the impedance of a series RLC circuit at resonance?
    A. High, as compared to the circuit resistance
    B. Approximately equal to capacitive reactance
    C. Approximately equal to inductive reactance
    D. Approximately equal to circuit resistance

E5A03: D. The magnitude of the impedance of a series RLC circuit at resonance is approximately equal to circuit resistance.

Copyright © Mometrix Media. You have been licensed one copy of this document for personal use only. Any other reproduction or redistribution is strictly prohibited. All rights reserved.

What is the magnitude of the impedance of a circuit with a resistor, an inductor and a capacitor all in parallel, at resonance?

A. Approximately equal to circuit resistance
B. Approximately equal to inductive reactance
C. Low, as compared to the circuit resistance
D. Approximately equal to capacitive reactance

E5A04: A. The magnitude of the impedance of a circuit with a resistor, an inductor and a capacitor all in parallel, at resonance is approximately equal to circuit resistance.

What is the magnitude of the current at the input of a series RLC circuit as the frequency goes through resonance?

A. Minimum
B. Maximum
C. R/L
D. L/R

E5A05: B. The magnitude of the current at the input of a series RLC circuit as the frequency goes through resonance is at maximum.

What is the magnitude of the circulating current within the components of a parallel LC circuit at resonance?

A. It is at a minimum
B. It is at a maximum
C. It equals 1 divided by the quantity 2 times Pi, multiplied by the square root of inductance L multiplied by capacitance C
D. It equals 2 multiplied by Pi, multiplied by frequency, multiplied by inductance

E5A06: B. The magnitude of the circulating current within the components of a parallel LC circuit at resonance is at a maximum.

What is the magnitude of the current at the input of a parallel RLC circuit at resonance?

A. Minimum
B. Maximum
C. R/L
D. L/R

E5A07: A. The magnitude of the current at the input of a parallel RLC circuit at resonance is at a minimum.

What is the phase relationship between the current through and the voltage across a series resonant circuit at resonance?

A. The voltage leads the current by 90 degrees
B. The current leads the voltage by 90 degrees
C. The voltage and current are in phase
D. The voltage and current are 180 degrees out of phase

E5A08: C. In a series resonant circuit at resonance, the voltage and current are in phase.

Copyright © Mometrix Media. You have been licensed one copy of this document for personal use only. Any other reproduction or redistribution is strictly prohibited. All rights reserved.

How is the Q of an RLC parallel resonant circuit calculated?
    A. Reactance of either the inductance or capacitance divided by the resistance
    B. Reactance of either the inductance or capacitance multiplied by the resistance
    C. Resistance divided by the reactance of either the inductance or capacitance
    D. Reactance of the inductance multiplied by the reactance of the capacitance

E5A09: C. The Q of an RLC parallel resonant circuit is calculated by dividing the resistance by the reactance of either the inductance or capacitance.

How is the Q of an RLC series resonant circuit calculated?
    A. Reactance of either the inductance or capacitance divided by the resistance
    B. Reactance of either the inductance or capacitance times the resistance
    C. Resistance divided by the reactance of either the inductance or capacitance
    D. Reactance of the inductance times the reactance of the capacitance

E5A10: A. The Q of an RLC series resonant circuit is calculated by dividing the reactance of either the inductance or capacitance by the resistance.

What is the half-power bandwidth of a parallel resonant circuit that has a resonant frequency of 7.1 MHz and a Q of 150?
    A. 157.8 Hz
    B. 315.6 Hz
    C. 47.3 kHz
    D. 23.67 kHz

E5A11: C. The half-power bandwidth of a parallel resonant circuit that has a resonant frequency of 7.1 MHz and a Q of 150 is 47.3 kHz.

What is the half-power bandwidth of a parallel resonant circuit that has a resonant frequency of 3.7 MHz and a Q of 118?
    A. 436.6 kHz
    B. 218.3 kHz
    C. 31.4 kHz
    D. 15.7 kHz

E5A12: C. The half-power bandwidth of a parallel resonant circuit that has a resonant frequency of 3.7 MHz and a Q of 118 is 31.4 kHz.

What is an effect of increasing Q in a resonant circuit?
    A. Fewer components are needed for the same performance
    B. Parasitic effects are minimized
    C. Internal voltages and circulating currents increase
    D. Phase shift can become uncontrolled

E5A13: Increasing Q in a resonant circuit can cause internal voltages and circulating currents to increase.

Copyright © Mometrix Media. You have been licensed one copy of this document for personal use only. Any other reproduction or redistribution is strictly prohibited. All rights reserved.

What is the resonant frequency of a series RLC circuit if R is 22 ohms, L is 50 microhenrys and C is 40 picofarads?

A. 44.72 MHz
B. 22.36 MHz
C. 3.56 MHz
D. 1.78 MHz

E5A14: C. The resonant frequency of a series RLC circuit if R is 22 ohms, L is 50 microhenrys and C is 40 picofarads is 3.56 MHz.

Which of the following can increase Q for inductors and capacitors?

A. Lower losses
B. Lower reactance
C. Lower self-resonant frequency
D. Higher self-resonant frequency

E5A15: A. Lower losses can increase Q for inductors and capacitors.

What is the resonant frequency of a parallel RLC circuit if R is 33 ohms, L is 50 microhenrys and C is 10 picofarads?

A. 23.5 MHz
B. 23.5 kHz
C. 7.12 kHz
D. 7.12 MHz

E5A16: D. The resonant frequency of a parallel RLC circuit with R = 33 ohms, L = 50 microhenrys and C = 10 picofarads, is 7.12 MHz.

What is the result of increasing the Q of an impedance-matching circuit?

A. Matching bandwidth is decreased
B. Matching bandwidth is increased
C. Matching range is increased
D. It has no effect on impedance matching

E5A17: A. Increasing the Q of an impedance-matching circuit will decrease the matching bandwidth.

E5B – Time constants and phase relationships: RLC time constants; definition; time constants in RL and RC circuits; phase angle between voltage and current; phase angles of series RLC; phase angle of inductance vs susceptance; admittance and susceptance

What is the term for the time required for the capacitor in an RC circuit to be charged to 63.2% of the applied voltage?

A. An exponential rate of one
B. One time constant
C. One exponential period
D. A time factor of one

E5B01: B. A time-constant is the time required for the capacitor in an RC circuit to be charged to 63.2% of the applied voltage.

Copyright © Mometrix Media. You have been licensed one copy of this document for personal use only. Any other reproduction or redistribution is strictly prohibited. All rights reserved.

What is the term for the time it takes for a charged capacitor in an RC circuit to discharge to 36.8% of its initial voltage?
A. One discharge period
B. An exponential discharge rate of one
C. A discharge factor of one
D. One time constant

E5B02: D. A time-constant is the time it takes for a charged capacitor in an RC circuit to discharge to 36.8% of its initial voltage.

What happens to the phase angle of a reactance when it is converted to a susceptance?
A. It is unchanged
B. The sign is reversed
C. It is shifted by 90 degrees
D. The susceptance phase angle is the inverse of the reactance phase angle

E5B03: B. The sign of a phase angle of a reactance is reversed when it is converted to a susceptance.

What is the time constant of a circuit having two 220 microfarad capacitors and two 1 megohm resistors, all in parallel?
A. 55 seconds
B. 110 seconds
C. 440 seconds
D. 220 seconds

E5B04: D. The time constant of a circuit having two 220 microfarad capacitors and two 1 megohm resistors, all in parallel, is 220 seconds.

What happens to the magnitude of a reactance when it is converted to a susceptance?
A. It is unchanged
B. The sign is reversed
C. It is shifted by 90 degrees
D. The magnitude of the susceptance is the reciprocal of the magnitude of the reactance

E5B05: D. When a reactance is converted to a susceptance, the magnitude of the susceptance is the reciprocal of the magnitude of the reactance.

What is susceptance?
A. The magnetic impedance of a circuit
B. The ratio of magnetic field to electric field
C. The inverse of reactance
D. A measure of the efficiency of a transformer

E5B06: C. Susceptance is the inverse of reactance.

What is the phase angle between the voltage across and the current through a series RLC circuit if X_C is 500 ohms, R is 1 kilohm, and X_L is 250 ohms?
A. 68.2 degrees with the voltage leading the current
B. 14.0 degrees with the voltage leading the current
C. 14.0 degrees with the voltage lagging the current
D. 68.2 degrees with the voltage lagging the current

Copyright © Mometrix Media. You have been licensed one copy of this document for personal use only. Any other reproduction or redistribution is strictly prohibited. All rights reserved.

E5B07: C. The phase angle of a series RLC circuit with X_C = 500 ohms, R = 1 kilohm, and X_L = 250 ohms is 14.0 degrees with the voltage lagging the current.

What is the phase angle between the voltage across and the current through a series RLC circuit if X_C is 100 ohms, R is 100 ohms, and X_L is 75 ohms?
    A. 14 degrees with the voltage lagging the current
    B. 14 degrees with the voltage leading the current
    C. 76 degrees with the voltage leading the current
    D. 76 degrees with the voltage lagging the current

E5B08: A. The phase angle of a series RLC circuit with X_C = 100 ohms, R = 100 ohms, and X_L = 75 ohms is 14 degrees with the voltage lagging the current.

What is the relationship between the current through a capacitor and the voltage across a capacitor?
    A. Voltage and current are in phase
    B. Voltage and current are 180 degrees out of phase
    C. Voltage leads current by 90 degrees
    D. Current leads voltage by 90 degrees

E5B09: D. In a capacitor, current leads voltage by 90 degrees.

What is the relationship between the current through an inductor and the voltage across an inductor?
    A. Voltage leads current by 90 degrees
    B. Current leads voltage by 90 degrees
    C. Voltage and current are 180 degrees out of phase
    D. Voltage and current are in phase

E5B10: A. In an inductor, voltage leads current by 90 degrees.

What is the phase angle between the voltage across and the current through a series RLC circuit if X_C is 25 ohms, R is 100 ohms, and X_L is 50 ohms?
    A. 14 degrees with the voltage lagging the current
    B. 14 degrees with the voltage leading the current
    C. 76 degrees with the voltage lagging the current
    D. 76 degrees with the voltage leading the current

E5B11: B. The phase angle of a series RLC circuit with X_C = 25 ohms, R = 100 ohms, and X_L = 50 ohms is 14 degrees with the voltage leading the current.

What is admittance?
    A. The inverse of impedance
    B. The term for the gain of a field effect transistor
    C. The turns ratio of a transformer
    D. The unit used for Q factor

E5B12: A. Admittance is the inverse of impedance.

Copyright © Mometrix Media. You have been licensed one copy of this document for personal use only. Any other reproduction or redistribution is strictly prohibited. All rights reserved.

What letter is commonly used to represent susceptance?
    A. G
    B. X
    C. Y
    D. B

E5B13: D. the letter 'B' is commonly used to represent susceptance.

E5C – Coordinate systems and phasors in electronics: Rectangular Coordinates; Polar Coordinates; Phasors

Which of the following represents a capacitive reactance in rectangular notation?
    A. –jX
    B. +jX
    C. X
    D. Omega

E5C01: A. "–jX" represents a capacitive reactance in rectangular notation.

How are impedances described in polar coordinates?
    A. By X and R values
    B. By real and imaginary parts
    C. By phase angle and amplitude
    D. By Y and G values

E5C02: C. Impedances are described by phase angle and amplitude in polar coordinates.

Which of the following represents an inductive reactance in polar coordinates?
    A. A positive real part
    B. A negative real part
    C. A positive phase angle
    D. A negative phase angle

E5C03: C. A positive phase angle represents an inductive reactance in polar coordinates.

Which of the following represents a capacitive reactance in polar coordinates?
    A. A positive real part
    B. A negative real part
    C. A positive phase angle
    D. A negative phase angle

E5C04: D. A negative phase angle represents a capacitive reactance in polar coordinates.

What is the name of the diagram used to show the phase relationship between impedances at a given frequency?
    A. Venn diagram
    B. Near field diagram
    C. Phasor diagram
    D. Far field diagram

Copyright © Mometrix Media. You have been licensed one copy of this document for personal use only. Any other reproduction or redistribution is strictly prohibited. All rights reserved.

E5C05: C. A phasor diagram is used to show the phase relationship between impedances at a given frequency.

What does the impedance 50–j25 represent?
    A. 50 ohms resistance in series with 25 ohms inductive reactance
    B. 50 ohms resistance in series with 25 ohms capacitive reactance
    C. 25 ohms resistance in series with 50 ohms inductive reactance
    D. 25 ohms resistance in series with 50 ohms capacitive reactance

E5C06: B. The impedance 50–j25 represents 50 ohms resistance in series with 25 ohms capacitive reactance.

What is a vector?
    A. The value of a quantity that changes over time
    B. A quantity with both magnitude and an angular component
    C. The inverse of the tangent function
    D. The inverse of the sine function

E5C07: B. A vector is a quantity with both magnitude and an angular component.

What coordinate system is often used to display the phase angle of a circuit containing resistance, inductive and/or capacitive reactance?
    A. Maidenhead grid
    B. Faraday grid
    C. Elliptical coordinates
    D. Polar coordinates

E5C08: D. Polar coordinates are often used to display the phase angle of a circuit containing resistance, inductive and/or capacitive reactance.

When using rectangular coordinates to graph the impedance of a circuit, what does the horizontal axis represent?
    A. Resistive component
    B. Reactive component
    C. The sum of the reactive and resistive components
    D. The difference between the resistive and reactive components

E5C09: A. When using rectangular coordinates to graph the impedance of a circuit, the horizontal axis represents the resistive component.

When using rectangular coordinates to graph the impedance of a circuit, what does the vertical axis represent?
    A. Resistive component
    B. Reactive component
    C. The sum of the reactive and resistive components
    D. The difference between the resistive and reactive components

E5C10: B. When using rectangular coordinates to graph the impedance of a circuit, the vertical axis represents the reactive component.

Copyright © Mometrix Media. You have been licensed one copy of this document for personal use only. Any other reproduction or redistribution is strictly prohibited. All rights reserved.

What do the two numbers that are used to define a point on a graph using rectangular coordinates represent?
   A. The magnitude and phase of the point
   B. The sine and cosine values
   C. The coordinate values along the horizontal and vertical axes
   D. The tangent and cotangent values

E5C11: C. The two numbers that are used to define a point on a graph using rectangular coordinates represent the coordinate values along the horizontal and vertical axes.

If you plot the impedance of a circuit using the rectangular coordinate system and find the impedance point falls on the right side of the graph on the horizontal axis, what do you know about the circuit?
   A. It has to be a direct current circuit
   B. It contains resistance and capacitive reactance
   C. It contains resistance and inductive reactance
   D. It is equivalent to a pure resistance

E5C12: D. If you plot the impedance of a circuit using the rectangular coordinate system and find the impedance point falls on the right side of the graph on the horizontal axis, you know the circuit is equivalent to a pure resistance.

What coordinate system is often used to display the resistive, inductive, and/or capacitive reactance components of impedance?
   A. Maidenhead grid
   B. Faraday grid
   C. Elliptical coordinates
   D. Rectangular coordinates

E5C13: D. Rectangular coordinates are used to display the resistive, inductive, and/or capacitive reactance components of impedance.

Which point on Figure E5-2 best represents the impedance of a series circuit consisting of a 400 ohm resistor and a 38 picofarad capacitor at 14 MHz?
   A. Point 2
   B. Point 4
   C. Point 5
   D. Point 6

E5C14: B. Point 4 on Figure E5-2 best represents the impedance of a series circuit consisting of a 400 ohm resistor and a 38 picofarad capacitor at 14 MHz.

Which point in Figure E5-2 best represents the impedance of a series circuit consisting of a 300 ohm resistor and an 18 microhenry inductor at 3.505 MHz?
   A. Point 1
   B. Point 3
   C. Point 7
   D. Point 8

E5C15: B. Point 3 on Figure E5-2 best represents the impedance of a series circuit consisting of a 300 ohm resistor and an 18 microhenry inductor at 3.505 MHz.

Copyright © Mometrix Media. You have been licensed one copy of this document for personal use only. Any other reproduction or redistribution is strictly prohibited. All rights reserved.

Which point on Figure E5-2 best represents the impedance of a series circuit consisting of a 300 ohm resistor and a 19 picofarad capacitor at 21.200 MHz?
    A. Point 1
    B. Point 3
    C. Point 7
    D. Point 8

E5C16: A. Point 1 on Figure E5-2 best represents the impedance of a series circuit consisting of a 300 ohm resistor and a 19 picofarad capacitor at 21.200 MHz.

Which point on Figure E5-2 best represents the impedance of a series circuit consisting of a 300 ohm resistor, a 0.64-microhenry inductor and an 85-picofarad capacitor at 24.900 MHz?
    A. Point 1
    B. Point 3
    C. Point 5
    D. Point 8

E5C17: D. Point 8 on Figure E5-2 best represents the impedance of a series circuit consisting of a 300 ohm resistor, a 0.64-microhenry inductor and an 85-picofarad capacitor at 24.900 MHz.

E5D – AC and RF energy in real circuits: skin effect; electrostatic and electromagnetic fields; reactive power; power factor; electrical length of conductors at UHF and microwave frequencies

What is the result of skin effect?
    A. As frequency increases, RF current flows in a thinner layer of the conductor, closer to the surface
    B. As frequency decreases, RF current flows in a thinner layer of the conductor, closer to the surface
    C. Thermal effects on the surface of the conductor increase the impedance
    D. Thermal effects on the surface of the conductor decrease the impedance

E5D01: A. As a result of skin effect, as frequency increases, RF current flows in a thinner layer of the conductor, closer to the surface.

Why is it important to keep lead lengths short for components used in circuits for VHF and above?
    A. To increase the thermal time constant
    B. To avoid unwanted inductive reactance
    C. To maintain component lifetime
    D. All of these choices are correct

E5D02: B. It is important to keep lead lengths short for components used in circuits for VHF and above to avoid unwanted inductive reactance.

What is microstrip?
    A. Lightweight transmission line made of common zip cord
    B. Miniature coax used for low power applications
    C. Short lengths of coax mounted on printed circuit boards to minimize time delay between microwave circuits
    D. Precision-printed circuit conductors above a ground plane that provide constant impedance interconnects at microwave frequencies

Copyright © Mometrix Media. You have been licensed one copy of this document for personal use only. Any other reproduction or redistribution is strictly prohibited. All rights reserved.

E5D03: D. Microstrip is precision-printed circuit conductors above a ground plane that provide constant impedance interconnects at microwave frequencies

Why are short connections necessary at microwave frequencies?
    A. To increase neutralizing resistance
    B. To reduce phase shift along the connection
    C. Because of ground reflections
    D. To reduce noise figure

E5D04: B. Short connections are necessary at microwave frequencies to reduce phase shift along the connection.

Which parasitic characteristic increases with conductor length?
    A. Inductance
    B. Permeability
    C. Permittivity
    D. Malleability

E5D05: A. Inductance increases with conductor length.

In what direction is the magnetic field oriented about a conductor in relation to the direction of electron flow?
    A. In the same direction as the current
    B. In a direction opposite to the current
    C. In all directions; omni-directional
    D. In a direction determined by the left-hand rule

E5D06: D. the magnetic field is oriented in a direction determined by the left-hand rule about a conductor in relation to the direction of electron flow.

What determines the strength of the magnetic field around a conductor?
    A. The resistance divided by the current
    B. The ratio of the current to the resistance
    C. The diameter of the conductor
    D. The amount of current flowing through the conductor

E5D07: D. The amount of current flowing through a conductor determines the strength of the magnetic field around it.

What type of energy is stored in an electromagnetic or electrostatic field?
    A. Electromechanical energy
    B. Potential energy
    C. Thermodynamic energy
    D. Kinetic energy

E5D08: B. Potential energy is stored in an electromagnetic or electrostatic field.

Copyright © Mometrix Media. You have been licensed one copy of this document for personal use only. Any other reproduction or redistribution is strictly prohibited. All rights reserved.

What happens to reactive power in an AC circuit that has both ideal inductors and ideal capacitors?
  A. It is dissipated as heat in the circuit
  B. It is repeatedly exchanged between the associated magnetic and electric fields, but is not dissipated
  C. It is dissipated as kinetic energy in the circuit
  D. It is dissipated in the formation of inductive and capacitive fields

E5D09: B. Reactive power in an AC circuit that has both ideal inductors and ideal capacitors is repeatedly exchanged between the associated magnetic and electric fields, but is not dissipated.

How can the true power be determined in an AC circuit where the voltage and current are out of phase?
  A. By multiplying the apparent power times the power factor
  B. By dividing the reactive power by the power factor
  C. By dividing the apparent power by the power factor
  D. By multiplying the reactive power times the power factor

E5D10: A. True power in an out-of-phase AC circuit can be determined by multiplying the apparent power times the power factor.

What is the power factor of an R-L circuit having a 60 degree phase angle between the voltage and the current?
  A. 1.414
  B. 0.866
  C. 0.5
  D. 1.73

E5D11: C. The power factor of an R-L circuit having a 60 degree phase angle between the voltage and the current is 0.5.

How many watts are consumed in a circuit having a power factor of 0.2 if the input is 100-VAC at 4 amperes?
  A. 400 watts
  B. 80 watts
  C. 2000 watts
  D. 50 watts

E5D12:B. 80 watts are consumed in a circuit having a power factor of 0.2 and an input of 100-VAC at 4 amperes.

How much power is consumed in a circuit consisting of a 100 ohm resistor in series with a 100 ohm inductive reactance drawing 1 ampere?
  A. 70.7 Watts
  B. 100 Watts
  C. 141.4 Watts
  D. 200 Watts

E5D13: B. 100 Watts are consumed in a circuit consisting of a 100 ohm resistor in series with a 100 ohm inductive reactance drawing 1 ampere.

Copyright © Mometrix Media. You have been licensed one copy of this document for personal use only. Any other reproduction or redistribution is strictly prohibited. All rights reserved.

What is reactive power?
    A. Wattless, nonproductive power
    B. Power consumed in wire resistance in an inductor
    C. Power lost because of capacitor leakage
    D. Power consumed in circuit Q

E5D14: A. Reactive power is wattless, nonproductive power.

What is the power factor of an R-L circuit having a 45 degree phase angle between the voltage and the current?
    A. 0.866
    B. 1.0
    C. 0.5
    D. 0.707

E5D15: D. The power factor of an R-L circuit having a 45 degree phase angle between the voltage and the current is 0.707.

What is the power factor of an R-L circuit having a 30 degree phase angle between the voltage and the current?
    A. 1.73
    B. 0.5
    C. 0.866
    D. 0.577

E5D16: C. The power factor of an R-L circuit having a 30 degree phase angle between the voltage and the current is 0.866.

How many watts are consumed in a circuit having a power factor of 0.6 if the input is 200VAC at 5 amperes?
    A. 200 watts
    B. 1000 watts
    C. 1600 watts
    D. 600 watts

E5D17: D. 600watts are consumed in a circuit having a power factor of 0.6 if the input is 200VAC at 5 amperes.

How many watts are consumed in a circuit having a power factor of 0.71 if the apparent power is 500VA?
    A. 704 W
    B. 355 W
    C. 252 W
    D. 1.42 mW

E5D18: B. 355 watts are consumed in a circuit having a power factor of 0.71 if the apparent power is 500VA.

Copyright © Mometrix Media. You have been licensed one copy of this document for personal use only. Any other reproduction or redistribution is strictly prohibited. All rights reserved.

E6 – Circuit Components

E6A – Semiconductor materials and devices: semiconductor materials; germanium, silicon, P-type, N-type; transistor types: NPN, PNP, junction, field-effect transistors: enhancement mode; depletion mode; MOS; CMOS; N-channel; P-channel

In what application is gallium arsenide used as a semiconductor material in preference to germanium or silicon?
    A. In high-current rectifier circuits
    B. In high-power audio circuits
    C. In microwave circuits
    D. In very low frequency RF circuits

E6A01: C. Gallium arsenide is used as a semiconductor material in preference to germanium or silicon in microwave circuits.

Which of the following semiconductor materials contains excess free electrons?
    A. N-type
    B. P-type
    C. Bipolar
    D. Insulated gate

E6A02: A. N-type semiconductor materials contain excess free electrons.

Why does a PN-junction diode not conduct current when reverse biased?
    A. Only P-type semiconductor material can conduct current
    B. Only N-type semiconductor material can conduct current
    C. Holes in P-type material and electrons in the N-type material are separated by the applied voltage, widening the depletion region
    D. Excess holes in P-type material combine with the electrons in N-type material, converting the entire diode into an insulator

E6A03: C. A PN-junction diode does not conduct current when reverse biased because holes in P-type material and electrons in the N-type material are separated by the applied voltage, widening the depletion region.

What is the name given to an impurity atom that adds holes to a semiconductor crystal structure?
    A. Insulator impurity
    B. N-type impurity
    C. Acceptor impurity
    D. Donor impurity

E6A04: C. Acceptor impurities are atoms that add holes to a semiconductor crystal structure.

What is the alpha of a bipolar junction transistor?
    A. The change of collector current with respect to base current
    B. The change of base current with respect to collector current
    C. The change of collector current with respect to emitter current
    D. The change of collector current with respect to gate current

Copyright © Mometrix Media. You have been licensed one copy of this document for personal use only. Any other reproduction or redistribution is strictly prohibited. All rights reserved.

E6A05: C. The alpha of a bipolar junction transistor is the change in collector current with respect to emitter current.

What is the beta of a bipolar junction transistor?
    A. The frequency at which the current gain is reduced to 1
    B. The change in collector current with respect to base current
    C. The breakdown voltage of the base to collector junction
    D. The switching speed of the transistor

E6A06: B. The beta of a bipolar junction transistor is the change in collector current with respect to the base current.

Which of the following indicates that a silicon NPN junction transistor is biased on?
    A. Base-to-emitter resistance of approximately 6 to 7 ohms
    B. Base-to-emitter resistance of approximately 0.6 to 0.7 ohms
    C. Base-to-emitter voltage of approximately 6 to 7 volts
    D. Base-to-emitter voltage of approximately 0.6 to 0.7 volts

E6A07: D. A base-to-emitter voltage of approximately 0.6 to 0.7 volts would indicate that a silicon NPN junction transistor is biased on.

What term indicates the frequency at which the grounded-base current gain of a transistor has decreased to 0.7 of the gain obtainable at 1 kHz?
    A. Corner frequency
    B. Alpha rejection frequency
    C. Beta cutoff frequency
    D. Alpha cutoff frequency

E6A08: D. Alpha cutoff frequency is the frequency at which the grounded-base current gain of a transistor has decreased to 0.7 of the gain obtainable at 1 kHz.

What is a depletion-mode FET?
    A. An FET that exhibits a current flow between source and drain when no gate voltage is applied
    B. An FET that has no current flow between source and drain when no gate voltage is applied
    C. Any FET without a channel
    D. Any FET for which holes are the majority carriers

E6A09: A. A depletion-mode FET is an FET that exhibits a current flow between source and drain when no gate voltage is applied.

In Figure E6-2, what is the schematic symbol for an N-channel dual-gate MOSFET?
    A. 2
    B. 4
    C. 5
    D. 6

E6A10: B. In Figure E6-2, the schematic symbol for an N-channel dual-gate MOSFET is 4.

Copyright © Mometrix Media. You have been licensed one copy of this document for personal use only. Any other reproduction or redistribution is strictly prohibited. All rights reserved.

In Figure E6-2, what is the schematic symbol for a P-channel junction FET?
    A. 1
    B. 2
    C. 3
    D. 6

E6A11: A. In Figure E6-2, the schematic symbol for a P-channel junction FET is 1.

Why do many MOSFET devices have internally connected Zener diodes on the gates?
    A. To provide a voltage reference for the correct amount of reverse-bias gate voltage
    B. To protect the substrate from excessive voltages
    C. To keep the gate voltage within specifications and prevent the device from overheating
    D. To reduce the chance of the gate insulation being punctured by static discharges or excessive voltages

E6A12: D. Many MOSFET devices have internally connected Zener diodes on the gates to reduce the chance of the gate insulation being punctured by static discharges or excessive voltages.

What do the initials CMOS stand for?
    A. Common Mode Oscillating System
    B. Complementary Mica-Oxide Silicon
    C. Complementary Metal-Oxide Semiconductor
    D. Common Mode Organic Silicon

E6A13: C. CMOS stands for Complementary Metal-Oxide Semiconductor.

How does DC input impedance at the gate of a field-effect transistor compare with the DC input impedance of a bipolar transistor?
    A. They are both low impedance
    B. An FET has low input impedance; a bipolar transistor has high input impedance
    C. An FET has high input impedance; a bipolar transistor has low input impedance
    D. They are both high impedance

E6A14: C. An FET has high input impedance; a bipolar transistor has low input impedance.

Which semiconductor material contains excess holes in the outer shell of electrons?
    A. N-type
    B. P-type
    C. Superconductor-type
    D. Bipolar-type

E6A15: B. P-type semiconductor materials contain excess holes in the outer shell of electrons.

What are the majority charge carriers in N-type semiconductor material?
    A. Holes
    B. Free electrons
    C. Free protons
    D. Free neutrons

E6A16: B.

Copyright © Mometrix Media. You have been licensed one copy of this document for personal use only. Any other reproduction or redistribution is strictly prohibited. All rights reserved.

What are the names of the three terminals of a field-effect transistor?
A. Gate 1, gate 2, drain
B. Emitter, base, collector
C. Emitter, base 1, base 2
D. Gate, drain, source

E6A17: D. The three terminals of a field-effect transistor are called the gate, drain, and source.

E6B – Diodes

What is the most useful characteristic of a Zener diode?
A. A constant current drop under conditions of varying voltage
B. A constant voltage drop under conditions of varying current
C. A negative resistance region
D. An internal capacitance that varies with the applied voltage

E6B01: B. Zener diodes are most useful because they have a constant voltage drop under conditions of varying current.

What is an important characteristic of a Schottky diode as compared to an ordinary silicon diode when used as a power supply rectifier?
A. Much higher reverse voltage breakdown
B. Controlled reverse avalanche voltage
C. Enhanced carrier retention time
D. Less forward voltage drop

E6B02: D. Schottky diodes can be more useful than ordinary diodes in some applications because they have less forward voltage drop.

What special type of diode is capable of both amplification and oscillation?
A. Point contact
B. Zener
C. Tunnel
D. Junction

E6B03: C. Tunnel diodes are capable of both amplification and oscillation.

What type of semiconductor device is designed for use as a voltage-controlled capacitor?
A. Varactor diode
B. Tunnel diode
C. Silicon-controlled rectifier
D. Zener diode

E6B04: A. Varactor diode are designed for use as voltage-controlled capacitors.

What characteristic of a PIN diode makes it useful as an RF switch or attenuator?
A. Extremely high reverse breakdown voltage
B. Ability to dissipate large amounts of power
C. Reverse bias controls its forward voltage drop
D. A large region of intrinsic material

Copyright © Mometrix Media. You have been licensed one copy of this document for personal use only. Any other reproduction or redistribution is strictly prohibited. All rights reserved.

E6B05: D. The large region of intrinsic material in a PIN diode makes it useful as an RF switch or attenuator.

Which of the following is a common use of a hot-carrier diode?
    A. As balanced mixers in FM generation
    B. As a variable capacitance in an automatic frequency control circuit
    C. As a constant voltage reference in a power supply
    D. As a VHF/UHF mixer or detector

E6B06: D. Hot-carrier diodes are often used as VHF/UHF mixers or detectors.

What is the failure mechanism when a junction diode fails due to excessive current?
    A. Excessive inverse voltage
    B. Excessive junction temperature
    C. Insufficient forward voltage
    D. Charge carrier depletion

E6B07: B. When a junction diode fails due to excessive current, it is called an excessive junction temperature failure.

Which of the following describes a type of semiconductor diode?
    A. Metal-semiconductor junction
    B. Electrolytic rectifier
    C. CMOS-field effect
    D. Thermionic emission diode

E6B08: A. Metal-semiconductor junctions are used to make Schottky diodes.

What is a common use for point contact diodes?
    A. As a constant current source
    B. As a constant voltage source
    C. As an RF detector
    D. As a high voltage rectifier

E6B09: C. Point contact diodes are used as RF detectors.

In Figure E6-3, what is the schematic symbol for a light-emitting diode?
    A. 1
    B. 5
    C. 6
    D. 7

E6B10: B. In Figure E6-3, the schematic symbol for a light-emitting diode is 5.

What is used to control the attenuation of RF signals by a PIN diode?
    A. Forward DC bias current
    B. A sub-harmonic pump signal
    C. Reverse voltage larger than the RF signal
    D. Capacitance of an RF coupling capacitor

E6B11: A. Forward DC bias current is used to control the attenuation of RF signals by a PIN diode.

Copyright © Mometrix Media. You have been licensed one copy of this document for personal use only. Any other reproduction or redistribution is strictly prohibited. All rights reserved.

What is one common use for PIN diodes?
  A. As a constant current source
  B. As a constant voltage source
  C. As an RF switch
  D. As a high voltage rectifier

E6B12: C. PIN diodes are commonly used as RF switches.

What type of bias is required for an LED to emit light?
  A. Reverse bias
  B. Forward bias
  C. Zero bias
  D. Inductive bias

E6B13: B. Forward bias is required for an LED to emit light.

E6C – Digital ICs: Families of digital ICs; gates; Programmable Logic Devices (PLDs)

What is the function of hysteresis in a comparator?
  A. To prevent input noise from causing unstable output signals
  B. To allow the comparator to be used with AC input signal
  C. To cause the output to change states continually
  D. To increase the sensitivity

E6C01: A. Hysteresis in a comparator prevents input noise from causing unstable output signals.

What happens when the level of a comparator's input signal crosses the threshold?
  A. The IC input can be damaged
  B. The comparator changes its output state
  C. The comparator enters latch-up
  D. The feedback loop becomes unstable

E6C02: B. When the level of a comparator's input signal crosses the threshold, the comparator changes its output state.

What is tri-state logic?
  A. Logic devices with 0, 1, and high impedance output states
  B. Logic devices that utilize ternary math
  C. Low power logic devices designed to operate at 3 volts
  D. Proprietary logic devices manufactured by Tri-State Devices

E6C03: A. Tri-state logic devices have 0, 1, and high impedance output states.

What is the primary advantage of tri-state logic?
  A. Low power consumption
  B. Ability to connect many device outputs to a common bus
  C. High speed operation
  D. More efficient arithmetic operations

Copyright © Mometrix Media. You have been licensed one copy of this document for personal use only. Any other reproduction or redistribution is strictly prohibited. All rights reserved.

E6C04: B. The primary advantage of tri-state logic is the ability to connect many device outputs to a common bus.

What is an advantage of CMOS logic devices over TTL devices?
    A. Differential output capability
    B. Lower distortion
    C. Immune to damage from static discharge
    D. Lower power consumption

E6C05: D. An advantage of CMOS logic devices over TTL devices is lower power consumption.

Why do CMOS digital integrated circuits have high immunity to noise on the input signal or power supply?
    A. Larger bypass capacitors are used in CMOS circuit design
    B. The input switching threshold is about two times the power supply voltage
    C. The input switching threshold is about one-half the power supply voltage
    D. Input signals are stronger

E6C06: C. CMOS digital integrated circuits have high immunity to noise on the input signal because the input switching threshold is about one-half the power supply voltage.

What best describes a pull-up or pull-down resistor?
    A. A resistor in a keying circuit used to reduce key clicks
    B. A resistor connected to the positive or negative supply line used to establish a voltage when an input or output is an open circuit
    C. A resistor that insures that an oscillator frequency does not drive lower over time
    D. A resistor connected to an op-amp output that only functions when the logic output is false

E6C07: B. Pull-up or pull-down resistors are connected to the positive or negative supply line and used to establish a voltage when an input or output is an open circuit.

In Figure E6-5, what is the schematic symbol for a NAND gate?
    A. 1
    B. 2
    C. 3
    D. 4

E6C08: B. In Figure E6-5, the schematic symbol for a NAND gate is 2.

What is a Programmable Logic Device (PLD)?
    A. A device to control industrial equipment
    B. A programmable collection of logic gates and circuits in a single integrated circuit
    C. Programmable equipment used for testing digital logic integrated circuits
    D. An algorithm for simulating logic functions during circuit design

E6C09: B. A PLD is a programmable collection of logic gates and circuits in a single integrated circuit.

In Figure E6-5, what is the schematic symbol for a NOR gate?
    A. 1
    B. 2
    C. 3
    D. 4

Copyright © Mometrix Media. You have been licensed one copy of this document for personal use only. Any other reproduction or redistribution is strictly prohibited. All rights reserved.

E6C10: D. In Figure E6-5, the schematic symbol for a NOR gate is 4.

In Figure E6-5, what is the schematic symbol for the NOT operation (inverter)?
    A. 2
    B. 4
    C. 5
    D. 6

E6C11: C. In Figure E6-5, the schematic symbol for the NOT operation is 5.

What is BiCMOS logic?
    A. A logic device with two CMOS circuits per package
    B. A FET logic family based on bimetallic semiconductors
    C. A logic family based on bismuth CMOS devices
    D. An integrated circuit logic family using both bipolar and CMOS transistors

E6C12: D. BiCMOS logic is an integrated circuit logic family using both bipolar and CMOS transistors.

Which of the following is an advantage of BiCMOS logic?
    A. Its simplicity results in much less expensive devices than standard CMOS
    B. It is totally immune to electrostatic damage
    C. It has the high input impedance of CMOS and the low output impedance of bipolar transistors
    D. All of these choices are correct

E6C13: C. BiCMOS logic has the advantage of high input impedance and low output impedance.

What is the primary advantage of using a Programmable Gate Array (PGA) in a logic circuit?
    A. Many similar gates are less expensive than a mixture of gate types
    B. Complex logic functions can be created in a single integrated circuit
    C. A PGA contains its own internal power supply
    D. All of these choices are correct

E6C14: B. The primary advantage of using a Programmable Gate Array (PGA) in a logic circuit is that complex logic functions can be created in a single integrated circuit.

E6D – Toroidal and Solenoidal Inductors: permeability, core material, selecting, winding; transformers; Piezoelectric devices

How many turns will be required to produce a 5-microhenry inductor using a powdered-iron toroidal core that has an inductance index (A L) value of 40 microhenrys/100 turns?
    A. 35 turns
    B. 13 turns
    C. 79 turns
    D. 141 turns

E6D01: A. 35 turns will be required to produce a 5-microhenry inductor using a powdered-iron toroidal core that has an inductance index (A L) value of 40 microhenrys/100 turns.

Copyright © Mometrix Media. You have been licensed one copy of this document for personal use only. Any other reproduction or redistribution is strictly prohibited. All rights reserved.

What is the equivalent circuit of a quartz crystal?
  A. Motional capacitance, motional inductance, and loss resistance in series, all in parallel with a
  shunt capacitor representing electrode and stray capacitance
  B. Motional capacitance, motional inductance, loss resistance, and a capacitor representing electrode
  and stray capacitance all in parallel
  C. Motional capacitance, motional inductance, loss resistance, and a capacitor representing electrode
  and stray capacitance all in series
  D. Motional inductance and loss resistance in series, paralleled with motional capacitance and a
  capacitor representing electrode and stray capacitance

E6D02: A. The equivalent circuit of a quartz crystal is motional capacitance, motional inductance, and
loss resistance in series, all in parallel with a shunt capacitor representing electrode and stray
capacitance.

Which of the following is an aspect of the piezoelectric effect?
  A. Mechanical deformation of material by the application of a voltage
  B. Mechanical deformation of material by the application of a magnetic field
  C. Generation of electrical energy in the presence of light
  D. Increased conductivity in the presence of light

E6D03: A. The piezoelectric effect is mechanical deformation of material by the application of a voltage.

Which materials are commonly used as a slug core in a variable inductor?
  A. Polystyrene and polyethylene
  B. Ferrite and brass
  C. Teflon and Delrin
  D. Cobalt and aluminum

E6D04: B. Ferrite and brass are commonly used as slug cores in variable inductors.

What is one reason for using ferrite cores rather than powdered-iron in an inductor?
  A. Ferrite toroids generally have lower initial permeability
  B. Ferrite toroids generally have better temperature stability
  C. Ferrite toroids generally require fewer turns to produce a given inductance value
  D. Ferrite toroids are easier to use with surface mount technology

E6D05: C. Ferrite toroids generally require fewer turns than powdered-iron to produce a given
inductance value.

What core material property determines the inductance of a toroidal inductor?
  A. Thermal impedance
  B. Resistance
  C. Reactivity
  D. Permeability

E6D06: D. Permeability of the core material determines the inductance of a toroidal inductor.

Copyright © Mometrix Media. You have been licensed one copy of this document for personal use only. Any other reproduction or redistribution is strictly prohibited. All rights reserved.

What is the usable frequency range of inductors that use toroidal cores, assuming a correct selection of core material for the frequency being used?
    A. From a few kHz to no more than 30 MHz
    B. From less than 20 Hz to approximately 300 MHz
    C. From approximately 10 Hz to no more than 3000 kHz
    D. From about 100 kHz to at least 1000 GHz

E6D07: B. Inductors that use toroidal cores range from less than 20 Hz to approximately 300 MHz.

What is one reason for using powdered-iron cores rather than ferrite cores in an inductor?
    A. Powdered-iron cores generally have greater initial permeability
    B. Powdered-iron cores generally maintain their characteristics at higher currents
    C. Powdered-iron cores generally require fewer turns to produce a given inductance
    D. Powdered-iron cores use smaller diameter wire for the same inductance

E6D08: B. Powdered-iron cores generally maintain their characteristics at higher currents than ferrite cores.

What devices are commonly used as VHF and UHF parasitic suppressors at the input and output terminals of a transistor HF amplifier?
    A. Electrolytic capacitors
    B. Butterworth filters
    C. Ferrite beads
    D. Steel-core toroids

E6D09: C. Ferrite beads are commonly used as VHF and UHF parasitic suppressors at the input and output terminals of transistor HF amplifiers.

What is a primary advantage of using a toroidal core instead of a solenoidal core in an inductor?
    A. Toroidal cores confine most of the magnetic field within the core material
    B. Toroidal cores make it easier to couple the magnetic energy into other components
    C. Toroidal cores exhibit greater hysteresis
    D. Toroidal cores have lower Q characteristics

E6D10: A. Toroidal cores confine most of the magnetic field within the core material, while solenoidal cores do not.

How many turns will be required to produce a 1-mH inductor using a core that has an inductance index (A L) value of 523 millihenrys/1000 turns?
    A. 2 turns
    B. 4 turns
    C. 43 turns
    D. 229 turns

E6D11: C. 43 turns will be required to produce a 1-mH inductor using a core that has an inductance index (A L) value of 523 millihenrys/1000 turns.

What is the definition of saturation in a ferrite core inductor?
    A. The inductor windings are over coupled
    B. The inductor's voltage rating is exceeded causing a flashover
    C. The ability of the inductor's core to store magnetic energy has been exceeded
    D. Adjacent inductors become over-coupled

Copyright © Mometrix Media. You have been licensed one copy of this document for personal use only. Any other reproduction or redistribution is strictly prohibited. All rights reserved.

E6D12: C. Saturation in a ferrite core inductor is when the ability of the inductor's core to store magnetic energy has been exceeded.

What is the primary cause of inductor self-resonance?
    A. Inter-turn capacitance
    B. The skin effect
    C. Inductive kickback
    D. Non-linear core hysteresis

E6D13: A. Inter-turn capacitance is the primary cause of inductor self-resonance.

Which type of slug material decreases inductance when inserted into a coil?
    A. Ceramic
    B. Brass
    C. Ferrite
    D. Powdered-iron

E6D14: B. Brass slug material decreases inductance when inserted into a coil.

What is current in the primary winding of a transformer called if no load is attached to the secondary?
    A. Magnetizing current
    B. Direct current
    C. Excitation current
    D. Stabilizing current

E6D15: A. Current in the primary winding of a transformer is called magnetizing current when no load is attached to the secondary.

What is the common name for a capacitor connected across a transformer secondary that is used to absorb transient voltage spikes?
    A. Clipper capacitor
    B. Trimmer capacitor
    C. Feedback capacitor
    D. Snubber capacitor

E6D16: D. A capacitor connected across a transformer secondary that is used to absorb transient voltage spikes is called a snubber capacitor.

Why should core saturation of a conventional impedance matching transformer be avoided?
    A. Harmonics and distortion could result
    B. Magnetic flux would increase with frequency
    C. RF susceptance would increase
    D. Temporary changes of the core permeability could result

E6D17: A. Core saturation of a conventional impedance matching transformer should be avoided because harmonics and distortion could result.

Copyright © Mometrix Media. You have been licensed one copy of this document for personal use only. Any other reproduction or redistribution is strictly prohibited. All rights reserved.

E6E – Analog ICs: MMICs, CCDs, Device packages

Which of the following is true of a charge-coupled device (CCD)?
A. Its phase shift changes rapidly with frequency
B. It is a CMOS analog-to-digital converter
C. It samples an analog signal and passes it in stages from the input to the output
D. It is used in a battery charger circuit

E6E01: C. A charge-coupled device (CCD) samples an analog signal and passes it in stages from the input to the output.

Which of the following device packages is a through-hole type?
A. DIP
B. PLCC
C. Ball grid array
D. SOT

E6E02: A. DIP is a type of through-hole device packaging.

Which of the following materials is likely to provide the highest frequency of operation when used in MMICs?
A. Silicon
B. Silicon nitride
C. Silicon dioxide
D. Gallium nitride

E6E03: D. Gallium nitride is likely to provide the highest frequency of operation when used in MMICs.

Which is the most common input and output impedance of circuits that use MMICs?
A. 50 ohms
B. 300 ohms
C. 450 ohms
D. 10 ohms

E6E04: A. 50 ohms is the most common input and output impedance of circuits that use MMICs.

Which of the following noise figure values is typical of a low-noise UHF preamplifier?
A. 2 dB
B. -10 dB
C. 44 dBm
D. -20 dBm

E6E05: A. 2 dB is a typical noise value of a low-noise UHF preamplifier.

What characteristics of the MMIC make it a popular choice for VHF through microwave circuits?
A. The ability to retrieve information from a single signal even in the presence of other strong signals
B. Plate current that is controlled by a control grid
C. Nearly infinite gain, very high input impedance, and very low output impedance
D. Controlled gain, low noise figure, and constant input and output impedance over the specified frequency range

Copyright © Mometrix Media. You have been licensed one copy of this document for personal use only. Any other reproduction or redistribution is strictly prohibited. All rights reserved.

E6E06: D. MMICs have controlled gain, low noise figures, and constant input and output impedances over the specified frequency range, making them popular for VHF through microwave circuits.

Which of the following is typically used to construct a MMIC-based microwave amplifier?
    A. Ground-plane construction
    B. Microstrip construction
    C. Point-to-point construction
    D. Wave-soldering construction

E6E07: B. Microstrip construction is typically used to construct a MMIC-based microwave amplifier.

How is voltage from a power supply normally furnished to the most common type of monolithic microwave integrated circuit (MMIC)?
    A. Through a resistor and/or RF choke connected to the amplifier output lead
    B. MMICs require no operating bias
    C. Through a capacitor and RF choke connected to the amplifier input lead
    D. Directly to the bias voltage (VCC IN) lead

E6E08: A. Power supplies are normally connected to MMICs through a resistor and/or RF choke connected to the amplifier output lead.

Which of the following component package types would be most suitable for use at frequencies above the HF range?
    A. TO-220
    B. Axial lead
    C. Radial lead
    D. Surface mount

E6E09: D. Components in surface mount packaging are most suitable for use at frequencies above the HF range.

What is the packaging technique in which leadless components are soldered directly to circuit boards?
    A. Direct soldering
    B. Virtual lead mounting
    C. Stripped lead
    D. Surface mount

E6E10: D. Surface mount is the packaging technique in which leadless components are soldered directly to circuit boards.

What is a characteristic of DIP packaging used for integrated circuits?
    A. Package mounts in a direct inverted position
    B. Low leakage doubly insulated package
    C. Two chips in each package (Dual In Package)
    D. A total of two rows of connecting pins placed on opposite sides of the package (Dual In-line Package)

E6E11: DIP packaging for ICs is a total of two rows of connecting pins placed on opposite sides of the package.

Copyright © Mometrix Media. You have been licensed one copy of this document for personal use only. Any other reproduction or redistribution is strictly prohibited. All rights reserved.

Why are high-power RF amplifier ICs and transistors sometimes mounted in ceramic packages?
- A. High-voltage insulating ability
- B. Better dissipation of heat
- C. Enhanced sensitivity to light
- D. To provide a low-pass frequency response

E6E12: B. High-power RF amplifier ICs and transistors sometimes mounted in ceramic packages for better dissipation of heat.

E6F – Optical components: photoconductive principles and effects, photovoltaic systems, optical couplers, optical sensors, and optoisolators; LCDs

What is photoconductivity?
- A. The conversion of photon energy to electromotive energy
- B. The increased conductivity of an illuminated semiconductor
- C. The conversion of electromotive energy to photon energy
- D. The decreased conductivity of an illuminated semiconductor

E6F01: B. Photoconductivity is the increased conductivity of an illuminated semiconductor.

What happens to the conductivity of a photoconductive material when light shines on it?
- A. It increases
- B. It decreases
- C. It stays the same
- D. It becomes unstable

E6F02: A. Photoconductive material becomes more conductive when light shines on it.

What is the most common configuration of an optoisolator or optocoupler?
- A. A lens and a photomultiplier
- B. A frequency modulated helium-neon laser
- C. An amplitude modulated helium-neon laser
- D. An LED and a phototransistor

E6F03: D. Optoisolators and optocouplers are most often used as LEDs and phototransistors, respectively.

What is the photovoltaic effect?
- A. The conversion of voltage to current when exposed to light
- B. The conversion of light to electrical energy
- C. The conversion of electrical energy to mechanical energy
- D. The tendency of a battery to discharge when used outside

E6F04: B. The photovoltaic effect is the conversion of light to electrical energy.

Which describes an optical shaft encoder?
- A. A device which detects rotation of a control by interrupting a light source with a patterned wheel
- B. A device which measures the strength of a beam of light using analog to digital conversion
- C. A digital encryption device often used to encrypt spacecraft control signals
- D. A device for generating RTTY signals by means of a rotating light source

Copyright © Mometrix Media. You have been licensed one copy of this document for personal use only. Any other reproduction or redistribution is strictly prohibited. All rights reserved.

E6F05: A. An optical shaft encoder is a device which detects rotation of a control by interrupting a light source with a patterned wheel.

Which of these materials is affected the most by photoconductivity?
    A. A crystalline semiconductor
    B. An ordinary metal
    C. A heavy metal
    D. A liquid semiconductor

E6F06: A. Crystalline semiconductors are most affected by photoconductivity.

What is a solid state relay?
    A. A relay using transistors to drive the relay coil
    B. A device that uses semiconductors to implement the functions of an electromechanical relay
    C. A mechanical relay that latches in the on or off state each time it is pulsed
    D. A passive delay line

E6F07: B. A solid state relay is a device that uses semiconductors to implement the functions of an electromechanical relay.

Why are optoisolators often used in conjunction with solid state circuits when switching 120VAC?
    A. Optoisolators provide a low impedance link between a control circuit and a power circuit
    B. Optoisolators provide impedance matching between the control circuit and power circuit
    C. Optoisolators provide a very high degree of electrical isolation between a control circuit and the circuit being switched
    D. Optoisolators eliminate the effects of reflected light in the control circuit

E6F08: C. Optoisolators are often used in conjunction with solid state circuits when switching 120VAC because they provide a very high degree of electrical isolation between a control circuit and the circuit being switched.

What is the efficiency of a photovoltaic cell?
    A. The output RF power divided by the input DC power
    B. The effective payback period
    C. The open-circuit voltage divided by the short-circuit current under full illumination
    D. The relative fraction of light that is converted to current

E6F09: D. The efficiency of a photovoltaic cell is the relative fraction of light that is converted to current.

What is the most common type of photovoltaic cell used for electrical power generation?
    A. Selenium
    B. Silicon
    C. Cadmium Sulfide
    D. Copper oxide

E6F10: B. The most common type of photovoltaic cell used for electrical power generation is silicon.

What is the approximate open-circuit voltage produced by a fully-illuminated silicon photovoltaic cell?
    A. 0.1 V
    B. 0.5 V
    C. 1.5 V
    D. 12 V

Copyright © Mometrix Media. You have been licensed one copy of this document for personal use only. Any other reproduction or redistribution is strictly prohibited. All rights reserved.

E6F11:B. The approximate open-circuit voltage produced by a fully-illuminated silicon photovoltaic cell is 0.5 V.

What absorbs the energy from light falling on a photovoltaic cell?
    A. Protons
    B. Photons
    C. Electrons
    D. Holes

E6F12: C. Electrons absorb the energy from light falling on photovoltaic cells.

What is a liquid crystal display (LCD)?
    A. A modern replacement for a quartz crystal oscillator which displays its fundamental frequency
    B. A display utilizing a crystalline liquid and polarizing filters which becomes opaque when voltage is applied
    C. A frequency-determining unit for a transmitter or receiver
    D. A display that uses a glowing liquid to remain brightly lit in dim light

E6F13: B. A liquid crystal display is a display utilizing a crystalline liquid and polarizing filters which become opaque when voltage is applied.

Which of the following is true of LCD displays?
    A. They are hard to view in high ambient light conditions
    B. They may be hard to view through polarized lenses
    C. They only display alphanumeric symbols
    D. All of these choices are correct

E6F14: B. LCD displays may be hard to view through polarized lenses.

E7 – Practical Circuits

E7A – Digital circuits: digital circuit principles and logic circuits: classes of logic elements; positive and negative logic; frequency dividers; truth tables

Which is a bi-stable circuit?
    A. An "AND" gate
    B. An "OR" gate
    C. A flip-flop
    D. A clock

E7A01: C. Flip-flops are bi-stable circuits.

What is the function of a decade counter digital IC?
    A. It produces one output pulse for every ten input pulses
    B. It decodes a decimal number for display on a seven segment LED display
    C. It produces ten output pulses for every input pulse
    D. It adds two decimal numbers together

E7A02: A. Decade counters produce one output pulse for every ten input pulses.

- 436 -

Copyright © Mometrix Media. You have been licensed one copy of this document for personal use only. Any other reproduction or redistribution is strictly prohibited. All rights reserved.

Which of the following can divide the frequency of a pulse train by 2?
    A. An XOR gate
    B. A flip-flop
    C. An OR gate
    D. A multiplexer

E7A03: B. Flip-flops can divide the frequency of a pulse train by 2.

How many flip-flops are required to divide a signal frequency by 4?
    A. 1
    B. 2
    C. 4
    D. 8

E7A04: B. Two flip-flops are required to divide a signal frequency by 4.

Which of the following is a circuit that continuously alternates between two states without an external clock?
    A. Monostable multivibrator
    B. J-K flip-flop
    C. T flip-flop
    D. Astable multivibrator

E7A05: D. Astable multivibrators continuously alternate between two states without an external clock.

What is a characteristic of a monostable multivibrator?
    A. It switches momentarily to the opposite binary state and then returns to its original state after a set time
    B. It produces a continuous square wave oscillating between 1 and 0
    C. It stores one bit of data in either a 0 or 1 state
    D. It maintains a constant output voltage, regardless of variations in the input voltage

E7A06: A. monostable multivibrators switch momentarily to the opposite binary state and then return to their original state after a set time.

What logical operation does a NAND gate perform?
    A. It produces logic "0" at its output only when all inputs are logic "0"
    B. It produces logic "1" at its output only when all inputs are logic "1"
    C. It produces logic "0" at its output if some but not all inputs are logic "1"
    D. It produces logic "0" at its output only when all inputs are logic "1"

E7A07: D. NAND gates produce a logic "0" at their output only when all inputs are logic "1".

What logical operation does an OR gate perform?
    A. It produces logic "1" at its output if any or all inputs are logic "1"
    B. It produces logic "0" at its output if all inputs are logic "1"
    C. It only produces logic "0" at its output when all inputs are logic "1"
    D. It produces logic "1" at its output if all inputs are logic "0"

E7A08: A. OR gates produce logic "1" at their output if any or all inputs are logic "1".

Copyright © Mometrix Media. You have been licensed one copy of this document for personal use only. Any other reproduction or redistribution is strictly prohibited. All rights reserved.

What logical operation is performed by an exclusive NOR gate?
  A. It produces logic "0" at its output only if all inputs are logic "0"
  B. It produces logic "1" at its output only if all inputs are logic "1"
  C. It produces logic "0" at its output if any single input is logic "1"
  D. It produces logic "1" at its output if any single input is logic "1"

E7A09: C. Exclusive NOR gates produce logic "0" at their output if any single input is logic "1".

What is a truth table?
  A. A table of logic symbols that indicate the high logic states of an op-amp
  B. A diagram showing logic states when the digital device output is true
  C. A list of inputs and corresponding outputs for a digital device
  D. A table of logic symbols that indicate the logic states of an op-amp

E7A10: C. A truth table is a list of inputs and corresponding outputs for a digital device.

What type of logic defines "1" as a high voltage?
  A. Reverse Logic
  B. Assertive Logic
  C. Negative Logic
  D. Positive Logic

E7A11: D. Positive Logic defines "1" as a high voltage.

What type of logic defines "0" as a high voltage?
  A. Reverse Logic
  B. Assertive Logic
  C. Negative Logic
  D. Positive Logic

E7A12: C. Negative Logic defines "0" as a high voltage.

E7B – Amplifiers: Class of operation; vacuum tube and solid-state circuits; distortion and intermodulation; spurious and parasitic suppression; microwave amplifiers; switching-type amplifiers

For what portion of a signal cycle does a Class AB amplifier operate?
  A. More than 180 degrees but less than 360 degrees
  B. Exactly 180 degrees
  C. The entire cycle
  D. Less than 180 degrees

E7B01: A. A class AB amplifier operates on more than 180 degrees but less than 360 degrees of a signal cycle.

What is a Class D amplifier?
  A. A type of amplifier that uses switching technology to achieve high efficiency
  B. A low power amplifier that uses a differential amplifier for improved linearity
  C. An amplifier that uses drift-mode FETs for high efficiency
  D. A frequency doubling amplifier

Copyright © Mometrix Media. You have been licensed one copy of this document for personal use only. Any other reproduction or redistribution is strictly prohibited. All rights reserved.

E7B02: A. A class D amplifier uses switching technology to achieve high efficiency.

Which of the following components form the output of a class D amplifier circuit?
    A. A low-pass filter to remove switching signal components
    B. A high-pass filter to compensate for low gain at low frequencies
    C. A matched load resistor to prevent damage by switching transients
    D. A temperature compensating load resistor to improve linearity

E7B03: A. A low-pass filter to removes switching signal components from the output of a class D amplifier.

Where on the load line of a Class A common emitter amplifier would bias normally be set?
    A. Approximately half-way between saturation and cutoff
    B. Where the load line intersects the voltage axis
    C. At a point where the bias resistor equals the load resistor
    D. At a point where the load line intersects the zero bias current curve

E7B04: A. Bias would normally be set approximately half-way between saturation and cutoff for a class A common emitter amplifier.

What can be done to prevent unwanted oscillations in an RF power amplifier?
    A. Tune the stage for maximum SWR
    B. Tune both the input and output for maximum power
    C. Install parasitic suppressors and/or neutralize the stage
    D. Use a phase inverter in the output filter

E7B05: C. Installing parasitic suppressors and/or neutralizing the stage can prevent unwanted oscillations in an RF power amplifier.

Which of the following amplifier types reduces or eliminates even order harmonics?
    A. Push-push
    B. Push-pull
    C. Class C
    D. Class AB

E7B06: B. Push-pull amplifiers reduce or eliminate even order harmonics.

Which of the following is a likely result when a Class C amplifier is used to amplify a single-sideband phone signal?
    A. Reduced intermodulation products
    B. Increased overall intelligibility
    C. Signal inversion
    D. Signal distortion and excessive bandwidth

E7B07: D. Signal distortion and excessive bandwidth can result from a class C amplifier being used to amplify a single-sideband phone signal.

Copyright © Mometrix Media. You have been licensed one copy of this document for personal use only. Any other reproduction or redistribution is strictly prohibited. All rights reserved.

How can an RF power amplifier be neutralized?
- A. By increasing the driving power
- B. By reducing the driving power
- C. By feeding a 180-degree out-of-phase portion of the output back to the input
- D. By feeding an in-phase component of the output back to the input

E7B08: C. An RF power amplifier can be neutralized by feeding a 180-degree out-of-phase portion of the output back to the input.

Which of the following describes how the loading and tuning capacitors are to be adjusted when tuning a vacuum tube RF power amplifier that employs a Pi-network output circuit?
- A. The loading capacitor is set to maximum capacitance and the tuning capacitor is adjusted for minimum allowable plate current
- B. The tuning capacitor is set to maximum capacitance and the loading capacitor is adjusted for minimum plate permissible current
- C. The loading capacitor is adjusted to minimum plate current while alternately adjusting the tuning capacitor for maximum allowable plate current
- D. The tuning capacitor is adjusted for minimum plate current, and the loading capacitor is adjusted for maximum permissible plate current

E7B09: D. When tuning a vacuum tube RF power amplifier that employs a Pi-network output circuit, the tuning capacitor is adjusted for minimum plate current, and the loading capacitor is adjusted for maximum permissible plate current.

In Figure E7-1, what is the purpose of R1 and R2?
- A. Load resistors
- B. Fixed bias
- C. Self bias
- D. Feedback

E7B10: B. In Figure E7-1, R1 and R2 are used as a fixed bias.

In Figure E7-1, what is the purpose of R3?
- A. Fixed bias
- B. Emitter bypass
- C. Output load resistor
- D. Self bias

E7B11: D. In Figure E7-1, R3 is a self-bias.

What type of amplifier circuit is shown in Figure E7-1?
- A. Common base
- B. Common collector
- C. Common emitter
- D. Emitter follower

E7B12: C. A common emitter amplifier is shown in Figure E7-1.

Copyright © Mometrix Media. You have been licensed one copy of this document for personal use only. Any other reproduction or redistribution is strictly prohibited. All rights reserved.

In Figure E7-2, what is the purpose of R?
A. Emitter load
B. Fixed bias
C. Collector load
D. Voltage regulation

E7B13: A. In Figure E7-2, R is an emitter load.

Why are switching amplifiers more efficient than linear amplifiers?
A. Switching amplifiers operate at higher voltages
B. The power transistor is at saturation or cut-off most of the time, resulting in low power dissipation
C. Linear amplifiers have high gain resulting in higher harmonic content
D. Switching amplifiers use push-pull circuits

E7B14: B. Switching amplifiers are more efficient than linear amplifiers because the power transistor is at saturation or cut-off most of the time, resulting in low power dissipation.

What is one way to prevent thermal runaway in a bipolar transistor amplifier?
A. Neutralization
B. Select transistors with high beta
C. Use a resistor in series with the emitter
D. All of these choices are correct

E7B15: C. Using a resistor in series with the emitter is one way to prevent thermal runaway in a bipolar transistor amplifier

What is the effect of intermodulation products in a linear power amplifier?
A. Transmission of spurious signals
B. Creation of parasitic oscillations
C. Low efficiency
D. All of these choices are correct

E7B16: A. Intermodulation products result in transmission of spurious signals in a linear power amplifier.

Why are odd-order rather than even-order intermodulation distortion products of concern in linear power amplifiers?
A. Because they are relatively close in frequency to the desired signal
B. Because they are relatively far in frequency from the desired signal
C. Because they invert the sidebands causing distortion
D. Because they maintain the sidebands, thus causing multiple duplicate signals

E7B17: A. Odd-order intermodulation distortion products are of concern in linear power amplifiers because they are relatively close in frequency to the desired signal.

What is a characteristic of a grounded-grid amplifier?
A. High power gain
B. High filament voltage
C. Low input impedance
D. Low bandwidth

Copyright © Mometrix Media. You have been licensed one copy of this document for personal use only. Any other reproduction or redistribution is strictly prohibited. All rights reserved.

E7B18: C. Grounded-grid amplifiers have low input impedance.

E7C – Filters and matching networks: types of networks; types of filters; filter applications; filter characteristics; impedance matching; DSP filtering

How are the capacitors and inductors of a low-pass filter Pi-network arranged between the network's input and output?
    A. Two inductors are in series between the input and output, and a capacitor is connected between the two inductors and ground
    B. Two capacitors are in series between the input and output, and an inductor is connected between the two capacitors and ground
    C. An inductor is connected between the input and ground, another inductor is connected between the output and ground, and a capacitor is connected between the input and output
    D. A capacitor is connected between the input and ground, another capacitor is connected between the output and ground, and an inductor is connected between input and output

E7C01: D. In a low-pass filter Pi-network, a capacitor is connected between the input and ground, another capacitor is connected between the output and ground, and an inductor is connected between input and output.

Which of the following is a property of a T-network with series capacitors and a parallel shunt inductor?
    A. It is a low-pass filter
    B. It is a band-pass filter
    C. It is a high-pass filter
    D. It is a notch filter

E7C02: C. A T-network with series capacitors and a parallel shunt inductor is a high-pass filter.

What advantage does a Pi-L-network have over a regular Pi-network for impedance matching between the final amplifier of a vacuum-tube transmitter and an antenna?
    A. Greater harmonic suppression
    B. Higher efficiency
    C. Lower losses
    D. Greater transformation range

E7C03: A. A Pi-L-network has greater harmonic suppression than a regular Pi-network for impedance matching between the final amplifier of a vacuum-tube transmitter and an antenna.

How does an impedance-matching circuit transform a complex impedance to a resistive impedance?
    A. It introduces negative resistance to cancel the resistive part of impedance
    B. It introduces transconductance to cancel the reactive part of impedance
    C. It cancels the reactive part of the impedance and changes the resistive part to a desired value
    D. Network resistances are substituted for load resistances and reactances are matched to the resistances

E7C04: C. An impedance-matching circuit cancels the reactive part of the impedance and changes the resistive part to a desired value.

Copyright © Mometrix Media. You have been licensed one copy of this document for personal use only. Any other reproduction or redistribution is strictly prohibited. All rights reserved.

Which filter type is described as having ripple in the passband and a sharp cutoff?
    A. A Butterworth filter
    B. An active LC filter
    C. A passive op-amp filter
    D. A Chebyshev filter

E7C05: A Chebyshev filter is described as having ripple in the passband and a sharp cutoff.

What are the distinguishing features of an elliptical filter?
    A. Gradual passband rolloff with minimal stop band ripple
    B. Extremely flat response over its pass band with gradually rounded stop band corners
    C. Extremely sharp cutoff with one or more notches in the stop band
    D. Gradual passband rolloff with extreme stop band ripple

E7C06: C. An elliptical filter has an extremely sharp cutoff with one or more notches in the stop band.

What kind of filter would you use to attenuate an interfering carrier signal while receiving an SSB transmission?
    A. A band-pass filter
    B. A notch filter
    C. A Pi-network filter
    D. An all-pass filter

E7C07: B. A notch filer could be used to attenuate an interfering carrier signal while receiving an SSB transmission.

Which of the following factors has the greatest effect in helping determine the bandwidth and response shape of a crystal ladder filter?
    A. The relative frequencies of the individual crystals
    B. The DC voltage applied to the quartz crystal
    C. The gain of the RF stage preceding the filter
    D. The amplitude of the signals passing through the filter

E7C08: A. The relative frequencies of the individual crystals have the greatest effect in helping determine the bandwidth and response shape of a crystal ladder filter.

What is a Jones filter as used as part of an HF receiver IF stage?
    A. An automatic notch filter
    B. A variable bandwidth crystal lattice filter
    C. A special filter that emphasizes image responses
    D. A filter that removes impulse noise

E7C09: B. A Jones filter as used as part of an HF receiver IF stage is a variable bandwidth crystal lattice filter.

Which of the following filters would be the best choice for use in a 2 meter repeater duplexer?
    A. A crystal filter
    B. A cavity filter
    C. A DSP filter
    D. An L-C filter

E7C10: B. A cavity filter would be the best choice for use in a 2 meter repeater duplexer.

Copyright © Mometrix Media. You have been licensed one copy of this document for personal use only. Any other reproduction or redistribution is strictly prohibited. All rights reserved.

Which of the following is the common name for a filter network which is equivalent to two L-networks connected back-to-back with the two inductors in series and the capacitors in shunt at the input and output?
- A. Pi-L
- B. Cascode
- C. Omega
- D. Pi

E7C11: D. A Pi-network is equivalent to two L-networks connected back-to-back with the two inductors in series and the capacitors in shunt at the input and output.

Which describes a Pi-L-network used for matching a vacuum tube final amplifier to a 50 ohm unbalanced output?
- A. A Phase Inverter Load network
- B. A Pi-network with an additional series inductor on the output
- C. A network with only three discrete parts
- D. A matching network in which all components are isolated from ground

E7C12: B. A Pi-network with an additional series inductor on the output could be used to match a vacuum tube final amplifier to a 50 ohm unbalanced output.

What is one advantage of a Pi-matching network over an L-matching network consisting of a single inductor and a single capacitor?
- A. The Q of Pi-networks can be varied depending on the component values chosen
- B. L-networks cannot perform impedance transformation
- C. Pi-networks have fewer components
- D. Pi-networks are designed for balanced input and output

E7C13: A. An advantage of a Pi-matching network over an L-matching network consisting of a single inductor and a single capacitor is that the Q of Pi-networks can be varied depending on the component values chosen.

Which mode is most affected by non-linear phase response in a receiver IF filter?
- A. Meteor scatter
- B. Single-Sideband voice
- C. Digital
- D. Video

E7C14: C. Digital mode is most affected by non-linear phase response in a receiver IF filter.

What is a crystal lattice filter?
- A. A power supply filter made with interlaced quartz crystals
- B. An audio filter made with four quartz crystals that resonate at 1kHz intervals
- C. A filter with wide bandwidth and shallow skirts made using quartz crystals
- D. A filter with narrow bandwidth and steep skirts made using quartz crystals

E7C15: D. A crystal lattice filter is a filter with narrow bandwidth and steep skirts made using quartz crystals.

Copyright © Mometrix Media. You have been licensed one copy of this document for personal use only. Any other reproduction or redistribution is strictly prohibited. All rights reserved.

E7D – Power supplies and voltage regulators; Solar array charge controllers

What is one characteristic of a linear electronic voltage regulator?
    A. It has a ramp voltage as its output
    B. It eliminates the need for a pass transistor
    C. The control element duty cycle is proportional to the line or load conditions
    D. The conduction of a control element is varied to maintain a constant output voltage

E7D01: D. A linear electronic voltage regulator varies the conduction of a control element to maintain a constant output voltage.

What is one characteristic of a switching electronic voltage regulator?
    A. The resistance of a control element is varied in direct proportion to the line voltage or load current
    B. It is generally less efficient than a linear regulator
    C. The controlled device's duty cycle is changed to produce a constant average output voltage
    D. It gives a ramp voltage at its output

E7D02: C. A switching electronic voltage regulator changes the duty cycle of the controlled device to produce a constant average output voltage.

What device is typically used as a stable reference voltage in a linear voltage regulator?
    A. A Zener diode
    B. A tunnel diode
    C. An SCR
    D. A varactor diode

E7D03: A. A Zener diode is typically used as a stable reference voltage in a linear voltage regulator.

Which of the following types of linear voltage regulator usually make the most efficient use of the primary power source?
    A. A series current source
    B. A series regulator
    C. A shunt regulator
    D. A shunt current source

E7D04: B. A series linear voltage regulator usually makes the most efficient use of the primary power source.

Which of the following types of linear voltage regulator places a constant load on the unregulated voltage source?
    A. A constant current source
    B. A series regulator
    C. A shunt current source
    D. A shunt regulator

E7D05: D. A shunt regulator places a constant load on the unregulated voltage source.

Copyright © Mometrix Media. You have been licensed one copy of this document for personal use only. Any other reproduction or redistribution is strictly prohibited. All rights reserved.

What is the purpose of Q1 in the circuit shown in Figure E7-3?
  A. It provides negative feedback to improve regulation
  B. It provides a constant load for the voltage source
  C. It increases the current-handling capability of the regulator
  D. It provides D1 with current

E7D06: C. The purpose of Q1 in the circuit shown in Figure E7-3 is increasing the current-handling capability of the regulator.

What is the purpose of C2 in the circuit shown in Figure E7-3?
  A. It bypasses hum around D1
  B. It is a brute force filter for the output
  C. To self-resonate at the hum frequency
  D. To provide fixed DC bias for Q1

E7D07: A. The purpose of C2 in the circuit shown in Figure E7-3 is bypassing hum around D1.

What type of circuit is shown in Figure E7-3?
  A. Switching voltage regulator
  B. Grounded emitter amplifier
  C. Linear voltage regulator
  D. Emitter follower

E7D08: C. A linear voltage regulator is shown in Figure E7-3.

What is the main reason to use a charge controller with a solar power system?
  A. Prevention of battery undercharge
  B. Control of electrolyte levels during battery discharge
  C. Prevention of battery damage due to overcharge
  D. Matching of day and night charge rates

E7D09: C. The main reason to use a charge controller with a solar power system is to prevent battery damage due to overcharging.

What is the primary reason that a high-frequency switching type high voltage power supply can be both less expensive and lighter in weight than a conventional power supply?
  A. The inverter design does not require any output filtering
  B. It uses a diode bridge rectifier for increased output
  C. The high frequency inverter design uses much smaller transformers and filter components for an equivalent power output
  D. It uses a large power factor compensation capacitor to create free power from the unused portion of the AC cycle

E7D10: C. The primary reason that a high-frequency switching type high voltage power supply can be both less expensive and lighter in weight than a conventional power supply is that the high frequency inverter design uses much smaller transformers and filter components for an equivalent power output.

Copyright © Mometrix Media. You have been licensed one copy of this document for personal use only. Any other reproduction or redistribution is strictly prohibited. All rights reserved.

What circuit element is controlled by a series analog voltage regulator to maintain a constant output voltage?

A. Reference voltage
B. Switching inductance
C. Error amplifier
D. Pass transistor

E7D11: D. A pass transistor is controlled by a series analog voltage regulator to maintain a constant output voltage.

What is the drop-out voltage of an analog voltage regulator?

A. Minimum input voltage for rated power dissipation
B. Maximum amount that the output voltage drops when the input voltage is varied over its specified range
C. Minimum input-to-output voltage required to maintain regulation
D. Maximum amount that the output voltage may decrease at rated load

E7D12: C. The drop-out voltage of an analog voltage regulator is the minimum input-to-output voltage required to maintain regulation.

What is the equation for calculating power dissipation by a series connected linear voltage regulator?

A. Input voltage multiplied by input current
B. Input voltage divided by output current
C. Voltage difference from input to output multiplied by output current
D. Output voltage multiplied by output current

E7D13: C. The equation for calculating power dissipation by a series connected linear voltage regulator is voltage difference from input to output multiplied by output current.

What is one purpose of a "bleeder" resistor in a conventional unregulated power supply?

A. To cut down on waste heat generated by the power supply
B. To balance the low-voltage filament windings
C. To improve output voltage regulation
D. To boost the amount of output current

E7D14: C. A "bleeder" resistor in a conventional unregulated power supply serves to improve output voltage regulation.

What is the purpose of a "step-start" circuit in a high voltage power supply?

A. To provide a dual-voltage output for reduced power applications
B. To compensate for variations of the incoming line voltage
C. To allow for remote control of the power supply
D. To allow the filter capacitors to charge gradually

E7D15: D. A "step-start" circuit in a high voltage power supply serves to allow the filter capacitors to charge gradually.

Copyright © Mometrix Media. You have been licensed one copy of this document for personal use only. Any other reproduction or redistribution is strictly prohibited. All rights reserved.

When several electrolytic filter capacitors are connected in series to increase the operating voltage of a power supply filter circuit, why should resistors be connected across each capacitor?
    A. To equalize, as much as possible, the voltage drop across each capacitor
    B. To provide a safety bleeder to discharge the capacitors when the supply is off
    C. To provide a minimum load current to reduce voltage excursions at light loads
    D. All of these choices are correct

E7D16: D. When several electrolytic filter capacitors are connected in series in a power supply filter circuit, resistors connected across each capacitor help to equalize the voltage drop across each capacitor, provide a safety bleeder to discharge the capacitors when the supply is off, and provide a minimum load current to reduce voltage excursions at light loads.

E7E – Modulation and demodulation: reactance, phase and balanced modulators; detectors; mixer stages

Which of the following can be used to generate FM phone emissions?
    A. A balanced modulator on the audio amplifier
    B. A reactance modulator on the oscillator
    C. A reactance modulator on the final amplifier
    D. A balanced modulator on the oscillator

E7E01: B. A reactance modulator on the oscillator can be used to generate FM phone emissions.

What is the function of a reactance modulator?
    A. To produce PM signals by using an electrically variable resistance
    B. To produce AM signals by using an electrically variable inductance or capacitance
    C. To produce AM signals by using an electrically variable resistance
    D. To produce PM signals by using an electrically variable inductance or capacitance

E7E02: D. A reactance modulator produces PM signals by using an electrically variable inductance or capacitance.

How does an analog phase modulator function?
    A. By varying the tuning of a microphone preamplifier to produce PM signals
    B. By varying the tuning of an amplifier tank circuit to produce AM signals
    C. By varying the tuning of an amplifier tank circuit to produce PM signals
    D. By varying the tuning of a microphone preamplifier to produce AM signals

E7E03: C. An analog phase modulator functions by varying the tuning of an amplifier tank circuit to produce PM signals.

What is one way a single-sideband phone signal can be generated?
    A. By using a balanced modulator followed by a filter
    B. By using a reactance modulator followed by a mixer
    C. By using a loop modulator followed by a mixer
    D. By driving a product detector with a DSB signal

E7E04: A. A single-sideband phone signal can be generated by using a balanced modulator followed by a filter.

Copyright © Mometrix Media. You have been licensed one copy of this document for personal use only. Any other reproduction or redistribution is strictly prohibited. All rights reserved.

What circuit is added to an FM transmitter to boost the higher audio frequencies?
    A. A de-emphasis network
    B. A heterodyne suppressor
    C. An audio prescaler
    D. A pre-emphasis network

E7E05: D. A pre-emphasis network can be added to an FM transmitter to boost the higher audio frequencies.

Why is de-emphasis commonly used in FM communications receivers?
    A. For compatibility with transmitters using phase modulation
    B. To reduce impulse noise reception
    C. For higher efficiency
    D. To remove third-order distortion products

E7E06: A. De-emphasis is commonly used in FM communications receivers for compatibility with transmitters using phase modulation.

What is meant by the term baseband in radio communications?
    A. The lowest frequency band that the transmitter or receiver covers
    B. The frequency components present in the modulating signal
    C. The unmodulated bandwidth of the transmitted signal
    D. The basic oscillator frequency in an FM transmitter that is multiplied to increase the deviation and carrier frequency

E7E07: B. Baseband is the frequency components present in the modulating signal.

What are the principal frequencies that appear at the output of a mixer circuit?
    A. Two and four times the original frequency
    B. The sum, difference and square root of the input frequencies
    C. The two input frequencies along with their sum and difference frequencies
    D. 1.414 and 0.707 times the input frequency

E7E08: C. The principal frequencies that appear at the output of a mixer circuit are the two input frequencies along with their sum and difference frequencies.

What occurs when an excessive amount of signal energy reaches a mixer circuit?
    A. Spurious mixer products are generated
    B. Mixer blanking occurs
    C. Automatic limiting occurs
    D. A beat frequency is generated

E7E09: A. When an excessive amount of signal energy reaches a mixer circuit, spurious mixer products are generated.

How does a diode detector function?
    A. By rectification and filtering of RF signals
    B. By breakdown of the Zener voltage
    C. By mixing signals with noise in the transition region of the diode
    D. By sensing the change of reactance in the diode with respect to frequency

E7E10: A. A diode detector functions by rectifying and filtering of RF signals.

Copyright © Mometrix Media. You have been licensed one copy of this document for personal use only. Any other reproduction or redistribution is strictly prohibited. All rights reserved.

Which type of detector is used for demodulating SSB signals?
    A. Discriminator
    B. Phase detector
    C. Product detector
    D. Phase comparator

E7E11: C. A product detector is used for demodulating SSB signals.

What is a frequency discriminator stage in a FM receiver?
    A. An FM generator circuit
    B. A circuit for filtering two closely adjacent signals
    C. An automatic band-switching circuit
    D. A circuit for detecting FM signals

E7E12: D. A frequency discriminator stage in a FM receiver is a circuit for detecting FM signals.

E7F – DSP filtering and other operations; Software Defined Radio Fundamentals; DSP modulation and demodulation

What is meant by direct digital conversion as applied to software defined radios?
    A. Software is converted from source code to object code during operation of the receiver
    B. Incoming RF is converted to a control voltage for a voltage controlled oscillator
    C. Incoming RF is digitized by an analog-to-digital converter without being mixed with a local oscillator signal
    D. A switching mixer is used to generate I and Q signals directly from the RF input

E7F01: Direct digital conversion is when incoming RF is digitized by an analog-to-digital converter without being mixed with a local oscillator signal.

What kind of digital signal processing audio filter is used to remove unwanted noise from a received SSB signal?
    A. An adaptive filter
    B. A crystal-lattice filter
    C. A Hilbert-transform filter
    D. A phase-inverting filter

E7F02: A. An adaptive filter is used to remove unwanted noise from a received SSB signal.

What type of digital signal processing filter is used to generate an SSB signal?
    A. An adaptive filter
    B. A notch filter
    C. A Hilbert-transform filter
    D. An elliptical filter

E7F03: A Hilbert-transform filter is used to generate an SSB signal.

Copyright © Mometrix Media. You have been licensed one copy of this document for personal use only. Any other reproduction or redistribution is strictly prohibited. All rights reserved.

What is a common method of generating an SSB signal using digital signal processing?
A. Mixing products are converted to voltages and subtracted by adder circuits
B. A frequency synthesizer removes the unwanted sidebands
C. Emulation of quartz crystal filter characteristics
D. Combine signals with a quadrature phase relationship

E7F04: D. Combining signals with a quadrature phase relationshipis a common method of generating an SSB signal.

How frequently must an analog signal be sampled by an analog-to-digital converter so that the signal can be accurately reproduced?
A. At half the rate of the highest frequency component of the signal
B. At twice the rate of the highest frequency component of the signal
C. At the same rate as the highest frequency component of the signal
D. At four times the rate of the highest frequency component of the signal

E7F05: B. An analog signal be sampled at twice the rate of the highest frequency component of the signal by an analog-to-digital converter.

What is the minimum number of bits required for an analog-to-digital converter to sample a signal with a range of 1 volt at a resolution of 1 millivolt?
A. 4 bits
B. 6 bits
C. 8 bits
D. 10 bits

E7F06: D. The minimum number of bits required for an analog-to-digital converter to sample a signal with a range of 1 volt at a resolution of 1 millivolt is 10.

What function can a Fast Fourier Transform perform?
A. Converting analog signals to digital form
B. Converting digital signals to analog form
C. Converting digital signals from the time domain to the frequency domain
D. Converting 8-bit data to 16 bit data

E7F07: C. A Fast Fourier Transform can convert digital signals from the time domain to the frequency domain.

What is the function of decimation with regard to digital filters?
A. Converting data to binary code decimal form
B. Reducing the effective sample rate by removing samples
C. Attenuating the signal
D. Removing unnecessary significant digits

E7F08: B. Decimation is reducing the effective sample rate by removing samples.

Why is an anti-aliasing digital filter required in a digital decimator?
A. It removes high-frequency signal components which would otherwise be reproduced as lower frequency components
B. It peaks the response of the decimator, improving bandwidth
C. It removes low frequency signal components to eliminate the need for DC restoration
D. It notches out the sampling frequency to avoid sampling errors

Copyright © Mometrix Media. You have been licensed one copy of this document for personal use only. Any other reproduction or redistribution is strictly prohibited. All rights reserved.

E7F09: A. An anti-aliasing digital filter is required in a digital decimator to remove high-frequency signal components which would otherwise be reproduced as lower frequency components.

What aspect of receiver analog-to-digital conversion determines the maximum receive bandwidth of a Direct Digital Conversion SDR?
   A. Sample rate
   B. Sample width in bits
   C. Sample clock phase noise
   D. Processor latency

E7F10: A. Sample rate determines the maximum receive bandwidth of a Direct Digital Conversion SDR.

What sets the minimum detectable signal level for an SDR in the absence of atmospheric or thermal noise?
   A. Sample clock phase noise
   B. Reference voltage level and sample width in bits
   C. Data storage transfer rate
   D. Missing codes and jitter

E7F11: B. Reference voltage level and sample width in bits sets the minimum detectable signal level for an SDR in the absence of atmospheric or thermal noise.

What digital process is applied to I and Q signals in order to recover the baseband modulation information?
   A. Fast Fourier Transform
   B. Decimation
   C. Signal conditioning
   D. Quadrature mixing

E7F12: A. Fast Fourier Transforms are performed on I and Q signals in order to recover the baseband modulation information.

What is the function of taps in a digital signal processing filter?
   A. To reduce excess signal pressure levels
   B. Provide access for debugging software
   C. Select the point at which baseband signals are generated
   D. Provide incremental signal delays for filter algorithms

E7F13: D. Taps in a digital signal processing filter provide incremental signal delays for filter algorithms.

Which of the following would allow a digital signal processing filter to create a sharper filter response?
   A. Higher data rate
   B. More taps
   C. Complex phasor representations
   D. Double-precision math routines

E7F14: B. Having more taps would allow a digital signal processing filter to create a sharper filter response.

Copyright © Mometrix Media. You have been licensed one copy of this document for personal use only. Any other reproduction or redistribution is strictly prohibited. All rights reserved.

Which of the following is an advantage of a Finite Impulse Response (FIR) filter vs an Infinite Impulse Response (IIR) digital filter?
  A. FIR filters delay all frequency components of the signal by the same amount
  B. FIR filters are easier to implement for a given set of passband rolloff requirements
  C. FIR filters can respond faster to impulses
  D. All of these choices are correct

E7F15: A. FIR filters delay all frequency components of the signal by the same amount, as opposed to IIR filters.

How might the sampling rate of an existing digital signal be adjusted by a factor of 3/4?
  A. Change the gain by a factor of 3/4
  B. Multiply each sample value by a factor of 3/4
  C. Add 3 to each input value and subtract 4 from each output value
  D. Interpolate by a factor of three, then decimate by a factor of four

E7F16: D. The sampling rate of an existing digital signal could be adjusted by a factor of ¾ by interpolating by a factor of three, then decimating by a factor of four.

What do the letters I and Q in I/Q Modulation represent?
  A. Inactive and Quiescent
  B. Instantaneous and Quasi-stable
  C. Instantaneous and Quenched
  D. In-phase and Quadrature

E7F17: D. The letters I and Q in I/Q Modulation represent In-phase and Quadrature.

E7G – Active filters and op-amp circuits: active audio filters; characteristics; basic circuit design; operational amplifiers

What is the typical output impedance of an integrated circuit op-amp?
  A. Very low
  B. Very high
  C. 100 ohms
  D. 1000 ohms

E7G01: A. The typical output impedance of an integrated circuit op-amp is very low.

What is the effect of ringing in a filter?
  A. An echo caused by a long time delay
  B. A reduction in high frequency response
  C. Partial cancellation of the signal over a range of frequencies
  D. Undesired oscillations added to the desired signal

E7G02: D. The effect of ringing in a filter is undesired oscillations added to the desired signal.

Copyright © Mometrix Media. You have been licensed one copy of this document for personal use only. Any other reproduction or redistribution is strictly prohibited. All rights reserved.

What is the typical input impedance of an integrated circuit op-amp?
    A. 100 ohms
    B. 1000 ohms
    C. Very low
    D. Very high

E7G03: D. The typical input impedance of an integrated circuit op-amp is very high.

What is meant by the term op-amp input offset voltage?
    A. The output voltage of the op-amp minus its input voltage
    B. The difference between the output voltage of the op-amp and the input voltage required in the immediately following stage
    C. The differential input voltage needed to bring the open loop output voltage to zero
    D. The potential between the amplifier input terminals of the op-amp in an open loop condition

E7G04: C. Op-amp input offset voltage is the differential input voltage needed to bring the open loop output voltage to zero.

How can unwanted ringing and audio instability be prevented in a multi-section op-amp RC audio filter circuit?
    A. Restrict both gain and Q
    B. Restrict gain but increase Q
    C. Restrict Q but increase gain
    D. Increase both gain and Q

E7G05:A. Ringing and audio instability be prevented in a multi-section op-amp RC audio filter circuit by restricting both gain and Q.

Which of the following is the most appropriate use of an op-amp active filter?
    A. As a high-pass filter used to block RFI at the input to receivers
    B. As a low-pass filter used between a transmitter and a transmission line
    C. For smoothing power supply output
    D. As an audio filter in a receiver

E7G06:D. The most appropriate use of an op-amp active filter is as an audio filter in a receiver.

What magnitude of voltage gain can be expected from the circuit in Figure E7-4 when R1 is 10 ohms and RF is 470 ohms?
    A. 0.21
    B. 94
    C. 47
    D. 24

E7G07: C. The voltage gain from the circuit in Figure E7-4 when R1 is 10 ohms and RF is 470 ohms should be 47.

How does the gain of an ideal operational amplifier vary with frequency?
    A. It increases linearly with increasing frequency
    B. It decreases linearly with increasing frequency
    C. It decreases logarithmically with increasing frequency
    D. It does not vary with frequency

Copyright © Mometrix Media. You have been licensed one copy of this document for personal use only. Any other reproduction or redistribution is strictly prohibited. All rights reserved.

E7G08: D. The gain of an ideal operational amplifier does not vary with frequency.

What will be the output voltage of the circuit shown in Figure E7-4 if R1 is 1000 ohms, RF is 10,000 ohms, and 0.23 volts DC is applied to the input?
    A. 0.23 volts
    B. 2.3 volts
    C. -0.23 volts
    D. -2.3 volts

E7G09: D. The output voltage of the circuit shown in Figure E7-4 when R1 is 1000 ohms, RF is 10,000 ohms, and 0.23 volts DC is applied to the input is -2.3 volts.

What absolute voltage gain can be expected from the circuit in Figure E7-4 when R1 is 1800 ohms and RF is 68 kilohms?
    A. 1
    B. 0.03
    C. 38
    D. 76

E7G10: C. A voltage gain of 38 can be expected from the circuit in Figure E7-4 when R1 is 1800 ohms and RF is 68 kilohms.

What absolute voltage gain can be expected from the circuit in Figure E7-4 when R1 is 3300 ohms and RF is 47 kilohms?
    A. 28
    B. 14
    C. 7
    D. 0.07

E7G11: B. An absolute voltage gain of 14 can be expected from the circuit in Figure E7-4 when R1 is 3300 ohms and RF is 47 kilohms.

What is an integrated circuit operational amplifier?
    A. A high-gain, direct-coupled differential amplifier with very high input impedance and very low output impedance
    B. A digital audio amplifier whose characteristics are determined by components external to the amplifier
    C. An amplifier used to increase the average output of frequency modulated amateur signals to the legal limit
    D. A RF amplifier used in the UHF and microwave regions

E7G12: A. An integrated circuit operational amplifier is a high-gain, direct-coupled differential amplifier with very high input impedance and very low output impedance.

Copyright © Mometrix Media. You have been licensed one copy of this document for personal use only. Any other reproduction or redistribution is strictly prohibited. All rights reserved.

E7H – Oscillators and signal sources: types of oscillators; synthesizers and phase-locked loops; direct digital synthesizers; stabilizing thermal drift; microphonics; high accuracy oscillators

What are three oscillator circuits used in Amateur Radio equipment?
  A. Taft, Pierce and negative feedback
  B. Pierce, Fenner and Beane
  C. Taft, Hartley and Pierce
  D. Colpitts, Hartley and Pierce

E7H01: D. Colpitts, Hartley and Pierce are all types of oscillator circuits used in Amateur Radio equipment.

Which describes a microphonic?
  A. An IC used for amplifying microphone signals
  B. Distortion caused by RF pickup on the microphone cable
  C. Changes in oscillator frequency due to mechanical vibration
  D. Excess loading of the microphone by an oscillator

E7H02: C. A microphonic is a change in oscillator frequency due to mechanical vibration.

How is positive feedback supplied in a Hartley oscillator?
  A. Through a tapped coil
  B. Through a capacitive divider
  C. Through link coupling
  D. Through a neutralizing capacitor

E7H03: A. Positive feedback is supplied through a tapped coil in a Hartley oscillator.

How is positive feedback supplied in a Colpitts oscillator?
  A. Through a tapped coil
  B. Through link coupling
  C. Through a capacitive divider
  D. Through a neutralizing capacitor

E7H04: C. Positive feedback is supplied through a capacitive divider in a Colpitts oscillator.

How is positive feedback supplied in a Pierce oscillator?
  A. Through a tapped coil
  B. Through link coupling
  C. Through a neutralizing capacitor
  D. Through a quartz crystal

E7H05: D. Positive feedback is supplied through a quartz crystal in a Pierce oscillator.

Which of the following oscillator circuits are commonly used in VFOs?
  A. Pierce and Zener
  B. Colpitts and Hartley
  C. Armstrong and deForest
  D. Negative feedback and balanced feedback

Copyright © Mometrix Media. You have been licensed one copy of this document for personal use only. Any other reproduction or redistribution is strictly prohibited. All rights reserved.

E7H06: B. Colpitts and Hartley oscillator circuits are commonly used in VFOs.

How can an oscillator's microphonic responses be reduced?
    A. Use of NP0 capacitors
    B. Eliminating noise on the oscillator's power supply
    C. Using the oscillator only for CW and digital signals
    D. Mechanically isolating the oscillator circuitry from its enclosure

E7H07: D. An oscillator's microphonic responses can be reduced by mechanically isolating the oscillator circuitry from its enclosure.

Which of the following components can be used to reduce thermal drift in crystal oscillators?
    A. NP0 capacitors
    B. Toroidal inductors
    C. Wirewound resistors
    D. Non-inductive resistors

E7H08: A. NP0 capacitors can be used to reduce thermal drift in crystal oscillators.

What type of frequency synthesizer circuit uses a phase accumulator, lookup table, digital to analog converter, and a low-pass anti-alias filter?
    A. A direct digital synthesizer
    B. A hybrid synthesizer
    C. A phase locked loop synthesizer
    D. A diode-switching matrix synthesizer

E7H09: A. A direct digital synthesizer uses a phase accumulator, lookup table, digital to analog converter, and a low-pass anti-alias filter.

What information is contained in the lookup table of a direct digital frequency synthesizer?
    A. The phase relationship between a reference oscillator and the output waveform
    B. The amplitude values that represent a sine-wave output
    C. The phase relationship between a voltage-controlled oscillator and the output waveform
    D. The synthesizer frequency limits and frequency values stored in the radio memories

E7H10: B. The amplitude values that represent a sine-wave output are contained in the lookup table of a direct digital frequency synthesizer.

What are the major spectral impurity components of direct digital synthesizers?
    A. Broadband noise
    B. Digital conversion noise
    C. Spurious signals at discrete frequencies
    D. Nyquist limit noise

E7H11: C. The major spectral impurity components of direct digital synthesizers are spurious signals at discrete frequencies.

Copyright © Mometrix Media. You have been licensed one copy of this document for personal use only. Any other reproduction or redistribution is strictly prohibited. All rights reserved.

Which of the following must be done to ensure that a crystal oscillator provides the frequency specified by the crystal manufacturer?

    A. Provide the crystal with a specified parallel inductance
    B. Provide the crystal with a specified parallel capacitance
    C. Bias the crystal at a specified voltage
    D. Bias the crystal at a specified current

E7H12: B. A crystal oscillator must be provided with a specified parallel capacitance to ensure that it provides the frequency specified by the manufacturer.

Which of the following is a technique for providing highly accurate and stable oscillators needed for microwave transmission and reception?

    A. Use a GPS signal reference
    B. Use a rubidium stabilized reference oscillator
    C. Use a temperature-controlled high Q dielectric resonator
    D. All of these choices are correct

E7H13: D. GPS signal references, rubidium stabilized reference oscillators, temperature-controlled high Q dielectric resonators can be used for providing highly accurate and stable oscillators needed for microwave transmission and reception.

What is a phase-locked loop circuit?

    A. An electronic servo loop consisting of a ratio detector, reactance modulator, and voltage-controlled oscillator
    B. An electronic circuit also known as a monostable multivibrator
    C. An electronic servo loop consisting of a phase detector, a low-pass filter, a voltage-controlled oscillator, and a stable reference oscillator
    D. An electronic circuit consisting of a precision push-pull amplifier with a differential input

E7H14: C. A phase-locked loop circuit is an electronic servo loop consisting of a phase detector, a low-pass filter, a voltage-controlled oscillator, and a stable reference oscillator.

Which of these functions can be performed by a phase-locked loop?

    A. Wide-band AF and RF power amplification
    B. Comparison of two digital input signals, digital pulse counter
    C. Photovoltaic conversion, optical coupling
    D. Frequency synthesis, FM demodulation

E7H15: D. A phase-locked loop can perform frequency synthesis and FM demodulation.

E8 – Signals and Emissions

Copyright © Mometrix Media. You have been licensed one copy of this document for personal use only. Any other reproduction or redistribution is strictly prohibited. All rights reserved.

E8A – AC waveforms: sine, square, sawtooth and irregular waveforms; AC measurements; average and PEP of RF signals; Fourier analysis; Analog to digital conversion: Digital to Analog conversion

What is the name of the process that shows that a square wave is made up of a sine wave plus all of its odd harmonics?
- A. Fourier analysis
- B. Vector analysis
- C. Numerical analysis
- D. Differential analysis

E8A01: A. Fourier analysis shows that a square wave is made up of a sine wave plus all of its odd harmonics.

What type of wave has a rise time significantly faster than its fall time (or vice versa)?
- A. A cosine wave
- B. A square wave
- C. A sawtooth wave
- D. A sine wave

E8A02: C. A sawtooth wave has a rise time significantly faster than its fall time (or vice versa).

What type of wave does a Fourier analysis show to be made up of sine waves of a given fundamental frequency plus all of its harmonics?
- A. A sawtooth wave
- B. A square wave
- C. A sine wave
- D. A cosine wave

E8A03: A. Fourier analysis shows sawtooth waves to be made up of sine waves of a given fundamental frequency plus all of its harmonics.

What is "dither" with respect to analog to digital converters?
- A. An abnormal condition where the converter cannot settle on a value to represent the signal
- B. A small amount of noise added to the input signal to allow more precise representation of a signal over time
- C. An error caused by irregular quantization step size
- D. A method of decimation by randomly skipping samples

E8A04: B. "Dither" in analog to digital converters is a small amount of noise added to the input signal to allow more precise representation of a signal over time.

What would be the most accurate way of measuring the RMS voltage of a complex waveform?
- A. By using a grid dip meter
- B. By measuring the voltage with a D'Arsonval meter
- C. By using an absorption wave meter
- D. By measuring the heating effect in a known resistor

E8A05: D. The most accurate way of measuring the RMS voltage of a complex waveform would be measuring the heating effect in a known resistor.

Copyright © Mometrix Media. You have been licensed one copy of this document for personal use only. Any other reproduction or redistribution is strictly prohibited. All rights reserved.

What is the approximate ratio of PEP-to-average power in a typical single-sideband phone signal?
- A. 2.5 to 1
- B. 25 to 1
- C. 1 to 1
- D. 100 to 1

E8A06: A. The approximate ratio of PEP-to-average power in a typical single-sideband phone signal is 2.5 to 1.

What determines the PEP-to-average power ratio of a single-sideband phone signal?
- A. The frequency of the modulating signal
- B. The characteristics of the modulating signal
- C. The degree of carrier suppression
- D. The amplifier gain

E8A07: B. The characteristics of the modulating signal determine the PEP-to-average power ratio of a single-sideband phone signal.

Why would a direct or flash conversion analog-to-digital converter be useful for a software-defined radio?
- A. Very low power consumption decreases frequency drift
- B. Immunity to out of sequence coding reduces spurious responses
- C. Very high speed allows digitizing high frequencies
- D. All of these choices are correct

E8A08: C. A direct or flash conversion analog-to-digital converter would be useful for a software-defined radio because the very high speed allows digitizing high frequencies.

How many levels can an analog-to-digital converter with 8 bit resolution encode?
- A. 8
- B. 8 multiplied by the gain of the input amplifier
- C. 256 divided by the gain of the input amplifier
- D. 256

E8A09: D. An analog-to-digital converter with 8 bit resolution can encode 256 levels.

What is the purpose of a low pass filter used in conjunction with a digital-to-analog converter?
- A. Lower the input bandwidth to increase the effective resolution
- B. Improve accuracy by removing out of sequence codes from the input
- C. Remove harmonics from the output caused by the discrete analog levels generated
- D. All of these choices are correct

E8A10: C. A low pass filter used in conjunction with a digital-to-analog converter serves to remove harmonics from the output caused by the discrete analog levels generated.

What type of information can be conveyed using digital waveforms?
- A. Human speech
- B. Video signals
- C. Data
- D. All of these choices are correct

E8A11: D. Human speech, video signals, and data can all be conveyed using digital waveforms.

Copyright © Mometrix Media. You have been licensed one copy of this document for personal use only. Any other reproduction or redistribution is strictly prohibited. All rights reserved.

What is an advantage of using digital signals instead of analog signals to convey the same information?
A. Less complex circuitry is required for digital signal generation and detection
B. Digital signals always occupy a narrower bandwidth
C. Digital signals can be regenerated multiple times without error
D. All of these choices are correct

E8A12: C. An advantage of using digital signals instead of analog signals to convey the same information is that digital signals can be regenerated multiple times without error.

Which of these methods is commonly used to convert analog signals to digital signals?
A. Sequential sampling
B. Harmonic regeneration
C. Level shifting
D. Phase reversal

E8A13: A. Sequential sampling is commonly used to convert analog signals to digital signals.

E8B – Modulation and demodulation: modulation methods; modulation index and deviation ratio; frequency and time division multiplexing; Orthogonal Frequency Division Multiplexing

What is the term for the ratio between the frequency deviation of an RF carrier wave and the modulating frequency of its corresponding FM-phone signal?
A. FM compressibility
B. Quieting index
C. Percentage of modulation
D. Modulation index

E8B01: D. The ratio between the frequency deviation of an RF carrier wave and the modulating frequency of its corresponding FM-phone signal is the modulation index.

How does the modulation index of a phase-modulated emission vary with RF carrier frequency (the modulated frequency)?
A. It increases as the RF carrier frequency increases
B. It decreases as the RF carrier frequency increases
C. It varies with the square root of the RF carrier frequency
D. It does not depend on the RF carrier frequency

E8B02: D. The modulation index of a phase-modulated emission does not depend on the RF carrier frequency.

What is the modulation index of an FM-phone signal having a maximum frequency deviation of 3000 Hz either side of the carrier frequency when the modulating frequency is 1000 Hz?
A. 3
B. 0.3
C. 3000
D. 1000

Copyright © Mometrix Media. You have been licensed one copy of this document for personal use only. Any other reproduction or redistribution is strictly prohibited. All rights reserved.

E8B03: A. The modulation index of an FM-phone signal having a maximum frequency deviation of 3000 Hz either side of the carrier frequency when the modulating frequency is 1000 Hz is 3.

What is the modulation index of an FM-phone signal having a maximum carrier deviation of plus or minus 6 kHz when modulated with a 2 kHz modulating frequency?
    A. 6000
    B. 3
    C. 2000
    D. 1/3

E8B04: B. The modulation index of an FM-phone signal having a maximum carrier deviation of plus or minus 6 kHz when modulated with a 2 kHz modulating frequency is 3.

What is the deviation ratio of an FM-phone signal having a maximum frequency swing of plus-or-minus 5 kHz when the maximum modulation frequency is 3 kHz?
    A. 60
    B. 0.167
    C. 0.6
    D. 1.67

E8B05: D. The deviation ratio of an FM-phone signal having a maximum frequency swing of plus-or-minus 5 kHz when the maximum modulation frequency is 3 kHz is 1.67.

What is the deviation ratio of an FM-phone signal having a maximum frequency swing of plus or minus 7.5 kHz when the maximum modulation frequency is 3.5 kHz?
    A. 2.14
    B. 0.214
    C. 0.47
    D. 47

E8B06: A. The deviation ratio of an FM-phone signal having a maximum frequency swing of plus or minus 7.5 kHz when the maximum modulation frequency is 3.5 kHz is 2.14.

Orthogonal Frequency Division Multiplexing is a technique used for which type of amateur communication?
    A. High speed digital modes
    B. Extremely low-power contacts
    C. EME
    D. OFDM signals are not allowed on amateur bands

E8B07: A. Orthogonal Frequency Division Multiplexing is a technique used for high speed digital modes of amateur communication.

What describes Orthogonal Frequency Division Multiplexing?
    A. A frequency modulation technique which uses non-harmonically related frequencies
    B. A bandwidth compression technique using Fourier transforms
    C. A digital mode for narrow band, slow speed transmissions
    D. A digital modulation technique using subcarriers at frequencies chosen to avoid intersymbol interference

E8B08: D. Orthogonal Frequency Division Multiplexing is a digital modulation technique using subcarriers at frequencies chosen to avoid intersymbol interference.

Copyright © Mometrix Media. You have been licensed one copy of this document for personal use only. Any other reproduction or redistribution is strictly prohibited. All rights reserved.

What is meant by deviation ratio?
    A. The ratio of the audio modulating frequency to the center carrier frequency
    B. The ratio of the maximum carrier frequency deviation to the highest audio modulating frequency
    C. The ratio of the carrier center frequency to the audio modulating frequency
    D. The ratio of the highest audio modulating frequency to the average audio modulating frequency

E8B09: B. Deviation ratio is the ratio of the maximum carrier frequency deviation to the highest audio modulating frequency.

What describes frequency division multiplexing?
    A. The transmitted signal jumps from band to band at a predetermined rate
    B. Two or more information streams are merged into a baseband, which then modulates the transmitter
    C. The transmitted signal is divided into packets of information
    D. Two or more information streams are merged into a digital combiner, which then pulse position modulates the transmitter

E8B10: B. Frequency division multiplexing is when two or more information streams are merged into a baseband, which then modulates the transmitter.

What is digital time division multiplexing?
    A. Two or more data streams are assigned to discrete sub-carriers on an FM transmitter
    B. Two or more signals are arranged to share discrete time slots of a data transmission
    C. Two or more data streams share the same channel by transmitting time of transmission as the sub-carrier
    D. Two or more signals are quadrature modulated to increase bandwidth efficiency

E8B11: B. Digital time division multiplexing is when two or more signals are arranged to share discrete time slots of a data transmission.

E8C – Digital signals: digital communication modes; information rate vs bandwidth; error correction

How is Forward Error Correction implemented?
    A. By the receiving station repeating each block of three data characters
    B. By transmitting a special algorithm to the receiving station along with the data characters
    C. By transmitting extra data that may be used to detect and correct transmission errors
    D. By varying the frequency shift of the transmitted signal according to a predefined algorithm

E8C01: C. Forward Error Correction is implemented by transmitting extra data that may be used to detect and correct transmission errors.

What is the definition of symbol rate in a digital transmission?
    A. The number of control characters in a message packet
    B. The duration of each bit in a message sent over the air
    C. The rate at which the waveform of a transmitted signal changes to convey information
    D. The number of characters carried per second by the station-to-station link

Copyright © Mometrix Media. You have been licensed one copy of this document for personal use only. Any other reproduction or redistribution is strictly prohibited. All rights reserved.

E8C02: C. Symbol rate in a digital transmission is the rate at which the waveform of a transmitted signal changes to convey information.

When performing phase shift keying, why is it advantageous to shift phase precisely at the zero crossing of the RF carrier?
A. This results in the least possible transmitted bandwidth for the particular mode
B. It is easier to demodulate with a conventional, non-synchronous detector
C. It improves carrier suppression
D. All of these choices are correct

E8C03: A. When performing phase shift keying, it is advantageous to shift phase precisely at the zero crossing of the RF carrier because it results in the least possible transmitted bandwidth for the particular mode.

What technique is used to minimize the bandwidth requirements of a PSK31 signal?
A. Zero-sum character encoding
B. Reed-Solomon character encoding
C. Use of sinusoidal data pulses
D. Use of trapezoidal data pulses

E8C04: C. Use of sinusoidal data pulses helps minimize the bandwidth requirements of a PSK31 signal.

What is the necessary bandwidth of a 13-WPM international Morse code transmission?
A. Approximately 13 Hz
B. Approximately 26 Hz
C. Approximately 52 Hz
D. Approximately 104 Hz

E8C05: C. A 13-WPM international Morse code transmission requires a bandwidth of approximately 52 Hz.

What is the necessary bandwidth of a 170-hertz shift, 300-baud ASCII transmission?
A. 0.1 Hz
B. 0.3 kHz
C. 0.5 kHz
D. 1.0 kHz

E8C06: C. A 170-hertz shift, 300-baud ASCII transmission requires a bandwidth of 0.5 kHz.

What is the necessary bandwidth of a 4800-Hz frequency shift, 9600-baud ASCII FM transmission?
A. 15.36 kHz
B. 9.6 kHz
C. 4.8 kHz
D. 5.76 kHz

E8C07: A. A 4800-Hz frequency shift, 9600-baud ASCII FM transmission requires a bandwidth of 15.36 kHz.

Copyright © Mometrix Media. You have been licensed one copy of this document for personal use only. Any other reproduction or redistribution is strictly prohibited. All rights reserved.

How does ARQ accomplish error correction?
    A. Special binary codes provide automatic correction
    B. Special polynomial codes provide automatic correction
    C. If errors are detected, redundant data is substituted
    D. If errors are detected, a retransmission is requested

E8C08: D. ARQ accomplishes error correction by requesting a retransmission if errors are detected.

Which is the name of a digital code where each preceding or following character changes by only one bit?
    A. Binary Coded Decimal Code
    B. Extended Binary Coded Decimal Interchange Code
    C. Excess 3 code
    D. Gray code

E8C09: D. In Gray code, each preceding or following character changes by only one bit.

What is an advantage of Gray code in digital communications where symbols are transmitted as multiple bits?
    A. It increases security
    B. It has more possible states than simple binary
    C. It has more resolution than simple binary
    D. It facilitates error detection

E8C10: D. An advantage of Gray code in digital communications is that it facilitates error detection.

What is the relationship between symbol rate and baud?
    A. They are the same
    B. Baud is twice the symbol rate
    C. Symbol rate is only used for packet-based modes
    D. Baud is only used for RTTY

E8C11: A. symbol rate and baud are the same.

E8D – Keying defects and overmodulation of digital signals; digital codes; spread spectrum

Why are received spread spectrum signals resistant to interference?
    A. Signals not using the spread spectrum algorithm are suppressed in the receiver
    B. The high power used by a spread spectrum transmitter keeps its signal from being easily overpowered
    C. The receiver is always equipped with a digital blanker
    D. If interference is detected by the receiver it will signal the transmitter to change frequencies

E8D01: A. Received spread spectrum signals are resistant to interference because signals not using the spread spectrum algorithm are suppressed in the receiver.

Copyright © Mometrix Media. You have been licensed one copy of this document for personal use only. Any other reproduction or redistribution is strictly prohibited. All rights reserved.

What spread spectrum communications technique uses a high speed binary bit stream to shift the phase of an RF carrier?
    A. Frequency hopping
    B. Direct sequence
    C. Binary phase-shift keying
    D. Phase compandored spread spectrum

E8D02: B. Direct sequence uses a high speed binary bit stream to shift the phase of an RF carrier.

How does the spread spectrum technique of frequency hopping work?
    A. If interference is detected by the receiver it will signal the transmitter to change frequencies
    B. If interference is detected by the receiver it will signal the transmitter to wait until the frequency is clear
    C. A pseudo-random binary bit stream is used to shift the phase of an RF carrier very rapidly in a particular sequence
    D. The frequency of the transmitted signal is changed very rapidly according to a particular sequence also used by the receiving station

E8D03: D. In frequency hopping, the frequency of the transmitted signal is changed very rapidly according to a particular sequence also used by the receiving station.

What is the primary effect of extremely short rise or fall time on a CW signal?
    A. More difficult to copy
    B. The generation of RF harmonics
    C. The generation of key clicks
    D. Limits data speed

E8D04: C. Extremely short rise or fall time on a CW signal lead to the generation of key clicks.

What is the most common method of reducing key clicks?
    A. Increase keying waveform rise and fall times
    B. Low-pass filters at the transmitter output
    C. Reduce keying waveform rise and fall times
    D. High-pass filters at the transmitter output

E8D05: A. The most common method of reducing key clicks is increasing keying waveform rise and fall times.

Which of the following indicates likely overmodulation of an AFSK signal such as PSK or MFSK?
    A. High reflected power
    B. Strong ALC action
    C. Harmonics on higher bands
    D. Rapid signal fading

E8D06: B. Strong ALC action indicates likely overmodulation of an AFSK signal such as PSK or MFSK.

What is a common cause of overmodulation of AFSK signals?
    A. Excessive numbers of retries
    B. Ground loops
    C. Bit errors in the modem
    D. Excessive transmit audio levels

Copyright © Mometrix Media. You have been licensed one copy of this document for personal use only. Any other reproduction or redistribution is strictly prohibited. All rights reserved.

E8D07: D. A common cause of overmodulation of AFSK signals is excessive transmit audio levels.

What parameter might indicate that excessively high input levels are causing distortion in an AFSK signal?
    A. Signal to noise ratio
    B. Baud rate
    C. Repeat Request Rate (RRR)
    D. Intermodulation Distortion (IMD)

E8D08: D. Intermodulation Distortion (IMD) might indicate that excessively high input levels are causing distortion in an AFSK signal.

What is considered a good minimum IMD level for an idling PSK signal?
    A. +10 dB
    B. +15 dB
    C. -20 dB
    D. -30 dB

E8D09: D. A good minimum IMD level for an idling PSK signal is -30 dB.

What are some of the differences between the Baudot digital code and ASCII?
    A. Baudot uses 4 data bits per character, ASCII uses 7 or 8; Baudot uses 1 character as a letters/figures shift code, ASCII has no letters/figures code
    B. Baudot uses 5 data bits per character, ASCII uses 7 or 8; Baudot uses 2 characters as letters/figures shift codes, ASCII has no letters/figures shift code
    C. Baudot uses 6 data bits per character, ASCII uses 7 or 8; Baudot has no letters/figures shift code, ASCII uses 2 letters/figures shift codes
    D. Baudot uses 7 data bits per character, ASCII uses 8; Baudot has no letters/figures shift code, ASCII uses 2 letters/figures shift codes

E8D10: B. Baudot uses 5 data bits per character, ASCII uses 7 or 8; Baudot uses 2 characters as letters/figures shift codes, ASCII has no letters/figures shift code.

What is one advantage of using ASCII code for data communications?
    A. It includes built in error correction features
    B. It contains fewer information bits per character than any other code
    C. It is possible to transmit both upper and lower case text
    D. It uses one character as a shift code to send numeric and special characters

E8D11: C. An advantage of using ASCII code for data communications is that it is possible to transmit both upper and lower case text.

What is the advantage of including a parity bit with an ASCII character stream?
    A. Faster transmission rate
    B. The signal can overpower interfering signals
    C. Foreign language characters can be sent
    D. Some types of errors can be detected

E8D12: D. By including a parity bit with an ASCII character stream, some types of errors can be detected.

E9 – Antennas and Transmission Lines

Copyright © Mometrix Media. You have been licensed one copy of this document for personal use only. Any other reproduction or redistribution is strictly prohibited. All rights reserved.

E9A – Basic Antenna parameters: radiation resistance, gain, beamwidth, efficiency, beamwidth; effective radiated power, polarization

What describes an isotropic antenna?
  A. A grounded antenna used to measure earth conductivity
  B. A horizontally polarized antenna used to compare Yagi antennas
  C. A theoretical antenna used as a reference for antenna gain
  D. A spacecraft antenna used to direct signals toward the earth

E9A01: C. An isotropic antenna is a theoretical antenna used as a reference for antenna gain.

What antenna has no gain in any direction?
  A. Quarter-wave vertical
  B. Yagi
  C. Half-wave dipole
  D. Isotropic antenna

E9A02: D. An isotropic antenna has no gain in any direction.

Why would one need to know the feed point impedance of an antenna?
  A. To match impedances in order to minimize standing wave ratio on the transmission line
  B. To measure the near-field radiation density from a transmitting antenna
  C. To calculate the front-to-side ratio of the antenna
  D. To calculate the front-to-back ratio of the antenna

E9A03: A. Knowing the feed point impedance of an antenna allows one to match impedances in order to minimize standing wave ratio on the transmission line.

Which of the following factors may affect the feed point impedance of an antenna?
  A. Transmission-line length
  B. Antenna height, conductor length/diameter ratio and location of nearby conductive objects
  C. The settings of an antenna tuner at the transmitter
  D. Sunspot activity and time of day

E9A04: B. Antenna height, conductor length/diameter ratio and location of nearby conductive objects may affect the feed point impedance of an antenna.

What is included in the total resistance of an antenna system?
  A. Radiation resistance plus space impedance
  B. Radiation resistance plus transmission resistance
  C. Transmission-line resistance plus radiation resistance
  D. Radiation resistance plus ohmic resistance

E9A05: D. Radiation resistance plus ohmic resistance is included in the total resistance of an antenna system.

How does the beamwidth of an antenna vary as the gain is increased?
  A. It increases geometrically
  B. It increases arithmetically
  C. It is essentially unaffected
  D. It decreases

Copyright © Mometrix Media. You have been licensed one copy of this document for personal use only. Any other reproduction or redistribution is strictly prohibited. All rights reserved.

E9A06: D. The beamwidth of an antenna decreases as the gain is increased.

What is meant by antenna gain?
    A. The ratio of the radiated signal strength of an antenna in the direction of maximum radiation to that of a reference antenna
    B. The ratio of the signal in the forward direction to that in the opposite direction
    C. The ratio of the amount of power radiated by an antenna compared to the transmitter output power
    D. The final amplifier gain minus the transmission line losses

E9A07: A. Antenna gain is the ratio of the radiated signal strength of an antenna in the direction of maximum radiation to that of a reference antenna.

What is meant by antenna bandwidth?
    A. Antenna length divided by the number of elements
    B. The frequency range over which an antenna satisfies a performance requirement
    C. The angle between the half-power radiation points
    D. The angle formed between two imaginary lines drawn through the element ends

E9A08: B. Antenna bandwidth is the frequency range over which an antenna satisfies a performance requirement.

How is antenna efficiency calculated?
    A. (radiation resistance / transmission resistance) x 100 per cent
    B. (radiation resistance / total resistance) x 100 per cent
    C. (total resistance / radiation resistance) x 100 per cent
    D. (effective radiated power / transmitter output) x 100 percent

E9A09: B. Antenna efficiency is calculated by (radiation resistance / total resistance) x 100 per cent.

Which of the following choices is a way to improve the efficiency of a ground-mounted quarter-wave vertical antenna?
    A. Install a good radial system
    B. Isolate the coax shield from ground
    C. Shorten the radiating element
    D. Reduce the diameter of the radiating element

E9A10: A. Installing a good radial system can improve the efficiency of a ground-mounted quarter-wave vertical antenna.

Which of the following factors determines ground losses for a ground-mounted vertical antenna operating in the 3 MHz to 30 MHz range?
    A. The standing wave ratio
    B. Distance from the transmitter
    C. Soil conductivity
    D. Take-off angle

E9A11: C. Soil conductivity determines ground losses for a ground-mounted vertical antenna operating in the 3 MHz to 30 MHz range.

Copyright © Mometrix Media. You have been licensed one copy of this document for personal use only. Any other reproduction or redistribution is strictly prohibited. All rights reserved.

How much gain does an antenna have compared to a 1/2-wavelength dipole when it has 6 dB gain over an isotropic antenna?
  A. 3.85 dB
  B. 6.0 dB
  C. 8.15 dB
  D. 2.79 dB

E9A12: A. An antenna has a gain of 3.85 dB compared to a 1/2-wavelength dipole when it has 6 dB gain over an isotropic antenna.

How much gain does an antenna have compared to a 1/2-wavelength dipole when it has 12 dB gain over an isotropic antenna?
  A. 6.17 dB
  B. 9.85 dB
  C. 12.5 dB
  D. 14.15 dB

E9A13: B. An antenna has a gain of 9.85 dB compared to a 1/2-wavelength dipole when it has 12 dB gain over an isotropic antenna.

What is meant by the radiation resistance of an antenna?
  A. The combined losses of the antenna elements and feed line
  B. The specific impedance of the antenna
  C. The value of a resistance that would dissipate the same amount of power as that radiated from an antenna
  D. The resistance in the atmosphere that an antenna must overcome to be able to radiate a signal

E9A14: C. The radiation resistance of an antenna is the value of a resistance that would dissipate the same amount of power as that radiated from an antenna.

What is the effective radiated power relative to a dipole of a repeater station with 150 watts transmitter power output, 2 dB feed line loss, 2.2 dB duplexer loss, and 7 dBd antenna gain?
  A. 1977 watts
  B. 78.7 watts
  C. 420 watts
  D. 286 watts

E9A15: D. The effective radiated power relative to a dipole of a repeater station with 150 watts transmitter power output, 2 dB feed line loss, 2.2 dB duplexer loss, and 7 dBd antenna gain is 286 watts.

What is the effective radiated power relative to a dipole of a repeater station with 200 watts transmitter power output, 4 dB feed line loss, 3.2 dB duplexer loss, 0.8 dB circulator loss, and 10 dBd antenna gain?
  A. 317 watts
  B. 2000 watts
  C. 126 watts
  D. 300 watts

E9A16: A. The effective radiated power relative to a dipole of a repeater station with 200 watts transmitter power output, 4 dB feed line loss, 3.2 dB duplexer loss, 0.8 dB circulator loss, and 10 dBd antenna gain is 317 watts.

Copyright © Mometrix Media. You have been licensed one copy of this document for personal use only. Any other reproduction or redistribution is strictly prohibited. All rights reserved.

What is the effective radiated power of a repeater station with 200 watts transmitter power output, 2 dB feed line loss, 2.8 dB duplexer loss, 1.2 dB circulator loss, and 7 dBi antenna gain?
- A. 159 watts
- B. 252 watts
- C. 632 watts
- D. 63.2 watts

E9A17: B. The effective radiated power of a repeater station with 200 watts transmitter power output, 2 dB feed line loss, 2.8 dB duplexer loss, 1.2 dB circulator loss, and 7 dBi antenna gain is 252 watts.

What term describes station output, taking into account all gains and losses?
- A. Power factor
- B. Half-power bandwidth
- C. Effective radiated power
- D. Apparent power

E9A18: C. Effective radiated power describes station output, taking into account all gains and losses.

E9B – Antenna patterns: E and H plane patterns; gain as a function of pattern; antenna design

In the antenna radiation pattern shown in Figure E9-1, what is the 3 dB beam-width?
- A. 75 degrees
- B. 50 degrees
- C. 25 degrees
- D. 30 degrees

E9B01: B. In the antenna radiation pattern shown in Figure E9-1, the 3 dB beam-width is 50 degrees.

In the antenna radiation pattern shown in Figure E9-1, what is the front-to-back ratio?
- A. 36 dB
- B. 18 dB
- C. 24 dB
- D. 14 dB

E9B02: B. In the antenna radiation pattern shown in Figure E9-1, the front-to-back ratio is 18 dB.

In the antenna radiation pattern shown in Figure E9-1, what is the front-to-side ratio?
- A. 12 dB
- B. 14 dB
- C. 18 dB
- D. 24 dB

E9B03: B. In the antenna radiation pattern shown in Figure E9-1, the front-to-side ratio is 14 dB.

Copyright © Mometrix Media. You have been licensed one copy of this document for personal use only. Any other reproduction or redistribution is strictly prohibited. All rights reserved.

What may occur when a directional antenna is operated at different frequencies within the band for which it was designed?

A. Feed point impedance may become negative
B. The E-field and H-field patterns may reverse
C. Element spacing limits could be exceeded
D. The gain may change depending on frequency

E9B04: D. The gain may change depending on frequency if a directional antenna is operated at different frequencies within the band for which it was designed.

What type of antenna pattern over real ground is shown in Figure E9-2?

A. Elevation
B. Azimuth
C. Radiation resistance
D. Polarization

E9B05: A. An elevation antenna pattern over real ground is shown in Figure E9-2.

What is the elevation angle of peak response in the antenna radiation pattern shown in Figure E9-2?

A. 45 degrees
B. 75 degrees
C. 7.5 degrees
D. 25 degrees

E9B06: C. The elevation angle of peak response in the antenna radiation pattern shown in Figure E9-2 is 7.5 degrees.

How does the total amount of radiation emitted by a directional gain antenna compare with the total amount of radiation emitted from an isotropic antenna, assuming each is driven by the same amount of power?

A. The total amount of radiation from the directional antenna is increased by the gain of the antenna
B. The total amount of radiation from the directional antenna is stronger by its front-to-back ratio
C. They are the same
D. The radiation from the isotropic antenna is 2.15 dB stronger than that from the directional antenna

E9B07: C. The total amount of radiation emitted by a directional gain antenna is equal to the total amount of radiation emitted from an isotropic antenna, assuming each is driven by the same amount of power.

How can the approximate beam-width in a given plane of a directional antenna be determined?

A. Note the two points where the signal strength of the antenna is 3 dB less than maximum and compute the angular difference
B. Measure the ratio of the signal strengths of the radiated power lobes from the front and rear of the antenna
C. Draw two imaginary lines through the ends of the elements and measure the angle between the lines
D. Measure the ratio of the signal strengths of the radiated power lobes from the front and side of the antenna

Copyright © Mometrix Media. You have been licensed one copy of this document for personal use only. Any other reproduction or redistribution is strictly prohibited. All rights reserved.

E9B08: A. The approximate beam-width in a given plane of a directional antenna be determined by noting the two points where the signal strength of the antenna is 3 dB less than maximum and computing the angular difference.

What type of computer program technique is commonly used for modeling antennas?
    A. Graphical analysis
    B. Method of Moments
    C. Mutual impedance analysis
    D. Calculus differentiation with respect to physical properties

E9B09: B. Method of Moments is a type of computer program technique commonly used for modeling antennas.

What is the principle of a Method of Moments analysis?
    A. A wire is modeled as a series of segments, each having a uniform value of current
    B. A wire is modeled as a single sine-wave current generator
    C. A wire is modeled as a series of points, each having a distinct location in space
    D. A wire is modeled as a series of segments, each having a distinct value of voltage across it

E9B10: A. In Method of Moments analysis, a wire is modeled as a series of segments, each having a uniform value of current.

What is a disadvantage of decreasing the number of wire segments in an antenna model below the guideline of 10 segments per half-wavelength?
    A. Ground conductivity will not be accurately modeled
    B. The resulting design will favor radiation of harmonic energy
    C. The computed feed point impedance may be incorrect
    D. The antenna will become mechanically unstable

E9B11: C. Decreasing the number of wire segments in an antenna model below the guideline of 10 segments per half-wavelength may result in the computed feed point impedance being incorrect.

What is the far field of an antenna?
    A. The region of the ionosphere where radiated power is not refracted
    B. The region where radiated power dissipates over a specified time period
    C. The region where radiated field strengths are obstructed by objects of reflection
    D. The region where the shape of the antenna pattern is independent of distance

E9B12: D. The far field of an antenna is the region where the shape of the antenna pattern is independent of distance.

What does the abbreviation NEC stand for when applied to antenna modeling programs?
    A. Next Element Comparison
    B. Numerical Electromagnetic Code
    C. National Electrical Code
    D. Numeric Electrical Computation

E9B13: B. NEC in antenna modeling programs stands for Numerical Electromagnetic Code.

Copyright © Mometrix Media. You have been licensed one copy of this document for personal use only. Any other reproduction or redistribution is strictly prohibited. All rights reserved.

What type of information can be obtained by submitting the details of a proposed new antenna to a modeling program?

A. SWR vs frequency charts
B. Polar plots of the far field elevation and azimuth patterns
C. Antenna gain
D. All of these choices are correct

E9B14: D. Submitting the details of a proposed new antenna to a modeling program can provide one with SWR vs. frequency charts, polar plots of the far field elevation and azimuth patterns, and antenna gain.

What is the front-to-back ratio of the radiation pattern shown in Figure E9-2?

A. 15 dB
B. 28 dB
C. 3 dB
D. 24 dB

E9B15: B. The front-to-back ratio of the radiation pattern shown in Figure E9-2 is 28 dB.

How many elevation lobes appear in the forward direction of the antenna radiation pattern shown in Figure E9-2?

A. 4
B. 3
C. 1
D. 7

E9B16: A. 4 elevation lobes appear in the forward direction of the antenna radiation pattern shown in Figure E9-2.

E9C – Wire and phased array antennas: rhombic antennas; effects of ground reflections; e-off angles; Practical wire antennas: Zepps, OCFD, loops

What is the radiation pattern of two 1/4-wavelength vertical antennas spaced 1/2-wavelength apart and fed 180 degrees out of phase?

A. Cardioid
B. Omni-directional
C. A figure-8 broadside to the axis of the array
D. A figure-8 oriented along the axis of the array

E9C01: D. The radiation pattern of two 1/4-wavelength vertical antennas spaced 1/2-wavelength apart and fed 180 degrees out of phase is a figure-8 oriented along the axis of the array.

What is the radiation pattern of two 1/4 wavelength vertical antennas spaced 1/4 wavelength apart and fed 90 degrees out of phase?

A. Cardioid
B. A figure-8 end-fire along the axis of the array
C. A figure-8 broadside to the axis of the array
D. Omni-directional

Copyright © Mometrix Media. You have been licensed one copy of this document for personal use only. Any other reproduction or redistribution is strictly prohibited. All rights reserved.

E9C02: A. The radiation pattern of two 1/4 wavelength vertical antennas spaced 1/4 wavelength apart and fed 90 degrees out of phase is a cardioid.

What is the radiation pattern of two 1/4 wavelength vertical antennas spaced a 1/2 wavelength apart and fed in phase?
    A. Omni-directional
    B. Cardioid
    C. A Figure-8 broadside to the axis of the array
    D. A Figure-8 end-fire along the axis of the array

E9C03: C. the radiation pattern of two 1/4 wavelength vertical antennas spaced a 1/2 wavelength apart and fed in phase is a figure-8 broadside to the axis of the array.

What happens to the radiation pattern of an unterminated long wire antenna as the wire length is increased?
    A. The lobes become more perpendicular to the wire
    B. The lobes align more in the direction of the wire
    C. The vertical angle increases
    D. The front-to-back ratio decreases

E9C04: B. The lobes of the radiation pattern align more in the direction of the wire as wire length is increased.

What is an OCFD antenna?
    A. A dipole feed approximately 1/3 the way from one end with a 4:1 balun to provide multiband operation
    B. A remotely tunable dipole antenna using orthogonally controlled frequency diversity
    C. An eight band dipole antenna using octophase filters
    D. A multiband dipole antenna using one-way circular polarization for frequency diversity

E9C05: A. An OCFD antenna is a dipole feed approximately 1/3 the way from one end with a 4:1 balun to provide multiband operation.

What is the effect of a terminating resistor on a rhombic antenna?
    A. It reflects the standing waves on the antenna elements back to the transmitter
    B. It changes the radiation pattern from bidirectional to unidirectional
    C. It changes the radiation pattern from horizontal to vertical polarization
    D. It decreases the ground loss

E9C06: B. A terminating resistor on a rhombic antenna changes the radiation pattern from bidirectional to unidirectional.

What is the approximate feed point impedance at the center of a two-wire folded dipole antenna?
    A. 300 ohms
    B. 72 ohms
    C. 50 ohms
    D. 450 ohms

E9C07: A. The approximate feed point impedance at the center of a two-wire folded dipole antenna is 300 ohms.

Copyright © Mometrix Media. You have been licensed one copy of this document for personal use only. Any other reproduction or redistribution is strictly prohibited. All rights reserved.

What is a folded dipole antenna?
    A. A dipole one-quarter wavelength long
    B. A type of ground-plane antenna
    C. A dipole consisting of one wavelength of wire forming a very thin loop
    D. A dipole configured to provide forward gain

E9C08: C. A folded dipole antenna is a dipole consisting of one wavelength of wire forming a very thin loop.

What is a G5RV antenna?
    A. A multi-band dipole antenna fed with coax and a balun through a selected length of open wire transmission line
    B. A multi-band trap antenna
    C. A phased array antenna consisting of multiple loops
    D. A wide band dipole using shorted coaxial cable for the radiating elements and fed with a 4:1 balun

E9C09: A. A G5RV antenna is a multi-band dipole antenna fed with coax and a balun through a selected length of open wire transmission line.

Which of the following describes a Zepp antenna?
    A. A dipole constructed from zip cord
    B. An end fed dipole antenna
    C. An omni-directional antenna commonly used for satellite communications
    D. A vertical array capable of quickly changing the direction of maximum radiation by changing phasing lines

E9C10: B. A Zepp antenna is an end-fed dipole antenna.

How is the far-field elevation pattern of a vertically polarized antenna affected by being mounted over seawater versus rocky ground?
    A. The low-angle radiation decreases
    B. The high-angle radiation increases
    C. Both the high-angle and low-angle radiation decrease
    D. The low-angle radiation increases

E9C11: D. A vertically polarized antenna mounted over seawater would have more low-angle radiation than one mounted over rocky ground.

Which of the following describes an extended double Zepp antenna?
    A. A wideband vertical antenna constructed from precisely tapered aluminum tubing
    B. A portable antenna erected using two push support poles
    C. A center fed 1.25 wavelength antenna (two 5/8 wave elements in phase)
    D. An end fed folded dipole antenna

E9C12: C. An extended double Zepp antenna is a center-fed 1.25 wavelength antenna (two 5/8 wave elements in phase).

What is the main effect of placing a vertical antenna over an imperfect ground?
    A. It causes increased SWR
    B. It changes the impedance angle of the matching network
    C. It reduces low-angle radiation
    D. It reduces losses in the radiating portion of the antenna

Copyright © Mometrix Media. You have been licensed one copy of this document for personal use only. Any other reproduction or redistribution is strictly prohibited. All rights reserved.

E9C13: C. placing a vertical antenna over an imperfect ground results in a reduction of low-angle radiation.

How does the performance of a horizontally polarized antenna mounted on the side of a hill compare with the same antenna mounted on flat ground?
    A. The main lobe takeoff angle increases in the downhill direction
    B. The main lobe takeoff angle decreases in the downhill direction
    C. The horizontal beam width decreases in the downhill direction
    D. The horizontal beam width increases in the uphill direction

E9C14: B. A horizontally polarized antenna mounted on the side of a hill would have a decreased main lobe takeoff angle in the downhill direction compared to same antenna mounted on flat ground.

How does the radiation pattern of a horizontally polarized 3-element beam antenna vary with its height above ground?
    A. The main lobe takeoff angle increases with increasing height
    B. The main lobe takeoff angle decreases with increasing height
    C. The horizontal beam width increases with height
    D. The horizontal beam width decreases with height

E9C15: B. The main lobe takeoff angle of a horizontally polarized 3-element beam antenna decreases with increasing height above ground.

E9D – Directional antennas: gain; Yagi Antennas; losses; SWR bandwidth; antenna efficiency; shortened and mobile antennas; RF Grounding

How does the gain of an ideal parabolic dish antenna change when the operating frequency is doubled?
    A. Gain does not change
    B. Gain is multiplied by 0.707
    C. Gain increases by 6 dB
    D. Gain increases by 3 dB

E9D01: C. The gain of an ideal parabolic dish antenna increases by 6 dB when the operating frequency is doubled.

How can linearly polarized Yagi antennas be used to produce circular polarization?
    A. Stack two Yagis fed 90 degrees out of phase to form an array with the respective elements in parallel planes
    B. Stack two Yagis fed in phase to form an array with the respective elements in parallel planes
    C. Arrange two Yagis perpendicular to each other with the driven elements at the same point on the boom fed 90 degrees out of phase
    D. Arrange two Yagis collinear to each other with the driven elements fed 180 degrees out of phase

E9D02: C. Placing two Yagis perpendicular to each other with the driven elements at the same point on the boom fed 90 degrees out of phase would result in circular polarization.

Copyright © Mometrix Media. You have been licensed one copy of this document for personal use only. Any other reproduction or redistribution is strictly prohibited. All rights reserved.

Where should a high Q loading coil be placed to minimize losses in a shortened vertical antenna?
    A. Near the center of the vertical radiator
    B. As low as possible on the vertical radiator
    C. As close to the transmitter as possible
    D. At a voltage node

E9D03: A. A high Q loading coil should be placed near the center of the vertical radiator to minimize losses in a shortened vertical antenna.

Why should an HF mobile antenna loading coil have a high ratio of reactance to resistance?
    A. To swamp out harmonics
    B. To maximize losses
    C. To minimize losses
    D. To minimize the Q

E9D04: C. An IIF mobile antenna loading coil should have a high ratio of reactance to resistance to minimize losses.

What is a disadvantage of using a multiband trapped antenna?
    A. It might radiate harmonics
    B. It radiates the harmonics and fundamental equally well
    C. It is too sharply directional at lower frequencies
    D. It must be neutralized

E9D05: A. A disadvantage of using a multiband trapped antenna is that it might radiate harmonics.

What happens to the bandwidth of an antenna as it is shortened through the use of loading coils?
    A. It is increased
    B. It is decreased
    C. No change occurs
    D. It becomes flat

E9D06: B. As an antenna is shortened through the use of loading coils, the bandwidth decreases.

What is an advantage of using top loading in a shortened HF vertical antenna?
    A. Lower Q
    B. Greater structural strength
    C. Higher losses
    D. Improved radiation efficiency

E9D07: D. Using top loading in a shortened HF vertical antenna results in improved radiation efficiency.

What happens as the Q of an antenna increases?
    A. SWR bandwidth increases
    B. SWR bandwidth decreases
    C. Gain is reduced
    D. More common-mode current is present on the feed line

E9D08: B. As the Q of an antenna increases, SWR bandwidth decreases.

Copyright © Mometrix Media. You have been licensed one copy of this document for personal use only. Any other reproduction or redistribution is strictly prohibited. All rights reserved.

What is the function of a loading coil used as part of an HF mobile antenna?
A. To increase the SWR bandwidth
B. To lower the losses
C. To lower the Q
D. To cancel capacitive reactance

E9D09: D. Loading coils used in HF mobile antennas cancel capacitive reactance.

What happens to feed point impedance at the base of a fixed length HF mobile antenna as the frequency of operation is lowered?
A. The radiation resistance decreases and the capacitive reactance decreases
B. The radiation resistance decreases and the capacitive reactance increases
C. The radiation resistance increases and the capacitive reactance decreases
D. The radiation resistance increases and the capacitive reactance increases

E9D10: B. As the frequency of operation is lowered for a fixed-length HF mobile antenna, the radiation resistance decreases and the capacitive reactance increases.

Which of the following types of conductors would be best for minimizing losses in a station's RF ground system?
A. A resistive wire, such as spark plug wire
B. A wide flat copper strap
C. A cable with six or seven 18 gauge conductors in parallel
D. A single 12 gauge or 10 gauge stainless steel wire

E9D11: B. A wide flat copper strap would be best for minimizing losses in a station's RF ground system.

Which of the following would provide the best RF ground for your station?
A. A 50 ohm resistor connected to ground
B. An electrically short connection to a metal water pipe
C. An electrically short connection to 3 or 4 interconnected ground rods driven into the Earth
D. An electrically short connection to 3 or 4 interconnected ground rods via a series RF choke

E9D12: C. An electrically short connection to 3 or 4 interconnected ground rods driven into the Earth would provide the best RF ground for your station.

What usually occurs if a Yagi antenna is designed solely for maximum forward gain?
A. The front-to-back ratio increases
B. The front-to-back ratio decreases
C. The frequency response is widened over the whole frequency band
D. The SWR is reduced

E9D13: B. If a Yagi antenna is designed solely for maximum forward gain, it usually has a low front-to-back ratio.

Copyright © Mometrix Media. You have been licensed one copy of this document for personal use only. Any other reproduction or redistribution is strictly prohibited. All rights reserved.

E9E – Matching: matching antennas to feed lines; phasing lines; power dividers

What system matches a higher impedance transmission line to a lower impedance antenna by connecting the line to the driven element in two places spaced a fraction of a wavelength each side of element center?
- A. The gamma matching system
- B. The delta matching system
- C. The omega matching system
- D. The stub matching system

E9E01: B. The delta matching system matches a higher impedance transmission line to a lower impedance antenna by connecting the line to the driven element in two places spaced a fraction of a wavelength each side of element center.

What is the name of an antenna matching system that matches an unbalanced feed line to an antenna by feeding the driven element both at the center of the element and at a fraction of a wavelength to one side of center?
- A. The gamma match
- B. The delta match
- C. The epsilon match
- D. The stub match

E9E02: A. The gamma match matches an unbalanced feed line to an antenna by feeding the driven element both at the center of the element and at a fraction of a wavelength to one side of center.

What is the name of the matching system that uses a section of transmission line connected in parallel with the feed line at or near the feed point?
- A. The gamma match
- B. The delta match
- C. The omega match
- D. The stub match

E9E03: D. The stub match uses a section of transmission line connected in parallel with the feed line at or near the feed point.

What is the purpose of the series capacitor in a gamma-type antenna matching network?
- A. To provide DC isolation between the feed line and the antenna
- B. To cancel the inductive reactance of the matching network
- C. To provide a rejection notch that prevents the radiation of harmonics
- D. To transform the antenna impedance to a higher value

E9E04: B. The series capacitor in a gamma-type antenna matching network serves to cancel the inductive reactance of the matching network.

How must the driven element in a 3-element Yagi be tuned to use a hairpin matching system?
- A. The driven element reactance must be capacitive
- B. The driven element reactance must be inductive
- C. The driven element resonance must be lower than the operating frequency
- D. The driven element radiation resistance must be higher than the characteristic impedance of the transmission line

Copyright © Mometrix Media. You have been licensed one copy of this document for personal use only. Any other reproduction or redistribution is strictly prohibited. All rights reserved.

E9E05: A. The driven element in a 3-element Yagi must be tuned to have capacitive reactance to use a hairpin matching system.

What is the equivalent lumped-constant network for a hairpin matching system of a 3-element Yagi?
    A. Pi-network
    B. Pi-L-network
    C. A shunt inductor
    D. A series capacitor

E9E06: C. A shunt inductor is the equivalent lumped-constant network for a hairpin matching system of a 3-element Yagi.

What term best describes the interactions at the load end of a mismatched transmission line?
    A. Characteristic impedance
    B. Reflection coefficient
    C. Velocity factor
    D. Dielectric constant

E9E07: B. Reflection coefficient is the term most applicable to the interactions at the load end of a mismatched transmission line.

Which of the following measurements is characteristic of a mismatched transmission line?
    A. An SWR less than 1:1
    B. A reflection coefficient greater than 1
    C. A dielectric constant greater than 1
    D. An SWR greater than 1:1

E9E08: D. A mismatched transmission line would have a SWR greater than 1:1.

Which of these matching systems is an effective method of connecting a 50 ohm coaxial cable feed line to a grounded tower so it can be used as a vertical antenna?
    A. Double-bazooka match
    B. Hairpin match
    C. Gamma match
    D. All of these choices are correct

E9E09: C. Gamma match is an effective method of connecting a 50 ohm coaxial cable feed line to a grounded tower so it can be used as a vertical antenna.

Which of these choices is an effective way to match an antenna with a 100 ohm feed point impedance to a 50 ohm coaxial cable feed line?
    A. Connect a 1/4-wavelength open stub of 300 ohm twin-lead in parallel with the coaxial feed line where it connects to the antenna
    B. Insert a 1/2 wavelength piece of 300 ohm twin-lead in series between the antenna terminals and the 50 ohm feed cable
    C. Insert a 1/4-wavelength piece of 75 ohm coaxial cable transmission line in series between the antenna terminals and the 50 ohm feed cable
    D. Connect 1/2 wavelength shorted stub of 75 ohm cable in parallel with the 50 ohm cable where it attaches to the antenna

E9E10: C. Inserting a 1/4-wavelength piece of 75 ohm coaxial cable transmission line in series between the antenna terminals and the 50 ohm feed cable would be an effective way to match their impedances.

Copyright © Mometrix Media. You have been licensed one copy of this document for personal use only. Any other reproduction or redistribution is strictly prohibited. All rights reserved.

What is an effective way of matching a feed line to a VHF or UHF antenna when the impedances of both the antenna and feed line are unknown?

    A. Use a 50 ohm 1:1 balun between the antenna and feed line

    B. Use the universal stub matching technique

    C. Connect a series-resonant LC network across the antenna feed terminals

    D. Connect a parallel-resonant LC network across the antenna feed terminals

E9E11: B. The universal stub matching technique can be used to match unknown impedances.

What is the primary purpose of a phasing line when used with an antenna having multiple driven elements?

    A. It ensures that each driven element operates in concert with the others to create the desired antenna pattern

    B. It prevents reflected power from traveling back down the feed line and causing harmonic radiation from the transmitter

    C. It allows single-band antennas to operate on other bands

    D. It makes sure the antenna has a low-angle radiation pattern

E9E12: A. A phasing line ensures that each driven element operates in concert with the others to create the desired antenna pattern.

What is a use for a Wilkinson divider?

    A. It divides the operating frequency of a transmitter signal so it can be used on a lower frequency band

    B. It is used to feed high-impedance antennas from a low-impedance source

    C. It is used to divide power equally between two 50 ohm loads while maintaining 50 ohm input impedance

    D. It is used to feed low-impedance loads from a high-impedance source

E9E13: C. A Wilkinson divider divides the operating frequency of a transmitter signal so it can be used on a lower frequency band.

E9F – Transmission lines: characteristics of open and shorted feed lines; 1/8 wavelength; 1/4 wavelength; 1/2 wavelength; feed lines: coax versus open-wire; velocity factor; electrical length; coaxial cable dielectrics; velocity factor

What is the velocity factor of a transmission line?

    A. The ratio of the characteristic impedance of the line to the terminating impedance

    B. The index of shielding for coaxial cable

    C. The velocity of the wave in the transmission line multiplied by the velocity of light in a vacuum

    D. The velocity of the wave in the transmission line divided by the velocity of light in a vacuum

E9F01: D. The velocity factor of a transmission line is the velocity of the wave in the transmission line divided by the velocity of light in a vacuum.

Copyright © Mometrix Media. You have been licensed one copy of this document for personal use only. Any other reproduction or redistribution is strictly prohibited. All rights reserved.

Which of the following determines the velocity factor of a transmission line?
    A. The termination impedance
    B. The line length
    C. Dielectric materials used in the line
    D. The center conductor resistivity

E9F02: C. The dielectric materials used determine the velocity factor of a transmission line.

Why is the physical length of a coaxial cable transmission line shorter than its electrical length?
    A. Skin effect is less pronounced in the coaxial cable
    B. The characteristic impedance is higher in a parallel feed line
    C. The surge impedance is higher in a parallel feed line
    D. Electrical signals move more slowly in a coaxial cable than in air

E9F03: D. The physical length of a coaxial cable is shorter than its electrical length because electrical signals move more slowly in a coaxial cable than in air.

What is the typical velocity factor for a coaxial cable with solid polyethylene dielectric?
    A. 2.70
    B. 0.66
    C. 0.30
    D. 0.10

E9F04: B. Coaxial cables with solid polyethylene dielectrics usually have a velocity factor of 0.66.

What is the approximate physical length of a solid polyethylene dielectric coaxial transmission line that is electrically one-quarter wavelength long at 14.1 MHz?
    A. 20 meters
    B. 2.3 meters
    C. 3.5 meters
    D. 0.2 meters

E9F05: C. A solid polyethylene dielectric coaxial transmission line that is electrically one-quarter wavelength long at 14.1 MHz has an approximate physical length of 3.5 meters.

What is the approximate physical length of an air-insulated, parallel conductor transmission line that is electrically one-half wavelength long at 14.10 MHz?
    A. 15 meters
    B. 20 meters
    C. 10 meters
    D. 71 meters

E9F06: C. An air-insulated, parallel conductor transmission line that is electrically one-half wavelength long at 14.10 MHz has an approximate physical length of 10 meters.

How does ladder line compare to small-diameter coaxial cable such as RG-58 at 50 MHz?
    A. Lower loss
    B. Higher SWR
    C. Smaller reflection coefficient
    D. Lower velocity factor

E9F07: A. Ladder line has lower loss than small-diameter coaxial cable such as RG-58 at 50 MHz.

Copyright © Mometrix Media. You have been licensed one copy of this document for personal use only. Any other reproduction or redistribution is strictly prohibited. All rights reserved.

What is the term for the ratio of the actual speed at which a signal travels through a transmission line to the speed of light in a vacuum?
    A. Velocity factor
    B. Characteristic impedance
    C. Surge impedance
    D. Standing wave ratio

E9F08: A. Velocity factor is the term for the ratio of the actual speed at which a signal travels through a transmission line to the speed of light in a vacuum.

What is the approximate physical length of a solid polyethylene dielectric coaxial transmission line that is electrically one-quarter wavelength long at 7.2 MHz?
    A. 10 meters
    B. 6.9 meters
    C. 24 meters
    D. 50 meters

E9F09: B. A solid polyethylene dielectric coaxial transmission line that is electrically one-quarter wavelength long at 7.2 MHz has an approximate physical length of 6.9 meters.

What impedance does a 1/8 wavelength transmission line present to a generator when the line is shorted at the far end?
    A. A capacitive reactance
    B. The same as the characteristic impedance of the line
    C. An inductive reactance
    D. The same as the input impedance to the final generator stage

E9F10: C. A 1/8 wavelength transmission line presents an inductive reactance to a generator when the line is shorted at the far end.

What impedance does a 1/8 wavelength transmission line present to a generator when the line is open at the far end?
    A. The same as the characteristic impedance of the line
    B. An inductive reactance
    C. A capacitive reactance
    D. The same as the input impedance of the final generator stage

E9F11: C. A 1/8 wavelength transmission line presents a capacitive reactance to a generator when the line is open at the far end.

What impedance does a 1/4 wavelength transmission line present to a generator when the line is open at the far end?
    A. The same as the characteristic impedance of the line
    B. The same as the input impedance to the generator
    C. Very high impedance
    D. Very low impedance

E9F12: D. A 1/4 wavelength transmission line presents a very low impedance to a generator when the line is open at the far end.

Copyright © Mometrix Media. You have been licensed one copy of this document for personal use only. Any other reproduction or redistribution is strictly prohibited. All rights reserved.

What impedance does a 1/4 wavelength transmission line present to a generator when the line is shorted at the far end?
    A. Very high impedance
    B. Very low impedance
    C. The same as the characteristic impedance of the transmission line
    D. The same as the generator output impedance

E9F13: A. A 1/4 wavelength transmission line presents a very high impedance to a generator when the line is shorted at the far end.

What impedance does a 1/2 wavelength transmission line present to a generator when the line is shorted at the far end?
    A. Very high impedance
    B. Very low impedance
    C. The same as the characteristic impedance of the line
    D. The same as the output impedance of the generator

E9F14: B. A 1/2 wavelength transmission line presents a very low impedance to a generator when the line is shorted at the far end.

What impedance does a 1/2 wavelength transmission line present to a generator when the line is open at the far end?
    A. Very high impedance
    B. Very low impedance
    C. The same as the characteristic impedance of the line
    D. The same as the output impedance of the generator

E9F15: A. A 1/2 wavelength transmission line presents a very high impedance to a generator when the line is open at the far end.

Which of the following is a significant difference between foam dielectric coaxial cable and solid dielectric cable, assuming all other parameters are the same?
    A. Foam dielectric has lower safe operating voltage limits
    B. Foam dielectric has lower loss per unit of length
    C. Foam dielectric has higher velocity factor
    D. All of these choices are correct

E9F16: Foam dielectric cable has lower safe operating voltage limits, lower loss per unit of length, and higher velocity factor than solid dielectric cable, assuming all other parameters are the same.

E9G – The Smith chart

Which of the following can be calculated using a Smith chart?
    A. Impedance along transmission lines
    B. Radiation resistance
    C. Antenna radiation pattern
    D. Radio propagation

E9G01: A. Impedance along transmission lines can be calculated using a Smith chart.

Copyright © Mometrix Media. You have been licensed one copy of this document for personal use only. Any other reproduction or redistribution is strictly prohibited. All rights reserved.

What type of coordinate system is used in a Smith chart?
    A. Voltage circles and current arcs
    B. Resistance circles and reactance arcs
    C. Voltage lines and current chords
    D. Resistance lines and reactance chords

E9G02: B. Resistance circles and reactance arcs are used in Smith charts.

Which of the following is often determined using a Smith chart?
    A. Beam headings and radiation patterns
    B. Satellite azimuth and elevation bearings
    C. Impedance and SWR values in transmission lines
    D. Trigonometric functions

E9G03: C. Impedance and SWR values in transmission lines are often determined using a Smith chart.

What are the two families of circles and arcs that make up a Smith chart?
    A. Resistance and voltage
    B. Reactance and voltage
    C. Resistance and reactance
    D. Voltage and impedance

E9G04: C. Resistance and reactance are the two families of circles and arcs that make up a Smith chart.

What type of chart is shown in Figure E9-3?
    A. Smith chart
    B. Free space radiation directivity chart
    C. Elevation angle radiation pattern chart
    D. Azimuth angle radiation pattern chart

E9G05: A. A Smith chart is shown in Figure E9-3.

On the Smith chart shown in Figure E9-3, what is the name for the large outer circle on which the reactance arcs terminate?
    A. Prime axis
    B. Reactance axis
    C. Impedance axis
    D. Polar axis

E9G06: B. The large outer circle on which the reactance arcs terminate is the reactance axis in Figure E9-3.

On the Smith chart shown in Figure E9-3, what is the only straight line shown?
    A. The reactance axis
    B. The current axis
    C. The voltage axis
    D. The resistance axis

E9G07: D. On the Smith chart shown in Figure E9-3, the only straight line shown is the resistance axis.

Copyright © Mometrix Media. You have been licensed one copy of this document for personal use only. Any other reproduction or redistribution is strictly prohibited. All rights reserved.

What is the process of normalization with regard to a Smith chart?
  A. Reassigning resistance values with regard to the reactance axis
  B. Reassigning reactance values with regard to the resistance axis
  C. Reassigning impedance values with regard to the prime center
  D. Reassigning prime center with regard to the reactance axis

E9G08: C. Normalization with regard to a Smith chart is the process of reassigning reactance values with regard to the resistance axis.

What third family of circles is often added to a Smith chart during the process of solving problems?
  A. Standing wave ratio circles
  B. Antenna-length circles
  C. Coaxial-length circles
  D. Radiation-pattern circles

E9G09: A. Standing wave ratio circles are often added to a Smith chart during the process of solving problems.

What do the arcs on a Smith chart represent?
  A. Frequency
  B. SWR
  C. Points with constant resistance
  D. Points with constant reactance

E9G10: D. The arcs on a Smith chart represent points with constant reactance.

How are the wavelength scales on a Smith chart calibrated?
  A. In fractions of transmission line electrical frequency
  B. In fractions of transmission line electrical wavelength
  C. In fractions of antenna electrical wavelength
  D. In fractions of antenna electrical frequency

E9G11: B. The wavelength scales on a Smith chart are calibrated in fractions of transmission line electrical wavelength.

E9H – Receiving Antennas: radio direction finding antennas; Beverage Antennas; specialized receiving antennas; longwire receiving antennas

When constructing a Beverage antenna, which of the following factors should be included in the design to achieve good performance at the desired frequency?
  A. Its overall length must not exceed 1/4 wavelength
  B. It must be mounted more than 1 wavelength above ground
  C. It should be configured as a four-sided loop
  D. It should be one or more wavelengths long

E9H01: D. Beverage antennas should be one or more wavelengths long.

Copyright © Mometrix Media. You have been licensed one copy of this document for personal use only. Any other reproduction or redistribution is strictly prohibited. All rights reserved.

Which is generally true for low band (160 meter and 80 meter) receiving antennas?
    A. Atmospheric noise is so high that gain over a dipole is not important
    B. They must be erected at least 1/2 wavelength above the ground to attain good directivity
    C. Low loss coax transmission line is essential for good performance
    D. All of these choices are correct

E9H02: A. The gain of low band (160 meter and 80 meter) receiving antennas is not usually measured with respect to a dipole because atmospheric noise is so high.

What is an advantage of using a shielded loop antenna for direction finding?
    A. It automatically cancels ignition noise in mobile installations
    B. It is electro statically balanced against ground, giving better nulls
    C. It eliminates tracking errors caused by strong out-of-band signals
    D. It allows stations to communicate without giving away their position

E9H04: B. An advantage of using a shielded loop antenna for direction finding is that it is electrostatically balanced against ground, giving better nulls.

What is the main drawback of a wire-loop antenna for direction finding?
    A. It has a bidirectional pattern
    B. It is non-rotatable
    C. It receives equally well in all directions
    D. It is practical for use only on VHF bands

E9H05: A. The main drawback of a wire-loop antenna for direction finding is that it has a bidirectional pattern.

What is the triangulation method of direction finding?
    A. The geometric angles of sky waves from the source are used to determine its position
    B. A fixed receiving station plots three headings to the signal source
    C. Antenna headings from several different receiving locations are used to locate the signal source
    D. A fixed receiving station uses three different antennas to plot the location of the signal source

E9H06: C. The triangulation method of direction finding involves using antenna headings from several different receiving locations to locate the signal source.

Why is it advisable to use an RF attenuator on a receiver being used for direction finding?
    A. It narrows the bandwidth of the received signal to improve signal to noise ratio
    B. It compensates for the effects of an isotropic antenna, thereby improving directivity
    C. It reduces loss of received signals caused by antenna pattern nulls, thereby increasing sensitivity
    D. It prevents receiver overload which could make it difficult to determine peaks or nulls

E9H07: D. An RF attenuator on a receiver being used for direction finding prevents receiver overload.

What is the function of a sense antenna?
    A. It modifies the pattern of a DF antenna array to provide a null in one direction
    B. It increases the sensitivity of a DF antenna array
    C. It allows DF antennas to receive signals at different vertical angles
    D. It provides diversity reception that cancels multipath signals

E9H08: A. A sense antenna modifies the pattern of a DF antenna array to provide a null in one direction.

Copyright © Mometrix Media. You have been licensed one copy of this document for personal use only. Any other reproduction or redistribution is strictly prohibited. All rights reserved.

Which of the following describes the construction of a receiving loop antenna?
A. A large circularly polarized antenna
B. A small coil of wire tightly wound around a toroidal ferrite core
C. One or more turns of wire wound in the shape of a large open coil
D. A vertical antenna coupled to a feed line through an inductive loop of wire

E9H09: C. A receiving loop antenna is one or more turns of wire wound in the shape of a large open coil.

How can the output voltage of a multiple turn receiving loop antenna be increased?
A. By reducing the permeability of the loop shield
B. By increasing the number of wire turns in the loop and reducing the area of the loop structure
C. By winding adjacent turns in opposing directions
D. By increasing either the number of wire turns in the loop or the area of the loop structure or both

E9H10: D. The output voltage of a multiple turn receiving loop antenna can be increased by increasing either the number of wire turns in the loop or the area of the loop structure or both.

What characteristic of a cardioid pattern antenna is useful for direction finding?
A. A very sharp peak
B. A very sharp single null
C. Broad band response
D. High-radiation angle

E9H11: B. The very sharp single null part of a cardioid pattern antenna is useful for direction finding.

E0 – Safety

E0A – Safety: amateur radio safety practices; RF radiation hazards; hazardous materials; grounding

What is the primary function of an external earth connection or ground rod?
A. Reduce received noise
B. Lightning protection
C. Reduce RF current flow between pieces of equipment
D. Reduce RFI to telephones and home entertainment systems

E0A01: B. The primary function of an external earth connection or ground rod is lightning protection.

When evaluating RF exposure levels from your station at a neighbor's home, what must you do?
A. Make sure signals from your station are less than the controlled MPE limits
B. Make sure signals from your station are less than the uncontrolled MPE limits
C. You need only evaluate exposure levels on your own property
D. Advise your neighbors of the results of your tests

E0A02: B. You must make sure signals from your station are less than the uncontrolled MPE limits.

Copyright © Mometrix Media. You have been licensed one copy of this document for personal use only. Any other reproduction or redistribution is strictly prohibited. All rights reserved.

Which of the following would be a practical way to estimate whether the RF fields produced by an amateur radio station are within permissible MPE limits?
    A. Use a calibrated antenna analyzer
    B. Use a hand calculator plus Smith-chart equations to calculate the fields
    C. Use an antenna modeling program to calculate field strength at accessible locations
    D. All of the choices are correct

E0A03: C. Using an antenna modeling program to calculate field strength at accessible locations is a practical way to estimate whether the RF fields produced by an amateur radio station are within permissible MPE limits.

When evaluating a site with multiple transmitters operating at the same time, the operators and licensees of which transmitters are responsible for mitigating over-exposure situations?
    A. Only the most powerful transmitter
    B. Only commercial transmitters
    C. Each transmitter that produces 5 percent or more of its MPE limit at accessible locations
    D. Each transmitter operating with a duty-cycle greater than 50 percent

E0A04: C. When evaluating a site with multiple transmitters operating at the same time, the operators and licensees of each transmitter that produces 5 percent or more of its MPE limit at accessible locations are responsible for mitigating over-exposure situations.

What is one of the potential hazards of using microwaves in the amateur radio bands?
    A. Microwaves are ionizing radiation
    B. The high gain antennas commonly used can result in high exposure levels
    C. Microwaves often travel long distances by ionospheric reflection
    D. The extremely high frequency energy can damage the joints of antenna structures

E0A05: B. One of the potential hazards of using microwaves in the amateur radio bands is that the high gain antennas commonly used can result in high exposure levels.

Why are there separate electric (E) and magnetic (H) field MPE limits?
    A. The body reacts to electromagnetic radiation from both the E and H fields
    B. Ground reflections and scattering make the field impedance vary with location
    C. E field and H field radiation intensity peaks can occur at different locations
    D. All of these choices are correct

E0A06: D. There are multiple reasons why there are separate electric (E) and magnetic (H) field MPE limits, including different body reactions, varying field impedance due to ground reflections and scattering, and different radiation intensity peaks.

How may dangerous levels of carbon monoxide from an emergency generator be detected?
    A. By the odor
    B. Only with a carbon monoxide detector
    C. Any ordinary smoke detector can be used
    D. By the yellowish appearance of the gas

E0A07: B. Dangerous levels of carbon monoxide from an emergency generator can be detected only with a carbon monoxide detector.

Copyright © Mometrix Media. You have been licensed one copy of this document for personal use only. Any other reproduction or redistribution is strictly prohibited. All rights reserved.

What does SAR measure?
   A. Synthetic Aperture Ratio of the human body
   B. Signal Amplification Rating
   C. The rate at which RF energy is absorbed by the body
   D. The rate of RF energy reflected from stationary terrain

E0A08: C. SAR measures the rate at which RF energy is absorbed by the body.

Which insulating material commonly used as a thermal conductor for some types of electronic devices is extremely toxic if broken or crushed and the particles are accidentally inhaled?
   A. Mica
   B. Zinc oxide
   C. Beryllium Oxide
   D. Uranium Hexafluoride

E0A09: C. Beryllium Oxide is extremely toxic if broken or crushed and the particles are accidentally inhaled.

What toxic material may be present in some electronic components such as high voltage capacitors and transformers?
   A. Polychlorinated Biphenyls
   B. Polyethylene
   C. Polytetrafluorethylene
   D. Polymorphic silicon

E0A10: A. Polychlorinated biphenyls may be present in some electronic components such as high voltage capacitors and transformers.

Which of the following injuries can result from using high-power UHF or microwave transmitters?
   A. Hearing loss caused by high voltage corona discharge
   B. Blood clotting from the intense magnetic field
   C. Localized heating of the body from RF exposure in excess of the MPE limits
   D. Ingestion of ozone gas from the cooling system

E0A11: C. Localized heating of the body can occur from RF exposure in excess of the MPE limits.

Copyright © Mometrix Media. You have been licensed one copy of this document for personal use only. Any other reproduction or redistribution is strictly prohibited. All rights reserved.

Extra Class Practice Test 1

Practice Questions

1. When using a transceiver that displays the carrier frequency of phone signals, which of the following displayed frequencies represents the highest frequency at which a properly adjusted USB emission will be totally within the band?
    a. The exact upper band edge
    b. 300 Hz below the upper band edge
    c. 1 kHz below the upper band edge
    d. 3 kHz below the upper band edge

2. Which of the following constitutes a spurious emission?
    a. An amateur station transmission made at random without the proper call sign identification
    b. A signal transmitted to prevent its detection by any station other than the intended recipient
    c. Any transmitted signal that unintentionally interferes with another licensed radio station
    d. An emission outside its necessary bandwidth that can be reduced or eliminated without affecting the information transmitted

3. What is a remotely controlled station?
    a. A station operated away from its regular home location
    b. A station controlled by someone other than the licensee
    c. A station operating under automatic control
    d. A station controlled indirectly through a control link

4. What is the definition of the term telemetry?
    a. One-way transmission of measurements at a distance from the measuring instrument
    b. Two-way radiotelephone transmissions in excess of 1000 feet
    c. Two-way single channel transmissions of data
    d. One-way transmission that initiates, modifies, or terminates the functions of a device at a distance

5. What is the minimum number of qualified VEs required to administer an Element 4 amateur operator license examination?
    a. 5
    b. 2
    c. 4
    d. 3

6. On what frequencies are spread spectrum transmissions permitted?
    a. Only on amateur frequencies above 50 MHz
    b. Only on amateur frequencies above 222 MHz
    c. Only on amateur frequencies above 420 MHz
    d. Only on amateur frequencies above 144 MHz

7. What is the direction of an ascending pass for an amateur satellite?
    a. From west to east
    b. From east to west
    c. From south to north
    d. From north to south

Copyright © Mometrix Media. You have been licensed one copy of this document for personal use only. Any other reproduction or redistribution is strictly prohibited. All rights reserved.

8. How many times per second is a new frame transmitted in a fast-scan (NTSC) television system?
   a. 30
   b. 60
   c. 90
   d. 120

9. Which of the following is true about contest operating?
   a. Operators are permitted to make contacts even if they do not submit a log
   b. Interference to other amateurs is unavoidable and therefore acceptable
   c. It is mandatory to transmit the call sign of the station being worked as part of every transmission to that station
   d. Every contest requires a signal report in the exchange

10. Which of the following digital modes is especially designed for use for meteor scatter signals?
    a. WSPR
    b. FSK441
    c. Hellschreiber
    d. APRS

11. Which type of modulation is common for data emissions below 30 MHz?
    a. DTMF tones modulating an FM signal
    b. FSK
    c. Pulse modulation
    d. Spread spectrum

12. What is the approximate maximum separation measured along the surface of the Earth between two stations communicating by Moon bounce?
    a. 500 miles, if the Moon is at perigee
    b. 2000 miles, if the Moon is at apogee
    c. 5000 miles, if the Moon is at perigee
    d. 12,000 miles, if the Moon is visible by both stations

13. What is transequatorial propagation?
    a. Propagation between two mid-latitude points at approximately the same distance north and south of the magnetic equator
    b. Propagation between any two points located on the magnetic equator
    c. Propagation between two continents by way of ducts along the magnetic equator
    d. Propagation between two stations at the same latitude

14. What does the term ray tracing describe in regard to radio communications?
    a. The process in which an electronic display presents a pattern
    b. Modeling a radio wave's path through the ionosphere
    c. Determining the radiation pattern from an array of antennas
    d. Evaluating high voltage sources for X-Rays

15. Which of the following parameter determines the bandwidth of a digital or computer-based oscilloscope?
    a. Input capacitance
    b. Input impedance
    c. Sampling rate
    d. Sample resolution

Copyright © Mometrix Media. You have been licensed one copy of this document for personal use only. Any other reproduction or redistribution is strictly prohibited. All rights reserved.

16. Which of the following factors most affects the accuracy of a frequency counter?
    a. Input attenuator accuracy
    b. Time base accuracy
    c. Decade divider accuracy
    d. Temperature coefficient of the logic

17. What is an effect of excessive phase noise in the local oscillator section of a receiver?
    a. It limits the receiver's ability to receive strong signals
    b. It reduces receiver sensitivity
    c. It decreases receiver third-order intermodulation distortion dynamic range
    d. It can cause strong signals on nearby frequencies to interfere with reception of weak signals

18. What is meant by the blocking dynamic range of a receiver?
    a. The difference in dB between the noise floor and the level of an incoming signal which will cause 1 dB of gain compression
    b. The minimum difference in dB between the levels of two FM signals which will cause one signal to block the other
    c. The difference in dB between the noise floor and the third order intercept point
    d. The minimum difference in dB between two signals which produce third order intermodulation products greater than the noise floor

19. Which of the following types of receiver noise can often be reduced by use of a receiver noise blanker?
    a. Ignition noise
    b. Broadband white noise
    c. Heterodyne interference
    d. All of these choices are correct

20. What can cause the voltage across reactances in series to be larger than the voltage applied to them?
    a. Resonance
    b. Capacitance
    c. Conductance
    d. Resistance

21. What is the term for the time required for the capacitor in an RC circuit to be charged to 63.2% of the applied voltage?
    a. An exponential rate of one
    b. One time constant
    c. One exponential period
    d. A time factor of one

22. Which of the following represents a capacitive reactance in rectangular notation?
    a. $-jX$
    b. $+jX$
    c. X
    d. Omega

23. What is the result of skin effect?
    a. As frequency increases, RF current flows in a thinner layer of the conductor, closer to the surface
    b. As frequency decreases, RF current flows in a thinner layer of the conductor, closer to the surface
    c. Thermal effects on the surface of the conductor increase the impedance
    d. Thermal effects on the surface of the conductor decrease the impedance

Copyright © Mometrix Media. You have been licensed one copy of this document for personal use only. Any other reproduction or redistribution is strictly prohibited. All rights reserved.

24. In what application is gallium arsenide used as a semiconductor material in preference to germanium or silicon?
    a. In high-current rectifier circuits
    b. In high-power audio circuits
    c. In microwave circuits
    d. In very low frequency RF circuits

25. What is the most useful characteristic of a Zener diode?
    a. A constant current drop under conditions of varying voltage
    b. A constant voltage drop under conditions of varying current
    c. A negative resistance region
    d. An internal capacitance that varies with the applied voltage

26. What is the function of hysteresis in a comparator?
    a. To prevent input noise from causing unstable output signals
    b. To allow the comparator to be used with AC input signal
    c. To cause the output to change states continually
    d. To increase the sensitivity

27. How many turns will be required to produce a 5-microhenry inductor using a powdered-iron toroidal core that has an inductance index (A L) value of 40 microhenrys/100 turns?
    a. 35 turns
    b. 13 turns
    c. 79 turns
    d. 141 turns

28. Which of the following is true of a charge-coupled device (CCD)?
    a. Its phase shift changes rapidly with frequency
    b. It is a CMOS analog-to-digital converter
    c. It samples an analog signal and passes it in stages from the input to the output
    d. It is used in a battery charger circuit

29. What is photoconductivity?
    a. The conversion of photon energy to electromotive energy
    b. The increased conductivity of an illuminated semiconductor
    c. The conversion of electromotive energy to photon energy
    d. The decreased conductivity of an illuminated semiconductor

30. Which is a bi-stable circuit?
    a. An "AND" gate
    b. An "OR" gate
    c. A flip-flop
    d. A clock

31. For what portion of a signal cycle does a Class AB amplifier operate?
    a. More than 180 degrees but less than 360 degrees
    b. Exactly 180 degrees
    c. The entire cycle
    d. Less than 180 degrees

- 495 -

Copyright © Mometrix Media. You have been licensed one copy of this document for personal use only. Any other reproduction or redistribution is strictly prohibited. All rights reserved.

32. How are the capacitors and inductors of a low-pass filter Pi-network arranged between the network's input and output?
    a. Two inductors are in series between the input and output, and a capacitor is connected between the two inductors and ground
    b. Two capacitors are in series between the input and output, and an inductor is connected between the two capacitors and ground
    c. An inductor is connected between the input and ground, another inductor is connected between the output and ground, and a capacitor is connected between the input and output
    d. A capacitor is connected between the input and ground, another capacitor is connected between the output and ground, and an inductor is connected between input and output

33. What is one characteristic of a linear electronic voltage regulator?
    a. It has a ramp voltage as its output
    b. It eliminates the need for a pass transistor
    c. The control element duty cycle is proportional to the line or load conditions
    d. The conduction of a control element is varied to maintain a constant output voltage

34. Which of the following can be used to generate FM phone emissions?
    a. A balanced modulator on the audio amplifier
    b. A reactance modulator on the oscillator
    c. A reactance modulator on the final amplifier
    d. A balanced modulator on the oscillator

35. What is meant by direct digital conversion as applied to software defined radios?
    a. Software is converted from source code to object code during operation of the receiver
    b. Incoming RF is converted to a control voltage for a voltage controlled oscillator
    c. Incoming RF is digitized by an analog-to-digital converter without being mixed with a local oscillator signal
    d. A switching mixer is used to generate I and Q signals directly from the RF input

36. What is the typical output impedance of an integrated circuit op-amp?
    a. Very low
    b. Very high
    c. 100 ohms
    d. 1000 ohms

37. What are three oscillator circuits used in Amateur Radio equipment?
    a. Taft, Pierce and negative feedback
    b. Pierce, Fenner and Beane
    c. Taft, Hartley and Pierce
    d. Colpitts, Hartley and Pierce

38. What is the name of the process that shows that a square wave is made up of a sine wave plus all of its odd harmonics?
    a. Fourier analysis
    b. Vector analysis
    c. Numerical analysis
    d. Differential analysis

Copyright © Mometrix Media. You have been licensed one copy of this document for personal use only. Any other reproduction or redistribution is strictly prohibited. All rights reserved.

39. What is the term for the ratio between the frequency deviation of an RF carrier wave and the modulating frequency of its corresponding FM-phone signal?
   a. FM compressibility
   b. Quieting index
   c. Percentage of modulation
   d. Modulation index

40. How is Forward Error Correction implemented?
   a. By the receiving station repeating each block of three data characters
   b. By transmitting a special algorithm to the receiving station along with the data characters
   c. By transmitting extra data that may be used to detect and correct transmission errors
   d. By varying the frequency shift of the transmitted signal according to a predefined algorithm

41. Why are received spread spectrum signals resistant to interference?
   a. Signals not using the spread spectrum algorithm are suppressed in the receiver
   b. The high power used by a spread spectrum transmitter keeps its signal from being easily overpowered
   c. The receiver is always equipped with a digital blanker
   d. If interference is detected by the receiver it will signal the transmitter to change frequencies

42. What describes an isotropic antenna?
   a. A grounded antenna used to measure earth conductivity
   b. A horizontally polarized antenna used to compare Yagi antennas
   c. A theoretical antenna used as a reference for antenna gain
   d. A spacecraft antenna used to direct signals toward the earth

43. In the antenna radiation pattern shown in Figure E9-1 (located at the end of the guide), what is the 3 dB beam-width?
   a. 75 degrees
   b. 50 degrees
   c. 25 degrees
   d. 30 degrees

44. What is the radiation pattern of two 1/4-wavelength vertical antennas spaced 1/2-wavelength apart and fed 180 degrees out of phase?
   a. Cardioid
   b. Omni-directional
   c. A figure-8 broadside to the axis of the array
   d. A figure-8 oriented along the axis of the array

45. How does the gain of an ideal parabolic dish antenna change when the operating frequency is doubled?
   a. Gain does not change
   b. Gain is multiplied by 0.707
   c. Gain increases by 6 dB
   d. Gain increases by 3 dB

Copyright © Mometrix Media. You have been licensed one copy of this document for personal use only. Any other reproduction or redistribution is strictly prohibited. All rights reserved.

46. What system matches a higher impedance transmission line to a lower impedance antenna by connecting the line to the driven element in two places spaced a fraction of a wavelength each side of element center?
    a. The gamma matching system
    b. The delta matching system
    c. The omega matching system
    d. The stub matching system

47. What is the velocity factor of a transmission line?
    a. The ratio of the characteristic impedance of the line to the terminating impedance
    b. The index of shielding for coaxial cable
    c. The velocity of the wave in the transmission line multiplied by the velocity of light in a vacuum
    d. The velocity of the wave in the transmission line divided by the velocity of light in a vacuum

48. Which of the following can be calculated using a Smith chart?
    a. Impedance along transmission lines
    b. Radiation resistance
    c. Antenna radiation pattern
    d. Radio propagation

49. When constructing a Beverage antenna, which of the following factors should be included in the design to achieve good performance at the desired frequency?
    a. Its overall length must not exceed 1/4 wavelength
    b. It must be mounted more than 1 wavelength above ground
    c. It should be configured as a four-sided loop
    d. It should be one or more wavelengths long

50. What is the primary function of an external earth connection or ground rod?
    a. Reduce received noise
    b. Lightning protection
    c. Reduce RF current flow between pieces of equipment
    d. Reduce RFI to telephones and home entertainment systems

Copyright © Mometrix Media. You have been licensed one copy of this document for personal use only. Any other reproduction or redistribution is strictly prohibited. All rights reserved.

Answers and Explanations

1. **D:** The highest frequency at which a properly adjusted USB emission will be totally within the band is 3 kHz below the upper band edge.

2. **D:** A spurious emission is an emission outside its necessary bandwidth that can be reduced or eliminated without affecting the information transmitted.

3. **D:** A remotely controlled station is a station controlled indirectly through a control link.

4. **A.** Telemetry is one-way transmission of measurements at a distance from the measuring instrument.

5. **D:** The minimum number of qualified VEs required to administer an Element 4 amateur operator license examination is 3.

6. **B:** spread spectrum transmissions are permitted only on amateur frequencies above 222 MHz.

7. **C:** An amateur satellite goes from south to north in an ascending pass.

8. **A:** A new frame transmitted 30 times per second in a fast-scan (NTSC) television system.

9. **A:** In contest operating, operators are permitted to make contacts even if they do not submit a log.

10. **B:** The FSK441 digital mode is especially designed for use for meteor scatter signals.

11. **B:** FSK modulation is common for data emissions below 30 MHz.

12. **D:** The approximate maximum separation measured along the surface of the Earth between two stations communicating by Moon bounce is 12,000 miles, if the Moon is visible by both stations.

13. **A:** Transequatorial propagation is propagation between two mid-latitude points at approximately the same distance north and south of the magnetic equator.

14. **B:** Ray tracing is modeling a radio wave's path through the ionosphere.

15. **C:** Sampling rate determines the bandwidth of a digital or computer-based oscilloscope.

16. **B:** Time base accuracy most affects the overall accuracy of a frequency counter.

17. **D:** Excessive phase noise in the local oscillator section of a receiver can cause strong signals on nearby frequencies to interfere with reception of weak signals.

18. **A:** The blocking dynamic range of a receiver is the difference in dB between the noise floor and the level of an incoming signal which will cause 1 dB of gain compression

19. **A:** Ignition noise can often be reduced by use of a receiver noise blanker.

20. **A:** Resonance can cause the voltage across reactances in series to be larger than the voltage applied to them.

21. **B:** A time-constant is the time required for the capacitor in an RC circuit to be charged to 63.2% of the applied voltage.

22. **A:** "–jX" represents a capacitive reactance in rectangular notation.

Copyright © Mometrix Media. You have been licensed one copy of this document for personal use only. Any other reproduction or redistribution is strictly prohibited. All rights reserved.

23. A: As a result of skin effect, as frequency increases, RF current flows in a thinner layer of the conductor, closer to the surface.

24. C: Gallium arsenide is used as a semiconductor material in preference to germanium or silicon in microwave circuits.

25. B: Zener diodes are most useful because they have a constant voltage drop under conditions of varying current.

26. A: Hysteresis in a comparator prevents input noise from causing unstable output signals.

27. A: 35 turns will be required to produce a 5-microhenry inductor using a powdered-iron toroidal core that has an inductance index (A L) value of 40 microhenrys/100 turns.

28. C: A charge-coupled device (CCD) samples an analog signal and passes it in stages from the input to the output.

29. B: Photoconductivity is the increased conductivity of an illuminated semiconductor.

30. C: Flip-flops are bi-stable circuits.

31. A: A class AB amplifier operates on more than 180 degrees but less than 360 degrees of a signal cycle.

32. D: In a low-pass filter Pi-network, a capacitor is connected between the input and ground, another capacitor is connected between the output and ground, and an inductor is connected between input and output.

33. D: A linear electronic voltage regulator varies the conduction of a control element to maintain a constant output voltage.

34. B: A reactance modulator on the oscillator can be used to generate FM phone emissions.

35. C: Direct digital conversion is when incoming RF is digitized by an analog-to-digital converter without being mixed with a local oscillator signal.

36. A: The typical output impedance of an integrated circuit op-amp is very low.

37. D: Colpitts, Hartley and Pierce are all types of oscillator circuits used in Amateur Radio equipment.

38. A: Fourier analysis shows that a square wave is made up of a sine wave plus all of its odd harmonics.

39. D: The ratio between the frequency deviation of an RF carrier wave and the modulating frequency of its corresponding FM-phone signal is the modulation index.

40. C: Forward Error Correction is implemented by transmitting extra data that may be used to detect and correct transmission errors.

41. A: Received spread spectrum signals are resistant to interference because signals not using the spread spectrum algorithm are suppressed in the receiver.

42. C: An isotropic antenna is a theoretical antenna used as a reference for antenna gain.

43. B: In the antenna radiation pattern shown in Figure E9-1, the 3 dB beam-width is 50 degrees.

Copyright © Mometrix Media. You have been licensed one copy of this document for personal use only. Any other reproduction or redistribution is strictly prohibited. All rights reserved.

44. D: The radiation pattern of two 1/4-wavelength vertical antennas spaced 1/2-wavelength apart and fed 180 degrees out of phase is a figure-8 oriented along the axis of the array.

45. C: The gain of an ideal parabolic dish antenna increases by 6 dB when the operating frequency is doubled.

46. B: The delta matching system matches a higher impedance transmission line to a lower impedance antenna by connecting the line to the driven element in two places spaced a fraction of a wavelength each side of element center.

47. D: The velocity factor of a transmission line is the velocity of the wave in the transmission line divided by the velocity of light in a vacuum.

48. A: Impedance along transmission lines can be calculated using a Smith chart.

49. D: Beverage antennas should be one or more wavelengths long.

50. B: The primary function of an external earth connection or ground rod is lightning protection.

Copyright © Mometrix Media. You have been licensed one copy of this document for personal use only. Any other reproduction or redistribution is strictly prohibited. All rights reserved.

Extra Class Practice Test 2

Practice Questions

1. When using a transceiver that displays the carrier frequency of phone signals, which of the following displayed frequencies represents the lowest frequency at which a properly adjusted LSB emission will be totally within the band?
    a. The exact lower band edge
    b. 300 Hz above the lower band edge
    c. 1 kHz above the lower band edge
    d. 3 kHz above the lower band edge

2. Which of the following factors might cause the physical location of an amateur station apparatus or antenna structure to be restricted?
    a. The location is near an area of political conflict
    b. The location is of geographical or horticultural importance
    c. The location is in an ITU Zone designated for coordination with one or more foreign governments
    d. The location is of environmental importance or significant in American history, architecture, or culture

3. What is meant by automatic control of a station?
    a. The use of devices and procedures for control so that the control operator does not have to be present at a control point
    b. A station operating with its output power controlled automatically
    c. Remotely controlling a station's antenna pattern through a directional control link
    d. The use of a control link between a control point and a locally controlled station

4. What is the amateur satellite service?
    a. A radio navigation service using satellites for the purpose of self training, intercommunication and technical studies carried out by amateurs
    b. A spacecraft launching service for amateur-built satellites
    c. A radio communications service using amateur radio stations on satellites
    d. A radio communications service using stations on Earth satellites for public service broadcast

5. Where are the questions for all written U.S. amateur license examinations listed?
    a. In FCC Part 97
    b. In a question pool maintained by the FCC
    c. In a question pool maintained by all the VECs
    d. In the appropriate FCC Report and Order

6. What privileges are authorized in the U.S. to persons holding an amateur service license granted by the Government of Canada?
    a. None, they must obtain a U.S. license
    b. All privileges of the Extra Class license
    c. The operating terms and conditions of the Canadian amateur service license, not to exceed U.S. Extra Class privileges
    d. Full privileges, up to and including those of the Extra Class License, on the 80, 40, 20, 15, and 10 meter bands

Copyright © Mometrix Media. You have been licensed one copy of this document for personal use only. Any other reproduction or redistribution is strictly prohibited. All rights reserved.

7. What is the direction of a descending pass for an amateur satellite?
   a. From north to south
   b. From west to east
   c. From east to west
   d. From south to north

8. How many horizontal lines make up a fast-scan (NTSC) television frame?
   a. 30
   b. 60
   c. 525
   d. 1080

9. Which of the following best describes the term self-spotting in regards to HF contest operating?
   a. The generally prohibited practice of posting one's own call sign and frequency on a spotting network
   b. The acceptable practice of manually posting the call signs of stations on a spotting network
   c. A manual technique for rapidly zero beating or tuning to a station's frequency before calling that station
   d. An automatic method for rapidly zero beating or tuning to a station's frequency before calling that station

10. Which of the following is a good technique for making meteor scatter contacts?
    a. 15 second timed transmission sequences with stations alternating based on location
    b. Use of high speed CW or digital modes
    c. Short transmission with rapidly repeated call signs and signal reports
    d. All of these choices are correct

11. What do the letters FEC mean as they relate to digital operation?
    a. Forward Error Correction
    b. First Error Correction
    c. Fatal Error Correction
    d. Final Error Correction

12. What characterizes libration fading of an EME signal?
    a. A slow change in the pitch of the CW signal
    b. A fluttery irregular fading
    c. A gradual loss of signal as the Sun rises
    d. The returning echo is several Hertz lower in frequency than the transmitted signal

13. What is the approximate maximum range for signals using transequatorial propagation?
    a. 1000 miles
    b. 2500 miles
    c. 5000 miles
    d. 7500 miles

14. What is indicated by a rising A or K index?
    a. Increasing disruption of the geomagnetic field
    b. Decreasing disruption of the geomagnetic field
    c. Higher levels of solar UV radiation
    d. An increase in the critical frequency

Copyright © Mometrix Media. You have been licensed one copy of this document for personal use only. Any other reproduction or redistribution is strictly prohibited. All rights reserved.

15. Which of the following parameters would a spectrum analyzer display on the vertical and horizontal axes?
    a. RF amplitude and time
    b. RF amplitude and frequency
    c. SWR and frequency
    d. SWR and time

16. What is an advantage of using a bridge circuit to measure impedance?
    a. It provides an excellent match under all conditions
    b. It is relatively immune to drift in the signal generator source
    c. It is very precise in obtaining a signal null
    d. It can display results directly in Smith chart format

17. Which of the following portions of a receiver can be effective in eliminating image signal interference?
    a. A front-end filter or pre-selector
    b. A narrow IF filter
    c. A notch filter
    d. A properly adjusted product detector

18. Which of the following describes two problems caused by poor dynamic range in a communications receiver?
    a. Cross-modulation of the desired signal and desensitization from strong adjacent signals
    b. Oscillator instability requiring frequent retuning and loss of ability to recover the opposite sideband
    c. Cross-modulation of the desired signal and insufficient audio power to operate the speaker
    d. Oscillator instability and severe audio distortion of all but the strongest received signals

19. Which of the following types of receiver noise can often be reduced with a DSP noise filter?
    a. Broadband white noise
    b. Ignition noise
    c. Power line noise
    d. All of these choices are correct

20. What is resonance in an electrical circuit?
    a. The highest frequency that will pass current
    b. The lowest frequency that will pass current
    c. The frequency at which the capacitive reactance equals the inductive reactance
    d. The frequency at which the reactive impedance equals the resistive impedance

21. What is the term for the time it takes for a charged capacitor in an RC circuit to discharge to 36.8% of its initial voltage?
    a. One discharge period
    b. An exponential discharge rate of one
    c. A discharge factor of one
    d. One time constant

22. How are impedances described in polar coordinates?
    a. By X and R values
    b. By real and imaginary parts
    c. By phase angle and amplitude
    d. By Y and G values

- 504 -

Copyright © Mometrix Media. You have been licensed one copy of this document for personal use only. Any other reproduction or redistribution is strictly prohibited. All rights reserved.

23. Why is it important to keep lead lengths short for components used in circuits for VHF and above?
    a. To increase the thermal time constant
    b. To avoid unwanted inductive reactance
    c. To maintain component lifetime
    d. All of these choices are correct

24. Which of the following semiconductor materials contains excess free electrons?
    a. N-type
    b. P-type
    c. Bipolar
    d. Insulated gate

25. What is an important characteristic of a Schottky diode as compared to an ordinary silicon diode when used as a power supply rectifier?
    a. Much higher reverse voltage breakdown
    b. Controlled reverse avalanche voltage
    c. Enhanced carrier retention time
    d. Less forward voltage drop

26. What happens when the level of a comparator's input signal crosses the threshold?
    a. The IC input can be damaged
    b. The comparator changes its output state
    c. The comparator enters latch-up
    d. The feedback loop becomes unstable

27. What is the equivalent circuit of a quartz crystal?
    a. Motional capacitance, motional inductance, and loss resistance in series, all in parallel with a shunt capacitor representing electrode and stray capacitance
    b. Motional capacitance, motional inductance, loss resistance, and a capacitor representing electrode and stray capacitance all in parallel
    c. Motional capacitance, motional inductance, loss resistance, and a capacitor representing electrode and stray capacitance all in series
    d. Motional inductance and loss resistance in series, paralleled with motional capacitance and a capacitor representing electrode and stray capacitance

28. Which of the following device packages is a through-hole type?
    a. DIP
    b. PLCC
    c. Ball grid array
    d. SOT

29. What happens to the conductivity of a photoconductive material when light shines on it?
    a. It increases
    b. It decreases
    c. It stays the same
    d. It becomes unstable

Copyright © Mometrix Media. You have been licensed one copy of this document for personal use only. Any other reproduction or redistribution is strictly prohibited. All rights reserved.

30. What is the function of a decade counter digital IC?
   a. It produces one output pulse for every ten input pulses
   b. It decodes a decimal number for display on a seven segment LED display
   c. It produces ten output pulses for every input pulse
   d. It adds two decimal numbers together

31. What is a Class D amplifier?
   a. A type of amplifier that uses switching technology to achieve high efficiency
   b. A low power amplifier that uses a differential amplifier for improved linearity
   c. An amplifier that uses drift-mode FETs for high efficiency
   d. A frequency doubling amplifier

32. Which of the following is a property of a T-network with series capacitors and a parallel shunt inductor?
   a. It is a low-pass filter
   b. It is a band-pass filter
   c. It is a high-pass filter
   d. It is a notch filter

33. What is one characteristic of a switching electronic voltage regulator?
   a. The resistance of a control element is varied in direct proportion to the line voltage or load current
   b. It is generally less efficient than a linear regulator
   c. The controlled device's duty cycle is changed to produce a constant average output voltage
   d. It gives a ramp voltage at its output

34. What is the function of a reactance modulator?
   a. To produce PM signals by using an electrically variable resistance
   b. To produce AM signals by using an electrically variable inductance or capacitance
   c. To produce AM signals by using an electrically variable resistance
   d. To produce PM signals by using an electrically variable inductance or capacitance

35. What kind of digital signal processing audio filter is used to remove unwanted noise from a received SSB signal?
   a. An adaptive filter
   b. A crystal-lattice filter
   c. A Hilbert-transform filter
   d. A phase-inverting filter

36. What is the effect of ringing in a filter?
   a. An echo caused by a long time delay
   b. A reduction in high frequency response
   c. Partial cancellation of the signal over a range of frequencies
   d. Undesired oscillations added to the desired signal

37. Which describes a microphonic?
   a. An IC used for amplifying microphone signals
   b. Distortion caused by RF pickup on the microphone cable
   c. Changes in oscillator frequency due to mechanical vibration
   d. Excess loading of the microphone by an oscillator

Copyright © Mometrix Media. You have been licensed one copy of this document for personal use only. Any other reproduction or redistribution is strictly prohibited. All rights reserved.

38. What type of wave has a rise time significantly faster than its fall time (or vice versa)?
   a. A cosine wave
   b. A square wave
   c. A sawtooth wave
   d. A sine wave

39. How does the modulation index of a phase-modulated emission vary with RF carrier frequency (the modulated frequency)?
   a. It increases as the RF carrier frequency increases
   b. It decreases as the RF carrier frequency increases
   c. It varies with the square root of the RF carrier frequency
   d. It does not depend on the RF carrier frequency

40. What is the definition of symbol rate in a digital transmission?
   a. The number of control characters in a message packet
   b. The duration of each bit in a message sent over the air
   c. The rate at which the waveform of a transmitted signal changes to convey information
   d. The number of characters carried per second by the station-to-station link

41. What spread spectrum communications technique uses a high speed binary bit stream to shift the phase of an RF carrier?
   a. Frequency hopping
   b. Direct sequence
   c. Binary phase-shift keying
   d. Phase compandored spread spectrum

42. What antenna has no gain in any direction?
   a. Quarter-wave vertical
   b. Yagi
   c. Half-wave dipole
   d. Isotropic antenna

43. In the antenna radiation pattern shown in Figure E9-1 (located at the end of the guide), what is the front-to-back ratio?
   a. 36 dB
   b. 18 dB
   c. 24 dB
   d. 14 dB

44. What is the radiation pattern of two 1/4 wavelength vertical antennas spaced 1/4 wavelength apart and fed 90 degrees out of phase?
   a. Cardioid
   b. A figure-8 end-fire along the axis of the array
   c. A figure-8 broadside to the axis of the array
   d. Omni-directional

Copyright © Mometrix Media. You have been licensed one copy of this document for personal use only. Any other reproduction or redistribution is strictly prohibited. All rights reserved.

45. How can linearly polarized Yagi antennas be used to produce circular polarization?
   a. Stack two Yagis fed 90 degrees out of phase to form an array with the respective elements in parallel planes
   b. Stack two Yagis fed in phase to form an array with the respective elements in parallel planes
   c. Arrange two Yagis perpendicular to each other with the driven elements at the same point on the boom fed 90 degrees out of phase
   d. Arrange two Yagis collinear to each other with the driven elements fed 180 degrees out of phase

46. What is the name of an antenna matching system that matches an unbalanced feed line to an antenna by feeding the driven element both at the center of the element and at a fraction of a wavelength to one side of center?
   a. The gamma match
   b. The delta match
   c. The epsilon match
   d. The stub match

47. Which of the following determines the velocity factor of a transmission line?
   a. The termination impedance
   b. The line length
   c. Dielectric materials used in the line
   d. The center conductor resistivity

48. What type of coordinate system is used in a Smith chart?
   a. Voltage circles and current arcs
   b. Resistance circles and reactance arcs
   c. Voltage lines and current chords
   d. Resistance lines and reactance chords

49. Which is generally true for low band (160 meter and 80 meter) receiving antennas?
   a. Atmospheric noise is so high that gain over a dipole is not important
   b. They must be erected at least 1/2 wavelength above the ground to attain good directivity
   c. Low loss coax transmission line is essential for good performance
   d. All of these choices are correct

50. When evaluating RF exposure levels from your station at a neighbor's home, what must you do?
   a. Make sure signals from your station are less than the controlled MPE limits
   b. Make sure signals from your station are less than the uncontrolled MPE limits
   c. You need only evaluate exposure levels on your own property
   d. Advise your neighbors of the results of your tests

Copyright © Mometrix Media. You have been licensed one copy of this document for personal use only. Any other reproduction or redistribution is strictly prohibited. All rights reserved.

Answers and Explanations

1. D: The lowest frequency at which a properly adjusted LSB emission will be totally within the band is 3 kHz above the lower band edge.

2. D: If the location of an amateur station apparatus or antenna structure is of environmental importance or significant in American history, architecture, or culture, it may be restricted.

3. A: Automatic control of a station is the use of devices and procedures for control so that the control operator does not have to be present at a control point.

4. C: The amateur satellite service is a radio communications service using amateur radio stations on satellites.

5. C: The questions for all written U.S. amateur license examinations listed are in a question pool maintained by all the VECs.

6. C: Persons in the US holding an amateur service license granted by the Government of Canada are granted the operating terms and conditions of the Canadian amateur service license, not to exceed U.S. Extra Class privileges.

7. A: An amateur satellite goes from north to south in a descending pass.

8. C: There are 525 horizontal lines in a fast-scan (NTSC) television frame.

9. A: In HF contest operating, self-spotting is the generally prohibited practice of posting one's own call sign and frequency on a spotting network.

10. D: Good techniques for making meteor scatter contacts include 15 second timed transmission sequences with stations alternating based on location, use of high speed CW or digital modes, and short transmissions with rapidly repeated call signs and signal reports.

11. A: The letters FEC in digital operation mean Forward Error Correction.

12. B: A fluttery irregular fading characterizes libration fading of an EME signal.

13. C: The approximate maximum range for signals using transequatorial propagation is 5000 miles.

14. A: A rising A or K index indicates increasing disruption of the geomagnetic field.

15. B: A spectrum analyzer would display RF amplitude and frequency on the vertical and horizontal axes, respectively.

16. C: An advantage of using a bridge circuit to measure impedance is that it is very precise in obtaining a signal null.

17. A: A front-end filter or pre-selector can be effective in eliminating image signal interference.

18. A: Cross-modulation of the desired signal and desensitization from strong adjacent signals are both problems caused by poor dynamic range in a communications receiver.

19. D: Broadband white noise, ignition noise, and power line noise can often be reduced with a DSP noise filter.

Copyright © Mometrix Media. You have been licensed one copy of this document for personal use only. Any other reproduction or redistribution is strictly prohibited. All rights reserved.

20. C: Resonance in an electrical circuit is the frequency at which the capacitive reactance equals the inductive reactance.

21. D: A time-constant is the time it takes for a charged capacitor in an RC circuit to discharge to 36.8% of its initial voltage.

22. C: Impedances are described by phase angle and amplitude in polar coordinates.

23. B: It is important to keep lead lengths short for components used in circuits for VHF and above to avoid unwanted inductive reactance.

24. A: N-type semiconductor materials contain excess free electrons.

25. D: Schottky diodes can be more useful than ordinary diodes in some applications because they have less forward voltage drop.

26. B: When the level of a comparator's input signal crosses the threshold, the comparator changes its output state.

27. A: The equivalent circuit of a quartz crystal is motional capacitance, motional inductance, and loss resistance in series, all in parallel with a shunt capacitor representing electrode and stray capacitance.

28. A: DIP is a type of through-hole device packaging.

29. A: Photoconductive material becomes more conductive when light shines on it.

30. A: Decade counters produce one output pulse for every ten input pulses.

31. A: A class D amplifier uses switching technology to achieve high efficiency.

32. C: A T-network with series capacitors and a parallel shunt inductor is a high-pass filter.

33. C: A switching electronic voltage regulator changes the duty cycle of the controlled device to produce a constant average output voltage.

34. D: A reactance modulator produces PM signals by using an electrically variable inductance or capacitance.

35. A: An adaptive filter is used to remove unwanted noise from a received SSB signal.

36. D: The effect of ringing in a filter is undesired oscillations added to the desired signal.

37. C: A microphonic is a change in oscillator frequency due to mechanical vibration.

38. C: A sawtooth wave has a rise time significantly faster than its fall time (or vice versa).

39. D: The modulation index of a phase-modulated emission does not depend on the RF carrier frequency.

40. C: Symbol rate in a digital transmission is the rate at which the waveform of a transmitted signal changes to convey information.

41. B: Direct sequence uses a high speed binary bit stream to shift the phase of an RF carrier.

42. D: An isotropic antenna has no gain in any direction.

43. B: In the antenna radiation pattern shown in Figure E9-1, the front-to-back ratio is 18 dB.

Copyright © Mometrix Media. You have been licensed one copy of this document for personal use only. Any other reproduction or redistribution is strictly prohibited. All rights reserved.

44. A: The radiation pattern of two 1/4 wavelength vertical antennas spaced 1/4 wavelength apart and fed 90 degrees out of phase is a cardioid.

45. C: Placing two Yagis perpendicular to each other with the driven elements at the same point on the boom fed 90 degrees out of phase would result in circular polarization.

46. A: The gamma match matches an unbalanced feed line to an antenna by feeding the driven element both at the center of the element and at a fraction of a wavelength to one side of center.

47. C: The dielectric materials used determine the velocity factor of a transmission line.

48. B: Resistance circles and reactance arcs are used in Smith charts.

49. A: The gain of low band (160 meter and 80 meter) receiving antennas is not usually measured with respect to a dipole because atmospheric noise is so high.

50. B: You must make sure signals from your station are less than the uncontrolled MPE limits.

Copyright © Mometrix Media. You have been licensed one copy of this document for personal use only. Any other reproduction or redistribution is strictly prohibited. All rights reserved.

Extra Class Practice Test 3

Practice Questions

1. With your transceiver displaying the carrier frequency of phone signals, you hear a station calling CQ on 14.349 MHz USB. Is it legal to return the call using upper sideband on the same frequency?
    a. Yes, because you were not the station calling CQ
    b. Yes, because the displayed frequency is within the 20 meter band
    c. No, the sideband will extend beyond the band edge
    d. No, U.S. stations are not permitted to use phone emissions above 14.340 MHz

2. Within what distance must an amateur station protect an FCC monitoring facility from harmful interference?
    a. 1 mile
    b. 3 miles
    c. 10 miles
    d. 30 miles

3. How do the control operator responsibilities of a station under automatic control differ from one under local control?
    a. Under local control there is no control operator
    b. Under automatic control the control operator is not required to be present at the control point
    c. Under automatic control there is no control operator
    d. Under local control a control operator is not required to be present at a control point

4. What is a telecommand station in the amateur satellite service?
    a. An amateur station located on the Earth's surface for communication with other Earth stations by means of Earth satellites
    b. An amateur station that transmits communications to initiate, modify or terminate functions of a space station
    c. An amateur station located more than 50 km above the Earth's surface
    d. An amateur station that transmits telemetry consisting of measurements of upper atmosphere

5. What is a Volunteer Examiner Coordinator?
    a. A person who has volunteered to administer amateur operator license examinations
    b. A person who has volunteered to prepare amateur operator license examinations
    c. An organization that has entered into an agreement with the FCC to coordinate amateur operator license examinations
    d. The person who has entered into an agreement with the FCC to be the VE session manager

6. Under what circumstances may a dealer sell an external RF power amplifier capable of operation below 144 MHz if it has not been granted FCC certification?
    a. It was purchased in used condition from an amateur operator and is sold to another amateur operator for use at that operator's station
    b. The equipment dealer assembled it from a kit
    c. It was imported from a manufacturer in a country that does not require certification of RF power amplifiers
    d. It was imported from a manufacturer in another country and was certificated by that country's government

Copyright © Mometrix Media. You have been licensed one copy of this document for personal use only. Any other reproduction or redistribution is strictly prohibited. All rights reserved.

7. What is the orbital period of an Earth satellite?
    a. The point of maximum height of a satellite's orbit
    b. The point of minimum height of a satellite's orbit
    c. The time it takes for a satellite to complete one revolution around the Earth
    d. The time it takes for a satellite to travel from perigee to apogee

8. How is an interlaced scanning pattern generated in a fast-scan (NTSC) television system?
    a. By scanning two fields simultaneously
    b. By scanning each field from bottom to top
    c. By scanning lines from left to right in one field and right to left in the next
    d. By scanning odd numbered lines in one field and even numbered lines in the next

9. From which of the following bands is amateur radio contesting generally excluded?
    a. 30 m
    b. 6 m
    c. 2 m
    d. 33 cm

10. Which of the following digital modes is especially useful for EME communications?
    a. FSK441
    b. PACTOR III
    c. Olivia
    d. JT65

11. How is the timing of JT65 contacts organized?
    a. By exchanging ACK/NAK packets
    b. Stations take turns on alternate days
    c. Alternating transmissions at 1 minute intervals
    d. It depends on the lunar phase

12. When scheduling EME contacts, which of these conditions will generally result in the least path loss?
    a. When the Moon is at perigee
    b. When the Moon is full
    c. When the Moon is at apogee
    d. When the MUF is above 30 MHz

13. What is the best time of day for transequatorial propagation?
    a. Morning
    b. Noon
    c. Afternoon or early evening
    d. Late at night

14. Which of the following signal paths is most likely to experience high levels of absorption when the A index or K index is elevated?
    a. Transequatorial propagation
    b. Polar paths
    c. Sporadic-E
    d. NVIS

Copyright © Mometrix Media. You have been licensed one copy of this document for personal use only. Any other reproduction or redistribution is strictly prohibited. All rights reserved.

15. Which of the following test instrument is used to display spurious signals and/or intermodulation distortion products in an SSB transmitter?
    a. A wattmeter
    b. A spectrum analyzer
    c. A logic analyzer
    d. A time-domain reflectometer

16. If a frequency counter with a specified accuracy of +/- 1.0 ppm reads 146,520,000 Hz, what is the most the actual frequency being measured could differ from the reading?
    a. 165.2 Hz
    b. 14.652 kHz
    c. 146.52 Hz
    d. 1.4652 MHz

17. What is the term for the blocking of one FM phone signal by another, stronger FM phone signal?
    a. Desensitization
    b. Cross-modulation interference
    c. Capture effect
    d. Frequency discrimination

18. How can intermodulation interference between two repeaters occur?
    a. When the repeaters are in close proximity and the signals cause feedback in the final amplifier of one or both transmitters
    b. When the repeaters are in close proximity and the signals mix in the final amplifier of one or both transmitters
    c. When the signals from the transmitters are reflected out of phase from airplanes passing overhead
    d. When the signals from the transmitters are reflected in phase from airplanes passing overhead

19. Which of the following signals might a receiver noise blanker be able to remove from desired signals?
    a. Signals which are constant at all IF levels
    b. Signals which appear across a wide bandwidth
    c. Signals which appear at one IF but not another
    d. Signals which have a sharply peaked frequency distribution

20. What is the magnitude of the impedance of a series RLC circuit at resonance?
    a. High, as compared to the circuit resistance
    b. Approximately equal to capacitive reactance
    c. Approximately equal to inductive reactance
    d. Approximately equal to circuit resistance

21. What happens to the phase angle of a reactance when it is converted to a susceptance?
    a. It is unchanged
    b. The sign is reversed
    c. It is shifted by 90 degrees
    d. The susceptance phase angle is the inverse of the reactance phase angle

22. Which of the following represents an inductive reactance in polar coordinates?
    a. A positive real part
    b. A negative real part
    c. A positive phase angle
    d. A negative phase angle

- 514 -

Copyright © Mometrix Media. You have been licensed one copy of this document for personal use only. Any other reproduction or redistribution is strictly prohibited. All rights reserved.

23. What is microstrip?
    a. Lightweight transmission line made of common zip cord
    b. Miniature coax used for low power applications
    c. Short lengths of coax mounted on printed circuit boards to minimize time delay between microwave circuits
    d. Precision-printed circuit conductors above a ground plane that provide constant impedance interconnects at microwave frequencies

24. Why does a PN-junction diode not conduct current when reverse biased?
    a. Only P-type semiconductor material can conduct current
    b. Only N-type semiconductor material can conduct current
    c. Holes in P-type material and electrons in the N-type material are separated by the applied voltage, widening the depletion region
    d. Excess holes in P-type material combine with the electrons in N-type material, converting the entire diode into an insulator

25. What special type of diode is capable of both amplification and oscillation?
    a. Point contact
    b. Zener
    c. Tunnel
    d. Junction

26. What is tri-state logic?
    a. Logic devices with 0, 1, and high impedance output states
    b. Logic devices that utilize ternary math
    c. Low power logic devices designed to operate at 3 volts
    d. Proprietary logic devices manufactured by Tri-State Devices

27. Which of the following is an aspect of the piezoelectric effect?
    a. Mechanical deformation of material by the application of a voltage
    b. Mechanical deformation of material by the application of a magnetic field
    c. Generation of electrical energy in the presence of light
    d. Increased conductivity in the presence of light

28. Which of the following materials is likely to provide the highest frequency of operation when used in MMICs?
    a. Silicon
    b. Silicon nitride
    c. Silicon dioxide
    d. Gallium nitride

29. What is the most common configuration of an optoisolator or optocoupler?
    a. A lens and a photomultiplier
    b. A frequency modulated helium-neon laser
    c. An amplitude modulated helium-neon laser
    d. An LED and a phototransistor

Copyright © Mometrix Media. You have been licensed one copy of this document for personal use only. Any other reproduction or redistribution is strictly prohibited. All rights reserved.

30. Which of the following can divide the frequency of a pulse train by 2?
    a. An XOR gate
    b. A flip-flop
    c. An OR gate
    d. A multiplexer

31. Which of the following components form the output of a class D amplifier circuit?
    a. A low-pass filter to remove switching signal components
    b. A high-pass filter to compensate for low gain at low frequencies
    c. A matched load resistor to prevent damage by switching transients
    d. A temperature compensating load resistor to improve linearity

32. What advantage does a Pi-L-network have over a regular Pi-network for impedance matching between the final amplifier of a vacuum-tube transmitter and an antenna?
    a. Greater harmonic suppression
    b. Higher efficiency
    c. Lower losses
    d. Greater transformation range

33. What device is typically used as a stable reference voltage in a linear voltage regulator?
    a. A Zener diode
    b. A tunnel diode
    c. An SCR
    d. A varactor diode

34. How does an analog phase modulator function?
    a. By varying the tuning of a microphone preamplifier to produce PM signals
    b. By varying the tuning of an amplifier tank circuit to produce AM signals
    c. By varying the tuning of an amplifier tank circuit to produce PM signals
    d. By varying the tuning of a microphone preamplifier to produce AM signals

35. What type of digital signal processing filter is used to generate an SSB signal?
    a. An adaptive filter
    b. A notch filter
    c. A Hilbert-transform filter
    d. An elliptical filter

36. What is the typical input impedance of an integrated circuit op-amp?
    a. 100 ohms
    b. 1000 ohms
    c. Very low
    d. Very high

37. How is positive feedback supplied in a Hartley oscillator?
    a. Through a tapped coil
    b. Through a capacitive divider
    c. Through link coupling
    d. Through a neutralizing capacitor

Copyright © Mometrix Media. You have been licensed one copy of this document for personal use only. Any other reproduction or redistribution is strictly prohibited. All rights reserved.

38. What type of wave does a Fourier analysis show to be made up of sine waves of a given fundamental frequency plus all of its harmonics?
    a. A sawtooth wave
    b. A square wave
    c. A sine wave
    d. A cosine wave

39. What is the modulation index of an FM-phone signal having a maximum frequency deviation of 3000 Hz either side of the carrier frequency when the modulating frequency is 1000 Hz?
    a. 3
    b. 0.3
    c. 3000
    d. 1000

40. When performing phase shift keying, why is it advantageous to shift phase precisely at the zero crossing of the RF carrier?
    a. This results in the least possible transmitted bandwidth for the particular mode
    b. It is easier to demodulate with a conventional, non-synchronous detector
    c. It improves carrier suppression
    d. All of these choices are correct

41. How does the spread spectrum technique of frequency hopping work?
    a. If interference is detected by the receiver it will signal the transmitter to change frequencies
    b. If interference is detected by the receiver it will signal the transmitter to wait until the frequency is clear
    c. A pseudo-random binary bit stream is used to shift the phase of an RF carrier very rapidly in a particular sequence
    d. The frequency of the transmitted signal is changed very rapidly according to a particular sequence also used by the receiving station

42. Why would one need to know the feed point impedance of an antenna?
    a. To match impedances in order to minimize standing wave ratio on the transmission line
    b. To measure the near-field radiation density from a transmitting antenna
    c. To calculate the front-to-side ratio of the antenna
    d. To calculate the front-to-back ratio of the antenna

43. In the antenna radiation pattern shown in Figure E9-1 (located at the end of the guide), what is the front-to-side ratio?
    a. 12 dB
    b. 14 dB
    c. 18 dB
    d. 24 dB

44. What is the radiation pattern of two 1/4 wavelength vertical antennas spaced a 1/2 wavelength apart and fed in phase?
    a. Omni-directional
    b. Cardioid
    c. A Figure-8 broadside to the axis of the array
    d. A Figure-8 end-fire along the axis of the array

Copyright © Mometrix Media. You have been licensed one copy of this document for personal use only. Any other reproduction or redistribution is strictly prohibited. All rights reserved.

45. Where should a high Q loading coil be placed to minimize losses in a shortened vertical antenna?
    a. Near the center of the vertical radiator
    b. As low as possible on the vertical radiator
    c. As close to the transmitter as possible
    d. At a voltage node

46. What is the name of the matching system that uses a section of transmission line connected in parallel with the feed line at or near the feed point?
    a. The gamma match
    b. The delta match
    c. The omega match
    d. The stub match

47. Why is the physical length of a coaxial cable transmission line shorter than its electrical length?
    a. Skin effect is less pronounced in the coaxial cable
    b. The characteristic impedance is higher in a parallel feed line
    c. The surge impedance is higher in a parallel feed line
    d. Electrical signals move more slowly in a coaxial cable than in air

48. Which of the following is often determined using a Smith chart?
    a. Beam headings and radiation patterns
    b. Satellite azimuth and elevation bearings
    c. Impedance and SWR values in transmission lines
    d. Trigonometric functions

49. What is an advantage of using a shielded loop antenna for direction finding?
    a. It automatically cancels ignition noise in mobile installations
    b. It is electro statically balanced against ground, giving better nulls
    c. It eliminates tracking errors caused by strong out-of-band signals
    d. It allows stations to communicate without giving away their position

50. Which of the following would be a practical way to estimate whether the RF fields produced by an amateur radio station are within permissible MPE limits?
    a. Use a calibrated antenna analyzer
    b. Use a hand calculator plus Smith-chart equations to calculate the fields
    c. Use an antenna modeling program to calculate field strength at accessible locations
    d. All of the choices are correct

Copyright © Mometrix Media. You have been licensed one copy of this document for personal use only. Any other reproduction or redistribution is strictly prohibited. All rights reserved.

Answers and Explanations

1. C: It is not legal respond using USB on 14.349 MHz because the sideband will extend beyond the band edge.

2. A: An amateur station located within 1 mile (1600 m) of an FCC monitoring facility must protect it from harmful interference.

3. B: The control operator does not have to be present at a station under automatic control.

4. B: A telecommand station in the amateur satellite service is an amateur station that transmits communications to initiate, modify or terminate functions of a space station.

5. C: A Volunteer Examiner Coordinator is an organization that has entered into an agreement with the FCC to coordinate amateur operator license examinations.

6. A: A dealer may sell an external RF power amplifier capable of operation below 144 MHz if it has not been granted FCC certification if it was purchased in used condition from an amateur operator and is sold to another amateur operator for use at that operator's station.

7. C: The orbital period of an Earth satellite is the time it takes for a satellite to complete one revolution around the Earth.

8. D: In a fast-scan (NTSC) television system, an interlaced scanning pattern is generated by scanning odd numbered lines in one field and even numbered lines in the next.

9. A: Amateur radio contesting is generally excluded from the 30 meter band.

10. D: The JT65 digital mode is especially useful for EME communications.

11. C: The timing of JT65 contacts is organized by alternating transmissions at 1 minute intervals.

12. A: Scheduling EME contacts when the Moon is at perigee will generally result in the least path loss.

13. C: The best time of day for transequatorial propagation is afternoon or early evening.

14. B: Polar paths are more likely to experience high levels of absorption when the A index or K index is elevated than transequatorial propagation, sporadic-E propagation, and NVIS propagation.

15. B: A spectrum analyzer is used to display spurious signals and/or intermodulation distortion products in an SSB transmitter.

16. C: The most the actual frequency being measured could differ from the reading would be 146.52 Hz.

17. C: Capture effect is the term for the blocking of one FM phone signal by another, stronger FM phone signal.

18. B: Intermodulation interference between two repeaters can occur when the repeaters are in close proximity and the signals mix in the final amplifier of one or both transmitters.

19. B: A receiver noise blanker might be able to remove signals which appear across a wide bandwidth from desired signals.

20. D: The magnitude of the impedance of a series RLC circuit at resonance is approximately equal to circuit resistance.

Copyright © Mometrix Media. You have been licensed one copy of this document for personal use only. Any other reproduction or redistribution is strictly prohibited. All rights reserved.

21. B: The sign of a phase angle of a reactance is reversed when it is converted to a susceptance.

22. C: A positive phase angle represents an inductive reactance in polar coordinates.

23. D: Microstrip is precision-printed circuit conductors above a ground plane that provide constant impedance interconnects at microwave frequencies

24. C: A PN-junction diode does not conduct current when reverse biased because holes in P-type material and electrons in the N-type material are separated by the applied voltage, widening the depletion region.

25. C: Tunnel diodes are capable of both amplification and oscillation.

26. A: Tri-state logic devices have 0, 1, and high impedance output states.

27. A: The piezoelectric effect is mechanical deformation of material by the application of a voltage.

28. D: Gallium nitride is likely to provide the highest frequency of operation when used in MMICs.

29. D: Optoisolators and optocouplers are most often used as LEDs and phototransistors, respectively.

30. B: Flip-flops can divide the frequency of a pulse train by 2.

31. A: A low-pass filter to removes switching signal components from the output of a class D amplifier.

32. A: A Pi-L-network has greater harmonic suppression than a regular Pi-network for impedance matching between the final amplifier of a vacuum-tube transmitter and an antenna.

33. A: A Zener diode is typically used as a stable reference voltage in a linear voltage regulator.

34. C: An analog phase modulator functions by varying the tuning of an amplifier tank circuit to produce PM signals.

35. C: A Hilbert-transform filter is used to generate an SSB signal.

36. D: The typical input impedance of an integrated circuit op-amp is very high.

37. A: Positive feedback is supplied through a tapped coil in a Hartley oscillator.

38. A: Fourier analysis shows sawtooth waves to be made up of sine waves of a given fundamental frequency plus all of its harmonics.

39. A: The modulation index of an FM-phone signal having a maximum frequency deviation of 3000 Hz either side of the carrier frequency when the modulating frequency is 1000 Hz is 3.

40. A: When performing phase shift keying, it is advantageous to shift phase precisely at the zero crossing of the RF carrier because it results in the least possible transmitted bandwidth for the particular mode.

41. D: In frequency hopping, the frequency of the transmitted signal is changed very rapidly according to a particular sequence also used by the receiving station.

42. A: Knowing the feed point impedance of an antenna allows one to match impedances in order to minimize standing wave ratio on the transmission line.

43. B: In the antenna radiation pattern shown in Figure E9-1, the front-to-side ratio is 14 dB.

Copyright © Mometrix Media. You have been licensed one copy of this document for personal use only. Any other reproduction or redistribution is strictly prohibited. All rights reserved.

44. C: The radiation pattern of two 1/4 wavelength vertical antennas spaced a 1/2 wavelength apart and fed in phase is a figure-8 broadside to the axis of the array.

45. A: A high Q loading coil should be placed near the center of the vertical radiator to minimize losses in a shortened vertical antenna.

46. D: The stub match uses a section of transmission line connected in parallel with the feed line at or near the feed point.

47. D: The physical length of a coaxial cable is shorter than its electrical length because electrical signals move more slowly in a coaxial cable than in air.

48. C: Impedance and SWR values in transmission lines are often determined using a Smith chart.

49. B: An advantage of using a shielded loop antenna for direction finding is that it is electrostatically balanced against ground, giving better nulls.

50. C: Using an antenna modeling program to calculate field strength at accessible locations is a practical way to estimate whether the RF fields produced by an amateur radio station are within permissible MPE limits.

Copyright © Mometrix Media. You have been licensed one copy of this document for personal use only. Any other reproduction or redistribution is strictly prohibited. All rights reserved.

Extra Class Practice Test 4

Practice Questions

1. With your transceiver displaying the carrier frequency of phone signals, you hear a DX station calling CQ on 3.601 MHz LSB. Is it legal to return the call using lower sideband on the same frequency?
    a. Yes, because the DX station initiated the contact
    b. Yes, because the displayed frequency is within the 75 meter phone band segment
    c. No, the sideband will extend beyond the edge of the phone band segment
    d. No, U.S. stations are not permitted to use phone emissions below 3.610 MHz

2. What must be done before placing an amateur station within an officially designated wilderness area or wildlife preserve, or an area listed in the National Register of Historical Places?
    a. A proposal must be submitted to the National Park Service
    b. A letter of intent must be filed with the National Audubon Society
    c. An Environmental Assessment must be submitted to the FCC
    d. A form FSD-15 must be submitted to the Department of the Interior

3. What is meant by IARP?
    a. An international amateur radio permit that allows U.S. amateurs to operate in certain countries of the Americas
    b. The internal amateur radio practices policy of the FCC
    c. An indication of increased antenna reflected power
    d. A forecast of intermittent aurora radio propagation

4. What is an Earth station in the amateur satellite service?
    a. An amateur station within 50 km of the Earth's surface intended for communications with amateur stations by means of objects in space
    b. An amateur station that is not able to communicate using amateur satellites
    c. An amateur station that transmits telemetry consisting of measurement of upper atmosphere
    d. Any amateur station on the surface of the Earth

5. Which of the following best describes the Volunteer Examiner accreditation process?
    a. Each General, Advanced and Amateur Extra Class operator is automatically accredited as a VE when the license is granted
    b. The amateur operator applying must pass a VE examination administered by the FCC Enforcement Bureau
    c. The prospective VE obtains accreditation from the FCC
    d. The procedure by which a VEC confirms that the VE applicant meets FCC requirements to serve as an examiner

6. Which of the following geographic descriptions approximately describes "Line A"?
    a. A line roughly parallel to and south of the U.S.-Canadian border
    b. A line roughly parallel to and west of the U.S. Atlantic coastline
    c. A line roughly parallel to and north of the U.S.-Mexican border and Gulf coastline
    d. A line roughly parallel to and east of the U.S. Pacific coastline

Copyright © Mometrix Media. You have been licensed one copy of this document for personal use only. Any other reproduction or redistribution is strictly prohibited. All rights reserved.

7. What is meant by the term mode as applied to an amateur radio satellite?
   a. The type of signals that can be relayed through the satellite
   b. The satellite's uplink and downlink frequency bands
   c. The satellite's orientation with respect to the Earth
   d. Whether the satellite is in a polar or equatorial orbit

8. What is blanking in a video signal?
   a. Synchronization of the horizontal and vertical sync pulses
   b. Turning off the scanning beam while it is traveling from right to left or from bottom to top
   c. Turning off the scanning beam at the conclusion of a transmission
   d. Transmitting a black and white test pattern

9. What type of transmission is most often used for a ham radio mesh network?
   a. Spread spectrum in the 2.4 GHz band
   b. Multiple Frequency Shift Keying in the 10 GHz band
   c. Store and forward on the 440 MHz band
   d. Frequency division multiplex in the 24 GHz band

10. What is the purpose of digital store-and-forward functions on an Amateur Radio satellite?
    a. To upload operational software for the transponder
    b. To delay download of telemetry between satellites
    c. To store digital messages in the satellite for later download by other stations
    d. To relay messages between satellites

11. What is indicated when one of the ellipses in an FSK crossed-ellipse display suddenly disappears?
    a. Selective fading has occurred
    b. One of the signal filters is saturated
    c. The receiver has drifted 5 kHz from the desired receive frequency
    d. The mark and space signal have been inverted

12. What do Hepburn maps predict?
    a. Sporadic E propagation
    b. Locations of auroral reflecting zones
    c. Likelihood of rain-scatter along cold or warm fronts
    d. Probability of tropospheric propagation

13. What is meant by the terms extraordinary and ordinary waves?
    a. Extraordinary waves describe rare long skip propagation compared to ordinary waves which travel shorter distances
    b. Independent waves created in the ionosphere that are elliptically polarized
    c. Long path and short path waves
    d. Refracted rays and reflected waves

14. What does the value of Bz (B sub Z) represent?
    a. Geomagnetic field stability
    b. Critical frequency for vertical transmissions
    c. Direction and strength of the interplanetary magnetic field
    d. Duration of long-delayed echoes

Copyright © Mometrix Media. You have been licensed one copy of this document for personal use only. Any other reproduction or redistribution is strictly prohibited. All rights reserved.

15. What determines the upper frequency limit for a computer sound-card-based oscilloscope program?
    a. Analog-to-digital conversion speed of the soundcard
    b. Amount of memory on the soundcard
    c. Q of the interface of the interface circuit
    d. All of these choices are correct

16. If a frequency counter with a specified accuracy of +/- 0.1 ppm reads 146,520,000 Hz, what is the most the actual frequency being measured could differ from the reading?
    a. 14.652 Hz
    b. 0.1 MHz
    c. 1.4652 Hz
    d. 1.4652 kHz

17. How is the noise figure of a receiver defined?
    a. The ratio of atmospheric noise to phase noise
    b. The ratio of the noise bandwidth in Hertz to the theoretical bandwidth of a resistive network
    c. The ratio of thermal noise to atmospheric noise
    d. The ratio in dB of the noise generated by the receiver to the theoretical minimum noise

18. Which of the following may reduce or eliminate intermodulation interference in a repeater caused by another transmitter operating in close proximity?
    a. A band-pass filter in the feed line between the transmitter and receiver
    b. A properly terminated circulator at the output of the transmitter
    c. A Class C final amplifier
    d. A Class D final amplifier

19. How can conducted and radiated noise caused by an automobile alternator be suppressed?
    a. By installing filter capacitors in series with the DC power lead and a blocking capacitor in the field lead
    b. By installing a noise suppression resistor and a blocking capacitor in both leads
    c. By installing a high-pass filter in series with the radio's power lead and a low-pass filter in parallel with the field lead
    d. By connecting the radio's power leads directly to the battery and by installing coaxial capacitors in line with the alternator leads

20. What is the magnitude of the impedance of a circuit with a resistor, an inductor and a capacitor all in parallel, at resonance?
    a. Approximately equal to circuit resistance
    b. Approximately equal to inductive reactance
    c. Low, as compared to the circuit resistance
    d. Approximately equal to capacitive reactance

21. What is the time constant of a circuit having two 220 microfarad capacitors and two 1 megohm resistors, all in parallel?
    a. 55 seconds
    b. 110 seconds
    c. 440 seconds
    d. 220 seconds

Copyright © Mometrix Media. You have been licensed one copy of this document for personal use only. Any other reproduction or redistribution is strictly prohibited. All rights reserved.

22. Which of the following represents a capacitive reactance in polar coordinates?
    a. A positive real part
    b. A negative real part
    c. A positive phase angle
    d. A negative phase angle

23. Why are short connections necessary at microwave frequencies?
    a. To increase neutralizing resistance
    b. To reduce phase shift along the connection
    c. Because of ground reflections
    d. To reduce noise figure

24. What is the name given to an impurity atom that adds holes to a semiconductor crystal structure?
    a. Insulator impurity
    b. N-type impurity
    c. Acceptor impurity
    d. Donor impurity

25. What type of semiconductor device is designed for use as a voltage-controlled capacitor?
    a. Varactor diode
    b. Tunnel diode
    c. Silicon-controlled rectifier
    d. Zener diode

26. What is the primary advantage of tri-state logic?
    a. Low power consumption
    b. Ability to connect many device outputs to a common bus
    c. High speed operation
    d. More efficient arithmetic operations

27. Which materials are commonly used as a slug core in a variable inductor?
    a. Polystyrene and polyethylene
    b. Ferrite and brass
    c. Teflon and Delrin
    d. Cobalt and aluminum

28. Which is the most common input and output impedance of circuits that use MMICs?
    a. 50 ohms
    b. 300 ohms
    c. 450 ohms
    d. 10 ohms

29. What is the photovoltaic effect?
    a. The conversion of voltage to current when exposed to light
    b. The conversion of light to electrical energy
    c. The conversion of electrical energy to mechanical energy
    d. The tendency of a battery to discharge when used outside

Copyright © Mometrix Media. You have been licensed one copy of this document for personal use only. Any other reproduction or redistribution is strictly prohibited. All rights reserved.

30. How many flip-flops are required to divide a signal frequency by 4?
    a. 1
    b. 2
    c. 4
    d. 8

31. Where on the load line of a Class A common emitter amplifier would bias normally be set?
    a. Approximately half-way between saturation and cutoff
    b. Where the load line intersects the voltage axis
    c. At a point where the bias resistor equals the load resistor
    d. At a point where the load line intersects the zero bias current curve

32. How does an impedance-matching circuit transform a complex impedance to a resistive impedance?
    a. It introduces negative resistance to cancel the resistive part of impedance
    b. It introduces transconductance to cancel the reactive part of impedance
    c. It cancels the reactive part of the impedance and changes the resistive part to a desired value
    d. Network resistances are substituted for load resistances and reactances are matched to the resistances

33. Which of the following types of linear voltage regulator usually make the most efficient use of the primary power source?
    a. A series current source
    b. A series regulator
    c. A shunt regulator
    d. A shunt current source

34. What is one way a single-sideband phone signal can be generated?
    a. By using a balanced modulator followed by a filter
    b. By using a reactance modulator followed by a mixer
    c. By using a loop modulator followed by a mixer
    d. By driving a product detector with a DSB signal

35. What is a common method of generating an SSB signal using digital signal processing?
    a. Mixing products are converted to voltages and subtracted by adder circuits
    b. A frequency synthesizer removes the unwanted sidebands
    c. Emulation of quartz crystal filter characteristics
    d. Combine signals with a quadrature phase relationship

36. What is meant by the term op-amp input offset voltage?
    a. The output voltage of the op-amp minus its input voltage
    b. The difference between the output voltage of the op-amp and the input voltage required in the immediately following stage
    c. The differential input voltage needed to bring the open loop output voltage to zero
    d. The potential between the amplifier input terminals of the op-amp in an open loop condition

37. How is positive feedback supplied in a Colpitts oscillator?
    a. Through a tapped coil
    b. Through link coupling
    c. Through a capacitive divider
    d. Through a neutralizing capacitor

Copyright © Mometrix Media. You have been licensed one copy of this document for personal use only. Any other reproduction or redistribution is strictly prohibited. All rights reserved.

38. What is "dither" with respect to analog to digital converters?
    a. An abnormal condition where the converter cannot settle on a value to represent the signal
    b. A small amount of noise added to the input signal to allow more precise representation of a signal over time
    c. An error caused by irregular quantization step size
    d. A method of decimation by randomly skipping samples

39. What is the modulation index of an FM-phone signal having a maximum carrier deviation of plus or minus 6 kHz when modulated with a 2 kHz modulating frequency?
    a. 6000
    b. 3
    c. 2000
    d. 1/3

40. What technique is used to minimize the bandwidth requirements of a PSK31 signal?
    a. Zero-sum character encoding
    b. Reed-Solomon character encoding
    c. Use of sinusoidal data pulses
    d. Use of trapezoidal data pulses

41. What is the primary effect of extremely short rise or fall time on a CW signal?
    a. More difficult to copy
    b. The generation of RF harmonics
    c. The generation of key clicks
    d. Limits data speed

42. Which of the following factors may affect the feed point impedance of an antenna?
    a. Transmission-line length
    b. Antenna height, conductor length/diameter ratio and location of nearby conductive objects
    c. The settings of an antenna tuner at the transmitter
    d. Sunspot activity and time of day

43. What may occur when a directional antenna is operated at different frequencies within the band for which it was designed?
    a. Feed point impedance may become negative
    b. The E-field and H-field patterns may reverse
    c. Element spacing limits could be exceeded
    d. The gain may change depending on frequency

44. What happens to the radiation pattern of an unterminated long wire antenna as the wire length is increased?
    a. The lobes become more perpendicular to the wire
    b. The lobes align more in the direction of the wire
    c. The vertical angle increases
    d. The front-to-back ratio decreases

45. Why should an HF mobile antenna loading coil have a high ratio of reactance to resistance?
    a. To swamp out harmonics
    b. To maximize losses
    c. To minimize losses
    d. To minimize the Q

Copyright © Mometrix Media. You have been licensed one copy of this document for personal use only. Any other reproduction or redistribution is strictly prohibited. All rights reserved.

46. What is the purpose of the series capacitor in a gamma-type antenna matching network?
    a. To provide DC isolation between the feed line and the antenna
    b. To cancel the inductive reactance of the matching network
    c. To provide a rejection notch that prevents the radiation of harmonics
    d. To transform the antenna impedance to a higher value

47. What is the typical velocity factor for a coaxial cable with solid polyethylene dielectric?
    a. 2.70
    b. 0.66
    c. 0.30
    d. 0.10

48. What are the two families of circles and arcs that make up a Smith chart?
    a. Resistance and voltage
    b. Reactance and voltage
    c. Resistance and reactance
    d. Voltage and impedance

49. What is the main drawback of a wire-loop antenna for direction finding?
    a. It has a bidirectional pattern
    b. It is non-rotatable
    c. It receives equally well in all directions
    d. It is practical for use only on VHF bands

50. When evaluating a site with multiple transmitters operating at the same time, the operators and licensees of which transmitters are responsible for mitigating over-exposure situations?
    a. Only the most powerful transmitter
    b. Only commercial transmitters
    c. Each transmitter that produces 5 percent or more of its MPE limit at accessible locations
    d. Each transmitter operating with a duty-cycle greater than 50 percent

Copyright © Mometrix Media. You have been licensed one copy of this document for personal use only. Any other reproduction or redistribution is strictly prohibited. All rights reserved.

Answers and Explanations

1. C: It is not legal to respond using LSB on 3.601 MHz because the sideband will extend beyond the edge of the phone band segment.

2. C: Before placing an amateur station within an officially designated wilderness area or wildlife preserve, or an area listed in the National Register of Historical Places, an Environmental Assessment must be submitted to the FCC.

3. A: IARP is an international amateur radio permit that allows U.S. amateurs to operate in certain countries of the Americas.

4. A: An Earth station in the amateur satellite service is an amateur station within 50 km of the Earth's surface intended for communications with amateur stations by means of objects in space.

5. D: The Volunteer Examiner accreditation process is the procedure by which a VEC confirms that the VE applicant meets FCC requirements to serve as an examiner.

6. A: "Line A" is a line roughly parallel to and south of the U.S.-Canadian border.

7. B: The term mode as applied to an amateur radio satellite refers to the satellite's uplink and downlink frequency bands.

8. B: Blanking in a video signal is turning off the scanning beam while it is traveling from right to left or from bottom to top.

9. A: Spread spectrum in the 2.4 GHz band is most often used for a ham radio mesh network.

10. C: The purpose of digital store-and-forward functions on an Amateur Radio satellite is to store digital messages in the satellite for later download by other stations.

11. A: When one of the ellipses in an FSK crossed-ellipse display suddenly disappears, it means selective fading has occurred.

12. D: Hepburn maps predict the probability of tropospheric propagation.

13. B: Extraordinary and ordinary waves are independent waves created in the ionosphere that are elliptically polarized.

14. C: Bz represents the direction and strength of the interplanetary magnetic field.

15. A: The analog-to-digital conversion speed of the sound card determines the upper frequency limit of a computer sound-card-based oscilloscope program.

16. A: The most the actual frequency being measured could differ from the reading would be 14.652 Hz.

17. D: The noise figure of a receiver is defined as the ratio in dB of the noise generated by the receiver to the theoretical minimum noise.

18. B: A properly terminated circulator at the output of the transmitter may reduce or eliminate intermodulation interference in a repeater caused by another transmitter operating in close proximity.

Copyright © Mometrix Media. You have been licensed one copy of this document for personal use only. Any other reproduction or redistribution is strictly prohibited. All rights reserved.

19. D: Conducted and radiated noise caused by an automobile alternator can be suppressed by connecting the radio's power leads directly to the battery and by installing coaxial capacitors in line with the alternator leads.

20. A: The magnitude of the impedance of a circuit with a resistor, an inductor and a capacitor all in parallel, at resonance is approximately equal to circuit resistance.

21. D: The time constant of a circuit having two 220 microfarad capacitors and two 1 megohm resistors, all in parallel, is 220 seconds.

22. D: A negative phase angle represents a capacitive reactance in polar coordinates.

23. B: Short connections are necessary at microwave frequencies to reduce phase shift along the connection.

24. C: Acceptor impurities are atoms that add holes to a semiconductor crystal structure.

25. A: Varactor diode are designed for use as voltage-controlled capacitors.

26. B: The primary advantage of tri-state logic is the ability to connect many device outputs to a common bus.

27. B: Ferrite and brass are commonly used as slug cores in variable inductors.

28. A: 50 ohms is the most common input and output impedance of circuits that use MMICs.

29. B: The photovoltaic effect is the conversion of light to electrical energy.

30. B: Two flip-flops are required to divide a signal frequency by 4.

31. A: Bias would normally be set approximately half-way between saturation and cutoff for a class A common emitter amplifier.

32. C: An impedance-matching circuit cancels the reactive part of the impedance and changes the resistive part to a desired value.

33. B: A series linear voltage regulator usually makes the most efficient use of the primary power source.

34. A: A single-sideband phone signal can be generated by using a balanced modulator followed by a filter.

35. D: Combining signals with a quadrature phase relationshipis a common method of generating an SSB signal.

36. C: Op-amp input offset voltage is the differential input voltage needed to bring the open loop output voltage to zero.

37. C: Positive feedback is supplied through a capacitive divider in a Colpitts oscillator.

38. B: "Dither" in analog to digital converters is a small amount of noise added to the input signal to allow more precise representation of a signal over time.

Copyright © Mometrix Media. You have been licensed one copy of this document for personal use only. Any other reproduction or redistribution is strictly prohibited. All rights reserved.

39. B: The modulation index of an FM-phone signal having a maximum carrier deviation of plus or minus 6 kHz when modulated with a 2 kHz modulating frequency is 3.

40. C: Use of sinusoidal data pulses helps minimize the bandwidth requirements of a PSK31 signal.

41. C: Extremely short rise or fall time on a CW signal lead to the generation of key clicks.

42. B: Antenna height, conductor length/diameter ratio and location of nearby conductive objects may affect the feed point impedance of an antenna.

43. D: The gain may change depending on frequency if a directional antenna is operated at different frequencies within the band for which it was designed.

44. B: The lobes of the radiation pattern align more in the direction of the wire as wire length is increased.

45. C: An HF mobile antenna loading coil should have a high ratio of reactance to resistance to minimize losses.

46. B: The series capacitor in a gamma-type antenna matching network serves to cancel the inductive reactance of the matching network.

47. B: Coaxial cables with solid polyethylene dielectrics usually have a velocity factor of 0.66.

48. C: Resistance and reactance are the two families of circles and arcs that make up a Smith chart.

49. A: The main drawback of a wire-loop antenna for direction finding is that it has a bidirectional pattern.

50. C: When evaluating a site with multiple transmitters operating at the same time, the operators and licensees of each transmitter that produces 5 percent or more of its MPE limit at accessible locations are responsible for mitigating over-exposure situations.

Copyright © Mometrix Media. You have been licensed one copy of this document for personal use only. Any other reproduction or redistribution is strictly prohibited. All rights reserved.

Extra Class Practice Test 5

Practice Questions

1. What is the maximum power output permitted on the 60-meter band?
    a. 50 watts PEP effective radiated power relative to an isotropic radiator
    b. 50 watts PEP effective radiated power relative to a dipole
    c. 100 watts PEP effective radiated power relative to the gain of a half-wave dipole
    d. 100 watts PEP effective radiated power relative to an isotropic radiator

2. What is the National Radio Quiet Zone?
    a. An area in Puerto Rico surrounding the Arecibo Radio Telescope
    b. An area in New Mexico surrounding the White Sands Test Area
    c. An area surrounding the National Radio Astronomy Observatory
    d. An area in Florida surrounding Cape Canaveral

3. When may an automatically controlled station originate third party communications?
    a. Never
    b. Only when transmitting RTTY or data emissions
    c. When agreed upon by the sending or receiving station
    d. When approved by the National Telecommunication and Information Administration

4. What class of licensee is authorized to be the control operator of a space station?
    a. All except Technician Class
    b. Only General, Advanced or Amateur Extra Class
    c. Any class with appropriate operator privileges
    d. Only Amateur Extra Class

5. What is the minimum passing score on amateur operator license examinations?
    a. Minimum passing score of 70%
    b. Minimum passing score of 74%
    c. Minimum passing score of 80%
    d. Minimum passing score of 77%

6. Amateur stations may not transmit in which of the following frequency segments if they are located in the contiguous 48 states and north of Line A?
    a. 440 MHz – 450 MHz
    b. 53 MHz – 54 MHz
    c. 222 MHz – 223 MHz
    d. 420 MHz – 430 MHz

7. What do the letters in a satellite's mode designator specify?
    a. Power limits for uplink and downlink transmissions
    b. The location of the ground control station
    c. The polarization of uplink and downlink signals
    d. The uplink and downlink frequency ranges

Copyright © Mometrix Media. You have been licensed one copy of this document for personal use only. Any other reproduction or redistribution is strictly prohibited. All rights reserved.

8. Which of the following is an advantage of using vestigial sideband for standard fast- scan TV transmissions?
    a. The vestigial sideband carries the audio information
    b. The vestigial sideband contains chroma information
    c. Vestigial sideband reduces bandwidth while allowing for simple video detector circuitry
    d. Vestigial sideband provides high frequency emphasis to sharpen the picture

9. What is the function of a DX QSL Manager?
    a. To allocate frequencies for DXpeditions
    b. To handle the receiving and sending of confirmation cards for a DX station
    c. To run a net to allow many stations to contact a rare DX station
    d. To relay calls to and from a DX station

10. Which of the following techniques is normally used by low Earth orbiting digital satellites to relay messages around the world?
    a. Digipeating
    b. Store-and-forward
    c. Multi-satellite relaying
    d. Node hopping

11. Which type of digital mode does not support keyboard-to-keyboard operation?
    a. Winlink
    b. RTTY
    c. PSK31
    d. MFSK

12. Tropospheric propagation of microwave signals often occurs along what weather related structure?
    a. Gray-line
    b. Lightning discharges
    c. Warm and cold fronts
    d. Sprites and jets

13. Which amateur bands typically support long-path propagation?
    a. 160 meters to 40 meters
    b. 30 meters to 10 meters
    c. 160 meters to 10 meters
    d. 6 meters to 2 meters

14. What orientation of Bz (B sub z) increases the likelihood that incoming particles from the Sun will cause disturbed conditions?
    a. Southward
    b. Northward
    c. Eastward
    d. Westward

15. What might be an advantage of a digital vs. an analog oscilloscope?
    a. Automatic amplitude and frequency numerical readout
    b. Storage of traces for future reference
    c. Manipulation of time base after trace capture
    d. All of these choices are correct

Copyright © Mometrix Media. You have been licensed one copy of this document for personal use only. Any other reproduction or redistribution is strictly prohibited. All rights reserved.

16. If a frequency counter with a specified accuracy of +/- 10 ppm reads 146,520,000 Hz, what is the most the actual frequency being measured could differ from the reading?
    a. 146.52 Hz
    b. 10 Hz
    c. 146.52 kHz
    d. 1465.20 Hz

17. What does a value of -174 dBm/Hz represent with regard to the noise floor of a receiver?
    a. The minimum detectable signal as a function of receive frequency
    b. The theoretical noise at the input of a perfect receiver at room temperature
    c. The noise figure of a 1 Hz bandwidth receiver
    d. The galactic noise contribution to minimum detectable signal

18. What transmitter frequencies would cause an intermodulation-product signal in a receiver tuned to 146.70 MHz when a nearby station transmits on 146.52 MHz?
    a. 146.34 MHz and 146.61 MHz
    b. 146.88 MHz and 146.34 MHz
    c. 146.10 MHz and 147.30 MHz
    d. 173.35 MHz and 139.40 MHz

19. How can noise from an electric motor be suppressed?
    a. By installing a high pass filter in series with the motor's power leads
    b. By installing a brute-force AC-line filter in series with the motor leads
    c. By installing a bypass capacitor in series with the motor leads
    d. By using a ground-fault current interrupter in the circuit used to power the motor

20. What is the magnitude of the current at the input of a series RLC circuit as the frequency goes through resonance?
    a. Minimum
    b. Maximum
    c. R/L
    d. L/R

21. What happens to the magnitude of a reactance when it is converted to a susceptance?
    a. It is unchanged
    b. The sign is reversed
    c. It is shifted by 90 degrees
    d. The magnitude of the susceptance is the reciprocal of the magnitude of the reactance

22. What is the name of the diagram used to show the phase relationship between impedances at a given frequency?
    a. Venn diagram
    b. Near field diagram
    c. Phasor diagram
    d. Far field diagram

23. Which parasitic characteristic increases with conductor length?
    a. Inductance
    b. Permeability
    c. Permittivity
    d. Malleability

Copyright © Mometrix Media. You have been licensed one copy of this document for personal use only. Any other reproduction or redistribution is strictly prohibited. All rights reserved.

24. What is the alpha of a bipolar junction transistor?
    a. The change of collector current with respect to base current
    b. The change of base current with respect to collector current
    c. The change of collector current with respect to emitter current
    d. The change of collector current with respect to gate current

25. What characteristic of a PIN diode makes it useful as an RF switch or attenuator?
    a. Extremely high reverse breakdown voltage
    b. Ability to dissipate large amounts of power
    c. Reverse bias controls its forward voltage drop
    d. A large region of intrinsic material

26. What is an advantage of CMOS logic devices over TTL devices?
    a. Differential output capability
    b. Lower distortion
    c. Immune to damage from static discharge
    d. Lower power consumption

27. What is one reason for using ferrite cores rather than powdered-iron in an inductor?
    a. Ferrite toroids generally have lower initial permeability
    b. Ferrite toroids generally have better temperature stability
    c. Ferrite toroids generally require fewer turns to produce a given inductance value
    d. Ferrite toroids are easier to use with surface mount technology

28. Which of the following noise figure values is typical of a low-noise UHF preamplifier?
    a. 2 dB
    b. -10 dB
    c. 44 dBm
    d. -20 dBm

29. Which describes an optical shaft encoder?
    a. A device which detects rotation of a control by interrupting a light source with a patterned wheel
    b. A device which measures the strength of a beam of light using analog to digital conversion
    c. A digital encryption device often used to encrypt spacecraft control signals
    d. A device for generating RTTY signals by means of a rotating light source

30. Which of the following is a circuit that continuously alternates between two states without an external clock?
    a. Monostable multivibrator
    b. J-K flip-flop
    c. T flip-flop
    d. Astable multivibrator

31. What can be done to prevent unwanted oscillations in an RF power amplifier?
    a. Tune the stage for maximum SWR
    b. Tune both the input and output for maximum power
    c. Install parasitic suppressors and/or neutralize the stage
    d. Use a phase inverter in the output filter

Copyright © Mometrix Media. You have been licensed one copy of this document for personal use only. Any other reproduction or redistribution is strictly prohibited. All rights reserved.

32. Which filter type is described as having ripple in the passband and a sharp cutoff?
    a. A Butterworth filter
    b. An active LC filter
    c. A passive op-amp filter
    d. A Chebyshev filter

33. Which of the following types of linear voltage regulator places a constant load on the unregulated voltage source?
    a. A constant current source
    b. A series regulator
    c. A shunt current source
    d. A shunt regulator

34. What circuit is added to an FM transmitter to boost the higher audio frequencies?
    a. A de-emphasis network
    b. A heterodyne suppressor
    c. An audio prescaler
    d. A pre-emphasis network

35. How frequently must an analog signal be sampled by an analog-to-digital converter so that the signal can be accurately reproduced?
    a. At half the rate of the highest frequency component of the signal
    b. At twice the rate of the highest frequency component of the signal
    c. At the same rate as the highest frequency component of the signal
    d. At four times the rate of the highest frequency component of the signal

36. How can unwanted ringing and audio instability be prevented in a multi-section op-amp RC audio filter circuit?
    a. Restrict both gain and Q
    b. Restrict gain but increase Q
    c. Restrict Q but increase gain
    d. Increase both gain and Q

37. How is positive feedback supplied in a Pierce oscillator?
    a. Through a tapped coil
    b. Through link coupling
    c. Through a neutralizing capacitor
    d. Through a quartz crystal

38. What would be the most accurate way of measuring the RMS voltage of a complex waveform?
    a. By using a grid dip meter
    b. By measuring the voltage with a D'Arsonval meter
    c. By using an absorption wave meter
    d. By measuring the heating effect in a known resistor

39. What is the deviation ratio of an FM-phone signal having a maximum frequency swing of plus-or-minus 5 kHz when the maximum modulation frequency is 3 kHz?
    a. 60
    b. 0.167
    c. 0.6
    d. 1.67

Copyright © Mometrix Media. You have been licensed one copy of this document for personal use only. Any other reproduction or redistribution is strictly prohibited. All rights reserved.

40. What is the necessary bandwidth of a 13-WPM international Morse code transmission?
   a. Approximately 13 Hz
   b. Approximately 26 Hz
   c. Approximately 52 Hz
   d. Approximately 104 Hz

41. What is the most common method of reducing key clicks?
   a. Increase keying waveform rise and fall times
   b. Low-pass filters at the transmitter output
   c. Reduce keying waveform rise and fall times
   d. High-pass filters at the transmitter output

42. What is included in the total resistance of an antenna system?
   a. Radiation resistance plus space impedance
   b. Radiation resistance plus transmission resistance
   c. Transmission-line resistance plus radiation resistance
   d. Radiation resistance plus ohmic resistance

43. What type of antenna pattern over real ground is shown in Figure E9-2 (located at the end of the guide)?
   a. Elevation
   b. Azimuth
   c. Radiation resistance
   d. Polarization

44. What is an OCFD antenna?
   a. A dipole feed approximately 1/3 the way from one end with a 4:1 balun to provide multiband operation
   b. A remotely tunable dipole antenna using orthogonally controlled frequency diversity
   c. An eight band dipole antenna using octophase filters
   d. A multiband dipole antenna using one-way circular polarization for frequency diversity

45. What is a disadvantage of using a multiband trapped antenna?
   a. It might radiate harmonics
   b. It radiates the harmonics and fundamental equally well
   c. It is too sharply directional at lower frequencies
   d. It must be neutralized

46. How must the driven element in a 3-element Yagi be tuned to use a hairpin matching system?
   a. The driven element reactance must be capacitive
   b. The driven element reactance must be inductive
   c. The driven element resonance must be lower than the operating frequency
   d. The driven element radiation resistance must be higher than the characteristic impedance of the transmission line

47. What is the approximate physical length of a solid polyethylene dielectric coaxial transmission line that is electrically one-quarter wavelength long at 14.1 MHz?
   a. 20 meters
   b. 2.3 meters
   c. 3.5 meters
   d. 0.2 meters

Copyright © Mometrix Media. You have been licensed one copy of this document for personal use only. Any other reproduction or redistribution is strictly prohibited. All rights reserved.

48. What type of chart is shown in Figure E9-3 (located at the end of the guide)?
    a. Smith chart
    b. Free space radiation directivity chart
    c. Elevation angle radiation pattern chart
    d. Azimuth angle radiation pattern chart

49. What is the triangulation method of direction finding?
    a. The geometric angles of sky waves from the source are used to determine its position
    b. A fixed receiving station plots three headings to the signal source
    c. Antenna headings from several different receiving locations are used to locate the signal source
    d. A fixed receiving station uses three different antennas to plot the location of the signal source

50. What is one of the potential hazards of using microwaves in the amateur radio bands?
    a. Microwaves are ionizing radiation
    b. The high gain antennas commonly used can result in high exposure levels
    c. Microwaves often travel long distances by ionospheric reflection
    d. The extremely high frequency energy can damage the joints of antenna structures

Copyright © Mometrix Media. You have been licensed one copy of this document for personal use only. Any other reproduction or redistribution is strictly prohibited. All rights reserved.

Answers and Explanations

1. C: The maximum power output permitted on the 60-meter band is 100 W PEP relative to a half-wave dipole. Before March 3, 2012, the maximum was 50 W.

2. C: The National Radio Quiet Zone is an area surrounding the National Radio Astronomy Observatory.

3. A: An automatically controlled station may never originate third party communications.

4. C: Any license class with appropriate operator privileges is authorized to be the control operator of a space station.

5. B: The minimum passing score on amateur operator license examinations is 74%.

6. D: Amateur stations may not transmit on frequencies between 222 MHz and 223 MHz if they are located in the contiguous 48 states and north of Line A.

7. D: The letters in a satellite's mode designator specify the uplink and downlink frequency ranges.

8. C: An advantage of using vestigial sideband for standard fast- scan TV transmissions is reducing bandwidth while allowing for simple video detector circuitry.

9. B: A DX QSL Manager handles the receiving and sending of confirmation cards for a DX station.

10. B: Store-and-forward is a technique used by low Earth orbiting digital satellites to relay messages around the world.

11. A: Winlink does not support keyboard-to-keyboard operation.

12. C: Tropospheric propagation of microwave signals often occurs along warm and cold fronts.

13. C: The amateur 160 m and 10 m bands typically support long-path propagation.

14. A: A southward orientation of Bz increases the likelihood that incoming particles from the Sun will cause disturbed conditions.

15. D: Digital oscilloscopes have many advantages over analog oscilloscopes, including automatic amplitude and frequency readouts, onboard storage of traces, and manipulation of time bases after trace capture.

16. D: The most the actual frequency being measured could differ from the reading would be 1465.20 Hz.

17. B: A value of -174 dBm/Hz represents the theoretical noise at the input of a perfect receiver at room temperature.

18. A: 146.34 MHz and 146.61 MHz frequencies would cause an intermodulation-product signal in a receiver tuned to 146.70 MHz when a nearby station transmits on 146.52 MHz.

19. B: Noise from an electric motor can be suppressed by installing a brute-force AC-line filter in series with the motor leads.

20. B: The magnitude of the current at the input of a series RLC circuit as the frequency goes through resonance is at maximum.

Copyright © Mometrix Media. You have been licensed one copy of this document for personal use only. Any other reproduction or redistribution is strictly prohibited. All rights reserved.

21. D: When a reactance is converted to a susceptance, the magnitude of the susceptance is the reciprocal of the magnitude of the reactance.

22. C: A phasor diagram is used to show the phase relationship between impedances at a given frequency.

23. A: Inductance increases with conductor length.

24. C: The alpha of a bipolar junction transistor is the change in collector current with respect to emitter current.

25. D: The large region of intrinsic material in a PIN diode makes it useful as an RF switch or attenuator.

26. D: An advantage of CMOS logic devices over TTL devices is lower power consumption.

27. C: Ferrite toroids generally require fewer turns than powdered-iron to produce a given inductance value.

28. A: 2 dB is a typical noise value of a low-noise UHF preamplifier.

29. A: An optical shaft encoder is a device which detects rotation of a control by interrupting a light source with a patterned wheel.

30. D: Astable multivibrators continuously alternate between two states without an external clock.

31. C: Installing parasitic suppressors and/or neutralizing the stage can prevent unwanted oscillations in an RF power amplifier.

32. D: A Chebyshev filter is described as having ripple in the passband and a sharp cutoff.

33. D: A shunt regulator places a constant load on the unregulated voltage source.

34. D: A pre-emphasis network can be added to an FM transmitter to boost the higher audio frequencies.

35. B: An analog signal be sampled at twice the rate of the highest frequency component of the signal by an analog-to-digital converter.

36. A: Ringing and audio instability be prevented in a multi-section op-amp RC audio filter circuit by restricting both gain and Q.

37. D: Positive feedback is supplied through a quartz crystal in a Pierce oscillator.

38. D: The most accurate way of measuring the RMS voltage of a complex waveform would be measuring the heating effect in a known resistor.

39. D: The deviation ratio of an FM-phone signal having a maximum frequency swing of plus-or-minus 5 kHz when the maximum modulation frequency is 3 kHz is 1.67.

40. C: A 13-WPM international Morse code transmission requires a bandwidth of approximately 52 Hz.

41. A: The most common method of reducing key clicks is increasing keying waveform rise and fall times.

42. D: Radiation resistance plus ohmic resistance is included in the total resistance of an antenna system.

43. A: An elevation antenna pattern over real ground is shown in Figure E9-2.

Copyright © Mometrix Media. You have been licensed one copy of this document for personal use only. Any other reproduction or redistribution is strictly prohibited. All rights reserved.

44. A: An OCFD antenna is a dipole feed approximately 1/3 the way from one end with a 4:1 balun to provide multiband operation.

45. A: A disadvantage of using a multiband trapped antenna is that it might radiate harmonics.

46. A: The driven element in a 3-element Yagi must be tuned to have capacitive reactance to use a hairpin matching system.

47. C: A solid polyethylene dielectric coaxial transmission line that is electrically one-quarter wavelength long at 14.1 MHz has an approximate physical length of 3.5 meters.

48. A: A Smith chart is shown in Figure E9-3.

49. C: The triangulation method of direction finding involves using antenna headings from several different receiving locations to locate the signal source.

50. B: One of the potential hazards of using microwaves in the amateur radio bands is that the high gain antennas commonly used can result in high exposure levels.

Copyright © Mometrix Media. You have been licensed one copy of this document for personal use only. Any other reproduction or redistribution is strictly prohibited. All rights reserved.

Extra Class Practice Test 6

Practice Questions

1. Where must the carrier frequency of a CW signal be set to comply with FCC rules for 60-meter operation?
    a. At the lowest frequency of the channel
    b. At the center frequency of the channel
    c. At the highest frequency of the channel
    d. On any frequency where the signal's sidebands are within the channel

2. Which of the following additional rules apply if you are installing an amateur station antenna at a site at or near a public use airport?
    a. You may have to notify the Federal Aviation Administration and register it with the FCC as required by Part 17 of FCC rules
    b. No special rules apply if your antenna structure will be less than 300 feet in height
    c. You must file an Environmental Impact Statement with the EPA before construction begins
    d. You must obtain a construction permit from the airport zoning authority

3. Which of the following statements concerning remotely controlled amateur stations is true?
    a. Only Extra Class operators may be the control operator of a remote station
    b. A control operator need not be present at the control point
    c. A control operator must be present at the control point
    d. Repeater and auxiliary stations may not be remotely controlled

4. Which of the following is a requirement of a space station?
    a. The space station must be capable of terminating transmissions by telecommand when directed by the FCC
    b. The space station must cease all transmissions after 5 years
    c. The space station must be capable of changing its orbit whenever such a change is ordered by NASA
    d. All of these choices are correct

5. Who is responsible for the proper conduct and necessary supervision during an amateur operator license examination session?
    a. The VEC coordinating the session
    b. The FCC
    c. Each administering VE
    d. The VE session manager

6. Under what circumstances might the FCC issue a Special Temporary Authority (STA) to an amateur station?
    a. To provide for experimental amateur communications
    b. To allow regular operation on Land Mobile channels
    c. To provide additional spectrum for personal use
    d. To provide temporary operation while awaiting normal licensing

Copyright © Mometrix Media. You have been licensed one copy of this document for personal use only. Any other reproduction or redistribution is strictly prohibited. All rights reserved.

7. On what band would a satellite receive signals if it were operating in mode U/V?
   a. 435 MHz – 438 MHz
   b. 144 MHz – 146 MHz
   c. 50.0 MHz – 50.2 MHz
   d. 29.5 MHz – 29.7 MHz

8. What is vestigial sideband modulation?
   a. Amplitude modulation in which one complete sideband and a portion of the other are transmitted
   b. A type of modulation in which one sideband is inverted
   c. Narrow-band FM modulation achieved by filtering one sideband from the audio before frequency modulating the carrier
   d. Spread spectrum modulation achieved by applying FM modulation following single sideband amplitude modulation

9. During a VHF/UHF contest, in which band segment would you expect to find the highest level of activity?
   a. At the top of each band, usually in a segment reserved for contests
   b. In the middle of each band, usually on the national calling frequency
   c. In the weak signal segment of the band, with most of the activity near the calling frequency
   d. In the middle of the band, usually 25 kHz above the national calling frequency

10. Which of the following describes a method of establishing EME contacts?
    a. Time synchronous transmissions alternately from each station
    b. Storing and forwarding digital messages
    c. Judging optimum transmission times by monitoring beacons reflected from the Moon
    d. High speed CW identification to avoid fading

11. What is the most common data rate used for HF packet?
    a. 48 baud
    b. 110 baud
    c. 300 baud
    d. 1200 baud

12. Which of the following is required for microwave propagation via rain scatter?
    a. Rain droplets must be electrically charged
    b. Rain droplets must be within the E layer
    c. The rain must be within radio range of both stations
    d. All of these choices are correct

13. Which of the following amateur bands most frequently provides long-path propagation?
    a. 80 meters
    b. 20 meters
    c. 10 meters
    d. 6 meters

14. By how much does the VHF/UHF radio horizon distance exceed the geometric horizon?
    a. By approximately 15 percent of the distance
    b. By approximately twice the distance
    c. By approximately 50 percent of the distance
    d. By approximately four times the distance

Copyright © Mometrix Media. You have been licensed one copy of this document for personal use only. Any other reproduction or redistribution is strictly prohibited. All rights reserved.

15. What is the effect of aliasing in a digital or computer-based oscilloscope?
    a. False signals are displayed
    b. All signals will have a DC offset
    c. Calibration of the vertical scale is no longer valid
    d. False triggering occurs

16. How much power is being absorbed by the load when a directional power meter connected between a transmitter and a terminating load reads 100 watts forward power and 25 watts reflected power?
    a. 100 watts
    b. 125 watts
    c. 25 watts
    d. 75 watts

17. A CW receiver with the AGC off has an equivalent input noise power density of -174 dBm/Hz. What would be the level of an unmodulated carrier input to this receiver that would yield an audio output SNR of 0 dB in a 400 Hz noise bandwidth?
    a. -174 dBm
    b. -164 dBm
    c. -155 dBm
    d. -148 dBm

18. What is the term for unwanted signals generated by the mixing of two or more signals?
    a. Amplifier desensitization
    b. Neutralization
    c. Adjacent channel interference
    d. Intermodulation interference

19. What is a major cause of atmospheric static?
    a. Solar radio frequency emissions
    b. Thunderstorms
    c. Geomagnetic storms
    d. Meteor showers

20. What is the magnitude of the circulating current within the components of a parallel LC circuit at resonance?
    a. It is at a minimum
    b. It is at a maximum
    c. It equals 1 divided by the quantity 2 times Pi, multiplied by the square root of inductance L multiplied by capacitance C
    d. It equals 2 multiplied by Pi, multiplied by frequency, multiplied by inductance

21. What is susceptance?
    a. The magnetic impedance of a circuit
    b. The ratio of magnetic field to electric field
    c. The inverse of reactance
    d. A measure of the efficiency of a transformer

22. What does the impedance 50–j25 represent?
    a. 50 ohms resistance in series with 25 ohms inductive reactance
    b. 50 ohms resistance in series with 25 ohms capacitive reactance
    c. 25 ohms resistance in series with 50 ohms inductive reactance
    d. 25 ohms resistance in series with 50 ohms capacitive reactance

Copyright © Mometrix Media. You have been licensed one copy of this document for personal use only. Any other reproduction or redistribution is strictly prohibited. All rights reserved.

23. In what direction is the magnetic field oriented about a conductor in relation to the direction of electron flow?
    a. In the same direction as the current
    b. In a direction opposite to the current
    c. In all directions; omni-directional
    d. In a direction determined by the left-hand rule

24. What is the beta of a bipolar junction transistor?
    a. The frequency at which the current gain is reduced to 1
    b. The change in collector current with respect to base current
    c. The breakdown voltage of the base to collector junction
    d. The switching speed of the transistor

25. Which of the following is a common use of a hot-carrier diode?
    a. As balanced mixers in FM generation
    b. As a variable capacitance in an automatic frequency control circuit
    c. As a constant voltage reference in a power supply
    d. As a VHF/UHF mixer or detector

26. Why do CMOS digital integrated circuits have high immunity to noise on the input signal or power supply?
    a. Larger bypass capacitors are used in CMOS circuit design
    b. The input switching threshold is about two times the power supply voltage
    c. The input switching threshold is about one-half the power supply voltage
    d. Input signals are stronger

27. What core material property determines the inductance of a toroidal inductor?
    a. Thermal impedance
    b. Resistance
    c. Reactivity
    d. Permeability

28. What characteristics of the MMIC make it a popular choice for VHF through microwave circuits?
    a. The ability to retrieve information from a single signal even in the presence of other strong signals
    b. Plate current that is controlled by a control grid
    c. Nearly infinite gain, very high input impedance, and very low output impedance
    d. Controlled gain, low noise figure, and constant input and output impedance over the specified frequency range

29. Which of these materials is affected the most by photoconductivity?
    a. A crystalline semiconductor
    b. An ordinary metal
    c. A heavy metal
    d. A liquid semiconductor

30. What is a characteristic of a monostable multivibrator?
    a. It switches momentarily to the opposite binary state and then returns to its original state after a set time
    b. It produces a continuous square wave oscillating between 1 and 0
    c. It stores one bit of data in either a 0 or 1 state
    d. It maintains a constant output voltage, regardless of variations in the input voltage

- 545 -

Copyright © Mometrix Media. You have been licensed one copy of this document for personal use only. Any other reproduction or redistribution is strictly prohibited. All rights reserved.

31. Which of the following amplifier types reduces or eliminates even order harmonics?
    a. Push-push
    b. Push-pull
    c. Class C
    d. Class AB

32. What are the distinguishing features of an elliptical filter?
    a. Gradual passband rolloff with minimal stop band ripple
    b. Extremely flat response over its pass band with gradually rounded stop band corners
    c. Extremely sharp cutoff with one or more notches in the stop band
    d. Gradual passband rolloff with extreme stop band ripple

33. What is the purpose of Q1 in the circuit shown in Figure E7-3 (located at the end of the guide)?
    a. It provides negative feedback to improve regulation
    b. It provides a constant load for the voltage source
    c. It increases the current-handling capability of the regulator
    d. It provides D1 with current

34. Why is de-emphasis commonly used in FM communications receivers?
    a. For compatibility with transmitters using phase modulation
    b. To reduce impulse noise reception
    c. For higher efficiency
    d. To remove third-order distortion products

35. What is the minimum number of bits required for an analog-to-digital converter to sample a signal with a range of 1 volt at a resolution of 1 millivolt?
    a. 4 bits
    b. 6 bits
    c. 8 bits
    d. 10 bits

36. Which of the following is the most appropriate use of an op-amp active filter?
    a. As a high-pass filter used to block RFI at the input to receivers
    b. As a low-pass filter used between a transmitter and a transmission line
    c. For smoothing power supply output
    d. As an audio filter in a receiver

37. Which of the following oscillator circuits are commonly used in VFOs?
    a. Pierce and Zener
    b. Colpitts and Hartley
    c. Armstrong and deForest
    d. Negative feedback and balanced feedback

38. What is the approximate ratio of PEP-to-average power in a typical single-sideband phone signal?
    a. 2.5 to 1
    b. 25 to 1
    c. 1 to 1
    d. 100 to 1

Copyright © Mometrix Media. You have been licensed one copy of this document for personal use only. Any other reproduction or redistribution is strictly prohibited. All rights reserved.

39. What is the deviation ratio of an FM-phone signal having a maximum frequency swing of plus or minus 7.5 kHz when the maximum modulation frequency is 3.5 kHz?
    a. 2.14
    b. 0.214
    c. 0.47
    d. 47

40. What is the necessary bandwidth of a 170-hertz shift, 300-baud ASCII transmission?
    a. 0.1 Hz
    b. 0.3 kHz
    c. 0.5 kHz
    d. 1.0 kHz

41. Which of the following indicates likely overmodulation of an AFSK signal such as PSK or MFSK?
    a. High reflected power
    b. Strong ALC action
    c. Harmonics on higher bands
    d. Rapid signal fading

42. How does the beamwidth of an antenna vary as the gain is increased?
    a. It increases geometrically
    b. It increases arithmetically
    c. It is essentially unaffected
    d. It decreases

43. What is the elevation angle of peak response in the antenna radiation pattern shown in Figure E9-2 (located at the end of the guide)?
    a. 45 degrees
    b. 75 degrees
    c. 7.5 degrees
    d. 25 degrees

44. What is the effect of a terminating resistor on a rhombic antenna?
    a. It reflects the standing waves on the antenna elements back to the transmitter
    b. It changes the radiation pattern from bidirectional to unidirectional
    c. It changes the radiation pattern from horizontal to vertical polarization
    d. It decreases the ground loss

45. What happens to the bandwidth of an antenna as it is shortened through the use of loading coils?
    a. It is increased
    b. It is decreased
    c. No change occurs
    d. It becomes flat

46. What is the equivalent lumped-constant network for a hairpin matching system of a 3-element Yagi?
    a. Pi-network
    b. Pi-L-network
    c. A shunt inductor
    d. A series capacitor

Copyright © Mometrix Media. You have been licensed one copy of this document for personal use only. Any other reproduction or redistribution is strictly prohibited. All rights reserved.

47. What is the approximate physical length of an air-insulated, parallel conductor transmission line that is electrically one-half wavelength long at 14.10 MHz?
    a. 15 meters
    b. 20 meters
    c. 10 meters
    d. 71 meters

48. On the Smith chart shown in Figure E9-3 (located at the end of the guide), what is the name for the large outer circle on which the reactance arcs terminate?
    a. Prime axis
    b. Reactance axis
    c. Impedance axis
    d. Polar axis

49. Why is it advisable to use an RF attenuator on a receiver being used for direction finding?
    a. It narrows the bandwidth of the received signal to improve signal to noise ratio
    b. It compensates for the effects of an isotropic antenna, thereby improving directivity
    c. It reduces loss of received signals caused by antenna pattern nulls, thereby increasing sensitivity
    d. It prevents receiver overload which could make it difficult to determine peaks or nulls

50. Why are there separate electric (E) and magnetic (H) field MPE limits?
    a. The body reacts to electromagnetic radiation from both the E and H fields
    b. Ground reflections and scattering make the field impedance vary with location
    c. E field and H field radiation intensity peaks can occur at different locations
    d. All of these choices are correct

Copyright © Mometrix Media. You have been licensed one copy of this document for personal use only. Any other reproduction or redistribution is strictly prohibited. All rights reserved.

Answers and Explanations

1. B: The carrier frequency of a CW signal must be set at the center frequency of the channel to comply with FCC rules.

2. A: If installing an amateur station antenna at a site at or near a public use airport, you may have to notify the Federal Aviation Administration and register it with the FCC as required by Part 17 of FCC rules.

3. C: A control operator must be present at the control point of a remotely controlled amateur station.

4. A: A space station must be capable of terminating transmissions by telecommand when directed by the FCC.

5. C: Each administering VE is responsible for the proper conduct and necessary supervision during an amateur operator license examination session.

6. A: The FCC might issue a Special Temporary Authority (STA) to an amateur station to provide for experimental amateur communications.

7. A: A satellite would receive signals between 435 MHz and 438 MHz if it were operating in mode U/V.

8. A: Vestigial sideband modulation is amplitude modulation in which one complete sideband and a portion of the other are transmitted.

9. C: During a VHF/UHF contest, you would expect to find the highest activity in the weak signal segment of the band, with most of the activity near the calling frequency.

10. A: Establishing EME contacts can be done by timing synchronous transmissions alternately from each station.

11. C: The most common data rate used for HF packets is 300 baud.

12. C: For microwave propagation via rain scatter, the rain must be within radio range of both stations.

13. B: The amateur 20 meter band supports long-path propagation more frequently than the 6, 10, or 80 meter bands.

14. A: The VHF/UHF radio horizon distance exceeds the geometric horizon by approximately 15 percent of the distance.

15. A: Aliasing in a digital or computer-based oscilloscope means that false signals are being displayed.

16. D: 75 watts of power are being absorbed by the load when a directional power meter connected between a transmitter and a terminating load reads 100 watts forward power and 25 watts reflected power.

17. D: -148 dBm is the level of an unmodulated carrier input to this receiver that would yield an audio output SNR of 0 dB in a 400 Hz noise bandwidth.

18. D: Intermodulation interference is an unwanted signal generated by the mixing of two or more signals.

Copyright © Mometrix Media. You have been licensed one copy of this document for personal use only. Any other reproduction or redistribution is strictly prohibited. All rights reserved.

19. B: Thunderstorms are a major cause of atmospheric static.

20. B: The magnitude of the circulating current within the components of a parallel LC circuit at resonance is at a maximum.

21. C: Susceptance is the inverse of reactance.

22. B: The impedance 50–j25 represents 50 ohms resistance in series with 25 ohms capacitive reactance.

23. D: the magnetic field is oriented in a direction determined by the left-hand rule about a conductor in relation to the direction of electron flow.

24. B: The beta of a bipolar junction transistor is the change in collector current with respect to the base current.

25. D: Hot-carrier diodes are often used as VHF/UHF mixers or detectors.

26. C: CMOS digital integrated circuits have high immunity to noise on the input signal because the input switching threshold is about one-half the power supply voltage.

27. D: Permeability of the core material determines the inductance of a toroidal inductor.

28. D: MMICs have controlled gain, low noise figures, and constant input and output impedances over the specified frequency range, making them popular for VHF through microwave circuits.

29. A: Crystalline semiconductors are most affected by photoconductivity.

30. A: monostable multivibrators switch momentarily to the opposite binary state and then return to their original state after a set time.

31. B: Push-pull amplifiers reduce or eliminate even order harmonics.

32. C: An elliptical filter has an extremely sharp cutoff with one or more notches in the stop band.

33. C: The purpose of Q1 in the circuit shown in Figure E7-3 is increasing the current-handling capability of the regulator.

21. C: Susceptance is the inverse of reactance.

22. B: The impedance 50–j25 represents 50 ohms resistance in series with 25 ohms capacitive reactance.

23. D: the magnetic field is oriented in a direction determined by the left-hand rule about a conductor in relation to the direction of electron flow.

24. B: The beta of a bipolar junction transistor is the change in collector current with respect to the base current.

25. D: Hot-carrier diodes are often used as VHF/UHF mixers or detectors.

Copyright © Mometrix Media. You have been licensed one copy of this document for personal use only. Any other reproduction or redistribution is strictly prohibited. All rights reserved.

26. C: CMOS digital integrated circuits have high immunity to noise on the input signal because the input switching threshold is about one-half the power supply voltage.

27. D: Permeability of the core material determines the inductance of a toroidal inductor.

28. D: MMICs have controlled gain, low noise figures, and constant input and output impedances over the specified frequency range, making them popular for VHF through microwave circuits.

29. A: Crystalline semiconductors are most affected by photoconductivity.

30. A: Monostable multivibrators switch momentarily to the opposite binary state and then return to their original state after a set time.

31. B: Push-pull amplifiers reduce or eliminate even order harmonics.

32. C: An elliptical filter has an extremely sharp cutoff with one or more notches in the stop band.

33. C: The purpose of Q1 in the circuit shown in Figure E7-3 is increasing the current-handling capability of the regulator.

34. A: De-emphasis is commonly used in FM communications receivers for compatibility with transmitters using phase modulation.

35. D: The minimum number of bits required for an analog-to-digital converter to sample a signal with a range of 1 volt at a resolution of 1 millivolt is 10.

36. D: The most appropriate use of an op-amp active filter is as an audio filter in a receiver.

37. B: Colpitts and Hartley oscillator circuits are commonly used in VFOs.

38. A: The approximate ratio of PEP-to-average power in a typical single-sideband phone signal is 2.5 to 1.

39. A: The deviation ratio of an FM-phone signal having a maximum frequency swing of plus or minus 7.5 kHz when the maximum modulation frequency is 3.5 kHz is 2.14.

40. C: A 170-hertz shift, 300-baud ASCII transmission requires a bandwidth of 0.5 kHz.

41. B: Strong ALC action indicates likely overmodulation of an AFSK signal such as PSK or MFSK.

42. D: The beamwidth of an antenna decreases as the gain is increased.

43. C: The elevation angle of peak response in the antenna radiation pattern shown in Figure E9-2 is 7.5 degrees.

44. B: A terminating resistor on a rhombic antenna changes the radiation pattern from bidirectional to unidirectional.

45. B: As an antenna is shortened through the use of loading coils, the bandwidth decreases.

46. C: A shunt inductor is the equivalent lumped-constant network for a hairpin matching system of a 3-element Yagi.

Copyright © Mometrix Media. You have been licensed one copy of this document for personal use only. Any other reproduction or redistribution is strictly prohibited. All rights reserved.

47. C: An air-insulated, parallel conductor transmission line that is electrically one-half wavelength long at 14.10 MHz has an approximate physical length of 10 meters.

48. B: The large outer circle on which the reactance arcs terminate is the reactance axis in Figure E9-3.

49. D: An RF attenuator on a receiver being used for direction finding prevents receiver overload.

50. D: There are multiple reasons why there are separate electric (E) and magnetic (H) field MPE limits, including different body reactions, varying field impedance due to ground reflections and scattering, and different radiation intensity peaks.

Copyright © Mometrix Media. You have been licensed one copy of this document for personal use only. Any other reproduction or redistribution is strictly prohibited. All rights reserved.

Extra Class Practice Test 7

Practice Questions

1. Which amateur band requires transmission on specific channels rather than on a range of frequencies?
    a. 12 meter band
    b. 17 meter band
    c. 30 meter band
    d. 60 meter band

2. What is the highest modulation index permitted at the highest modulation frequency for angle modulation below 29.0 MHz?
    a. 0.5
    b. 1.0
    c. 2.0
    d. 3.0

3. What is meant by local control?
    a. Controlling a station through a local auxiliary link
    b. Automatically manipulating local station controls
    c. Direct manipulation of the transmitter by a control operator
    d. Controlling a repeater using a portable handheld transceiver

4. Which amateur service HF bands have frequencies authorized for space stations?
    a. Only the 40 m, 20 m, 17 m, 15 m, 12 m and 10 m bands
    b. Only the 40 m, 20 m, 17 m, 15 m and 10 m bands
    c. Only the 40 m, 30 m, 20 m, 15 m, 12 m and 10 m bands
    d. All HF bands

5. What should a VE do if a candidate fails to comply with the examiner's instructions during an amateur operator license examination?
    a. Warn the candidate that continued failure to comply will result in termination of the examination
    b. Immediately terminate the candidate's examination
    c. Allow the candidate to complete the examination, but invalidate the results
    d. Immediately terminate everyone's examination and close the session

6. When may an amateur station send a message to a business?
    a. When the total money involved does not exceed $25
    b. When the control operator is employed by the FCC or another government agency
    c. When transmitting international third-party communications
    d. When neither the amateur nor his or her employer has a pecuniary interest in the communications

7. Which of the following types of signals can be relayed through a linear transponder?
    a. FM and CW
    b. SSB and SSTV
    c. PSK and Packet
    d. All of these choices are correct

Copyright © Mometrix Media. You have been licensed one copy of this document for personal use only. Any other reproduction or redistribution is strictly prohibited. All rights reserved.

8. What is the name of the signal component that carries color information in NTSC video?
   a. Luminance
   b. Chroma
   c. Hue
   d. Spectral Intensity

9. What is the Cabrillo format?
   a. A standard for submission of electronic contest logs
   b. A method of exchanging information during a contest QSO
   c. The most common set of contest rules
   d. The rules of order for meetings between contest sponsors

10. What digital protocol is used by APRS?
   a. PACTOR
   b. 802.11
   c. AX.25
   d. AMTOR

11. What is the typical bandwidth of a properly modulated MFSK16 signal?
   a. 31 Hz
   b. 316 Hz
   c. 550 Hz
   d. 2.16 kHz

12. Atmospheric ducts capable of propagating microwave signals often form over what geographic feature?
   a. Mountain ranges
   b. Forests
   c. Bodies of water
   d. Urban areas

13. Which of the following could account for hearing an echo on the received signal of a distant station?
   a. High D layer absorption
   b. Meteor scatter
   c. Transmit frequency is higher than the MUF
   d. Receipt of a signal by more than one path

14. Which of the following descriptors indicates the greatest solar flare intensity?
   a. Class A
   b. Class B
   c. Class M
   d. Class X

15. Which of the following is an advantage of using an antenna analyzer compared to an SWR bridge to measure antenna SWR?
   a. Antenna analyzers automatically tune your antenna for resonance
   b. Antenna analyzers do not need an external RF source
   c. Antenna analyzers display a time-varying representation of the modulation envelope
   d. All of these choices are correct

Copyright © Mometrix Media. You have been licensed one copy of this document for personal use only. Any other reproduction or redistribution is strictly prohibited. All rights reserved.

16. What do the subscripts of S parameters represent?
   a. The port or ports at which measurements are made
   b. The relative time between measurements
   c. Relative quality of the data
   d. Frequency order of the measurements

17. What does the MDS of a receiver represent?
   a. The meter display sensitivity
   b. The minimum discernible signal
   c. The multiplex distortion stability
   d. The maximum detectable spectrum

18. Which describes the most significant effect of an off-frequency signal when it is causing cross-modulation interference to a desired signal?
   a. A large increase in background noise
   b. A reduction in apparent signal strength
   c. The desired signal can no longer be heard
   d. The off-frequency unwanted signal is heard in addition to the desired signal

19. How can you determine if line noise interference is being generated within your home?
   a. By checking the power line voltage with a time domain reflectometer
   b. By observing the AC power line waveform with an oscilloscope
   c. By turning off the AC power line main circuit breaker and listening on a battery operated radio
   d. By observing the AC power line voltage with a spectrum analyzer

20. What is the magnitude of the current at the input of a parallel RLC circuit at resonance?
   a. Minimum
   b. Maximum
   c. R/L
   d. L/R

21. What is the phase angle between the voltage across and the current through a series RLC circuit if X_C is 500 ohms, R is 1 kilohm, and X_L is 250 ohms?
   a. 68.2 degrees with the voltage leading the current
   b. 14.0 degrees with the voltage leading the current
   c. 14.0 degrees with the voltage lagging the current
   d. 68.2 degrees with the voltage lagging the current

22. What is a vector?
   a. The value of a quantity that changes over time
   b. A quantity with both magnitude and an angular component
   c. The inverse of the tangent function
   d. The inverse of the sine function

23. What determines the strength of the magnetic field around a conductor?
   a. The resistance divided by the current
   b. The ratio of the current to the resistance
   c. The diameter of the conductor
   d. The amount of current flowing through the conductor

Copyright © Mometrix Media. You have been licensed one copy of this document for personal use only. Any other reproduction or redistribution is strictly prohibited. All rights reserved.

24. Which of the following indicates that a silicon NPN junction transistor is biased on?
    a. Base-to-emitter resistance of approximately 6 to 7 ohms
    b. Base-to-emitter resistance of approximately 0.6 to 0.7 ohms
    c. Base-to-emitter voltage of approximately 6 to 7 volts
    d. Base-to-emitter voltage of approximately 0.6 to 0.7 volts

25. What is the failure mechanism when a junction diode fails due to excessive current?
    a. Excessive inverse voltage
    b. Excessive junction temperature
    c. Insufficient forward voltage
    d. Charge carrier depletion

26. What best describes a pull-up or pull-down resistor?
    a. A resistor in a keying circuit used to reduce key clicks
    b. A resistor connected to the positive or negative supply line used to establish a voltage when an input or output is an open circuit
    c. A resistor that insures that an oscillator frequency does not drive lower over time
    d. A resistor connected to an op-amp output that only functions when the logic output is false

27. What is the usable frequency range of inductors that use toroidal cores, assuming a correct selection of core material for the frequency being used?
    a. From a few kHz to no more than 30 MHz
    b. From less than 20 Hz to approximately 300 MHz
    c. From approximately 10 Hz to no more than 3000 kHz
    d. From about 100 kHz to at least 1000 GHz

28. Which of the following is typically used to construct a MMIC-based microwave amplifier?
    a. Ground-plane construction
    b. Microstrip construction
    c. Point-to-point construction
    d. Wave-soldering construction

29. What is a solid state relay?
    a. A relay using transistors to drive the relay coil
    b. A device that uses semiconductors to implement the functions of an electromechanical relay
    c. A mechanical relay that latches in the on or off state each time it is pulsed
    d. A passive delay line

30. What logical operation does a NAND gate perform?
    a. It produces logic "0" at its output only when all inputs are logic "0"
    b. It produces logic "1" at its output only when all inputs are logic "1"
    c. It produces logic "0" at its output if some but not all inputs are logic "1"
    d. It produces logic "0" at its output only when all inputs are logic "1"

31. Which of the following is a likely result when a Class C amplifier is used to amplify a single-sideband phone signal?
    a. Reduced intermodulation products
    b. Increased overall intelligibility
    c. Signal inversion
    d. Signal distortion and excessive bandwidth

Copyright © Mometrix Media. You have been licensed one copy of this document for personal use only. Any other reproduction or redistribution is strictly prohibited. All rights reserved.

32. What kind of filter would you use to attenuate an interfering carrier signal while receiving an SSB transmission?
   a. A band-pass filter
   b. A notch filter
   c. A Pi-network filter
   d. An all-pass filter

33. What is the purpose of C2 in the circuit shown in Figure E7-3 (located at the end of the guide)?
   a. It bypasses hum around D1
   b. It is a brute force filter for the output
   c. To self-resonate at the hum frequency
   d. To provide fixed DC bias for Q1

34. What is meant by the term baseband in radio communications?
   a. The lowest frequency band that the transmitter or receiver covers
   b. The frequency components present in the modulating signal
   c. The unmodulated bandwidth of the transmitted signal
   d. The basic oscillator frequency in an FM transmitter that is multiplied to increase the deviation and carrier frequency

35. What function can a Fast Fourier Transform perform?
   a. Converting analog signals to digital form
   b. Converting digital signals to analog form
   c. Converting digital signals from the time domain to the frequency domain
   d. Converting 8-bit data to 16 bit data

36. What magnitude of voltage gain can be expected from the circuit in Figure E7-4 (located at the end of the guide) when R1 is 10 ohms and RF is 470 ohms?
   a. 0.21
   b. 94
   c. 47
   d. 24

37. How can an oscillator's microphonic responses be reduced?
   a. Use of NP0 capacitors
   b. Eliminating noise on the oscillator's power supply
   c. Using the oscillator only for CW and digital signals
   d. Mechanically isolating the oscillator circuitry from its enclosure

38. What determines the PEP-to-average power ratio of a single-sideband phone signal?
   a. The frequency of the modulating signal
   b. The characteristics of the modulating signal
   c. The degree of carrier suppression
   d. The amplifier gain

39. Orthogonal Frequency Division Multiplexing is a technique used for which type of amateur communication?
   a. High speed digital modes
   b. Extremely low-power contacts
   c. EME
   d. OFDM signals are not allowed on amateur bands

Copyright © Mometrix Media. You have been licensed one copy of this document for personal use only. Any other reproduction or redistribution is strictly prohibited. All rights reserved.

40. What is the necessary bandwidth of a 4800-Hz frequency shift, 9600-baud ASCII FM transmission?
    a. 15.36 kHz
    b. 9.6 kHz
    c. 4.8 kHz
    d. 5.76 kHz

41. What is a common cause of overmodulation of AFSK signals?
    a. Excessive numbers of retries
    b. Ground loops
    c. Bit errors in the modem
    d. Excessive transmit audio levels

42. How does the beamwidth of an antenna vary as the gain is increased?
    a. It increases geometrically
    b. It increases arithmetically
    c. It is essentially unaffected
    d. It decreases

43. How does the total amount of radiation emitted by a directional gain antenna compare with the total amount of radiation emitted from an isotropic antenna, assuming each is driven by the same amount of power?
    a. The total amount of radiation from the directional antenna is increased by the gain of the antenna
    b. The total amount of radiation from the directional antenna is stronger by its front-to-back ratio
    c. They are the same
    d. The radiation from the isotropic antenna is 2.15 dB stronger than that from the directional antenna

44. What is the approximate feed point impedance at the center of a two-wire folded dipole antenna?
    a. 300 ohms
    b. 72 ohms
    c. 50 ohms
    d. 450 ohms

45. What is an advantage of using top loading in a shortened HF vertical antenna?
    a. Lower Q
    b. Greater structural strength
    c. Higher losses
    d. Improved radiation efficiency

46. What term best describes the interactions at the load end of a mismatched transmission line?
    a. Characteristic impedance
    b. Reflection coefficient
    c. Velocity factor
    d. Dielectric constant

47. How does ladder line compare to small-diameter coaxial cable such as RG-58 at 50 MHz?
    a. Lower loss
    b. Higher SWR
    c. Smaller reflection coefficient
    d. Lower velocity factor

Copyright © Mometrix Media. You have been licensed one copy of this document for personal use only. Any other reproduction or redistribution is strictly prohibited. All rights reserved.

48. On the Smith chart shown in Figure E9-3 (located at the end of the guide), what is the only straight line shown?
   a. The reactance axis
   b. The current axis
   c. The voltage axis
   d. The resistance axis

49. What is the function of a sense antenna?
   a. It modifies the pattern of a DF antenna array to provide a null in one direction
   b. It increases the sensitivity of a DF antenna array
   c. It allows DF antennas to receive signals at different vertical angles
   d. It provides diversity reception that cancels multipath signals

50. How may dangerous levels of carbon monoxide from an emergency generator be detected?
   a. By the odor
   b. Only with a carbon monoxide detector
   c. Any ordinary smoke detector can be used
   d. By the yellowish appearance of the gas

Copyright © Mometrix Media. You have been licensed one copy of this document for personal use only. Any other reproduction or redistribution is strictly prohibited. All rights reserved.

Answers and Explanations

1. D: The 60-meter band requires transmission on specific channels rather than on a range of frequencies.

2. B: The highest modulation index permitted at the highest modulation frequency for angle modulation below 29.0 MHz is 1.0.

3. C: Local control is direct manipulation of the transmitter by a control operator.

4. A: Only the 40 m, 20 m, 17 m, 15 m, 12 m and 10 m bands have frequencies authorized for space stations.

5. B: If a candidate fails to comply with the examiner's instructions during an amateur operator license examination, the VE should immediately terminate the candidate's examination.

6. D: An amateur station may send a message to a business when neither the amateur nor his or her employer has a pecuniary interest in the communications.

7. D: FM, CW, SSB, SSTV, PSK, and Packet signals can all be relayed through a linear transponder.

8. B: The signal component that carries color information in NTSC video is chroma.

9. A: The Cabrillo format is a standard for submission of electronic contest logs.

10. C: The AX.25 digital protocol is used by APRS.

11. B: The typical bandwidth of a properly modulated MFSK16 signal is 316 Hz.

12. C: Atmospheric ducts capable of propagating microwave signals often form over bodies of water.

13. D: Receipt of a signal by more than one path could account for hearing an echo on the received signal of a distant station.

14. D: A class X descriptor indicates the greatest solar flare intensity.

15. B: An advantage of using an antenna analyzer compared to an SWR bridge to measure antenna SWR is that antenna analyzers do not need an external RF source.

16. A: The subscripts of S parameters represent the port or ports at which measurements are made.

17. B: The MDS of a receiver represents the minimum discernible signal.

18. D: When an off-frequency signal is causing cross-modulation interference to a desired signal, the off-frequency signal is heard in addition to the desired signal.

19. C: You can determine if line noise interference is being generated within your home by turning off the AC power line main circuit breaker and listening on a battery operated radio.

20. A: The magnitude of the current at the input of a parallel RLC circuit at resonance is at a minimum.

21. C: The phase angle of a series RLC circuit with X_C = 500 ohms, R = 1 kilohm, and X_L = 250 ohms is 14.0 degrees with the voltage lagging the current.

22. B: A vector is a quantity with both magnitude and an angular component.

Copyright © Mometrix Media. You have been licensed one copy of this document for personal use only. Any other reproduction or redistribution is strictly prohibited. All rights reserved.

23. D: The amount of current flowing through a conductor determines the strength of the magnetic field around it.

24. D: A base-to-emitter voltage of approximately 0.6 to 0.7 volts would indicate that a silicon NPN junction transistor is biased on.

25. B: When a junction diode fails due to excessive current, it is called an excessive junction temperature failure.

26. B: Pull-up or pull-down resistors are connected to the positive or negative supply line and used to establish a voltage when an input or output is an open circuit.

27. B: Inductors that use toroidal cores range from less than 20 Hz to approximately 300 MHz.

28. B: Microstrip construction is typically used to construct a MMIC-based microwave amplifier.

29. B: A solid state relay is a device that uses semiconductors to implement the functions of an electromechanical relay.

30. D: NAND gates produce a logic "0" at their output only when all inputs are logic "1".

31. D: Signal distortion and excessive bandwidth can result from a class C amplifier being used to amplify a single-sideband phone signal.

32. B: A notch filer could be used to attenuate an interfering carrier signal while receiving an SSB transmission.

33. A: The purpose of C2 in the circuit shown in Figure E7-3 is bypassing hum around D1.

34. B: Baseband is the frequency components present in the modulating signal.

35. C: A Fast Fourier Transform can convert digital signals from the time domain to the frequency domain.

36. C: The voltage gain from the circuit in Figure E7-4 when R1 is 10 ohms and RF is 470 ohms should be 47.

37. D: An oscillator's microphonic responses can be reduced by mechanically isolating the oscillator circuitry from its enclosure.

38. B: The characteristics of the modulating signal determine the PEP-to-average power ratio of a single-sideband phone signal.

39. A: Orthogonal Frequency Division Multiplexing is a technique used for high speed digital modes of amateur communication.

40. A: A 4800-Hz frequency shift, 9600-baud ASCII FM transmission requires a bandwidth of 15.36 kHz.

41. D: A common cause of overmodulation of AFSK signals is excessive transmit audio levels.

42. D: The beamwidth of an antenna decreases as the gain is increased.

43. C: The total amount of radiation emitted by a directional gain antenna is equal to the total amount of radiation emitted from an isotropic antenna, assuming each is driven by the same amount of power.

44. A: The approximate feed point impedance at the center of a two-wire folded dipole antenna is 300 ohms.

Copyright © Mometrix Media. You have been licensed one copy of this document for personal use only. Any other reproduction or redistribution is strictly prohibited. All rights reserved.

45. D: Using top loading in a shortened HF vertical antenna results in improved radiation efficiency.

46. B: Reflection coefficient is the term most applicable to the interactions at the load end of a mismatched transmission line.

47. A: Ladder line has lower loss than small-diameter coaxial cable such as RG-58 at 50 MHz.

48. D: On the Smith chart shown in Figure E9-3, the only straight line shown is the resistance axis.

49. A: A sense antenna modifies the pattern of a DF antenna array to provide a null in one direction.

50. B: Dangerous levels of carbon monoxide from an emergency generator can be detected only with a carbon monoxide detector.

Copyright © Mometrix Media. You have been licensed one copy of this document for personal use only. Any other reproduction or redistribution is strictly prohibited. All rights reserved.

Extra Class Practice Test 8

Practice Questions

1. If a station in a message forwarding system inadvertently forwards a message that is in violation of FCC rules, who is primarily accountable for the rules violation?
    a. The control operator of the packet bulletin board station
    b. The control operator of the originating station
    c. The control operators of all the stations in the system
    d. The control operators of all the stations in the system not authenticating the source from which they accept communications

2. What limitations may the FCC place on an amateur station if its signal causes interference to domestic broadcast reception, assuming that the receivers involved are of good engineering design?
    a. The amateur station must cease operation
    b. The amateur station must cease operation on all frequencies below 30 MHz
    c. The amateur station must cease operation on all frequencies above 30 MHz
    d. The amateur station must avoid transmitting during certain hours on frequencies that cause the interference

3. What is the maximum permissible duration of a remotely controlled station's transmissions if its control link malfunctions?
    a. 30 seconds
    b. 3 minutes
    c. 5 minutes
    d. 10 minutes

4. Which VHF amateur service bands have frequencies available for space stations?
    a. 6 meters and 2 meters
    b. 6 meters, 2 meters, and 1.25 meters
    c. 2 meters and 1.25 meters
    d. 2 meters

5. To which of the following examinees may a VE not administer an examination?
    a. Employees of the VE
    b. Friends of the VE
    c. Relatives of the VE as listed in the FCC rules
    d. All of these choices are correct

6. Which of the following types of amateur station communications are prohibited?
    a. Communications transmitted for hire or material compensation, except as otherwise provided in the rules
    b. Communications that have a political content, except as allowed by the Fairness Doctrine
    c. Communications that have a religious content
    d. Communications in a language other than English

Copyright © Mometrix Media. You have been licensed one copy of this document for personal use only. Any other reproduction or redistribution is strictly prohibited. All rights reserved.

7. Why should effective radiated power to a satellite which uses a linear transponder be limited?
    a. To prevent creating errors in the satellite telemetry
    b. To avoid reducing the downlink power to all other users
    c. To prevent the satellite from emitting out-of-band signals
    d. To avoid interfering with terrestrial QSOs

8. Which of the following is a common method of transmitting accompanying audio with amateur fast-scan television?
    a. Frequency-modulated sub-carrier
    b. A separate VHF or UHF audio link
    c. Frequency modulation of the video carrier
    d. All of these choices are correct

9. Which of the following contacts may be confirmed through the U.S. QSL bureau system?
    a. Special event contacts between stations in the U.S.
    b. Contacts between a U.S. station and a non-U.S. station
    c. Repeater contacts between U.S. club members
    d. Contacts using tactical call signs

10. What type of packet frame is used to transmit APRS beacon data?
    a. Unnumbered Information
    b. Disconnect
    c. Acknowledgement
    d. Connect

11. Which of the following HF digital modes can be used to transfer binary files?
    a. Hellschreiber
    b. PACTOR
    c. RTTY
    d. AMTOR

12. When a meteor strikes the Earth's atmosphere, a cylindrical region of free electrons is formed at what layer of the ionosphere?
    a. The E layer
    b. The F1 layer
    c. The F2 layer
    d. The D layer

13. What type of HF propagation is probably occurring if radio signals travel along the terminator between daylight and darkness?
    a. Transequatorial
    b. Sporadic-E
    c. Long-path
    d. Gray-line

14. What does the space weather term G5 mean?
    a. An extreme geomagnetic storm
    b. Very low solar activity
    c. Moderate solar wind
    d. Waning sunspot numbers

Copyright © Mometrix Media. You have been licensed one copy of this document for personal use only. Any other reproduction or redistribution is strictly prohibited. All rights reserved.

15. Which of the following instruments would be best for measuring the SWR of a beam antenna?
    a. A spectrum analyzer
    b. A Q meter
    c. An ohmmeter
    d. An antenna analyzer

16. Which of the following is a characteristic of a good DC voltmeter?
    a. High reluctance input
    b. Low reluctance input
    c. High impedance input
    d. Low impedance input

17. An SDR receiver is overloaded when input signals exceed what level?
    a. One-half the maximum sample rate
    b. One-half the maximum sampling buffer size
    c. The maximum count value of the analog-to-digital converter
    d. The reference voltage of the analog-to-digital converter

18. What causes intermodulation in an electronic circuit?
    a. Too little gain
    b. Lack of neutralization
    c. Nonlinear circuits or devices
    d. Positive feedback

19. What type of signal is picked up by electrical wiring near a radio antenna?
    a. A common-mode signal at the frequency of the radio transmitter
    b. An electrical-sparking signal
    c. A differential-mode signal at the AC power line frequency
    d. Harmonics of the AC power line frequency

20. What is the phase relationship between the current through and the voltage across a series resonant circuit at resonance?
    a. The voltage leads the current by 90 degrees
    b. The current leads the voltage by 90 degrees
    c. The voltage and current are in phase
    d. The voltage and current are 180 degrees out of phase

21. What is the phase angle between the voltage across and the current through a series RLC circuit if X_C is 100 ohms, R is 100 ohms, and X_L is 75 ohms?
    a. 14 degrees with the voltage lagging the current
    b. 14 degrees with the voltage leading the current
    c. 76 degrees with the voltage leading the current
    d. 76 degrees with the voltage lagging the current

22. What coordinate system is often used to display the phase angle of a circuit containing resistance, inductive and/or capacitive reactance?
    a. Maidenhead grid
    b. Faraday grid
    c. Elliptical coordinates
    d. Polar coordinates

Copyright © Mometrix Media. You have been licensed one copy of this document for personal use only. Any other reproduction or redistribution is strictly prohibited. All rights reserved.

23. What type of energy is stored in an electromagnetic or electrostatic field?
   a. Electromechanical energy
   b. Potential energy
   c. Thermodynamic energy
   d. Kinetic energy

24. What term indicates the frequency at which the grounded-base current gain of a transistor has decreased to 0.7 of the gain obtainable at 1 kHz?
   a. Corner frequency
   b. Alpha rejection frequency
   c. Beta cutoff frequency
   d. Alpha cutoff frequency

25. Which of the following describes a type of semiconductor diode?
   a. Metal-semiconductor junction
   b. Electrolytic rectifier
   c. CMOS-field effect
   d. Thermionic emission diode

26. In Figure E6-5 (located at the end of the guide), what is the schematic symbol for a NAND gate?
   a. 1
   b. 2
   c. 3
   d. 4

27. What is one reason for using powdered-iron cores rather than ferrite cores in an inductor?
   a. Powdered-iron cores generally have greater initial permeability
   b. Powdered-iron cores generally maintain their characteristics at higher currents
   c. Powdered-iron cores generally require fewer turns to produce a given inductance
   d. Powdered-iron cores use smaller diameter wire for the same inductance

28. How is voltage from a power supply normally furnished to the most common type of monolithic microwave integrated circuit (MMIC)?
   a. Through a resistor and/or RF choke connected to the amplifier output lead
   b. MMICs require no operating bias
   c. Through a capacitor and RF choke connected to the amplifier input lead
   d. Directly to the bias voltage (VCC IN) lead

29. Why are optoisolators often used in conjunction with solid state circuits when switching 120VAC?
   a. Optoisolators provide a low impedance link between a control circuit and a power circuit
   b. Optoisolators provide impedance matching between the control circuit and power circuit
   c. Optoisolators provide a very high degree of electrical isolation between a control circuit and the circuit being switched
   d. Optoisolators eliminate the effects of reflected light in the control circuit

30. What logical operation does an OR gate perform?
   a. It produces logic "1" at its output if any or all inputs are logic "1"
   b. It produces logic "0" at its output if all inputs are logic "1"
   c. It only produces logic "0" at its output when all inputs are logic "1"
   d. It produces logic "1" at its output if all inputs are logic "0"

Copyright © Mometrix Media. You have been licensed one copy of this document for personal use only. Any other reproduction or redistribution is strictly prohibited. All rights reserved.

31. How can an RF power amplifier be neutralized?
    a. By increasing the driving power
    b. By reducing the driving power
    c. By feeding a 180-degree out-of-phase portion of the output back to the input
    d. By feeding an in-phase component of the output back to the input

32. Which of the following factors has the greatest effect in helping determine the bandwidth and response shape of a crystal ladder filter?
    a. The relative frequencies of the individual crystals
    b. The DC voltage applied to the quartz crystal
    c. The gain of the RF stage preceding the filter
    d. The amplitude of the signals passing through the filter

33. What type of circuit is shown in Figure E7-3 (located at the end of the guide)?
    a. Switching voltage regulator
    b. Grounded emitter amplifier
    c. Linear voltage regulator
    d. Emitter follower

34. What are the principal frequencies that appear at the output of a mixer circuit?
    a. Two and four times the original frequency
    b. The sum, difference and square root of the input frequencies
    c. The two input frequencies along with their sum and difference frequencies
    d. 1.414 and 0.707 times the input frequency

35. What is the function of decimation with regard to digital filters?
    a. Converting data to binary code decimal form
    b. Reducing the effective sample rate by removing samples
    c. Attenuating the signal
    d. Removing unnecessary significant digits

36. How does the gain of an ideal operational amplifier vary with frequency?
    a. It increases linearly with increasing frequency
    b. It decreases linearly with increasing frequency
    c. It decreases logarithmically with increasing frequency
    d. It does not vary with frequency

37. Which of the following components can be used to reduce thermal drift in crystal oscillators?
    a. NP0 capacitors
    b. Toroidal inductors
    c. Wirewound resistors
    d. Non-inductive resistors

38. Why would a direct or flash conversion analog-to-digital converter be useful for a software-defined radio?
    a. Very low power consumption decreases frequency drift
    b. Immunity to out of sequence coding reduces spurious responses
    c. Very high speed allows digitizing high frequencies
    d. All of these choices are correct

Copyright © Mometrix Media. You have been licensed one copy of this document for personal use only. Any other reproduction or redistribution is strictly prohibited. All rights reserved.

39. What describes Orthogonal Frequency Division Multiplexing?
   a. A frequency modulation technique which uses non-harmonically related frequencies
   b. A bandwidth compression technique using Fourier transforms
   c. A digital mode for narrow band, slow speed transmissions
   d. A digital modulation technique using subcarriers at frequencies chosen to avoid intersymbol interference

40. How does ARQ accomplish error correction?
   a. Special binary codes provide automatic correction
   b. Special polynomial codes provide automatic correction
   c. If errors are detected, redundant data is substituted
   d. If errors are detected, a retransmission is requested

41. What parameter might indicate that excessively high input levels are causing distortion in an AFSK signal?
   a. Signal to noise ratio
   b. Baud rate
   c. Repeat Request Rate (RRR)
   d. Intermodulation Distortion (IMD)

42. What is meant by antenna gain?
   a. The ratio of the radiated signal strength of an antenna in the direction of maximum radiation to that of a reference antenna
   b. The ratio of the signal in the forward direction to that in the opposite direction
   c. The ratio of the amount of power radiated by an antenna compared to the transmitter output power
   d. The final amplifier gain minus the transmission line losses

43. How can the approximate beam-width in a given plane of a directional antenna be determined?
   a. Note the two points where the signal strength of the antenna is 3 dB less than maximum and compute the angular difference
   b. Measure the ratio of the signal strengths of the radiated power lobes from the front and rear of the antenna
   c. Draw two imaginary lines through the ends of the elements and measure the angle between the lines
   d. Measure the ratio of the signal strengths of the radiated power lobes from the front and side of the antenna

44. What is a folded dipole antenna?
   a. A dipole one-quarter wavelength long
   b. A type of ground-plane antenna
   c. A dipole consisting of one wavelength of wire forming a very thin loop
   d. A dipole configured to provide forward gain

45. What happens as the Q of an antenna increases?
   a. SWR bandwidth increases
   b. SWR bandwidth decreases
   c. Gain is reduced
   d. More common-mode current is present on the feed line

Copyright © Mometrix Media. You have been licensed one copy of this document for personal use only. Any other reproduction or redistribution is strictly prohibited. All rights reserved.

46. Which of the following measurements is characteristic of a mismatched transmission line?
    a. An SWR less than 1:1
    b. A reflection coefficient greater than 1
    c. A dielectric constant greater than 1
    d. An SWR greater than 1:1

47. What is the term for the ratio of the actual speed at which a signal travels through a transmission line to the speed of light in a vacuum?
    a. Velocity factor
    b. Characteristic impedance
    c. Surge impedance
    d. Standing wave ratio

48. What is the process of normalization with regard to a Smith chart?
    a. Reassigning resistance values with regard to the reactance axis
    b. Reassigning reactance values with regard to the resistance axis
    c. Reassigning impedance values with regard to the prime center
    d. Reassigning prime center with regard to the reactance axis

49. Which of the following describes the construction of a receiving loop antenna?
    a. A large circularly polarized antenna
    b. A small coil of wire tightly wound around a toroidal ferrite core
    c. One or more turns of wire wound in the shape of a large open coil
    d. A vertical antenna coupled to a feed line through an inductive loop of wire

50. What does SAR measure?
    a. Synthetic Aperture Ratio of the human body
    b. Signal Amplification Rating
    c. The rate at which RF energy is absorbed by the body
    d. The rate of RF energy reflected from stationary terrain

Copyright © Mometrix Media. You have been licensed one copy of this document for personal use only. Any other reproduction or redistribution is strictly prohibited. All rights reserved.

Answers and Explanations

1. B: The control operator of the originating station is primarily accountable if a forwarded message violates FCC rules.

2. D: If an amateur station causes interference to domestic broadcast reception, the FCC may require that the station avoid transmitting during certain hours on frequencies that cause the interference.

3. B: The maximum permissible duration of a remotely controlled station's transmissions if its control link malfunctions is 3 minutes.

4. D: The 2-meter amateur service bands have frequencies available for space stations.

5. C: A VE may not administer an examination to his or her own relatives, as listed in the FCC rules.

6. A: Amateur station communications transmitted for hire or material compensation are prohibited, except as otherwise provided in the rules.

7. B: Effective radiated power should be limited to a satellite which uses a linear transponder to avoid reducing the downlink power to all other users.

8. D: Frequency-modulated sub-carriers, separate VHF or UHF audio links, and frequency modulation of the video carrier are all common methods of transmitting accompanying audio with amateur fast-scan television.

9. B: Contacts between a U.S. station and a non-U.S. station may be confirmed through the U.S. QSL bureau system.

10. A: Unnumbered Information packet frames are used to transmit APRS beacon data.

11. B: PACTOR can be used to transfer binary files.

12. A: When a meteor strikes the Earth's atmosphere, a cylindrical region of free electrons is formed at the E layer of the ionosphere.

13. D: Gray-line HF propagation is probably occurring if radio signals travel along the terminator between daylight and darkness.

14. A: The space weather term G5 indicates an extreme geomagnetic storm.

15. D: An antenna analyzer would be best for measuring the SWR of a beam antenna.

16. C: High impedance input is a characteristic of a good DC voltmeter.

17. C: An SDR receiver is overloaded when input signals exceed the maximum count value of the analog-to-digital converter.

18. C: Nonlinear circuits or devices cause intermodulation in an electronic circuit.

19. A: A common-mode signal at the frequency of the radio transmitter is picked up by electrical wiring near a radio antenna.

Copyright © Mometrix Media. You have been licensed one copy of this document for personal use only. Any other reproduction or redistribution is strictly prohibited. All rights reserved.

20. C: In a series resonant circuit at resonance, the voltage and current are in phase.

21. A: The phase angle of a series RLC circuit with X_C = 100 ohms, R = 100 ohms, and X_L = 75 ohms is 14 degrees with the voltage lagging the current.

22. D: Polar coordinates are often used to display the phase angle of a circuit containing resistance, inductive and/or capacitive reactance.

23. B: Potential energy is stored in an electromagnetic or electrostatic field.

24. D: Alpha cutoff frequency is the frequency at which the grounded-base current gain of a transistor has decreased to 0.7 of the gain obtainable at 1 kHz.

25. A: Metal-semiconductor junctions are used to make Schottky diodes.

26. B: In Figure E6-5, the schematic symbol for a NAND gate is 2.

27. B: Powdered-iron cores generally maintain their characteristics at higher currents than ferrite cores.

28. A: Power supplies are normally connected to MMICs through a resistor and/or RF choke connected to the amplifier output lead.

29. C: Optoisolators are often used in conjunction with solid state circuits when switching 120VAC because they provide a very high degree of electrical isolation between a control circuit and the circuit being switched.

30. A: OR gates produce logic "1" at their output if any or all inputs are logic "1".

31. C: An RF power amplifier can be neutralized by feeding a 180-degree out-of-phase portion of the output back to the input.

32. A: The relative frequencies of the individual crystals have the greatest effect in helping determine the bandwidth and response shape of a crystal ladder filter.

33. C: A linear voltage regulator is shown in Figure E7-3.

34. C: The principal frequencies that appear at the output of a mixer circuit are the two input frequencies along with their sum and difference frequencies.

35. B: Decimation is reducing the effective sample rate by removing samples.

36. D: The gain of an ideal operational amplifier does not vary with frequency.

37. A: NP0 capacitors can be used to reduce thermal drift in crystal oscillators.

38. C: A direct or flash conversion analog-to-digital converter would be useful for a software-defined radio because the very high speed allows digitizing high frequencies.

39. D: Orthogonal Frequency Division Multiplexing is a digital modulation technique using subcarriers at frequencies chosen to avoid intersymbol interference.

40. D: ARQ accomplishes error correction by requesting a retransmission if errors are detected.

Copyright © Mometrix Media. You have been licensed one copy of this document for personal use only. Any other reproduction or redistribution is strictly prohibited. All rights reserved.

41. D: Intermodulation Distortion (IMD) might indicate that excessively high input levels are causing distortion in an AFSK signal.

42. A: Antenna gain is the ratio of the radiated signal strength of an antenna in the direction of maximum radiation to that of a reference antenna.

43. A: The approximate beam-width in a given plane of a directional antenna be determined by noting the two points where the signal strength of the antenna is 3 dB less than maximum and computing the angular difference.

44. C: A folded dipole antenna is a dipole consisting of one wavelength of wire forming a very thin loop.

45. B: As the Q of an antenna increases, SWR bandwidth decreases.

46. D: A mismatched transmission line would have a SWR greater than 1:1.

47. A: Velocity factor is the term for the ratio of the actual speed at which a signal travels through a transmission line to the speed of light in a vacuum.

48. C: Normalization with regard to a Smith chart is the process of reassigning reactance values with regard to the resistance axis.

49. C: A receiving loop antenna is one or more turns of wire wound in the shape of a large open coil.

50. C: SAR measures the rate at which RF energy is absorbed by the body.

Copyright © Mometrix Media. You have been licensed one copy of this document for personal use only. Any other reproduction or redistribution is strictly prohibited. All rights reserved.

Extra Class Practice Test 9

Practice Questions

1. What is the first action you should take if your digital message forwarding station inadvertently forwards a communication that violates FCC rules?
    a. Discontinue forwarding the communication as soon as you become aware of it
    b. Notify the originating station that the communication does not comply with FCC rules
    c. Notify the nearest FCC Field Engineer's office
    d. Discontinue forwarding all messages

2. Which amateur stations may be operated under RACES rules?
    a. Only those club stations licensed to Amateur Extra class operators
    b. Any FCC-licensed amateur station except a Technician class
    c. Any FCC-licensed amateur station certified by the responsible civil defense organization for the area served
    d. Any FCC-licensed amateur station participating in the Military Auxiliary Radio System (MARS)

3. Which of these ranges of frequencies is available for an automatically controlled repeater operating below 30 MHz?
    a. 18.110 MHz – 18.168 MHz
    b. 24.940 MHz – 24.990 MHz
    c. 10.100 MHz – 10.150 MHz
    d. 29.500 MHz – 29.700 MHz

4. Which UHF amateur service bands have frequencies available for a space station?
    a. 70 cm only
    b. 70 cm and 13 cm
    c. 70 cm and 33 cm
    d. 33 cm and 13 cm

5. What may be the penalty for a VE who fraudulently administers or certifies an examination?
    a. Revocation of the VE's amateur station license grant and the suspension of the VE's amateur operator license grant
    b. A fine of up to $1000 per occurrence
    c. A sentence of up to one year in prison
    d. All of these choices are correct

6. Which of the following conditions apply when transmitting spread spectrum emission?
    a. A station transmitting SS emission must not cause harmful interference to other stations employing other authorized emissions
    b. The transmitting station must be in an area regulated by the FCC or in a country that permits SS emissions
    c. The transmission must not be used to obscure the meaning of any communication
    d. All of these choices are correct

Copyright © Mometrix Media. You have been licensed one copy of this document for personal use only. Any other reproduction or redistribution is strictly prohibited. All rights reserved.

7. What do the terms L band and S band specify with regard to satellite communications?
    a. The 23 centimeter and 13 centimeter bands
    b. The 2 meter and 70 centimeter bands
    c. FM and Digital Store-and-Forward systems
    d. Which sideband to use

8. What hardware, other than a receiver with SSB capability and a suitable computer, is needed to decode SSTV using Digital Radio Mondiale (DRM)?
    a. A special IF converter
    b. A special front end limiter
    c. A special notch filter to remove synchronization pulses
    d. No other hardware is needed

9. What type of equipment is commonly used to implement a ham radio mesh network?
    a. A 2 meter VHF transceiver with a 1200 baud modem
    b. An optical cable connection between the USB ports of 2 separate computers
    c. A standard wireless router running custom software
    d. A 440 MHz transceiver with a 9600 baud modem

10. Which of these digital modes has the fastest data throughput under clear communication conditions?
    a. AMTOR
    b. 170 Hz shift, 45 baud RTTY
    c. PSK31
    d. 300 baud packet

11. Which of the following HF digital modes uses variable-length coding for bandwidth efficiency?
    a. RTTY
    b. PACTOR
    c. MT63
    d. PSK31

12. Which of the following frequency ranges is most suited for meteor scatter communications?
    a. 1.8 MHz – 1.9 MHz
    b. 10 MHz – 14 MHz
    c. 28 MHz – 148 MHz
    d. 220 MHz – 450 MHz

13. At what time of year is Sporadic E propagation most likely to occur?
    a. Around the solstices, especially the summer solstice
    b. Around the solstices, especially the winter solstice
    c. Around the equinoxes, especially the spring equinox
    d. Around the equinoxes, especially the fall equinox

14. How does the intensity of an X3 flare compare to that of an X2 flare?
    a. 10 percent greater
    b. 50 percent greater
    c. Twice as great
    d. Four times as great

Copyright © Mometrix Media. You have been licensed one copy of this document for personal use only. Any other reproduction or redistribution is strictly prohibited. All rights reserved.

15. When using a computer's soundcard input to digitize signals, what is the highest frequency signal that can be digitized without aliasing?
    a. The same as the sample rate
    b. One-half the sample rate
    c. One-tenth the sample rate
    d. It depends on how the data is stored internally

16. What is indicated if the current reading on an RF ammeter placed in series with the antenna feed line of a transmitter increases as the transmitter is tuned to resonance?
    a. There is possibly a short to ground in the feed line
    b. The transmitter is not properly neutralized
    c. There is an impedance mismatch between the antenna and feed line
    d. There is more power going into the antenna

17. Which of the following choices is a good reason for selecting a high frequency for the design of the IF in a conventional HF or VHF communications receiver?
    a. Fewer components in the receiver
    b. Reduced drift
    c. Easier for front-end circuitry to eliminate image responses
    d. Improved receiver noise figure

18. What is the purpose of the preselector in a communications receiver?
    a. To store often-used frequencies
    b. To provide a range of AGC time constants
    c. To increase rejection of unwanted signals
    d. To allow selection of the optimum RF amplifier device

19. What undesirable effect can occur when using an IF noise blanker?
    a. Received audio in the speech range might have an echo effect
    b. The audio frequency bandwidth of the received signal might be compressed
    c. Nearby signals may appear to be excessively wide even if they meet emission standards
    d. FM signals can no longer be demodulated

20. How is the Q of an RLC parallel resonant circuit calculated?
    a. Reactance of either the inductance or capacitance divided by the resistance
    b. Reactance of either the inductance or capacitance multiplied by the resistance
    c. Resistance divided by the reactance of either the inductance or capacitance
    d. Reactance of the inductance multiplied by the reactance of the capacitance

21. What is the relationship between the current through a capacitor and the voltage across a capacitor?
    a. Voltage and current are in phase
    b. Voltage and current are 180 degrees out of phase
    c. Voltage leads current by 90 degrees
    d. Current leads voltage by 90 degrees

22. When using rectangular coordinates to graph the impedance of a circuit, what does the horizontal axis represent?
    a. Resistive component
    b. Reactive component
    c. The sum of the reactive and resistive components
    d. The difference between the resistive and reactive components

Copyright © Mometrix Media. You have been licensed one copy of this document for personal use only. Any other reproduction or redistribution is strictly prohibited. All rights reserved.

23. What happens to reactive power in an AC circuit that has both ideal inductors and ideal capacitors?
    a. It is dissipated as heat in the circuit
    b. It is repeatedly exchanged between the associated magnetic and electric fields, but is not dissipated
    c. It is dissipated as kinetic energy in the circuit
    d. It is dissipated in the formation of inductive and capacitive fields

24. What is a depletion-mode FET?
    a. An FET that exhibits a current flow between source and drain when no gate voltage is applied
    b. An FET that has no current flow between source and drain when no gate voltage is applied
    c. Any FET without a channel
    d. Any FET for which holes are the majority carriers

25. What is a common use for point contact diodes?
    a. As a constant current source
    b. As a constant voltage source
    c. As an RF detector
    d. As a high voltage rectifier

26. What is a Programmable Logic Device (PLD)?
    a. A device to control industrial equipment
    b. A programmable collection of logic gates and circuits in a single integrated circuit
    c. Programmable equipment used for testing digital logic integrated circuits
    d. An algorithm for simulating logic functions during circuit design

27. What devices are commonly used as VHF and UHF parasitic suppressors at the input and output terminals of a transistor HF amplifier?
    a. Electrolytic capacitors
    b. Butterworth filters
    c. Ferrite beads
    d. Steel-core toroids

28. Which of the following component package types would be most suitable for use at frequencies above the HF range?
    a. TO-220
    b. Axial lead
    c. Radial lead
    d. Surface mount

29. What is the efficiency of a photovoltaic cell?
    a. The output RF power divided by the input DC power
    b. The effective payback period
    c. The open-circuit voltage divided by the short-circuit current under full illumination
    d. The relative fraction of light that is converted to current

30. What logical operation is performed by an exclusive NOR gate?
    a. It produces logic "0" at its output only if all inputs are logic "0"
    b. It produces logic "1" at its output only if all inputs are logic "1"
    c. It produces logic "0" at its output if any single input is logic "1"
    d. It produces logic "1" at its output if any single input is logic "1"

Copyright © Mometrix Media. You have been licensed one copy of this document for personal use only. Any other reproduction or redistribution is strictly prohibited. All rights reserved.

31. Which of the following describes how the loading and tuning capacitors are to be adjusted when tuning a vacuum tube RF power amplifier that employs a Pi-network output circuit?
    a. The loading capacitor is set to maximum capacitance and the tuning capacitor is adjusted for minimum allowable plate current
    b. The tuning capacitor is set to maximum capacitance and the loading capacitor is adjusted for minimum plate permissible current
    c. The loading capacitor is adjusted to minimum plate current while alternately adjusting the tuning capacitor for maximum allowable plate current
    d. The tuning capacitor is adjusted for minimum plate current, and the loading capacitor is adjusted for maximum permissible plate current

32. What is a Jones filter as used as part of an HF receiver IF stage?
    a. An automatic notch filter
    b. A variable bandwidth crystal lattice filter
    c. A special filter that emphasizes image responses
    d. A filter that removes impulse noise

33. What is the main reason to use a charge controller with a solar power system?
    a. Prevention of battery undercharge
    b. Control of electrolyte levels during battery discharge
    c. Prevention of battery damage due to overcharge
    d. Matching of day and night charge rates

34. What occurs when an excessive amount of signal energy reaches a mixer circuit?
    a. Spurious mixer products are generated
    b. Mixer blanking occurs
    c. Automatic limiting occurs
    d. A beat frequency is generated

35. Why is an anti-aliasing digital filter required in a digital decimator?
    a. It removes high-frequency signal components which would otherwise be reproduced as lower frequency components
    b. It peaks the response of the decimator, improving bandwidth
    c. It removes low frequency signal components to eliminate the need for DC restoration
    d. It notches out the sampling frequency to avoid sampling errors

36. What will be the output voltage of the circuit shown in Figure E7-4 (located at the end of the guide) if R1 is 1000 ohms, RF is 10,000 ohms, and 0.23 volts DC is applied to the input?
    a. 0.23 volts
    b. 2.3 volts
    c. -0.23 volts
    d. -2.3 volts

37. What type of frequency synthesizer circuit uses a phase accumulator, lookup table, digital to analog converter, and a low-pass anti-alias filter?
    a. A direct digital synthesizer
    b. A hybrid synthesizer
    c. A phase locked loop synthesizer
    d. A diode-switching matrix synthesizer

Copyright © Mometrix Media. You have been licensed one copy of this document for personal use only. Any other reproduction or redistribution is strictly prohibited. All rights reserved.

38. How many levels can an analog-to-digital converter with 8 bit resolution encode?
    a. 8
    b. 8 multiplied by the gain of the input amplifier
    c. 256 divided by the gain of the input amplifier
    d. 256

39. What is meant by deviation ratio?
    a. The ratio of the audio modulating frequency to the center carrier frequency
    b. The ratio of the maximum carrier frequency deviation to the highest audio modulating frequency
    c. The ratio of the carrier center frequency to the audio modulating frequency
    d. The ratio of the highest audio modulating frequency to the average audio modulating frequency

40. Which is the name of a digital code where each preceding or following character changes by only one bit?
    a. Binary Coded Decimal Code
    b. Extended Binary Coded Decimal Interchange Code
    c. Excess 3 code
    d. Gray code

41. What is considered a good minimum IMD level for an idling PSK signal?
    a. +10 dB
    b. +15 dB
    c. -20 dB
    d. -30 dB

42. What is meant by antenna bandwidth?
    a. Antenna length divided by the number of elements
    b. The frequency range over which an antenna satisfies a performance requirement
    c. The angle between the half-power radiation points
    d. The angle formed between two imaginary lines drawn through the element ends

43. What type of computer program technique is commonly used for modeling antennas?
    a. Graphical analysis
    b. Method of Moments
    c. Mutual impedance analysis
    d. Calculus differentiation with respect to physical properties

44. What is a G5RV antenna?
    a. A multi-band dipole antenna fed with coax and a balun through a selected length of open wire transmission line
    b. A multi-band trap antenna
    c. A phased array antenna consisting of multiple loops
    d. A wide band dipole using shorted coaxial cable for the radiating elements and fed with a 4:1 balun

45. What is the function of a loading coil used as part of an HF mobile antenna?
    a. To increase the SWR bandwidth
    b. To lower the losses
    c. To lower the Q
    d. To cancel capacitive reactance

Copyright © Mometrix Media. You have been licensed one copy of this document for personal use only. Any other reproduction or redistribution is strictly prohibited. All rights reserved.

46. Which of these matching systems is an effective method of connecting a 50 ohm coaxial cable feed line to a grounded tower so it can be used as a vertical antenna?
    a. Double-bazooka match
    b. Hairpin match
    c. Gamma match
    d. All of these choices are correct

47. What is the approximate physical length of a solid polyethylene dielectric coaxial transmission line that is electrically one-quarter wavelength long at 7.2 MHz?
    a. 10 meters
    b. 6.9 meters
    c. 24 meters
    d. 50 meters

48. What third family of circles is often added to a Smith chart during the process of solving problems?
    a. Standing wave ratio circles
    b. Antenna-length circles
    c. Coaxial-length circles
    d. Radiation-pattern circles

49. How can the output voltage of a multiple turn receiving loop antenna be increased?
    a. By reducing the permeability of the loop shield
    b. By increasing the number of wire turns in the loop and reducing the area of the loop structure
    c. By winding adjacent turns in opposing directions
    d. By increasing either the number of wire turns in the loop or the area of the loop structure or both

50. Which insulating material commonly used as a thermal conductor for some types of electronic devices is extremely toxic if broken or crushed and the particles are accidentally inhaled?
    a. Mica
    b. Zinc oxide
    c. Beryllium Oxide
    d. Uranium Hexafluoride

Copyright © Mometrix Media. You have been licensed one copy of this document for personal use only. Any other reproduction or redistribution is strictly prohibited. All rights reserved.

Answers and Explanations

1. A: If your digital message forwarding station inadvertently forwards a communication that violates FCC rules, the first thing you should do is stop forwarding the message.

2. C: Any FCC-licensed amateur station certified by the responsible civil defense organization for the area served may be operated under RACES rules.

3. D: An automatically controlled repeater operating below 30 MHz may operate between 29.500 MHz and 29.700 MHz.

4. B: The 70 cm and 13 cm amateur service bands have frequencies available for space stations.

5. A: A VE who fraudulently administers or certifies an examination may be subject to revocation of his or her amateur station license grant and suspension of his or her amateur operator license grant.

6. D: When transmitting spread spectrum emission, the station must not cause harmful interference to other stations employing other authorized emissions, the transmitting station must be in an area regulated by the FCC or in a country that permits SS emissions, and the transmission must not be used to obscure the meaning of any communication.

7. A: The terms L band and S band specify the 23 centimeter and 13 centimeter bands, respectively, with regard to satellite communications.

8. D: The only hardware required to decode SSTV using Digital Radio Mondiale (DRM) is a receiver with SSB capability and a suitable computer.

9. C: Standard wireless routers running custom software are commonly used to implement ham radio mesh networks.

10. D: 300 baud packets are faster than PSK31, 170 Hz shift, 45 baud RTTY, and AMTOR under clear communication conditions.

11. D: PSK31 uses variable-length coding for bandwidth efficiency.

12. C: The 28 MHz – 148 MHz range is better suited for meteor scatter communications than 1.8 MHz – 1.9 MHz, 10 MHz – 14 MHz, or 220 MHz – 450 MHz.

13. A: Sporadic E propagation most likely to occur around the solstices, especially the summer solstice.

14. C: An X3 flare is twice as great as an X2 flare.

15. B: When using a computer's soundcard input to digitize signals, the highest frequency signal that can be digitized without aliasing is one-half the sample rate.

16. D: If the current reading on an RF ammeter placed in series with the antenna feed line of a transmitter increases as the transmitter is tuned to resonance, it indicates there is more power going into the antenna.

17. C: It is a good reason to select a high frequency for the design of the IF in a conventional HF or VHF communications receiver because it makes it easier for front-end circuitry to eliminate image responses.

18. C: The purpose of the preselector in a communications receiver is to increase rejection of unwanted signals.

Copyright © Mometrix Media. You have been licensed one copy of this document for personal use only. Any other reproduction or redistribution is strictly prohibited. All rights reserved.

19. C: When using an IF noise blanker, nearby signals may appear to be excessively wide even if they meet emission standards.

20. C: The Q of an RLC parallel resonant circuit is calculated by dividing the resistance by the reactance of either the inductance or capacitance.

21. D: In a capacitor, current leads voltage by 90 degrees.

22. A: When using rectangular coordinates to graph the impedance of a circuit, the horizontal axis represents the resistive component.

23. B: Reactive power in an AC circuit that has both ideal inductors and ideal capacitors is repeatedly exchanged between the associated magnetic and electric fields, but is not dissipated.

24. A: A depletion-mode FET is an FET that exhibits a current flow between source and drain when no gate voltage is applied.

25. C: Point contact diodes are used as RF detectors.

26. B: A PLD is a programmable collection of logic gates and circuits in a single integrated circuit.

27. C: Ferrite beads are commonly used as VHF and UHF parasitic suppressors at the input and output terminals of transistor HF amplifiers.

28. D: Components in surface mount packaging are most suitable for use at frequencies above the HF range.

29. D: The efficiency of a photovoltaic cell is the relative fraction of light that is converted to current.

30. C: Exclusive NOR gates produce logic "0" at their output if any single input is logic "1".

31. D: When tuning a vacuum tube RF power amplifier that employs a Pi-network output circuit, the tuning capacitor is adjusted for minimum plate current, and the loading capacitor is adjusted for maximum permissible plate current.

32. B: A Jones filter as used as part of an HF receiver IF stage is a variable bandwidth crystal lattice filter.

33. C: The main reason to use a charge controller with a solar power system is to prevent battery damage due to overcharging.

34. A: When an excessive amount of signal energy reaches a mixer circuit, spurious mixer products are generated.

35. A: An anti-aliasing digital filter is required in a digital decimator to remove high-frequency signal components which would otherwise be reproduced as lower frequency components.

36. D: The output voltage of the circuit shown in Figure E7-4 when R1 is 1000 ohms, RF is 10,000 ohms, and 0.23 volts DC is applied to the input is -2.3 volts.

37. A: A direct digital synthesizer uses a phase accumulator, lookup table, digital to analog converter, and a low-pass anti-alias filter.

38. D: An analog-to-digital converter with 8 bit resolution can encode 256 levels.

39. B: Deviation ratio is the ratio of the maximum carrier frequency deviation to the highest audio modulating frequency.

Copyright © Mometrix Media. You have been licensed one copy of this document for personal use only. Any other reproduction or redistribution is strictly prohibited. All rights reserved.

40. D: In Gray code, each preceding or following character changes by only one bit.

41. D: A good minimum IMD level for an idling PSK signal is -30 dB.

42. B: Antenna bandwidth is the frequency range over which an antenna satisfies a performance requirement.

43. B: Method of Moments is a type of computer program technique commonly used for modeling antennas.

44. A: A G5RV antenna is a multi-band dipole antenna fed with coax and a balun through a selected length of open wire transmission line.

45. D: Loading coils used in HF mobile antennas cancel capacitive reactance.

46. C: Gamma match is an effective method of connecting a 50 ohm coaxial cable feed line to a grounded tower so it can be used as a vertical antenna.

47. B: A solid polyethylene dielectric coaxial transmission line that is electrically one-quarter wavelength long at 7.2 MHz has an approximate physical length of 6.9 meters.

48. A: Standing wave ratio circles are often added to a Smith chart during the process of solving problems.

49. D: The output voltage of a multiple turn receiving loop antenna can be increased by increasing either the number of wire turns in the loop or the area of the loop structure or both.

50. C: Beryllium Oxide is extremely toxic if broken or crushed and the particles are accidentally inhaled.

Copyright © Mometrix Media. You have been licensed one copy of this document for personal use only. Any other reproduction or redistribution is strictly prohibited. All rights reserved.

Extra Class Practice Test 10

Practice Questions

1. If an amateur station is installed aboard a ship or aircraft, what condition must be met before the station is operated?
    a. Its operation must be approved by the master of the ship or the pilot in command of the aircraft
    b. The amateur station operator must agree not to transmit when the main radio of the ship or aircraft is in use
    c. The amateur station must have a power supply that is completely independent of the main ship or aircraft power supply
    d. The amateur operator must have an FCC Marine or Aircraft endorsement on his or her amateur license

2. What frequencies are authorized to an amateur station operating under RACES rules?
    a. All amateur service frequencies authorized to the control operator
    b. Specific segments in the amateur service MF, HF, VHF and UHF bands
    c. Specific local government channels
    d. Military Auxiliary Radio System (MARS) channels

3. What types of amateur stations may automatically retransmit the radio signals of other amateur stations?
    a. Only beacon, repeater or space stations
    b. Only auxiliary, repeater or space stations
    c. Only earth stations, repeater stations or model craft
    d. Only auxiliary, beacon or space stations

4. Which amateur stations are eligible to be telecommand stations?
    a. Any amateur station designated by NASA
    b. Any amateur station so designated by the space station licensee, subject to the privileges of the class of operator license held by the control operator
    c. Any amateur station so designated by the ITU
    d. All of these choices are correct

5. What must the administering VEs do after the administration of a successful examination for an amateur operator license?
    a. They must collect and send the documents to the NCVEC for grading
    b. They must collect and submit the documents to the coordinating VEC for grading
    c. They must submit the application document to the coordinating VEC according to the coordinating VEC instructions
    d. They must collect and send the documents to the FCC according to instructions

6. What is the maximum permitted transmitter peak envelope power for an amateur station transmitting spread spectrum communications?
    a. 1 W
    b. 1.5 W
    c. 10 W
    d. 1.5 kW

Copyright © Mometrix Media. You have been licensed one copy of this document for personal use only. Any other reproduction or redistribution is strictly prohibited. All rights reserved.

7. Why may the received signal from an amateur satellite exhibit a rapidly repeating fading effect?
   a. Because the satellite is spinning
   b. Because of ionospheric absorption
   c. Because of the satellite's low orbital altitude
   d. Because of the Doppler Effect

8. Which of the following is an acceptable bandwidth for Digital Radio Mondiale (DRM) based voice or SSTV digital transmissions made on the HF amateur bands?
   a. 3 KHz
   b. 10 KHz
   c. 15 KHz
   d. 20 KHz

9. Why might a DX station state that they are listening on another frequency?
   a. Because the DX station may be transmitting on a frequency that is prohibited to some responding stations
   b. To separate the calling stations from the DX station
   c. To improve operating efficiency by reducing interference
   d. All of these choices are correct

10. How can an APRS station be used to help support a public service communications activity?
    a. An APRS station with an emergency medical technician can automatically transmit medical data to the nearest hospital
    b. APRS stations with General Personnel Scanners can automatically relay the participant numbers and time as they pass the check points
    c. An APRS station with a GPS unit can automatically transmit information to show a mobile station's position during the event
    d. All of these choices are correct

11. Which of these digital modes has the narrowest bandwidth?
    a. MFSK16
    b. 170 Hz shift, 45 baud RTTY
    c. PSK31
    d. 300-baud packet

12. Which type of atmospheric structure can create a path for microwave propagation?
    a. The jet stream
    b. Temperature inversion
    c. Wind shear
    d. Dust devil

13. What is the cause of gray-line propagation?
    a. At midday, the Sun super heats the ionosphere causing increased refraction of radio waves
    b. At twilight and sunrise, D-layer absorption is low while E-layer and F-layer propagation remains high
    c. In darkness, solar absorption drops greatly while atmospheric ionization remains steady
    d. At mid-afternoon, the Sun heats the ionosphere decreasing radio wave refraction and the MUF

Copyright © Mometrix Media. You have been licensed one copy of this document for personal use only. Any other reproduction or redistribution is strictly prohibited. All rights reserved.

14. What does the 304A solar parameter measure?
    a. The ratio of X-Ray flux to radio flux, correlated to sunspot number
    b. UV emissions at 304 angstroms, correlated to solar flux index
    c. The solar wind velocity at 304 degrees from the solar equator, correlated to solar activity
    d. The solar emission at 304 GHz, correlated to X-Ray flare levels

15. Which of the following displays multiple digital signal states simultaneously?
    a. Network analyzer
    b. Bit error rate tester
    c. Modulation monitor
    d. Logic analyzer

16. Which of the following describes a method to measure intermodulation distortion in an SSB transmitter?
    a. Modulate the transmitter with two non-harmonically related radio frequencies and observe the RF output with a spectrum analyzer
    b. Modulate the transmitter with two non-harmonically related audio frequencies and observe the RF output with a spectrum analyzer
    c. Modulate the transmitter with two harmonically related audio frequencies and observe the RF output with a peak reading wattmeter
    d. Modulate the transmitter with two harmonically related audio frequencies and observe the RF output with a logic analyzer

17. Which of the following is a desirable amount of selectivity for an amateur RTTY HF receiver?
    a. 100 Hz
    b. 300 Hz
    c. 6000 Hz
    d. 2400 Hz

18. What does a third-order intercept level of 40 dBm mean with respect to receiver performance?
    a. Signals less than 40 dBm will not generate audible third-order intermodulation products
    b. The receiver can tolerate signals up to 40 dB above the noise floor without producing third-order intermodulation products
    c. A pair of 40 dBm signals will theoretically generate a third-order intermodulation product with the same level as the input signals
    d. A pair of 1 mW input signals will produce a third-order intermodulation product which is 40 dB stronger than the input signal

19. What is a common characteristic of interference caused by a touch controlled electrical device?
    a. The interfering signal sounds like AC hum on an AM receiver or a carrier modulated by 60 Hz hum on a SSB or CW receiver
    b. The interfering signal may drift slowly across the HF spectrum
    c. The interfering signal can be several kHz in width and usually repeats at regular intervals across a HF band
    d. All of these choices are correct

20. How is the Q of an RLC series resonant circuit calculated?
    a. Reactance of either the inductance or capacitance divided by the resistance
    b. Reactance of either the inductance or capacitance times the resistance
    c. Resistance divided by the reactance of either the inductance or capacitance
    d. Reactance of the inductance times the reactance of the capacitance

Copyright © Mometrix Media. You have been licensed one copy of this document for personal use only. Any other reproduction or redistribution is strictly prohibited. All rights reserved.

21. What is the relationship between the current through an inductor and the voltage across an inductor?
    a. Voltage leads current by 90 degrees
    b. Current leads voltage by 90 degrees
    c. Voltage and current are 180 degrees out of phase
    d. Voltage and current are in phase

22. When using rectangular coordinates to graph the impedance of a circuit, what does the vertical axis represent?
    a. Resistive component
    b. Reactive component
    c. The sum of the reactive and resistive components
    d. The difference between the resistive and reactive components

23. How can the true power be determined in an AC circuit where the voltage and current are out of phase?
    a. By multiplying the apparent power times the power factor
    b. By dividing the reactive power by the power factor
    c. By dividing the apparent power by the power factor
    d. By multiplying the reactive power times the power factor

24. In Figure E6-2 (located at the end of the guide), what is the schematic symbol for an N-channel dual-gate MOSFET?
    a. 2
    b. 4
    c. 5
    d. 6

25. In Figure E6-3 (located at the end of the guide), what is the schematic symbol for a light-emitting diode?
    a. 1
    b. 5
    c. 6
    d. 7

26. In Figure E6-5 (located at the end of the guide), what is the schematic symbol for a NOR gate?
    a. 1
    b. 2
    c. 3
    d. 4

27. What is a primary advantage of using a toroidal core instead of a solenoidal core in an inductor?
    a. Toroidal cores confine most of the magnetic field within the core material
    b. Toroidal cores make it easier to couple the magnetic energy into other components
    c. Toroidal cores exhibit greater hysteresis
    d. Toroidal cores have lower Q characteristics

Copyright © Mometrix Media. You have been licensed one copy of this document for personal use only. Any other reproduction or redistribution is strictly prohibited. All rights reserved.

28. What is the packaging technique in which leadless components are soldered directly to circuit boards?
	a. Direct soldering
	b. Virtual lead mounting
	c. Stripped lead
	d. Surface mount

29. What is the most common type of photovoltaic cell used for electrical power generation?
	a. Selenium
	b. Silicon
	c. Cadmium Sulfide
	d. Copper oxide

30. What is a truth table?
	a. A table of logic symbols that indicate the high logic states of an op-amp
	b. A diagram showing logic states when the digital device output is true
	c. A list of inputs and corresponding outputs for a digital device
	d. A table of logic symbols that indicate the logic states of an op-amp

31. In Figure E7-1 (located at the end of the guide), what is the purpose of R1 and R2?
	a. Load resistors
	b. Fixed bias
	c. Self bias
	d. Feedback

32. Which of the following filters would be the best choice for use in a 2 meter repeater duplexer?
	a. A crystal filter
	b. A cavity filter
	c. A DSP filter
	d. An L-C filter

33. What is the primary reason that a high-frequency switching type high voltage power supply can be both less expensive and lighter in weight than a conventional power supply?
	a. The inverter design does not require any output filtering
	b. It uses a diode bridge rectifier for increased output
	c. The high frequency inverter design uses much smaller transformers and filter components for an equivalent power output
	d. It uses a large power factor compensation capacitor to create free power from the unused portion of the AC cycle

34. How does a diode detector function?
	a. By rectification and filtering of RF signals
	b. By breakdown of the Zener voltage
	c. By mixing signals with noise in the transition region of the diode
	d. By sensing the change of reactance in the diode with respect to frequency

35. What aspect of receiver analog-to-digital conversion determines the maximum receive bandwidth of a Direct Digital Conversion SDR?
	a. Sample rate
	b. Sample width in bits
	c. Sample clock phase noise
	d. Processor latency

Copyright © Mometrix Media. You have been licensed one copy of this document for personal use only. Any other reproduction or redistribution is strictly prohibited. All rights reserved.

36. What absolute voltage gain can be expected from the circuit in Figure E7-4 (located at the end of the guide) when R1 is 1800 ohms and RF is 68 kilohms?
   a. 1
   b. 0.03
   c. 38
   d. 76

37. What information is contained in the lookup table of a direct digital frequency synthesizer?
   a. The phase relationship between a reference oscillator and the output waveform
   b. The amplitude values that represent a sine-wave output
   c. The phase relationship between a voltage-controlled oscillator and the output waveform
   d. The synthesizer frequency limits and frequency values stored in the radio memories

38. What is the purpose of a low pass filter used in conjunction with a digital-to-analog converter?
   a. Lower the input bandwidth to increase the effective resolution
   b. Improve accuracy by removing out of sequence codes from the input
   c. Remove harmonics from the output caused by the discrete analog levels generated
   d. All of these choices are correct

39. What describes frequency division multiplexing?
   a. The transmitted signal jumps from band to band at a predetermined rate
   b. Two or more information streams are merged into a baseband, which then modulates the transmitter
   c. The transmitted signal is divided into packets of information
   d. Two or more information streams are merged into a digital combiner, which then pulse position modulates the transmitter

40. What is an advantage of Gray code in digital communications where symbols are transmitted as multiple bits?
   a. It increases security
   b. It has more possible states than simple binary
   c. It has more resolution than simple binary
   d. It facilitates error detection

41. What are some of the differences between the Baudot digital code and ASCII?
   a. Baudot uses 4 data bits per character, ASCII uses 7 or 8; Baudot uses 1 character as a letters/figures shift code, ASCII has no letters/figures code
   b. Baudot uses 5 data bits per character, ASCII uses 7 or 8; Baudot uses 2 characters as letters/figures shift codes, ASCII has no letters/figures shift code
   c. Baudot uses 6 data bits per character, ASCII uses 7 or 8; Baudot has no letters/figures shift code, ASCII uses 2 letters/figures shift codes
   d. Baudot uses 7 data bits per character, ASCII uses 8; Baudot has no letters/figures shift code, ASCII uses 2 letters/figures shift codes

42. How is antenna efficiency calculated?
   a. (radiation resistance / transmission resistance) x 100 per cent
   b. (radiation resistance / total resistance) x 100 per cent
   c. (total resistance / radiation resistance) x 100 per cent
   d. (effective radiated power / transmitter output) x 100 percent

Copyright © Mometrix Media. You have been licensed one copy of this document for personal use only. Any other reproduction or redistribution is strictly prohibited. All rights reserved.

43. What is the principle of a Method of Moments analysis?
    a. A wire is modeled as a series of segments, each having a uniform value of current
    b. A wire is modeled as a single sine-wave current generator
    c. A wire is modeled as a series of points, each having a distinct location in space
    d. A wire is modeled as a series of segments, each having a distinct value of voltage across it

44. Which of the following describes a Zepp antenna?
    a. A dipole constructed from zip cord
    b. An end fed dipole antenna
    c. An omni-directional antenna commonly used for satellite communications
    d. A vertical array capable of quickly changing the direction of maximum radiation by changing phasing lines

45. What happens to feed point impedance at the base of a fixed length HF mobile antenna as the frequency of operation is lowered?
    a. The radiation resistance decreases and the capacitive reactance decreases
    b. The radiation resistance decreases and the capacitive reactance increases
    c. The radiation resistance increases and the capacitive reactance decreases
    d. The radiation resistance increases and the capacitive reactance increases

46. Which of these choices is an effective way to match an antenna with a 100 ohm feed point impedance to a 50 ohm coaxial cable feed line?
    a. Connect a 1/4-wavelength open stub of 300 ohm twin-lead in parallel with the coaxial feed line where it connects to the antenna
    b. Insert a 1/2 wavelength piece of 300 ohm twin-lead in series between the antenna terminals and the 50 ohm feed cable
    c. Insert a 1/4-wavelength piece of 75 ohm coaxial cable transmission line in series between the antenna terminals and the 50 ohm feed cable
    d. Connect 1/2 wavelength shorted stub of 75 ohm cable in parallel with the 50 ohm cable where it attaches to the antenna

47. What impedance does a 1/8 wavelength transmission line present to a generator when the line is shorted at the far end?
    a. A capacitive reactance
    b. The same as the characteristic impedance of the line
    c. An inductive reactance
    d. The same as the input impedance to the final generator stage

48. What do the arcs on a Smith chart represent?
    a. Frequency
    b. SWR
    c. Points with constant resistance
    d. Points with constant reactance

49. What characteristic of a cardioid pattern antenna is useful for direction finding?
    a. A very sharp peak
    b. A very sharp single null
    c. Broad band response
    d. High-radiation angle

Copyright © Mometrix Media. You have been licensed one copy of this document for personal use only. Any other reproduction or redistribution is strictly prohibited. All rights reserved.

50. What toxic material may be present in some electronic components such as high voltage capacitors and transformers?
    a. Polychlorinated Biphenyls
    b. Polyethylene
    c. Polytetrafluorethylene
    d. Polymorphic silicon

Copyright © Mometrix Media. You have been licensed one copy of this document for personal use only. Any other reproduction or redistribution is strictly prohibited. All rights reserved.

Answers and Explanations

1. A: Amateur stations aboard ships or aircraft do not need special endorsement so long as permission is obtained from the captain or pilot of the craft, and all applicable rules are followed.

2. A: An amateur station operating under RACES rules may use all amateur service frequencies authorized to the control operator.

3. B: Only auxiliary, repeater or space stations may automatically retransmit the radio signals of other amateur stations.

4. B: Any amateur station so designated by the space station licensee is eligible to be a telecommand station, subject to the privileges of the class of operator license held by the control operator.

5. C: The administering VEs must submit the application document to the coordinating VEC according to the coordinating VEC's instructions after the administration of a successful examination for an amateur operator license.

6. C: The maximum permitted transmitter peak envelope power for an amateur station transmitting spread spectrum communications is 10 W.

7. A: The received signal from an amateur satellite may exhibit a rapidly repeating fading effect because the satellite is spinning.

8. A: 3 KHz is an acceptable bandwidth for Digital Radio Mondiale (DRM) based voice or SSTV digital transmissions made on the HF amateur bands.

9. D: A DX station may state that they are listening on another frequency for a number of reasons, including because they may be transmitting on a frequency that is prohibited to some responding stations, to separate the calling stations from the DX station, and to improve operating efficiency by reducing interference.

10. C: An APRS station can help support a public service communications activity by automatically transmitting information to show a mobile station's position during the event.

11. C: PSK31 has lower bandwidth than MFSK16, 170 Hz shift, 45 baud RTTY, and 300-baud packets.

12. B: Temperature inversion can create a path for microwave propagation.

13. B: The cause of gray-line propagation is low D-layer absorption and high E-layer and F-layer propagation at twilight and sunrise.

14. B: The 304A solar parameter measures UV emissions at 304 angstroms, correlated to solar flux index.

15. D: A logic analyzer displays multiple digital signal states simultaneously.

16. B: Intermodulation distortion in an SSB transmitter can be measured by modulating the transmitter with two non-harmonically related audio frequencies and observing the RF output with a spectrum analyzer.

17. B: 300 Hz is a desirable amount of selectivity for an amateur RTTY HF receiver.

Copyright © Mometrix Media. You have been licensed one copy of this document for personal use only. Any other reproduction or redistribution is strictly prohibited. All rights reserved.

18. C: A third-order intercept level of 40 dBm means that a pair of 40 dBm signals will theoretically generate a third-order intermodulation product with the same level as the input signals.

19. D: Touch-controlled electrical devices may cause interference that sounds like AC hum on an AM receiver or a carrier modulated by 60 Hz hum on a SSB or CW receiver, interference that drifts slowly across the HF spectrum, and interference that can be several kHz in width and repeats at regular intervals across a HF band.

20. A: The Q of an RLC series resonant circuit is calculated by dividing the reactance of either the inductance or capacitance by the resistance.

21. A: In an inductor, voltage leads current by 90 degrees.

22. B: When using rectangular coordinates to graph the impedance of a circuit, the vertical axis represents the reactive component.

23. A: True power in an out-of-phase AC circuit can be determined by multiplying the apparent power times the power factor.

24. B: In Figure E6-2, the schematic symbol for an N-channel dual-gate MOSFET is 4.

25. B: In Figure E6-3, the schematic symbol for a light-emitting diode is 5.

26. D: In Figure E6-5, the schematic symbol for a NOR gate is 4.

27. A: Toroidal cores confine most of the magnetic field within the core material, while solenoidal cores do not.

28. D: Surface mount is the packaging technique in which leadless components are soldered directly to circuit boards.

29. B: The most common type of photovoltaic cell used for electrical power generation is silicon.

30. C: A truth table is a list of inputs and corresponding outputs for a digital device.

31. B: In Figure E7-1, R1 and R2 are used as a fixed bias.

32. B: A cavity filter would be the best choice for use in a 2 meter repeater duplexer.

33. C: The primary reason that a high-frequency switching type high voltage power supply can be both less expensive and lighter in weight than a conventional power supply is that the high frequency inverter design uses much smaller transformers and filter components for an equivalent power output.

34. A: A diode detector functions by rectifying and filtering of RF signals.

35. A: Sample rate determines the maximum receive bandwidth of a Direct Digital Conversion SDR.

36. C: A voltage gain of 38 can be expected from the circuit in Figure E7-4 when R1 is 1800 ohms and RF is 68 kilohms.

Copyright © Mometrix Media. You have been licensed one copy of this document for personal use only. Any other reproduction or redistribution is strictly prohibited. All rights reserved.

37. B: The amplitude values that represent a sine-wave output are contained in the lookup table of a direct digital frequency synthesizer.

38. C: A low pass filter used in conjunction with a digital-to-analog converter serves to remove harmonics from the output caused by the discrete analog levels generated.

39. B: Frequency division multiplexing is when two or more information streams are merged into a baseband, which then modulates the transmitter.

40. D: An advantage of Gray code in digital communications is that it facilitates error detection.

41. B: Baudot uses 5 data bits per character, ASCII uses 7 or 8; Baudot uses 2 characters as letters/figures shift codes, ASCII has no letters/figures shift code.

42. B: Antenna efficiency is calculated by (radiation resistance / total resistance) x 100 per cent.

43. A: In Method of Moments analysis, a wire is modeled as a series of segments, each having a uniform value of current.

44. B: A Zepp antenna is an end-fed dipole antenna.

45. B: As the frequency of operation is lowered for a fixed-length HF mobile antenna, the radiation resistance decreases and the capacitive reactance increases.

46. C: Inserting a 1/4-wavelength piece of 75 ohm coaxial cable transmission line in series between the antenna terminals and the 50 ohm feed cable would be an effective way to match their impedances.

47. C: A 1/8 wavelength transmission line presents an inductive reactance to a generator when the line is shorted at the far end.

48. D: The arcs on a Smith chart represent points with constant reactance.

49. B: The very sharp single null part of a cardioid pattern antenna is useful for direction finding.

50. A: Polychlorinated biphenyls may be present in some electronic components such as high voltage capacitors and transformers.

Copyright © Mometrix Media. You have been licensed one copy of this document for personal use only. Any other reproduction or redistribution is strictly prohibited. All rights reserved.

Technician Class Figures

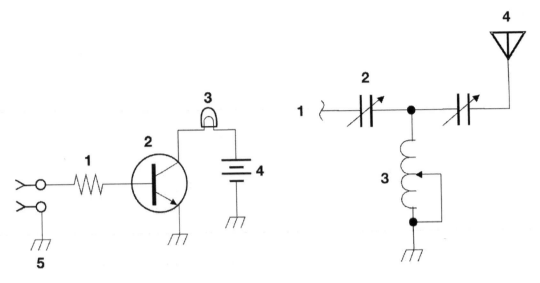

Figure T-1

Figure T-3

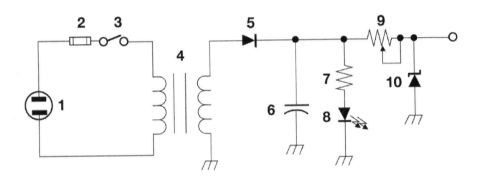

Figure T-2

Copyright © Mometrix Media. You have been licensed one copy of this document for personal use only. Any other reproduction or redistribution is strictly prohibited. All rights reserved.

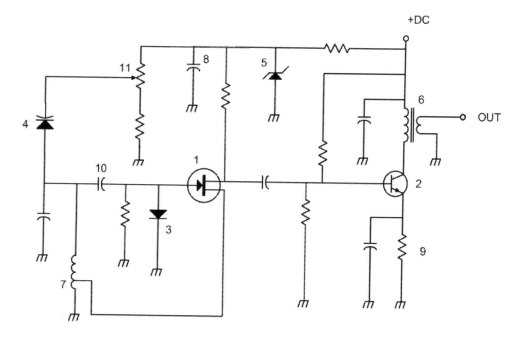

Figure G7-1

Copyright © Mometrix Media. You have been licensed one copy of this document for personal use only. Any other reproduction or redistribution is strictly prohibited. All rights reserved.

Extra Class Figures

Figure E5-2

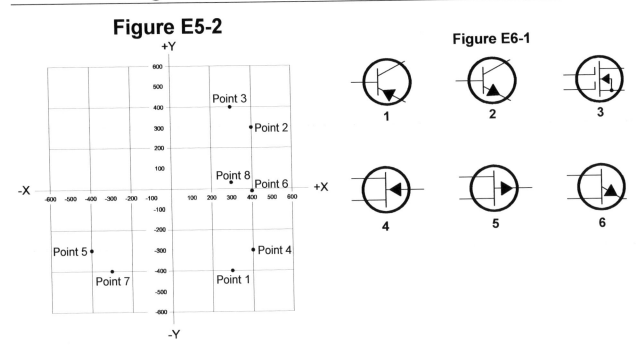

Figure E6-1

Figure E6-2

Figure E6-3

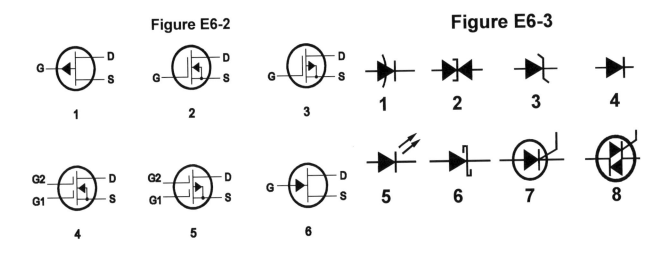

Copyright © Mometrix Media. You have been licensed one copy of this document for personal use only. Any other reproduction or redistribution is strictly prohibited. All rights reserved.

Figure E6-5

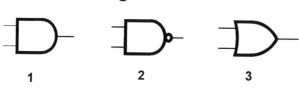

1   2   3

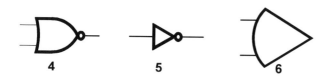

4   5   6

Figure E7-1

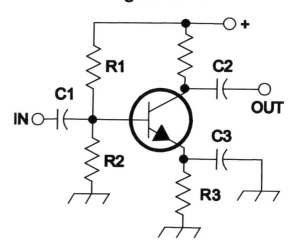

Figure E7-2

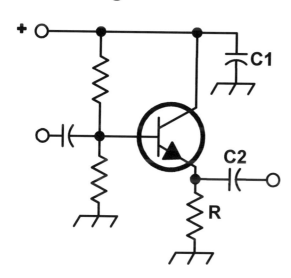

Figure E7- 3

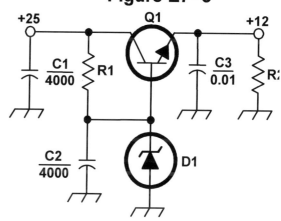

Copyright © Mometrix Media. You have been licensed one copy of this document for personal use only. Any other reproduction or redistribution is strictly prohibited. All rights reserved.

Figure E7-4

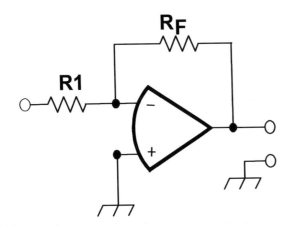

Figure E9-1

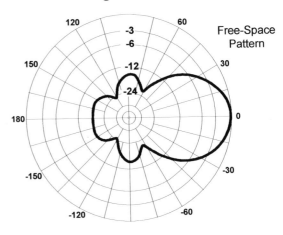

Figure E9-2

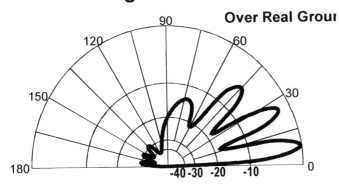

Figure E9-3

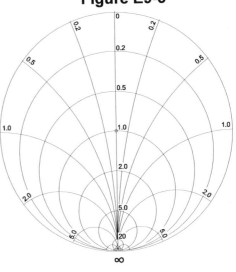

Additional Bonus Material

Due to our efforts to try to keep this book to a manageable length, we've created a link that will give you access to all of your additional bonus material.

Please visit http://www.mometrix.com/bonus948/hamradiotech, http://www.mometrix.com/bonus948/hamradiogen, or http://www.mometrix.com/bonus948/hamradioextra to access the information.

Copyright © Mometrix Media. You have been licensed one copy of this document for personal use only. Any other reproduction or redistribution is strictly prohibited. All rights reserved.

15414312R10338

Made in the USA
Middletown, DE
21 November 2018